MW00379383

Gramophone
75th
ANNIVERSARY

The illustration on the right is a framed copy of part of Schumann's Piano Quintet, on Vocalion A-0162, played by The London String Quartet with Mrs Ethel Hobday. The text of the inscription is as follows:

First Gramophone Congress, July 9, 1925

ISLE OF JETHOU – C.I.

This record which was first played by me in the month of March 1922 may be considered the founder of ***The Gramophone***. It was the first to teach me what the gramophone could do. Mr Robin Legge, the musical critic of *The Daily Telegraph* hearing my enthusiasm asked me to write an article for his page. That article provoked such a wide reponse from readers that I determined to found a magazine, *Floreat*.

Compton Mackenzie

First Gramophone Congress July 9. 1925

ISLE OF JETHOU - C.I.

This record which was first played to me in the month of March 1922 may be considered the founder of The Gramophone. It was the first to teach me what the gramophone could do. Mr Robin Legge, the musical critic of the Daily Telegraph hearing my enthusiasm asked me to write an article for his page. That article provoked such a wide response from readers that I determined to found a magazine. Floreat!

Compton Mackenzie

First published in Great Britain in 1998 by
Gramophone Publications Limited

Production Editor Mark Walker
Designer Dinah Lone
Production Dermot Jones

Gramophone Publications Limited
135 Greenford Road,
Sudbury Hill,
Harrow,
Middlesex HA1 3YD,
Great Britain

Colour origination by Derek Croxson Limited,
The Island, Moor Road, Chesham, Buckinghamshire,
HP5 1NZ

Printed and bound in England by William Clowes
Limited, Beccles, Suffolk, NR34 9QE

First edition

British Library Cataloguing in Publication Data.
A catalogue record for this book is available from
The British Library

ISBN 0 902470 99 X

Author's note

On many occasions people have asked when the title of our publication would be brought up to date. In the days of LP the gramophone became a record player, and with the advent of CD the word 'gramophone' receded even further into the mists of time. But parallel with these developments the magazine's title increasingly gained world recognition and is now seen as being synonymous with the role which it fulfils in respect of recorded classical music. However, it was recognized that in many cases references to the magazine omitted the definite article, and we also became progressively more aware of the difficulty of incorporating the definite article into a suitable design for the magazine's logo. Therefore, in June 1969 the definite article was dropped, hence the apparent inconsistency in references to the title of the magazine in the pages which follow.

In writing and editing this 75-year survey I have sought the views of many friends and colleagues to whom I am greatly indebted, as I am to Mark Walker, my Production Editor, who has been a tower of strength and reliability. I am also grateful to the various record companies for the provision of photographic material (duly credited) which has supplemented that which exists in *Gramophone*'s archives.

In any literary work associated with the gramophone the inclusion, or otherwise, of record numbers is invariably a matter of some debate. Spanning such a substantial part of the Industry's history, with many famous recordings appearing and reappearing over the years in various formats, it has been decided to indicate only the original UK issuing company and, where possible, the date of first review in *Gramophone*.

For recollections of the earliest days I have drawn, with thanks, on four autobiographical works: Compton Mackenzie's ten-volume *My Life and Times* (Chatto & Windus, 1963-1971)[1], his *My Record of Music* (Hutchinson, 1955)[2], Faith Mackenzie's *More Than I Should* (Collins, 1940)[3] and *Christopher Stone Speaking* (Elkin Matthews, 1933)[4], together with Andro Linklater's biography of Mackenzie, *Compton Mackenzie: A Life* (Chatto & Windus, 1987)[5].

Beyond this I have referred to nearly 900 issues of the magazine, from which we have also selected a number of items to support and illustrate the narrative. In many cases it has been necessary to edit these items to suit the context in which they have been used.

Sudbury Hill,
Harrow, Middlesex

ACP
December 1997

Contents

Foreword

Harold C. Schonberg

Harold C. Schonberg was for 20 years the senior music critic of *The New York Times* and the first music critic to be awarded the Pulitzer Prize. He first contributed to *The Gramophone* in November 1947

You will, I hope, excuse the autobiographical elements in this preface to Anthony Pollard's history of ***Gramophone***, but for years I have been part of the family, with memories that go back to the Second World War.

It was early in 1943, and I was a Yank in England, at the American staging area in Stone. Most of my fellow shavetails (newly commissioned second lieutenants) wondered what was in store for them. But not I. I had picked up the phone, got a Brit to show me where to put the tuppence and other coins into the slot, and I called Cecil Pollard in Kenton.

I called Cecil Pollard, because in New York I had been working for Peter Hugh Reed as assistant editor of the *American Music Lover*, then the only classical music review magazine in America. Assistant editor sounds very grand; but there were only the two of us to do much of the reviewing, and we wrote articles under our own names and a variety of pseudonyms. We had some outside reviewers who sent in their stuff, but the magazine was put out just by the two of us. So I cleaned the windows, swept the floors, and polished up the handles of the big brass doors, learning a lot about the business as I went along.

When I got my orders for England I phoned Mr Reed and he told me to get in touch with Cecil Pollard, his opposite number in England who ran ***The Gramophone***. Naturally I knew the magazine. It was required reading when it arrived at the *American Music Lover* office.

So now that I was in England I immediately wangled a three-day pass and took the train to London after talking with Cecil. He had told me how to get to his home. "Come for dinner", he urged. Indeed yes. And so it came to pass that I met the amiable, affable Cecil Pollard (most people called him "Polly", a name I could never bring myself to use). We hit it off very well. Also present was his wife Nellie and son Anthony, about 14 as I remember it, in love with Spitfires. There were Spitfire models all over the place.

It was a lovely evening, full of talk about music, records and the record industry. I had gossip to relate about the American side of things – only Victor and Columbia in those days. I was impressed by ***The Gramophone*** operation as Cecil described it to me. My magazine had been pretty much happy-go-lucky (yet it is still very much alive as *The American Record Guide*, a bi-monthly published in Cincinnati). Cecil was obviously a sharp businessman, unlike Peter Hugh Reed who was a dreamer, a charming raconteur (I adored the man) and entirely disorganized.

On later visits I was overwhelmed by ***The Gramophone***'s record library, which had just about every British record issued since 1923. Cecil was nice enough to let me browse, and I was able to hear some wonderful things that had never been released in the States.

But as the D-Day build-up started, and I was racing all over England doing this and that, we lost contact. We kept in touch by mail. Back in America after the war, I became a critic on the now-defunct *New York Sun*. That was in 1946, and the following year Cecil Pollard invited me to write a monthly "Letter from America" for ***The Gramophone***. This continued to 1960, when the pressure of my newspaper work at *The New York Times* necessitated a halt.

Of course I kept in touch with Cecil during those "Letter from America" years, and with his son Anthony on his visits to New York, and when the mantle passed to him. I have read every issue of ***Gramophone*** since 1940, and I have watched it grow and prosper under the Pollards. These days it is a much more glamorous publication than it was 50 years ago, embracing as it does colour printing and all the joys of modern technology. Yet, basically, it remains the most prestigious publication of its kind because of its strong reviewing staff. That is still the *raison d'être* of ***Gramophone***.

Now comes Anthony Pollard's book about ***Gramophone*** and its world. Tony has been part of the British classical recording scene for decades, as was his father before him. Here we will find, in effect, a history of the British recording industry as experienced by a participant. It goes from acoustic records to CDs, from Dame Nellie Melba to Dame Kiri, from Compton Mackenzie and Fred Gaisberg and Edward Lewis to John Culshaw, Walter Legge and the other makers and shakers of the industry. In its way ***Gramophone*** has also been among the makers and shakers of the industry, and it has grown as the industry has grown. Anthony Pollard's reminiscences, along with other contributions to this book, will help explain the phenomenon that started with Thomas Edison and his miraculous invention in 1877.

The Gramophone

Edited by COMPTON MACKENZIE

Contents

Vol. I. No. 1 APRIL *(for May)* 1923 Monthly 6d.

Gramophone a reminiscence

Introduction

Anthony Pollard

This is the story of a magazine – ***Gramophone***. It was the brainchild of one man, Compton Mackenzie, who almost single-handedly produced the first issue from a little island called Herm in the Channel Islands. That first issue appeared on April 20th, 1923 and the magazine has now completed 75 years of continuous publication.

In endeavouring to recount the story of those 75 years, which reflect also the changing pattern of the Record Industry itself, I have turned the pages of every issue of the magazine and referred to a range of autobiographical and biographical material related to the four people who were to shape the history of the Company. There have also been Minute Books, reports, correspondence and financial accounts which, together with my own personal involvement of over 50 years, have enabled me to draw together many of the threads of this fascinating story.

Research, particularly of the early years, has occasionally produced conflicting accounts of certain events and I have attempted to resolve these given the information and knowledge available to me, but the nature of my task has been such that errors may have arisen, and facts and individuals omitted: for this I would hasten to apologize.

However, whilst the endeavours of those original pioneers will never be forgotten, it is to all those members of the Company who over the years have maintained and developed the traditions and philosophy of the magazine that credit is now due. The production of a magazine such as ***Gramophone*** calls for the integration of the skills of a varied group of people to work successfully as a team, and in that respect we have indeed been fortunate.

I believe that today Compton Mackenzie would happily recognize his 75-year-old paper boat and, with great pride, wish it a fair wind and calm sea as it sails towards its Centenary.

How it all began

TELEPHONE: HOP. 4900

THE GRAMOPHONE

Edited by
COMPTON MACKENZIE

Publishing Offices:
48 Hatfield Street,
S.E.1

Editorial Office:
Isle of Herm,
Channel Islands

Vol. I. APRIL, 1923 No. 1

Prologue

IO SONO IL PROLOGO.—An apology is due to the public for inflicting upon it another review, but I should not be doing so unless I were persuaded that many of the numerous possessors of gramophones will welcome an organ of candid opinion. The critical policy of THE GRAMOPHONE will be largely personal, and as such it will be honest but not infallible, while the errors we make will be mostly on the side of kindness. If we endorse what a firm claims for its goods in our advertisement columns, we shall endorse that claim because we believe it to be justified.

The instruments on which all records sent for us to review are tested are the Orchestraphone sold by the Gramophone Exchange, an horizontal grand of His Master's Voice, and an Adams model of the Vocalion Company. The soundboxes used are the H.M.V. Exhibition No. 2, a Vocalion, a Realistic, an Ultone, a Superphone, a Sonat, and a Three Muses. If the maker of any other soundbox likes to send us his product for trial, we shall use it in competition with the others; but no opinion will be passed on any soundbox sent to us before a three months' trial. We shall try each month to keep pace with the records issued; but we hope that our readers will accept these preliminary reviews as provisional; and every three months we shall deal very critically with the output of the preceding quarter.

I have received many kind promises of support from distinguished writers; and if I find that the sales warrant me in supposing that gramophone enthusiasts want the kind of review THE GRAMOPHONE will set out to be, I can promise them that I will do my best to ensure their obtaining the finest opinions procurable.

We shall have nothing to do with Wireless in these columns. Our policy will be to encourage the recording companies to build up for generations to come a great library of good music. I do not want to waste time in announcing what we are going to do in future numbers, because I do not know yet if there is any real need for this review at all. We shall write as servants of the public, and if we sometimes take upon ourselves a certain freedom of speech in dealing with our masters, such freedom of speech is the privilege of all good servants.

Andiam! Incominciate!

Compton Mackenzie

1922-1928

A *Gramophone* chronology

1922-1928

1922

September

- Compton Mackenzie contributes an article entitled "The Gramophone" to *The Daily Telegraph*.

1923

March

- First recording made by the Royal Family – King George V and Queen Mary at Buckingham Palace.

April

- Compton Mackenzie founds ***The Gramophone*** (***TG***) on the island of Herm.
- Louis Sterling becomes MD of the Columbia Graphophone Company.

Louis Sterling

June

- First recording of a complete string quartet – Brahms's Op. 51 No. 1 by the Catterall Quartet for HMV.

July

- ***TG*** opens offices at 25 Newman Street, London.
- Compton Mackenzie moves from Herm to Jethou.

September

- *The Radio Times* first published following the beginning of regular broadcasting from 2LO, London Station of The British Broadcasting Company in November 1922.

November

- Gustav Holst completes the recording of his *Planets* Suite with the LSO for Columbia.

December

- Alec Robertson's first contribution to ***TG***.

Alec Robertson

1924

April

- First recording of a British symphony by Vocalion – Sir John McEwen's *Solway* with Cuthbert Whitemore and the Aeolian Orchestra.

May

- H. C. Harrison of Western Electric is granted patent for electrical recording.

June

- ***TG*** organizes Steinway Hall tests.
- Herman Klein, opera critic, joins ***TG***.

Herman Klein

July

- First complete recording of an opera in English made by HMV – Puccini's *Madam Butterfly* with Rosina Buckmann in the title-role and Tudor Davies as Pinkerton.

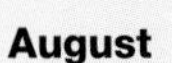

August

- Edward "Chick" Fowler joins The Gramophone Company.

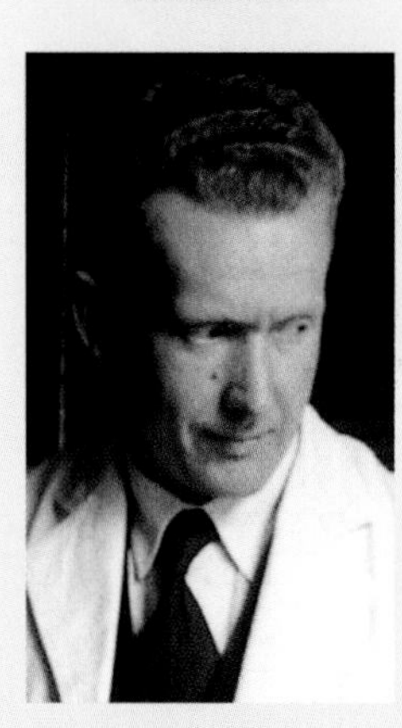

Edward "Chick" Fowler
Photo EMI

September

- ***TG*** moves to 58 Frith Street, London.
- Percy Wilson's first contribution to ***TG***.

October

- First Electrical Process record made by The Gramophone Company at Hayes – King Henry V's Prayer, read by Mr Pack – using B.E.G. Mittell's system.

November

- The Expert Committee is formed at the instigation of Christopher Stone.

Percy Wilson

1925

February

- W. S. Barrell joins the Columbia Graphophone Company as Chief Engineer to Recording Dept.
- W. A. Chislett contributes his first reviews to ***TG***.

W. A. Chislett

March

- The American Victor company electrically record Alfred Cortot playing Chopin's Impromptu No. 2 in F sharp, Op. 36 at their Camden studios.

May

- W. R. Anderson's first contribution to ***TG***.

June

- First Western Electric process recording made by HMV in the UK – *Ah! Ha!* by Jack Hylton and his Band.

July

- ***TG*** organizes a Congress at The Central Hall, Westminster – forerunner of today's audio exhibitions.

The Gramophone, July, 1928

ROYAL OPERA COVENT GARDEN
EVA TURNER
NEW RECORDS NOW READY
NEW RECORDS NOW READY
EVA TURNER – The British Soprano who has created such a furore in "Turandot" and "Aida" on her debut at Covent Garden
Records EXCLUSIVELY for COLUMBIA
ELECTRIC RECORDING
Columbia New Process RECORDS
WITHOUT SCRATCH

On August 30th, 1924 a company was formed in Guernsey to formalize the business affairs associated with the publication of *The Gramophone*. The Bank of Liverpool & Martins Ltd. was later to become Martins Bank Ltd., and eventually Barclays Bank plc. The Company's account has not moved since its formation

Minutes of a Meeting held at 11.30 a.m. on Saturday 30th August 1924 at No. 6 New Street, Guernsey, Channel Islands.

Present: Compton Mackenzie, Capt. D.W. Parish, Victor G. Carey, Basil Leng, Miss Nellie Boyle, W.H. Weston and one other.

It was resolved:

1. To register a private company under the Guernsey Company Law 1908 with the title of "Gramophone (Publications) Limited", with its registered office at No. 6 New Street, Guernsey, Channel Islands.

2. To appoint the following officers:
(a) Managing Director: C.R. Stone
(b) Ordinary Directors: Compton Mackenzie & Capt. D.W. Parish.

3. Open an account with the Bank of Liverpool & Martins Ltd. 68 Lombard Street, London, E.C. in the name of "Gramophone (Publications) Limited", cheques to be signed by at least one director and the secretary.

4. To take over rent agreement, telephone agreement, assurance policy and all other agreements now held in the name of C.R. Stone regarding "The Gramophone" magazine.

5. To leave all editorial & administrative matters in the hands of the London Board of Directors (C.R. Stone & D.W. Parish) until the next meeting.

October

- Rice and Kellogg introduce a dynamic loudspeaker.

December

- Electrical recording comes into general use, four years after Columbia had first made experimental attempts in Westminster Abbey during the burial service for the Unknown Warrior in November 1920. The first release of an electrically recorded symphony, made by HMV, is Tchaikovsky's No. 4 with Sir Landon Ronald and the Royal Albert Hall Orchestra.
- 78rpm turntable speed standardized.

1926

March

- Cecil Pollard joins *TG* as Business Manager.

May

- First actual performance recording by HMV at The Royal Opera House, Covent Garden – Boito's *Mefistofele* with Chaliapin in the title-role.

June

- Melba's Covent Garden farewell appearance recorded live by HMV.

July

- First recording by the Casals/Cortot/Thibaud trio of Schubert's Piano Trio in B flat, D898 by HMV.

August

- W. W. Townsley joins Barnett Samuel, predecessor of Decca.

December

- Kenneth Wilkinson joins World Echo Record Company and later Crystalate.

Références
EMI
BEETHOVEN : "Erzherzogtrio"
"Archduke" Trio
Trio "l'Archiduc"
SCHUBERT : Klaviertrio B-dur
Piano Trio in B flat major
Trio avec piano
en si bémol majeur D. 898
ALFRED CORTOT
JACQUES THIBAUD
PABLO CASALS

- Brunswick introduce the Panatrope, the first all-electric gramophone.

1927

March

- Walter Legge joins The Gramophone Company.
- To mark the centenary of Beethoven's death, Columbia release the first complete set of symphonies.
- Victor introduces the first record-changing phonograph.

Walter Legge *Photo EMI*

May

- Columbia make first electrical recording of a complete opera in English – Leoncavallo's *Pagliacci* with the British National Opera Company.

July

- Christopher Stone begins broadcasting for the BBC.

July/August

- Columbia make the first-ever recordings in the Festspielhaus, Bayreuth of excerpts from *The Ring* and *Parsifal*.

August

- David Bicknell joins The Gramophone Company, Artists Department.

September

- John Whittle joins The Gramophone Company, Advertisement Department.
- HMV record excerpts from public performances during the Three Choirs Festival in Hereford Cathedral.

David Bicknell *Photo EMI*

October

- Edison introduces 40-minute long-playing discs in the USA.
- Première of *The Jazz Singer*, first commercially successful talking picture.

1928

August

- Atterberg's Symphony No. 6 wins the Schubert Memorial Prize – Columbia record the work with Beecham and issue the results prior to the public première. This was the first known instance of such an occurrence.

How it all began

Anthony Pollard

In the course of his lifetime Compton Mackenzie wrote over 100 books, always endeavouring to work to a background of music – a lapse of concentration could easily be resolved from the enjoyment of a Chopin waltz, rather than the thought of a looming financial crisis. In the early 1920s he held the Crown lease on two of the Channel Islands, Herm and Jethou, and found himself in a quandary concerning the financial wisdom of perpetuating such an arrangement. Somewhat depressed and anxious, he was in London in February 1922, and believing that a defiant piece of extravagance was a tonic for such a mood, took himself into the Aeolian company's Bond Street showrooms and signed a hire-purchase agreement for an Aeolian organ (a pianola with stops), arranging for its delivery to Herm. At the time they had no catalogue of the rolls available for the machine but promised that this would be forwarded within a few days.

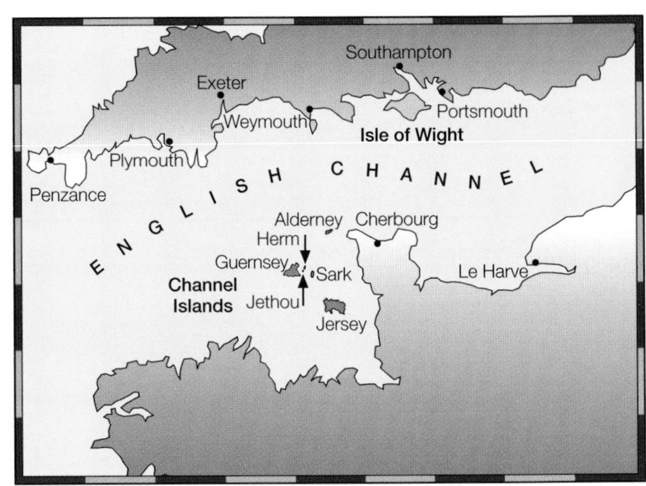

Compton Mackenzie's house on Jethou

When the catalogue arrived Mackenzie found that it contained none of the classical works which he recalled from past acquaintance but simply a selection of musical comedies and other light music. He therefore advised the company that in the circumstances he must cancel the order, only to be told that the terms of the hire-purchase agreement made this impossible. Would he consider taking a gramophone in lieu of the organ? To this he replied that nothing would induce him to have a gramophone. He had owned one 12 years previously in Cornwall and apart from some records by Caruso and Harry Lauder he thought it was useless. However, ultimately he had no alternative and accepted a Hepplewhite model Vocalion gramophone together with some of their records.

Eventually the machine arrived in Herm and he played first a shortened version of Schumann's Piano Quintet. His surprise was such that he asked Robertson, his boatman, what other record companies there were? "There's HMV. That's the biggest." "What's HMV stand for?" Trying not to look surprised at Mackenzie's ignorance, Robertson replied, "His Master's Voice".

From that beginning Mackenzie obtained the HMV, Columbia and Vocalion catalogues and, at a cost of about £400, had within two months purchased a collection of over 1,200 discs. These were mainly of items which could each be accommodated on a single disc: the HMV

An example of the HMV Celebrity Catalogue

The following is an extract from Compton Mackenzie's original article on the gramophone, which appeared in the weekly "Music of the Day" column of *The Daily Telegraph* on Saturday, September 2nd 1922. It was the positive response to this piece that prompted Mackenzie to launch a magazine devoted to the subject

THE GRAMOPHONE

By Compton Mackenzie

I have only recently discovered the gramophone. Until lately I supposed it to be nothing but a detestable interruption of conversation and country peace, the golf of sound. Gramophony was a noise to me rather more unpleasant than would be the combined sounds of a child running a hoop-stick along a railing, a dentist's drill, a cat trying to get out of a basket in a railway carriage, and a nursemaid humming upon a comb wrapped in tissue paper.

To be sure, I knew that there were such alleviations as the records of Caruso; but inasmuch as friends who produced one of these records nearly always produced Tosti's *Ideale* or Tosti's *Addio*, I came to think that the choice was a small one. I had heard old records of Mischa Elman: but violin records ten years ago were very different from what they are now. In those days the squeak of a bat would have been almost as audible. As for the bands and orchestras of those days – but let us forget them, although I regret to add that "His Master's Voice" still allows currency to some ancient outrages upon music. There is a ghastly record of Brahms's *Hungarian Dance* in D minor played by Joachim which is only fit for a museum, and even there should never be played. However, it is ungrateful to speak of such when nowadays the same company has given us that first [actually the fifth] *Hungarian Dance* divinely played by Kreisler and as perfectly rendered.

My own instrument is what is called the Hepplewhite model of Aeolian Vocalion, and I confidently affirm that neither that nor the Adam model of the same make are surpassed by any other instrument, cost it three times as much. With equal confidence I affirm that it is folly to spend, let us say, £35 upon an instrument when for another £15 the perfect instrument can be obtained. Anybody who can afford to pay £35 by monthly instalments can afford to pay £50, and anyone who can afford £50 for an instrument can afford to pay the extra amount for good records, even if they have fewer of them.

catalogue contained only one complete symphony (Beethoven's Fifth by Nikisch and the Berlin Philharmonic Orchestra on four double-sided discs) with only a few snippets of chamber music. The strength of the catalogue was in the Celebrity section, which featured recordings by artists such as Backhaus, Chaliapin, Caruso, Galli-Curci, Kreisler, McCormack and Melba. The Columbia catalogue contained no symphonies but a better selection of chamber music. He quickly realized that there was a need to ventilate the whole question of recorded classical music and was fortunate in being asked by Robin Legge, music critic of *The Daily Telegraph*, to write an article on the subject. This appeared on September 2nd, 1922 and as a result of the response Compton Mackenzie decided to launch *The Gramophone*.

The decision is made

Now the real problems had to be faced. Mackenzie was clear in his mind of the need for such a magazine: the gramophone was the ideal means of developing a far wider public appreciation of good music but the record companies had to be encouraged in their endeavours and the buying-public made aware of all that was happening. At this time there were one or two trade papers but nothing directed specifically towards the serious listener.

The British Broadcasting Company transmitter on 2LO had started in the London area on November 14th, 1922, with Birmingham and Manchester following the next day, and John Reith (later Lord Reith) – who was to set the standard which would later be emulated by the world's broadcasting organizations – was appointed General Manager on December 30th. For many this seemed to ring the death-knell of the gramophone record business but not for Mackenzie who, in assessing his fellow-Scot, was of the opinion that a well-controlled broadcasting company would ultimately benefit music and the record business.

Financial backing was needed for his venture and Mackenzie turned to his brother-in-law Christopher Stone to put up the other half of £1,000. Stone ridiculed the idea, depicting the inevitable development of radio with listeners being able to select at will from dozens of alternative programmes.

Mackenzie, however, clung to his belief and encouraged by Walter Yeomans, head of the Education Department of The Gramophone Company (HMV), he met Alfred Clark, Managing Director of the company in his office at Hayes, Middlesex. Clark was both friendly and helpful but even so Mackenzie felt afterwards that he viewed the whole project as a bubble blown by an enthusiastic amateur. None the less, he promised three pages of

Walter Yeomans of The Gramophone Company

Alfred Clark, Managing Director of The Gramophone Company *Photo EMI*

In April 1973, as part of the magazine's Golden Jubilee celebrations, Roger Wimbush looked back 50 years at other events in the year of *The Gramophone*'s launch

1 9 2 3

1923, the year in which ***The Gramophone*** was born was typical of post-war Britain. Although the *Charleston* was still two years away and it was another year before the first Labour Prime Minister kissed hands, the 'bright young people' were painting the town and political crises were ever present, both in respect of personalities and policies.

While the *jeunesse dorée* jazzed through the London night and moralists denounced what today we would call 'unisex' (Oxford bags, the Eton crop, short skirts and flat chests), the Labour Exchanges were faced with nearly two million unemployed. In fact one in twenty-eight of the population of England and Wales was in receipt of Poor Law Relief. Milk was 6d. [2½ p] a quart, rising later in the year to 8d., and *The Times* went up from 1½ d. to 2d. At the same time, the *Times Literary Supplement* fell from 6d. to 3d., which must have pleased the Senior Common Rooms, if it made little impact in the Public Reading Rooms, where the few 'sits vac' advertisements were assiduously followed up.

Not, then, the most propitious time to launch a paper dealing with what some would call an extravagance and others a foolishness. Yet there were, as always, plenty of delights. Broadcasting was getting under way after its first year, and a sensational example of progress took place at Southwark County Court, where quill pens were abolished after 150 years of use. Wembley Stadium saw its first Cup Final, when an estimated crowd of 200,000 gave the authorities a fright (Bolton Wanderers beat West Ham United 2–0), Yorkshire were County Cricket Champions, Suzanne Lenglen won the Women's Singles at Wimbledon. Hobbs scored his one hundredth century, and Oxford not only won the Boat Race but beat Cambridge at Lord's by an innings and 227 runs!

May 4th was the hottest day since 1871, but in July the temperature was up to 84 degrees in the shade. Thunderstorms were ferocious, floods shut schools and factories, and a Channel gale wrecked a train between Folkestone and Dover. President Warren Harding of the United States died and Margaret Bondfield became the first woman Chairman of the TUC. Soon afterwards she was to become the first woman in the Cabinet. Tutankhamun's tomb was opened and *The Beggar's Opera* ended a run of three-and-a-half years at the Lyric Theatre, Hammersmith. The tercentenaries of Byrd and Weelkes were duly celebrated, and London saw its first neon lighting, picking out the outline of the Coliseum. 123 railway companies were grouped into the LMS, LNER, GWR and SR, but travellers on the Metropolitan still had the benefit of first-class Pullman travel out of Baker Street, and indeed first class was to remain on the Inner Circle until 1940. London buses (then properly called omnibuses) were open-topped. Above all, 1923 was the healthiest year in our history up to that time, so perhaps the auguries for a new birth were brighter than contemporaries might have supposed.

advertising per month – two for HMV and one for the popularly-priced Zonophone label – at seven guineas each [£7·35]. He then added, "And we shan't object to you calling your paper *The Gramophone*". "Why should you?" Mackenzie asked in astonishment. "Well, it is a proprietary title, you know," he replied with a smile. Mackenzie then made approaches to Herbert Ridout, publicity manager of the Columbia Graphophone Company, and to Vocalion Records – both of whom promised advertisement support and review records.

The first issue

So it was, immediately following the New Year celebrations of 1923, on the little island of Herm (no more than one-and-a-half miles long by half- a - mile wide and some four miles off the East coast of Guernsey in the Channel Islands), that Compton Mackenzie set about producing the first issue of ***The Gramophone***. Fortuitously, in the preceding December, a flute-playing Subaltern from his Aegean Intelligence days – John Hope-Johnstone – had arrived for an extended stay on the island and soon found himself more than well occupied.

The West coast of Herm, with Mackenzie's house in the centre, as seen from Jethou

Mackenzie's life seemed to consist of a series of financial crises only staved off by writing yet another book; thus in the early part of 1923 he was working on his new novel, *The Old Man of the Sea*, during the evening and early into the morning whilst listening to gramophone records played either by his wife Faith or his secretary Nellie Boyte, and then after sleeping until around 11am he would commence work on the magazine.

A collection of miniature scores was purchased to establish, among other things, the exact nature of the cuts which disfigured the majority of recordings of any work of substance – a practice which incensed Mackenzie. Hope-Johnstone went to London to secure the advertisement bookings and with Yeomans's help arranged for the printing of the magazine with Hudson & Kearns who, until one of their directors found out, also provided an office at 48 Hatfield Street, London SE1.

It was not surprising that the first issue was late: it had been intended to publish on April 1st but it was the 20th before it appeared. With a print run of 6,000 copies it consisted of 28 pages plus cover. There were nine pages of advertisements (which included the promised HMV, Columbia and Vocalion support – the first pair to be a constant and happy presence in the years ahead) whilst the 21 pages of text were written principally by the Mackenzies, Hope-Johnstone and the pianist Mark Hambourg. Mackenzie had written 11 pages under his own name and the initials CM and Z; Faith Mackenzie (as F Sharp) had written an article on "Good Singing"; Hope-Johnstone (as James Caskett) had reviewed the latest records; Hambourg had written about piano recording. Walter Yeomans (as Warren Monk) had written about a Royal record and there was also a long piece on Gramophone Societies.

As it happened only half of the copies were sold and so for the second (June) issue the print order was reduced to 3,000 copies. Needless to say, this went out of print almost immediately and became one of the rarest editions of the magazine. A further 'office' address was provided for this June issue at the home of Cyril Storey, a friend of Walter Yeomans, at 28 Stockwell Park Crescent, SW9, but given the volume of mail coming through his letter-box it was clear that a more permanent arrangement had to be made.

A London office is opened

Mackenzie's marriage to Faith was not the easiest and for much of their lives they tended to go their separate ways. Before settling on Herm in December 1920, Mackenzie had for seven years leased "Casa Solitaria" on Capri and Faith had remained there until the end of 1922 when she joined Mackenzie on Herm. This arrangement did not prove to be a success and she was therefore happy when, following Christopher Stone's change of heart and decision to support the venture, it was agreed that the two of them should establish a permanent office for the magazine in London.

Premises were leased on July 9th, 1923 at 25 Newman Street, providing office space as well as accommodation for Faith, whilst Christopher Stone was to travel daily from his home, Peppers Farm, Ashurst in Sussex. It was from Newman Street that the third (August) issue was produced and it would be fair to say that with a basic administrative structure in place the immediate future now looked a little more stable.

Mackenzie's genius

Financial affairs bedevilled Mackenzie for the greater part of his life. He was accused, even by his wife Faith, of writing pot-boilers to support his life-style, and this was undoubtedly

Christopher Stone, and Faith Compton Mackenzie at a wedding in the mid-1930s

The Gramophone, April, 1923 — 20

REVIEW *of* APRIL RECORDS

HIS MASTER'S VOICE.—D.683.—D.684.—**Brandenburg Concerto in G,** and **Air on the G String.**

The most important place among the April records must be given to the first record which has been made of an orchestral piece by Bach. It is surprising that the Brandenburg Concerti and the Orchestral Suites, which are so admirably suited to the recording room, have not been given us before. Bach's genius was perhaps best able to express itself in vocal and orchestral works. A polyphonic style is not naturally adapted to a key-board instrument, on which it is difficult if not impossible to bring out the inside voices. In this concerto, written for nine instruments, he is at his best, and the records must be considered as the most important rendering of Bach that is available on the gramophone.

The recording is of the highest quality, and the only criticism I have to offer of Mr. Goossens' conducting is that perhaps he allows his youthful exuberance rather to run away with him. The orchestra used, though considerably larger than that for which the concerto was written, is by no means large, and it is no doubt partly due to this wise limitation of size that the result is so clear and comprehensible. It would be an interesting experiment to record one of these concerti with the very small chamber orchestra of the period at which they were written.

HIS MASTER'S VOICE.—05714.—**Paderewski** (Pianoforte). **Hungarian Rhapsody, No. 10** (Liszt).

To anyone who has really heard Paderewski play the news that he has returned to the recording room will seem an event of the greatest importance. Those who know his playing only through the medium of the gramophone will be less interested, for they will remember the old records and how tedious they were to listen to—like an orchestra of banjos. But while Paderewski has been in the desert the technique of recording has improved, and his own has not declined nor his genius. He is still in most ways the greatest of living pianists, and he shows his powers to perfection in this Hungarian Rhapsody. Liszt was eminently a writer of pianistic music. He and Chopin, each in his own way, understood the possibilities of the piano as no one else has understood them. He has been reproached with turning the piano into an orchestra, but he showed that it was one of the characteristics of the piano that it could be turned into an orchestra, and half the later writers have imitated him. As recording this is one of the most successful reproductions of the piano tone. There is still just a trace of the old twang we know so well, but a judicious choice of needle and soundbox will reduce it, so that if one sits at a reasonable distance it is almost as if Paderewski himself were playing, not quite on a Steinway perhaps, but on that home-grown instrument which has done duty on most London concert platforms. And of how many piano records can one say so much ?

COLUMBIA.—L.1467, L.1468.—**Danzas Fantasticas** (Turina); **New Queen's Hall Orchestra conducted by Sir Henry Wood.**

Both Sir Henry Wood and the Columbia company are to be commended for these records of a composer almost unknown in this country. It is a relief to find conductors deserting the beaten track, even when they give us less charming things than these dances. For certain orchestral pieces creep into our collections like dry-rot. I take out a record of, say, the "Volga Boatmen's Song," and on the back I find "Coppelia," or of the Intermezzi from "Carmen," and without the least in the world wanting it, I find "Sylvia." It would be amusing to make a list of all the records available of the "Coppelia" and "Sylvia" music, the "Midsummer Night's Dream" overture and the Peer Gynt suite; and probably the end is not yet. The "Danzas Fantasticas" are unlike anything else that has been recorded. The Spanish idiom is unfamiliar in England, and these two excellent records of dances, which are really fantastic and really Spanish, should be in every representative collection of orchestral records. It is difficult to choose between the two, but on the whole I think I prefer the "Exaltacion."

HIS MASTER'S VOICE.—2-053208.—**Galli-Curci** (Soprano). **Un bel di Vedremo** from "**Madame Butterfly**" (Puccini).

One of the most solid grounds I have for facing the coming of old age with equanimity is the reasonable hope that I shall spend it listening to as many records of la diva Galli-Curci's voice as there are of Caruso's. With nearly 200 of her records old age will hold few terrors. It will be the coloratura records that I shall prefer. I shall want to hear her sing "Casta Diva" and the "Queen of the Night," music from the "Magic Flute" as well as those she has already sung so divinely—"Come per me sereno," "Ah non credea mirarti," "Una voce poco fa" and the rest. After the really shameful parsimony of the Master's Voice company during the first three months of 1923, I was a trifle disappointed to get "Un bel di vedremo," but when I listen to her exquisite singing of it I am almost persuaded to think she is equally perfect in this more dramatic style as in pure coloratura—almost persuaded, but not quite. It is an enchanting record, but I feel sure that I shall be even more enchanted when I hear "Casta Diva" or the "Queen of the Night" aria.

COLUMBIA.—1470.—**Prelude in A major ; Etude in G flat** (Chopin) ; **Prelude to Choral** (Bach-Busoni) ; **Scotch Slip** (Beethoven) ; **Busoni** (Piano).

No pianist expresses a more interesting personality than Busoni—interesting and disquieting. He has not the temperament of a Paderewski. It is a cynical and formidable intellect that deigns to communicate with us. Music, we feel, is one of the many possibilities of an exceptionally gifted intelligence, as painting was of Leonardo da Vinci. This man might have been a saint or a criminal or a mathematician ; it happens that he is a musician. His personality survives even the double mechanism of the piano and the gramophone. This record is particularly welcome as, owing to his serious illness, admirers have been disappointed of a concert he was to have given. The record represents the latest development of piano recording ; the scratch is almost entirely eliminated and the reproduction of the piano tone is much ahead of anything possible until recently.

The Instruments of the Orchestra :

COLUMBIA.—3198.—**Violin, Viola, 'Cello, Piccolo, Flute, Oboe.**

COLUMBIA.—3199.—**Cor Anglais, Clarinet, Bass Clarinet, Bassoon, Contra-Bassoon, French Horn.**

COLUMBIA.—3200.—**Trumpet, Cornet, Trombone, Bass Trombone, Tuba.**

It might be argued that too close an acquaintance with the technical details would be apt to interfere with our appreciation of music, that the proper attitude ought to be one of mere passivity, that the listener should allow the waves of sound to break over him without any effort to analyse or even think about what it is that affects him. Actually most of us are so constituted that unless our minds have something to occupy them while listening to music, our attention is apt to wander into a world of day-dreams where only the most rudimentary consciousness of the music survives. A certain preoccupation with the methods by which the musician produces his effects is the best corrective of this tendency to go wool-gathering. With even a moderate amount of study anyone with an average ear can acquire sufficient practical knowledge of harmony to recognise the commoner individual chords and modulations and to identify the various instruments of the orchestra. It is as an aid to the latter of these two studies that the records under review are designed and very well designed. The principle adopted is to play the same piece of music on each of the different instruments. It is true that the result on some of the instruments sounds rather odd—one would hardly expect a phrase to be equally suited to the bass tuba and the piccolo—but the method is I think on the whole the best for making clear the exact differences of timbre between the instruments. There exists another set of records made on the plan of choosing for each instrument a passage written to bring out its characteristic qualities. The enthusiastic and enterprising student is recommended to acquire both.

true. He had obtained the Crown lease to Herm and Jethou without really appreciating that the expenditure required was beyond his means; as a result he found himself negotiating the sale of Herm to Sir Percival Perry at much the same time as he was endeavouring to launch ***The Gramophone***, and in fact in July 1923 he moved across to Jethou, where he was to live until 1930. His biographer, Andro Linklater, estimated that in the three years during which he occupied Herm the island had consumed about £23,000 (or £345,000 in present-day money). In that time he wrote two books a year which should have earned him a minimum of £7,000 annually – free of tax, since Herm was not subject to UK taxes – but events conspired to reduce this figure substantially. As if this was not enough he was also trying to support his mother, Virginia Compton, who was on the verge of bankruptcy as a result

The island of Jethou with Guernsey in the background

The house on Jethou (1993) with Guernsey in the background

February 1924

EDITORIAL NOTES

The Editor has blandly expressed his intention of not contributing to the February and March numbers of ***The Gramophone***, on the ground that he exceeded the time-limit of his leisure so seriously over the Quarterly Review of Records in the January number that he is confronted with the unavoidable demands of the novel which he is now writing, and must on no account be disturbed till he has finished it. There is nothing for his faithful but incompetent Helots in the London Office to do but to apologize to our readers on his behalf, and to assure them that though he cannot write for this nor, probably, for the next number of ***The Gramophone***, nor yet answer any of his correspondents personally, he will continue his Musical Autobiography in the April number, and will accompany or follow the next instalment of it with articles on Chamber Music Records and on the Caruso Records.

If this is the Editor's idea of "gradually eliminating the personal element" from the pages of ***The Gramophone***, he has strangely mistaken the temper of his London staff. There are at least two sides to every question, and if Mr Compton Mackenzie glories in the independence of his island home at Jethou, and prides himself upon his immunity from the cares and fogs of London, and from the assaults of outraged readers and gramophonic bores, he will have to submit to the indiscretions of those equally independent henchmen who slave at 25 Newman Street. It is an opportunity which they cannot resist. Regardless of the consequences the incompetent Helots become, in a flash, formidable Robots.

Yevonde's portrait of Compton Mackenzie in the early 1920s

We therefore beg to present to you, gentle reader, a portrait of the Editor. You may like to have it as much as we think you will – or you may not. But that is immaterial. It is our gesture of malicious independence. The portrait is at any rate a good one, worthy of the great Yevonde; but we wish that it had been possible to obtain a photograph of the Editor in his kilt – somewhat in the style of a Raeburn – with the rocky background of his island; pipe in mouth, with one hand winding up his Orchestraphone, with the other commanding the waves to silence: his sheep-dog at his feet greedily devouring the latest number of ***The Gramophone***.

July 9th, 1925

THE GRAMOPHONE CONGRESS

This was the second of Compton Mackenzie's presentations and it took place in the Central Hall, Westminster – an all-day event running from 10am to 10.30pm. It was opened by Sir Richard Terry and attracted some 2,000 people. The Central Hall was occupied by a static exhibition supported by some 11 manufacturers, and between 5.30pm and 10.30pm the smaller Caxton Hall was used for a series of listening tests, using a range of acoustic reproducers, on which the audience were invited to vote.

The Gold Medal was won by the Orchorsol Junior – a table model priced at £10. The Silver went to the Dousona – a pedestal model at nine Guineas [£9·45] – and the Bronze to the EMG Model B at £25.

Stands in the Central Hall for the NGS and *The Gramophone*. Christopher Stone is seen, centre, holding a piece of paper

The Award presented to the Orchorsol Company in the form of a gold disc – suitably inscribed on one side and grooved on the other. Another 'first' for *The Gramophone*?

The Gramophone, October, 1925

In LIVERPOOL you can hear the Orchorsol at DAVIS' MUSIC STORES, 3, The Arcade, Lord Street.

In MANCHESTER you can hear the Orchorsol at MAURICE JOHNSTONE'S 100, Deansgate.

1200

models of the

ORCHORSOL

The Gold Medal Gramophone

have been sold and are giving perfect satisfaction in one thousand, two hundred homes all over the World—in the British Isles, in far Australia, Egypt, India, Ceylon, Penang and Jamaica the Orchorsol is their cherished possession, the chosen Gramophone for its unique musical performance. Perfect reproduction free from the slightest suggestion of the mechanical. One thousand, two hundred! A small number if mass production were the process, but remember, each Orchorsol is carefully made by hand and tested for days before despatch. Well-seasoned figured Oak or specially selected Mahogany is used for the handsome cabinets, the best British motor is fitted, and the correct co-ordination of the Sound Box, the Orchorsol Patent Tone Arm and Orchorsol Patent Amplifier, make an instrument recognised the best for the true reproduction of all classes of music.

Winners of Highest Honours at "The Gramophone" Tests, 1924 and 1925.

The consistent success of the Orchorsol in open competition sets up a record unequalled by any other Gramophone in the World. It is an achievement of which we are justifiably proud and convincing proof of the performance of the Orchorsol. If you have not heard it, let us send you a model on approval. There is no obligation save a few shillings return carriage (free in London) if you are not convinced of its superiority after 7 days' test.

THE ORCHORSOL MODELS.

Orchorsol Junior, Oak	£10 0 0
Model D.7, Oak	£15 15 0
,, C.8 Mahogany	£19 10 0
,, C.12 ,, ...	£36 15 0
,, E.10 ,, ...	£52 10 0

Any model purchasable on convenient "out of income" terms.

Model C 12.

Solid Mahogany Cabinet. Section with shelves stores 72 records in albums. Collaro Double Spring Motor, patent automatic stop. Height 42 ins. Width 19 ins. Depth 20½ ins.

35 Guineas.

ORCHORSOL GRAMOPHONE Co.
149, South Lambeth Road, London, S.W.8.
Telephone: Brixton 223.

of the failure of her repertory company in the Grand Theatre, Nottingham. Mackenzie even considered returning to the stage as a means of helping her.

To launch a magazine such as ***The Gramophone*** in those circumstances said an enormous amount for the calibre of the man, but one can also understand why, having set the wheels in motion, he was anxious to concentrate on matters of strategy rather than involve himself with the day-to-day operation of the business. As if to emphasize this point he was writing to Stone towards the end of 1923 saying, "My main object is to make ***The Gramophone*** by the end of 1925 a property that will bring in a reasonable income for you and Faith"[5].

Throughout his life he displayed an innate understanding of the enormous value of publicity and constantly turned this to ***The Gramophone***'s advantage. Initially, there was the article in *The Daily Telegraph*, then on June 14th, 1924 he instituted an evening of gramophone tests in London's Steinway Hall before a capacity audience of 400 enthusiasts who listened to a panel of judges, ranging from Percy Scholes to Marie Novello, Alec Robertson and Francis Brett Young, evaluating a series of reproducers which included the EMG (making its début), the Algraphone and a Decca portable. This exercise was repeated the following year when on July 9th a Gramophone Congress was held in the Central Hall,

Westminster from 10am to 10.30pm which attracted over 2,000 people. These two events were the forerunners of today's Audio Shows.

For many years he wrote regular articles in the national press discussing the latest gramophone records, always insisting that he was credited as Editor of *The Gramophone*. He also made the same stipulation when, on June 12th, 1924, he became the first person to present a formal programme of gramophone records on 2LO. It was suggested later that these broadcasts should become a regular feature but Mackenzie demurred, given the logistics of travelling from the Channel Islands. However, he did suggest that Christopher Stone should undertake these programmes, with initially the same credits to *The Gramophone*: these commenced on July 7th, 1927 and for the next 25 years were to establish Stone as one of the country's best-known broadcasters.

Beyond this there were his stimulating and often controversial editorials, together with the regular competitions with which he enlivened the pages, to say nothing of his pioneering launch of the National Gramophonic Society in 1924. At the end of that year he was briefly in London and wrote to Faith who was then back in Capri, "Our beloved *Gramophone* is getting all the credit for the music the recording companies are giving us. I must say I do feel a little proud of what we have managed to do in eighteen months"[1].

As the years progressed the paper's emphasis had to be more professional and progressively much of the 'enthusiastic amateur' approach was lost. This was regretted by many readers but it eased the conscience of the new professional contributors who often felt ill-at-ease with Mackenzie's opinions. He said on many occasions that had he listened to the experts he would never have started the magazine and confident in his success he wrote, "Fortunately I have been granted exceptional rapidity of assimilation ... I have also been granted normality of experience. It may be that in a certain number of months I shall accomplish in the adventures of taste what the average man accomplishes in the same number of years, but he and I are going to reach the same goal ultimately and the only difference is that I get there first." Thus spoke a man who believed in himself and his chosen vocation.

December 1923 **Editorial**

EDITORIAL INDEPENDENCE

I want to emphasize very strongly the complete independence of *The Gramophone*. I have heard rumours that we are subsidised by this or that large firm. I can assure my readers that the only person who subsidises this paper is myself. And I should like to emphasize once more the complete dissociation of the editorial staff from the advertisement staff. As critics we are not less fallible than all critics. We are apt to praise too highly and condemn too severely; but at any rate our praise and our blame are completely independent of our advertising columns. We are not a paper for the Trade. We are a paper for the Public; and I have myself been a servant of the public too long not to be aware by now of my responsibilities. At the same time I am in no danger of forgetting my very deep obligations to the Trade, and if in the future our paper can continue to be what I venture to hope that it is now, a real link between the Trade and the Public, I shall count it as a success.

In wishing both our readers and our advertisers a very merry and musical Christmas, I should like to add my personal thanks for the kindness and generosity of both, because, indeed, they have touched me very deeply. Nor must I (nor you, readers) forget to thank the staff and the contributors, who have given their services for nothing, or next door to nothing, and thus enabled me to preserve my independence of any financial help. If each reader will get us one new subscriber during the next year, I shall be able to pay both staff and contributors and myself. And at the same time, what is much more important, our influence will be *quadrupled*. You know what that will mean.

October 1923

PHYSICAL JERKS

We have received the "Birley Daily Physical Fitness" gramophone record (price 6s. [30p], including chart). It provides instructions and music for six minutes of physical jerks, one minute to each exercise, and after testing them on the office staff we can recommend Capt. Birley's exercises and methods as simple, effective and intelligible to even a beginner. Thus does the gramophone record spread its influence and help to the most grotesque moments of our daily life.

Price increases and further changes

Returning to those formative months in *The Gramophone*'s history one can see that editorially the concept was working well and from September 1923 there was steady progress both in terms of circulation and advertising sales. Even so, with overheads at a minimum

February 1924 **Correspondence**

WARPED RECORDS

This week I received from Chicago a most admirable portable gramophone, about which I shall soon have something to say. As usual with portables, the turntable is for a 10-inch record, but, of course, it will take a 12-inch record provided that the 12-inch record is absolutely true. I got out one of my albums of Galli-Curci, as I always do when any novelty arrives, and by chance put on Proch's *Air and Variations*. After listening for a moment it struck me that the variations were taking possession of the air, and I discovered that the record was warped and was therefore clicking against the side of the instrument. The next record was all right, the next four clicked. I began to choose records at random, and I found that about 60 per cent clicked. Why should some records warp and not others? Mine are all kept in the same way. The worst is yet to come. I picked up the Proch record to see where is was warped, and though I pressed it very lightly it broke in half, which put me in a damnable temper. I hope, Sir, that you will take the earliest possible opportunity to prefer a strong indictment against the recording companies on this count. In order to pay for a record of Galli-Curci I have to sell four copies of a novel, and I think I deserve one that is not warped. Suppose you were a warped critic?

Compton Mackenzie
Isle of Jethou, C.I.

Christopher Stone was writing, "We had no money for anything. No one took any salary and we all worked like slaves"[4]. A situation such as that could not persist indefinitely and in parallel with a 100 per cent increase in the cover price to one shilling [5p] in June 1924, there were also increases applied to the advertisement rates.

On August 30th, 1924 it was agreed to register a company, Gramophone (Publications) Limited, at 6 New Street, Guernsey, for the specific purpose of publishing the magazine. Christopher Stone was the Managing Director with Compton Mackenzie and Douglas Woodbine-Parrish (who had also invested capital in the Company) as his co-directors. For the next few months the business of the Company progressed satisfactorily and with the introduction of a number of ancillary publications ("Gramophone Tips", "The Book of Translations", etc.), the launch of the National Gramophonic Society [p. 44] and the introduction of "The Lifebelt" [p. 216], the financial situation began to improve. It was even proposed that the Company should undertake publication of the Dairy Shorthorn Association's journal!

In October 1924 Kemp, Chatteris, Nicholl, Sendall & Company were appointed as the Company's auditors and whilst an interim report in January 1925 suggested that their preliminary checking of the Company's accounts had been satisfactory, within 12 months they indicated "serious defalcations" on the part of the Company Secretary (who was dismissed on February 4th, 1926), together with a generally unsatisfactory financial situation. As Mackenzie was to write in 1967, "A young accountant from our firm of auditors gave a rather disturbing picture of the financial side of ***The Gramophone***. To our gratified surprise he said he would leave his own job and work for the paper in whose future he had confidence. In 1926 Cecil Pollard became business manager, and the position ***The Gramophone*** holds today is due to his enthusiasm, integrity and skill"[1]. Thus began an association with the Pollard family which currently spans three generations.

Cecil Pollard at the time of joining the Company in 1926

The magazine develops with the Industry

At the same time as ***The Gramophone*** was gradually finding its feet the record industry was evolving techniques which would provide the basis for the continuing development of the shellac disc over the next 25 years.

Whilst it was understandable that in the first issue of the magazine Mackenzie should refer to surface scratch – one of the bugbears of all shellac disc users – it was most percipient that he should write the following: "In my opinion by far the most encouraging product of the first quarter of 1923 is the new wax that the Columbia Company are using for all its records. When playing with the loudest needle I possess, the Cleopatra, there is less

August 1923 **Editorial**

If I were a despot, I would summon before me the leading chemists of the day; I would immure them in a completely equpped laboratory, and I would give them two years to eliminate the scratch from gramophone records.

Sir Compton Mackenzie

"Novelist, autobiographer and connoisseur of life", as his obituary in *The Times* put it, Compton Mackenzie was already a well-known figure by the time he came to launch *The Gramophone* in 1923

Compton Mackenzie in the "Pitchpine" room, Jethou

He was born Edward Montague Compton Mackenzie on January 17th, 1883 to a theatrical family – his father was actor/manager Edward Compton, whose own father, Charles Mackenzie, had taken the stage name of Henry Compton; his mother was the actress Virginia Bateman; his birthplace was West Hartlepool where his parents were currently on tour. After attending St Paul's School, he read History at Magdalen College, Oxford, and it was at Oxford that he met his future brother-in-law and co-editor of ***The Gramophone***, Christopher Stone.

His first novel was *The Passionate Elopement*, followed by many others including *Carnival*, *Sinister Street*, *Guy and Pauline* (1915), *Sylvia Scarlett* (1918) and *Sylvia and Michael* (1919). By 1914 he was regarded as one of the most promising of the young generation of English novelists whose most prominent member was D. H. Lawrence. Many of his later novels, however, were confessedly 'pot-boilers' or light comedies, the most famous of which, *Whisky Galore* (1947), was memorably filmed by Ealing Studios in 1949. Of all his vast output of novels, plays, histories, biographies, essays, children's stories and ten volumes of autobiography – over 100 in all – only three 'Scottish' novels are currently in print: *Monarch of the Glen*, *Whisky Galore* and *Rival Monster* (all published in a "Highland Omnibus" by Penguin).

During the First World War he was with the Royal Marines at Gallipoli, and then served as an intelligence officer in the Aegean (he was appointed head of counter-espionage in Athens under the codename "Z") – experiences that he later revealed in *Greek Memories*, the publication of which resulted in him being prosecuted under the Official Secrets Act in 1933.

Mackenzie moved several times during his life, and had a taste for islands. He and his wife Faith (sister of Christopher Stone) lived successively on the Italian island of Capri, the Channel Islands of Herm and Jethou, where he founded ***The Gramophone***, and the Hebridean island of Barra, where he espoused the cause of Scottish nationalism. In his final years he commuted between Edinburgh and his French house, Pradelles, Les Arques, Lot.

He married Faith in 1905 and after her death in 1960 he married twice more: first to Christina MacSween in 1962, and, after her death the following year, he married her sister Lilian in 1965.

He was knighted in 1952, and received several other honours including an honorary LLD from Glasgow University and a C.Lit from the Royal Society of Literature; in addition, he was the President of the Siamese Cat Club and also found time to be President of the Croquet Association. As guest presenter of the Wexford Gramophone Society in 1950 he suggested they put on live performances instead of just playing recordings of operas, and the Wexford Opera Festival was born the following year. As his obituary in *The Times* summed him up, Compton Mackenzie "began as an infant prodigy and ended as an octogenarian with the gaiety and undimmed zest for life of a teenager". He died on November 30th, 1972.

Extracts from Compton Mackenzie's "Musical Autobiography"

In the first issue of the magazine, the Editor Compton Mackenzie embarked on the serialization of his "Musical Autobiography", not, he noted, from motives of "vanity and egotism", but because he regarded himself as "a great sinner and like St Augustine of Hippo I feel I ought to pillory myself as a warning and an encouragement to the public". Opinionated and occasionally pompous, the memoir is always redeemed by a string of vivid anecdotes, the author's unfailing literary charm and a dash of self-deprecating wit.

April 1923

My earliest recollection of music dates to a month or so before my second birthday; and I hear, more remotely fine than the squeak of a bat, the faint crooning of nursery rhymes. But the pictures of those nursery rhymes are much more vivid to me now than the tunes to which they were sung; and I fancy that I must have soon tired of the singing, because before I was two years old I had learnt them all by heart and preferred reading them to myself to having them sung.

My first memory of a musical instrument is of the Pan-pipes played by a Punch and Judy showman at Lowestoft, followed immediately by the appearance of Punch, an apparition that affected me with such horror that I was led shrieking from the sands. The sound of Pan-pipes still affects me with a foreboding of some sinister event about to happen; and even now I never get from the cor anglais or the oboe the pastoral atmosphere I ought to get. Very soon after this experience with the pipes, on being taken to church by my mother for the first time in the town of West Hartlepool, where nearly three years earlier I had been born, I was invited by her to be silent and to listen to the organ.

"Organ?" I repeated incredulously; "Organ, but where is the monkey?"

This story is by now a desiccated chestnut, but I was the genuine originator of it. Clearly at that period sound did not mean much unless accompanied by some outward pictorial symbol.

Compton Mackenzie at the helm of his boat, "Watch Me", at Herm

Later, in London, Mackenzie recalls how music became a means of restoring his youthful self-confidence when his nurse, "who resembled the witch in *Hänsel and Gretel* or *Rapunzel*", made him take solitary walks through Earl's Court:

I used to support myself against my various terrors of being captured by gypsies, Fagins, and circus-proprietors by humming to myself all the way, and I am pretty sure that the song I hummed most was one called *White wings, they never grow weary*, which gave me my first spiritual uplift. *Hi-Tiddly-Hi-Ti* was a favourite about this period and was usefully optimistic; then there was *Get your hair cut*, which had a frightening second line: "There's a barber round the corner, and he's waiting for the order". This, I remember, struck me as an appalling thought, and the melody, which was a catchy one, gave me little pleasure in consequence. My enemies the reed pipes appeared again, played now by an extraordinary old man who wore a moleskin cap with no peak, a bright red waistcoat, and a very long tailcoat. But the strangest thing about him was that he was covered with white rats and mice. I was perfectly certain that he was the Pied Piper of Hamelin, and I expected every moment to be charmed away by his playing to that mysterious cave from which the children of Hamelin never returned. Even to this day there is a certain type of clean-shaven old gentleman with silvery stubble on his chin who affects me with a kind of sub-conscious fright.

September 1923

Whilst Mackenzie was an undergraduate at Oxford he rarely listened to music. Finally a day came when he resolved to make an effort towards musical appreciation:

When I left Oxford I went to live at Burford, where I spent a year in strict seclusion, only broken by going up to Oxford to rehearse and act in *The Clouds* of Aristophanes. The music for this was written by Sir Hubert Parry, and I believe that it contained some delightful parodies on modern music to accord with the spirit of Aristophanes' mockery of contemporary taste. It may have been my inability to appreciate the point of that music which made me wonder if it were not time that I applied some of my diversified energy to acquiring a taste and knowledge of music. I remember Sir Hubert Parry coming in to have tea with me one dusky afternoon. He was motoring down to Gloucestershire and stopped in Burford on the way. He sat down suddenly at the piano and began to play what I think must have been a skit on the music of Debussy's *Pelléas and Mélisande*. I know that we had been talking about Maeterlinck and that I had read him part of a parody I had just written, at which he

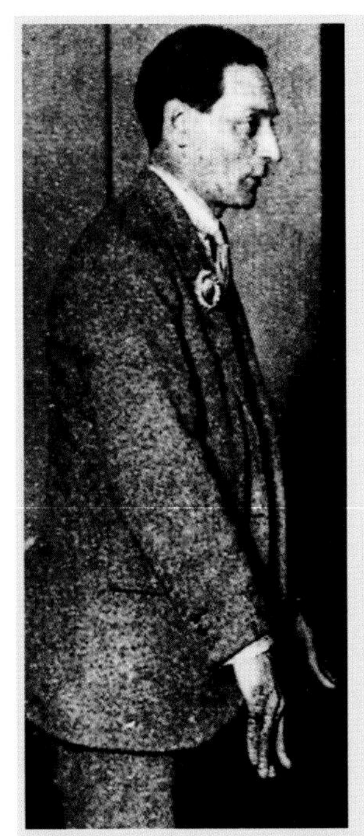

Compton Mackenzie addressing the Gramophone Congress, July 1925

had laughed heartily. It was so cold in the hall of "Lady Ham" that Parry would not take off his fur coat, but sat thumping away on the piano and roaring with laughter at some musical joke which, of course, I could not understand. It struck me then how kindly he had laughed at my jokes about Maeterlinck, and I felt ashamed that I could not appreciate his jokes. I believe that this was the actual moment when I decided that I had got to learn something about music. What a delightful man he was, and it was so surprising to hear somebody who looked and talked like an Admiral eloquent about music and literature.

November 1923

Remembrance of his first visit to the Promenade concerts, then held at Queen's Hall under Sir Henry Wood's direction, elicited a comparison between then (1903) and now (1923):

I write these words fresh from revisiting the Promenade concerts after a long interval of years. Beyond the fact that it now costs twice as much to stand in the Promenade as in days gone by, and that I could no longer perceive an egg-headed oboe player whose humptiness-and-dumptiness was always curiously accentuated by the expression forced upon it by his instrument I could detect no change. The very coffee that was served in the bar during the interval might have been brewed twenty years ago and warmed up for the evening. As for Sir Henry Wood he looked if anything younger than twenty years ago; and when one evening Sir Edward Elgar's thrilling arrangement of Bach's great fugue in C minor for orchestra was applauded and applauded again and Sir Henry Wood turning to the audience announced that he would have great pleasure in giving an encore of the piece in a few days' time, I felt that if he had announced that he would have great pleasure in giving an encore of the fugue five hundred years hence, he would not have been overestimating either his longevity or his youthfulness. I suddenly remember that there is one great change in the orchestra which I have only just realized, and that is the introduction of a number of women in the strings. I cannot pretend that this innovation delights me any more than it delights me to see Oxford profaned – I will use no weaker word – by petticoated undergraduates who ride ungracefully on bicycles and wear black sponge-bags upon their heads. If women are going to play in orchestras, I do wish that they would not wear low-necked dresses and leave their arms bare, for by so doing they destroy all the beautiful black and white austerity that ought to make an orchestra resemble an immense pianoforte come to life. Incidentally I noticed with disapproval that several of the male players were dressed more suitably for golf than for music. This may seem fractious criticism: but the loss of external decorum implies a deplorable indifference to form which is our besetting sin in modern art. I should not mind the orchestra's donning tweeds, or even pyjamas, to play most contemporary music; but I do strongly object to Bach in anything but the orthodox black and white of evening-dress.

Compton Mackenzie and Hamlet at Herm

July 1924

After a dissertation on humour, and Beethoven's dramatic gifts, the Autobiography concludes with some strictures on a 'modern' composer:

I owe Strauss a particlar grudge. Soon after I had been enjoying the [Beethoven] C minor orchestrally, it was my misfortune to hear one of the first performances in England of *Till Eulenspiegel's Merry Pranks*. I heard the same audience that cheered the C minor cheer what seemed to me a pandemonium of unpleasant noise. I read the programme and was infuriated by what it claimed that the music was doing. Do I not recall that a twirl on the oboe represented the rope being put around Till's neck? Bah! I would as soon spend an afternoon listening to three little boys each trying to outbelch the other. My experience of Strauss discouraged me, for my enjoyment of the Fifth Symphony was beginning to appear as an accident. However, I made one more attempt and went to hear the *Eroica* which I had already played over to myself many times on the Aeolian. It bored me to death. It was as if the cacophony of Strauss had cast upon me an evil spell. It is strange to think that when after an interval of twenty years I heard *Till Eulenspiegel's Merry Pranks* for the second time it seemed to me just a string of tawdry and very obvious melodies. I wonder at what point in those twenty years I should have enjoyed that symphonic poem. I shall never know. I passed it as a train passes a striking bit of scenery in the night.

scratch on the new Columbia records than there used to be on their old records with the softest needle in existence. Moreover, what scratch there is has no quality of harshness, and is not much more than the light crackle of a gently burning fire. The two records they have produced of the Léner Quartet of Budapest are really superb (Columbia); apart from the almost noiseless wax, the recording is magnificent and the interpretation of a linked sweetness."

This immediately prompted a telephone call from Columbia's Herbert Ridout who asked, for reasons he could not disclose, that for the next four months no reference should be made to this reduction in surface noise on their records. On the basis that no one else seemed to have noticed the difference this was a frustrating request, but Mackenzie acceded until on September 14th, 1923 the new Columbia "Grafonola" was launched by Sir Henry Wood before an audience of 400 at The Connaught

December 1925 **News**

REVIEWS

The number of records issued seems to increase. Columbia and HMV between them are responsible for about a hundred a month, while Parlophones and Vocalions are not far behind. Now Polydors have entered the lists, so to speak; and more space is claimed by the reviewers. We try to deal fairly with all the records sent in; and it should be clearly understood that if a record is not mentioned it may be assumed to be not worth buying. This applies equally to records which are not sent to *The Gramophone* for review; for all the makers of records have been invited to submit their wares to our reviewers; and if some have declined the invitation, or have ceased to accept it, our readers are justified in drawing a logical inference; and since the object of *The Gramophone* from the outset has been to help the public to buy wisely, without fear or favour, it strengthens our power for good whenever a reader declines to consider the purchase of any record which has not at the least been mentioned in the reviews.

***The Gramophone* very quickly established itself as a forum for the exchange of views, as the following correspondence indicates**

DAME CLARA BUTT AND HMV

September 1923

I would be obliged if you would give the following letter prominence in your paper:

In their May supplement The Gramophone Co. Ltd., listed a record of mine, *Il segreto*. This record was made about twelve years ago and was never passed by me as fit for publication and in my opinion it is not so.

More recently The Gramophone Co. have listed in their July supplement a record by me, *Caro mio ben*, which was one of the first records I made for that Company about sixteen years ago.

Announced as these records are among others in The Gramophone Co.'s monthly supplements, I feel that despite any reference to the date on which they were recorded, the greater proportion of the public may accept them as representing my present work.

It is eight years now since I made any records for The Gramophone Co., as during those eight years my services for new recordings have been exclusively retained by the Columbia Graphophone Co., Ltd., whose records of mine I consider are the best reproductions of my voice.

I desire the general public and your readers in particular to understand that the above-mentioned records are issued at this time without my consent, and I would ask my public not to judge me by these records.

Clara Butt-Rumford
London, NW3

October 1923

In the September number of *The Gramophone* you published a letter from Dame Clara Butt, referring to certain records made by her, recently issued by us, from which the impression might be formed that they were so brought out as new recordings by this artist.

As a matter of fact, we were particularly careful to make it clear that this was not the case, and the following statement was printed in our May Supplement:

"Special interest attaches to this record (*Il segreto per esser felici*) as it was made by Dame Clara Butt in Germany before the War, and the 'master' record, which was detained by the German authorities, has only recently been handed over to us."

Dame Clara Butt also states that the record of *Caro mio ben* which we issued in July, was one of the first she made for us, but upon reference to our books, we find that it was recorded in Berlin at the same time as *Il segreto per esser felici* and a few other titles, the 'master' records of which were detained by the German authorities.

With regard to the quality of the recordings referred to, our experts are too jealous of the reputation of the Company to pass any record for issue which does not reach the very high standard we have set, and the public, who, after all, must be the final judges, have accorded the records such an enthusiastic reception as leaves no doubt about their being in thorough agreement with the opinion of our experts.

W. Manson *Manager (English Branch)*
The Gramophone Co. Ltd. Hayes, Middx.

The Gramophone, October, 1923

Rooms. At the same time they introduced their "New Process" shellac discs (a new 'core' to the disc) and it was this Mackenzie had recognized in his April review. Understandably, Columbia were anxious that the introduction of new technology did not totally invalidate their existing catalogue, and within two years a similar situation was to face all companies as they introduced electric recording.

The early issues of the magazine quickly established it as a forum for the exchange of views on a wide range of subjects hitherto unrepresented. Matters of repertoire and artists on the one hand but, perhaps surprising to today's readers, a far greater general interest in the whole question of actually reproducing the records. The 'technology' involved was simple and comprehensible to all, and the wide variation in the quality of sound was easily recognized. It therefore followed that there was much discussion about the relative merits of the various reproducers and sound-boxes, the durability of the spring-driven motors, the various types of needles, the use of special horns, etc. With the publication in September and October 1924 of two articles on needle alignment by Percy Wilson, as relevant in the 1980s as they were in the 1920s [p. 246], *The Gramophone* established a more professional approach to technical matters, thus paralleling the changes which were taking place elsewhere in the magazine.

The Expert Committee

Percy Wilson, who but for a break during the war years served as technical adviser from 1924 to 1966, established the Expert Committee in November 1924 at the suggestion of Christopher Stone. Initially, this consisted of H. F. V. Little (at the time chief chemist of Thorium Ltd., a contributor to the magazine and an opera buff), George Webb (a builder whose hobby was gramophones), C. L. Balmain (designer of gramophone horns and Deputy Controller of H. M. Stationery Office) and Lionel Gilman and William Wild (neither specifically qualified but both writers of forceful letters to the Editor!). Later, with the coming of electric recording, four additional members were co-opted from the National Physical Laboratory at Teddington and all were to become heads of their respective departments – Heat, Electricity, Metrology and Acoustics. Thus the Expert Committee was ideally equipped to guide the editors and the readers through the complex months ahead when electric recording and reproduction would replace the old and trusted acoustic techniques. For everyone this was to be a major milestone.

Mackenzie wrote, "By the beginning of 1928 it was clear that the old sound-box was doomed and that its place would soon be taken everywhere by the electric pick-up. No doubt, for a time the old battles would be waged by the supporters of this or that pickup but the introduction of electricity would put many of us out of the contest at the start. I looked at my big Balmain horn – the old Balmain pagoda as I used to call it – which glided along in a bath of mercury and had given me the best reproduction available as yet with the various sound-boxes whose merits and demerits were for ever discussed. I looked at the Lifebelt sadly, recognizing that soon its day would be past. P. Wilson, who had come down to Jethou as the representative of our Expert Committee

When *The Gramophone* celebrated its Silver Jubilee on June 16th, 1948 Percy Wilson (left) was reunited with two members of the Expert Committee, William Wild (centre) and George Webb (right)

and had endorsed my enthusiasm about that little gadget [p. 216], had gone over completely to electric reproduction. I felt I must try to follow him, but though I wrote with apparent light-heartedness about the future I knew that some of the fun of the gramophone for me was gone, because I should never be able to understand how a pickup worked"[2].

Frith Street

By September 1924 the growing size of the operation necessitated a move to new offices at 58 Frith Street in the south-west corner of Soho Square. In the June 1925 issue Christopher Stone wrote, "A year ago the London office was in a fourth-floor maisonette in Newman Street, but now at 58 Frith Street one wonders how we ever managed at all at Newman Street. On the ground floor, with a fine basement, in an eighteenth-century house containing remarkable mantle-pieces and a staircase with a beautiful top-light, the offices are convenient and adequate. We have good neighbours – a restaurant on one side, a picture gallery on the other. Mozart once lodged in Frith Street and already we are beginning to convince ourselves that it must have been at Number Fifty-eight. But the Editor says that it was Number Seven." (Actually the Editor was wrong, later references in the February 1926 issue indicated that in 1764 the Mozarts lodged at No. 21 Thrift Street, the original name of Frith Street. No. 21 was rebuilt in 1858.)

This photograph shows one of the offices at 58 Frith Street, the London office of the magazine from September 1924 until September 1929 when it was moved to 10a Soho Square

A kilted Compton Mackenzie with his Balmain gramophone

The end of the 1920s

The remaining years were by no means uneventful as the editors developed the magazine and endeavoured to project it in the directions indicated by both the readers and the various manufacturers.

Until the early 1970s the repertoire covered in the pages of *The Gramophone* embraced the total output of the record industry. For much of that time music was not subject to the divisions which we know today, and whilst the reviews favoured the 'serious' repertoire there was substantial coverage of popular music, and eventually of "Jazz and Swing". In the circumstances it was not surprising that comprehensive coverage had soon to give way to a degree of selectivity.

Herman Klein

W. R. Anderson

The all-important panel of contributors was progressively strengthened and an early acquisition had been Herman Klein who was then the doyen of opera critics and probably the greatest living authority on the art of singing. He had heard Tietjens in 1866 and was a close friend of Benedict (who had met Beethoven). He was the principal opera critic from June 1924 until his death in March 1934. Other names appeared which were to grace our pages for years to come – they included Alec Robertson, W. R. Anderson, Peter Latham, W. A. Chislett, W. S. Meadmore, Roger Wimbush, C. M. Crabtree, P. G. Hurst and Richard Holt. Beyond this the editors were now able to attract articles from more than just the eminent men of letters who had supported Mackenzie at the outset. Artists such as Anthony Bernard, Josef Lhevinne, George Baker, Gracie Fields, Joseph Szigeti, John Barbirolli and

C. M. Crabtree

Christopher Stone

Joint Editor of *The Gramophone* and brother-in-law of Compton Mackenzie, Christopher Reynolds Stone was born on September 19th, 1882. He was the youngest son of The Revd Edward Daniel Stone, an assistant master at Eton who later founded his own school, "Stonehouse" at Broadstairs in Kent. Stone was educated at Eton and Christ Church College, Oxford, where he was a scholar, graduating in 1905. At Oxford he met Compton Mackenzie, then an undergraduate at Magdalen College, and for a time they shared "Lady Ham", a house in Burford. In 1908 Stone married Mrs Alyce Chinnery, a widow some 20 years his senior, and devoted himself to writing. His first novel, *Scars*, was published in 1907, followed by *The Noise of Life* (1910), *They Also Serve* (1910), *The Shoe of a Horse* (1912) and a volume of poetry and prose, *Lusus* (1909)

In his office in Soho Square

In September 1914 he enlisted as a private in the 16th Battalion, The Middlesex Regiment (Public Schools Battalion), and in the following year was commissioned as a Second Lieutenant in the 22nd Battalion, Royal Fusiliers. He was awarded the Distinguished Service Order and the Military Cross for acts of gallantry, was three times mentioned in dispatches, and had been promoted to Major, Second-in-Command by February 1918, when the regiment was disbanded. He was then appointed to the staff of the 99th Infantry Brigade, and finished the war as Aide-de-Camp to Major-General Pereira, Commanding Officer of the 2nd Division.

Christopher Stone, an inveterate pipe-smoker

After the war, Stone resumed his writing career, finishing a novel he had begun in 1914 – *The Rigour of the Game* (1920) – and publishing two more based on his wartime experiences – *The Valley of Indecision* (1920) and *Flying Buttresses* (1921). He also wrote *BB* (1919), a memoir of his former Commanding Officer, Randle Barnet-Barker, and edited the *History of the 22nd Battalion, Royal Fusiliers* (1923).

It was whilst he was acting as London Editor for *The Gramophone* that Stone was approached by the BBC to present a programme of gramophone records (the offer was initially made to Compton Mackenzie, but given the logistics of travelling from the Channel Islands he demurred). Stone's first broadcast, on July 7th, 1927, attracted some 6,000 letters from listeners and led to his later being known as "the first disc-jockey" – a title which he disliked. As his obituary in *The Times* was to put it, "he set a fashion in broadcasting and pioneered the curious and exclusive profession based on the simple act of spinning a disc on a turntable and talking amiably and informatively about it". Because of his refusal to use a script, Stone's microphone manner was refreshingly informal, much helped by his endearing habit of making mistakes on air. *The Times* obituarist commented: "He faced the once unfamiliar microphone with a happy blend of casualness, tolerance and good humour, which British audiences by nature found most engaging." Stone said later, "I never had any words written down. I insisted on being free to meander along in my own fashion and tell a few personal stories prompted by the records I played".

Stone became a radio celebrity in the 1930s, and was paid the grand sum of £5,000 a year by Radio Luxembourg – an arrangement, however, that resulted in him being dropped from the BBC in 1935, although he resumed his BBC work in 1939, and also appeared on television in the 1950s: his final record programmes were made for the South African Broadcasting Corporation in the mid-1950s. He published an autobiography, *Christopher Stone Speaking*, in 1933.

Stone's wife, Alyce, died in 1945, and he eventually retired to Eton; he died on May 22nd, 1965 aged 82.

In the June 1927 issue Christopher Stone offered this portrait of life on Compton Mackenzie's island

AT JETHOU

At the last moment the Editor has failed with the review of records which should have appeared in this number. As usual, illness is the cause, and this has followed a time of severe strain. One assumes that, as in the early days of ***The Gramophone***, so now our readers like to hear the personal aspect of our activities, and will regard with an indulgent eye the domestic picture presented herewith and a brief description of a visit which I paid to Jethou. I arrived at Guernsey in time to see the last performance of *The School for Scandal* by the newly-formed amateur society of the island. The Editor was not only playing Charles Surface, but had been directing the rehearsals for weeks beforehand; and the performance was, as *The Tatler* said, "unquestionably one of the best amateur productions anywhere of recent years". The credit was very largely his.

The next day we crossed to the island of Jethou, and I was able to enjoy two things which I had never seen before – the garden in all its glory and the new library, which the carpenter – a genius of a carpenter – had built during the last twelve months. It is completely lined with books, which give it an atmosphere of having been lived in for ages; as many books as there are gramophone records perhaps, enough to fill a life-time with fine music and fine literature.

While staying on the island I never knew what time or day it was. There were clocks which ticked and newspapers galore; but the times and dates which they suggested had no relevance. Meals appeared every now and then; one talked and walked in what seemed a timeless daylight; at one moment we were summoned to the top of the island to take part in sports, at another we were dancing in the library to the gramophone; at another the Editor was reading his new play to us; at another lying prone on a couch listening to the test prints of the NGS Ravel records. But whatever happened it was perfect weather, perfect companionship, perfect food; even the army of Siamese cats seemed a natural feature of the quiet fantastic island; and when, in the banality of the London office I remember the race of the tide between Crevichon and Jethou and the cry of the oyster catchers in the night, the view of Herm and Sark from the wood, and the foison of the walled garden in still sunlight, I wonder why we ever get any editorial contributions to ***The Gramophone***.

Christopher Stone, Compton Mackenzie, Félicité Ross (Stone's step-daughter) and Faith Compton Mackenzie in the Library built by MacDonald, Mackenzie's boat-man

Faith Compton Mackenzie

Wife of Compton Mackenzie and sister of Christopher Stone, Faith assisted her brother in the London office of *The Gramophone* and contributed to the magazine under the pseudonym F Sharp

She was born on February 28th, 1878 and was five years older than her husband, who ascribed the success of their long marriage to "the ability of each to lead his or her life in mutual respect based on years of friendship". An accomplished pianist, Gerald Moore described her as the best accompanist he had ever known. Another interest was acting, and before her marriage she had toured in the United States and in London had played at the Avenue Theatre with Charles Hawtrey. She also took up drawing and sculpture, before writing novels, biographies, three volumes of autobiography and many contributions to *The Gramophone*, including a series of essays on Rossini, Donizetti, Bellini and Verdi. She died on July 9th, 1960 at the age of 82.

Alec Robertson, in the obituary he wrote for the August 1960 issue of the magazine described her thus: "This tall, handsome and gracious woman was one of those rare people who took a vital interest in the doings of her large and assorted company of men and women friends, but rarely talked about herself. Sir Compton once told me that she might well have made her name as a pianist, and she shared her musical gifts with two other members of her family, Frank and Lucy Stone, one a cellist, the other a violinist. Sir Compton mentions in his book, *My Record of Music*, that their playing of Mendelssohn's Piano Trio in D minor first showed him how enjoyable chamber music could be. I do not remember Faith ever talking about her piano playing, but she could not conceal the fact that she was an excellent writer. Among her books were biographies of *Christina of Sweden*, *Marie Mancini* and *William Cory*, three very enjoyable autobiographcial volumes, *As Much As I Dare*, *More Than I Should* and *Always Afternoon*, and *The Crooked Wall*, one of a number of novels, which won a choice from The Book Society.

Faith Compton Mackenzie on the Shiants, Hebrides

Faith Compton Mackenzie at *The Gramophone*'s Silver Jubilee party in June 1948

"When we talked about Italy, and especially about her music and her people, Faith shed her reserve and curious elusiveness and we ended our conversation, usually, in a passion of nostalgia."

Faith Compton Mackenzie provided this charming portrait of gramophonic evenings at "Casa Solitaria" on Capri for the March 1925 number of the magazine

IL FOX

DANCING AT CAPRI

By F Sharp

In Capri there is only one danceable wooden floor as far as I know, and that is seldom available, owing to its owner's absence for ten months in the year. So we dance on the tiles, so to speak. Italian houses generally have tiled floors, and our studio is no exception, but the floor is so well laid that it is possible to dance almost as smoothly as on parquet, though it is, of course, heavier. A little French chalk, however, does wonders.

Outside the studio is a large terrace which is really the roof of the rest of the house. Here we sit under the moon, and dance too, but the terrace surface is incurably rough. However, it is not bad to dance under an open sky with great limestone cliffs towering above you and the Tyrrhenian sea lapping the rocks three hundred sheer feet below – in the solitary house set in the very arms of nature at its most impressive, and sometimes most terrifying. White and austere it faces bravely as the rocks the fierce onslaught of the elements. Wild south-west winds have screamed and crashed round its casements, hailstones bigger than cherries have stampeded against its panes – thunder, deafening as cannon, has rolled and echoed, roared and re-echoed round the vast cliffs.

All the more wonderful, therefore, is the undisturbed calm in which this house is wrapped for so many months of the year, and no one who has danced here in the midst of such fantastic beauty is ever likely to forget it, bathed in moonlight or crowned with dazzling stars.

The 'surface noise' of the gramophone is drowned in the shrill of *grilli*, those mysterious insects whose ecstatic chant recalls the pre-war after-theatre hour, and fills the mountain side with a clamour of unsatisfied cab whistles. I call it a chant – but I believe it is done with the hind legs. At any rate it is effective, and if we could express ourselves as clearly in the dance we should do well enough!

"Casa Solitaria", Capri

Some wear sandals and bare feet, rather a dangerous proceeding unless you are very sure of your partner – and some are vain or polite enough to carry evening shoes and change from the rope soles that you must wear along the mountain path that leads to the house. Rope shoes are not elegant, but they are less tiring on the tiled floor than the thin evening sole which is generally affected by owners of the fine ankles which Mr Harry Melvill so justly admires. No one wants to wear stiff collars and 'boiled' shirts in Capri – they are symbols of conventions we come to Capri to forget. Men are best and happiest in white, women in whatever they feel like wearing. It is never a 'dance' – we just dance, and often till sunrise, because on moonlit nights the dawn is so imperceptible that before we know what is happening the sun is up and the moon is setting, very large and pink over a silent sea that seems to be a solid mass of emeralds, rubies and sapphires, with a fire-opal here and there. A school of dolphins will sometimes appear down below at dawn and make a contemptuous display of indolent grace which makes us feel rather painstaking and fussy.

Cecil Pollard

Cecil Pollard in 1952

Cecil Pollard, whose business acumen played such a crucial role in the success of ***The Gramophone***, was born in London on April 28th, 1899, the eldest son of the family (he had a younger brother and two sisters). He left school aged 14 and went to work as a messenger boy and clerk. In 1917 he enlisted in the Artists' Rifles, and was later commissioned in the Queen's Royal West Surrey Regiment, before being invalided out of the army the following year. In 1925 he married Nellie Elizabeth Goddard, and was articled to an accounting firm, where he qualified as ACA. After carrying out an audit of ***The Gramophone***, he was invited to join the Company as business manager in 1926, where he remained until his death on September 14th, 1965 at the age of 66. Ownership of the company passed into the hands of the Pollard family in 1950, where it remains with his son Anthony and his grandson, Christopher. His main leisure pursuits were golf and gardening.

Compton Mackenzie paid him this tribute in the October 1965 issue: "His most remarkable achievement was the way he carried ***The Gramophone*** through the last war. I still marvel at it. To the very end of that long illness borne with much courage Cecil Pollard kept his hand on the financial tiller. He was regarded with the greatest respect by everybody in the gramophone world, and I know that the men who direct the destinies of the gramophone will feel almost as sharp a sense of personal loss as I feel myself. The greatest penalty of old age is to outlive friends we have loved."

The following month Roger Wimbush wrote, "as an old contributor perhaps I may be allowed to express what I am sure must be in the minds of those colleagues who knew Cecil Pollard. He was, of course, a management man, but he knew better than anybody that the success of a paper like ***The Gramophone*** ultimately depends on the level of its critical writing. Not only did he make it his business to engage eminent music critics but, what was equally important, he maintained the liveliest interest in them. He saw to it that ***The Gramophone*** was a good paper to work for, and he has left us with a personal legacy of friendship as well as an established journal, which is respected throughout the world".

Malcolm Sargent wrote of their various interests: Stanley Chapple (Vocalion) talked about the making of records: the subject of syncopation and 'jazz' was aired by Jack Hylton, Fred Elizalde and Bert Ambrose: and Alfred Clark, Managing Director of The Gramophone Company spoke about "Forty years of the gramophone". In October and November 1928 there was also the first article (in two parts) to be written in the magazine by the young Walter Legge on his idol, Titta Ruffo. (In a letter to me in January 1978, a year before his death, Legge wrote of a recent visit to Ruffo's son in Rome and as a result asked if I could let him have photocopies of the article, "the first piece I ever wrote ... It was very long – two instalments – and I was the proudest youngster in Christendom to see my name in print in your columns, and a week or two later to receive a cheque signed by Christopher [Stone].")

The Expert Committee were contributing monthly reports on the latest electric reproducers, discussing recording speeds and conducting tests on 18 different types of steel needles with magnified photographs showing varying degrees of tip wear, etc., whilst Percy Wilson wrote frankly about the technical shortcomings of reproducing electric recordings.

The correspondence columns were always a source of interest and controversy, and it now became clear just how far the influence of the magazine was spreading outside of the UK, with readers writing from Australia, Baluchistan, Canada, China, France, Greece, Hong Kong, India, New Zealand, North and South America, Romania, South Africa and Spain. And for the December 1927 issue the basic cover was replaced by a three-colour design incorporating a drawing of Harlequin and Columbine – a sign of things to come.

Developments prior to 1939

1929-1938

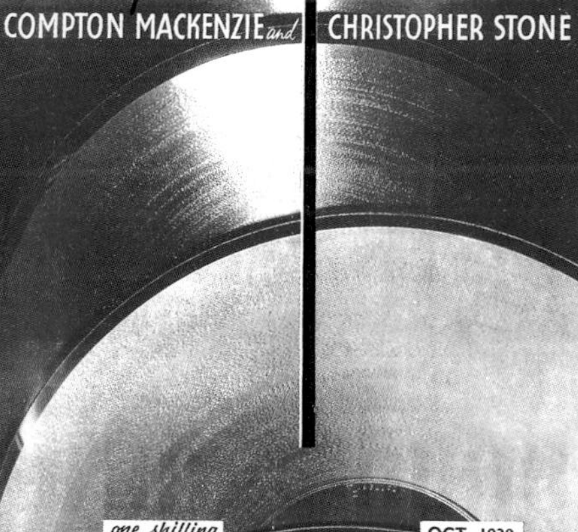

A *Gramophone* chronology

1929-1938

1929

January

- RCA acquires the Victor Talking Machine Company.

March

- Alan Blumlein joins the Technical Department of the Columbia Graphophone Company.

April

- G. W. Cook joins the Technical Department of the Columbia Graphophone Company.

July

- C. H. Thomas joins the Columbia Graphophone Company.
- First release of recordings from The Decca Record Company, under the direction of Edward Lewis, which include Delius's *Sea Drift* with Roy Henderson, Grainger's *Jutish Melody* and *Offenbach's Orpheus in the Underworld* Overture.

September

- *TG* moves to 10a Soho Square.
- L. G. Wood joins The Gramophone Company.

November

- Gilbert Wilson, brother of Percy, appointed Technical Editor of *TG*.
- Edison Company cease issue of cylinder and diamond discs.

C. H.Thomas *Photo EMI*

L. G. Wood *Photo EMI*

Gilbert Wilson

The Gramophone, February, 1929

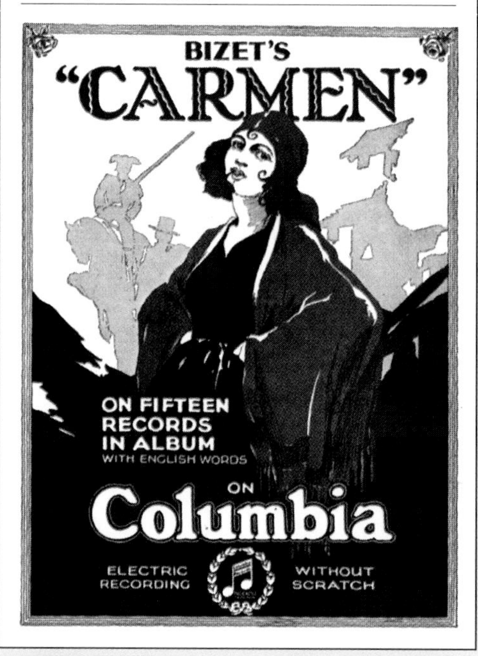

BIZET'S
"CARMEN"
ON FIFTEEN RECORDS IN ALBUM
WITH ENGLISH WORDS
ON
Columbia
ELECTRIC RECORDING
WITHOUT SCRATCH

1930

May

- First release in Columbia's "History of Music" series, eventually comprising five sets containing 40 10-inch 78rpm discs.

June

- Edgar Jackson joins *TG* to review jazz records.

September

- Alfred Clark becomes Chairman of The Gramophone Company, while still retaining his position as MD.

October

- Formation of the BBC Symphony Orchestra, the first permanent London orchestra since the foundation of the London Symphony Orchestra in 1904. The new orchestra make their début in the Queen's Hall.

December

- Compton Mackenzie leaves Jethou.

1931

April

- The Gramophone Company and the Columbia Graphophone Company merge to form Electric and Musical Industries Limited – EMI. Louis Sterling is appointed MD and Alfred Clark Chairman.
- HMV introduce the first of their Society Editions, conceived by Walter Legge – Elena Gerhardt singing Wolf Lieder.

September/November

- RCA launch a short-lived series of 10- and 12-inch 33⅓rpm discs in USA. These include Beethoven's Symphony No. 5 with Stokowski and the Philadelphia Orchestra – the first symphony to be specially recorded for this medium.

November

- EMI open their new Abbey Road Studios (Chief Engineer, W. S. Barrell; Manager, W. S. Purser) with Elgar conducting the LSO.

December

- A. D. Blumlein (EMI) takes out British Patent No. 394, 325 embracing all aspects of two-channel stereo recording.

Alan Blumlein *Photo EMI*

1932

- Garrard introduce first separate automatic record-changer, model RCI.
- Bell Laboratories use "Oscar", a tailor's dummy, to make binaural recordings.

February

- Christopher Stone appointed Co-Editor of *TG*.

April

- BASF and AEG, in collaboration with Fritz Pfleumer, produce magnetic tape in Germany.

May

- Harry Sarton joins Decca as A&R Manager.

October

- First concert by the newly formed London Philharmonic Orchestra under Beecham in Queen's Hall.

1933

February

- First American symphony recorded by American Columbia – Roy Harris's Symphony No. 1 by Koussevitzky and the Boston Symphony Orchestra.

The Gramophone, December, 1929

May

- Robin Legge, music critic, dies.

September

- Anna Instone joins BBC Gramophone Department.

1934

January

- Beecham and the LPO make experimental stereo recording for EMI of Mozart's *Jupiter* Symphony, using Blumlein's system.

March

- Herman Klein dies aged 78.

The Gramophone, August, 1929

An Important Announcement

We wish to draw the attention of all Zonophone enthusiasts to the fact that we are now including each month in our supplementary lists a number of electrical re-recordings of records which have proved consistent favourites as old recordings in our catalogue. These re-issues can be accepted as the last word in brilliance and style, and the artistes in every case are of typically high repute.

MANUFACTURED AT HAYES, MIDDLESEX, BY THE GRAMOPHONE CO. LTD. (HIS MASTER'S VOICE)
THE BRITISH ZONOPHONE COMPANY LTD., HAYES, MIDDLESEX

June

- HMV make the first recordings in the new Glyndebourne Opera House with concerted items from Morart's *Le nozze di Figaro* under Fritz Busch, with the arias being recorded the following year.

The Gramophone, March, 1930

August

- Decca Records Inc., a subsidiary of The Decca Record Company, founded in New York.

October

- RCA introduce the first record club in USA.
- The term 'high fidelity' comes into use in record and equipment advertisements.
- First release in series "L'Anthologie Sonore" in France which eventually comprised over 150 78rpm discs.

1935

- George Fenwick, who joined The Gramophone Company in 1911, working in the Cabinet Factory, is appointed manager of the famous 363 Oxford Street showrooms.

October

- Decca record their first complete opera, Purcell's *Dido and Aeneas*, with 20-year-old Nancy Evans in the title-role.

George Fenwick

The Gramophone, May, 1930

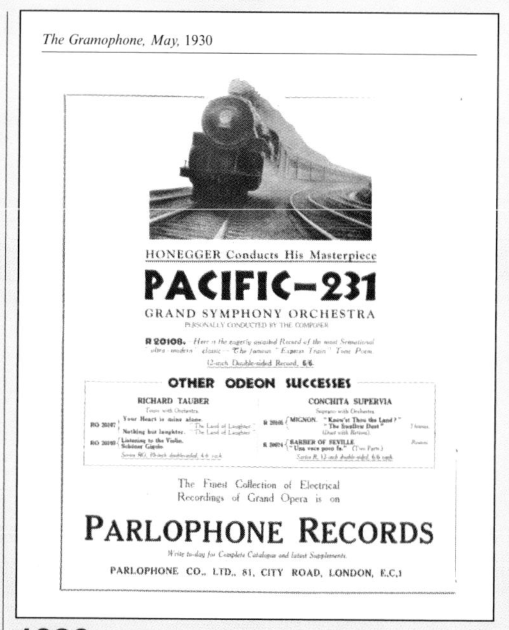

1936

July

- National Federation of Gramophone Societies (later Federation of Recorded Music Societies) formed by W. W. Johnson and F. E. Young.

November

- BASF record Beecham and the LPO in concert at Ludwigshafen on magnetic tape.
- The British Broadcasting Corporation opens the world's first regular television service from Alexandra Palace, London.
- The first edition of *The Gramophone Shop Encyclopedia of Recorded Music* by R. D. Darrell is published. Further editions appear in 1942 and 1948.

1937

March

- Decca purchase the Crystalate Company, and with it their recording studios at 165 Broadhurst Gardens, West Hampstead, together with two engineers, Arthur Haddy and Kenneth Wilkinson.

November

- Beecham makes the first classical recording by an English conductor in Berlin – Mozart's *Die Zauberflöte*, recorded by HMV. (Bandleader Jack Hylton had recorded there in November 1927.)

1938

January

- Mahler's Symphony No. 9 with Walter and the Vienna Philharmonic Orchestra recorded by HMV at a public concert in Vienna, prior to the Anschluss in March 1938.

November

- First NFGS "High Leigh" Conference.

December

- Columbia Broadcasting System (CBS) acquires the American Recording Company.

Developments prior to 1939

Compton Mackenzie in his office overlooking the trees in the centre of Soho Square during the summer of 1936

Soho Square and *Vox* - 1929

In writing his Prologue to the first issue of *The Gramophone* Mackenzie had said, "We shall have nothing to do with Wireless in these columns", and broadly speaking he had remained true to his word. None the less, Mackenzie was concerned at the attitude of the press towards the BBC and felt that John Reith needed support if he was to succeed in maintaining the necessary standards. Therefore, in October 1929 Mackenzie launched a fortnightly entitled *Vox* under the editorship of Christopher Grieve (better-known as the poet Hugh MacDiarmid). Unfortunately the venture failed, Mackenzie later believing that it was premature, and a year later all that remained of *Vox* and two other alternative titles registered at the same time – *The Radio Critic* and *The Broadcast Review* – was the incorporation of their names in the masthead of *The Gramophone*. The publication of *Vox* had also necessitated a move to larger offices at 10a Soho Square and these became the home of *The Gramophone* from September 1929 until shortly after the outbreak of the Second World War.

A new approach to recording

Many of the issues raised by contributors and correspondents in the early editions of the magazine were to run as a constant thread during the coming years, some to be resolved by developing technology, others to remain as a bone of contention to the present day. In May 1929 Joseph Szigeti told of recording the Brahms Violin Concerto with Sir Hamilton Harty in Manchester, the sessions for nine sides taking "the best part of three mornings". With an hour to spare at the end of the final session Szigeti suggested making some "luxury" records, with the barest pauses after each side, only to realize when later

The front cover of the first issue of *Vox* which consisted of 32 pages, plus cover, and used a number of *The Gramophone*'s contributors, including W. R. Anderson and Herman Klein

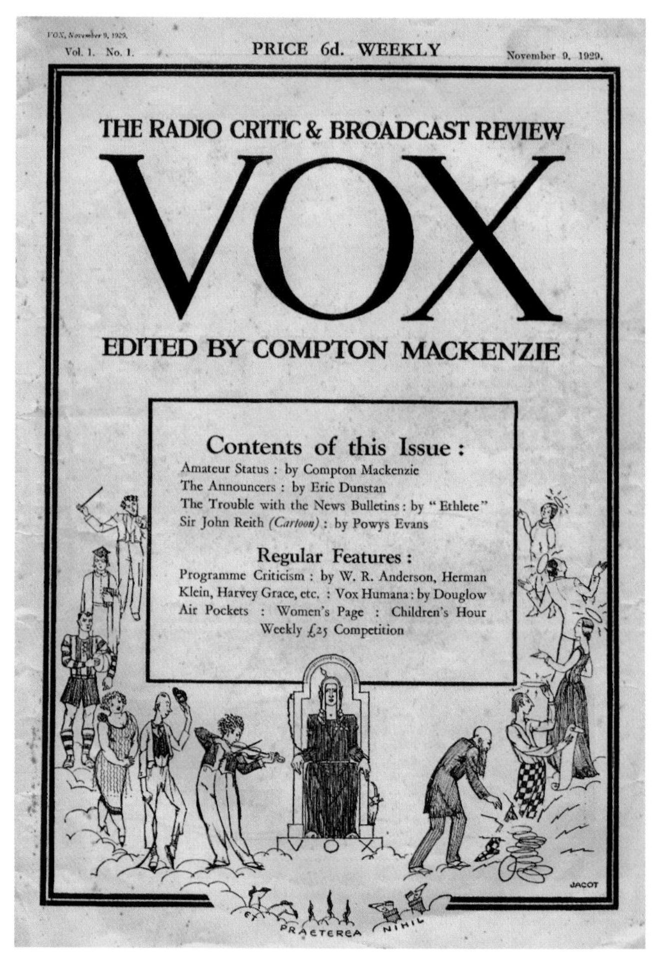

VOX, November 9, 1929.
Vol. 1. No. 1.

PRICE 6d. WEEKLY

November 9, 1929.

THE RADIO CRITIC & BROADCAST REVIEW

VOX

EDITED BY COMPTON MACKENZIE

Contents of this Issue:

Amateur Status : by Compton Mackenzie
The Announcers : by Eric Dunstan
The Trouble with the News Bulletins : by "Ethlete"
Sir John Reith *(Cartoon)* : by Powys Evans

Regular Features:

Programme Criticism : by W. R. Anderson, Herman Klein, Harvey Grace, etc. : Vox Humana : by Douglow
Air Pockets : Women's Page : Children's Hour
Weekly £25 Competition

Columbia's advertisement for Szigeti's "luxury" Brahms Violin Concerto

evaluating the 'tests' that nearly all those which he chose were from the "luxury" session. He wrote, "Indeed, my idea of a studio Utopia is a place where gramophone records are taken like snapshots, I imagine myself surrounded by a battalion of recording machines, one of which will surely give the perfect result; one machine perhaps making a test whilst one is keeping a permanent record of that test. The number of machines employed would eliminate the present unnerving waits between sides".

In this case he did not have to wait too long for his studio Utopia: a report in the June 1934 issue commented, "The latest development in recording long works deserves a note. The two turntables now installed in recording studios enable an orchestra to record a symphony, for instance, as in a concert performance without stopping at the end of every four minutes and repeating that 'side' again and rehearsing the next bit, and so on, till the urge and life of a real performance were jeopardized".

The arrival of Decca

Notwithstanding the economic problems of the late-1920s the record industry had made good progress, particularly with the introduction of electric recording in 1925 and the subsequent development of electric reproduction. Shares in the Columbia Graphophone Company, under the guidance of Louis Sterling, had risen from 11s. [55p] in 1923 to peak at nearly £20 in 1929, with The Gramophone Company stock, and that of a number of other smaller companies, performing nearly as well. Against this background a young stockbroker, Edward Lewis, was invited to handle the flotation of the Barnett Samuel Company, makers of the famous Decca portable gramophone, and in September 1928 the company was floated as The Decca Gramophone Company.

Edward (later Sir Edward) Lewis *From a portrait in oils by Henry Carr R.P. 1956*

Lewis was struck at the outset by the fact "that a company manufacturing gramophones but not records was rather like one making razors but not the consumable blades" (*No CIC*, E. R. Lewis, 1956 – privately published). It followed that when he noticed the Duophone Company, who operated a record factory at Shannon Corner on the Kingston By-pass, were in financial difficulties he recommended to the Decca directors that they should consider the possibility of taking over the plant as

April 1929 **Editorial**

ARS GRATIA ARTIS

Dr Malcolm Sargent, at the age of thirty-three, has just refused to play the cinema organ for half an hour every day at 12s. 9d. [63p] a minute. This shows a more genuine horror of the instrument than even I could have fancied possible in these days of hard struggling for economic existence. What puzzles me, however, even more than Dr Sargent's devotion to art is why it should be worth while for a West End cinema theatre to pay £7,000 a year to any man, whatever his acrobatic and musical ability, to play their organ three times daily throughout the year for ten minutes at a session. I really should very much like to know the name of the cinema theatre which was prepared to offer this price, and I think Dr Sargent owes it to his professional brethren with lower ideals than himself to reveal the name. Art for art's sake is not so rare as many people imagine. At the same time, Dr Malcolm Sargent has set a standard of self-denial which will make us examine his gramophone records with particular attention in the future, and if he should swerve one inch from the right road to the summit of Parnassus we shall not be able to let the slip pass unnoticed. Meanwhile, I commend to his attention the version we lately had from HMV under his baton of Quilter's *Children's Overture*, which was a heavy-handed affair and not up to the standard which we shall expect from him in the future.

The Gramophone, August, 1929

a going concern and virtually overnight enter the record business. Their lack of enthusiasm resulted in Lewis forming a syndicate in January 1929 to purchase the factory and subsequently The Decca Gramophone Company. Thus, in June 1929 the first Decca records were announced, with Walter Yeomans joining the company from The Gramophone Company. In September the Stock Exchange slump hit the market and to all intents and purposes the record boom was over. Many of the smaller record companies were to go out of business and on April 21st, 1931 the Columbia and Gramophone companies amalgamated to form Electric and Musical Industries Ltd. (later EMI), with Alfred Clark as Chairman and Louis Sterling as Managing Director.

Company finances - The 1930s

The trading problems of the late 1920s and 1930s came as a cruel blow to my father who, having inherited a deficit of £1,268 on the accounts for 1925, managed to turn this round to a profit of £87 by the end of 1927, adding another £1,688 in 1928. Sadly, the costs of the ill-fated *Vox* resulted in losses in 1929 and 1930 and in addition the Company was also saddled with excess office space for the next few years. In fact, the period up to the end of 1939 could only be described as a struggle. In 1931 the Directors reported, "From these and other figures it is clear that expenses have been reduced to counterbalance the loss of revenue which is entirely due to general trade depression. So far as ***The Gramophone*** and the NGS are concerned we cannot hope to effect any further substantial reductions , and if we succeed in disposing of the *Vox* offices this year the relief (£400-£500) will be considerable since it is this burden combined with the difficulty of collecting money owed to us which has made the maintenance of a balance at the bank increasingly precarious. So far as cash is concerned we are living from hand to mouth and have only a deposit of £250 to fall back upon in an emergency.

"The position of the Company is however relatively strong and has been considerably strengthened during the last year. It has no serious competitor and as soon as the gramophone and radio trade revive a large increase in revenue may be confidently anticipated.

"The joint Editors wish to place on record their deep appreciation of the sound financial organization of Mr C. L. Pollard, which has enabled the paper to weather the storm; in recognition of his services Mr Pollard has been appointed a Director in place of Mr D. W. Parrish who retired last year."

The loss of revenue continued up to the end of 1939 by which time the figures were down by some 48 per cent. In commenting on the accounts in December 1938 the Directors stated, "In perusing the Accounts now before you it will be seen that during the year the Company has made a profit of £23 0s. 5d. It is unfortunately not large enough to completely wipe out the 1937 loss. During the year the Company had anticipated saving approximately £300 on printing, but the new printers broke their contract after five issues. Another printer – Gibbs & Bamforth of St Albans – was prepared to take this over at an inclusive charge of £95 per issue with the option of increasing to £100 per issue after the first three months. It was ultimately agreed to pay them £98 per issue on a three years contract." The printing of ***The Gramophone*** remained with Gibbs & Bamforth and their successors for the next 42 years.

Jazz and Swing

Apart from a shrinking number of advertisers these problems were not reflected in the pages of the magazine and from December 1929 it even sported a multi-coloured front cover. In June 1930 the contributors' ranks were strengthened by the addition of Edgar Jackson (founding editor of *The Melody Maker* in January 1926, leaving in November 1929) who for 28 years was to edit his own review section of the magazine – originally "Dance and Popular Rhythmic", then "Swing Music" and ultimately "Jazz and Swing". Given the increasing interest in this area of the repertoire, and its support from a wide range of advertisers, the decision was a good one, but Jackson was never easily contained within the editorial concept of the magazine. Christopher Stone supported him,

Compton Mackenzie did not. His literary style was 'racy' but his judgement was good and he was respected by those who understood the genre and were anxious to see its advancement. One such was John Hammond, who later played a major role in the American music business. Following his early contributions to Jackson's pages in *The Gramophone*, he recorded Joseph Szigeti and introduced both the Budapest String Quartet and Goddard Lieberson to American Columbia. However, his real interest lay in the field of jazz and he discovered artists such as Billie Holiday, Count Basie, Teddy Wilson, Bob Dylan and his future brother-in-law Benny Goodman. He died in July 1987 at the age of 76. Jackson also worked with the American critic Leonard Feather (who died in October 1994) and together they established the detailed 'personnels' which became so much a part of the original "Jazz and Swing" reviews. Edgar Jackson retired from his reviewing role in May 1958 but continued his association with the Company's *Popular Record Catalogue* which he had compiled from the start in 1953, handing over to Albert McCarthy in 1966. He died on August 31st, 1967 at the age of 72.

Edgar Jackson *Photo Flair*

JAZZ PERSONNEL

Humphrey Lyttelton and his Band

****Hopfrog* (Lyttelton) (Parlophone CE12891)
****Snake Rag* (Joe "King" Oliver) (Parlophone CE12890)
(Parlophone R3286 – 4s. 8d.)
****Ice Cream* (Johnson, Moll, King) (Parlophone CE12908)
****Froggy Moore* (Morton, Spikes) (Parlophone CE12909)
(Parlophone R3292 – 4s. 8d.)

12890/1 – **Lyttelton** (cornet) with **Wally Fawkes, Ian Christie** (clarts); **Keith Christie** (tmb); **George Webb** (pno); **"Buddy" Vallis** (bjo); **John Wright** (bass); **George Hopkinson** (dms). March 29th, 1950.

12908/9 – As above. April 26th, 1950.

This valuable element of the "Jazz and Swing" reviews was developed over the years by Edgar Jackson and Leonard Feather (the former collecting the European data, the latter the American), it then being used by both in the course of their respective reviewing activities.

The Lyttelton data above, from the June 1950 issue, covered two 78rpm releases. Sides were given a maximum of five stars and in addition to the titles showed composer(s), original recording company and matrix number: there were also details of the issuing company (not always the same as the recording company), the record catalogue number and price. Then followed the personnel details, keyed by matrix number, and the recording date.

Publication of these personnels was phased-out in May 1958 by which time the information had become an integral part of the LP sleeve-note.

Society issues

In the UK the young Walter Legge developed Compton Mackenzie's ideas in respect of the National Gramophonic Society and in October 1931 HMV launched through the pages of *The Gramophone* the Hugo Wolf Society [p. 46]. This called for 500 subscribers at 30s. [£1.50] for an initial album of six double-sided 12-inch 78s. Mackenzie gave it his total endorsement in the October editorial but the following month, when there was a suggestion of a lack of support, he wrote, "I was depressed to learn that the response had not been too encouraging. It will really be grotesque if 500 people out of 50 million cannot manage to find thirty shillings a year to possess records of the greatest living singers singing some of the world's greatest songs. Should the Hugo Wolf Society fail to become an established fact I shall feel that I have suffered the most humiliating rebuff of my career. No doubt rebuffs are good for people, but good though they may be for individuals, they are very bad for art; and if lovers of the gramophone never intend to venture beyond the familiar ground on which they

Walter Legge, responsible for the inter-war EMI Society Issues *Photo EMI*

now amuse themselves, this means inevitably that the gramophone will return to the state of a mechanical toy from which we had, perhaps rashly, supposed it had been promoted.

"He who smokes twenty gaspers a day, let him smoke eighteen and subscribe to ten songs by Hugo Wolf, for gaspers are the enemy of the throat, and Hugo Wolf songs are not. Even if the individual music-lover be not convinced that he will get his money's worth in enjoyment out of the Hugo Wolf songs, let him remember that the failure to bring into existence this particular Society will set a full stop to the formation of any other societies."

Gilbert Wilson, Christopher Stone and the comedienne Annette Mills at *The Gramophone*'s Silver Jubilee celebration on June 16th, 1948

Happily, by December the crisis was over and only 30 more subscribers were needed. Amazingly, Mr F. Fujita of Tokyo had rallied support in Japan and produced 111 subscribers! Elena Gerhardt had already recorded the first album and copies were to be ready before Christmas. There followed a series of famous 'society' recordings which featured the works of Beethoven, Bach, Brahms, François Couperin, Delius, Handel, Haydn, Kilpinen, Mahler, Mozart, Scarlatti, Schubert, Sibelius and Wolf, where the sales were guaranteed in advance and satisfied the somewhat parlous financial state of the Industry. There was, of course, an undertaking to subscribers that these would be 'limited editions' and ironically there was soon to be agonizing by those who could not afford to take up the offer at the time and therefore missed an issue. Mackenzie supported the record companies in the view that these releases should not be re-pressed and it was interesting that some 29 years later agreement was sought, through the pages of the magazine, for the LP reissue in the UK of the Beethoven/Schnabel recordings.

What is this high fidelity?

During the latter part of 1929 Christopher Stone appointed Percy Wilson's younger brother Gilbert as Technical Editor, whilst PW contributed a regular feature entitled "Technical Talk". As electrical reproduction began to dominate the market so the Expert Committee was phased-out and each month the magazine ran detailed technical reports on the latest record players, radiograms, loudspeakers, motors, radios (even push-button models), and the new television sets when the system was introduced in the London area in 1936. Percy Wilson also wrote a series of articles entitled, "What is this High Fidelity?" (December 1935 – August 1936), following which Mackenzie wrote in his Editorial for September 1936, "In common with, I am sure, most of our readers I have been reading with the greatest interest P. Wilson's articles on high fidelity in recording and reproduction, and I want to ask him to tell us what prospect he sees of reproducing on the gramophone what I will call the diffusion of the orchestra. It has become reasonably 'stereoscopic' but it still remains imprisoned. In the old days I used to dream of a super-gramophone with half a dozen horns and six synchronized discs, one of which would hold the woodwind, another the brass, another couple the strings, another the percussion, and another the solo instrument in a concerto, and I used to wonder if six horns like that would succeed in achieving diffusion. Of course such recording would be impossible for many reasons on our present discs, but would it be attainable by any method of recording of which we are aware at the present?". Percy Wilson replied the following month.

Archives and Federations

In February 1936 there was an open letter to the Editor from Gordon Bottomley calling for the foundation of a National Record Library. He wrote, "Does there exist anywhere any institution which is doing for gramophone records even a little of what our great libraries do for

October 1936

DIFFUSION

by Percy Wilson

Replying to Compton Mackenzie's queries the previous month, Percy Wilson contributed an article to the October 1936 issue in which he considered the possibility of what would eventually come to be known as stereophonic recording

I have never yet heard anything like perfect diffusion in reproduction. The nearest approach, I think, is in a large room with a Voigt domestic loudspeaker [p. 221]. But I am assured that such diffusion has been secured by using several microphones, each connected to its own amplifier and loudspeaker system, the loudspeakers being placed in the same relative positions as the microphones. Mr Voigt some months ago gave a remarkably good demonstration using two sound channels of this kind, but half a dozen is said to be better.

It appears then that phase effects as well as directional effects are important in this connection. Mr Mackenzie's idea of half a dozen horns and synchronized discs is by no means so fantastic as it may seem at first, though, of course, the demand that the discs should be synchronized is a difficult one to satisfy. It would not even be necessary for one horn and disc to hold the woodwind, another the percussion and so on as he imagines. Provided the horns are placed in the same relative positions as the original microphones in recording, the microphones could be allowed to pick up and transfer to the appropriate discs all the sounds that impinge on them. The resolution into the individual instruments of the orchestra would be performed by the ear in listening.

I remember an acoustic illusion of similar type, when I was first introduced, years ago, to the electrical reproducing equipment of a friend of mine. He was fortunate enough to have two lobbies leading from two of the *corners* of his drawing-room, the fireplace being in the wall between. He placed moving coil loudspeakers over the doors of the two lobbies so that they 'discharged' into the room at right angles, and each at 45 degrees to the fireplace wall. When I went in he switched on the amplifier which fed both speakers and asked me to say where the sound was coming from. I could only reply that it seemed to come from somewhere over the mantlepiece. The sound was not fully diffused because there was no phase-difference between the two sources, but the faculty of the ear to take two sources and combine them into a single auditory impression was entirely demonstrated.

I do not think there is any reason to doubt that by using multiple sources and multiple reproducers a perfectly diffused and stereoscopic quality can be secured. But I am not yet convinced that the same effect will not somehow and sometime be obtained in a much more simple and practical way.

books?" The answer was 'no', and it would be another 15 years before Patrick Saul was to launch what in 1955 would become The British Institute of Recorded Sound, ultimately in 1983 to be renamed the National Sound Archive, as part of The British Library.

From the very first issue of the magazine there had been support for the gramophone society movement and in September 1936 reference was made to the formation on July 25th of the National Federation of Gramophone Societies by W. W. Johnson and F. E. Young, both of the Gillingham Society. The Federation successfully drew together over 200 gramophone societies in the UK and, with the support of *The Gramophone*, hosted the High Leigh Conference over the weekend November 4th-7th, 1938. In the warmth of an Indian summer everyone who was anyone in the world of records and audio gathered with members of the Federation to discuss matters of mutual interest. The names today sound like a roll-call of the Industry and they included Fred Gaisberg (unofficial conference photographer), Walter Legge, Rex Palmer, William Purser, Richard Haigh, Herbert Ridout, Victor

The NFGS High Leigh Conference, November 1938. From the left: Cecil Pollard, Walter Yeomans (Decca), Alec Robertson, Faith Mackenzie, Christopher Stone, Fred Gaisberg (HMV), Vera Lovegrove (*TG*) and Anna Instone (BBC)

February 1934 **Editorial**

ELGAR'S THIRD SYMPHONY

It is good news to hear that Sir Edward Elgar is out of hospital, and we all sincerely hope that he will soon be well enough to resume his work on that Third Symphony. It is a satisfaction that in *The Gramophone* the denigration of Elgar's work which was fashionable for a few years has always been absent. Some superlative rubbish has been written about him by musical critics who confuse the whims of fashion with the canons of good taste. Already the fashion is beginning to swing round in Elgar's favour, and I have no doubt that his Third Symphony will restore him to a position of prominence in the shop-window of contemporary taste. However, that is not of very profound importance to a man like Elgar, whose ultimate position is so completely secure.

Sadly, Elgar died on February 23rd, 1934 without completing his Third Symphony. On his deathbed he is reported to have said of the incomplete sketches for the Symphony, "don't let anyone tinker with it". In a letter in the July 1975 issue, *Gramophone* contributor and musicologist Dr Roger Fiske discussed the subject

July 1975 **Correspondence**

Elgar left only twenty-five bars fully scored and fifteen to twenty minutes of music on two staves, fully harmonized, but with hardly any instrumental indications. Because this two-stave music was split between all four movements it would never be possible to salvage more than three or four minutes of continuous music from any one of them. 'Completion' will always be out of the question. He habitually wrote in sections, starting a new page for each new section and not numbering the pages. Thus, their order is in doubt.

When Elgar pleaded for no tinkering he must have meant he did not want anyone to complete the Symphony. I agree wholeheartedly; no one ever should.

I am equally sure that sooner or later someone is going to make audible Elgar's Third Symphony sketches, though it may not happen until all who knew Elgar personally are dead. Whether they like it or nor, great creative artists become public property, and I'm not at all sure that they have any right to dictate what posterity shall do about their lives and their works.

In October 1997, a reconstruction of the Symphony by Anthony Payne based on further research into extant sources was recorded by the BBC Symphony Orchestra conducted by Andrew Davis. It was premièred in February 1998 and a recording released by NMC.

Homewood, John Whittle, George Fenwick, Valentine Britten, Walter Yeomans, Arthur Haddy, Mick Ginn, Paul Voigt, Kathleen Imhof and Anna Instone. From *The Gramophone* there was Compton Mackenzie, Christopher Stone, Faith Mackenzie, Cecil Pollard, Percy and Gilbert Wilson, Alec Robertson and Roger Wimbush. The war would intervene before the next High Leigh Conference (March 16th-19th, 1951) but it would never again attract such a galaxy of industry stars.

Contributors and correspondents

The magazine enjoyed many eminent contributors. One such was Fred Gaisberg who was employed in America by Emile Berliner in 1893 and came to London to make the first European recordings for The Gramophone and Typewriter Company. It was he who made the famous Caruso recordings in Milan in 1902 which were believed by many to have established the gramophone as a serious instrument rather than as a toy. In May 1938 he wrote of the death of Chaliapin, and in September of the death of Sir Landon Ronald with whom he had worked since the early days of The Gramophone Company, recording particularly Adelina Patti and Sir Edward Elgar. He also wrote about Gigli (June and December) and Bruno Walter (January 1939).

Elsewhere in the magazine during the 1930s appeared the names of a number of correspondents and contributors who were to feature regularly in the years ahead – Cedric Wallis, Desmond Shawe-Taylor, George A. Brewster, David Hall, Canon Drummond, John Freestone, Moore Orr, Albert J. Franck, Harold Rosenthal, Lionel Salter, L. F. B. Gilhespy, K. S. Sorabji, Leo Riemens, Julian Morton Moses, Percy Scholes, Robert Bauer, Colin Shreve, Christopher le Fleming, Knud de Hegermann-Lindencrone, Roland Gelatt and G. J. Cuming – to name but a few.

Sir Landon Ronald who, with Fred Gaisberg, was responsible for many early HMV recordings. The photograph was taken in 1930 *Photo EMI*

Domestic matters

In February 1932 Christopher Stone became Co-Editor of *The Gramophone* with Compton Mackenzie. Given the fact that he had carried the lion's share of the work since the second issue this was a well-deserved tribute. Faith Mackenzie functioned as London Editor whilst Mackenzie himself contributed his regular editorials and devised a series of competitions guaranteed to keep the staff of the London office up to their ears in paper.

Robin Legge (no relation to Walter), who commissioned that crucial *Daily Telegraph* article and had given Mackenzie so much encouragement in the early days, died

April 1934

E L G A R

In April 1934, two months after Elgar's death, Compton Mackenzie wrote of an encounter with the composer in the billiards-room of the Savile Club back in 1923. Elgar had obviously heard about Mackenzie's new magazine and commented,

"I suppose you people using this magazine of yours (i.e. *The Gramophone*) have discovered that nothing I have written has the slightest value. However, you can say what you like about my music, for I am no longer interested in music. The only thing I am interested in nowadays is the microscope, and if you take my advice you will set to work to interest yourself in the microscope in order to prepare yourself by the contemplation of diatoms for the disillusionment which must come to every artist nowadays after he has reached sixty." He then told me that he was thinking of taking a steamer up the Amazon as far as Manaos, but that he should not go unless he could have a cabin entirely to himself. Among other remarks that recur to me from that conversation are that Busoni had the greatest musical mind of the time, that Schubert wrote too often in an exhausted key, and that when he was young he had once told his mother that he should feel he had done something in the world when a postcard addressed to him as Edward Elgar without an address reached him. This postcard had finally reached him from a South Sea island and given him great pleasure.

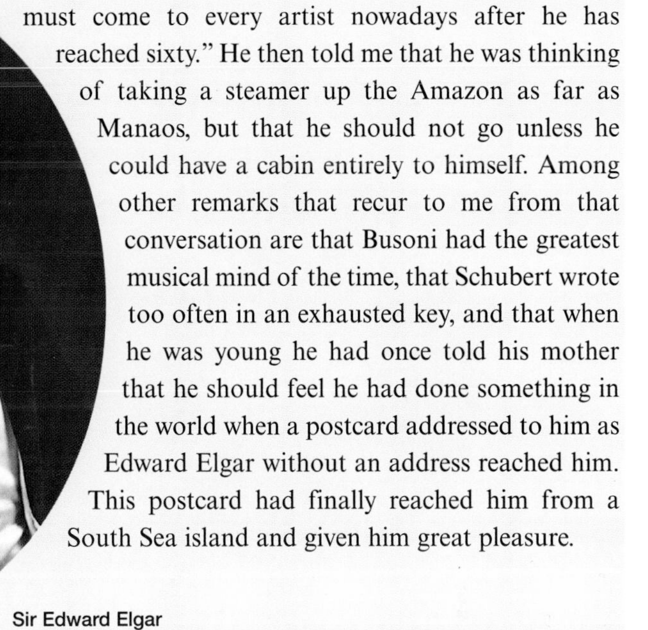

Sir Edward Elgar

Fred Gaisberg pours the coffee for Artur Schnabel in the Abbey Road Green Room – early 1930s *Photo EMI*

in May 1933 and the following year, on March 10th, 1934, Herman Klein died at the age of 78.

Another epoch came to a close at the end of May 1934 when Faith Mackenzie returned to Jethou to supervise the move of Mackenzie's records, which were eventually to go to his new home on the island of Barra in the Outer Hebrides. He had left Jethou at the end of 1930 but it was only now that the lease had been sold; in the July 1934 issue Faith Mackenzie wrote, "And now it is farewell to Jethou. Time to move on after ten years of it. Leave others to enjoy the fruits of so much work and thought; the garden, ten years ago a sad waste of bracken and woods, now glorious with enchanting rare flowers and shrubs; the long room designed so curiously to hold the books and records that accumulated month by month. The records! We unearthed some good things before we left, but there was a mass of pre-electric stuff really not fit to give away. What more dignified end could be devised for them than to be warmed gently on the stove and fluted to fantastic shapes and launched on to a milky sea carrying paper sails on a perfect evening in June. To join the floating puffins at their play, to race along the rushing tide and end perhaps at Alderney, perhaps even on the coast of Normandy! This was the fate of a small fleet that put out to sea on June the Eleventh, 1934."

During the 1930s Alec Robertson lived in a disused lighthouse at Winterton on the bleak East Anglian coast. The picture (1938) shows an 'editorial' meeting in the wind-blown sand dunes – from the left, Alec Robertson, Leslie Beck (role unknown), Walter Yeomans and Cecil Pollard, with Anthony Pollard in the foreground

RECORD SOCIETIES

by Malcolm Walker

The Gramophone, March, 1927

The National Gramophonic Society

was started three years ago by Compton Mackenzie under the auspices of THE GRAMOPHONE to do for recorded music what such organisations as the Medici Society have done for the printed word. By the voting of the members and with the help of an advisory committee of well-known musicians, a number of important works have been chosen and completely recorded by first-rate players.

N.G.S. Records hold their own in point of playing, recording and price with *any* gramophone records on the market.

Limited Membership

Membership is strictly limited, thus adding to these unique records the distinction of rarity which will be as greatly appreciated by the discerning amateur as the possession of a piece of Wedgwood by the ardent collector.

Forgotten Masterpieces

of Beethoven, Brahms, Mozart and Schubert are produced on these records. Works by the modern composers Elgar, Goossens and Vaughan Williams, with many other attractive short works, all unobtainable on any other record, are available to members.

How to join the N.G.S.

The subscription to the N.G.S. is *2s. 6d.*, except to annual subscribers to THE GRAMOPHONE who are *ipso facto* members. Send for fullest particulars and register your name and address as a member.

Address your letter to—

The Secretary,
NATIONAL GRAMOPHONIC SOCIETY
58, Frith Street, London, W.1. **Telephone: Regent 1383**

The National Gramophonic Society

In the September 1923 issue of *The Gramophone* Compton Mackenzie wrote: "For some time past I have had in my head a scheme that requires much thought before it can be considered a practical scheme.

The Music Society String Quartet with André Mangeot, Boris Pecker, John Barbirolli and Henry J. Besly

Briefly, my ambition is to incorporate a number of enthusiasts for good music on the gramophone in a society which will aim at achieving for gramophone music what such societies as the Medici have done for the reproduction of paintings and for the printed book. If I receive 500 postcards I will take the next step, which will be to start the society and give it a name". One of Mackenzie's musical advisers in this enterprise was Walter Wilson Cobbett, a distinguished chamber music lover and violinist, who himself would later sponsor a recording of the Schubert Quintet. The choice of works to be recorded was decided by the voting of members, who originally paid an annual subscription of 5s. [25p], and an advisory panel which included W. R. Anderson, Spencer Dyke, Alec Robertson, Peter Latham and Mackenzie himself.

THE NATIONAL GRAMOPHONIC SOCIETY

Can you spare Thirty Shillings a Quarter for six Chamber Music records?

If you can, and if you are with the Editor in the great fight which he has made for over a year in the cause of the highest class of recorded music, it is your duty as well as your privilege to be one of the Thousand Members.

Send 5/- (the annual subscription) to The Secretary, N.G.S., 58, Frith Street, London, W.1, and you will receive full particulars.

On October 9th, 1923 the National Gramophonic Society (NGS) was formed and the first release in early 1924 was the Spencer Dyke Quartet

The Gramophone, November, 1924

Beethoven's "Harp" Quartet
in E flat, Op. 74,
and
Debussy's Quartet in G
played by
THE SPENCER DYKE
STRING QUARTET
(SIX 12-INCH DOUBLE-SIDED
RECORDS IN ALL),

are now ready for distribution to Members of the National Gramophonic Society.

An analytical note by "N. P." is issued with each set.

Particulars from
The Secretary, N.G.S.,
58, Frith Street, London, W.1.

performing Beethoven's String Quartet in E flat, *Harp*, Op. 74, on three acoustically recorded 78rpm discs (numbered A, B and C). This was followed by the first-ever recording of the Debussy Quartet (D/F), and, shortly afterwards by the gramophone première on nine sides of Schoenberg's *Verklärte Nacht* in its original string sextet form (N/Q). Chamber music would form the basis of the label, which then proceeded to offer the clarinet quintets of Brahms (SS/WW) and Mozart (XX/AAA) with Frederick Thurston and Charles Draper as the respective soloists, Elgar's Piano Quintet (for which Mackenzie attempted to persuade the composer to take the keyboard part to no avail – NN/RR), Mozart's Oboe Quartet with Léon Goossens (R/S), Vaughan Williams's *Phantasy* Quintet with John Barbirolli as cellist in the Music Society Quartet (EEE/FFF) plus several string fantasias by Gibbons and Purcell. These pioneering recordings were made and manufactured for the NGS by the Aeolian company. Whilst membership was limited, advertisements promoting the NGS's activities appeared regularly in the pages of ***The Gramophone***.

The introduction of electrical recording in 1925 was to prove a headache for the NGS. Mackenzie always regretted that the Society had not adopted the new system earlier than 1927, for by the time of the Beethoven centenary that same year, the larger companies had moved into the area of chamber music, especially Columbia who released 12 quartets, performed by the Léner Quartet. In January 1928 the first orchestral recordings were made of Delius's *Summer night on the river* (NGS72), Debussy's *Danse sacrée et danse profane* with pianist Ethel Bartlett (NGS70/1) and Warlock's Serenade for strings (NGS75), all conducted by 28-year-old John Barbirolli in his conducting début on disc. Many years later Sir John (as he was then known) recalled to me how much he owed in the furtherance of his career from his activities with the National Gramophonic Society [p. 50].

Other notable and important recordings which were issued by the NGS included several works by Bax – the Oboe Quintet with its

Finding a bubble on an NGS record

A member of the NGS finding that the wrong records have been sent to him

Nicolas Medtner (right) with Capt. H. T. Binstead representing H. H. The Maharajah of Mysore, in 1948 at the time of the Medtner Society recordings. In the background is Faith Mackenzie

dedicatee Léon Goossens (NGS76/7) and the First String Quartet with the Marie Wilson Quartet (NGS153/5), Ravel's String Quartet by the International Quartet (whose recorded interpretation on NGS78/81 was handsomely endorsed by the composer), and a much regarded reading of Mozart's Piano and Wind Quintet, K452 with Kathleen Long (piano), and wind players Thurston, Goossens, Aubrey Brain and John Alexander (NGS121/3). One of the most unusual and enterprising recordings to be undertaken by the NGS was of Paul Juon's Chamber Symphony, Op. 27, a work scored for five strings, horn, oboe and piano (NGS144/6).

Sadly too few readers of ***The Gramophone*** supported the NGS: by 1927 it had just 241 members and the maximum barely exceeded 300. In his January 1929 editorial Mackenzie stated: "To be perfectly frank we are not getting the support from our readers on this side of the Atlantic that we get from the other. I fully recognize the growing embarrassment for the purse of the riches which the recording companies offer us every month, but there have been several occasions lately when I have had to ask myself whether there is still any real need for such a society as ours. It is beginning to look as if the greater and lesser recording companies were providing all the Chamber Music that the public at home can absorb, and it was with this feeling of uneasiness about the value of the NGS that I recently put out a 'feeler' in the matter of song recording. I should like to be able to announce that the response I received was more encouraging than it has been, but though several enthusiasts have acclaimed the idea and given us the benefit of their suggestions, the general response has not been lively enough to encourage us to proceed any further with this scheme at present. We are still receiving enough support for our publications of Chamber Music to warrant our continuing with them, but if we are merely going to record charming Quartets of Haydn and Mozart, which will inevitably sooner or later be given to us by the recording companies, I shall have to consider very seriously the value of our activities, which are, as may be imagined, a great additional strain upon an already overworked staff."

In November 1929 Mackenzie reported that a clearance sale of overstocked NGS recordings had been a complete sell-out in 48 hours! The following summer, the enterprise of the NGS's activities was recognized in the *New York Telegram* when it commented "The Society, a non-profit-making organization, makes the best of the unusual recordings" and it was noted that the *New York Times* had also been giving prominence to the objects and achievements of the Society.

The final NGS recording, made on March 24th and 28th, 1931, was of Warlock's poignant cycle *The Curlew*, with John Armstrong as soloist, conducted by Constant Lambert (NGS163/5). Although many of the recordings continued to be available for several years, the Society's active life was over.

The pioneering efforts of the National Gramophonic Society attracted this tribute from W. S. Meadmore in his article "Twenty-Five Years of ***The Gramophone***" (June 1948): "The NGS was active for eight years and I think had considerable influence in jockeying the recording companies to emulate its very high standard. It certainly was one factor which finally decided them to issue uncut works, not as an exceptional event, but as a normal proceeding".

Society Editions

The effects of the economic depression brought about a reassessment within the recording industry of how to present artistically important areas of the repertoire against less commercially viable returns. The then Editor of HMV's house magazine *The Voice*, the 26-year-old Walter Legge, put forward the idea of Society Editions, paid for in advance on a subscription basis. The initial set was of six double-sided 78rpm discs containing a representative selection of Lieder by Hugo Wolf, sung by Elena Gerhardt.

Five hundred subscribers were requested to pay £1.50 each for the set which would include notes, texts and translations by the critic Ernest Newman, and Mackenzie enthusiastically expounded the cause in his Editorial for October 1931. However, response from British readers was muted and had it not been for an enlightened body of Japanese record buyers the recordings would not have been undertaken. Mackenzie was able to state in December 1931 that all subscriptions (bar 30) had been taken up and the recordings made. He concluded "the good news has also reached us that a Beethoven

The Gramophone, May, 1942

Fred Smith has great pleasure in announcing exclusive records of Russian songs, sung by

ODA SLOBODSKAYA

TCHEREPNIN
I Would Have Kissed You

RACHMANINOFF
The Lilacs
How Lovely Here

TCHAIKOVSKY
The Golden Cornfields
So Soon Forgotten
Was not I Once Like a Tender Blade that Sprung
Had I only Known

CÉSAR CUI
The Statue

TANEIEV
My Heart is Throbbing
Nocturne
Dreams
In the Silence of the Night

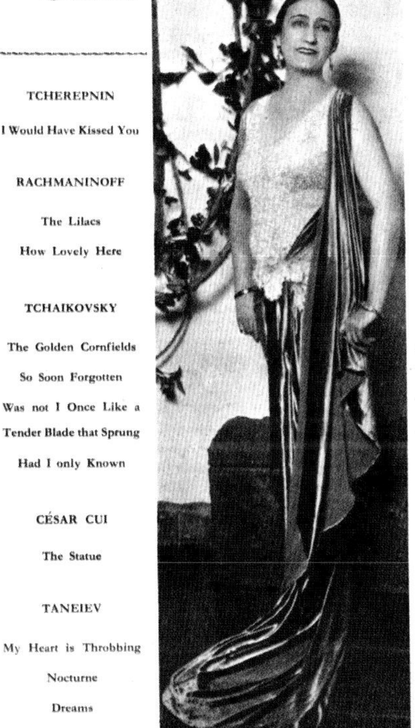

We are all thinking of Russia nowadays, and this issue of records comes timely, I think. But such superb songs, so superbly sung would be assured of a welcome whenever they might be heard.

The infinite care taken by Madame Slobodskaya at the recording sessions impressed me beyond words. Time and again she remade the waxes. Time and again she found faults where others had listened entranced. One realises by such an experience that the true artiste knows degrees even in perfection.

Many a devotee of singing is really a devotee of top notes. Truly the top must be served, and marvellously indeed does Slobodskaya serve them. But those rarer ones who listen to the whole, not merely to the part, will glow at the rich beauty of her middle register, the register which must carry the work.

I wish also to mention the accompaniments by Ivor Newton. It was quite evident at the sessions, and it is borne out by the records, that he measured his own part by the immensely exacting requirements of both the singer's voice and performance.

The four 12-inch records will be available about mid-May. Made by Decca they are exclusive to Rimington, Van Wyck, and are complete in album with booklet of English words. Price £1 19 6, inclusive of tax and post free

FREDK. T. SMITH

RIMINGTON, VAN WYCK LTD.

42-43, CRANBOURN STREET, LONDON, W.C.2. GERRARD 1171

Sonata Society on similar lines will be started early in the New Year" [p. 39].

In the decade of the 1930s, EMI through their HMV, Columbia and Parlophone labels, introduced Society Editions devoted to major works by Bach (13 volumes), Beethoven (19), Brahms (1), Couperin (1), Delius (3), English Music (2), Handel (1), Haydn (9), Kilpinen (1), Mahler (2), Mozart (15), Mussorgsky (1), Domenico Scarlatti (2), Schubert (2), Sibelius (4) and Wolf (6). They continued to introduce new Society Editions after 1945, the main one being devoted to Medtner (three volumes) who himself played his three Piano Concertos in addition to solo piano works. The young and enterprising Maharajah of Mysore was the moving force behind this project. The Delius Trust sponsored the composer's opera *A Village Romeo and Juliet* under Beecham in 1948 (two volumes). The majority of the pre-war sets were still available as ordinary catalogue items into the mid-1950s when classical 78rpm discs began to be deleted from the manufacturers' catalogues.

Similar Society Editions, though not on such an extensive scale, were produced by Joe Brogan of The Gramophone Shop, New York and included Maggie Teyte in French and Russian song, and the Swedish mezzo-soprano Lorri Lail in Lieder and other songs. The recordings were distributed in the UK by Fred Smith of Rimington Van Wyck, who also initiated Society releases by the soprano Oda Slobodskaya in Russian songs and Phyllis Sellick in a miscellany of French piano music and Tippett's Piano Sonata No. 1.

Following the introduction of the LP disc in the United States, RCA Victor began transferring and reissuing some of the Society Editions, most notably the Beethoven Piano Sonatas with Schnabel. In Britain the Beethoven Violin Sonatas with Kreisler were reissued on the "Great Recordings of the Century" series in 1958 and two of the Mozart operas had appeared two years earlier. However, a letter from a reader in the July 1961 issue of ***The Gramophone*** questioned why no LP issues had so far appeared in Britain of Schnabel's Beethoven Sonatas. The following month Alec Robertson explained that one subscriber to the original 78rpm sets had objected to the possible reissue of these recordings, on the grounds that the first two volumes at least were originally issued as limited editions, restricted to subscribers only. AR expressed the hope that other subscribers would waive their rights and agree to the reissue of these recordings, considering that the discs were available overseas and that the original albums, long since out of circulation, had little second-hand value. A most encouraging response was received from older readers of the magazine who supported AR's view, so that in November 1961 David Bicknell of EMI was able to announce a planned reissue of these historic Schnabel recordings in the ensuing months and years. Today these rightly famous recordings continue to adorn the catalogue.

Cecil Pollard in his Soho Square office in 1936. Behind him are the shelves containing part of the Company's record library

Later that year there was a break in Christopher Stone's relationship with the BBC and he was now to be heard on a number of the continental commercial stations who transmitted English language programmes to the UK. These included a regular Friday evening slot for ***The Gramophone*** on Radio Lyons. His broadcasting commitment being that much greater, Faith Mackenzie now assumed wider responsibilities as London Editor, facing up to some of the layout problems which had become apparent over the past few months and on which readers had been invited to comment. In fact, this was Edgar Jackson trying to modernize the appearance of the magazine and, as might have been expected, his ideas were rejected by the majority of readers, although some of the changes were retained in the light music section where they were thought to be apposite.

Now that the ties with the Channel Islands were severed it was decided to put the original company into liquidation and float a new one, General Gramophone Publications Limited, on the mainland: this was completed on December 30th, 1936. The word 'General' had to be inserted in the registered title to avoid any confusion with The Gramophone Company of Hayes.

As a writer, Compton Mackenzie's energy knew no bounds. He had no real interest in outdoor pursuits and, even though a Scotsman, believed golf to be a totally futile game. His 'safety valve' when he might have been driving himself too hard was sciatica and the onset of a crippling attack, often lasting for more than a week, ensured a necessary period of rest. When one of these attacks prevented him from writing his usual Editorial, Christopher Stone would stand-in but early in 1937, when Stone was no longer actively co-editing the magazine, Herbert Ridout was invited to fill the gap. Ridout had joined Louis Sterling and the Columbia Graphophone Company in 1906 and was to be associated with the record industry for nearly 40 years. Mackenzie had consulted him before starting the magazine and his 'stand-in' editorial of February 1937 provides an interesting picture of Mackenzie himself and the light in which ***The Gramophone*** was then seen by the record industry [p. 52].

February 1938 **News**

PITY THE POOR BURGLAR

Modern inventions are making it increasingly difficult for the old-fashioned art of house-breaking to flourish with any degree of comfort or safety. Witness the latest invention for catching the malefactor red-handed. As the burglar enters the house he sets off a silent alarm which puts into operation a strange instrument – a hybrid mixture of gramophone and telephone. Roughly, this is how it works. The burglar-alarm sets off the motor of the gramophone. At the same time an automatic finger dials "999" on a telephone so placed that when the operator answers the urgent call, he or she hears a voice, recorded on a special, soft disc, repeating firmly and untiringly, "Come to 13, Laburnum Shrubbery at once. A house-breaking incident has just taken place." These words – or the equivalent – are repeated for the length of a large disc playing for approximately ten minutes. "What happens if the burglar cuts the telephone wires?" They've thought of that too! This cunning device has its own special line concealed somewhere in the cellar or attic, and even as the burglar fondly imagines he has cut all communications with the outside world, the treacherous voice of our mechanical informer is summoning swift retribution. Who would be a burglar?

December 1939 **News**

LOUIS KENTNER'S RECORDINGS IN BUDAPEST

In an interview in the December 1939 issue, the pianist Louis Kentner recalled some of his earliest electrical recordings made for the Edison Bell Record Company in Budapest in 1928

Louis Kentner *Photo APR*

The electrical system had not then been generally accepted, and sessions were haphazard, far indeed different from the carefully planned sessions of today. For example, the piano was hired for the occasion from a neighbouring shop and proved to be a bad and out of tune instrument. So, one afternoon, I sat in front of this piano and played, with hardly a pause, the Brahms *Paganini* Variations, two Chopin *Impromptus*, two Debussy pieces and finally some modern pieces by Dohnányi and Kodály. All these were recorded from my first playings. Now I should have had to go through every composition at least half a dozen times before the recording people would have expressed satisfaction. These ghostly murmurs of my dead self would, I am sure, only distress me if I were to hear them again. But it is strange that I still meet people who have saved these records and are enthusiastic. But perhaps that is only their charming English politeness.

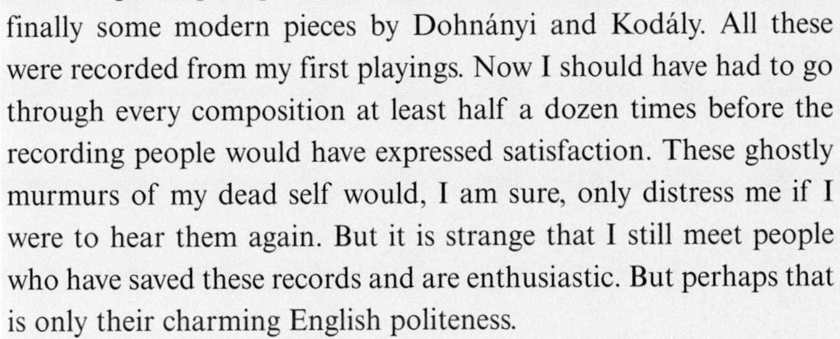

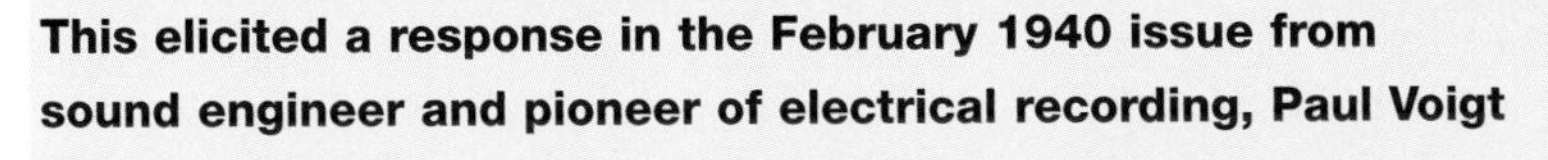

This elicited a response in the February 1940 issue from sound engineer and pioneer of electrical recording, Paul Voigt

February 1940 **Correspondence**

In the year 1928 I went on a recording expedition for Edison Bell Ltd., and spent a month in Budapest recording about two hundred titles.

On foreign expeditions, in the interests of economy, unnecessary rehearsal is to be avoided, and if the artists know their numbers well enough, it is even possible to record direct without any rehearsal in the studio.

My recordings in Budapest covered many different artists. Some were difficult to work with but one in particular, a promising young pianist, was very easy to work with and a number of good piano records were recorded with him. Although I have never been in contact with the said pianist since, I have followed with interest how Mr Louis Kentner (the pianist in question) has gradually achieved fame and is now one of the acknowledged experts.

In the report of an interview with Mr Kentner published in ***The Gramophone***, he evidently remembered the experimental nature of the apparatus and the manner in which the sessions were conducted. He is wrong, however, when he mentions that the piano was hired for the occasion of his visit. The same piano was, in fact, used for the whole of the period. I hold no brief for the instrument in question, but Mr Kentner need not fear that he would be distressed if he were to hear the records again.

His two Chopin *Impromptus* in particular were among the outstanding records in the Edison Bell catalogue for a long time afterwards and were almost invariably used in the Regent Street shop for demonstration purposes. The people who tell Mr Kentner that they are enthusiastic about those records are not just being polite. They have reason for their enthusiasm.

I am sending a copy of this letter to Mr Kentner with an invitation to pay me a visit in the near future to hear over modern reproducing equipment the records which I have still preserved from my visit to Budapest.

P. G. A. H. Voigt, B.Sc.
London, SE19

Trouble looming

With the storm clouds gathering in Europe a letter from a reader in Munich, published in the November 1938 issue, reflected a somewhat different view of the British Prime Minister, Neville Chamberlain, to that invariably handed-down by history. "Last week we had great days in Munich. You should have seen it! You can hardly imagine *how* popular Mr Chamberlain is here. One afternoon he visited a beergarden 'incognito' ... the result was when he left it one hour later some hundreds of people stood at the door of the beergarden to cry 'Heil, Chamberlain!'. Day and night thousands of people waited in front of the Regina Hotel to greet Mr Chamberlain and shout 'Heil!' to him. Whenever Mr Chamberlain came to the balcony people cried and cried and clapped hands. Mr Chamberlain smiled and smiled. The balcony was a garden of flowers. When Mr Chamberlain left Munich he gave all the flowers to Munich hospitals."

Against this background Mackenzie discussed in the Editorial for January 1939 the somewhat surprising rising pattern of record sales and took the opportunity of launching another of his competitions, this time asking for essays of up to 800 words on the subject,

On Toscanini's retirement as conductor of the New York Philharmonic Orchestra at the end of April 1936, the 36-year-old John Barbirolli was appointed to conduct ten weeks of the next season's concerts. In the October 1936 issue he contributed the following

A FEW REMINISCENCES

by John Barbirolli

Although I have little time for writing articles at present, I was unable to refuse the invitation of *The Gramophone*, which was responsible for my first orchestral recordings in the days of the National Gramophonic Society. Proud and happy as I am at the compliment which New York has paid me, I am deeply aware of the hard and difficult task which lies before me, and I hope that I shall not prove too unworthy of the honour which has been paid to British Music through me.

Please let me deprecate at once any talk that I am to be Toscanini's successor. With his going closes a great era in the history of the New York Philharmonic, and an official of the New York Philharmonic Society put the position in this way to a reporter in an interview. He said: "We feel that in inviting Mr Barbirolli we are making what may prove an interesting experiment. We realize he is young but we are faced with the necessity of discovering fresh talent, and from what we have heard of his conducting in England we have every reason to believe that our choice will be a happy one."

John Barbirolli in the 1930s

I hope so. Strangely enough this year is my Silver Jubilee as a public performer; it is almost exactly twenty-five years ago that I, a small boy of eleven, played the solo part in the Saint-Saëns Concerto at the Queen's Hall.

I continued my studies as a cellist, but my real ambition had always been to conduct. When I was sixteen I became a member of the Queen's Hall Orchestra, and it was good schooling to work my way through such a large repertoire of orchestral works. Round about this time I also played in the Carl Rosa Opera Company Orchestra, and soon after joined the Beecham Opera Company at Drury Lane: in fact I scorned no avenue that would teach me something about my job. In those days mechanical music was unknown in the theatre; wherever plays were performed there would be a small theatre orchestra. I played in one of these. There was not much to do, incidental music to plays had fallen into disuse; all we did was to play the people to and from the bar in the intervals. In the long waits between the act-intervals I studied scores. When the time came that I had the opportunity to conduct, all these early experiences, this knowledge of playing inside an orchestra were to stand me in good stead.

My first professional effort was in 1925 when I founded a chamber orchestra under the auspices of the Guild of Singers and Players. The orchestra was small but of fine quality, and it soon made some reputation for itself. It was with this orchestra that I made my first gramophonic recordings for the National Gramophonic Society with some Purcell and Delius pieces.

My first big concert opportunity came when, through the sudden indisposition of Sir Thomas Beecham, the London Symphony Orchestra sent for me, giving me forty-eight hours' notice to conduct the Elgar Second Symphony [on December 12th, 1927]. Casals was the soloist in the Haydn Concerto, and one incident I remember vividly. At rehearsal, after the first few introductory bars, I stopped the orchestra and made a few remarks. Casals leaned forward in his chair and said: "Listen to him. He knows." I was only a boy, and those few words coming from such a great artist touched me deeply. It was a wonderful thing for a man of his greatness to do: I shall never forget it. But then I have always cherished the thought that all really great men are simple and generous, and very rarely have I been disillusioned. It is certainly true of Casals and Kreisler, to mention but two.

The Queen's Hall was packed that night, and a memorable evening for me. Coming off the rostrum, after the closing bars of the Elgar, I found a little man on the platform who accosted me with the words: "Don't sign any gramophone contracts. See you tomorrow at ten. My name's Gaisberg – HMV". And that was the beginning of my association with HMV, and of a very delightful friendship with that great little man, Fred Gaisberg, an association that has lasted ever since.

I have not the slightest doubt that my recordings have helped to spread my name abroad. The Editor has asked me if I have any stories to tell of recordings, but modern recording has reached such a high standard that there is little time for anything but the job in hand, and consequently recording is a strain. One evening I was recording with Heifetz for three hours, during which time we made the whole of the Wieniawski Concerto and the *Rondo Capriccioso* of Saint-Saëns – that gives you an idea of what has to be done in a studio these days! The end of that session found us completely exhausted, and the lady had gone home with the key of the whisky cupboard. It was broken open!

I would not like to go to New York now without acknowledging my very real debt to my friends, the orchestral players of this country. From the day I left my seat among them to stand before them, our relations have been those of mutual respect and affection, and in the great honour that has come to me, I would like to feel they have a share.

June 1939

SPRING – AND A YOUNG MAN'S FANCY

By W. S. Meadmore

The broken sash

"In the Springtime, a young man's fancy ...". Poets have never tired of warning the moth-like male of the particular dangers of this time of the year. But you, reader, as a gramophone enthusiast, must beware of indulging in any such fancies which so inevitably lead to the altar and matrimony.

One day you will arrive home and find that instead of the old and well-beloved mistress, your gramophone, there is another, a wife, waiting for you. No man can serve two masters, to serve two mistresses is even more incredible. The first intoxication of honeymoon days having passed, you will wistfully think of the many happy hours formerly spent in your favourite gramophone shop, hunting for fresh treasure and trying over new records.

How long you will be able to stand this strain will naturally depend on your own temperament. But the evening will surely come when you will return home with a carrier bag, and that unfortunately not a plain cover, but with the name of your dealer writ large on it for all to see. So heavy is the bag that the string has cut into the bottom of your fingers. But that is nothing to the sinking feeling in your heart that you are over an hour late for dinner.

On entering the house you will at once be impressed with an unfamiliar atmosphere of coolness. You will be received with an unfriendly look. One glance has been enough for your wife. She knows what you have been up to and what the bag contains.

"What! More records?" she will exclaim in tones of icy disdain. She has at once conveyed to you that you have wasted money which could have been much more wisely and pleasurably spent on a female hat.

In bachelor days, with new records to be tried, you would not have troubled about food. Now you have to endure a tedious meal which has been spoilt by your lateness, and listen to frivolous domestic small talk with your mind already over-taxed and occupied as to the exact needle and sound-box to use for that marvellous Gigli record. Having gulped a cup of scalding coffee, it is with the furtiveness of a criminal that you steal out of the room and place the first record on the gramophone – a thrill you have impatiently waited for and anticipated ever since you left the gramophone shop.

"What! More records?" becomes a hateful refrain in the rhythm of your life; you become deceitful, dissemble, and watch the opportunity to smuggle new records into the house. When 'she' hears one of these for the first time and exclaims "that's a new one, isn't it?" you lie glibly and aver: "Oh, no. That's one I haven't played for a long time."

Thus your character deteriorates. From an honest gramophone enthusiast, unafraid to look any man in the face, you become shifty, evasive and even toy with the notion of selling your gramophone and record collection. Even the most perfervid of married gramophone enthusiasts have these dark moments and hear Beethoven's ominous and fateful knockings on the door. Not only is your character debased, but also your taste. Your wife is conventional, her likings are for light music. She detests modern music or anything she calls 'noisy', while gladly suffering the most cacophonous of dance records. Being a mere man you are obliged to resort to the subterfuge of only playing the records you really like on those rare occasions when she is away from home. It is like having an affair with another woman, the stolen moments are sweet enough, but it becomes increasingly difficult to hide your guilty and secret passion from the all-seeing eyes of your wife.

It would not be so bad if the monthly lists were not so disconcertingly attractive. Out of sheer devilry, or so it would seem, each month sees some old favourite of yours recorded which you have been wishing would be done for years. 'She' thinks you already have too many records, they take up far too much space, and 'she' cannot understand why you want more. Once you laughed – in your bachelor days – when you were watching an obviously newly married couple looking through a pile of second-hand records and you heard the young woman say: "I can't think what you want with new records when you already have at least a dozen at home!".

February 1937 **Editorial**

INSTEAD OF OUR USUAL EDITORIAL

Compton Mackenzie had an attack of sciatica and was unable to contribute an Editorial to the February 1937 issue. Faith Mackenzie, acting in Christopher Stone's absence, invited Herbert Ridout, who had worked in the Publicity Department of the Columbia Graphophone Company since 1906, to 'stand-in'

Mr Compton Mackenzie is ill. It is no empty platitude to say we are all sorry to hear this and wish him a speedy recovery. He is a type of worker to whom inactivity, for any reason, must be anathema. His working and sleeping hours must be, and probably are, planned to extract the utmost from each round of the clock. So it is pretty certain that he must chafe and rebel against an idleness enforced by illness – a rebellion that will probably increase as convalescence develops.

I remember quite distinctly the article in Robin Legge's Saturday music page of *The Daily Telegraph* signed by Compton Mackenzie [p. 15]. It was the outburst of one who had made a discovery. Frankly, to one like myself, who had for some years been connected with publicizing the gramophone and the music it offered, it was a little amusing. No doubt the amusement was shared by others in the industry.

What I – and others in similar positions in other companies – had been endeavouring to bring home to the public for years, had apparently fallen almost completely on stony ground. We had been trying to educate the public in the good music and first-rate artists by that time becoming identified with the gramophone. And here, out of the blue, came a popular novelist who had discovered the gramophone!

Little reckoning that it was likely to have any sequel, everybody thought it a very handsome and timely recognition of a form of home music that was genuinely endeavouring to earn the goodwill of music-lovers, obviously and utterly sincere in its enthusiasm – and with that tacit acknowledgement practically dismissed it. Why, indeed, should we do otherwise?

It was good propaganda for the gramophone, of course, but – well, just a drop in the oceans of publicity then beginning to rise to full flood. In a few weeks the article was all but forgotten. But if Mr Mackenzie had not impressed the industry with his initial writing upon the gramophone, it soon became clear that he had not said his last word, and clear, too, that his interest was no passing whim or fancy.

It seemed that the gramophone had 'got' him. Perhaps he realized that its potentialities were so vast that he was impelled to go farther. Be that as it may, it could only have been a few months later when the heads of the industry – Mr Alfred Clark and Mr Louis Sterling prominently among them – found themselves being asked to consider the possibilities of a new monthly devoted to the gramophone and to be edited by Mr Compton Mackenzie.

So *The Gramophone* magazine was born. I was in America when the first issue in its severe buff cover appeared, but I recall the shock I had when I realized that here was something which was not merely a sequel to Mr Mackenzie's journalistic 'squib' but what might well prove to be a force in gramophone propaganda. But if it was a brazenly bold venture it was a well-timed one, for it came at a moment when the first real technical improvements in gramophones and records were being made, side by side with the intensive cultural development of the material recorded.

Looking back, I think there were a lot of people in the industry who felt that the magazine could hardly succeed because it was so far above the heads of the class we had come to consider the gramophone public. The manufacturers themselves were still endeavouring to lift the musical standard, with better artists and better music, but it was pretty heavy going for them, and by the same token a magazine that had the same objective must find it equally difficult.

But that is where the personality of Mr Mackenzie came in. If a music critic or music journalist had essayed the production of such a paper, it would probably have shaped something like a collection of the (to me) somewhat abstruse leaflets that are given away with records. The founder of this magazine, however, was a novelist with a journalistic mind. He had the gift of writing down – not lowering his style but writing down – to the understanding of the ordinary individual. Reading his articles, it sometimes struck me that he must have switched off from working on some romantic part of a novel to write his gramophone *causerie*. They were not the stuffy product of a mind that thinks in movements, but of a lively, moving mind.

When he told his readers he liked a recording, he told why. He did not analyse the music as such, but frequently pictured the scene in which he first heard it, or the effect it had upon his emotions. He always insisted on the fact that it was recorded music – music of the gramophone – and made his readers feel that seeing it through his eyes, hearing it with his ears, they might reasonably enjoy it with him.

In founding this magazine, its editor gathered around him writers who, in the main, were men who had knowledge of the gramophone – and its limitations as well as its possibilities – in addition to a knowledge of music. The one therefore was tempered with the other and the editor took the head off the 'crocodile' and kept it more or less in the straight and (very) narrow gramophone-cum-music path. So, with a shrewdness that might be looked for

The Gramophone, April, 1929

more in a general journalist than in a novelist-editor, he dexterously maintained a high standard of readability, leavened with musical yeast just sufficiently technical to keep the reader feeling he was being elevated.

It has been one of my joys whenever Mr Mackenzie came to town from one of his remote islands, he almost always paid me a visit. His mission was always the same. He wanted first-hand information of developments; would ask what we thought of ***The Gramophone***; was it exercising any influence? And was there anything he could do to help?

On one of his visits, when talking of future plans, two projected operas were mentioned. Our visitor inquired what they were and whether we would issue them with the usual side-by-side Italian-English libretti. A moment's thought and then – "I think it might add to the interest if freer English translations were given. The usual singing translations are frequently so stiff and awful. The translator has to fit ugly English words in place of liquid singing Italian" – or words to that effect.

The suggestion was daring and I think Mr Mackenzie sensed our doubt as to its practicability. Then – "Well, I'd like to do them for you if you'll allow me."

And that is why you will find among the Columbia opera albums *La bohème* and *La traviata* each described as having a libretto of Italian text "with English prose translation by Compton Mackenzie". And, as a tip to readers of ***The Gramophone***, if you want to enjoy the stories of two famous operas, here in these shilling booklets is, not a stilted dialogue written in a form to make it singable, but Compton Mackenzzie at his best, making the plots live and thrill – the same cultured literary style, the same easy, beautiful flow of language, the same complete immersion in the characters, and the same precision and certainty of words that one finds in his novels. These are, I believe, the cheapest Compton Mackenzie books ever issued.

Let me tell you this. It may surprise you. Mr Mackenzie has made no big money out of the gramophone, or indeed (if the publisher allows me to say so) out of ***The Gramophone***. I know a little of the production costs of magazines, so I'm safe in saying that.

Why, then, has Mr Compton Mackenzie devoted all this time and money, lavished all this service, upon a subject (objective if you will) that could not, in the nature of things, be nearly so productive or remunerative as his other work – as he must have known from the beginning?

I could give you the answer in my own words, but it happens that, as I finish this, I have glanced at *Who's Who* for any clues it might afford as to his personality. And there, in simple words, I find the answer –

RECREATION: The gramophone, Editor of ***The Gramophone***.

"Why records are selling better and better". He described the response in May 1939 as an "unqualified success" with replies from all over the world. He had elicited the help of Fred Gaisberg and Richard Haigh (General Manager of HMV) as judges and the first prize went to John Freestone of Haywards Heath, later to be a regular contributor to the magazine.

During the coming weeks it was impossible to dismiss the inevitability of war and even before the declaration on September 3rd, 1939 the question had to be faced as to whether the record industry would continue and, even if it did, would there be any place for a publication such as *The Gramophone*? Beyond this it was generally believed that once war broke out London would be a prime target for enemy bombers and consequently many businesses were preparing to evacuate the capital. Compton Mackenzie was by now on Barra in the Outer Hebrides and in the autumn of 1938 Faith Mackenzie had moved to a small cottage at West Horrington, near Glastonbury in the West Country. Christopher Stone had a house at Wiston, near Steyning in Sussex, and my father was living at Kenton in Middlesex.

May 1939 **Editorial**

WHY RECORDS ARE SELLING BETTER AND BETTER

by John Freestone

In January 1939, Compton Mackenzie set readers a competition to "elicit their theories about the reason why records are selling better and better". The winner was judged to be John Freestone, who after the war became a regular contributor to the magazine

The last great boom in record sales was easy to understand. It was due largely to the introduction of electrical recording, and its end was caused partly by the Depression, and partly by the production on a large scale of really efficient and moderately priced wireless sets. For a time the novelty of radio proved a sufficient draw to affect badly the sales of records, but the many advantages of the gramophone came, in time, to be felt, and as a natural reaction, the sale of records increased once again. This is one cause, among many, of the revival in the record industry. It is not enough in itself, however, to account for the improvement of recent months, and we must look elsewhere for further reasons. None of these in itself may seem of outstanding importance, but the combined effect of all of them must be considerable. Remember, it may be necessary to go back several years for some of these, for the reaction of the public is slow.

During the 'boom' years, many people were playing their electrically recorded discs on machines designed for acoustical records, and consequently record wear was considerable. The early pickups were also heavy on records. Many of my friends at that time complained to me that the new records did not last as well as the old ones, and as a consequence their purchases decreased. These difficulties have now been overcome. More recent sound-boxes and pickups cause little wear.

In addtion many of the smaller companies who sold cheap records at uneconomic prices have disappeared and so the standard makes no longer have this competition to face. As a result they are able to issue records of a higher general standard.

A few years ago the musical film became popular and the general public found that grand opera, in suitable doses, was not so boring as they had imagined. Grace Moore introduced them to the entrance of Butterfly, "One fine day", "Sempre libera", and other famous excerpts from well-known operas. Deanna Durbin introduced Mozart's *Alleluia*, and Kiepura sang such numbers as "Che gelida manina", "Di quella pira" and "Celeste Aida". It takes a few years for the desire of music of this kind to gain a hold on the provincial public, but I am sure that opera, in any case, is very much in the ascendant. During their last visit to Brighton the Carl Rosa company played to packed houses, and the vast majority of the audiences were young people, of my own age, or even less. As a result of this increase in the number of music lovers the sale of records has naturally tended to improve. (The provincial opera lover must depend largely on records for his amusement.)

About a year ago HMV and Columbia introduced record players at popular prices, thus bringing a two-piece radiogram within the reach of all.

A number of new personalities of outstanding merit have recently come before the record buying public: Björling, Korjus, Flagstad, Lemnitz – to mention the first names that come to me.

The introduction of society issues has been a great boon to the companies concerned. They are able to satisfy the connoisseur, with the certainty of sufficient sales for their records. This has enabled them to play for greater safety in the general monthly lists.

One last point, the radio and gramophone firms have found it possible to offer efficient radiograms at a price little in advance of a wireless set alone, and many people have thus spent the little extra necessary to enable them to play records, and a new public has been reached.

All the points raised have, I feel, had their gradual effect on the sale of records, and it would seem probable that the present increase in sales may continue steadily for many months to come.

The Second World War

1939-1949

A *Gramophone* chronology

1939-1949

1939

- Goddard Lieberson joins CBS Masterworks as assistant to the Director.

January

- First releases on Louise Dyer's Oiseau-Lyre label reviewed in *TG*.

Goddard Lieberson *Photo Sony*

April

- Fred Gaisberg retires from The Gramophone Company after 49 years in the Industry and is succeeded as Artists Manager by David Bicknell who joined the company in 1927.

May

- Sir Louis Sterling retires as MD of EMI and Alfred Clark continues as MD/Chairman.

October

- *TG* offices move to 49 Ebrington Road, Kenton, Middlesex.

Fred Gaisberg

1940

- *Fantasia*, filmed by the Walt Disney Studio with a stereo soundtrack, is released.

September

- *TG* leaves 10a Soho Square, London but retains a small basement office in Russell Square.
- George Winkworth joins *TG* as part-time Advertisement Manager.

October

- Walter Yeomans of The Decca Record Company dies.
- The British Chancellor of the Exchequer introduces Purchase Tax on gramophone records. Initially 33⅓ per cent on the price to the retailer. A 6s. [30p] 12-inch 78rpm disc is increased to 7s. 4d. [36p].

1941

May

- Cecil Pollard appointed London Editor of *TG*.
- G. Howard-Sorrell joins *TG*'s reviewing team.

1942

April

- EMI take advertising space on front cover of *TG* – continuing until May 1969.

May

- W. S. Purser, ex-Columbia Technical Manager, dies and is succeeded by Charles B. Gregory – who joined Columbia in 1895 – as Manager of the EMI Studios, Abbey Road.

Charles Gregory *Photo EMI*

June

- Capitol Records Inc is founded in USA by Glenn Wallichs, Johnny Mercer and Buddy DeSylva.
- Alan Blumlein and two other EMI research engineers are killed when a Halifax bomber crashes in the Wye Valley whilst carrying out airborne centimetric radar research critical to the war effort.

August

- James Caesar Petrillo, head of the American Federation of Musicians (AFM), introduces a ban on most recording activities in USA.

1943

September/November

- First recording sponsored by the newly created British Council undertaken by EMI – Moeran's Symphony in G minor by Heward and the Hallé Orchestra.

1944

June

- Decca commence the use of "Full Frequency Range Recording"– *ffrr* (the actual announcement was made in June 1945 – "in use over the past 12 months", the first important release being Stravinsky's *Petrouchka* with Ansermet and the LPO in 1946). EMI had a similar system which had been used when recording Holst's *Planets* with Boult and the BBC SO in January 1945 but it was not publicized at the time.

November

- AFM ban on recording in the USA ends.

The Gramophone, July, 1945

ffrr
Decca
full frequency range recording, announced by Decca on June the 8th, has been in daily use in the Decca recording studios for the past twelve months. Decca Red Label records, made the ffrr way, demonstrate the unquestionable superiority of Decca full frequency range recording: the outcome of extensive pioneer research by Decca engineers making possible for the first time the recording of the full range of musical frequencies with all their overtones.

The Gramophone, May, 1946

Petrouchka—Ballet Suite (Igor Stravinsky)

Recorded at the Kingsway Hall, London. K 1388/92 (10 sides)
Automatic couplings AK 1388/92
Decca Red Label ffrr records 4/- (plus P.T.) Printed descriptive notes by the conductor are included.

Decca ffrr Living music

ONE SHILLING JULY, 1945

The Gramophone

Trade Office: Montague House Russell Square London, W.C.1 Telephone: Museum 8521

incorporating VOX, THE RADIO CRITIC and BROADCAST REVIEW

Edited by COMPTON MACKENZIE and CHRISTOPHER STONE

LONDON EDITOR - CECIL POLLARD

Editorial Office: 49 Ebrington Road Kenton, Harrow Middlesex Telephone: Wordsworth 2010

SATURN URANUS MARS VENUS MERCURY JUPITER NEPTUNE

THE PLANETS

Gustav Holst

Concert performances in complete form are very rare. With these records you can enjoy and become intimate with every detail of Holst's masterpiece. The Planets calls for the fullest resources of a large modern orchestra, and this latest achievement of "His Master's Voice" in collaboration with the British Council is an artistic triumph.

THE B.B.C. SYMPHONY ORCHESTRA
Conducted by SIR ADRIAN BOULT
The Planets Suite, Op.32. *Holst*
DB 6227-8, DBS 6229, DB 6230-3
Album No. 387. Auto. Couplings DBS 8994, DB 8995-9000
Recorded under the auspices of the British Council
(Full details will be found on page 11)

"HIS MASTER'S VOICE"

THE GRAMOPHONE COMPANY LTD., HAYES, MIDDLESEX

1945

April

- Alfred Clark becomes President of EMI with Sir Alexander Aikman as Chairman and Sir Ernest Fisk as MD.

June

- RCA in America release the first 78rpm records pressed in vinyl – $2 as opposed to $1 – a limited exercise not copied elsewhere at the time.

August

- Founding of the Philharmonia Orchestra by Walter Legge.

October

- First public appearance of the Philharmonia Orchestra in the Kingsway Hall under Beecham.

Sir Alexander Aikman (left), Sir Henry Wood and Alfred Clark, Chairman of EMI, in June 1944 *Photo EMI*

- George Mendelssohn founds Vox Records in New York.

W. S. Barrell

1946

January

- Charles B. Gregory dies and is succeeded as Manager of the EMI Abbey Road Studios by W. S. Barrell.

July

- Anthony Pollard joins *TG*.

September

- Alfred Clark resigns as President of EMI.
- EMI make their first recording with Karajan and the VPO – Beethoven's Symphony No. 8.
- Founding of the Royal Philharmonic Orchestra by Sir Thomas Beecham.

November

- John Culshaw joins The Decca Record Company.

1947

Dr Fred Hamel

- Limited introduction of magnetic tape for professional recording purposes.

August

- Deutsche Grammophon inaugurate their Archiv Produktion label under Dr Fred Hamel, initially covering the period from Gregorian Chant to circa 1800. The first recording was with Helmut Walcha at the small organ of the Church of St Jacobi, Lübeck.

1948

April

- ***TG*** Silver Jubilee is celebrated.

June

- The 33⅓ rpm long-playing record is introduced in the USA by Columbia Records Inc.

October

- Herbert Ridout dies.
- EMI introduce the use of magnetic tape for a number of their recording sessions.

November

- Lionel Salter joins ***TG***'s panel of reviewers.

1949

February

- 45rpm records introduced in the USA by RCA Victor.

April

- First release of Haydn Society 78s in the USA.

The Second World War

A view of The Round House, part of Christopher Stone's Wiston Old Rectory, which housed *The Gramophone* for a few weeks in 1939

Cecil Pollard's home at 49 Ebrington Road, Kenton in 1939. It was from the front ground-floor room that the magazine was produced from late-1939 until August 1951, and it was this view which in the summer of 1943 greeted a somewhat puzzled American soldier, Fred Lord II, who asked Cecil Pollard, pruning his roses in the front garden, if he could direct him to the offices of *The Gramophone*!

Soho Square to Kenton

The Soho Square office consisted of my father, Christopher Stone, William Hollamby, Gilbert Wilson, Allan Houghton and Vera Lovegrove. In August 1939 it was proposed to operate all but the trade circulation and subscription departments from Stone's house at Wiston in Sussex, and my father moved with my mother and myself to a cottage in the grounds. With the lease on Soho Square due to expire in September 1940 my father suggested that the remaining staff should endeavour to make alternative arrangements: Hollamby (who had joined the Company in 1924) went into the Royal Artillery and was later followed by Houghton (joined 1936) who went into the Royal Air Force, with Wilson going to a company involved with defence electronics.

Gilbert Wilson (left) with Christopher Stone in 1948

Nellie Pollard

Those early months of the Second World War were often referred to in Britain as "the phoney war" and it was not until the evacuation from France in May 1940 and the aerial Battle of Britain in September that things began to change. My father soon realized that the business could not be operated from the depths of Sussex and within a few weeks of the move in August 1939 he had established an office in a room of his house in Ebrington Road, Kenton. Initially, he was helped by his secretary, Vera Lovegrove, who had joined the Company in 1929, but early the following year she left on account of ill health (sadly to die on October 28th, 1942), and for the next six years he was assisted by my mother.

Up to this point there had been, in addition to Mackenzie's editorials, a fairly positive editorial input from either Stone or Faith Mackenzie. My father had been principally concerned with business affairs, but fortunately enough of the editorial decision-making had come his way to ensure that he could cope when, in the autumn of 1939, he found himself responsible for all the day-to-day functions of the Company, and in May 1941 he was appointed London Editor.

200th Issue

January 1940 marked the publication of the 200th issue of the magazine and in his editorial Mackenzie retold the story of its inception and paid tribute to my father, saying "We have been extremely happy in our relations with the gramophone industry and I know there is not a man on the business side who would not agree with me in giving the greater part of the credit for this to our Manager, Cecil Pollard, whose devotion over many years to the best interests of everybody concerned is beyond any ability of mine to convey in words".

The three main anchor-men of the reviewing team, Alec Robertson, W. R. Anderson and Edgar Jackson, remained in place throughout the war years and in May 1941 they were joined by Geoffrey Howard-Sorrell, who lived immediately opposite our house in Kenton; he took-over the "Miscellaneous and Dance" reviews from Roger Wimbush (who joined the Royal Norfolk Regiment) and also contributed a valuable series of technical articles until the return of Percy Wilson in September 1953. However, with a substantial reduction in the number of record releases, contributions by other familiar names such as W. A. Chislett and Harold Rosenthal (later to edit *Opera*) became less frequent. In July 1940 Herbert Ridout began a remarkable series of 39 articles recounting his involvement with the record industry between 1906 and 1931: in addition the 'golden-age' collectors were ably served by P. G. Hurst, and Clough (and Cuming) continued to monitor both record deletions and such foreign releases for which information reached them. Fred Gaisberg, who had retired from The Gramophone Company in April 1939, was also to become a more regular contributor, writing about those artists with whom he had worked (Patti, Menuhin, Toscanini, Pagliughi, Austral, Pachmann, Caruso, Dawson, etc.) and his successor, Walter Legge, also took up his pen to write a series of similar articles which would span the next 30 years.

The Correspondence columns provided news from servicemen at home and abroad giving their musical experiences in circumstances often very different to those which they had been accustomed in the past. Some were readers from happier days, such as Lt. James Robertson of the Royal Navy who was sadly killed at the age of 27 when HMS Barham was sunk on November 25th, 1941. His last letter to the Editor was dated November 6th. Later, from Italy, there were letters from the young Viscount Lascelles (later Lord Harewood) serving with The Brigade of Guards and from Ronald Phillips (a soldier serving in Italy who was instrumental in reinstating the San Carlo Opera in Naples after the Allied liberation and bringing Gigli and Gobbi to sing there – later he was to

Alec Robertson (centre) with Leonard Smith (EMI, left) and Lionel Salter in 1952

Fred Gaisberg (left) with some of his industry colleagues in 1948 – Mrs "Bill" Homewood (wife of Victor and past secretary to the Managing Director of EMI, Alfred Clark), William Sinkler Darby (employed by Berliner in 1895 and associated with Gaisberg in his early recording days), Arthur Clarke (veteran EMI recording engineer) and Victor Homewood (stand-in accompanist on some early HMV sessions and latterly EMI's Catalogue Manager)

found Collectors' Corner in Shaftesbury Avenue and Monmouth Street). In fact, letters came from every theatre of war, including military prison camps in Germany, suggesting that perhaps *The Gramophone* was playing its small part in the war effort.

A report and paper rationing

A report by Cecil Pollard to his fellow directors in August 1940 highlighted some of the problems of the day. "A year ago the Directors decided to make a 50% cut in their salaries owing to the war and the uncertainty which lay before them and the publication. At this date a few observations on the past and future would not be amiss.

"The circulation has now reached a level of 5,600 a month; this can be treated as net sales as returns are now made illegal by a recent government order. In September 1939 we printed 7,700 copies of which approximately one thousand were returned, the remaining thousand can be accounted for by loss of readers through military service and the inability to send copies to countries over-run by the Nazis.

"During the last few months the dealers have been finding business very difficult. Imhofs [a large record and instrument retailer in London] have ceased taking advertising space while others have reduced to half. As far as EMI and Decca are concerned it is hoped that they will maintain their present [page] space of five and one respectively. Owing to the shortage of material all radio firms are finding it difficult to produce new machines with the result that they cannot and do not wish to advertise.

"The printers, Messrs Gibbs & Bamforth, are still giving excellent service but like most firms their staff is being depleted owing to men joining up [for military service]. This with the frequent air raid warnings has slowed down considerably the production side. The decision to reduce the size of *The Gramophone* to 32 pages and cover, and the drop in the print order, shows a saving of approximately £37 per issue over last year. The average cost now being £60 per issue.

"When the war broke out we were lucky in having a good supply of paper in hand which cost 2½d. [1p] per lb. This stock will only last until January or February which will mean applying now for our third quota which will cost at least 5d. [2p] per lb, or £30 per issue. Estimated monthly income – Advertising £110, Sales and Subscriptions £135, Sundry Sales £5: making a total income of £250. Estimated monthly expenditure – Printing £60, Paper £30, Contributors £45, Salaries £88: making a total of £223. This leaves a balance in hand of £27 to meet Postage and Carriage £15, Rent £5 and the remaining £7 for telephone, general expenses, audit fee, insurance, etc."

As an island nation Britain could never be self-supporting and with the advent of war the importation of raw materials and finished goods had to run the gauntlet of enemy action against our vital shipping lanes. Economies were effected by rationing and controls, some of which were still to apply in the early 1950s. The availability of paper was a major factor and in his Editorial for July 1940 Mackenzie had written, "There is one matter in which we have already been obliged to take measures of curtailment, and that is the amount of paper which is available. What stock we have must be spread over as many months as possible or else we may find ourselves in a position to furnish our readers with everything that they expect to read in *The Gramophone* but without any paper to print it on. We are therefore starting to reduce the number of pages this month to a standard which we think we can maintain for many months to come, and must ask members of Gramophone Societies and the collectors of secondhand records to be content with the space still left to them. The first claim must always be that of the new records for review."

Traditionally, all newspapers and magazines were sold on a 'sale or return' basis, with full credit for the returns. A government order in January 1940 required that henceforth all such goods should be sold 'on firm sale' with no returns, and this was a precursor to the introduction of a form of paper rationing. Even though there was a requirement that advertising should occupy no more than 40 per cent of the publication, the result overall gave the publishers much better control over their sales and, with everyone being in the same position, profitability increased. Apart from a loss in 1939, the Company was able to show a trading profit throughout the wartime years – on average in the region of £300 per annum.

Space-saving and the front cover

In April 1942 the paper shortage gave rise to major changes in the appearance of the magazine: on the one hand a space-saving three-column layout was adopted overall and progressively the nine- and ten-point typefaces were reduced to eight and six point. Another change was to sell the lower portion of the front cover as advertising space and the option for this, and the outside back cover, was immediately taken up by EMI.

Later this was to have repercussions which were recorded in the Company's Minute Book. In September 1947 my father reported that he had received a letter from

The Gramophone
Edited by COMPTON MACKENZIE and CHRISTOPHER STONE
ONE SHILLING - MARCH 1942

ONE SHILLING APRIL 1942

The Gramophone

Trade Office: Montague House Russell Square London, W.C.1 Telephone: Museum 7745

Incorporating VOX, THE RADIO CRITIC and BROADCAST REVIEW
Edited by COMPTON MACKENZIE and CHRISTOPHER STONE
LONDON EDITOR - CECIL POLLARD

Editorial Office: 49 Ebrington Road Kenton, Harrow Middlesex Telephone: Wordsworth 2010

An announcement by

"HIS MASTER'S VOICE"

The list of new "His Master's Voice" records for April is considerably smaller than usual. The reason is merely that gramophone records, like other goods, are restricted by war-time conditions, and The Gramophone Company may find it necessary from time to time to meet the situation by temporarily restricting the new issues of "His Master's Voice" records. Within these limitations "His Master's Voice" will continue to offer you the GREATEST ARTISTS & FINEST RECORDING

THE GRAMOPHONE COMPANY LIMITED · HAYES · MIDDLESEX

The front cover changes to meet the need to save space. The EMI advertisement would remain until May 1969

The Decca Record Company (who had consistently supported the magazine with advertising, albeit at a lower level than EMI) requesting that they should be allowed advertising space on the front and back covers of the magazine. After discussion the Board agreed to this request and wrote accordingly to EMI terminating their 'until cancelled' contract with effect from the December 1947 issue, but indicating the Company's willingness to enter into another agreement for part of the space. EMI's Record Controller, C. H. Thomas (later to be the first Managing Director of EMI Records), suggested verbally that such action on the magazine's part could well result in the loss of all EMI advertising support. The Board, in reviewing the matter, instructed my father to continue negotiations on the lines laid down, which upheld the free and unbiased policy of the paper. In November, he reported that he had met both Mr Thomas of EMI and Mr F. E. Attwood, the Publicity Manager of Decca, in an endeavour to clear the deadlock; as a result he had also met Mr J. Gray, a Director of Decca, who advised him to leave matters as they were as at that time his company was not in a position to support the changes. As a result EMI continued to appear on the front cover until May 1969 when *The Gramophone* reinstated its own cover designs. With Decca's launch of LP in June 1950 they utilized a full-colour spread in the centre of the magazine.

Jimmy Gray, a Director of The Decca Record Company

Record Industry shortages

The record industry faced two specific shortages of raw materials. In the first place the special wax used in the 2-inch thick recording blanks came from Russia and in order to conserve the material the majority of records were cut on 'flow-coats' – glass discs with a relatively thin covering of wax. The older engineers, such as Arthur Clarke and Chick Fowler, maintained that they could never achieve the same quality with these substitutes which remained in use until the late-1940s when they were superseded first by acetates (although mainly for popular recordings) and then magnetic tape recording.

The other shortage, that of shellac which was a vital constituent of the 78rpm record, severely restricted the manufacture of the discs themselves. Shellac came from the Far East and its availability was curtailed as a result of the Japanese invasion of Malaya and Burma, as well as the problems of shipping such supplies as there were to the UK. From August 1942 onwards continual appeals were made for people to hand in their unwanted records for recycling, with initially two charities benefiting – The British Legion and The Great Ormond Street Hospital for Sick Children. Compton Mackenzie discussed this quite logically in his editorial of August 1942 but by June 1944 he was agonizing with readers on the problems of parting with much loved recordings. Parallel with this were appeals from ENSA (Entertainments National Service Association) in September 1942 for record players to use in military establishments, and in the following January from the Prime Minister for books and magazines for the Services – hand them in at any Post Office!

George Winkworth, *The Gramophone*'s Advertisement Manager from September 1940 until his death in May 1957

John Culshaw in the early 1950s *Photo Decca*

Lieutenant H. Schonberg, First Allied Airborne Army, with ETO ribbon, three battle stars and his glider trooper wings (1945)

Farewell to Soho Square and Walter Yeomans

With the termination of the Soho Square lease in September 1940, the trade counter and record library were transferred to Montague House in Russell Square: the subscription files going to Ebrington Road. The Russell Square office was opened for a few hours each week and presided over by George Winkworth, who had recently retired as Advertisement Manager of *The Sound Wave* and who was now to sell advertisement space in ***The Gramophone***.

In October came the sad news of Walter Yeomans's death from tuberculosis. He had played a major part in the early days of The Gramophone Company and also of The Decca Record Company which he had joined when it was started in 1929. Beyond this he had been a stalwart supporter of ***The Gramophone***, although as Mackenzie wrote in November 1940, "he never once suggested that preference should be shown to something in which he was interested. When he left HMV he went to Decca, where an enlightened policy gave him an opportunity to do all that was possible for British music". A few months before his death he had written, in confidence, to Mackenzie, "I want to pay 100% tribute to Pollard. He is a masterpiece. For him ***The Gramophone*** is his life's work. He spends incredible hours per week toiling away at the task of keeping ***The Gramophone*** vital and up to scratch. I see a good deal 'behind the scenes' and Pollard's unwavering loyalty, his devotion and his impartial enthusiasm is something I cannot find words to describe. Please believe all I say implicitly. Your London office is a Hall of Vitality. Over this Hall Pollard presides with grace, wisdom and understanding." (My father was never to read this tribute which appeared in Octave 8 of Mackenzie's *My Life and Times* published in 1969, four years after his death.)

On the cessation of hostilities PFC Fred Lord worked for *The Gramophone* for several months whilst awaiting a return passage to the USA (many US servicemen benefited from this enlightened attitude of the American Defense Department). He returned to Hunnemans, a real estate company in Boston and whilst he had no professional connection with the music business his nephew, Nathaniel Johnson, is currently responsible for RCA Victor's classical reissue programme. The picture, with Nellie Pollard, was taken in the garden of Ebrington Road in 1950. Fred Lord died in the spring of 1977

Cpl Jerry Pastene who wrote several articles for the magazine in the 1940s, conducted the Heidelburg SO following the city's liberation and who, though involved in the travel business, remained close to the music business on his return to the USA. He died in 1989

Early in 1943 Christopher Stone returned to the Army in a Public Relations capacity and was soon sent to North Africa. At home the build-up to the Allied landings on D-Day, June 6th, 1944, was in progress and a number of readers now in the Services availed themselves of the 'open-house' which my parents always kept at Ebrington Road. From many visitors there were a number of 'regulars' who became a part of the family and these included Sub-Lieutenant John Culshaw (Royal Navy, Fleet Air Arm), Lieutenant Harold C. Schonberg (US Army), Cpl Jerry Pastene (US Army) and PFC Fred Lord II (US Army). In return for the comforts of home, a pile of gramophone records and an occasional bed, they brought good company and, the Americans in particular, much appreciated food from their PX – a very up-market NAAFI.

The Gramophone at War

"It is not my desire to inflict upon readers of *The Gramophone* one superfluous word about the crisis which at the moment of writing is still at the height of its fever", wrote Compton Mackenzie in October 1938, referring to the possibility of war in Europe. However, when the war began a year later the magazine could not avoid being adversely affected by wartime restrictions, and inevitably these were reflected in the editorial pages. Most significantly, paper rationing altered the physical appearance of the magazine, steadily reducing its size, but other wartime conditions also necessitated frequent comment. These were to test severely Mackenzie's hopeful prediction, also in October 1938, that "readers of this paper will find in their gramophones one of the major alleviations of any bad times that may be ahead of us".

October 1939 **News**

F O R E W A R N E D

We went to press last month too early to draw attention to two ARP [Air Raid Precautions] records on HMV giving on separate but connected 'cuts' the wailing siren, the intermittent siren, the whistle, the rattle, the constant siren note, and the handbells. These were followed by another, "ARP signals, what they mean, what you do", wherein a man with a determined and not ingratiating voice explained the various noises. Whether anyone would dare to play any of these records within earshot of any unwitting stranger is doubtful, and it is to be hoped that they were really made for and used by instructors in ARP classes many months ago. [The records were never generally available but copies do exist in *Gramophone*'s library.]

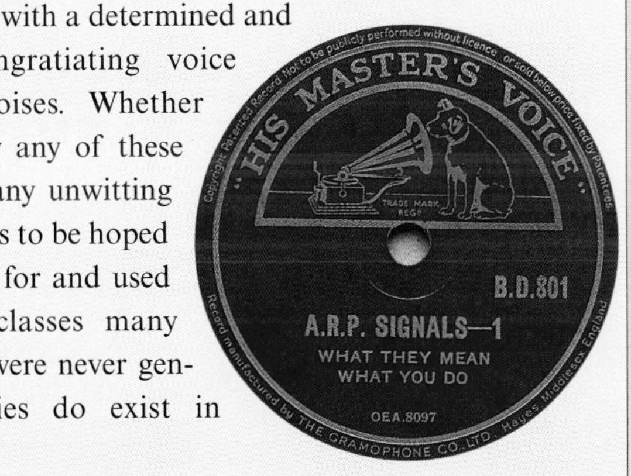

PLEASE NOTE

A Message to Readers & the Trade

It is our intention to continue publishing THE GRAMOPHONE each month, but owing to the transport delay and the likelihood of paper control there may be difficulty in obtaining copies. Therefore all readers of THE GRAMOPHONE are advised to place a regular order for the paper with their usual supplier now. (An order of this kind does not involve pre-payment.)

10a SOHO SQUARE, LONDON, W.1

The outbreak of war affected the availability of most commodities and the supply of paper, to a considerable extent dependent on imports, was at risk from the outset

Paper rationing

In printing, as in so many areas, the onset of war was greeted by a short-lived cessation of activity (also particularly true in the musical world, of course), wartime requirements and objectives taking time to be reflected in working practices. *The British and Colonial Printer* reported on September 14th, 1939: "In many offices work has fallen off almost to nothing. Other firms engaged one way or another in work of national importance are busy. Most firms have lost some of their workers to the armed forces." They went on to observe how Acts of Parliament and rationing "tickets" were being printed by the score, noting that every new regulation brought in its train other printed matter.

In a characteristically forthright editorial, also in the October 1939 issue, Compton Mackenzie passed on information he had received that record companies held enough unpublished material to maintain supplies for three years, and went on to make the following prophecy:

"I believe that the sales of records of great music will astound the recording companies, and it is in that belief that we who have carried on this paper for over sixteen years are determined not to let it die, even if it has to be reduced to a single sheet sent round to a handful of loyal and indomitable enthusiasts. Enquiries made among the trade reveal a determination to support us in our resolve to endure. We may have to reduce our size. We may have to appear in the middle of the month instead of in the beginning. We may have to keep our readers waiting for reviews of some records until the following month. We

GERMAN MUSIC

In the early days of the war, the Editor was asked about the propriety of buying records of German composers, or indeed of listening to German music at all. In June 1940 he wrote

I do not think it is necessary for me to argue the aesthetic side of this question. I have seen no signs this time of the pseudo-patriotism, which at the beginning of the last war tried to persuade people to refuse to listen to German music, merely because it was German music. On the other hand, commercially, German artists do not benefit by a penny from the sale of German records in this country, and copyright royalties are in abeyance. I hope when the war is over artists that were enemies will receive royalties now unpaid, for I think it would be a mean trick to make money at the artists' expense under the guise of patriotism. But those buying German records in England now need not worry about royalties being paid now. Remember too that all the records have been paid for out of British controlled funds and that the Germans receive no benefit. Moreover these recordings are essential in order to keep a German-made record out of export markets like South America or in other places where German-speaking communities are large.

The German propaganda broadcasts of Lord Haw-Haw (the English announcer who was eventually revealed as William Joyce and hung as a traitor after the war) caused further comment on this subject from Mackenzie in November 1940

Last autumn Lord Haw-Haw announced that Beethoven's music was being banned in this country. The other day the BBC related in the news-bulletin that the Germans had prohibited the playing of Chopin in Poland, and the next day this was contradicted with a good deal of unction by Lord Haw-Haw. On the evidence, I fancy that the BBC like Lord Haw-Haw earlier had had its leg – or should I say ear? – pulled. It is true that at the beginning of the last war a number of nitwits in this country thought it savoured of patriotism to plead for the prohibition of all German music so long as we were fighting Germany, but fortunately the body of public opinion was sound and these buffoons were crushed. I have noticed in one or two obscure provincial rags a revival of this imbecility in the correspondence columns during this war, but the banning of German music has never been mooted by any newspaper of repute, and we have no reason to fear that it ever will be. Surely there is enough genuine stupidity loose in the world at present without ourselves or the Germans inventing stupidities.

But by December 1940, Mackenzie was horrified to learn that the BBC proposed banning "old works that can be interpreted in terms of modern Germany (such as Brahms's *Triumphlied* and Wagner's *Siegfried*)" and insisting that "German and Italian songs must be sung in English or not at all". In his December 1940 editorial, subtitled "Lunatics at Large", Mackenzie wrote

A perusal of the correspondence columns in *The Radio Times* leaves one with the impression that lunatics preponderate in this country. We do not want any secondhand Nazis interfering with the art of this country, and we are not fighting this war for ambitious Jacks-in-office. An ass's bray is the same in English, German and Italian, but the beauty of a song depends on its being sung in the words to which it was set. Cannot the officials of the BBC understand that behaviour like this drags us down to the level of what we are fighting against? Fortunately we with our gramophones are independent of music on the wireless, and was I not right to warn you all a year before the war started that while it lasted your music would depend on your gramophones?

may have to issue an appeal for six-monthly subscriptions. Nevertheless we shall continue. Our printers have given us the assurance of their support. The general feeling of the trade is one of optimism. We have at least as much right to crave the patience, indulgence and sympathy of our readers as the BBC of their listeners, and I hope that in our own humble way we shall make less of a mess of it than the BBC have made of broadcasting and that ***The Gramophone*** will not assume the characteristics of a newspaper edited in one of the lower forms of a girls' school."

In the UK, control of paper was effected by the Paper Controller, a senior figure from the industry appointed by the Ministry of Supply. Though within the framework of a succession of regulations (75 by 1946) paper control was in essence secured by the industry through a system of voluntary economies and agreements. At least in the first instance regulations were framed to regulate prices, control exports, and, as far as the printing industry was concerned, secure the agreement of unions in a closely regulated industry. *The World's Paper Trade Review* (September 1939) called the resulting Schedule of Controlled Prices, "a historic document".

As far as general and specialist consumer magazines were concerned, the thrust of paper control was to discourage new business, reduce the quantity and quality of paper, and discourage or ban frivolous use, including limiting advertising. Its positive aspect was to assist the continuity of existing businesses. It was only later during the war that there was a life-threatening shortage of paper as far as *The Gramophone* was concerned, but with its longstanding supply arrangements it survived not least because of its place as an established part of an industry and its position as the customer base of one paper supplier, A. H. James & Co. Ltd.

In February 1940, an "explanation" of current regulations affecting the magazine was printed, outlining the repercussions of a decision by the Newspaper Proprietors and Newsagents, and urging readers to ensure delivery by subscribing:

> For two reasons it is possible that, during the coming months, readers who are not regular subscribers may find difficulty in obtaining *The Gramophone*.
>
> The first reason is that in wartime the demand for *The Gramophone* increases very considerably, from month to month, and the printing number is difficult to estimate.
>
> The second reason is that, owing to war restrictions, the Newspaper Proprietors and the Newsagents have decided that all issues of periodicals will be sold to the Newsagents on a non-returnable basis.
>
> The effect of this decision must be that Newsagents will be careful to order no more copies than they reckon to sell, and in some cases, owing to miscalculation, their supplies will not be equal to public demand.
>
> To make certain, therefore, that *The Gramophone* is delivered regularly, it is necessary to place a standing order with the local Newsagent. A postal subscription through a Newsagent or direct from this office of course does just as well.
>
> For subscribers desirous of having *The Gramophone* sent regularly to relatives or friends in the Fighting Forces, special terms have been arranged, and enquiries are now invited.
>
> Readers not already subscribing are advised, in their own interests, to place definite orders at once. A yearly subscription costs 14s., half-yearly 7s.

The Gramophone was able to continue publication despite being much reduced in size and a shadow of its peacetime healthy self. In July 1940, Mackenzie announced the beginning of a steady reduction in pages as a result of a decline in the availability of paper:

"What stock we have must be spread over as many months as possible or else we may find ourselves in a position to furnish our readers with everything that they expect to read in *The Gramophone* but without any paper to print it on. We are therefore starting to reduce the number of pages this month to a standard which we think we can maintain for many months to come, and must ask members of Gramophone Societies and the collectors of secondhand records to be content with the space still left to them. The first claim must always be that of the new records for review."

In April 1941, while acknowledging that circulation had "grown steadily" over the "last eighteen fateful months", he announced that the difficulty of getting paper made a further reduction in size imperative.

One only has to look at a bound set of *The Gramophone* to see the effect of the war, and while this was not entirely due to paper control but also to the contraction of the record industry under wartime conditions, a few simple statistics will make clear that this decline was cumulative during the war:

Issue	Editorial	Advertisements
January 1938	45	18
January 1939	44	18
September 1939	42	20
January 1940	27	12
January 1945	11	8

Volume XVII (1939-40) ran to 438 pages of editorial; by the next volume this had shrunk to 278. "Turn Table Talk" in May 1941 noted that:

"The slimming process continues inexorably and our Vol. XVIII [June 1940-May 1941] when bound will be as slim as our Vol. I. The paper control's new order brings our allowance down to a quarter of the pre-war standard instead of the present third; and that implies a decrease of four pages a month. We have decided, for printing and other reasons, to reduce this and every alternate issue by eight pages and maintain next month's issue and the August, October and December issues at the same size as last month; and to make further reductions of type to increase the contents of the meagre space."

By 1943-4, 1944-5 and 1945-6 this had become 150 pages each year. Thereafter it began to grow again, but slowly. Shortages were not quickly reversed, and in July 1945 Mackenzie fulminated against a perceived unfairness in the allocation of resources:

"Let us hope that the unfair treatment of the recording companies in the matter of shellac will soon be a thing of the past. I might add the same about the allotment of paper, which has been a scandal from the day war broke out. It is unsufficiently realized by the British public how many very stupid people are still enjoying too much

October 1939 **News**

Soho Square has its underground shelters, and at one corner of the square is an ARP post sandbagged and decorated with suitable *facetiae*. The occupants made a plea for a portable gramophone and some records to while away the raidless evenings and though we were able to supply a parcel of records we had no portable. Mr G. H. Russell of The Gramophone Exchange very gallantly came to our rescue and had a portable put into good order for our defenders.

power. The power granted to stupid people in time of war is not the least of its horrors."

Particularly in the years immediately after the war, examination of a run of back issues can show the tell-tale signs of paper difficulties, say the issues for December 1945 and April 1947 with the revealing 'browning' of lower quality paper; whereas for all the issues printed during the war the paper survives in remarkably good condition, a sure sign of a quality product even if economy standards were in force and the quantity reduced.

Even as late as February 1949, the magazine noted there was "still a waiting list" for copies:

"The fact that newsprint releases enable daily newspapers to be available unrestrictedly has given many dealers and would-be-readers of *The Gramophone* the impression that a similar position now applies to periodicals. This is not the case, and as the supply of this journal, owing to paper rationing, remains insufficient at present to meet the demand the patience of those who are still unable to obtain it regularly must continue to be invoked."

The control of paper for "magazines, periodicals and news bulletins" was not finally revoked until February 1950.

The collaboration of Lewis Foreman is gratefully acknowledged in the preparation of this report on Paper Rationing

April 1941 **News**

REPLACEMENT VALUE

There is a story told of an enthusiastic collector of old records, who had an air-raid shelter erected in his back garden, during his wife's absence from home. When she returned and attempted to enter the shelter, she found it choc-a-bloc with her husband's precious records. Protesting that surely her safety should be considered first, she was naturally indignant when her husband replied that the records were of great value, as they could not be replaced; leaving her to make the obvious inference!

Purchase Tax

On October 21st, 1940 a purchase tax on "luxury" goods was introduced for the express purpose of discouraging unnecessary spending during wartime. The tax was applied to the wholesale value of goods, including records which were initially taxed at 33⅓ per cent of the wholesale price. A few months earlier, in his June 1940 editorial, Compton Mackenzie had asked rhetorically, "whether gramophone records are one of those luxuries which the Chancellor of the Exchequer begged people not to buy". His reply being, "that if this country has sunk to conditions in which music and literature are to be stigmatized as luxuries the quicker we are shaken into sanity the better".

As it turned out, books were exempted from the tax because, as his detractors (including Mackenzie) believed, the religiously-minded Chancellor could not find a way to tax literature without also taxing the Bible. In response to the news that, apparently, records were indeed deemed to be "luxuries", Mackenzie delivered a characteristically trenchant diatribe against the Chancellor of the Exchequer, Sir Kingsley Wood and his "assault upon our culture" in his editorial for November 1940:

"I had hoped against hope until the last moment that Sir Kingsley Wood would reconsider his decision not to exempt gramophone records from the Purchase Tax. I avoided taking part in the protest against the taxation of books because there were plenty of eloquent writers willing and fortunately able to convince Sir Kingsley Wood that a tax on learning, imagination and wit was not the best of propaganda for the cause we sustain, and that a tax on the Holy Gospel is not the most lucid evidence of a Christian purpose. However, at the last minute a telephone call informs me that in spite of every effort behind the scenes the Chancellor of the Exchequer, thwarted of his desire to tax literature, is determined to tax music. He probably does not think, amiable and esurient and harassed little man, that he is taxing music when he places a thirty-three and a third per cent purchase tax on gramophone records and exempts printed music. He probably believes himself as much a friend of the Muses as Apollo himself, and one may be allowed to hope that if he did once grasp that the gramophone record is to music what the printed word is to literature, he would realize the crime he proposes to commit against art. Music lovers have no desire to shirk their patriotic obligations. Let Sir Kingsley Wood and his financial advisers demonstrate to them that the Purchase Tax on records will benefit the country materially enough to justify the deprivation it will entail, and music lovers will not grudge their deprivation, neither those who pay more for their records nor those who on account of the tax have to reduce their purchases of records by a third. Let Sir Kingsley Wood come to the microphone and tell the country that the men working in the gramophone factories are diverting labour and money and time from the great national effort and I am sure he will hear no more complaints; but he could not come to the microphone and say as much. Does Sir Kingsley Wood want to go down through time as a small-minded politician whose idea of financing a mundane catastrophe was to tax the most precious gifts of the human mind? I cannot believe it, but I will promise him that if he does I will do my humble best to immortalize this aspect of him in a book."

The new tax was levied upon the wholesale not the retail price. A letter from E. R. Lewis of Decca, also in the November 1940 issue, made clear the difficulty in which this situation placed retailers:

"I feel that the position of the shopkeepers under the Purchase Tax requires a certain amount of sympathetic consideration. Purchase Tax is returnable, not by the retailer subsequent to the sale of goods, but by the wholesaler subsequent to the purchase of the goods by the retailer. As a result, on all goods purchased after October 21st the retailer will, of necessity, pay the tax to the wholesaler despite the fact that the goods remain on his shelf. If, therefore, a retailer added the tax to goods purchased before October 21st he would be merely collecting the tax in advance from the public, which tax would be paid over to the wholesaler as he replaced the goods sold, and by the wholesaler to the Customs and Excise. Although, admittedly, the man in the street might feel that he was being fleeced by having to pay the tax on goods that he knew the retailer must have purchased without the addition of the tax, a careful consideration of the retailer's position puts quite a different complexion on the matter, and a retailer who finances his business with care and foresight may well feel that he is having his own throat cut, however much he may prefer to give the public the benefit of the lowest possible prices and snatch as much quick turnover as possible."

Resulting increases in prices were quoted inclusively in the magazine. Thus in the September 1940 issue a Columbia DX record was 4s. [20p]; by December it had become 4s. 10½ d. [24½ p]. Indeed one of the sure signs of taxation on records was the spread of odd ha'pennies on the prices of records.

Once the tax was imposed it could only go up, and in his June 1943 editorial, Mackenzie seized on the launch of the British Council subsidy of recordings of British music, to attack the Chancellor, remarking that, "it seems faintly idiotic that Sir Kingsley Wood should immediately proceed to increase the already outrageous tax on every kind of gramophone record, and thus on representative British music". He got much nearer the key issue when he added: "when he sat down after his Budget speech like an amiable prima donna to receive a shower of bouquets from his fellow-members of the House of Commons, somebody should have told him that between music and lipstick there is something more than a distinction without a difference.

April 1969 **Correspondence**

TAX INSANITY

This is the time of year we wait with grim faces for the Budget. Last year the Chancellor took another savage swipe at the record industry. In years before that the industry mounted a campaign to have Purchase Tax removed from discs. Have they given up the fight, like so many other people in this over-taxed country?

It just does not make sense that a book written by a Beatle is not subjected to tax, but a Beatle recording is taxed. It just does not make sense that public money should be used to subsidize orchestras and the recordings of some little-heard British music, only for that money to be mopped up by the Exchequer in the record shop.

It might be argued that because of the tax that record companies have been forced to tempt purchasers with an ever increasing range of lower priced discs. In itself this is a two-edged sword. As one of your reviewers pointed out recently, who is going to pay full price for a reissue of Segovia? Not me. But MCA may know otherwise. The real danger of taxation forcing down the price of discs is that fewer and fewer ventures like the Decca *Ring* or the current Philips Berlioz cycle will become economically possible.

I suggest that more people hear good music on disc these days than in the concert hall. Our present Government, which pretends to be aiming at giving people a fuller life, is in fact, by its continued savage attacks on the record industry, in the process of constricting that fuller life. There may be some justification for reasonable taxation – but ten shillings and sixpence on a standard classical recording is not reason, it's plain insanity.

Peter Baker
Polegate, Sussex

It would, and should have been, easy to exempt from this preposterous tax records of good music."

On April 15th, 1942 the tax had been increased to 66⅔ per cent of the wholesale price, then on April 13th, 1943 that figure rose to 100 per cent where it remained throughout the war until April 16th, 1946 when it was reduced to 33⅓ per cent once more. But the tax increased again, first to 50 per cent on November 13th, 1947 and then back to 66⅔ per cent on April 9th, 1948.

In his editorial for May 1949, Mackenzie calculated that, "Since the tax was first levied the music lovers of this country have paid £7,750,000 into the National Exchequer for the records they have bought and £5,250,000 for the record-playing devices they have bought – thirteen million pounds in all". In the following number, the Editor published in full a letter he had drafted which had been sent to the Chancellor "signed by a dozen eminent representatives of music and poetry" in which he again railed against the logic that refused to accord records the same privileged status as books, periodicals (or sheet music).

The Chancellor reportedly read the letter with "sympathy and interest", but much to Mackenzie's continuing disgust, predictably was unable "to propose any fresh relief from the Purchase Tax in present economic circumstances". Records were never able to achieve any special status in the eyes of future chancellors either.

A notice in the May 1953 issue indicated an unexpected, but welcome reduction in the tax to 50 per cent, to which was added the optimistic comment that "we can look forward to the day when the Chancellor will announce the complete abolition of the tax". Instead, the Chancellor increased the tax by a further 10 per cent to 60 per cent in his autumn Budget of 1955.

Prior to the spring Budget of 1959 the anti-tax campaign was renewed with the insertion of a lengthy statement in the March issue, signed by Dr Leslie Russell, Senior Musical Adviser to the London County Council, Mr. J. F. Lockwood, Chairman of Electric and Musical Industries Limited (EMI), and Mr. E. R. Lewis, Chairman of The Decca Record Company. Two months later in May a small concession was announced:

"As readers at home will already know the Chancellor of the Exchequer in his Budget proposals, announced on April 7th last, reduced the rate of Purchase Tax on gramophone records from 60 per cent to 50 per cent of the wholesale price. We feel sure that even this slight concession will be welcomed by all readers and we would acknowledge here the work of the British Phonograph Committee (a body sponsored by the British Gramophone Record Industry) and wish them continued success in their campaign against this most illogical tax."

The British Phonograph Committee (a forerunner of the British Phonographic Industry – BPI) issued the following statement in May 1960:

"We are profoundly disappointed. The case for the abolition of Purchase Tax on gramophone records is irrefutable. The case for a substantial reduction even in the present Budget was overwhelming. Following last year's Budget, the Chancellor of the Exchequer said he was unaware that the feeling of the House of Commons was so strong on this subject. Since then, by deputation and by a petition signed by 140 Members of Parliament of all Parties, including 20 Privy Councillors, he was made fully aware of the feelings of Parliament regarding this intolerable tax. Accepted by the public and industry as part of their patriotic duty in wartime, it is indefensible that 15 years after the cessation of the Second World War the tax has not been abolished and stands at a higher level than it was then."

The rate fell slowly, first to 45 per cent then to 25 per cent (in 1963), but continued to fluctuate. As a result of Government Emergency Measures it rose by ten per cent in August 1966, and in the Budget of April 1968 it rose from 27½ per cent to 50 per cent, and was also added to pre-recorded tapes (50 per cent) and tape recorders (33⅓ per cent).

In 1971 a full-price pop LP sold for £2·15, of which Purchase Tax accounted for 55p (almost 26 per cent of the purchase price), according to figures given by L. G. Wood, Group Director of EMI Records, in a lecture to the Royal Society which was subsequently published in the November 1971 issue of ***The Gramophone***. Eventually, Purchase Tax was abolished, only to be immediately replaced in April 1973 by Value Added Tax (VAT), initially at the rate of eight per cent. Unlike the old tax, VAT was levied on the retail instead of the wholesale price. The debate between books and records continued, however, for books were again zero rated from the outset.

Resale Price Maintenance, the system supported by the British Phonographic Industry which fixed the cost of records, was abandoned in August 1969 and henceforth manufacturers' recommended retail prices were quoted alongside reviews in the magazine. The recommended retail price system was discontinued in August 1980, to be replaced the next month in the magazine by price symbols, indicating not a specific price but a price category, e.g. full, medium or bargain price.

The collaboration of Lewis Foreman is gratefully acknowledged in the preparation of this report on Purchase Tax

Record salvage

In October 1939 Mackenzie had passed on to readers the information that "stocks, whether they be matrices of hitherto unpublished works of music or of the material with which to publish them, are sufficient to maintain for three years the standard of excellence which we have learnt to expect from the recording companies", and he predicted that "provided distribution does not fail, the sale of gramophone records will show a steady increase month by month." But by 1941 shortages of raw materials, specifically shellac which had to be imported, prompted the launch of the Record Salvage campaign. Gramophone enthusiasts were encouraged to hand in their old records for recycling.

A joint statement from The Gramophone Company (EMI) and The Decca Record Company, published in the February 1943 issue, made clear that the three-year stockpile of recordings was well and truly exhausted:

> The further maintenance of adequate record supplies will depend upon the goodwill and readiness of the public to return old and unwanted records, because only by this means will manufacture continue. We ask users not only to give up their old records but to encourage their friends who may no longer be interested, but who may have old records, to give them up also.
>
> Some millions of scrap records are needed. In the last ten years over one hundred million records have been sold and it should be possible for the quantity required to be returned by the public. It does not matter what condition the records are in provided they are not broken. All of them will be reground and aid in making new record material.

Such an appeal must have been the occasion for much soul-searching on the part of the readers of ***The Gramophone***, most of whom had spent many years building their collections. In June 1944, Mackenzie addressed this thorny problem:

"I shall be frank and say that I think most readers of ***The Gramophone*** have bought their records with the notion of building up a library of good music and therefore that I should esteem it unreasonable to invite them to disperse those libraries for the sake of providing light entertainment in hospitals, camps, war factories, canteens, gun-sites or forward positions on the battle fronts, in warships and in merchantmen. Such a sacrifice must be made only if the individual is prompted by his own sense of duty. I am not prepared to preach on the matter. Where readers may be able to help is in finding out where accumulations of genuinely unwanted records exist and telling the owners of such accumulations that they can obtain cash for them and at the same time help to entertain a community engaged in every form of service. The recording companies have maintained throughout the war a standard of production which in the circumstances is little short of miraculous. It is our job to do all that we can to help them."

August 1942 **News**

RECORD SALVAGE

You will shortly see this poster in every record dealer's window and you will hear and read of this scheme to recover obsolete records throughout England, Scotland and Wales.

The Reason

Apart from use in the home, records are needed for official purposes, for broadcasting programmes at home and overseas, for providing "Music While You Work" in war factories and entertainment in workers' canteens, social centres and in HM Forces.

To provide for these services old records are urgently needed for the manufacture of new records in order to reduce the consumption of shellac which is required for other purposes.

How You Can Help

Turn out every record you can spare of the makes asked for and give them to your nearest British Legion Branch (your Post Office will tell you where it is). By doing so you will be serving two good causes by one good action, as the proceeds from the sale of the salvage is being divided between the British Legion and the Hospital for Sick Children, Great Ormond Street, London.

October 1942 **News**

RECORD SALVAGE DRIVE

To speed the collection of old gramophone records for salvage, householders are asked to indicate that they have some records to give by placing one of the discs, or a record bag, in the window. A pencilled note "call after 7pm", or whatever is a convenient time for handing over the records, could be written on the record bag.

Recording artists handing in unwanted 78s at the British Legion HQ in London. The comedian Sandy Powell shakes hands with General Sir Ian Hamilton, behind him is Ann Stevens (a young HMV artist), Richard Tauber, the singer Anne Shelton, the Monk twins and the comedienne Nellie Wallace

L I L L I   M A R L E N E

This popular wartime song had lyrics by Hans Leip, a German soldier who had written them during the First World War, but it did not achieve its finished form until it was set to music in 1938 by composer Norbert Schultze. It was recorded by Danish singer Lale Andersen in 1939 and became a hit on both sides when it was broadcast to German troops in Africa in 1942. It was subsequently recorded several times in both German and English versions. Anne Shelton adopted it as the signature tune of her BBC radio show, *Introducing Anne*, and her recording sold over a million copies. (After the war it became associated with Marlene Dietrich.) Yet another recording of the song prompted the following comment from Compton Mackenzie

July 1944 **Editorial**

A paradox of this war is that the only song which has caught the fancy of our troops is a German song, *Lilli Marlene*. So far I think I like Turner Layton's performance on a 10-inch Columbia disc, the best of those I have heard. I understand the original singer was a woman. I wish one of our readers with the Mediterranean Forces would give us an authoritative account of when this song became popular. I am told that the BBC was much perturbed because our own troops in North Africa always insisted on tuning in to the German wireless for their light music, and that desperate efforts were made to provide an English singing sweetie to cut out her German rival. These legends grow, and before this legend grows any more I should be grateful for an authentic history of this episode. If in fact *Lilli Marlene* was the favourite song, does it not suggest that this infernal crooning by Cockneys with synthetic American accents, male and female, is not so popular as the BBC thinks it is. There is something which comes perilously near to degradation in the music put out on the BBC on most nights between 11 o'clock and midnight. Some of the songs in their performance, words and music, encourage the enemy to suppose there are still enough decadent nitwits in this country to enable him to get out of the mess he is in. We in this country know that such drooling sentimentality means nothing, but we cannot afford to mislead a nation like the German which takes a masochistic delight in being misled. I am glad that on the whole the recording companies have refrained from issuing the soggiest tripe with which we are fed by the wireless. The companion to *Lilli Marlene* on the other side of the Turner Layton disc is *In a Friendly Little Harbour*, which is as sweet as bread and milk used to be.

Correspondence

LETTERS FROM SERVICEMEN

October 1941

Hic Pars Militiae

Music has always had a place in the panoply of war, whether for its disciplined rhythm, for is exhilaration, or for its share in victory. More subtly, music can bring back the visions of a life worth fighting for, the bigness of a world beyond the reach of man's destruction.

The civilian turned soldier often yearns for the loves of his old life. His books, his painting, and his once familiar music are torn from him by the relentless nothingness, the absolute subjectivity of the military machine. The power of material forces and perhaps a deeper knowledge of the meaning of the words "fellow men" add depth to his understanding. Danger strengthens his character, pain modifies his intolerance and a little good emerges from the vast evil mass of hate and bestiality.

Some of us can remember the grandeur of Beethoven when the bombs were thundering down. We were grateful for the depth of the emotion which swallowed up our fear.

'Signals' had struggled for months to build up a radio gramophone worthy of its task, and now they had succeeded, encouraged by the enthusiasm and vision of their Commanding Officer. The crude hall vanished, the uniforms, usually so persistently uncomfortable, were forgotten. Only the music to measure remained. We were refreshed, reclothed in sanity. We had listened again to an orderly tumult of sound which we could match against the disorderly tumult of France. How small the war seemed in comparison. Man was greater than war. Man was master of his fate.

J. N. G.

June 1942

The Gramophone in "Stalag XXB"

As a reader of your magazine for many years you might be interested to hear of the gramophone conditions here. In May 1941, a supply of Decca Portables and records arrived. The records were Rex, Decca and Decca-Polydor. Needless to say they were received with great jubilation.

The machines and records were supplied to working camps of 100 men or more, 30 records (20 of 10-inch and ten of 12-inch) being the average. Unfortunately the supply of needles is a great difficulty, causing great wear owing to having to make each needle work until all semblance of point disappears. Also the record envelopes soon went west. The 12-inch records were mostly extremely classical – Beethoven, Bach, Mozart symphonies – and to make matters worse, usually only one record of each work was received at the working camp. A fit subject for a Bateman cartoon is the POW who wanted to listen to Bach. I personally have been told in no uncertain terms, just where to go when attempting it. The war cry is "Give us Bing". At the main camp of this Stalag is a large cabinet Electrola, bearing unmistakable signs of Hayes, Middlesex. All good wishes.

(Driver) M. C. Moore
Prisoners of War Camp,
Stalag XXB, Germany

June 1942

Organized recitals on a tanker

Perhaps your readers would be interested to know what the gramophone means to the men of the tanker fleet; I refer to this branch of the Merchant Navy because tankers spend less time in port than any other class of merchant ship, and officers and men are more than ever forced to rely upon their initiative to help break the long, weary spells of the 'watch below'.

We had an HMV table model gramophone fitted in the smoke-room, and a little over 100 records. At the beginning of the trip the machine was played in a desultory sort of manner, and very soon the stock favourites were in danger of being worn out; other records – mainly because of unattractive titles – had never been heard. We decided to adopt a more sensible attitude: the machine to be played for well-planned recitals only, on two evenings of each week; other nights, of course, it might be played as usual.

A 'gramophone master' was elected, his job being to arrange the programmes and give a few explanatory notes before each record. Poor fellow! What a time he had, hunting up scraps of information out of well-worn encyclopaedias! But we managed very well, and these two interludes each week, simple though they may seem on paper, meant a great deal to men who had not seen home-side in years, and foreign ports only at long intervals.

We had 'popular' evenings, 'musical tours', 'grand opera', 'comedy', 'jazz versus the classics' (please don't shudder, highbrows! We were 1,000 miles from land!) 'military and martial', 'sentimental' and so on.

One of our company possessed an old copy of *Punch*, which included a somewhat satirical sketch of the coat-of-arms of the "Inconsolable Company of Crooners". So we, too, formed an ICC with a rival "Austere Order of Opera and Orchestra". Every week we each put a few coppers in a battered old tobacco tin, labelled "Purchase of New Gramophone Records".

For me, one of the great moments of that trip was an occasion when we were passing the Gulf of Florida. It had been the most beautiful sunset it has been my lot to see. The apprentice had not yet blacked out and the last rich, orange glow from the sun poured through the open ports of the smoke-room. Our recital just beginning, we sat listening to a new record we had bought in the States – Louis Kentner playing Liszt's immortal *Hungarian Rhapsody*. Unforgettable!

R/O E. Rhodes
c/o Cockerline Co., Ltd, Filey, Yorks

May 1943

Issues received

I am writing this in the back of a three-ton truck somewhere in North Africa, with the First Army; although to avoid trouble with the Censor, I have given you my home address. A few days ago I received the December and January issues of ***The Gramophone*** and can assure you that they were most welcome. Having read them I have have passed them on to two other gramophiles in the regiment, so you will see that they are doing good service.

(Gnr.) Thomas Webber
As from Plymouth

January 1944

You lucky people

I am always delighted to get ***The Gramophone*** – the October issue has just come to hand, and I packed up duty immediately to read it through from cover to cover. What wonderful records you are getting at home! I'm longing to hear the new recordings by Hess, Teyte and Solomon. A new *Archduke* and what a trio of fine players! You lucky people! How I laugh at those who grudge the Purchase Tax! Those who fuss about such a trifle should be sent to West Africa, or to Italy, or to the jungles of New Guinea, far from their treasured records; there they would learn that you can't have the cake and eat it too, and they would realize that the joy of listening to music isn't measured in £. s. d.

We've got an antique HMV portable here, which breaks down once a week, but manages to churn out the *New World*, the Fifth, some Chopin by Murdoch, *Finlandia*, *In diesen heil'gen Hallen*, some Galli-Curci and *Wolsey's Wilde* by Landowska. It's impossible to increase our repertoire because the shops here have had no records for sale since 1940; and our last parcel of records from London is at the bottom of the Atlantic (and we had paid the Purchase Tax on them!). But time and repetition don't stale our precious discs; they make them even more precious.

R. J. Perfitt, Lieut., RNVR
Dakar, Senegal, French West Africa

December 1944

From Arakan paddy fields

Having just come out of the Arakan after spending nearly two years there, I can give an account of some of the musical activities which flourish in that jungled wilderness. Concert halls and cosy firesides just don't exist for the Arakan music lovers. They listen to their portable grams in broken-down bamboo huts, or in some quiet (?) corner of a paddy field – the music being heavily accompanied by the buzz of mosquitoes, zooming of flying beetles, and the maddening twitching in the undergrowth.

In the rear areas gram clubs hold at least one concert a week to quite large audiences. Programmes are mostly classical, containing an overture, symphony and concerto.

The forward areas possess very limited private record collections, but my unit did manage to gather once a week to discuss and listen to music. In one very forward unit a Signals officer delighted many of the jungle-weary boys by appearing with gram and records – now, unfortunately, in Jap hands.

The Army Educational Corps deserves praise in its setting up of record libraries in the Arakan and holding bi-weekly concerts for low and highbrows. Thanks to the men who give their interesting musical talks and help make the hearing of music possible in so desolate a place.

I have left behind me many music lovers who in every jungle, paddy field and basha form what must be the largest club of its kind – the Arakan Gram Club.

Arnold Levy (Signals)
Mhow, India

February 1945

All in the truck

Mr Levy's letter in your December issue has prompted us to write of our own musical experiences on the Western front. We disembarked on D + 21, with an HMV portable and 50 records. Being RASC the problem of carrying and housing them did not trouble us. Our first worry was acoustical – where to play? A consideration of the alternatives to the open air revealed a barn and a ransacked chapel. We chose the barn and our choice was a lucky one as it brought us a gift of needles, queer French needles with a collar, from a local family.

Later, when we moved to open country there was nothing for it but to dig ourselves a sound-chamber in the ground, a laborious task which occupied a week but was justified acoustically by results. A further move took us to similar terrain and another pit had to be dug. This attracted official notice, became a show-piece and received a visit from the Company Commander. After this publicity we contented ourselves with what orchards and farmyards offered to keep in (and keep out) sound, which wasn't much.

On one memorable occasion we gave a performance of Tchaikovsky's *Pathétique* in a bedroom of a farmhouse, to which we gained access by an upstairs window, as we believed the staircase to be mined. Perhaps our best performances were in a deserted fishmonger shop where, over a period of two weeks, we played our whole repertoire, now amounting to some 90 discs.

When in reach of towns we lost no opportunity of visiting local shops and in this way acquired an Imperial recording of the *Linz* by the Vienna Phil; the Haydn 86th on Polydor; a wartime recording of the first movement of the *Choral*, on Electra, by the Saxon State Orchestra under Böhm (we already had with us the HMV Stokowski recording); *Till Eulenspeigel* by the Brussels Conservatoire under Defauw, an *Ouverture à Grand Orchestre* by Mozart on HMV, and much more besides.

You may wonder if all this is acceptable to our immediate neighbours in the platoon. Although we cannot claim mass conversions, we have at least made them aware of the existence of something other than jive, and one or two hard cases are now heard whistling themes from the *Choral* and Third and Fifth. Such things as the *Nutcracker* Suite and Overtures are, of course, established favourites, and even *Petrushka* has its following.

In conclusion we should like to say, in traversing that desolated country which was the Falaise Gap, where the senses were constantly assailed by things unpleasant, how comforting it was to feel that we had immortality, in the shape of the *Choral*, with us in the truck.

L. Williams, Dvr., J. W. Taylor, Dvr., RASC
British Liberation Army

November 1986

RECORD COLLECTING IN 1940

A recollection by Ronald Hastings

And a dangerous hobby it could be, for reasons not connected with Nazi bombing which, in any case, was largely at night when we were back home playing our newly bought 78s behind black-out curtains, often turning the air blue because of audible scratches we had failed to detect up in London. The dangers were musical and medical, or biological.

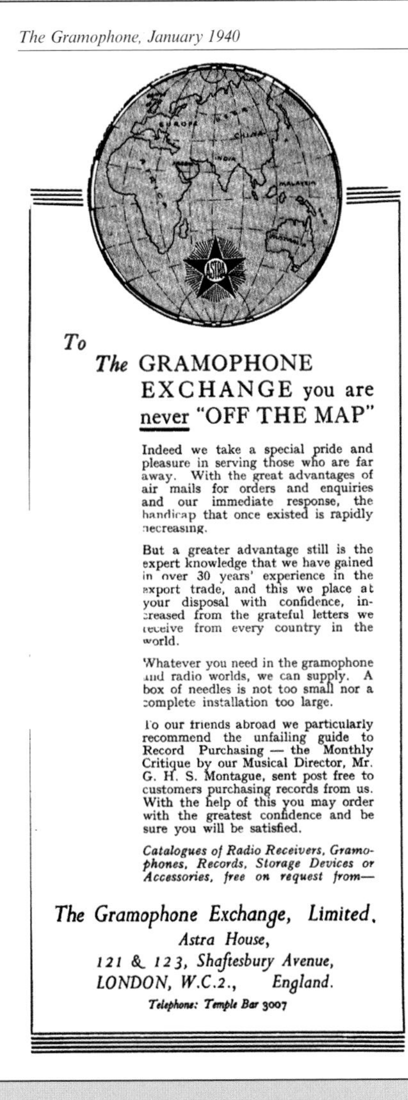

To
The GRAMOPHONE EXCHANGE you are never "OFF THE MAP"
Indeed we take a special pride and pleasure in serving those who are far away. With the great advantages of air mails for orders and enquiries and our immediate response, the handicap that once existed is rapidly decreasing.
But a greater advantage still is the expert knowledge that we have gained in over 30 years' experience in the export trade, and this we place at your disposal with confidence, increased from the grateful letters we receive from every country in the world.
Whatever you need in the gramophone and radio worlds, we can supply. A box of needles is not too small nor a complete installation too large.
To our friends abroad we particularly recommend the unfailing guide to Record Purchasing — the Monthly Critique by our Musical Director, Mr. G. H. S. Montague, sent post free to customers purchasing records from us. With the help of this you may order with the greatest confidence and be sure you will be satisfied.
Catalogues of Radio Receivers, Gramophones, Records, Storage Devices or Accessories, free on request from—
The Gramophone Exchange, Limited.
Astra House,
121 & 123, Shaftesbury Avenue,
LONDON, W.C.2., England.
Telephone: Temple Bar 3007

The Gramophone, January 1940

We bought for good, for ever, musically and technically. We had to look around, to search through piles of secondhand and deleted records, keeping a weather eye out for the favourite record of Compton Mackenzie – *La paloma* sung by Emilio de Gogorza, the acoustic 12-inch, not the electric ten, though I have that now and find it marvellous. But we had far more specialist shops and far more fun, tiring and headache-making though it was. Very good geographically too, finding out where all the back streets were, panhandling along our cobbled Klondike.

In 1940, my regular record gathering programme commenced with the purchase of a 1s. 6d. [5½ p] return workman's rail ticket very early on a Saturday morning. Then there followed a day of record hearing before returning with, usually, two new discs, carefully chosen after hearing as many as I thought I could get away with, and still be welcome in the same shops the following week.

Arriving at Charing Cross from Kent before 8am, so that the workman's ticket was still legal, one walked everywhere. First of all up to the old and great Gramophone Exchange, at that time in large, heavily wooden premises on two floors in upper Shaftesbury Avenue. At one time the main, ground floor was for new records, the basement for secondhand, but the two got mixed up over the years. "Pop" Russell ran it and tall Bill Snow sat by the window behind the counter. Some years later they moved to Wardour Street which I never liked so much. In both shops we were reluctant to take records in for sale to stern looking Mr Russell, but being careful buyers this happened very rarely. At the far end of the earlier shop were those listening booths, musical retreats we all loved so much, except when other people opened the door with the same inquiry you got in phone booths. They were our first encounter with the dreaded fibre needles. All records, of course, both here and in other shops, were played on marvellous gramophones with those huge horns into which the great golfer, Henry Cotton, used to say he liked to bury his head and listen to Caruso, "then I can't hear the phone".

Fibre needles were triangular, sometimes with a thinner, round shank which went into the soundbox. The triangular bit went on to the record and then wore out in next to no time. A single operatic side might just last before the point went, an ensemble hardly ever did. Screwed to the side of the booth was a chain, on the end of which was a pair of special scissors which was used to cut a new point. There was great joy when I discovered about thorn needles, particularly BCN (Burmese Colour Needles) in blue, green, red or fawn. These were an enormous improvement, both in lasting quality and in tone. Imhof's in New Oxford Street also sold longer, tougher, black thorns but they hadn't the same tonal attraction. To sharpen thorns at home (shops hardly ever went in for them in their booths) you grappled with either a flat, to-and-fro sharpener from Imhof's or a round one for BCNs, both using sandpaper and very hard on the forefinger and thumb.

For each record I intended to buy I reckoned to hear three. In this way much time passed, except at HMV – at that time a fine, classical shop at 363 Oxford Street – where they were a bit 'stuffy' if you played records right through and would often insist that you didn't. Heaven for me was when I discovered about the hidden EMG shop. This was tucked away in Grape Street, a small turning off Shaftesbury Avenue, so only a few yards from The Gramophone Exchange. At EMG you could buy only new discs, but they kept many records from the HMV and Columbia Special List and other foreign lists (notably the German and Italian) as well and, above all, would give you advice, the assistants knowing their repertoire – and knowing they knew it! I did not always agree with them on opera, which did not go down well, and still remember the lowered temperature when I took back to the counter Tito Schipa's two *Don Giovanni* arias on HMV DA963, saying I did not like his renderings, and much preferred Heddle Nash's!

EMG had much the same booths as The Gramophone Exchange, fibre needles too. The only snag was that the shop was so small. These two shops usually provided what I needed, but most times I would make it down to the more palatial HMV premises, and that's where the medical and biological dangers were encountered. All record booths, being small with doors that shut tightly to keep the noise in, were very uncomfortable after 15 minutes or so, but HMV's were the most hazardous. Theirs had another factor, an odd, electrical sort of smell which made you feel ill. On every visit I was glad to get out and would occasionally commit the unforgivable, leaving before hearing all I wanted.

The Gramophone, September, 1939

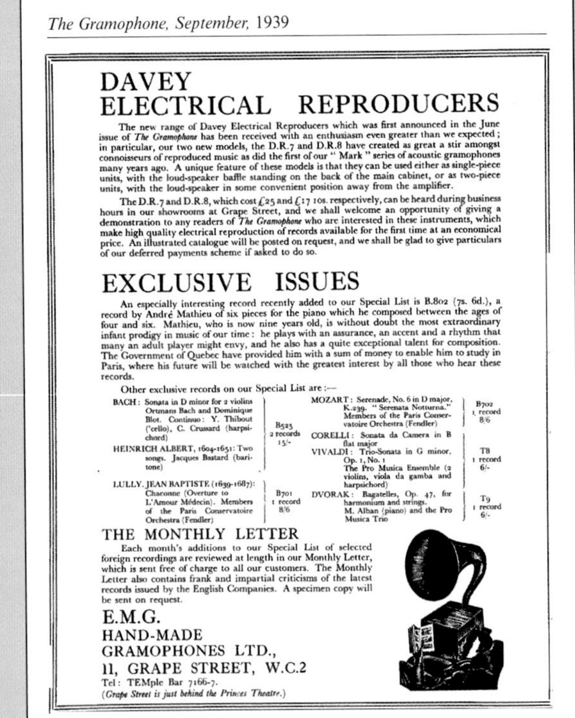

The Gramophone, October, 1939

IMHOF'S carrying on!

We are glad to inform our customers that our store is remaining open as usual from 9 a.m. to 6.30 p.m. daily. Now, more than ever, it will pay you to shop at Imhof's since we are completely equipped with adequate stocks to meet every radio and record requirement at the shortest notice. Order by post with confidence.

★

FOR YOUR SAFETY: Holborn Borough Council official A.R.P. shelter in basement.

Alfred Imhof Ltd., 112 New Oxford Street, W.C.1. Museum 5944

Despite being assailed by restrictions and moral dilemmas, *The Gramophone* survived this most trying period in its history. Following VE Day (Victory in Europe – May 8th, 1945), the Editor offered generous thanks in the June issue to all those whose support had enabled the magazine to continue

When I look back to the autumn of 1939 on what seemed then the almost insuperable task of keeping *The Gramophone* going through a war which I expected to last ten years I cannot find words to express my thanks to those who have made it possible not merely to maintain, but even considerably to improve, the stability of our paper. I know that shortage of paper and increase of price has had the paradoxical effect of making people buy more books and magazines and papers than ever before, but I think we have a right to believe that nobody would spend a shilling on a specialist publication like ours unless it was usefully serving enthusiasts whose enthusiasm for music that the gramophone gives had become keener than ever during the last six years.

My next thanks are due to the continuous and steady support which our advertisers have given us throughout the war. *Bis dat, qui cito dat*. He gives twice as much who gives quickly, and if our advertisers had been cautious at a time when caution would have been more than excusable I should not be writing this editorial for the first number of our 23rd volume.

Finally, I have to thank our staff and our printers for overcoming all the difficulties which our readers, themselves accustomed to the difficulties of these years, will easily imagine. In this connection I must pay a special tribute to Cecil Pollard who week in week out has devoted himself to the service of the paper, and now looks forward like myself to the time when we can fatten it up again.

The War ends – an end to rationing?

The war in Europe ceased on May 8th, 1945, and that in the Far East and Pacific on August 15th, 1945, but a number of years were to elapse before peacetime conditions would be restored in Britain. (Writing in 1997 it is hard to believe that on May 22nd, 1945 the Minister of Food announced further cuts in the ration for bacon, fats and soap but reassured everyone that the allowances would be "sufficient to maintain full health and vigour" – such was the price of victory.) In July 1946 Christopher Stone wrote, "Restrictions show little signs of being raised. *The Gramophone* itself had in its June issue for 1943 20 pages of 'matter', in June 1944 15, in June 1945 12 and this June 14; corresponding to publication of new recordings (excluding dance and miscellaneous) of roughly 13 works on single discs in 1943, six in 1944, ten in 1945 (not counting the special Victory supplement) and 12 last month. Ten years ago, in June 1936, *The Gramophone* had 46 pages of matter and reviews of – by similar rough calculations – 36 works or single records. In short there is as yet no sign of expansion towards normality."

Also, in July 1946, I joined the Company in time to help move the record library from Russell Square to Red Lion Square – a basement to basement job – before joining the Army. The following March a new London office was opened at 8 Barter Street, whilst the country was in total chaos on account of what was euphemistically referred to as the "fuel crisis" which resulted in publication delays far in excess of any experienced during the war.

Extract from the Minutes of a Board Meeting held at 14 Stafford St, W1 on Thursday, 8th August 1946 at 11.30am

The following matters were discussed and agreed:

2. That the Company engage A. C. Pollard as a Junior Clerk at a salary of £2 10. 0. per week.

The meeting closed at 12.15pm.

However, the issue for November 1947 was significant in that it contained the first editorial contribution from Lionel Salter – an article on the recorded music of Mendelssohn – who as I write is the magazine's longest-serving current contributor, and has had the questionable pleasure of working with all three generations of the Pollard family! His first record reviews appeared in November 1948. The November 1947 issue also saw the first "Letter from America" under Harold C. Schonberg's name – a feature which was to run for the next 12 years. In that first contribution HCS wrote, "The column inaugurates a monthly letter about news of American recordings. It is aimed primarily to inform rather than criticize. Here in America we are suffering an embarrassment of riches. Classical recordings are being issued in great quantity – far too great a quantity to discuss in detail, since a listing alone would saturate the space. I hasten to add that the quantity of American releases does not necessarily presuppose quality. There is still much shellac wasted, and there still is much duplication – two Shostakovich Ninths in recent months, reissues of Tchaikovsky and Beethoven symphonies, and so on."

Lionel Salter in 1945

THE FUEL CRISIS

February 1947 saw the worst weather since 1855, with heavy snow falls blocking roads and railway lines across the British Isles. The average daily temperature was the lowest recorded since 1841, and in many places did not rise above freezing. The weather caused great difficulties in the transport of coal from collieries to power stations; the situation was compounded by a lack of rolling-stock and problems in repairing railway engines after the war, and as a result stocks of coal at power stations fell below the minimum level of two weeks' consumption. A general restriction on electricity use was imposed by the Government-appointed fuel crisis committee. Power cuts hit both domestic users and industry: in London and the South-East there was a three-week curtailment which only ended on March 3rd when the Attlee administration announced that normal supplies would be restored to industry (domestic users had to wait even longer). The crisis caused publication delays for *The Gramophone* worse than any it had experienced during the war, as Christopher Stone explained to readers

March 1947 **Editorial**

Readers at home, whether old-timers or newcomers, will have accepted without surprise the week's delay in publication of our last number and the probable fortnight's delay of the present one: the misprints and omissions; and the news that the recording companies and radio manufacturers are doing their best but making few promises. Everything is topsy-turvy and when we recover our breath we shall hardly know whether to go on laughing at the muddle or to exert our healthy capacity for righteous indignation.

A good deal will depend on the weather.

Not so, perhaps, for our overseas readers, to whom the present plight of Great Britain may be a tedious memory by the time the February and March issues of *The Gramophone* reach them. We can only assure them that recording companies, advertisers, reviewing staff and printers have been straining every nerve not to sacrifice our traditional punctuality of publication and up-to-date reviews of records without the best effort that close co-operation can make.

MACKENZIE IN THE FAR EAST

In the autumn of 1945 Compton Mackenzie was invited by the Government of India to write a history of the country's contribution to the Second World War. Leaving London in October 1946 he travelled some 50,000 miles by sea, air, rail and road, visiting the battlefields where Indian servicemen fought – from the Western Desert to Burma, Malaya and Hong Kong. He was away for ten months and in 1948 published a diary of his journeys, *All Over the Place* (Chatto & Windus). In 1951 Volume 1 of his *Eastern Epic* was published (Chatto & Windus) but sadly the work was never completed.

In an editorial in August 1947 he described his visit to His Highness the Maharajah of Mysore and other places further East

August 1947 **Editorial**

Compton Mackenzie afloat on the Ganges (near Gandhi's home) in 1947

At the end of October last year I was the guest of His Highness the Maharajah in Mysore. The first thing he told me was that he had been a subscriber to ***The Gramophone*** ever since he first went to school in India in 1932, and that he possesses a complete set of the paper from the first number. Then he went on to talk about his desire to help in the recording of music which might not otherwise be recorded. To that desire he has already given practical expression by making it possible for gramophone enthusiasts to enjoy the works of Medtner, and I can assure readers that when they hear these records they will be very grateful to the Maharajah of Mysore.

Compton Mackenzie at Katmandu

Early in January I was staying in the Residency at Imphal. The house has been knocked about by Japanese bombers, but the orange trumpets of a great *Bignonia venusta* hide the damaged roof. On the first night I thought I was dreaming when I saw on a wardrobe in a corner of the war-scarred room an outsize EMG horn (or it may have been a Senior Expert) which the retiring Resident Mr Gimson had, regretfully I am sure, left behind him. I should find it hard to express in words

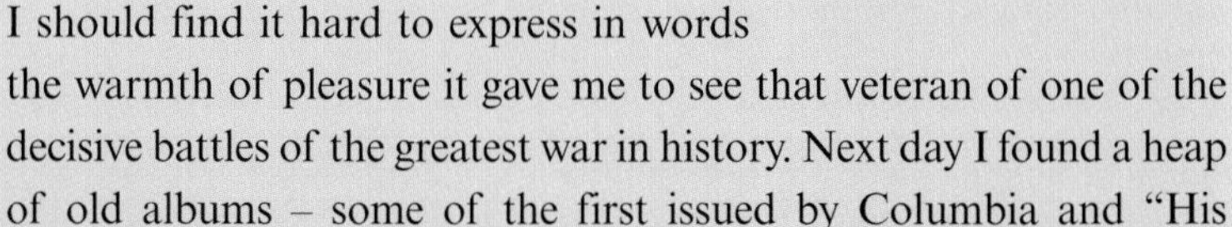

the warmth of pleasure it gave me to see that veteran of one of the decisive battles of the greatest war in history. Next day I found a heap of old albums – some of the first issued by Columbia and "His Master's Voice", and near them a packet of old numbers of ***The Gramophone*** . A month later I arrived in Rangoon just after one of the new Decolas on which I had the pleasure of hearing a concert of chamber music before taking part in the first Brains Trust ever held in Burma. This was under the auspices of the British Council. In Hong Kong I found people rather indignant because the British Council had not come there and brought a Decola with them.

Another thrill was to find in Katmandu, the most remote and inaccessible capital except Lhassa in all the East, the dog listening to his master's voice above a shop shuttered in the heat of noon. Hardly more than 200 Europeans have visited Nepal in 40 years, but as the photograph shows the HMV dog is there.

A wartime photograph of E. M. "Mick" Ginn who established the famous EMG marque in the inter-war years and later, in the 1950s, Expert Gramophones *Photo J. Ginn*

Compton Mackenzie at the Silver Jubilee party with Sir Louis Sterling (above) and Alfred Clark (left), both of whom had supported the magazine from the outset

The Gramophone's Silver Jubilee celebration at Canuto's restaurant in London on June 16th, 1948. Above is the only group picture of the three founders and Cecil Pollard (right), Faith Mackenzie, Compton Mackenzie and Christopher Stone

At the Silver Jubilee party: Cecil Pollard (left) with Peggy Holloway (who managed the Subscription Department for several years from the late 1940s); William Hollamby (who joined the company in 1924 but who, on Cecil Pollard's advice, branched out with much success after wartime military service); and Anthony Pollard, then enjoying Army life and still to decide if it was to be his career

Silver Jubilee

The 25th anniversary of *The Gramophone* was celebrated somewhat late (due to the Editor's absence in India) but in the June 1948 issue, W. S. Meadmore recounted the magazine's history in a six-page article, and on June 16th there was a celebration at Canuto's Restaurant in London which was attended by record company executives, composers and artists, contributors and staff. That same month it was agreed to appoint a new firm of accountants, Amsdon, Cossart & Wells and over the next 30 years the senior partner, Bert Wells, proved to be one of the Company's sagest advisers: happily today we are still advised by their successors, Baker Tilly, in the form of Len Speller. Later, on October 11th, came news of Herbert Ridout's death, another of those who had done so much to help the magazine in its earliest days.

The November 1948 issue contained the first of Edward Sackville-West's quarterly reviews, and in January 1951 he was to be joined by his colleague Desmond Shawe-Taylor in what would become a regular feature of the magazine, offering an opportunity to highlight important releases and provide, where necessary, a second opinion.

The 1940s closed with the tragic death of one of the record industry's great hopes for the future, the violinist Ginette Neveu, who was killed in an air crash at the age of 30. (This provoked much discussion among international classical artists as to the wisdom of air travel and was to recur with the deaths of Thibaud in September 1953 and Cantelli in November 1956.) Walter Legge wrote a moving tribute to Neveu in December 1949 – an issue still subject to the rigours of paper rationing.

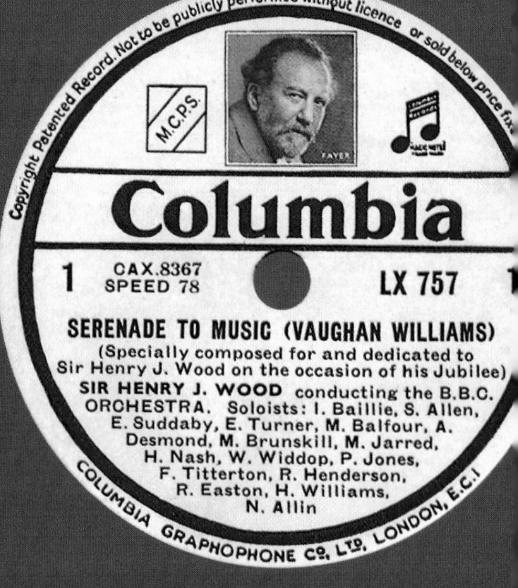

A selection of labels representing a few of the vocal 78s available on the HMV and Columbia catalogues

The Long-Playing record

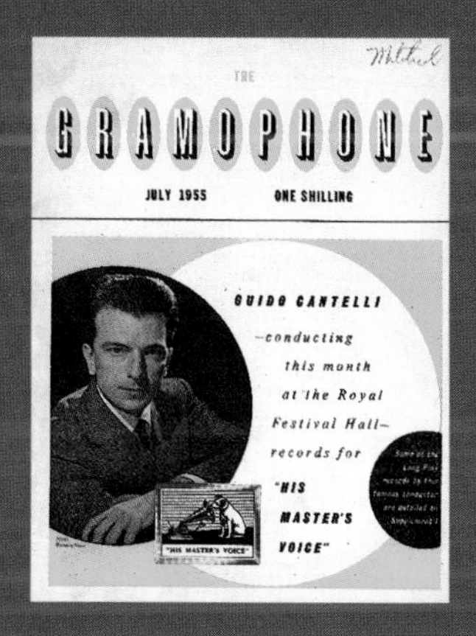

1950-1957

A *Gramophone* chronology

1950-1957

1950

- George R. Marek joins RCA as A&R Manager.
- Teldec is formed, a company jointly owned by Decca and Telefunken.
- Maurice Rosengarten becomes closely involved with Decca's classical catalogue.

Maurice Rosengarten
Photo Decca

January

- RCA Victor release LP records in the USA.
- First home tape recorders appear on the German market: UK follows 18 months later.

June

- Alfred Clark dies.
- Decca release its first 53 LP records in UK. The repertoire includes Beethoven's Symphony No. 5 (Schuricht and the Paris Conservatoire) and Piano Concerto No. 5 (Curzon/LPO/Szell) and Stravinsky's *Petrushka* (Ansermet and the Suisse Romande).
- Decca make their first opera in Vienna with the first-ever studio recording of Mozart's *Die Entführung aus dem Serail* with Krips and the VPO.

September

- First UK classical releases on Capitol label from Decca.

October

- The Nixa Record Company is established in the UK by Hilton Nixon – eventually to be called Pye Records.

Hilton Nixon

1951

- Founding of the embryo British Institute of Recorded Sound by Patrick Saul. Fully established in 1955 and in 1983 to become The British Library National Sound Archive.

February

- First UK classical LP releases on the Telefunken label from Decca.

April

- Harry Sarton, Decca Artists Manager, dies.

July

- Nixa release LPs under licence from various American companies, including Concert Hall, Lyricord, Renaissance and Period.

July/August

- First Bayreuth Festival since 1943. Decca/Telefunken record *Parsifal* with Knappertsbusch, and EMI *Die Meistersinger von Nürnberg* and Act 3 of *Die Walküre* with Karajan.

September

- Cecil Pollard moves from Kenton to Green Lane, Stanmore and *TG* editorial office goes with him.
- Death of the pioneering recording supervisor and impresario Fred Gaisberg who had originally worked for Berliner in 1893 and came to London to make the first European recordings for the gramophone. He was 78.

December

- Argo Record Company founded by Harley Usill and Alex Herbage – first 78rpm releases.
- First LP release on Allegro label from Oriole.
- Sir Ernest Fisk resigns as MD of EMI.

1952

February

- First UK release of Haydn Society recordings on Parlophone 78s.

May

- Publication of the first volume of *The World's Encyclopaedia of Recorded Music: 1925-51*, compiled by Clough and Cuming. Further supplements appeared in 1953 and 1957.

July

- Compton Mackenzie is knighted in Queen Elizabeth II's first Birthday Honours List.

October

- L. J. Brown appointed MD of EMI.
- EMI release the first 45rpm records in the UK in addition to their first LP releases.
- First Argo LP releases.

L. J. Brown *Photo EMI*

November

- Vox release LPs in UK.
- American Vanguard label available in UK on Nixa.

December

- First Monarch LP releases.

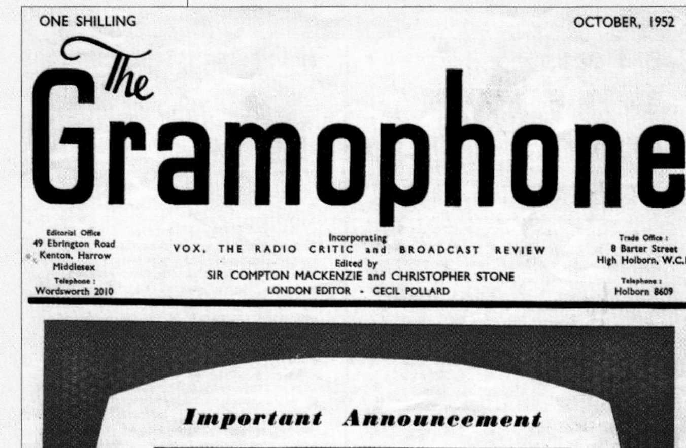

ONE SHILLING

OCTOBER, 1952

The Gramophone

Editorial Office
49 Ebrington Road
Kenton, Harrow
Middlesex
Telephone :
Wordsworth 2010

Incorporating
VOX, THE RADIO CRITIC and BROADCAST REVIEW
Edited by
SIR COMPTON MACKENZIE and CHRISTOPHER STONE
LONDON EDITOR - CECIL POLLARD

Trade Office :
8 Barter Street
High Holborn, W.C.1
Telephone :
Holborn 8609

Important Announcement

This issue contains details of the first

"HIS MASTER'S VOICE"

COLUMBIA

PARLOPHONE and M·G·M

Long Playing $33\frac{1}{3}$ *r.p.m. Records*

• NON-BREAKABLE • SUPERB RECORDING
• SILENT SURFACE

ANNOUNCEMENT BY E.M.I. SALES & SERVICE LTD · HAYES · MIDDLESEX

1953

- French Erato label founded by Philippe Loury.

January

- First Philips popular 78s of British origin issued. Material from American Columbia followed in March on transfer of this label from EMI to Philips.

March

- First commercial stereo/binuaural recordings on tape made in Symphony Hall, Boston by Emory Cook.

June

- First edition of *The Gramophone Long Playing Record Catalogue* compiled by Stanley Day, comprised 112 pages and listed some 1,400 LPs and around 250 45s, priced at 2s. 6d. [12½ p].
- EMI launch their "History of Music in Sound". Completed in 1959 the series eventually comprised 10 volumes on 27 LPs.

August

- H. F. V. Little dies.
- Supraphon release LPs in UK.

September

- G. Howard-Sorrell hands back the technical editorship of ***TG*** to Percy Wilson.
- EMI Records Division moves from Hayes to Great Castle Street, London.

October

- Westminster release LPs in UK.

November

- Decca undertake their first experimental stereo recordings with Mantovani and his Orchestra at their West Hampstead studios.
- Oiseau-Lyre release LPs in UK.

Geoffrey Howard-Sorrell

1954

January

- Pye Black Box record-player introduced.

February

- Peter Andry joins Decca.

April

- EMI introduce extended-play 45rpm discs.

May

- Decca make their first commercial stereo recording in Victoria Hall, Geneva – Rimsky-Korsakov's *Antar* with Ansermet and the Suisse Romande Orchestra.

Announcing...
INTERNATIONALLY FAMOUS ARTISTS
ON
PHILIPS
Minigroove 33⅓
LONG PLAYING RECORDS
PHILIPS
Philips long playing records are issued in a special pictorial cover (with descriptive notes)—an attractive 'picture gallery' effect that gives visual appeal to your collection.
Available at your local Record Dealer during JULY.

The Gramophone, July, 1954

June

- Joseph (later Sir Joseph) Lockwood joins EMI as Chief Executive.
- Mercury release LPs in the UK – distributed by Oriole Records.

July

- First Philips LP release.

July/August

- First recordings of complete operas in stereo made by Decca in Rome – Verdi's *La traviata* and *Otello*, and Puccini's *Manon Lescaut*, all with Tebaldi.

August

- Reg Pollard joins ***TG*** to become Advertisement Manager in 1957.

September

- EMI introduce 7½ ips pre-recorded reel-to-reel mono tapes.

October

- First Concert Artist LP release.
- RCA introduce "gruve-gard" LPs – raised rims and label areas.

November

- First Decca 45rpm releases.
- First Archiv/Heliodor LP release in the UK.

Christopher Stone (left) with Reg Pollard (1959)

- Gilbert Briggs (Wharfedale) and Peter Walker (Quad) give first Royal Festival Hall demonstration of live and recorded sound.

November/December

- Decca make the first commercial stereo recording in UK – Grieg's Piano Concerto with Winifred Atwell, Stanford Robinson and the LPO.

G. A. Briggs

P. J. Walker

1955

January

- ***TG*** joins Audit Bureau of Circulations.
- EMI acquire major interest in Capitol Records Inc.
- Emory Cook "Sounds of our Times" recordings released by Nixa.

February

- Deutsche Grammophon yellow label released in UK by Heliodor-Deutsche Grammophon Ltd.
- EMI's first commercial stereo recordings on tape, made in Kingsway Hall – Prokofiev's Symphonies Nos. 1 and 7 with Malko and the Philharmonia.

March

- Isabella Wallich, niece of Fred Gaisberg, launches the Delysé label.

April

- Joe Batten, recording pioneer originally with Edison Bell and later Columbia, dies.

Joe Batten (left) retired in October 1950 after 50 years in the record industry: with him is Arthur Clarke, EMI's Chief Recording Engineer, who had joined The Gramophone Company in 1908 *Photo EMI*

May

- Peter Dawson makes his final commercial recordings at EMI's Abbey Road Studios in stereo – the *Mandalay Scena* and *Clancy of the Overflow* with Mackerras and the LSO – over 50 years after his first cylinder recordings.

June

- Alec Robertson is appointed Music Editor of ***TG***.

October

- EMI release first "Stereosonic" 7½ips tapes in UK.

December

- First annual Critics' Choice feature in ***TG***.
- Amalgamations result in the formation of the Pye/Nixa label, to become Pye Records Ltd. in 1956.

1956

January

- First cover price increase for ***TG*** since June 1924, from 1s. [5p] to 1s. 6d. [7½ p].
- W. S. Barrell retires as Manager of EMI Studios, Abbey Road and is succeeded by Edward "Chick" Fowler, who joined HMV in 1924.
- World Record Club, the first UK record club, launched with Richard Attenborough (later Lord Attenborough) chairman of the selection committee.

April

- Mercury catalogue transfers to Pye Records in the UK.
- First European Audio Fair held in London at the Washington Hotel.

June

- First recordings made in UK by American engineers when Mercury undertook sessions with Barbirolli and the Hallé Orchestra in Manchester's Free Trade Hall. The works included the first recording of the new Vaughan Williams's Symphony No. 8 and Elgar's *Enigma* Variations.
- Record producers Victor Olof and Peter Andry leave Decca and move to EMI.

Victor Olof (left) and Peter Andry in the late 1950s

***TG*'s stand at the 1956 Audio Fair**

September

- Bhaskar Menon joins EMI as a management trainee.
- Gramophone turntables offering a fourth speed, 16⅔ rpm, now on the market but no discs so far.

October

- First recordings by a Soviet orchestra in Western Europe by DG – Tchaikovsky's Symphonies Nos. 5 and 6 with the Leningrad Philharmonic under Mravinsky.

December

- Karajan records Richard Strauss's *Der Rosenkavalier* for EMI at Abbey Road with Schwarzkopf as the Marschalin.

1957

January

- Erik Smith joins the Decca Classical Department.

February

- Geoffrey Horn's first contribution to ***TG***.

March

- Pye Records, in association with the British Council, record Tippett's *A child of our time* in Liverpool under Pritchard.

May

- George Winkworth, Advertisement Manager of ***TG***, dies.

June

- RCA Victor catalogue transferred in UK from EMI to Decca.
- Capitol label moves from Decca to EMI and introduces "Full Dimensional Sound" – FDS.

July

- Formation of EMI Records Ltd. – the first MD is C. H. Thomas.

September

- Quad Electrostatic loudspeaker introduced.

October

- Ray Minshull joins the Decca Classical Department.
- EMI introduce their "Great Recordings of the Century" series in UK.

November

- Argo acquired by Decca. They begin recording the complete works of William Shakespeare, completed in 1964 and totalling 137 LPs.

December

- W. S. Barrell retires from EMI.
- Dr Fred Hamel, who had directed the DG/Archiv label since 1947, dies: he is succeeded by Dr Hans Hickmann.

Dr Hans Hickmann
Photo DG

The Long-Playing record

From the earliest days of the record industry, playing-time had always been a consideration. In 1895 Berliner's single-sided 7-inch disc played for about two minutes: eventually, with the introduction of the single-sided 12-inch disc in 1903, this was increased to four-and-a-half minutes but this side-timing, with a few exceptions [p. 233], remained a constant factor for 78s over the next 60 years.

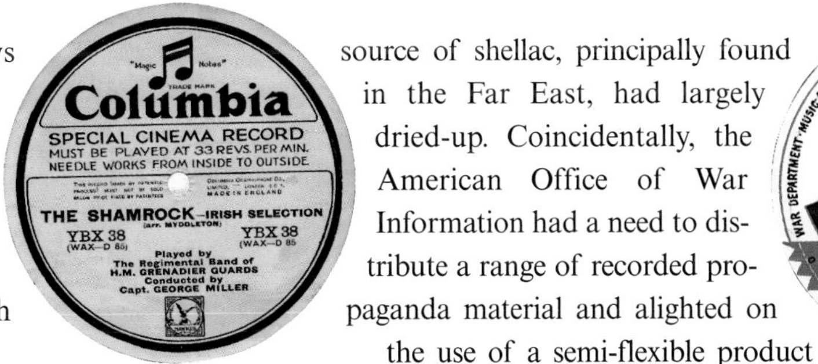

During the 1930s long-playing records were made for use in cinemas. These required special equipment and played from the inside to the outside at 33rpm

For popular repertoire this wasn't a problem but for the classical buyer there was considerable frustration in coping with fragmented symphonies, sonatas and concertos, etc. Various auto-changers carrying a stack of records were developed and multiple record sets were auto-coupled to allow the use of these devices. However they were pretty crude and often resulted in damaged records due to the operation of the changer or the inevitable wear of the steel reproducing needle itself.

The record industry was not blind to the problem: a company called Neophone had tried to develop a long-playing record as far back as 1905, Edison tried in 1926 and later, in 1931, there was another attempt, this time by RCA based on a speed of 33⅓ rpm. Clearly, some aspects of the technology were a long way from perfection but much also related to the inadequacy of the materials available for the manufacture of the disc itself. Traditionally, the gramophone record was made from shellac, carbon black and various fillers. During the Second World War the source of shellac, principally found in the Far East, had largely dried-up. Coincidentally, the American Office of War Information had a need to distribute a range of recorded propaganda material and alighted on the use of a semi-flexible product called Vinylite. Once the war was over it was this material which provided a key to the quest for a long-playing record. Dr Peter Goldmark, Director of Research for the Columbia Broadcasting System, had been charged with examining the whole question but it was not until 1946, in conjunction with William Bachman, Director of Research for the Columbia Recording Corp. (later Columbia Records Inc./CBS Records/Sony), that he was able to develop his final thinking.

A coarse-groove 78rpm "V Disc" pressed in Vinylite which could be played on standard equipment. Note Rudy Vallee's wartime role (c1943)

An EMI auto-changer of the 1930s

The Gramophone, December, 1952

An HMV advertisement extolling the virtues of the 7-inch 45rpm disc and player

Harold C. Schonberg's "Letter from America" commenced in November 1947 and he was therefore well placed to comment on 'the battle of the speeds' as it unfolded

LETTER FROM AMERICA

July 1949

To put it mildly, the record situation here at present is in a state of unbalance. Ever since the onslaught of 33s and 45s – although orthodox discs still are being pressed by Victor and Columbia – the public has been holding off, not knowing what to buy and as a result not buying much of anything. Some of the smaller companies are being forced to the wall, and many record dealers are feeling the squeeze. I don't know exactly how things are outside of New York City, but here most shellac discs in the major catalogues are being offered at a fifty per cent reduction in price. This reduction is not 'official' since no statement has been issued concerning a reduction in the price scale. Nevertheless there seems to be a dealers' urge to get rid of all stock; and I am told, reductions up to seventy per cent are being offered outside of New York.

August 1949

Victor's new little machine to handle the 45rpm discs is now on the American market. It is a short, compact mechanism with a fairly quick-acting changer, and can easily be incorporated into standard gramophone combinations. All of the Victor records are being pressed at 45rpm as well as the standard 78. The majority of record manufacturers, however, seem to be swinging to Columbia's 33⅓ long-playing discs, the latest being English Decca (*ffrr*).

On the whole, the Victor disc is of excellent quality. Curiously, for Vinylite discs, there often is surface noise. The frequency range is well up, though, the balance is generally good, and so far there has been a lack of distortion in the last quarter-inch of grooving. Some have complained that there is a deficiency of bass definition; that the records are cut to favour the majority of American console sets with their emphasis on bass. To a certain extent that is true, but proper equalization should take care of the bass curve.

October 1949

As far as the output of the two largest American recording companies – Victor and Columbia – is concerned, there is precious little to write about. Not since the war years has there been such a paucity of worthwhile releases, and the industry seems to be in a stabilizing period until the 33⅓ versus 45 controversy will be ironed out. At present, Columbia seems to have the better of it, since virtually every organization has cast its lot with long-playing discs, leaving Victor (with Capitol, which also is pressing 33⅓ discs as well as 45s and 78s) the sole representative of 45s. Ever-present are rumours of a settlement of some sort, such as a deal involving all popular music discs to be pressed at 45, all classical music at the long-playing 33⅓. There also are even more frightening rumours concerning the abandonment of disc recording in favour of tape mechanisms. These days, the conductor of a record review column is little more than a gossip columnist.

But while Victor and Columbia are reaching for each other's jugular veins, other companies are making hay, and one of the more interesting developments is the emergence of a few recording companies that may constitute a definite threat to V's and C's monopoly of the classical music field. Capitol Records, which is one of the largest popular-music companies, has added to its jazz catalogues the re-pressings of Telefunken records, and their first few releases are more than ambitious – they are well played and recorded, and in some cases present segments of the repertoire that most American companies ordinarily would not touch.

February 1950

In the most dignified of statements, issued on January 4th, Victor finally entered the long-playing record business. The general idea seemed to be that their 45rpm system had achieved "vast success ... nation-wide public acceptance ... the greatest advance in 50 years of recorded music ... a revolutionary advance", and that therefore, in addition, they were going to "make available its great artists and unsurpassed classical library on new and improved long-playing (33⅓ rpm) records". These discs are scheduled to hit the market on or about March 1st.

Although most of the statement was devoted to a eulogy of the 45rpm system, the implications are clear enough. The long-playing disc is here to stay, as far as classical music is concerned, and the chances are that the conventional 78rpm disc will be obsolete in a few years. So, probably, will be the 45rpm system. Right now they are obsolescent, and the Victor announcement will hasten their demise. Many people have held off purchasing an LP unit until they were sure that by doing so they would have the benefit of the Victor catalogue. Now the sales should spurt. Victor, too, has been having some trouble with artists. Beecham, for example, has just gone over to Columbia; and the long-playing policy of Victor should do much to pacify the other musicians under contract to them.

In the meantime, Columbia has been improving its process. Comparing shellac recordings with the LP equivalents, the balance is all toward the latter. Such things as the Mahler (Mitropoulis and the Minneapolis Orchestra) or the Third Act of *Walküre* (Traubel, Janssen, and the New York Philharmonic under Rodzinski), which originally were recorded in 1941 and 1945 respectively, sound amazingly better on LP. The *Walküre*, indeed, is as good an operatic recording, *qua* sound and balance, as I have ever heard.

One serious defect in the LP process, though, is the pitch waver evident on most of the piano discs. In some cases (e.g. Arrau's recording of Beethoven's *Waldstein*), it is so pronounced as to make the music almost impossible for a sensitive ear to stand, in others (the Firkušný recording of the Schumann *Phantasy*) it is less noticeable but still annoying. There have been some LP piano discs nearly perfect, though. The Renard recital mentioned last month, outside of one short section, was nearly perfect, and the Satie *Trois Morceaux en forme de poire* was superb throughout. Apparently the difficulty can be conquered.

It would be a shame if at this point, when the LP process is beginning to consolidate, American and British engineers fail to get together and work out a uniform standard of recording characteristics. Right now is the time for action; right now, while things are in a state of flux; right now, before everything becomes set.

March 1950

Although Victor has come out with the announcement that long-playing records will be in production by March, the industry is still feeling its way cautiously. Many experts had predicted that a 'deal' would be made: all classical records made by Columbia and Victor to be pressed on long-playing sides, all popular and semi-classical records on the 45rpm speed. There is no sign, however, that such an eventuality will happen, logical as the idea sounded. In the meantime, the smaller companies are making hay. The LP discs have been a wonderful boost for their business, and they are concentrating on aspects of the repertoire that the larger companies generally stay away from.

Nearly all of these are excellent recordings, with the best that the LP process has to offer – noiseless (virtually) surfaces, faithful instrumental balance, high fidelity. Some LP records are cut to fantastically high frequencies; so high, in fact, that a tone control circuit with several roll-off points is needed to handle them. Given the mechanical equipment, however, and given a decently pressed disc (the slightest off-centre pressing will raise havoc, especially with piano discs), the LP process offers much more than the shellac equivalent.

September 1950

The summer months have slightly slowed the unprecedented number of LP classical releases, though there is still enough abundance to make everybody happy. American collectors have been having a delirious time of it for over a year. Small companies rapidly spring up, each with the boast that they are presenting, or going to present, music that never before has been recorded, all engraved with matchless fidelity, unsurpassable clarity, incontestable artistry, etc., etc. Alas! Few of the newcomers are able to corral musicians who can compete with the high-priced artistry of our major concert figures. And yet, they often *do* present music that is a novelty, music that every real collector feels that he should have.

The sleeve of an early 10-inch Urania LP, manufactured by Columbia Records Inc.

The Columbia 33⅓ long-playing record was unveiled to the American press at the Waldorf-Astoria Hotel in New York on June 21st, 1948 by Edward Wallerstein, President of the company. He was flanked on the one side by an eight-foot stack of 78s and on the other by their LP equivalents, measuring little more than 15 inches in height. The impact of the vinyl disc, which played for 22 minutes per side with less surface noise than a 78, was positive but like many new developments there were teething troubles – the sound quality tended to be hard with wiry strings, and there was also evidence of wow and pre-echo.

The American public showed no signs of rushing to abandon their 78s, for apart from anything else the country's other major record company, RCA, had declined to share in Columbia's development of the LP and in fact launched the 7-inch 45rpm disc in competition in February 1949. Notwithstanding a relatively sophisticated high-speed changer, the 45rpm disc offered few advantages over the 78rpm disc – certainly not for any repertoire with a playing time in excess of four-and-a-half minutes. But the two companies were now joined in what became known as the 'battle of the speeds' – at the time one of America's most costly marketing contests.

Columbia continued to promote the LP and, by offering beneficial manufacturing facilities and waiving patent rights, encouraged a number of smaller labels to support the system. Eventually, in February 1950 RCA joined the LP bandwagon and just one year later Columbia began to release singles on 45s. Thus, the 'battle of the speeds' was resolved.

June 1950 **News**

LONG-PLAYING RECORDS

Decca have announced that LP records and the associated reproducers will be released during June and sample discs have already been received.

The equipment so far consists of two playing desks, a dual speed Deccalian and two Radiograms, both two-speed, one with autochange, a range that gives a wide choice to those who wish to sample the new discs.

For those who already have amplifiers or radiograms the minimum equipment for LP discs is either the 33A or 33B playing desk, which have single speed motors and microgroove pickups. The pickups are crystal types with sapphire stylus, no details of output being quoted so far. A further model, the 33C, is fitted with a Decca magnetic pickup, four different impedances being available to choice. The price of the 33A is £8 18s. 0d. whilst the 33B and C both cost £10 18s. 0d. all inclusive of tax.

The Deccalian, which seems basically the same as the existing model with the addition of a two-speed motor and interchangeable pickup heads, costs £37 16s. 0d., again tax paid. Both radiograms have the same specification being 5 valve, 3 waveband units in console cabinets. The 91 has a dual speed motor and costs £67 4s. 0d. inclusive, whilst the 92 with dual speed autochanger is priced at £75 inclusive.

Unfortunately no technical details of the records are available as yet so we have not been able to carry out any serious tests on the few we have received. We hope to obtain all the necessary data during the next few weeks and to get the extra equipment for our reviewers in time for them to try some of the new records before we go to press with the July issue.

LP comes to Britain

These developments in America did not pass unnoticed in the pages of the magazine but they had not aroused a great deal of interest among British readers. In part this was because in those days communications across the Atlantic were not what they are today, and beyond this British record buyers probably had more on their minds in the late 1940s than the introduction of a long-playing disc. The economy was beginning to recover and progressively we were shedding the rationing and restrictions of the wartime years but normality was still some way off.

At this time there were still only two record companies of any consequence in Great Britain – EMI, which encompassed the HMV, Columbia and Parlophone labels, and The Decca Record Company, the latter offering only a limited commercial challenge to the former. EMI had contractual ties with RCA and Columbia in America which dated back to the earliest days of the Industry. Decca, established as a record company as recently as 1929, had no such arrangements and as a much smaller company operated more flexibly.

Decca, having relinquished control of their American affiliate in 1939, re-established themselves in America as London Records Inc. in 1947, and by the autumn of 1949 were shipping British-manufactured LPs to America on the London label. With this experience they launched the LP in Great Britain in June 1950. It was a low-key affair and such publicity as there was, mainly in the pages of ***The Gramophone***, was precisely targeted and did not presuppose a sales avalanche. There had been no briefing of the magazine and in fact no review pressings had been received in time for discussion in the June issue. It was therefore perhaps unfortunate that the only comments in that issue, from AR, LS and a well-equipped reader (David James – *aka* Burnett James), were based upon a number of early American LPs of variable quality, the majority of which I had brought back to this country following a visit to America during the latter part of 1949. I had been working for Joe Brogan in The Gramophone Shop on East 48th Street, New York whilst endeavouring to assess the impact of LP on the US record market, as well as seeking further sales outlets for the magazine itself.

For EMI the situation was not quite so simple on account of their association with RCA and American Columbia, where conflicting interests existed until early in 1950. There had been a suggestion that they would follow the American companies in September 1949 but for various reasons this was rejected; a year later Sir Ernest Fisk, the Managing Director (who was to resign in December 1951), issued a Press Release which described the confused situation in the USA and went on to say, "It is hoped and

Sir Ernest Fisk (left) at the Royal Albert Hall in 1950 with Wilhelm Furtwängler

July 1950

STRAVINSKY. Petrouchka. L'Orchestre de la Suisse Romande (Ansermet).
Decca LXT2502 (12 in., 39s. 6d.).

Petrouchka, as then spelt, one of the most famous recordings in Decca's first LP release

This new recording of Stravinsky's masterpiece – which will become, I am sure, the first big landmark in the history of LP – lights up the orchestral colours with unprecedented vividness and perspective, and all the details of the score are wonderfully clear and excellently balanced. For this, the engineers must take much credit; though in the first scene (only) the strings lack amplitude of tone in comparison with the rest of the orchestra; and the disc surfaces could be quieter and less crackly in places. But obviously the greater part of our thanks goes to the orchestra and to Ansermet, one of the most clear-minded and sympathetic interpreters of Stravinsky of our generation; this performance has *atmosphere* over and above fine playing – listen to the Petrouchka's Room scene, in particular. I found myself mentally noting certain parts as high spots – the Russian dance; the Moor and the coconut; the Nursemaids and Coachmen – where both the playing and the recording were positively brilliant; but the standard in general is so high that it obviously behoves all record collectors to listen to the whole issue.

I feel it is unnecessary, at this stage, to recount the history of the composition of *Petrouchka* or the story of the ballet; and in any case, you will find it all on the back of the attractive cardboard record cover – a great step forward this, having a programme note available for every work recorded on LP. And how good it really is to be able to sit back and listen to the performance, knowing that the music will not be broken into every few minutes! LS

believed by most of the manufacturers in the USA that eventually the record business in that country will settle down to one speed only, but some time must be expected to elapse before that can be achieved. Electric and Musical Industries Ltd. ... have closely studied these new developments from their inception from all aspects including the technical, commercial and mechanical, and have been anxious to avoid causing any disruption in the record and instrument business in this country resulting in possible loss to wholesalers and retailers and possible confusion to record buyers. It is EMI's intention to keep in close touch with all aspects of these developments and to avoid major changes in this industry until the situation becomes more clarified. Consequently they believe it is essential in the interests of all parties concerned, and particularly in the interest of the buying public, not to issue records with speeds other than the standard 78rpm, unless and until they give to the trade six months prior notice." That notice came 18 months later, and EMI released their LPs (and the UK's first 45s) in October 1952, although it must be said that the delay resulted in much dismay within EMI itself.

However, in July 1950 Mackenzie was able to declare, "We have had to wait, what some people have thought was an unreasonably long time, for the long-playing record in this country, but at last here it is, and it is really gratifying to be able to affirm with complete conviction that it was worth waiting for. To Decca belongs the honour of being the first to issue it in this country, and if future records are as well chosen and as well made as the first few I have heard, and of course they will be, then without a doubt a new era for the gramophone has opened." He had listened to nine Decca LPs and there were also reviews of these, and others, from LS, WRA and RH. Yet, as Mackenzie was hailing a "new era for the gramophone" he was grieving at the death on June 16th of Alfred Clark and writing, "It is a melancholy coincidence that I should be saluting in this editorial another advance of the gramophone when the man who did perhaps more than

The first Bayreuth Festival after the Second World War took place in July and August 1951. EMI recorded the opening concert with Furtwängler conducting Beethoven's Symphony No. 9 in addition to Karajan directing Wagner's *Die Meistersinger von Nürnberg* and the *Ring* cycle, of which only Act 3 of *Die Walküre* was ever released.

Walter Legge (left), then International Artists' Manager for EMI, is seen arriving at London Airport (later Heathrow – note BOAC arrival/ departure buildings) and delivering some four miles of tape recorded at the Festival to B. E. G. Mittell, Managing Director of EMI Studios.

The Gramophone, December, 1951

The EMI *Meistersinger*, recorded by Walter Legge in Bayreuth during the summer of 1951, was released amazingly quickly on 34 12-inch Columbia 78s in December of the same year (it would be another 10 months before EMI released LPs). Decca had also recorded this opera in Vienna (with sessions in September 1950 and September 1951) and this was released on six LPs within a few weeks of the EMI version. Decca were quick to make the obvious point in their January 1952 advertisement, "six versus thirty-four".

The Gramophone, January, 1952

six *versus* **thirty-four!**

At last you can possess a complete performance of Wagner's *Die Meistersinger von Nürnberg** on six Decca long playing records — a set which employs all the resources of the Vienna State Opera to produce one of the most splendid achievements in operatic recording of our time. Heading the list of distinguished artists is Paul Schoeffler, whose Hans Sachs is probably the finest in the world today. Hilde Gueden is the delightful Eva, and the part of Pogner, her father, is sung by Otto Edelmann, one of the most distinguished of the younger generation of singers. Günther Treptow's Walther shows that there are still Helden-tenors who can combine robust tone and lyrical beauty in their singing, while Karl Dönch makes a suitably cantankerous Beckmesser. The minor roles are also excellently cast, and the orchestral playing by the Vienna Philharmonic Orchestra under the sensitive and experienced bâton of Hans Knappertsbusch reveals all the beauties of Wagner's score—beauties which are so abundant that the opera must be heard again and again if they are to be fully absorbed. That is why *Die Meistersinger* is an ideal work for the gramophone, especially when it occupies only six Decca long playing records as against thirty-four ordinary seventy-eights.

*We suggest you order this magnificent recording now so that you are sure of obtaining your copy immediately it becomes available. Decca ffrr Long Playing Records Nos. LXT 2659-64. Price £11 17s. 0d. For those who have already purchased Act II—issued a year ago Acts I and III are also available on five more Decca long playing records, Nos. LXT 2646-7 and LXT 2648-50. Price 39/6d. each record.

The above prices include cost of art container with notes, and Purchase Tax.

LONG PLAYING 33⅓ r.p.m. RECORDS

THE DECCA RECORD COMPANY LTD., 1-3 BRIXTON ROAD, LONDON, S.W.9

A

The original premises of The Gramophone Company in Maiden Lane, established in 1898

anybody to bring the gramophone from the headquarters it once shared with a typewriter in Maiden Lane to the position it occupies today has just passed away". Clark, originally Chairman and Managing Director of EMI, had resigned as President of the company in September 1946 and one may well wonder how different the EMI situation might have been if he had still been at the helm.

Decca respond

Decca took advantage of this situation and during the course of the next two years developed their reputation for technical quality and also broadened their artist roster. They marketed a range of LP reproducing equipment and established an "LP Advisory Panel" which helped to resolve the doubts of many who were contemplating conversion to the new medium. Even so, initially it was left to them to persuade the British record-buying public that the LP was the logical successor to the 78rpm disc, and there can be little doubt that they would have welcomed EMI's support in the campaign.

However, their Managing Director, Edward Lewis, had already shown himself to be a fighter and his sales campaign included some of the hardest-hitting advertisements ever to appear in the pages of *The Gramophone*. In the issue for November 1950 they depicted a cock crowing, then the next month an ostrich with its head stuck in the sand, and in January an advertisement referring to "the doubting Thomases" (a reference to C. H. Thomas who was then responsible for the day-to-day operation of EMI's UK record business). An advertisement in February 1951, "Dickie and the Ostrich", was a response from EMI under the guise of one of its then defunct companies, The Johnson Talking Machine Company, but by now the inference of the advertising was possibly beyond the understanding of those outside the Industry itself. None the less, Decca continued to run a unique series of advertisements for their LPs which included in January 1952 the famous "six versus thirty-four" copy which responded to EMI's release of *Die Meistersinger* on 34 12-inch 78s against Decca's six LPs. The most controversial advertisement came in November 1952 (the month following EMI's delayed entry into LP) which under the heading "Striding ahead" depicted a cavalier's boot about to descend on the artist's name which just happened to be 'Hayes'. Decca were quick to point out that the artist's name was Hayes but for many the message was clear. January 1953 saw the end of this particular campaign with another advertisement which reproduced some of the earlier adverts in the form of a series of New Year resolutions.

Edward (later Sir Edward) Lewis (left) and Sir Compton Mackenzie at a dinner given in September 1952 to celebrate the 21st Anniversary of Mr Lewis's appointment to the Decca Board *Photo Decca*

Battle of the adverts

These Decca advertisements, the work of their Advertising Manager, F. E. Attwood, were typical of their thrusting campaign in the early 1950s. Having successfully launched LP in Britain they were clearly "cock-a-hoop" but soon showed their irritation at EMI's attitude ("Tch! Tch! Tch!"), furthering the point in January 1951 ("Hoity-toity"). This advertisement referred to "the doubting Thomases", a clear reference to C. H. Thomas, EMI's Record Controller, and the following month, using the guise of one of their long-forgotten companies – The Johnson Talking Machine Company – EMI responded. For the next few months nothing exceptional happened, but in November 1952 (immediately following EMI's entry into LP) came the famous cavalier's boot about to descend on "Hayes". Attwood assured everyone that the artist's name (not previously, or subsequently, credited) was in fact Hayes. In January 1953 there were a number of New Year 'resolutions' after which their advertising continued with a succession of clever corporate advertisements which ran in addition to their regular 'new release' announcements. But the battle was over, and EMI and many others were safely on the LP bandwagon

The Gramophone, November, 1950

That's how we feel. But should we crow or shouldn't we? On the whole, we'd rather not. Still, you know, we have made two conquests: one of *quality*, the other of *time*. First there was ffrr alone (those dear old 78s), then, four months ago, came our wonderful L.P.s. ffrr plus long playing; two conquests that give the music-lover the best of both worlds—78s and 33⅓ L.P.s.

In addition, of course, there was the Decola, which instantly set a new and still unsurpassed standard of record reproduction, having a range of from thirty to fourteen thousand cycles per second. To-day even this range is greatly extended.

DECCA

THE DECCA RECORD COMPANY LTD. 1-3 BRIXTON ROAD LONDON S.W.9

The Gramophone, February, 1951

"Dickie and the Ostrich"

Dickie was a very small boy. Johnny was bigger. Johnny wanted to help Dickie but Dickie was frightened of the big boy Johnny. Dickie was very timid and used to put his head under the bedclothes. To comfort him, Dickie's mother told him stories about Father Christmas and about animals, particularly about a great big bird called an Ostrich—which Mother said put its head in the sand. One day a big man came from Africa and told Dickie the Ostrich does not put its head in the sand but can run very fast. Dickie was more frightened and that night he dreamed that an Ostrich ran after him at 50 miles an hour. Dickie fell out of bed crying.

Poor Little Dickie !!

ADVERTISEMENT OF

The Johnson Talking Machine Co., Ltd.

LONDON · ENGLAND

The Gramophone, December, 1950

TCH! TCH!! TCH!!!

You can't help feeling sorry for a poor deluded bird that sticks its head in the sand rather than face facts. Progress isn't going to wait for an ostrich. Long playing is progress. It had to come and it's here to stay — once you've heard it you'll understand why. You'll understand, too, why music-lovers who have invested in long playing wouldn't even consider going back to 78s. Up to twenty-five minutes' continuous, flawless, ffrr reproduction without having to turn the record and without the clatter and bang of an automatic changer — *poor* old ostrich!

By the way, the scantily-clothed gentlemen on the horizon are not being sold 'the three card trick'. Not on your life! They're enjoying Decca long playing in the neighbourhood of faraway Nairobi ... or, anyway, in one of the many foreign parts where Decca long playing records are already firmly established.

plus ffrr makes

DECCA

the world's finest record
★ To spread goodwill and be kind to all, especially to animals
Helping lame dogs over stiles, for instance

★ To go on making our records and reproducers better and better
★ To go on giving you recordings of the finest artists of today (and tomorrow)
THE DECCA RECORD COMPANY LTD., 1-3 BRIXTON ROAD, LONDON, S.W.9

The Gramophone, January, 1951

A maiden lady (all arsenic and old lace) has mentioned to us that, in her opinion, our last two advertisements have not been in keeping with our aspirations and high technical achievements. Maybe not. But we believe that they have drawn the attention of everybody — including the doubting Thomases and Thomasinas — to the unique character of Decca long playing records: up to twenty-five minutes' *uninterrupted* true ffrr reproduction from each side of a slim, surface-quiet, unbreakable twelve-inch record. Of course, if you already realise all these L.P. advantages it merely proves that the cockerel and the ostrich have done their jobs pretty well, doesn't it?

When all is said and done, it is your verdict that counts. And so we should be grateful if you would pass your own judgement on our achievement by asking your dealer to play you any Decca long playing record in which you are particularly interested. We believe that this will amply prove the success of our exclusive technique – Decca long playing plus *full frequency range recording.*

DECCA

If your dealer is unable to let you hear a long playing record will you please let us know — and we will talk to him like a father!

THE DECCA RECORD CO. LTD., 1-3 BRIXTON ROAD, LONDON, S.W.9

The Gramophone, November, 1952

13TH
14TH
15TH RELEASE
★ Not to blow our own trumpets (not too much, anyway)
★ To stop exterminating bug-bears (that's easy — we've almost completed that job, anyway!)
striding ahead...
Striding ahead, Decca presents the fifteenth long playing release. Now, the total of long playing ffrr records is 502*.
Following the galaxy of orchestral music found in our thirteenth release, the star items in the fifteenth are three complete operas. From the Paris Opéra-Comique, after their success with *Carmen* and *Manon*, comes *Lakmé*. The great trio of Puccini operas is completed with the issue of *Tosca*, recorded, like *La Bohème* and *Madama Butterfly*, at the Accademia di Santa Cecilia, Rome. Also from Rome, the long awaited recording of Verdi's *Aïda* introduces for the first time on Decca long playing records Ebe Stignani, the greatest Italian mezzo-soprano of our time, and Mario del Monaco, considered by many to be the finest dramatic tenor Italy has produced since the war.
Despite these obvious highlights, orchestral music is not neglected. There is, for instance, a fine performance of Sibelius' Fifth Symphony by Erik Tuxen and The Danish State Radio Symphony Orchestra. For lovers of chamber music, the release includes three more Beethoven Violin and Piano Sonatas (including the Kreutzer), played by that superb team Max Rostal and Franz Osborn, and the Shostakovitch Piano Quintet Op. 57.
Lastly, there is a fine collection of ballet music, among which *Le Cid* is notable for a brilliant recording which stands out even from the superb quality of other Decca L.P.'s.
DECCA
* The fourteenth release of Decca long playing ffrr records consisted of thirteen records of light music
HAYES

The Gramophone, January, 1953

RECORD CATALOGUES

by Malcolm Walker

Manufacturers' and cumulative catalogues

From the earliest days of the industry, every company issued its own catalogue listing the recordings which were currently available in their own individual countries: generally these appeared annually, with monthly supplements to keep them up to date. They were designed principally for the Trade although in later years some of the larger companies provided copies for sale to the public. The catalogues would list works by title interspersed with a summary of composers' works directing the reader to the relevant point in the artist section. As the industry was very much artist-orientated, there would be a special section devoted to the company's principal artists, with an illustration plus biographical detail as well as a list of their recordings. This continued virtually unchanged until 1940. Up to the early 1950s it was expected that the average record dealer would know his catalogues sufficiently well to be able to ascertain quickly the availability of any record for which he would be asked. It was the proud boast of George Fenwick, manager of the then-world-flagship HMV shop at 363 Oxford Street, London, that his sales assistants had no need even to refer to a catalogue, although to be fair it has to be said that the shop then stocked only EMI product.

George Fenwick, Manager of the HMV showrooms at 363 Oxford Street, from 1935 to 1961

Even in the 1930s, following the publication of the *Encyclopedia of the World's Best Recorded Music* (Gramophone Shop, New York, 1929), it was recognized that a cumulative catalogue, embracing all labels, would be useful and the first such publication was compiled in 1936 by R. D. Darrell – *The Gramophone Shop Encyclopedia of Recorded Music*, published by Joe Brogan of The Gramophone Shop in New York. Comprising 586 pages, the listings were by composer with appendices covering collections, addenda, language courses, diction and literature recordings, and a brief section devoted to national music and folk-songs. A revised and updated edition (with a total of 562 pages) appeared in 1942 published by Simon and Schuster with George Clark Leslie as Supervising Editor. A third edition appeared in 1948, now with Robert H. Reid as Editor. Consisting of 654 pages, it included for the first time an artists' index. These three volumes were solely concerned with listing 78rpm recordings. The mantle then passed to Francis F. Clough and Geoffrey J. Cuming who, with the support of The Decca Record Company Ltd., compiled *The World's Encyclopaedia of Recorded Music* (Sidgwick & Jackson) for publication in 1952.

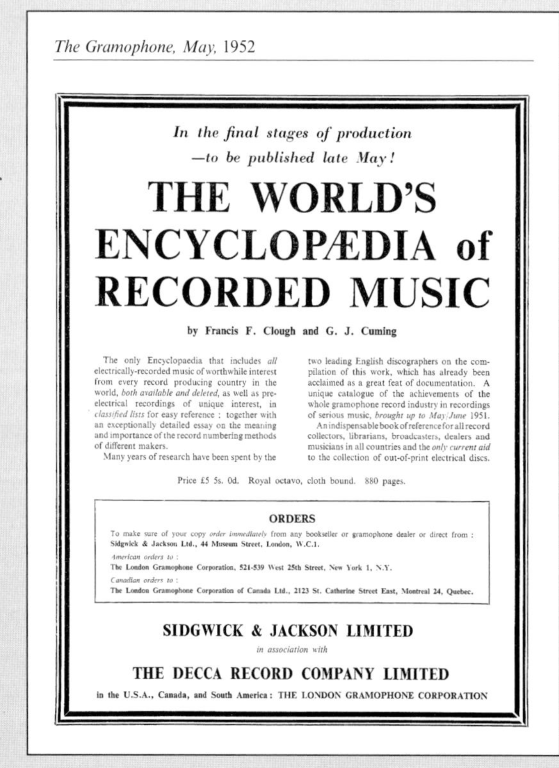

The Gramophone, May, 1952

In the final stages of production —to be published late May!

THE WORLD'S ENCYCLOPÆDIA of RECORDED MUSIC

by Francis F. Clough and G. J. Cuming

The only Encyclopaedia that includes *all* electrically-recorded music of worthwhile interest from every record producing country in the world, *both available and deleted*, as well as pre-electrical recordings of unique interest, in *classified lists* for easy reference: together with an exceptionally detailed essay on the meaning and importance of the record numbering methods of different makers.

Many years of research have been spent by the two leading English discographers on the compilation of this work, which has already been acclaimed as a great feat of documentation. A unique catalogue of the achievements of the whole gramophone record industry in recordings of serious music, *brought up to May/June* 1951.

An indispensable book of reference for all record collectors, librarians, broadcasters, dealers and musicians in all countries and the *only current aid* to the collection of out-of-print electrical discs.

Price £5 5s. 0d. Royal octavo, cloth bound. 880 pages.

ORDERS

To make sure of your copy *order immediately* from any bookseller or gramophone dealer or direct from: **Sidgwick & Jackson Ltd., 44 Museum Street, London, W.C.1.**

American orders to:
The London Gramophone Corporation, 521-539 West 25th Street, New York 1, N.Y.

Canadian orders to:
The London Gramophone Corporation of Canada Ltd., 2123 St. Catherine Street East, Montreal 24, Quebec.

SIDGWICK & JACKSON LIMITED

in association with

THE DECCA RECORD COMPANY LIMITED

in the U.S.A., Canada, and South America: THE LONDON GRAMOPHONE CORPORATION

WERM

The second edition of *The Gramophone Shop Encyclopedia* was reviewed in the March 1943 issue of ***The Gramophone*** and the following month a letter from Francis Clough stated that he and Geoffrey Cuming were, "occupied in collecting data and information to lead to the publication of a comprehensive discography on slightly different lines to those of the American publications" and asked for the assistance of readers in their objective. It now seems slightly ironic that they were asking for the loan of foreign catalogues in the midst of global war! In his Editorial of March 1950 Mackenzie again raised the subject of Clough's research and possible publication, and in the same issue Valentine Britten, the then BBC Gramophone Record Librarian, further endorsed the whole project. In July 1950 it was revealed that the first volume would be published by Sidgwick & Jackson. A whole page advertisement in the May 1952 issue announced publication later that month. Alec Robertson, in his enthusiastic review of the book in June 1952, remarked that the authors had "attempted to cover every record of permanent music issued since the advent of electrical recording up to April 1950, throughout the world" (although a number of rare and significant acoustically-made recordings were also included).

The first edition comprised 908 pages and listed recordings by composer. The first supplementary volume, published in 1953, and covering the years 1951-2, consisted of 284 pages of which ten were devoted to corrections to the first volume. The third volume, covering the years 1953-5 in 590 pages,

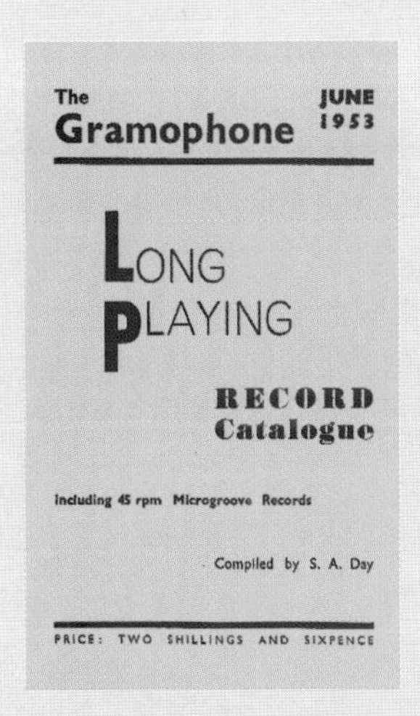

appeared in 1957 and turned out to be the last. Despite J. S. Knapp-Fisher, the Managing Director of Sidgwick & Jackson, writing to ask readers in September 1961 if any were able to "suggest an organization that might be prepared to subsidize this work", lack of financial support precluded the publication of a fourth volume. The entire project had been organized in their spare time by Clough, a solicitor living in Colwyn Bay and Cuming, a parson from Leicester. Eventually, spiralling costs and an increasing workload proved to be insurmountable difficulties, and they broke the news that work on a new volume had finally been suspended in a letter to ***The Gramophone*** in April 1965.

A further reprint of the original three volumes was noted by Roger Wimbush in November 1966 and in the following month Clough and Cuming announced that arrangements had been made with the British Institute of Recorded Sound (now the National Sound Archive, part of The British Library) to take over all the card-index entries which had been compiled since the publication of the third volume. The last major reprint of the three volumes took place in 1970 by Greenwood Press, Westport, Connecticut, USA.

In the area of vocal recordings Roberto Bauer had compiled *The New Catalogue of Historical Recordings*, 1898-1908/9 (originally published 1937, second edition from Sidgwick and Jackson in 1947, republished 1970) and there was also the *Collectors' Guide to American Recordings 1895-1925* by Julian Morton Moses (American Record Collectors' Exchange, 1949: republished 1993 by Monarch Record Enterprises, Dallas).

LP and CD catalogues

These books remain valuable research documents, charting much of the early recorded classical music, but the huge growth of the LP market called for something much more up to date and accessible to both the record dealer and collector.

The first such cumulative LP catalogue, listing all American LPs, was published in the autumn of 1949 by William F. Schwann in Boston, and this was followed in June 1953 by *The Gramophone LP Record Catalogue*, which also listed 7-inch 45rpm discs. Later, similar catalogues were produced in other countries, including the German *Bielefelder Katalogue*, first published in 1960, *Diapason* in France and Santandrea's *Catalogue generale dischi microsoli* in Italy.

Priced at 2s. 6d. [13p] *The Gramophone LP Record Catalogue* was compiled by Stanley Day, who would continue until 1975, when he was followed by Calum MacDonald until 1980, when compilation was undertaken by ***Gramophone***'s editorial department. The first edition (for which the demand far exceeded expectations bringing about an immediate reprint), covered 16 classical labels, 250 composers and some 1,500 LPs, all of which were available in the UK. The catalogue was up dated every quarter and spawned both the *Popular Record Catalogue* (1954-87, first compiled by Edgar Jackson, followed in time by Albert McCarthy, Arthur Jackson and, from 1984, Robert Seeley) and the *Spoken Word Catalogue* (1964-93, initially compiled by Cecil Bellamy).

Computer-based electronic compilation techniques were introduced in 1971, although sadly all the old LP data (which it had been hoped to convert) had to be jettisoned in 1985 following the introduction of new compilation programmes to produce *The Gramophone Compact Disc Digital Audio Guide and Catalogue*. Once again this was a quarterly publication, initially priced at 80p and originally including both classical and popular product. The first edition, published in September 1983, listed the works of 143 composers on 650 CDs on 27 different labels. It had indexes by composer, artist and catalogue number. Two separate catalogues, one devoted to LPs and cassettes, the other to CDs, continued to be published until June 1990. With effect from December 1990 the two publications were integrated, the page size being increased to match that of ***Gramophone*** and publication became twice yearly in June and December. The data is now held on an electronic database and serves a wide variety of uses within ***Gramophone***. As of January 1998 the database contained details of some 65,000 recordings featuring 67,000 works by more than 9,000 composers performed by over 45,000 artists issued by more than 1,300 different record companies.

Circulation and comparative reviewing

Margaret Pollard and her mother-in-law, Nellie Pollard, at the *Daily Herald*'s annual Brass Band Contest at the Royal Albert Hall in 1954

Whilst all this was happening the circulation of the magazine had gone from 24,100 in January 1950 to 42,750 by the end of 1953. Parallel with this the editorial department had been strengthened by the addition of Margaret Cleveland (my wife to-be) in an effort to cope with the increasing number of record reviews and the need to undertake comparative reviewing on a regular monthly basis. In this respect the magazine was ideally placed as it had always been a requirement that review records were returned to the Company's library and we were therefore in a position to provide a reviewer with all the material needed for the task. It was not an easy one, and in the course of time became increasingly complex, but at least the approach was positive and unequivocal.

Record catalogues and reviewers' equipment

With EMI's entry into LP we began to experience considerable difficulty in keeping track of all the new recordings and, in today's parlance, we needed a database which would supersede the manufacturers' annual catalogues and associated monthly supplements. One of our readers, Stanley Day, was also similarly concerned and suggested that we should publish a cumulative monthly listing of reviews in the magazine. Sadly, I could not see how the space could be found for this but suggested, as an alternative, a quarterly catalogue on the lines of the American Schwann. Day agreed in principle but on the understanding that he could produce something which was much more scholarly and comprehensive, and that it would include

This Decca advertisement features the equipment supplied to *The Gramophone*'s reviewers in 1950

Typical Unit-built Equipment

This combination comprises a Decca PA/VI high-fidelity amplifier and Decca corner speaker type CS3 or CS6, used with the Decca triple-speed player model 347/M, which is fitted with ffrr interchangeable magnetic pick-up heads with sapphire styli for 33⅓ r.p.m. long playing, 45 and 78 r.p.m. records.

Prices:		
	Corner speaker	£21.10.0
	347/M triple-speed player	£19.19.0
	PA/VI amplifier	£26. 5.0

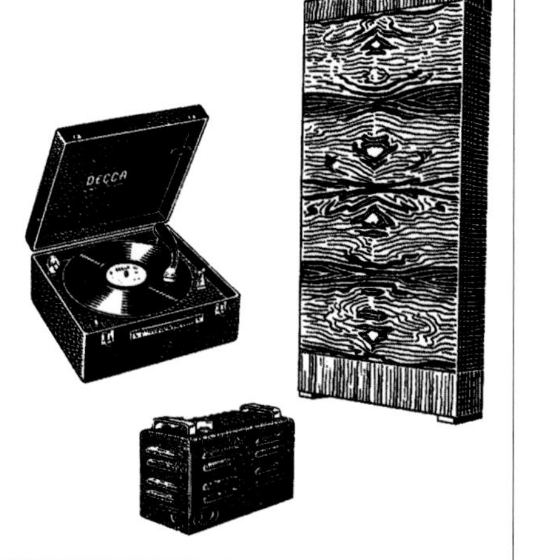

The June 1953 Coronation front cover used a reproduction of a bas-relief by Luc Della Robbia of a group of singers in the Musee di St Maria del Fiore in Florence

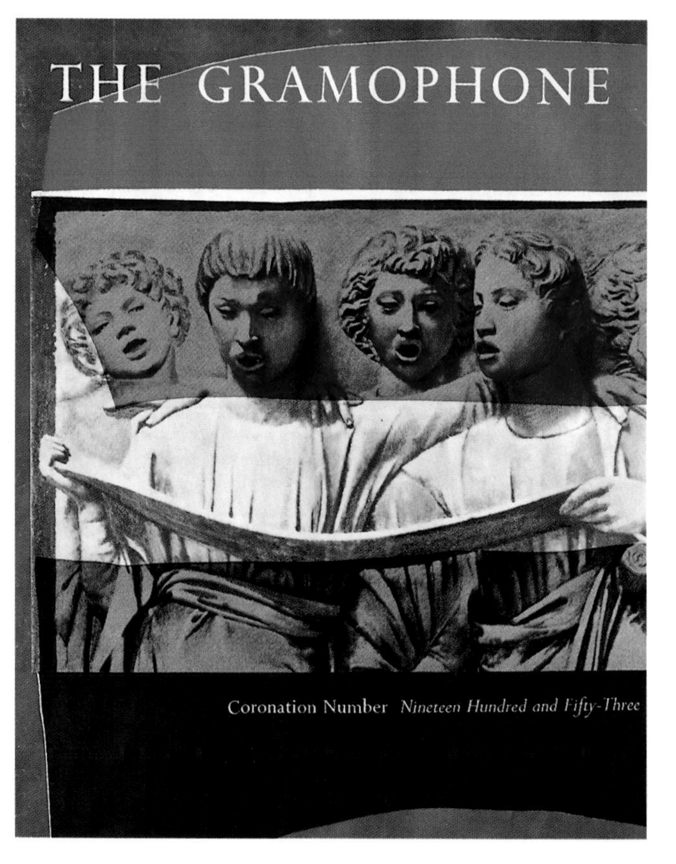

THE GRAMOPHONE
Coronation Number Nineteen Hundred and Fifty-Three

Arthur Haddy, at the time Manager of the Decca Recording Studios in Broadhurst Gardens, West Hampstead – later to be a Director of The Decca Record Company – was the powerhouse behind the technical excellence of their recordings, setting a standard which others endeavoured to emulate *Photo Decca*

review dates from ***The Gramophone***. My father's support of the venture was somewhat dampened by the reaction of George Fenwick, manager of HMV's store at 363 Oxford Street, who thought it was an interesting idea but pointed out that there would be no need of any copies in his store as the assistants were required to know the catalogue without reference to printed materials! None the less we went ahead and the first issue of *The Gramophone LP Record Catalogue* appeared in June 1953. Elsewhere we tell the story of the development of the various editions of these catalogues which were to sell in excess of 100,000 copies a year.

Shortly after the launch of LP, Arthur Haddy, head of Decca's West Hampstead studios, questioned the magazine's assessment of the recording quality of some of the new LPs. This had never been a problem with 78s but the finer tolerances experienced with LP undoubtedly called for a new approach and it was agreed to provide all our reviewers (at our own expense) with identical equipment, initially based on the range which Decca themselves were marketing. This resolved Arthur Haddy's problem and established for the future a criterion which would contribute to the excellence of the magazine's reviews.

In June 1953 ***The Gramophone*** celebrated the Coronation of Her Majesty Queen Elizabeth II with a varnished gold cover and plenty of colourful advertising within. The Editorial was written in the form of a loyal address by the Editor who, on July 8th, 1952, had been knighted in The Queen's first Birthday Honours List.

The following month Decca, trying to meet the need for a disc capable of accommodating some of the shorter works without packing them willy-nilly on to an LP, launched the 10-inch 33⅓ rpm Medium-Play disc which had a playing time of about nine minutes. The format was not copied elsewhere and with the increasing omnipotence of the LP, and the presence of the 45rpm extended-play disc (seven-and-a-half minutes per side – launched by EMI in April 1954 and in due course adopted by most companies) its life was relatively brief.

After some 12 years as a contributor, Geoffrey Howard-Sorrell handed back the technical editorship to Percy Wilson, who had been much involved in the early years with the Expert Committee and who, in September 1953, was to return for a final innings which would carry him up to February 1966. On the month of his return he was to write a farewell to his old friend and colleague H. F. V. Little who had died the previous month. Little, one of the original band of reviewers (who wrote under the pseudonym "Piccolo") and a member of the Expert Committee, was by profession a scientist and one of the pioneers of practical research into radioactive materials.

The Gramophone, June, 1954

Following the launch of their Extended-Play 45s in April 1954, EMI ran an extensive campaign to promote the discs. This proved very successful and they were adopted by the majority of labels

Price held for 30 years

The 32nd volume of the magazine commenced with the issue dated June 1954 and in his Editorial Sir Compton told readers how proud he was that following a cover-price increase from 6d. [2½ p] to 1s. [5p] in June 1924 it had been possible to maintain the price for the next 30 years. He suggested that much of the credit was due to the loyalty of the magazine's advertisers, "that loyalty has enabled us to concentrate upon advertisements bearing upon the gramophone and not to be tempted into accepting what is called national advertising, which means that every page in every number not only deserves to be read but *must* be read by everybody who wishes to keep in touch with the development of the gramophone". He also wrote of, "The smaller recording companies which have served good taste and are enjoying the practical

July 1955 **Correspondence**

I remember thirty-three years ago sitting in a café in Sheffield reading in *John O'London's Weekly* that Mr Compton Mackenzie was to start a new monthly devoted to the interests of gramophone enthusiasts. How eagerly I waited for that first number. I was not disappointed, the yellow cover with its classic design opened up a new world. In those days there was only the *Sound Wave* and *Talking Machine News* which commented on new records and any criticism they gave was mild in the extreme. How startlingly new, then, were **The Gramophone**'s reviews. Here was informed expression of views sometimes sharp and acrid. Here was a new standard, spirited, unafraid and with a delightful literary quality in the writing. My faith in the gramophone record as a serious medium of musical expression was at last confirmed.

I remember how it all began, though I suppose my experiences must be almost identical with others of my generation who returned from the 1914-18 war still in the bloom of youth, and with an unquenchable thirst for music. I soon found that listening to the piano transcriptions in the Star Folios of overtures and symphonic works just wasn't good enough, nor were the local Music Societies much help and in 1919 Subscription Concerts were few and Carl Rosa came once yearly. Therefore the would-be enquiring listener had perforce to search around for ways and means and possibilities.

I remember my first instrument. It was a Zonophone with a metal horn, but surprisingly enough this eventually gave an excellent account of itself with the addition of a Flex Diaphragm and fibre needles. Then came a table grand – not very satisfying; then a home-built, with Ultone tone arm, Ultone and Astra sound-boxes; and then in the mid-twenties an Orchorsol – in those days the last word, and with which I was well satisfied until the early thirties, when I acquired an EMG with exterior horn. This was the ultimate, it was also the end as far as acoustic reproduction was concerned.

I remember my first orchestral record, the *Scherzo* from Beethoven's Fifth conducted by Nikisch, and I can still remember how thrilling an interpretation it was. I remember my first Galli-Curci, a voice with a beautiful and unusual quality. Which reminds me that Sir Compton Mackenzie once wrote "with two hundred Galli-Curci records I could face old age with equanimity". It would be interesting to learn from Sir Compton if he still agrees? I doubt it! I remember my first chamber music venture, a snippet from the Schumann Quintet on Vocalion, what fascinating labels Vocalion had. I still have Scotney's *Caro nome* with its red-gold label. I remember the first Léner Quartet records, what an advance they were. For the first time one could hear the correct balance of the four instrumentalists.

I remember a thousand and one things about this hobby which has kept alive my unabated enthusiasm for nearly forty years! My other interests of painting and gardening pale almost into insignificance beside it.

H. P. Stones
Tunbridge Wells, Kent

appreciation of the public, and their success is one of the most favourable signs for the future". All sentiments which ring true today.

At the same time EMI gave notice of the deletion on January 1st, 1955 of a huge number of 78rpm records – although the last were not to go until March 1962. The industry's concern for the size of its catalogue was not exclusive to 78s: in America it had already been recognized that the 10-inch LP was not a success commercially and Harold Schonberg in his "Letter from America" (July 1954) reported that "record companies these days are busily engaged transferring the contents of 10-inch discs to single 12-inch LP sides, with a more-or-less-appropriate coupling for the work". This practice would be applied in the UK in the late 1960s.

The arrival of Deutsche Grammophon

Following Decca's launch of LP in June 1950, and Nixa's entry in July 1951 (with a range of small licensed labels from the USA) and then EMI's arrival in October 1952, there had been a progressive UK build-up of LP labels and these included Vox (November 1952), Supraphon (August 1953), Westminster (October 1953), Oiseau-Lyre (November 1953), Mercury (June 1954) and the giant Dutch electronics company Philips, later to be the major shareholder in the PolyGram Group and now licensee of the American Columbia catalogue (July 1954). However, in September 1954 an announcement concerning the formation of the Heliodor Record Company, a subsidiary of Deutsche Grammophon GmbH, ruffled a few feathers at EMI because the two companies had shared interests dating back to the turn of the century – though clouded in commercial terms by two wars.

In attempting to rebuild their business following the Second World War DGG had, with the support of Dr Ernst von Siemens – a director of the company bearing

The Gramophone, April, 1953

This 1953 EMG advertisement shows the 11 principal classical LP labels then currently available in the UK

The Gramophone, February, 1955

Deutsche Grammophon Gesellschaft

First Release
Available 1st February

LUDWIG VAN BEETHOVEN
Sonata for Violin and Pianoforte No. 1, D major, Opus 12/1
Sonata for Violin and Pianoforte No. 2, A major, Opus 12/2
Wolfgang Schneiderhan, Violin
Wilhelm Kempff, Pianoforte
12" LP DGM 18083

Schneiderhan

PETER TSCHAIKOVSKY
Symphony No. 6, B minor, Opus 74, "Pathétique"
The Berlin Philharmonic Orchestra
Conductor: Ferenc Fricsay
12" LP DGM 18104

Kempff

ROBERT SCHUMANN
Dichterliebe, Opus 48
Words by Heinrich Heine
Walther Ludwig, Tenor
Michael Raucheisen, Pianoforte
10" LP DG 16029

Ludwig

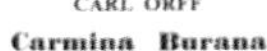

CARL ORFF
Carmina Burana
Elfride Trötschel, Soprano · Paul Kuen, Tenor
Hans Braun, Baritone · Karl Hoppe, Baritone
Choir and Orchestra of the Bayerischer Rundfunk
Conductor: Eugen Jochum
2-10" LPs DG 16045/6

Fricsay

Jochum

Retail Prices: 10" **DG** 27/3½d. (inc. P.T.), 12" **DGM** 36/5½d. (inc. P.T.)

HELIODOR RECORD COMPANY LIMITED, 8 CLARGES STREET, LONDON, W.1.
Subsidiary Company of the Deutsche Grammophon Gesellschaft m.b.H., Hannover

Staff of the newly established Heliodor Record Company taking afternoon tea in the late summer of 1954 at the "Compleat Angler" in Marlow, with the River Thames in the background. From the left: G. Steibelt (company secretary), Alex Herbage (A&R and Marketing), John Reid (Sales Manager – son of Hilton Nixon, founder of Nixa), Irma (secretary), Peter Lamb (editorial and advertising), a trainee from DGG Hanover, Friedel Schirmer and Werner Riemer (Managing Director) *Photo Herbage*

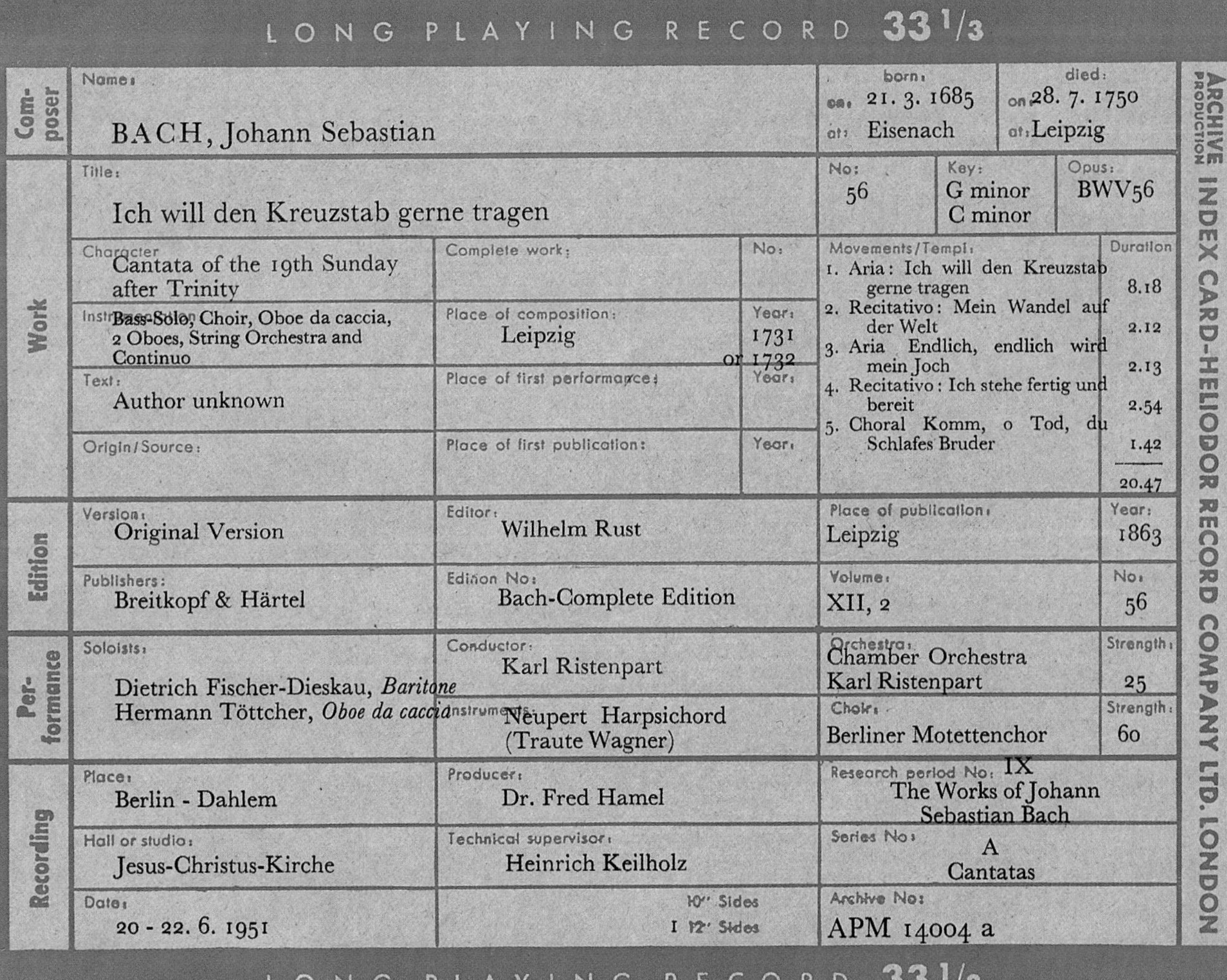

LONG PLAYING RECORD 33 1/3

ARCHIVE PRODUCTION INDEX CARD-HELIODOR RECORD COMPANY LTD. LONDON

Composer
Name: BACH, Johann Sebastian
born: ca. 21. 3. 1685 at: Eisenach
died: on 28. 7. 1750 at: Leipzig

Work
Title: Ich will den Kreuzstab gerne tragen
No: 56
Key: G minor, C minor
Opus: BWV56
Character: Cantata of the 19th Sunday after Trinity
Complete work:
No:
Instruments: Bass-Solo, Choir, Oboe da caccia, 2 Oboes, String Orchestra and Continuo
Place of composition: Leipzig
Year: 1731 or 1732
Text: Author unknown
Place of first performance:
Year:
Origin/Source:
Place of first publication:
Year:

Movements/Tempi:	Duration
1. Aria: Ich will den Kreuzstab gerne tragen	8.18
2. Recitativo: Mein Wandel auf der Welt	2.12
3. Aria Endlich, endlich wird mein Joch	2.13
4. Recitativo: Ich stehe fertig und bereit	2.54
5. Choral Komm, o Tod, du Schlafes Bruder	1.42
	20.47

Edition
Version: Original Version
Editor: Wilhelm Rust
Place of publication: Leipzig
Year: 1863
Publishers: Breitkopf & Härtel
Edition No: Bach-Complete Edition
Volume: XII, 2
No: 56

Performance
Soloists: Dietrich Fischer-Dieskau, *Baritone*; Hermann Töttcher, *Oboe da caccia*
Conductor: Karl Ristenpart
Orchestra: Chamber Orchestra Karl Ristenpart
Strength: 25
Instruments: Neupert Harpsichord (Traute Wagner)
Choir: Berliner Motettenchor
Strength: 60

Recording
Place: Berlin - Dahlem
Producer: Dr. Fred Hamel
Research period No: IX The Works of Johann Sebastian Bach
Hall or studio: Jesus-Christus-Kirche
Technical supervisor: Heinrich Keilholz
Series No: A Cantatas
Date: 20 - 22. 6. 1951
10" Sides
1 12" Sides
Archive No: APM 14004 a

LONG PLAYING RECORD 33 1/3

An early example of the Archiv Produktion Index Card (initially anglicized by Heliodor as Archive Production) which accompanied each recording and established a new standard for the presentation of such information. It was hailed by Lionel Salter, writing in the November 1954 issue of *The Gramophone*, as "the scholar's and encyclopaedist's dream".

DEUTSCHE GRAMMOPHON AND ARCHIV PRODUKTION

On October 24th, 1972, on the occasion of the 25th anniversary of Archiv Produktion, Dr Ernst von Siemens gave a speech at Nymphenburg near Munich in which he outlined the origins of the Archiv label

Dr Ernst von Siemens *Photo DG*

When somebody who since early childhood had been a passionate lover of the gramophone record, suddenly in 1941 – and thus in the middle of the war – acquires responsibility for the long renowned Deutsche Grammophon Gesellschaft, that's a great piece of luck for him. How did it come about? When the house of Siemens agreed with AEG that it would part with its interest in Telefunken, the Telefunken record label remained with the parent company. On the other hand Deutsche Grammophon, whose factory and repertoire Telefunken had acquired from its bankrupt estate, was allocated to us. And since I was responsible for electro-acoustics in the firm at the time, the care of the new child was entrusted to me. What was to be done? The moment was entirely unsuitable for a large-scale programme. Nevertheless, with us the word 'technology' had always been written large – and in this field it was possible even during the war to do something. We were able to get rather closer to our objective of bringing the record which was technically the best on to the market. It was more difficult to bring back the classical repertoire, which was responsible for the company's reputation, to its previous pitch. And the longer the war lasted, the greater became the problem.

ARCHIVE PRODUCTION

The Works of Johann Sebastian Bach

"ICH WILL DEN KREUZSTAB GERNE TRAGEN"

"ICH HABE GENUG"

APM 14004

When after the war we came to survey the surviving ruins, at least the factory in Hanover was remarkably well preserved. But what were the prospects for new recordings? German artists, or those of interest to us among them, were mostly forbidden to perform. International artists were unobtainable, and we for the time being were of no interest whatever to them. What was to be done? Luckily an exceptional personality had been advising the firm on marketing for some time: Hans Domizlaff. The problem fascinated him, and he recommended that we should depart completely from the well-trodden path and find a speciality at which we were competitive in the situation then obtaining.

Dr Fred Hamel *Photo DG*

After a thorough study of the market we reached the conclusion that for a German concern there was only one speciality in the record field to which foreign supremacy and the struggle for star artists were irrelevant: the good old German domestic music, or in fact periods of musical history before the era of Mozart. The initial programme was conceived as the revival of the artistic treasure of the eighteenth century, with preference being given to everything which could in the broadest sense be termed domestic music. As far as performance was concerned, the market value of important artists was to be ignored, and instead the earnest, scholarly character of an archive was to provide the opportunity for public propaganda for the gramophone record. Hence the plan for an 'Archiv' label.

First of all this entailed finding a suitable leader for the new project. In Dr Fred Hamel we found the man who brought to the new task not only the right academic qualifications but enthusiasm too. He set to work to draw up a programme of the periods in which Archiv Produktion should be active. He divided the whole time into ten – later 12 – research periods, which began with the Gregorian and ended with the eighteenth century.

It was important that Archiv Produktion recordings should fulfil the highest artistic and stylistic demands. The criterion was that the sound picture of past epochs should be approached as closely as possible, through the use of historic or reconstructed instruments, and the basing of recordings on original versions and first published editions.

When Dr Hamel was beginning to build up the repertoire the bicentenary of Johann Sebastian Bach's death (1950) was approaching. He thought that the most worthy way of setting production in motion would be through the publications of a number of Bach's works. In this respect it was useful that in 1947 Helmut Walcha had begun to record the works for organ, at first on the small organ of the Church of St Jakobi in Lübeck and later on the Schnitger organ in Cappel, under the technical supervision of Erich Thienhaus. This became the original recording by Archiv Produktion. But a start was also made with recordings of the cantatas so seldom heard, in which one of the collaborators was a very promising young baritone, by name Dietrich Fischer-Dieskau.

With lovingly chosen and prepared recordings, a beginning was also made in all the other research periods. Just before a recording of the 12 *Concerti grossi*, Op. 6 by Handel was to start, a harpsichord player was lacking. He was discovered at the last moment in the person of the new organist at the Markus-Kirche in Munich. I can still hear the expression of rapture with which the conductor of this production – Fritz Lehmann, who died so prematurely – described the art, and particularly in improvisation, of the young Karl Richter.

Were the assumptions which led to the creation of the Archiv label correct? Certainly the fear that we should not succeed in regaining a position in the world market was false. But 25 years ago who would have foreseen the German 'Wirtschaftswunder' ('economic miracle'), nowadays so gladly and so often criticized, and all its consequences? Who could have known then that Philips would decide to enter the record business and that one day the joining together of Philips and Deutsche Grammophon would give birth to a firm which – as is the case today – is one of the world's great record firms?

The Archiv label would long ago have been forgotten if it hadn't proved that it is in itself extremely hardy, and that it has brought the record a new market, not only for us; in short, it has met a genuine demand. I should hate to draw the conclusion that a catastrophe on the scale of 1945 was needed before new ideas could be brought to life. Anybody who like us is accustomed to look continually for new paths in technology would not wish to be satisfied either with well-worn ways alone for his fund of music. Furthermore, I have always argued passionately that great ideas were never born of penny-pinching accounting, and that we must also risk something for the extension of our repertoire.

Those were prophetic words from Ernst von Siemens and thanks to his initiative fresh impetus was given once again to the classical record business.

his name and the then owners of DGG – developed the Archiv label, a relatively low-cost, scholarly exercise which concentrated on German pre-Mozart repertoire and was designed initially for the European market and not likely to bring them into direct competition with the likes of EMI and Decca. The label was directed by Dr Fred Hamel, who joined the company in 1947, and his taste and vision set standards which in time were to be emulated by his successors all over the world. Sadly, he died on December 9th, 1957.

An early DGG sleeve

The UK introduction of the Archiv label in November 1954 was followed in February 1955 by the DG yellow label itself, offering mainstream classical repertoire performed by central European artists and orchestras: this was seen as an immediate threat by EMI and Decca, a situation which was compounded by a skilful DGG marketing operation.

Werner Riemer, Heliodor's Managing Director, had employed as his musical/marketing advisor Alex Herbage, originally with Decca and then in 1951 joint-founder with Harley Usill of the Argo Record Company. Herbage's first step was to establish from the pages of ***The Gramophone*** a list of the preferred LP versions of the core repertoire. He then evaluated these against the DGG equivalents and for Heliodor's initial releases selected only those recordings which were, in his opinion, superior to the magazine's existing recommendations. His judgement was good and the DGG yellow label was off to a flying start.

We join the ABC and survive a price increase

In June 1955 Sir Compton was happy to relate that the magazine's circulation in North America was in excess of 8,000 copies and suggested that "we can claim a larger circulation there than any other British monthly" – a claim which was not challenged. However, he was not so happy when in December he had to announce a price increase from 1s. [5p] to 1s. 6d. [7½ p]. It had been a matter of great pride that there had been no increase since June 1924 but the spiralling costs of print and paper had finally to be faced. In conclusion he wrote, "I hope we are not going to lose many readers in 1956, but, to be on the safe side, I wish a Merry Christmas to all in this last shillingsworth".

January 1955 **Editorial**

During the past twelve months the circulation of ***The Gramophone*** has risen from 42,750 in December 1953 to 57,000 in December 1954. This represents an increase in one year of more than the whole of our circulation ten years ago. This rise is a sign of the fantastic growth of the industry, particularly during the last two years. Once upon a time I was able to review every quarter all the records issued during the previous three months, apart from light entertainment and dance records, in four pages of leisurely talk. During 1953 ***The Gramophone*** devoted 186 pages to the section "Analytical Notes and First Reviews", and in 1954 these pages had increased to 258. In 1953 the number of 33⅓ records reviewed was 621. In 1954 this already formidable figure had rushed up to 1,011. Once upon a time we received a complete opera to review two or three times a year. I exaggerate. Not so often as that. In 1953 we received 17 complete operas for review, and during 1954 we received no less than 50! I dislike exclamation marks, but sometimes they are justified.

George Freshwater, Advertising Manager of EMI (1950)

For any publisher circulation figures are critical and particularly in those days when the all-important advertisement rate was invariably measured directly against the sale of the magazine. In December 1945 the print order was 12,200 – and given the continuing government restrictions in respect of 'returns' – this represented fairly accurately the actual sales figure on the assumption that newsagents were not going to throw copies to waste at their own expense. However, by December 1954 (and with the magazine still maintaining a 'no returns' policy) the print order had risen to 57,800. Such an increase tested the credulity of George Freshwater, Advertising Manager of EMI, who up to that time had grudgingly accepted the sight of a printer's invoice as evidence of the number of copies printed and sold. Freshwater had been involved in the UK with the development of an independent body known as the Audit Bureau of Circulations (ABC), whereby the publisher's sales figures would be authenticated by professional auditors, and he now insisted that ***The Gramophone*** join the ABC. Originally, the figures encompassed all sales, both in the UK and Overseas, and represented monthly averages seen over a half-year period. The figure for July to December 1955 (the period prior to the price increase) was 63,894 and that for the next half-year, January to June 1956 (after the price increase), was 66,979. Thus, Sir Compton's fears in respect of the price increase were unfounded and Freshwater probably rued the day he had suggested our joining the ABC, for no longer could he question the validity of our sales figures.

The December 1955 issue contained a new feature, "Critics' Choice", in which the magazine's 11 critics selected their six outstanding records of the year. (The feature is still an integral part of the magazine, but when it appeared in the March 1998 issue there were contributions from 41 critics.) The following month (January 1956) we instituted another feature which was to become a regular part of the magazine, the Index to Reviews.

American Columbia and RCA leave EMI

In 1953 the long association between American Columbia (later CBS and then Sony) and British Columbia came to an end, and in March the American catalogue was represented in the UK by Philips who had added record interests to their existing electronic activities. Similarly, RCA Victor (later BMG) was to separate from HMV and in June 1957 all new releases for the UK originated from Decca. Eventually, both CBS and RCA were to establish their own organizations in the UK (March 1965 and June 1969 respectively) and by then the ramifications of the record industry and its various labels, which for so many years had appeared immutable, was becoming so complex that it would require a book of its own to keep track of events. Sir Louis Sterling (who retired as Managing Director of EMI in May 1939) died on June 2nd, 1958 after making an enormous contribution to the British record industry and would certainly have been bemused by all the corporate changes.

The Gramophone, June, 1957

DECCA PRESENTS RCA RECORDS
RCA
Toscanini, Rubinstein, Horowitz, Heifetz, The Boston Pops Orchestra under Arthur Fiedler, Mario Lanza and Harry Belafonte . . . great names who are represented in the first release of RCA records. To the genius of these great artists is added the RCA 'New Orthophonic' high fidelity recording technique and Decca's unrivalled experience and skill in record manufacture.

Joseph (later Sir Joseph) Lockwood, at the time of his appointment to EMI, in conversation with Harry Bryan (right) Managing Director of Selecta Limited, main distributors for The Decca Record Company

June 1954 saw the arrival of a new Chief Executive at EMI, Joseph (later Sir Joseph) Lockwood, a miller by profession who undoubtedly was bemused by what he found in the record industry. However, he addressed himself to the many problems which then beset EMI and in the course of his 20-year association was to transform the company's record business, both in the UK and overseas.

Office moves and Staff

In September 1951 my father moved from Ebrington Road, Kenton to Green Lane, Stanmore where we located the Record Library and had an office for ourselves. For the next nine years the Company would operate with

From September 1951, Cecil and Anthony Pollard ran the editorial and financial elements of the Company from the top right-hand room of Cecil Pollard's home in Stanmore

June 1954

ARTURO TOSCANINI

by Harold C. Schonberg

Two hours before Toscanini's farewell broadcast concert with the NBC Symphony Orchestra there was doubt whether there was going to be a concert at all. At the rehearsal he had gone into a tantrum, thrown down his baton and called the whole thing off. Prior to that he had expressed worry about his memory, and had made a substitution on his all-Wagner programme, replacing the *Liebestod* with the *Tannhäuser* Bacchanale.

I happened to be home, listening to that final broadcast. During the *Tannhäuser* excerpts the tempos suddenly slowed and the texture began to thin out. Then the programme went off the air, "due to technical difficulties". The first few bars of Toscanini's recording of the Brahms First Symphony was played. After a few moments there was another pause, and the broadcast from Carnegie Hall was resumed.

The following day I learned what had happened. Toscanini had stopped conducting; at least, he stopped beating time. The orchestra was in a panic, and began taking cues from Frank Miller, the first cellist. Guido Cantelli, in the control room, became panic-stricken and feared that Toscanini was going to collapse. It was on his orders that the broadcast was interrupted. But then Toscanini recovered, picked up the beat and carried on. One wonders what thoughts were passing through his brain: the marvellous brain of an 87-year-old conductor who knew that this was the end of the greatest conducting career in history.

In the autumn of 1954 the Record Industry Ball was held in the Royal Albert Hall, with music from Ted Heath and his band. Although a success, the event was not repeated. The photograph shows Cecil and Anthony Pollard flanked by Goff and Nina Imhof of the long-established and famous music and instrument retailing business in London's New Oxford Street

February 1951

DINU LIPATTI

by Walter Legge

On December 2nd, 1950 Dinu Lipatti died. In the February 1951 issue, Walter Legge contributed a personal appreciation of the pianist in which he recalled a final 'Indian summer' of recording when a new medication briefly arrested the progress of Lipatti's fatal cancer

Dinu Lipatti
Photo EMI

In the last days of May [1950] I had a private letter from a Dr Dubois-Ferriére in Geneva urging me at once to organize an expedition to Geneva to record Dinu Lipatti. As his doctor he had administered injections of Cortison and the improvement was remarkable. Unfortunately, he explained, the treatment could not be continued for more than two months, and since this was the first time it had been tried for Lipatti's complaint he could give no promise of its permanence or continued efficacy, but he begged me as a friend of Lipatti's to stop at nothing to make recordings in Geneva possible while the improvement lasted.

Walter Legge with (from the left) Joan Hammond, Lady Jessie Wood and Isobel Baillie at the Henry Wood celebration luncheon in July 1944

Dr Dubois-Ferriére had already collected subscriptions from friends and admirers of Lipatti to present him with a new Steinway pianoforte from the Hamburg factory – a luxury Dinu had long wished to enjoy. But it was not a concert-grand, and I have a rooted objection to the lack of warm bass that seems inevitable in recordings made with short grands.

Those colleagues and friends who made those last Lipatti recordings possible have earned the gratitude of musicians and music lovers for decades, perhaps generations to come. W. S. Barrell, Director of EMI Studios, interrupted his holiday to find a suitable studio in Geneva. Radio-Geneva rearranged their programmes so that the studios should be available to us day and night. Paul Jecklin, Columbia's agent in Switzerland, bought from Steinway in Hamburg and had sent to Geneva the first of those fabulously beautiful post-war concert-grands to enter Switzerland, the instrument Lipatti had always wanted to use for recording. Our French company sent their superbly equipped new recording van directly from the Casals recordings in Prades.

W. S. Barrell (left), Director of the EMI Recording Studios with two of his technical colleagues – Dr G. F. Dutton and H. A. M. Clark *Photo EMI*

I found Dinu in better health and spirits than I had ever known him to enjoy. Friends had placed at his disposal a house standing in its own small park outside Geneva and a few minutes walk from the French frontier. We christened it "Haus Triebschenli" because it looked like a diminutive copy of Wagner's house on Lake Lucerne. Dinu loved the sun and the trees, and the weather smiled on us. For two radiant and blessed weeks the sun shone out of a clear blue sky and the thermometer settled itself comfortably in the nineties. Cortison had given him a ravenous appetite and restored his natural gaiety. Dinu laughed and made music. He had just heard the story of a great conductor, known among musicians for his nervous and seemingly undecided downbeat who, at the beginning of his first rehearsal with a famous Italian orchestra had been encouraged by a shout from the first contra-bass player "Corragio! Maestro, corragio!". Whenever an *arpeggio* in the Chopin *Valses* failed to come off with the desired clarity, accuracy and grace, Dinu stopped and called out either in apology or impatience "Arpeggio Maestro! arpeggio". It became a catch phrase which he cherished to the end. And when a legato passage was less smooth or chords less brilliant than he wanted it was always "Doigts de Maccaroni" – maccaroni fingers – the contemptuous epithet which he used on himself and his pupils for a lack of controlled strength in the fingers.

The recording van stood day and night beside the Radio-Geneva studios among lawns and well-kept rose beds in rural peace. Both new Steinways were in the studio, Jecklin's noble concert grand and Dinu's exquisitely sensitive short grand, his "virgin whom no other hands have caressed". We spent the first day satisfying ourselves by innumerable test recordings which piano to use, where it sounded best, which microphone to use and where to place it.

The recording of the Chopin *Valses* took nearly all of nine days, from three to seven hours a day. We worked as a rule from nine until lunch time and from half-past six or seven until ten or after. The first seven sessions were devoted to the *Valses*. Apart from all the other problems Lippati was particularly concerned with the fact that unlike the *Etudes*, which were composed in two batches, and the twenty-four *Preludes*, Chopin's *Valses*, although sometimes played as if they were written at one period of his life, belong together only by virtue of title and rhythm. To differentiate between these works of different periods, to avoid applying a personal range of nuances or mannerisms of rubato, was his constant preoccupation while studying and recording them. We decided, after seven sessions of *Valses*, that it would be refreshing to make a change from waltz rhythm and Chopin's texture, and to record some Bach. That evening he recorded Kempff's arrangement of a *Siciliana* and returned, not for the last time, to the old problem of *Jesu, Joy of man's desiring*. After six days eight of the *Valses* had been completed to the satisfaction of the most critical trio who ever sat in judgement on performances – Dinu, his wife, and I. At supper late that night we decided to devote the Sabbath, the next day, to Bach.

Sunday, July 9th, was the hottest and most memorable of all the days in that spell of incredible happiness. At nine in the morning we began Bach's B flat Partita and it was finished before lunch. Fearing that the effort of recording those four perfect sides – most of them were done some four or five times – would be too much for him I counselled cancelling the evening session, but Dinu would not hear of it: his sun was shining and he was going to make hay. At seven he started on the Mozart sonata. If ever a player was inspired it was Dinu that evening. Mozart and Bach were the composers nearest and dearest to his heart, and this was his first Mozart recording. The music came to an intensity of life rare, if not unique, in my experience. Phrases took on human form and character, living their exciting lives before the mind's eye as in a perfect performance of some unwritten opera. In no other way could he have demonstrated so convincingly his belief that even in his instrumental works Mozart was at heart a dramatic, an operatic composer. By ten o'clock the sonata was finished and now there was no stopping him; we must try to get the outstanding *Valses* while he was still in the mood. He recorded five, not all finally, and when shortly before midnight the exhausted engineers were trudging wearily in search of a meal, Dinu, the freshest of us all, played *Stormy weather*.

three small offices – Subscriptions at Ebrington Road, Trade Sales and Advertising in London, and Editorial and Financial from Stanmore. It was during this period that the family aspect of the Company was at its height when my father not only employed his brother Reg (to sell advertising), but also his sister Hylda (to work on accounts) and her husband Vic Dunbar (as Circulation Manager). Including my father, me and my wife, there were six family members out of a staff total of no more than ten and from time to time this produced quite interesting situations!

The end of an era

In January 1950, after my return from America, I succeeded my father as Company Secretary, but more to the point I worked with him on the editorial side of the magazine leaving him with more time to concentrate on the financial aspects of the Company, also hopefully providing him with an opportunity to relax a little after a period of ten years during which he had been 'all things to all men'. Our relationship was a happy one and he gave me every opportunity to develop a level of new editorial thinking which was necessary to accommodate the changes brought about by the long-playing record. In June 1958 I succeeded him as London Editor whilst he joined Sir Compton and Christopher Stone on the masthead as joint editors.

The two Christophers – with Stone in charge of an unusually quiet year-old Pollard (1958)

Faith Mackenzie's active role in the Company had ceased before the outbreak of the Second World War, Christopher Stone maintained an overall interest and most valuably read proofs whenever he could,

August 1956

LETTER FROM AMERICA

by Harold C. Schonberg

Ordinarily this Letter is typed in a smoke-filled room opening to the vista of a lovely chimney surrounded by a group of old flats. At this moment of typing, however, the following vista unfolds: a spacious green lawn; an oak so tall that the sky is pushing it sidewards; a cypress with grasping fingers right out of a Disney cartoon; roses pink and red and yellow; a triumphant flower border filled with specimens that a sidewalk-bred New Yorker cannot hope to identify. I am a little uneasy in such surroundings. I hear no traffic, and the birds make a noise that is positively thunderous; threatening, even. [HCS was writing from Anthony Pollard's house in Stanmore, north-west London.]

But it is good to be back in England after a lapse of twelve years. The last time, when I had more hair and less weight, England (as the saying then went) was kept from sinking into the sea only by the wartime barrage balloons holding it up. These days, of course, there are probably as many tourists as there were then soldiers. Not even one barrage balloon, however; and it is a thrill to see what Trafalgar Square looks like with light playing on the fountains. One wondered, during those black-out nights in 1943.

And it has been an educative experience to meet with some of ***The Gramophone*** critics. Up to now they have existed in my mind as a comprehensive set of initials bounded by the four sides of a magazine sheet. In more than one way they were a mystery. We American critics often have been somewhat disconcerted by the reception that some of our best-thought-of records have met in these pages. For many years we have respected and in many cases admired the reviewers of ***The Gramophone*** – admired them for their scholarship, for their painstaking treatment of the music, for the trouble they take to make comparative surveys; even, in some cases, for their writing ability. And yet, in so many instances, there is a mighty cleavage between American and British critics. We seem to hear the same things differently.

Now there is, of course, such a thing as a national school of criticism. Artists who cannot make headway in America may be received with enthusiasm in France; musicians whom the Press in England merely tolerate may make a big career in America. An orchestra that may suit American standards may be received with the utmost coolness in London; and several orchestras of European renown have failed to impress American audiences in recent years.

The point is that all critics and audiences bring to musical performances their own background and conditioning. We may like to think that criticism is an objective art – and it must be, up to a certain point – but at basis we hear with ears that are different from the ears of any person alive. Goodness knows that the problem is complicated enough in the concert hall. On records it is even worse, because our ears are completely at the mercy of the reproducing equipment upon which the record is played.

whilst Mackenzie rightly remained as the figure-head with my father briefing him in respect of the content of the Editorials which he continued to provide. However, the three original participants in the Company – Faith now in her early seventies and Mackenzie and Stone in their late sixties – had no family successors interested in the business and in view of my father's role in the Company (particularly the fact that without him it would have foundered on several occasions) they generously suggested that he should inherit their interests.

Thus, in December 1950 Service Contracts were drawn up in favour of all three, guaranteeing them fixed annual salaries for the remainder of their lives in exchange for their shareholdings which were transferred to the Pollard family. It was a matter of pride for my father and me that the sums paid under these agreements were always substantially in excess of the contracted requirements. Mackenzie's biographer, Andro Linklater, writing about Faith, said, "From 1950 her financial hardships gradually disappeared when it was agreed that the shares in ***The Gramophone*** held by her, Christopher and Monty should be commuted to annuities, with the magazine eventually passing to Cecil Pollard's son Anthony. Its rising circulation provided for all three of them an old age free from financial anxieties"[5].

And looking back at his years at the helm of the magazine, Mackenzie wrote in *My Record of Music* (1956), "I would that every crusader could have as happy an end to his fight as I have enjoyed"[2].

Stereo and beyond

1958-1969

A *Gramophone* chronology

1958-1969

1958

January

- Philips introduce Fontana, in part a reissue label.

March

- Decca move from the Brixton Road to new offices on London's Albert Embankment.

Decca's HQ on London's Albert Embankment *Photo Decca*

May

- Edgar Jackson, Jazz and Swing reviewer for ***TG***, stands down after 28 years.
- First review of the Quad Electrostatic loudspeaker by Percy Wilson.

June

- Anthony Pollard becomes London Editor of ***TG***.
- Pye Records release first commercial stereo LPs in the UK, including Beethoven's Symphonies Nos. 1 and 8 with Barbirolli and the Hallé Orchestra.
- Decca introduce first budget-price LPs in the UK with their Ace of Clubs label.
- Sir Louis Sterling dies aged 78.
- Beecham records Bizet's *Carmen* in Paris with Victoria de los Angeles in the title-role (the recording is completed in September 1959).

August

- G. W. Webb, chairman of the Expert Committee (1924-30), dies.

September

- Decca begin the first-ever studio recording of Wagner's *Ring – Das Rheingold* with Solti and VPO.
- Saga Records launched by Wilfred Banks and W. H. Barrington-Coupe: initially a mail-order operation.
- Name of Heliodor Record Company changed to Deutsche Grammophon (GB).

October

- Harmonia Mundi founded in France by Bernard Coutaz.
- EMI, Decca and DG release their first stereo LPs.
- Mercury label transfers from Pye to EMI.

December

- First complete stereo recording of an opera by a 20th-century British composer made by Decca – Britten's *Peter Grimes* with Peter Pears in the title-role and conducted by the composer.
- Oscar Preuss, Parlophone A&R Manager until 1955, dies aged 69.

Bernard Coutaz

The Gramophone, September, 1958

THIS MONTH'S NEW ISSUES

Brahms
Symphony No. 3 in F major, Op. 90
The Vienna Philharmonic Orchestra
conducted by **Karl Böhm**
ACL 14

FAMOUS OVERTURES BY ROSSINI
The thieving magpie *and* William Tell; Semiramis *and* The silken ladder
The Concertgebouw Orchestra
conducted by **Eduard van Beinum**
ACL 15

Richard Strauss
Till Eulenspiegel's lustige Streiche; Don Juan
The Vienna Philharmonic Orchestra
conducted by **Clemens Krauss**
ACL 16

ACE of CLUBS

12" LONG PLAYING
HIGH-FIDELITY
RECORDS
A DECCA PRODUCT
22/6
Tax paid, complete in pictorial sleeve

Already released

Beethoven
Symphony No. 5
Paris Conservatoire/Schuricht
ACL 1

Beethoven
Pastoral Symphony
London Philharmonic Orch/Kleiber
ACL 2

Tchaikovsky
Symphony No. 5
Hamburg Radio Symphony Orch/ Schmidt-Isserstedt
ACL 3

Mendelssohn
Violin Concerto in E minor
Campoli/LPO/van Beinum
Italian Symphony
Turin Symphony Orch/Rossi
ACL 4

Beethoven
Violin Concerto
Ricci/LPO/Boult
ACL 5

Rachmaninov
Piano Concerto No. 2
Katchen/NSO of London/Fistoulari
ACL 6

Rossini/Respighi
La Boutique Fantasque
LSO/Ansermet
ACL 7

Chopin
Les Sylphides
Tchaikovsky
Sleeping Beauty Suite
Paris Conservatoire/Désormière
ACL 8

Bizet
Carmen suite (a); L'Arlésienne suite (b)
LPO/Collins (a); van Beinum (b)
ACL 9

Tchaikovsky
1812 Overture; Hamlet—Fantasy overture
London Philharmonic Orch/Boult
ACL 10

Tchaikovsky
Romeo and Juliet—Fantasy overture (a); Capriccio italien (b)
(a) LPO/van Beinum
(b) Paris Conservatoire/Schuricht
ACL 11

MUSIC FROM SPAIN
Excerpts from: La vida breve (*Falla*), Danzas españolas (*Granados*), Iberia (*Albéniz*); La Procesión del Rocio (*Turina*)
Paris Conservatoire/Jorda
ACL 12

Franck
Symphony in D minor; Symphonic Variations (a)
Paris Conservatoire/Munch
(a) solo piano **Eileen Joyce**
ACL 13

FROM ALL RECORD DEALERS

ACE OF CLUBS RECORDS DECCA HOUSE ALBERT EMBANKMENT LONDON SE11

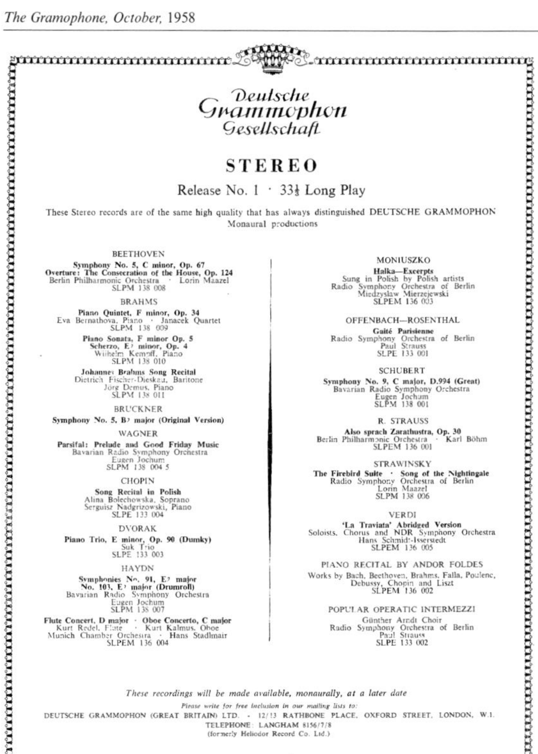

The Gramophone, October, 1958

Deutsche Grammophon Gesellschaft

STEREO

Release No. 1 · 33⅓ Long Play

These Stereo records are of the same high quality that has always distinguished DEUTSCHE GRAMMOPHON Monaural productions

BEETHOVEN
Symphony No. 5, C minor, Op. 67
Overture: The Consecration of the House, Op. 124
Berlin Philharmonic Orchestra · Lorin Maazel
SLPM 138 008

BRAHMS
Piano Quintet, F minor, Op. 34
Eva Bernathova, Piano · Janacek Quartet
SLPM 138 009

Piano Sonata, F minor Op. 5
Scherzo, E♭ minor, Op. 4
Wilhelm Kempff, Piano
SLPM 138 010

Johannes Brahms Song Recital
Dietrich Fischer-Dieskau, Baritone
Jörg Demus, Piano
SLPM 138 011

BRUCKNER
Symphony No. 5, B♭ major (Original Version)

WAGNER
Parsifal: Prelude and Good Friday Music
Bavarian Radio Symphony Orchestra
Eugen Jochum
SLPM 138 004 5

CHOPIN
Song Recital in Polish
Alina Bolechowska, Soprano
Serguisz Nadgrizowski, Piano
SLPE 133 004

DVORAK
Piano Trio, E minor, Op. 90 (Dumky)
Suk Trio
SLPE 133 003

HAYDN
Symphonies No. 91, E♭ major
No. 103, E♭ major (Drumroll)
Bavarian Radio Symphony Orchestra
Eugen Jochum
SLPM 138 007

Flute Concert, D major · Oboe Concerto, C major
Kurt Redel, Flute · Kurt Kalmus, Oboe
Munich Chamber Orchestra · Hans Stadlmair
SLPEM 136 004

MONIUSZKO
Halka—Excerpts
Sung in Polish by Polish artists
Radio Symphony Orchestra of Berlin
Miedzyslaw Mierzejewski
SLPEM 136 003

OFFENBACH—ROSENTHAL
Gaité Parisienne
Radio Symphony Orchestra of Berlin
Paul Strauss
SLPE 133 001

SCHUBERT
Symphony No. 9, C major, D.994 (Great)
Bavarian Radio Symphony Orchestra
Eugen Jochum
SLPM 138 001

R. STRAUSS
Also sprach Zarathustra, Op. 30
Berlin Philharmonic Orchestra · Karl Böhm
SLPEM 136 001

STRAWINSKY
The Firebird Suite · Song of the Nightingale
Radio Symphony Orchestra of Berlin
Lorin Maazel
SLPM 138 006

VERDI
'La Traviata' Abridged Version
Soloists, Chorus and NDR Symphony Orchestra
Hans Schmidt-Isserstedt
SLPEM 136 005

PIANO RECITAL BY ANDOR FOLDES
Works by Bach, Beethoven, Brahms, Falla, Poulenc, Debussy, Chopin and Liszt
SLPEM 136 002

POPULAR OPERATIC INTERMEZZI
Günther Arndt Choir
Radio Symphony Orchestra of Berlin
Paul Strauss
SLPE 133 002

These recordings will be made available, monaurally, at a later date

Please write for free inclusion in our mailing lists to:
DEUTSCHE GRAMMOPHON (GREAT BRITAIN) LTD. · 12/13 RATHBONE PLACE, OXFORD STREET, LONDON, W.1.
TELEPHONE: LANGHAM 8156/7/8
(formerly Heliodor Record Co. Ltd.)

1959

February

- E. M. Ginn, designer of the EMG acoustic gramophones, dies.

March

- Karajan makes first stereo recordings for DG (Strauss's *Ein Heldenleben* in Berlin) and Decca (Strauss's *Also sprach Zarathustra* in Vienna).
- Solti's recording of Wagner's *Das Rheingold*, recorded in September 1958, is released.
- Decca discontinue the production of 78rpm records.
- First "March LP Weekend Conference" organized by Kathleen and Ivan March in Blackpool.

Oscar Preuss (right) and Joe Batten on the occasion of the latter's retirement from EMI in October 1950

April

- American Audio Fidelity label available in the UK, with classical releases in September.

May

- L. G. Wood succeeds C. H. Thomas as MD of EMI Records.
- First releases on the Top Rank label.

June

- DG introduce the Heliodor bargain label in the UK.

September

- Garrard launch Magazine Tape Deck.
- SME launch their pickup arm.
- Nicolai Medal presented to the Decca Vienna recording crew by the VPO.

October

- John Gilbert, a contributor to *TG* for many years, joins as Audio Consultant.

November

- EMI introduce their budget-price "Concert Classics" label.

1960

January

- Maurice Rosengarten joins the Decca Board.
- First releases on the Lyrita label.
- First UK release at 16⅔ rpm on Top Rank label – tales by Edgar Alan Poe, reviewed in April 1960 – playing time 95 minutes.

April

- Associated Recordings market Westminster, Whitehall, Artia and Parliament labels in the UK.

July

- Lady Faith Compton Mackenzie dies at the age of 82.

August

- Top Rank label transferred to EMI.

October

- Associated Recordings market MK and Eros labels in the UK.

The Gramophone, May, 1959

TOP RANK
Extended and long play releases
12 inch Long Play Classical Recordings
Sir Adrian Boult conducting the Philharmonic Promenade Orchestra of London
Beethoven
Symphony No. 3 in E flat, Opus 55 ("Eroica") Coriolan Overture, Opus 62 XRC 6001 (32/2d inc. P.T.)
Symphony No. 5 in C. Minor, Opus 67 Leonora Overture, No. 3 Opus 72.B. XRC 6002 (32/2d inc. P.T.)
Symphony No. 6 in F, Opus 68 ("Pastoral") Fidelio Overture, Opus 72.C. XRC 6003 (32/2d inc. P.T.)
André Lardrot (Oboe) Felix Prohaska, Conductor of the Vienna State Opera, and the Chamber Orchestra
The Virtuoso Oboe
Concerto in C Major for Oboe and Orchestra—Haydn
Oboe Concerto in B Flat Major, Opus 7 No. 3—Albinoni
Concerto for Oboe and Strings, Cimarosa (arr. Benjamin)
Concerto in G Minor for Oboe and Strings—Handel
XRK 501 (39/9d inc. P.T.)
Hartford Symphony Chorale and Hartt Schola Cantorum. David Lloyd, tenor. Hartford Symphony Orchestra, Conductor Fritz Mahler.
Berlioz Requiem
Complete and as originally scored.
(Grande Messe des Morts—Opus 5).. XRK 502 and 503 (39/9d inc. P.T. each)
12 inch Long Play Popular Recordings
Knuckles O'Toole
"Honky Tonk Piano"—authentic renditions of all-time popular hit tunes...... "Ida," "Paper Doll," "If you knew Susie," "The sidewalks of New York". "Peg o' my heart," and many many others.... RX 3001 (32/2d inc. P.T.)
Paris Music Hall
The most delightful French melodies, all associated with the fabulous French Capital. The Paris Music Hall Orchestra, conducted by Mario Lazone. Vocals by Jacqueline Mille, Claude Bonheur and the Music Hall Boys......... RX 3003 (32/2d inc. P.T.)
Glenn Miller & His Orchestra (Vol. 1)
Exclusive compilation of his original 20th Century-Fox film soundtrack recordings. Complete numbers, extended tracks, in high fidelity—the great Miller band as it really was .... RX 3004 (32/2d inc. P.T.)
7 inch Extended Play Popular Recordings
I Want to Be Happy Cha Cha's
Enoch Light and the Light Brigade Sparkling arrangements of five hit cha-cha's ("Tea for Two", "I Want to be Happy", "Yes, Sir that's my Baby", "Lover", "The Sheik")........ JKR 8001 (10/11½ inc. P.T.)
LET'S GO!
Hot from the American hit parades TOP RANK rushes this extended play "special". Five tracks from the U.S. Top Ten by Buddy Killen and his Orchestra with vocals by Jimmy Lee, Johnny Hines and the Treetoppers...
"Don't take your gun to town," "The story of my love," "Tragedy," "Plain Jane" "She say (Oom dooby doom)". JKR 8008 (10/11½ inc. P.T.)
RANK RECORDS LTD. 38 SOUTH STREET. LONDON W.1.

1961

- First classical LP to sell in excess of one million copies worldwide – Tchaikovsky's Piano Concerto No. 1 with Van Cliburn on RCA.

January

- W. S. Barrell dies aged 70.

May

- First release of Pye-Nonesuch spoken word recordings.

June

- *TG* masthead shows Sir Compton Mackenzie and Christopher Stone as Founders and Cecil and Anthony Pollard as joint Editors.

July

- *TG* open offices at 379 Kenton Road and amalgamate Subscriptions from Ebrington Road and Editorial from Stanmore.

1962

- W. W. Townsley appointed to the Decca Board.

W. W. "Bill" Townsley (centre) with some of the Decca sales and marketing team in September 1970. From the left: Gerd Nathan (music cassettes), John Parry (repertoire), Maurice Roach (Advertising Manager), Fil Towers (sales), Colin Borland (Sales Manager), Graham Smith (sales) *Photo Decca*

February

- Decca introduce the Phase-4 label.

March

- Deletion of last EMI 78rpm records.
- Associated Recordings launch record club.

May

- Philips Records introduce the CBS label in the UK.

To launch their Phase-4 series Decca assembled this extravaganza of pseudo European and American marching bands with sound effects to suit, testing the extremes of stereo sound. The label comes from the American 'London' release

- EMI discontinue Top Rank label.

June

- Siemens and Philips combine their music businesses, Deutsche Grammophon Gesellschaft and Philips Phonographic Industries, by exchanging 50 per cent of each company's share. The venture is called DGG/PPI; both companies remain legally independent with their own repertoire.
- C. H. Thomas retires from EMI.

October

- EMI release "The Living Bible" on 12 LPs.

November

- Louise Hanson-Dyer, Australian-born founder of the Oiseau-Lyre label, dies.

Louise Hanson-Dyer

1963

January

- Sir Isaac Shoenberg, a Director of EMI responsible for the British high-definition television system developed by the company in the 1930s, and other developments associated with recording, dies aged 82.
- Audio Fidelity label transfers to Philips in the UK.

Sir Isaac Shoenberg *Photo EMI*

February

- DG release Karajan's version of Beethoven's symphonies with the Berlin Philharmonic Orchestra – the first occasion in which all nine works were planned and packaged as an integral set.

April

- Decca release Solti's recording of Wagner's *Parsifal* – the first studio version of the opera ever to be made.

June

- Philips introduce new Compact Cassette recorder at Berlin International Audio Fair.

July

- Victor Olof retires from EMI.

September

- RCA introduce "Dynagroove" recordings to the UK.

Victor Olof *Photo EMI*

1964

- Bhaskar Menon becomes Chairman and MD of EMI's Indian company.

January

- Mercury label transferred to Philips in the UK.

February

- Nonesuch Records formed in New York by Jac Holzmann.

Bhaskar Menon *Photo EMI*

April

- EMI and Decca confirm their intention to maintain a minimum resale price for their records.

June

- Walter Legge leaves EMI.

December

- John Borwick joins ***TG*** as Associate Technical Editor.

1965

- Lear introduce 8-track in-car cartridge in the USA.

February

- W. S. Meadmore dies aged 72.

March

- CBS (formerly American Columbia) commence independent operation in UK under the wing of Oriole Records, a CBS-owned company.

April

- Maurice Oberstein joins CBS UK from the USA.

May

- Christopher Stone dies aged 82.
- Saydisc founded by Gef and Genny Lucena.

Maurice Oberstein

July

- Barry Irving joins ***TG*** Advertisement Department.

August

- Joe Brogan, founder of The Gramophone Shop, New York, dies.

September

- Cecil Pollard dies aged 65.
- The "Music for Pleasure" label launched by Paul Hamlyn in association with EMI.

The Gramophone, October, 1965

NO HEADLINE COULD DO JUSTICE TO THE TREMENDOUS VALUE OFFERED BY EMI AND PAUL HAMLYN ON THEIR NEW JOINT LABEL

MUSIC FOR PLEASURE

Full details, including complete release list, overleaf

November

- Decca complete the first studio recording of Wagner's *Ring* with *Die Walküre*, featuring Solti and the VPO.

December

- Malcolm Walker joins ***TG*** as Assistant Editor.
- L. G. Wood joins the main board of EMI.

1966

February

- Percy Wilson retires as Technical Editor of ***TG*** and is succeeded by John Borwick, with John Gilbert continuing as Technical Consultant.

April

- Geoff Bridge becomes MD of EMI Records UK.

May

- Decca adopt the Dolby-A noise reduction system. The first sessions to utilize the system are held in Kingsway Hall, London – Mahler's Symphony No. 2 with Solti and the LSO.

July

- BBC radio commence regular stereo transmissions.

October

- UK introduction of Musicassettes by Philips and EMI.

The Gramophone, November, 1966

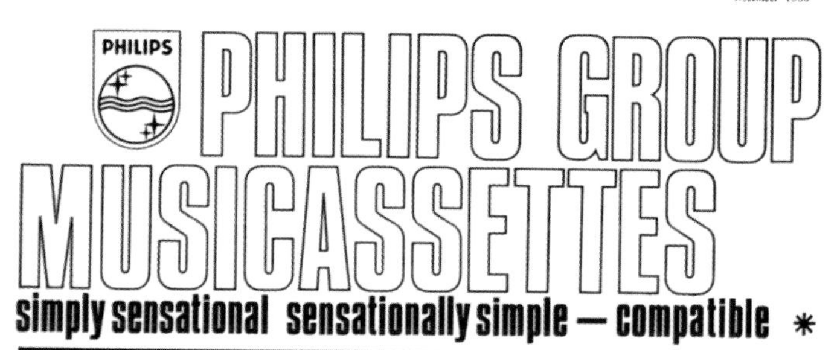

36 Advert
The GRAMOPHONE
November 1966
PHILIPS
PHILIPS GROUP
MUSICASSETTES
simply sensational sensationally simple — compatible ✱
Ready-recorded tape cassettes with the best of your favourite music can now be enjoyed wherever you are.
Musicassettes contain as much music listening time as a long-playing record and are permanent top value since the tape cannot be scratched or broken.
The unique dust-proof packaging prevents any wear and tear and even after playing a hundred times the sound will be as perfect as on the first day.
PLAY WHAT YOU LIKE! WHEN YOU LIKE! WHERE YOU LIKE!
THE GREGORY STRINGS
Joan Baez 5
Dusty Springfield
Ev'rything's coming up Dusty
Philips CPP1002
The Gregory Strings
To the memory of Kreisler
Fontana CFP4002
Joan Baez accompanying herself on the guitar
Joan Baez/5
Fontana CFF5000
Sung by Cleo Laine featuring the music of John Dankworth
Shakespeare and all that jazz
Fontana CFJ6000
The Walker Brothers Les Swingle Singers Luis Alberto del Parana y Los Paraguayos George Chisholm Robert Farnon and his Orchestra
Susan Maughan Frankie Vaughan Jerry Lee Lewis The Spencer Davis Group Tommy Kinsman and his Orchestra Rawicz and Landauer
Horst Jankowski's Orchestra and Chorus Harry Secombe John Hanson Xavier Cugat and his Orchestra The Les Reed Orchestra
The Band of the Scots Guards Woody Herman Oscar Peterson Trio The Modern Jazz Quartet Erroll Garner The Dutch Swing College Band
✱ these Stereo cassettes give genuine reproduction on Monaural equipment
WATCH FOR THE 1st CLASSICAL MUSICASSETTE RELEASE EARLY 1967
WRITE FOR LEAFLET GIVING FULL DETAILS OF THE WONDERFUL RANGE OF MUSICASSETTES TO —
PHILIPS GROUP RECORDS STANHOPE HOUSE STANHOPE PLACE LONDON W2

1967

January

- "Stereo 8" tape cartridges introduced to UK.
- First MIDEM (Marche International du Disque de l'Edition Musicale) held in Cannes.

February

- Ken East succeeds Geoff Bridge and becomes MD of EMI Records UK.

Ken East *Photo EMI*

- Live recording of Gerald Moore's farewell concert in London's Royal Festival Hall is made by EMI and released on LP three months later.

July

- EMI cease releasing LPs in both mono and stereo formats, other companies follow, although the Decca move did not come until March 1969.
- Decca delete all 10-inch LPs and discontinue their further production.
- The BBC introduce 625-line UHF colour television.

August

- Edgar Jackson dies aged 72.
- The Cleveland Orchestra under Szell becomes the first US orchestra to record in the UK while on a European tour. The recordings for CBS, made at EMI's Abbey Road Studios, include Mozart's Symphony No. 40.

October

- John Culshaw leaves Decca to join BBC-TV and is succeeded as Classical A&R Manager by Ray Minshull.
- Edward "Chick" Fowler retires from EMI Studios and is succeeded by Allen Stagg who had been MD of the International Broadcasting Company.

1968

May

- Nellie Pollard, Chairman of General Gramophone Publications Limited, publishers of ***TG***, dies aged 66.

July

- Freehold of 177-179 Kenton Road purchased by ***TG***.

September

- Dr Hans Hickmann, head of DG's Archiv label, dies. No successor is appointed until 1970.

October

- Pearl Records launched by Charles Haynes and John Waite.

John Waite (left) and Charles Haynes (right) *Photo Pearl*

1969

- G. W. Cook becomes General Manager of EMI Studios.

January

- Erik Smith leaves Decca and is appointed A&R Manager of Philips Classical Division.

June

- Definite article dropped from title ***Gramophone***. (References in this chronology now change from ***TG*** to ***G***.)

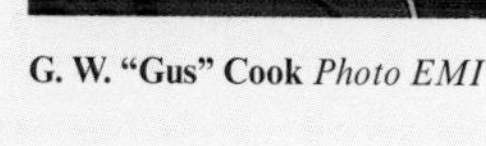

G. W. "Gus" Cook *Photo EMI*

- RCA Records commence independent operation in UK.
- Victor Olof's last sessions for EMI.

July

- Resale Price Maintenance is abolished on gramophone records.

August

- John Goldsmith launches the Unicorn label.

November

- Sir Joseph Lockwood stands down as CEO of EMI and is succeeded by John Read. He remains Chairman.
- ECM Records founded in Germany by Manfred Eicher.

Manfred Eicher *Photo ECM/Masotti*

Stereo and beyond

ALAN BLUMLEIN

On June 1st, 1977 a Greater London Council blue plaque was unveiled at 37 The Ridings, Ealing in West London, the home of Alan Blumlein who was killed on June 7th, 1942 at the age of 38

In December 1957 W. S. Barrell retired from EMI, having been associated with the company's recording activities since joining the Columbia Graphophone Company in 1925. In 1958-9 he contributed a series of articles to *The Gramophone* and in this extract he recalls Alan Blumlein's work in respect of stereo recording

The first stereo experiments

It was during 1932 that the late Alan Blumlein brought to Abbey Road some new equipment he had developed, having as its object, and I quote from Patent No. 394, 325 of December 1931, "to provide a sound recording, reproducing and/or transmission system whereby there is conveyed to the listener a realistic impression that the intelligence is being communicated to him over two acoustic paths in the same manner as he experiences in listening to everyday acoustic intercourse and this object embraces also the idea of conveying to the listener a true directional impression", in short, stereo. The reasoning and ideas expressed in this amazing document, while only now gaining wide currency, form the basis of all stereo recording today. I stress this point because sooner or later one of our foreign friends will undoubtedly claim to have invented stereo recording. In those days our only recording medium was the wax blank, so the two signals from the microphone system were fed to a complex cutter so arranged as to cut a single groove.

Several orchestral and other recordings were made under Blumlein's personal supervision, when the first thing to get us guessing was the 'appearance' of the new cut. Experienced operators were very expert in 'reading' a recorded wax by the shape of the wave and the appearance of the cut: but here was something quite new. One old hand described it as like a string of sausages – a very apt description.

These earliest records, being pressed in ordinary material of the era, suffered from excessive background noise, but even so the results were quite startling. Not only was one immediately aware of orchestral placement, but the feeling that the whole of the space between the two reproducing loudspeakers was filled with the orchestra was most impressive. It may seem odd that 25 years elapsed before we took up the subject again. Like many other things the principles could not be put into successful practice until the appropriate materials were available, and it has taken all this time to get them.

Alan and Doreen Blumlein on their Wedding Day, April 22nd, 1933 *Photo Simon Blumlein*

The stereo disc

Sir Malcolm Sargent (left), Isaac (later Sir Isaac) Shoenberg (EMI Director and Scientific Advisor) and L. J. Brown (EMI MD) at the Abbey Road Studios in April 1955 for the demonstration of "Stereosonic" tapes *Photo EMI*

In September 1936 Mackenzie had obliquely raised the question of stereo, asking Percy Wilson to develop his theories on the subject. Alan Blumlein's work for the Columbia Graphophone Company in the early 1930s was well known but technology and the availability of certain materials had to develop before his research could be applied in commercial terms. The use of tape recording in the late 1940s by the recording industry opened new doors and on April 4th, 1955 EMI demonstrated to the Press their "Stereosonic" tape records which were to go on to the market in October.

Notwithstanding the enormous advance in the reproduction of the original sound, which was apparent to all who heard these tapes, they made little commercial impact – principally because sound reproduction in the home was traditionally seen as disc-based by the consumer, whilst the Industry itself liked the convenient manufacture of the disc, as opposed to the complexity of tape duplication (time, cost, quality control, etc.).

However, in June 1956 Sir Compton was expressing concern relative to the development of the LP as a carrier for binaural sound (as he referred to stereo): "That binaural sound, or rather the development of binaural sound, will be the ordinary equipment of every gramophone owner in the future is certain, but it is still in the future". Clearly, Decca and EMI, who had both been researching all aspects of the stereo disc and in parallel building up a catalogue of stereo recordings on tape against the day when they would be needed, had no wish to upset the existing mono LP market which only six or seven years after the launch of LP was still gathering converts from the 78rpm disc.

Conscious of what was happening elsewhere in the Industry, EMI issued a policy statement in January 1958 indicating that they were in a position to launch stereo discs immediately but for the fact that there was no suitable reproducing equipment on the market "in a form and at a price acceptable to a worthwhile section of the public". The statement concluded by saying, "Although, therefore, it will probably be some years before stereo discs are available in the same wide range as ordinary monaural records ... the stage is almost set for a small but growing number to enter the market – probably in about twelve months time".

However, the situation changed when a Press demonstration of stereo discs was given by Pye Limited at the Waldorf Hotel in London on May 16th, 1958, followed immediately by the release of the records themselves, together with a range of reproducing equipment. This release of a limited number of rather poor stereo discs, by what at that time was one of the smaller companies in the British record industry, did little to enhance the image of the new product. However, neither EMI, Decca

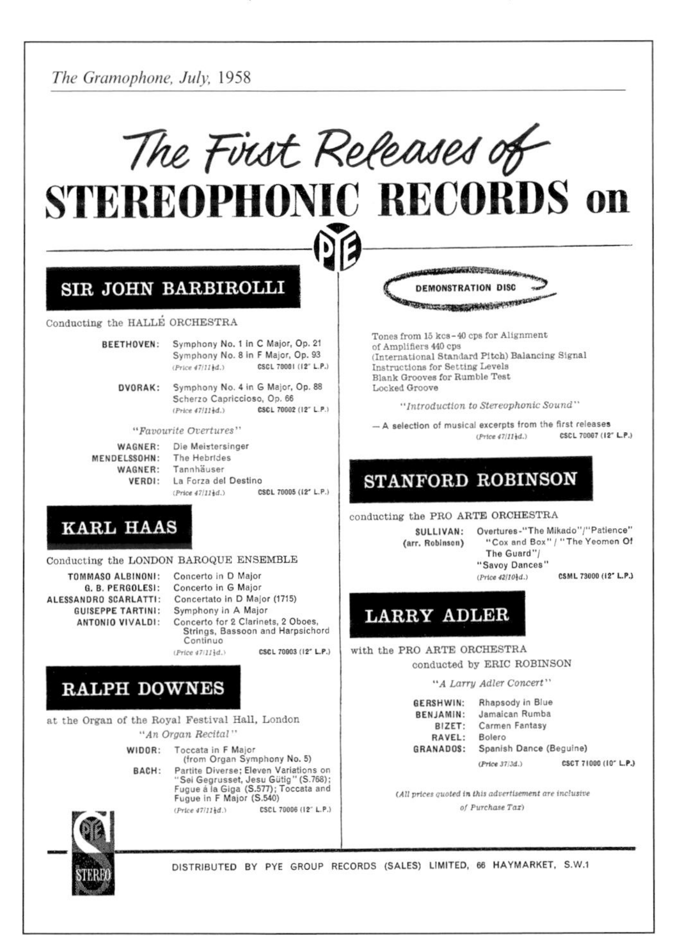

The Gramophone, July, 1958

Dr Hans-Werner Steinhausen, Technical Director of Deutsche Grammophon at the time of the introduction of the stereo disc, in conversation with Anthony Pollard in October 1972 *Photo DG*

or DG could ignore the situation which had been created and in October 1958 they marketed their first stereo discs.

Up to this point it was fair to say that the consumer felt reasonably secure within the framework of the Industry. After all, even the electrically-recorded 78rpm disc had enjoyed an exclusive life of some 25 years (and more if one included the acoustically-recorded product) and the introduction of LP in 1950 had not disturbed the relationship: with the flow of worthwhile 78s continuing for several years no one felt any coercion to convert to LP. In fact, in the mid- to late-1950s that conversion was still much in progress and, as a result, for all those who had adopted the mono LP the launch of a new disc requiring quite substantial reinvestment in the reproducing chain was rather unsettling. Seen from the 1990s one may wonder what all the fuss was about, but in the 1950s the music buyer had every reason to believe that his investment in the mono LP might have been good for much longer than was to be the case.

The 1960s – The market develops

After the excitement of the launch of both mono and stereo LPs in the previous decade, the 1960s proved in some respects to be a more static period. Huge investments in repertoire were being made by the major companies and there were few buyers who would argue

In the October 1958 issue, Trevor Harvey related his first impressions of stereo and the remarkably vivid sound heard on some stereo demonstration discs

STEREO – THE FIRST FEW DAYS

For the first few days of stereo listening I remained in what might be called the honeymoon stage. That is to say, I was as fascinated as any rabbit by railway trains and table tennis balls. Expresses thundered across my room, goods trains clanked from the opposite direction, my head jerked from side to side as I listened to a ping from this speaker, a pong from that. This stage, luckily for my neighbours, soon wore off. One bit of a demonstration disc still remains fun though, a recording of fire-engines leaving their headquarters, bells shrilling and clanging all over the place. The fun comes from watching the houses over the way and seeing the inhabitants throw up their windows to see the fire-engines. Most of them still do it after more than one playing of the record, though one old chap refuses to be drawn any more; he just looks a bit mystified and hovers near his window, just in case this time there really might be a fire somewhere. Stereo is certainly realistic all right.

One of the train recordings raises a pretty problem. It's on EMI's disc and they say it was made outside their factory at Hayes. The express thunders by from left to right at tremendous speed and as a recording it's a triumph. It must have been a down train, going from Paddington to the West, as you can tell if you know on which side of the line the Hayes factory lies. But here's the problem. Anyone who does much travelling on the Western Region line knows that it's just about there that their trains almost invariably slow down and dawdle around for a bit. I mean, how else could they count on being late at Reading? I've always known those EMI engineers to be very efficient: they must also be incredibly patient too, to have caught an express that rushes by as this one does.

The Gramophone, August, 1958

EMI

STEREOPHONIC EMI RECORDING

PIONEERS OF

STEREOPHONIC RECORDING

ANNOUNCE

A Stereophonic Demonstration Test Record

No. SDD.1 (12" double-sided LP 33⅓ r.p.m. record)

This record, which is intended for use only with stereophonic reproducing equipment, contains sound effects with linking narrative and eight widely varied musical illustrations, concluding with a metronome signal to ensure the correct balancing of the two loudspeakers. Sleeve notes contain useful technical information and instructions on the use of the metronome centring signal.

This record can be purchased from all record dealers. Price 47/11½d. including purchase tax.

EMI
'HIS MASTER'S VOICE'
CAPITOL
COLUMBIA
PARLOPHONE &
M-G-M RECORDS

The greatest recording organisation in the world

E.M.I. RECORDS LTD., 8-11 Great Castle Street, London W.1

July 1961 **Correspondence**

GIMMICK SELLING

I was dismayed to see in the current issue that the dreadful giveaway-gimmick is beginning to rear its ugly head even in the record industry. Those awful words "free gift" have already appeared and clearly the shadows of the cornflake and detergent packet loom in the background.

Just imagine the possibilities – LP sleeves with competitions on the back: "Fifty Stereograms *must* be won – Enter now!"; or what about offers: "Save 15 shillings on this real leatherette 25-record carrying case! Just fill in the enclosed form and post to us with a postal order for 18/9 plus the tokens from any three 12-inch Deliriophone extra long playing super-stereofidelity record sleeves". Or maybe just a band across the front announcing: "3/9 off!".

But seriously – are even the classical record-buying public so childish, or so penny-wise, that they have to be lured by some extra titbit (even if it is a print of a famous painting) to spend their money on something which is perfectly good, and may be extremely good value anyway? And is it too much to hope that the rest of the industry will not start falling over itself to follow suit?

J. C. Bretherton

Kintbury, Berks

March 1966 **News**

The Philips EL3300 has recently been featured as a car-borne music system and may be purchased complete with fittings to slide under a car dashboard. I am told that car tape players are already popular in the United States, being a standard fitting on some vehicles. They will certainly avoid the fading and interference troubles of car radios.

against the merits of stereo, which was now also enhancing the acceptance of LP in the popular market. Audio and record companies were advertising heavily in the magazine and throughout the decade the circulation averaged in excess of 71,600 copies per issue.

The Compact Cassette was launched by Philips in June 1963 and in October 1966 both EMI and Philips introduced a range of Musicassettes, but these were to have little initial impact on the market. In due course, the interest of classical buyers was to be activated by Decca's introduction of the Dolby-B noise suppression system in November 1970 and the subsequent use by various companies of improved tape formulations (chromium dioxide, etc.). For popular repertoire buyers (and many others) it was the development of the cassette's 'in-car' use, coupled with the Sony "Walkman", launched in Japan in July 1979 and in the UK in June 1980 (initially as the "Stowaway"), which provided the catalyst.

The Gramophone, June, 1961

The Gramophone, May, 1926

The nearest equivalent to a "Walkman" in 1926

February 1963 **Correspondence**

A PAT AND A KICK!

A sincere thanks to the recording industry in general for producing in the last year a great improvement in the quality of stereo records and an obvious desire to go on improving quality in the future.

But how many more times do we record collectors have to wait weeks, and sometimes months, for a copy of a record which is officially on release and reviewed with notices which would please even the most publicity-spoiled film star?

I am an extremely enthusiastic audiophile. I get the greatest pleasure from 'good' music, and great pleasure from a record which has got a stage further to realizing that impossible label 'perfect'. I have a great interest, too, in the production and general workings of the record industry and I expect it to be as good and efficient as any other industry.

Therefore, record industry, pull your socks up and don't advertise a record that isn't available (or one that is only available for a week and then disappears). You lose a lot of friends doing it (including record dealers!) and, anyway, it is in bad taste to create a demand by causing a famine.

Disappointed

Great Baddow, Essex

The Company expands

As the number of record releases increased, and the repertoire became more sophisticated, so it was necessary to enlarge the panel of reviewers and develop within their ranks more specialists. By the end of the decade there were 19 reviewers where in 1950 there had been four. Administratively, this posed a number of major problems and as a result new offices were opened in July 1961 at 379 Kenton Road to accommodate additional editorial staff and also the Subscription Department, which after nearly 22 years would now vacate the Ebrington Road address.

There was also a need to extend our coverage in the audio field and in December 1964 John Borwick joined us as Associate Technical Editor, succeeding Percy Wilson as Technical Editor in February 1966. John Gilbert continued as our Technical Consultant, a post which he had assumed in October 1959 and would occupy until his death on October 6th, 1993 at the age of 85.

John Gilbert (left) and John Borwick enjoying a quiet moment on *The Gramophone* stand at the London Audio Fair in 1969

It was in the 1960s that two other long-serving employees joined the Company – Barry Irving in July 1965 as assistant to the then Advertisement Manager, Reg Pollard (Cecil Pollard's brother, who had joined in August 1954, ultimately to succeed George Winkworth who died in May 1957), and Malcolm Walker who, in December 1965, joined as Assistant Editor of the magazine.

Barry Irving

In due course the need for even more office space became critical and from an administrative point of view it was now essential to have all departments of the Company under one roof (since 1946 the Advertisement and Circulation Departments had been operating from central London). Thus, in July 1968 the freehold of 177-179 Kenton Road was purchased and within a few months this would accommodate all the Company's employees for the next 27 years.

Malcolm Walker

It was also in June 1969 that the decision was taken to drop the definite article from the magazine's title and we now had to get used to calling ourselves *Gramophone*!

Ten years of LP

The tenth anniversary of the LP did not pass unnoticed in the pages of *The Gramophone* and in June 1960 there was a special feature on the "artistic achievement" by William Mann, and interviews by Arthur Jacobs with Sir Adrian Boult, Sir Yehudi Menuhin, Louis Kentner, Tito Gobbi,

Gramophone's offices at 177-179 Kenton Road

GRAMOPHONE
JUNE 1969 2/6
Karajan visits Great Britain this month
THIS ISSUE CONTAINS REVIEWS OF HIS LATEST RECORDINGS

The definite article is dropped and *Gramophone* has a new cover

Frederick Jackson and Léon Goossens. William Chislett viewed the situation "from both sides of the counter" and in the August issue Percy Wilson examined the "technical achievement". There were also contributions from the respective Chairmen of EMI and Decca. Joseph Lockwood of EMI commented that the Industry had tripled in size since the advent of LP and said, "we now see the standard long-playing record moving towards the wings, to allow the bright new star, stereo, to encompass the whole stage. Surprising in itself, the accomplishment within this short span is even more surprising, seen in relation to the fact that the gramophone record has been a national, indeed an international institution for more than 50 years. It is tempting to become complacent about our achievement but when we consider the influence that popular music, and the people who make it, exert over the younger generation, we cannot afford to be complacent – we have a great responsibility.

"In the field of serious music the past decade has produced achievements no less impressive. Recordings of the well-known works of the most popular composers are there in profusion: that we should expect, but the mine goes far, far deeper. Looking at EMI's own catalogue alone, works seldom, if ever, heard in public performance abound, often recorded several times by various of the world's greatest artists.

"It is the particular merit of *The Gramophone* and its contribution to the generally high standards of the Industry, that it lights a path through the galleries of this rich mine. Month by month it catalogues and analyses the products of the record companies. We all stand in debt to *The Gramophone*; the record buyers, the record dealer and the manufacturer. Its criticisms encourage us to maintain our standards – its praise helps us to sell our records and we welcome both results."

In the course of the same feature Edward Lewis of Decca recounted his earliest recollections of the system. "LP microgroove records were developed by the American Columbia Company and launched by

The Gramophone, June, 1960

ONLY
DECCA
can celebrate
10 YEARS OF LP THIS MONTH

In celebrating the 10th anniversary of the LP in Britain, Decca ensured that no one lost sight of their initial commitment

Joseph Lockwood *Photo EMI*

June 1960

In his interviews with six recording artists to mark the first ten years of LP, Arthur Jacobs asked: "Have you any wishes for the world of gramophone recording during the next ten years of LP?" To which Yehudi Menuhin replied

I would wish that with the perfection, the inevitably increasing complexity of the mechanical aura that surrounds the musical phrase, this very musical core and germ should not be lost sight of. Too often the hi-fi, the stereo amateurs, are bewildered by the trappings of music, and lose the sense of recognition of its content. Personally, I value the performance and the interpretation which it reveals far and away more than the particular achievement of hearing the overtones of a triangle or the spit of the oboe player, or the snort of the conductor.

I am concerned that, owing to the chase after the highest fractional overtones, by the time our recording techniques are perfected, only the dogs will be able to hear and appreciate the ultimate in hi-fi and stereo. I would like to keep something for the humans too.

Sir Edward Lewis in August 1976 making a presentation to W. W. "Bill" Townsley (left), his commercial Director, in celebration of his 50 years with Decca and its predecessor, Barnett Samuel
Photo Decca

them in the USA in 1948. I had my first demonstration by Edward Wallerstein, the then President of the Company, to whose courage and imagination the Industry is indebted, at his home in Westport, Connecticut, in the summer of 1949. The equipment used was a cheap record-player together with a radio receiver, and I was not much impressed. In fact I had been led to believe that it would be impossible to do justice to our Full Frequency Range Recordings (*ffrr*) on such microgroove records and that whilst the LP record might find acceptance in the USA, it probably had no great future elsewhere.

"It was not long, however, before I came to realize that here was the ideal medium for our own company, who were manufacturing records in England for shipment to the USA. Our engineers were also able, in a short space of time, to solve the technical difficulties which they had foreseen and our first LP records manufactured in England were on sale on the American market by September of that year. We ran into considerable production difficulties in the early stages, but by the end of the year these had been largely overcome.

"In the light of events, it seems that except for the introduction of LP records, the Industry would have dwindled. Certainly it could never have achieved anything like its present dimensions. The advantages of the LP record are so obvious now that there is no need to refer to them. The introduction of stereo is of course no overnight sensation as was the launching of LP records, but it does nevertheless represent yet another advance in the art of recording, and can be expected to prove a major contribution to the Industry during the next decade."

February 1964

"HIS MASTER'S VOICE"

Few trademarks are better known than the HMV dog and trumpet. In February 1964, Percy Wilson revealed the existence of at least one earlier manifestation of the famous Nipper logo which he had been shown by Dario Soria, Vice-President of RCA-Victor during a visit to the RCA laboratories in Princeton, New Jersey

TRADE-MARK.

No. 40,224. REGISTERED APR. 28, 1903.

VICTOR TALKING MACHINE CO.

TALKING MACHINES AND TALKING MACHINE PARTS.

WITNESSES: Edw. W. Vaill Jr.

PROPRIETOR: Victor Talking Machine Company by ... ATTORNEY

Another fascinating talk I had with Mr Soria related to the early history of the RCA-Victor Company at the beginning of the century. I had heard some of it before as it applied to The Gramophone Company over here; but I had not realized that the adoption of the Barraud dog picture as a trademark of both companies was not an inspired accident but the result of a deliberate search for a picture that would show "His Master's Voice". Who had the inspiration for the slogan I do not know, but it was certainly there before the picture. Mr Soria in fact showed me several engravings of attempts at illustration and gave me a copy of the one I reproduce herewith.

Record retailing and executives

Much of the success of the LP, be it mono or stereo, was attributable to the existence of a well-established national dealer system – some multiples but mainly independents – all of whom had a substantial knowledge of the various aspects of the record business. Companies such as EMG, Imhofs, Rimington Van Wyck, Gramophone Exchange, Murdochs, Keith Prowse, Collectors' Corner, H. C. Harridge, Saville Pianos, Henry Stave, Farringdon Records, The Recorderie, Duck Son & Pinker, Rushworths, Forsyths, Harlequin, Avgarde Gallery, Richmond Records, Chimes Music, Agate, Bruce Miller, Milsoms, Millers, Cloakes, Windows, Whitwams, Banks of York – to name but a few whose names conjure up memories of days past. Some are still happily serving the Industry, including the HMV emporium at 363 Oxford Street in London (although a planned move to larger premises immediately opposite is due in the near future). Opened in 1921, the store was presided over from 1935 to 1961 by George Fenwick, who had joined The Gramophone Company in 1911. It was a show-place for the company and, whilst their offices were still at Hayes (the Great Castle Street offices were not opened until 1953), was the London meeting point for all EMI's impor-

These 1951 advertisements from Murdochs, one of the larger multiples, epitomized the problem faced by many dealers in resolving the 78rpm/LP quandary

December 1966 **Correspondence**

THE GOOD OLD DAYS?

In August, September, October and December 1966, W. A. Chislett contributed four articles entitled "Sixty Years of Records" in which he recalled his experiences in the early days of recording. At the same time, Roger Wimbush, in his monthly "Here and There" column, continued his survey of early issues of the magazine: "Looking Back". Their reminiscences prompted a reader's letter in December

The reminiscences by Messrs. Chislett and Wimbush are a sheer delight. This is particularly so when their writings recall to mind the crudities to which our unsophistication in the search for perfection often led us. It seems to me that the whole business was much more exciting in the days of the phonograph's adolescence than it is today. One did not have to be an engineer or physicist or mathematician. Enjoyment of what was to be had was not contingent upon possession of a Ph.D. degree in music. Unworried by the fear which besets the phonophile of this era, that today's marvel may be obsolete tomorrow, we derived immense enjoyment from almost everything which came to hand. Not really uncritical, we were nevertheless not too troubled that eventual perfection still lay a long way off, and controversy subsisted on largely superficial considerations. That was fun because anyone could take a hand.

In these days discussion of phonographic matters by any persons other than 'authorities' suggests either the opinionated brashness of the ignorant or downright impudence. Thus 99·44 per cent of us now find ourselves in the outer darkness, ever unhappy that with each new 'advance', however infinitesimal, however imperceptible in the finished product – the sound – perfection becomes ever more remote, ever less attainable. Such satisfaction as is to be had comes from the belief that only the most advanced specifications are being realized in one's apparatus, even though the difference cannot be perceived. Somehow, it seems to me that sound loving has superseded music loving. No living music ever sounded like what issues from the vast bulk of records which inundate the current market.

Albert J. Franck
Richmond Hill, NY, USA

tant visitors. Fenwick, always immaculately dressed (as were his carefully selected assistants, all of whom were required to have music qualifications), claimed at the time that it was the finest and biggest record showroom in the world – and I don't recall anyone ever challenging that. Over the years he was to employ many people who would go on to serve the Industry in other capacities, and these included L. G. Wood and Walter Legge (the latter he almost sacked for throwing a chair at a colleague). Following a visit to America in 1949 he progressively introduced browser-boxes and self-service, but always insisted on the maintenance of the highest level of personal attention. He died on December 1st, 1985 at the age of 88.

"KEEPING TRACK"

Popular music in *The Gramophone* by Mark Walker

From the very earliest issues the magazine attempted to be as wide-ranging as possible in its coverage of recordings, featuring a round-up of dance records alongside the 'serious' classical releases, with reviews by "Peppering" (a pseudonym of Christopher Stone) and others of recordings by band-leaders such as Fred Elizalde, Jack Hylton, Paul Whiteman or Ambrose and the New Mayfair Dance Orchestra. With the addition of Edgar Jackson from *The Melody Maker* to the reviewing panel in June 1930, "Dance and Popular Rhythmic" received in-depth monthly coverage. Eventually, Edgar Jackson's reviews became "Jazz and Swing", while all other popular records were discussed under the rubric "Miscellaneous and Dance". Even during the severe paper rationing of the war years these reviews retained their allotted pages.

Bert Ambrose (centre) and his Mayfair Hotel Orchestra

Throughout the 1950s, "Miscellaneous and Dance" covered contemporary pop releases, which meant big bands such as Glenn Miller's or Ted Heath's, light orchestral music from Mantovani and Lawrence Welk, and singers such as Bing Crosby, Frank Sinatra and Doris Day. But the post-war phenomenon of a new popular music distinct from jazz caused problems for this middle-of-the-road coverage. The occasional mention of Tommy Steele, Anthony Newley and Lonnie Donegan, "our foremost 'commercial-folk' artist", in the late 1950s was a foretaste of things to come. With the arrival of the 'Beat Generation', *The Gramophone*'s popular music reviewers found themselves facing a growing generation gap, as this opening to September 1959's "Miscellaneous and Dance" reviews showed

Being one of those people that likes to lie back and savour what I listen to when I'm playing records for pleasure or review – not always the same thing by any means! – I found myself musing, when listening to Cliff Richard (Columbia) recording before a teenage audience in the Abbey Road Studios, that when the Beat Generation grows up, it will be heartily ashamed of itself, and that records such as these will provide irrefutable evidence of the temper of our times; the unintelligible and unintelligent mouthing to a twangy guitar, the pile-driver rhythm, the shrieks of rapture(?) coming in smack on cue, and the lesson in mass-hysteria that is given.

Coverage nevertheless remained broad, with sections devoted to Continental records, Folk-song and Blues written by regular reviewers John Oakland (actually the pseudonym of jazz critic Brian Rust) and Charles Fox, with occasional contributions from venerable British blues-man Alexis Korner. But, as the 1960s progressed, *The Gramophone*'s pop music column began to seem increasingly out of step with its subject-matter. Oakland confessed his difficulty in December 1961

I will mention Elvis Presley (RCA) and Cliff Richard (Columbia) mainly for the teenagers for whom they were designed; I must be getting old, because they make no sort of appeal to me, even though Mr Presley sings *Something for everybody*. "You should put yourself in the young fan's place when listening to these", said my wife, who can always see the other fellow's point of view (and sometimes mine); but though I tried, I just couldn't. It works the other way, too; I tried putting myself in an older listener's place while reviewing Jimmy Durante at the Copacabana (Columbia). Again I couldn't; and I don't think his audience found it easy either.

In the following March (1962), he attempted to come to terms with the latest teen dance craze

Twist! The biggest dance sensation since the Charleston, the Big Apple, the Jive, Rock 'n' Roll, according to your length of memory. I'm still struggling to emerge from a flood of singles and LPs of the music, actual or alleged, to which this latest manifestation of youth may be danced. (If dancing is the word: I've heard it described as "trying to dry yourself with an imaginary towel" and "trying to ward off a flock of birds with your elbows.")

The Beatles received their first mention, albeit a fleeting one, in the pages of *The Gramophone* in July 1963

Teenagers with plenty of money will surely rejoice that The Beatles, the Liverpudlians whose permanent address seems to be top of the Hit Parade, have an LP (Parlophone), and they may like to compare *Please please me* with the same song by the Kestrels on Piccadilly. Personally, I'd rather listen to Bryan Johnson ...

Their next appearance, in October, was even less auspicious. The unnamed single was *She loves me*

I didn't like either the singing or accompaniment on The Beatles's new single (Parlophone), but I thought I'd better mention its existence as there are several hundreds of thousands who apparently disagree with me.

"Editorial Notes" in the December 1963 issue added some hard figures to the new Beatles phenomenon

Britten and The Beatles

Possibly a strange combination – but they will long be remembered as the two highlights of 1963 for the British Record Industry.

For Decca, Benjamin Britten's *War Requiem* has probably broken all existing sales records for a classical release – over 200,000 records having been sold throughout the world in just over six months; and coupled with this the recording has rubbed shoulders with the idols of the 'pop' world in the American *Billboard* best selling charts for eight weeks – and this is modern music!

For EMI, The Beatles have been clocking up all kinds of records, and certainly the staff of the Company's Abbey Road studios and the police won't easily forget the recording sessions which produced their latest LP. Not only did their fans try to accompany them but they ordered over 280,000 copies of the LP before it was even on sale. In the words of EMI, "This is the first time that such a tremendous advance sales figure for an LP has been achieved in the history of the British Recording Industry. It is a further chapter in the fantastic story of The Beatles, whose sales figures for singles, EPs and LPs in the twelve months they have been recording now total over three million".

The band's next appearance in "Miscellaneous and Dance" (January 1964) found the reviewer gamely admitting to being a little out of touch

The event of last month was, of course, the issue of The Beatles's LP, orders for which exceeded a quarter of a million before it was even issued. I personally watched the eighth copy in a single morning – the day of release – being bought in a small village record shop, outside London. Why is it so popular that a quarter of a million teenagers cheerfully part with over thirty bob each for it? Being old enough to remember being castigated as a young lad for spending four whole shillings on one 78rpm (by an irate mother who thought no record was worth more than the eighteenpence Decca were charging for their pop singles then), I suppose I belong to the generation of utter squares who are physically unable to 'dig' The Beatles's message. I'll give you that they have a tremendous zest, drive, relentless vitality, yes; but I need more than that for my thirty-odd bob.

Their next few releases attracted no better. In August 1965 Oakland handed over reviewing duties to Peter Clayton after eight years of "watching the ever-changing scene of popular music". Oakland generously said of his successor that he was "much better qualified than I am to cope with current trends". The antiquated heading "Miscellaneous and Dance" was dropped in favour of the more trendy "Keeping Track". A change of title coincided with a change of style, racier and noticeably more appreciative of the merits of contemporary pop, although Clayton was no less acerbic when in the mood, saying of the Moody Blues in his October 1965 column, for example, that they "might be better described as the Pseudy Blues, for their music is not only derivative but tentative, so that their half-baked American sound is both tedious and feeble". The Beatles fared rather better in February 1966, however, but then the album under consideration was "Rubber Soul"

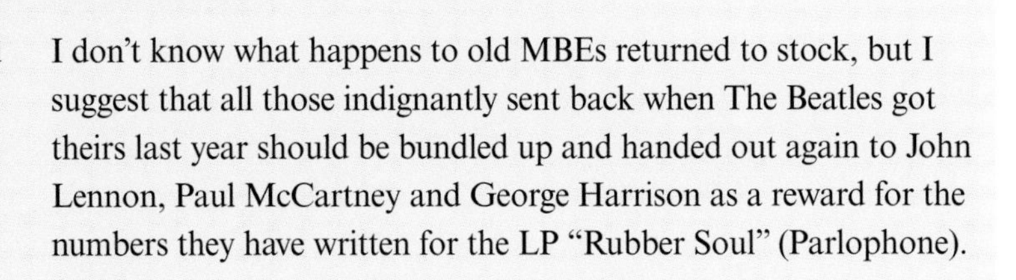

I don't know what happens to old MBEs returned to stock, but I suggest that all those indignantly sent back when The Beatles got theirs last year should be bundled up and handed out again to John Lennon, Paul McCartney and George Harrison as a reward for the numbers they have written for the LP "Rubber Soul" (Parlophone).

This is the best Beatles LP of all, for although it's full of their accustomed musical daring – shifting, disturbing harmonies, odd-length choruses – it's all on a subtler level than before; while in two songs, *Norwegian wood* and the exquisite *Michelle*, it has the two best things the Lennon-McCartney partnership has ever produced. There is something good to be said about almost every track; taken as a whole it's the best pop album I've ever had the pleasure of reviewing.

In October 1966 "Revolver" won equally enthusiastic praise from Clayton, who was well aware of the album's significance

It isn't easy to describe what's here, since much of it involves things which are either new to pop music or which are being properly applied for the first time, and which can't be helpfully compared with anything. In fact, the impression you get is not of any one sound or flavour, but simply of smoking hot newness with plenty of flaws and imperfections.

July 1967 saw the release of the most experimental Beatles album yet

"Sgt Pepper's Lonely Hearts Club Band" (Parlophone) is, like nearly everything The Beatles do, bizarre, wonderful, perverse, beautiful, exciting, provocative, exasperating, compassionate and mocking. More than either of their previous adventurous LPs – "Rubber Soul" and "Revolver" – you'll have to give this one time to grow on you. I think you will find it's worth it. You may at first be fascinated by, say, *Lucy in the sky with diamonds*, but that's just a string of pretty images which, if they mean anything at all, are important only to their creators. The marvellous tracks, to my mind, are the apparently simple ones, like *A little help from my friends*, and the astonishing *She's leaving home*, a documentary verse story of infinite knowingness and breathtaking melodic charm. There's plenty of electronic gimmickry on the record (the transistors are really overworked on the track the BBC has banned, *A day in the life*) but that isn't the heart of the thing. It's the combination of imagination, cheek and skill that makes this such a rewarding LP.

"Editorial Notes" in September 1967 provided some more figures

Beatles sales

By the end of the first week in August, UK sales of the "Sgt Pepper" LP had topped 500,000, and a similar figure was at hand for the single, *All you need is love*. Total world sales of The Beatles is now calculated at over 200 million singles (one LP = 6 singles, one EP = 2 singles).

By June 1968, Peter Clayton had moved on and a panel of other reviewers had taken over. Despite occasional complimentary notices of artists such as Eric Burdon or Fleetwood Mac (in the days when they were still a blues band), "Keeping Track" began to show signs of once again going off the rails as far as youth culture was concerned. Frank Sinatra, Peggy Lee and Mantovani were in, The Rolling Stones were definitely out, as a review of "Beggars' Banquet" in January 1969 demonstrated

The Rolling Stones *Photo Decca*

All critical criteria are virtually pointless, of course, where the recorded work of Mr Mick Jagger and his cohorts is concerned. The LP will sell an enormous number of copies all round the Western world, and the urgency to meet this reliable demand is detectable in the release instructions on the label copy of my pressing which states in bold capitals "As Soon As Possible Rush Rush Rush". No doubt all your teenage relatives have rushed for their copies already. I dutifully listened to the album, and can report only minimal musical content, lyrics which are unintelligible or uninspired, much that is grotesque, and one track, *Street fighting man*, that is downright unpleasant. Connoisseurs of modern youth may be drawn by titles like *Sympathy for the Devil*, *Stray cat blues* and *Factory girl*, and if they gather the full gist of each, I will be interested to hear from them.

The generation gap between *Gramophone* and the 'pop' record-buying public seemed to have become insurmountable. By the early 1970s coverage was concentrated once more upon pre-Rock 'n' Roll era staples such as Ted Heath and Syd Lawrence, with Geoff Love and the ubiquitous Mantovani also strongly favoured. The opening column was now subtitled "Middle-of-the-Road". Led Zeppelin's "Physical Graffiti" received a positive com-

ment in May 1975, as did Pink Floyd's "Wish You Were Here" (December 1975) but in June 1975 "Keeping Track" admitted its main interest and became "Easy Listening". There were, however, occasional experiments, such as William Mann (WSM) reviewing Rick Wakeman's pomp-rock 'cantata' *The Myths and Legends of King Arthur* in the Choral and Song section of the July 1975 issue (WSM was in fact much at home with the overall 'pop' repertoire: early in The Beatles' career, as chief music critic of *The Times*, he had upset much of the musical establishment by reviewing them in his pages). The pop reviews, reduced to only a column or two each month by the late 1970s, could never do more than scratch the surface, although the round-up of "Rock Albums", written by Peter Field, now gave generally sympathetic coverage to bands as diverse as ELO, The Bee Gees, Dr Hook, Status Quo, Blondie and Lynyrd Skynyrd. The entire "Easy Listening" section had ceased to appear every month by 1978, and the rock album round-ups continued only intermittently, although if they could not claim to be comprehensive, they were at least well-informed.

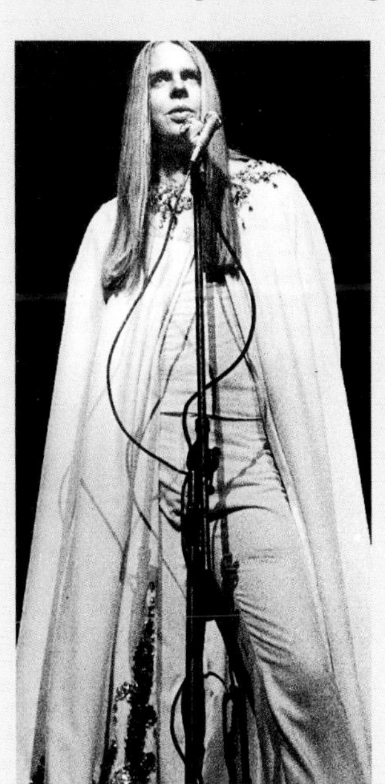

Rick Wakeman *Photo A&M*

The last Rock album column appeared in December 1980, with comments on new albums from artists including Jeff Beck, The Michael Schenker Group, AC/DC, Kate Bush and Stiff Little Fingers. "Easy Listening" cropped up for the last time in April 1982, thereafter its coverage was partially subsumed by the long-established light orchestral section, "Nights at the Round Table".

Ironically, perhaps, Paul McCartney (now Sir Paul) returned to the magazine's pages in 1997 in the guise of a 'classical' composer when his symphonic work *Standing Stone* was reviewed in the November issue.

One of the great supporters of 363 Oxford Street was C. H. Thomas who, having joined the Columbia Graphophone Company in July 1929, was to become the first Managing Director of EMI Records in July 1957. It was Thomas who guided the new Chief Executive, Joseph Lockwood, through the complicated web of the record industry when he arrived on the scene in 1954: he retired as a Divisional Director of EMI in June 1962 and died in November 1981. He had been succeeded as Managing Director of EMI Records in May 1959 by L. G. Wood, who joined The Gramophone Company in September 1929 and was later to take his seat on the EMI Board. Wood was a founder of the Industry association, The British Phonographic Industry, as well as serving with distinction on other related committees.

The 1960s saw the departure of two classical record producers who had indelibly stamped their mark on the Industry's history. Walter Legge joined The Gramophone Company in March 1927. He was an autocratic perfectionist, totally unwilling to accept anything other than the best and as such produced an extensive catalogue of superb

Joseph Lockwood with C. H. Thomas (centre) and Dame Eva Turner *Photo EMI*

recordings for EMI. It was typical of him that, in the absence of what he perceived as a first-class British orchestra, he founded the Philharmonia in August 1945. To everyone's great loss he resigned from EMI in June 1964 following a number of disagreements. He died on March 22nd, 1979 at the age of 72.

The other producer was John Culshaw who joined Decca in November 1946 and after a number of excursions established himself as a regular Decca producer in the mid-1950s. As a company, Decca were continually extending the boundaries of recording and this was a philosophy wellsuited to Culshaw's artistic outlook. This culminated in the recording of Wagner's *Ring* with Georg

September 1966

ON HAVING RECORDED THE RING

by John Culshaw

The release in November 1965 of *Die Walküre* conducted by Georg Solti marked the completion of the first recording of Wagner's *Ring* cycle. John Culshaw, Decca's Classical Recording Director and producer of the project, told the story of this monumental achievement in the September 1966 issue

If anyone had asked me when I joined Decca in 1946 whether I thought that some day I might be involved with the first complete *Ring* recording, the answer would have been "No". In those days of oven-baked waxes and 78rpm records, a complete *Ring* was unthinkable; and even with the advent of LP and stereo, it remained unthinkable to every company except Decca. Now that it is finished, let credit be given where it is most deserved. Artists, orchestra, technicians and administrators all contributed in their different ways to making the recorded *Ring*; but their work could not even have started if two men had not had the courage and imagination to take the huge financial risk involved. Decca made the *Ring* because its Chairman, Sir Edward Lewis, and Mr Maurice Rosengarten, the Director who has been responsible for the classical programme since its inception, approved a budget which gave the rest of us the artistic and technical licence to do the thing properly. Big ideas are fine, as Wagner knew, but they remain in a vacuum until money can give them a tangible, practical public form – which Wagner also knew. Sentimental hindsight suggests that the success Decca has had with the *Ring* was pre-ordained, but it was nothing of the sort. The night before we started *Rheingold* in 1958 I had dinner with Georg Solti in the Hotel Imperial in Vienna, and as we were leaving we bumped into a very distinguished colleague from the competition [Walter Legge], who asked us what we were about to record. We told him, for it was scarcely a secret in Vienna. "Very interesting," he said, "very nice. Of course, you won't sell any ..." He was not alone in thinking that, but he was wrong.

John Culshaw and Georg Solti *Photo Decca*

Over the years a very special sort of teamwork came into being, and I like to think that its unity set an example and developed an atmosphere in which creative work could flourish. The technical leader of the team was Gordon Parry, without whose energy, inspiration and dazzling combination of engineering and musical knowledge, the Decca *Ring* would have been a shadow of what it is. It was he who sold me on the idea of putting up *Rheingold* to our Directors in 1957; it was he who devised the bulk of the many technical innovations we have used along the way; and it was his idea that the story of how we recorded *Götterdämmerung* would make a fine television film, which eventually it did in Humphrey Burton's production for the BBC of *The Golden Ring*. He and his colleague Jimmy Brown have become experts in all sorts of special Wagnerian requirements, from the anvils of *Rheingold* to the magical transformation of a tenor into a baritone at the end of *Götterdämmerung*, Act 1. Once you become a recording producer you quickly learn that you are only as good as your engineers enable you to be, for without their co-operation and understanding there is little you can do.

We were lucky in other ways, too. In Jack Law we had a brilliant tape editor, who demonstrated time and time again that you can make the impossible possible if you try hard enough and have a good ear. Beyond him range all the other technicians who patiently steered the venture through the dubbing rooms and through the complicated business of processing. But none of this would have meant anything had we not been able to assemble the right artists and the right orchestra in the right place at the right time.

That is the heart of the matter. Given the money, anyone can record the *Ring* and do it badly. The basic strength of the Decca *Ring* is in its casting, which is why it has taken so many years to record. We did not compromise; if we could not have the artists we wanted, we were prepared to wait; we did not build it round a single star, and let the rest go hang. As time passed, the artists realized that to appear in the Decca *Ring* was much more than just another engagement in a recording studio, and the atmosphere of sheer professionalism and dramatic concentration which then came into being has no precedent in my experience.

At the helm was Georg Solti, whose energy, devotion, musicianship and dramatic sense kept up the intensity from first to last. We knew, when we met for each successive venture, that however neat and assured the schedule might look, we were inevitably in for one Viennese crisis after another, plus a running battle with the clock.

On September 28th, 1959 – much to the great surprise of all concerned – the Decca recording crew in Vienna were summoned before the assembled Vienna Philharmonic Orchestra and presented with the Nicolai Medal as a token of the Orchestra's appreciation of the team's work: previous recipients of the award had included Richard Strauss, Furtwängler, Krauss and Karajan. Believing that much of the team's success was due to Georg Solti they sent him a telegram telling him of the award but on hearing nothing from him Culshaw later asked him if he had received the telegram. "Oh, yes," he said, "but I thought it was a joke!". From the left, Gordon Parry, Christopher Raeburn, Karl Brugger, John Culshaw, James Brown (Decca), Prof. Otto Strasser, Prof. Helmut Wobisch and Prof. Walter Weller (VPO) *Photo Decca*

Solti's flexibility, which derives from years of experience in theatre and which is not the same thing as compromise, saved us from disaster time and time again. Neither *Siegfried* nor *Walküre* would have been finished at all had it not been for his determination not to accept defeat. Naturally, we have had our disagreements, and it seems to have astonished a lot of people who saw *The Golden Ring* that a recording producer would actually dare to argue with a distinguished conductor. But that is precisely what a producer is paid to do, in addition to creating an atmosphere in which all the artists can give their best. It is because Solti is not arrogant and vain, and because of his utter devotion to the music, that he is willing to take comment and criticism from our side of the fence, just as we listen very seriously when he finds something wrong with the sound we are producing. You cannot begin to record the *Ring* without accepting as a basis the simple fact that the music is far greater than any of the personalities involved in its performance, whatever medium you are working in.

We have not been short of personalities, however. We have had the great professionals, and as always it has been a joy to work with them. Birgit Nilsson, Hans Hotter, Wolfgang Windgassen, Kirsten Flagstad, Set Svanholm, Gustav Neidlinger, Gottlob Frick ... these are some of the people who, along with Solti, have given substance and a lifetime's experience to the Decca *Ring*. Yet there was never a trace of arrogance. I remember a worried Hans Hotter discussing with all of us the right inflexion for his phrase "Geh' hin, Knecht! Kniee vor Fricka!" at the end of *Walküre*, Act 2. He must have sung it hundreds of times on stage, but he was still ready to rethink and reinterpret: in other words, he was thinking about Wotan, not about Hotter.

The informal atmosphere of teamwork which we sought to create among ourselves may have helped to bring such artists together; certainly the apartment we inhabit in Vienna was an open house over the years. We had a galaxy of very distinguished visitors: sometimes there was Max Lorenz sitting in a Sofiensaal box, and often there was Ljuba Welitsch, for whom we bring kippers to Vienna. And we had a lot of jokes, because they are necessary to break the tension. Those who saw the television film will know that we produced Grane, Brünnhilde's horse, alive and kicking, at the appropriate moment in the Immolation scene. This was not 'staged' for television – we had planned it long before the television crew arrived, for it has become a sort of tradition to surprise Birgit Nilsson with something new in each opera she records. When at last we had finished *Siegfried* we sent Gustav Neidlinger, who lives near Stuttgart, the following cable: Return immediately to remake your part: studio cat ate the tape. Unfortunately, Gustav took it quite seriously and rang up at seven the next morning to say he would be coming on the first plane And once there was a completely unintentional joke when, having put Kurt Böhme in a very small and resonant room and told him to roar like the *Siegfried* Fafner so that we could test the sound, we promptly forgot him. He was found some 15 minutes later, still roaring at the top of his voice, by a bewildered Sofiensaal porter.

We lost some friends along the way. It was Kirsten Flagstad's fervent wish to be involved with our *Ring*, but fate allowed her the *Rheingold* Fricka and no more. (She was working on the *Walküre* Fricka and the *Götterdämmerung* Waltraute at the time of her death.) In the long sad years of her final illness she kept up a correspondence with me which gave all of us in Vienna a unique and privileged sort of confidence, for we were all terribly fond of her; we knew her as "Mum". After the first rough playback of the complete *Siegfried* I rang Georg Solti in London to tell him how pleased we were with it, and could not understand why he seemed so quiet. Then he said: "I suppose you haven't seen the papers. Kirsten died last night".

Those of us who have worked on the *Ring* are often asked, now that it is finished, whether we would like to start all over again. We would not, for one very good reason: the finest artists of our generation so far as Wagner is concerned have worked together to make this first recorded *Ring*; the best technicians and the best equipment have been at their disposal; and the management, not without understandable anxiety from time to time, has given all of us the freedom and authority to do our best. The first recorded *Ring* may not be the last in record history, but we like to think it has set a standard for the years to come.

January 1965 **News**

WORDS

I am sorry to see some critics now using the American word "podium" for "rostrum". Are we soon to have "concert master" for "leader"? A recent concert announcement referred to a *Sonata a cinque* by Handel. What on earth does that mean? Is it in five parts or for five players? Neither seems likely and it does nothing (for me at least) to identify the work. The Nixa recording of the Gabrielis talks about a "Ricercare del 12° tono a 7 voci". One is tempted to turn this into Fahrenheit. In the January 1924 issue of **The Gramophone** at which I have been looking I read in advertisements of the Ravel Septette and a Beethoven Quartette, which is tea-shoppe nonsense. Why these absurd feminine endings? It was sometimes said that people who called themselves artistes, quite plainly weren't.

Walter Legge with his wife, Elisabeth Schwarzkopf in the early 1970s *Photo EMI*

Solti, hailed at the time by many as the record industry's greatest achievement – and having witnessed much of the endeavour, the anguish and the triumph, it's a sentiment with which I fully concur. The recording was completed in 1966 and the story told by Culshaw in his book *Ring Resounding* (Secker and Warburg: 1967). After this the grass seemed greener elsewhere and in October 1967 Culshaw moved to the BBC as Head of Music (Television). He died on April 27th, 1980 at the tragically early age of 55.

With the completion of *The Ring*, Georg Solti and John Culshaw made a presentation to Northern dealers in the Grand Hotel, Manchester on November 7th, 1966. Arrangements for the event had been fraught with difficulties due to Solti's commitments but Sir Edward Lewis, the Chairman of Decca, agreed that the Decca Navigator company's private Airspeed "Ambassador" be used for the round-trip from Gatwick to Ringway (Manchester). The picture shows Anthony Pollard, Valerie and Georg Solti, John Culshaw and Jack Law (a member of Decca's Vienna recording team) on the tarmac at Ringway *Photo Decca*

Although totally different in nature and background, Legge and Culshaw made enormous contributions to the classical record industry during the course of their careers.

Ten years of stereo

In the 1960s not only were we able to review the first ten years of LP, but in June 1968 Edward Greenfield was able to look at the impact of ten years of stereo, commenting on the "smoothness" with which it had been introduced and quoting Ray Minshull, Classical Artists Manager of The Decca Record Company, who suggested that stereo had brought "a much bigger change than most people expected ... with stereo the gramophone has become much more of an entertainment that people can sit down to and enjoy". Greenfield also quoted John Warrack who, in assessing the first stereo records in November 1958, wrote "stereo places a much greater musical

Edward Greenfield (left) with EMI's respected classical producer, Suvi Raj Grubb (1973)

responsibility on the recording engineers who are going to have a more creative role than hitherto ... Perhaps the day is upon us when a like-minded conductor and engineer must work on the score together and reach full agreement on its interpretation before a note is played". In closing EG referred to the final chapter in John Culshaw's book *Ring Resounding* where a future scenario speculated "about developments towards combining vision with sound in our recorded repertory. With computer-help the listener (and viewer) might even be able to alter the vision at least as much as he can alter the sound of a record. He could virtually act as producer in his own opera performance".

Christopher Stone was a Fellow of the Royal Zoological Society and this picture from 1949 shows him with one of London Zoo's baby chimpanzees

June 1948 and two of *The Gramophone*'s earliest contributors, W. S. Meadmore (left) and Roger Wimbush (right), flank Fred Smith, redoubtable Managing Director of the London record dealer, Rimington Van Wyck, from September 1939 until his untimely death in February 1962

On the home front

In June 1961 the changed role of Sir Compton and Christopher Stone was acknowledged by showing them on the masthead as Founders, whilst my father and I became joint Editors. But for three of the pioneers the 1960s were to deal harshly: Faith Mackenzie died on July 9th, 1960; Christopher Stone died on May 22nd, 1965 and on September 14th of the same year my father died – to be followed two-and-a-half years later – on May 13th, 1968 – by my mother who was then Chairman of the Company. The decade also saw the loss of W. S. Meadmore, a regular contributor since 1927, who died in February 1965.

October 1968 **Correspondence**

ALFRED BRENDEL

I completely endorse the opinions of several of your reviewers of late as regards the pianist Alfred Brendel.

His recordings of Mozart, Beethoven, Schubert and Liszt have been superb for their musicianly finesse and intellectual grasp. I doubt that there have been finer performances on record of the Mozart concertos.

Surely it is time that some company rescued this remarkable pianist from the invariably second-rate accompanists and recordings with which he is inflicted. In fact, does anybody record him at all nowadays? All his recent releases have been reissues of recordings made up to ten or so years ago.

Gerald J. Fitzgerald
Melbourne, Australia

October 1969 **Correspondence**

"DER ROSENKAVALIER"

History, we know – because a great man said it – is bunk. But something rather unlikely happened on April 12th, 1926 which, as far as I can tell, is now entirely forgotten. Something that, in Cowper's words, has "now become a history little known".

A German film director, Robert Wiene, who had made a rather silly film called *The Cabinet of Dr Caligari* made a *silent* film of *Der Rosenkavalier*. One had seen silent versions of *I Pagliacci* and *Carmen*, but this was different. The silent *Rosenkavalier* was shown to London at the Tivoli in the Strand, and the usual orchestra of some twenty players (under the direction of Mr John Reynders) was "specially augmented" for the occasion. So much so that the wooden wall separating the orchestra from the audience was moved back to wipe out at least three rows of stalls. This was done because, on the first night only, Richard Strauss appeared in person to conduct. And what a night that was! The audience consisted of two factions – one, the avidly intense film enthusiasts who had come to see the latest work of the master Robert Wiene; two, the music lovers who had come to see Richard Strauss himself. There were curious results. On that first night the music, as far as the Tivoli management was concerned, took precedence, and this meant that when the conductor, in control of his own score, had the orchestra lagging behind the film, the film in the projection room was slowed up, and sometimes ran so slowly that one intermittently saw the blank screen while the sixteen-frames-a-second picture was projected at much less than the normal speed. But the film lovers, on seeing some particularly effective scene, would loudly applaud the cinematic result, and this drew loud sibilancies of "Sh!" from the musical part of the audience, whose remonstrances entirely drowned the music they were trying to hear. It did not actually come to blows, but the antagonism was declared. These two contending factions made a far livelier evening than, unfortunately, the film itself. But at the end the applause was all for Richard Strauss.

Richard Strauss in 1925

L. Withrington
Petts Wood, Kent

[Some readers may recall the issue in July 1926 of four 12-inch HMV 78s (D1094-7) which featured excerpts from *Der Rosenkavalier* played by the Augmented Tivoli Orchestra and conducted by the composer. The recording was made in the Queen's Hall and D1097 contains the Presentation March which was specially written by Richard Strauss to accompany this film presentation – *Ed.*]

Some personal thoughts

My principal source of research for these reminiscences has naturally been the magazine itself, and turning the pages of every individual issue has recalled events, many of which I remember well, and people, so many of whom are sadly no longer with us.

My editorial involvement with the magazine was always of the 'hands-on' type – in truth for much of the time there was no one else to do it! For instance, the monthly make-up of the issue in the early 1950s was always done in the quiet of the evening, working with my father at his home in Stanmore, with my mother bringing a reviving whisky and soda around nine o'clock and enquiring, "How much longer?". Generally, we would finish around 11pm and I would then drive to the printers in St Albans, a 30-minute journey, and hand the proceeds to the night staff. By the late-1950s I was doing the job on my own, generally over a weekend, and in all probability I made-up (with scissors and paste) something in excess of 350 issues of the magazine. Having read and edited the original manuscript, read the proofs, transferred the corrections to the made-up pages and finally passed the pages for press, I suppose it is understandable that many of those pages, as I turn them now, should have a distinctly familiar appearance.

EMI's advertisement contract for the front cover resulted in RCA prefacing their colour section within the April 1960 issue of the magazine with this mock front cover

1970-1979

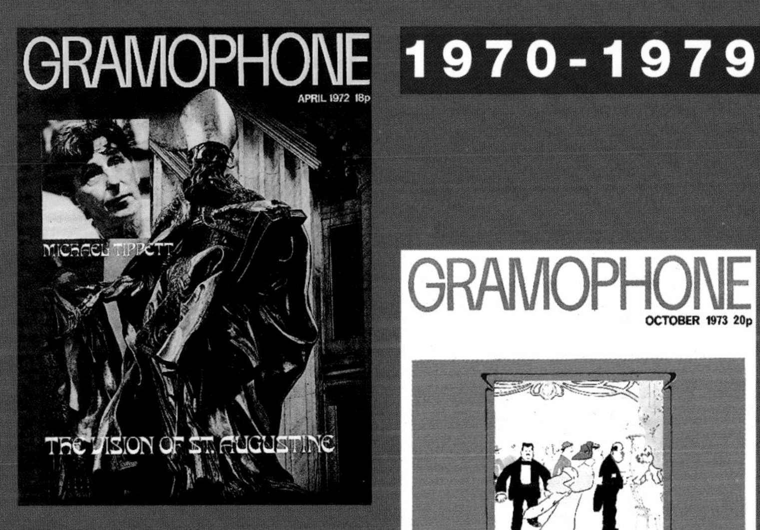

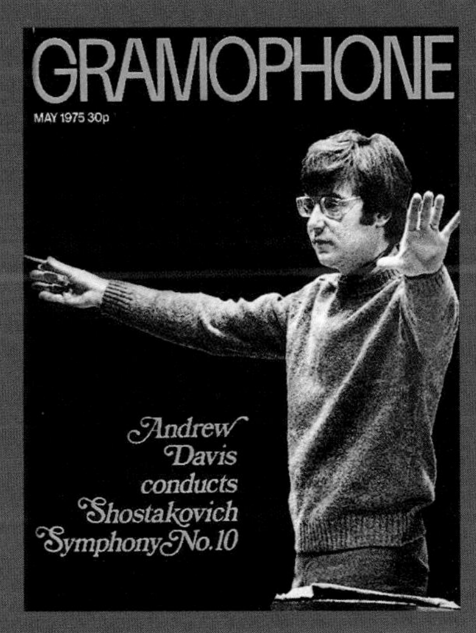

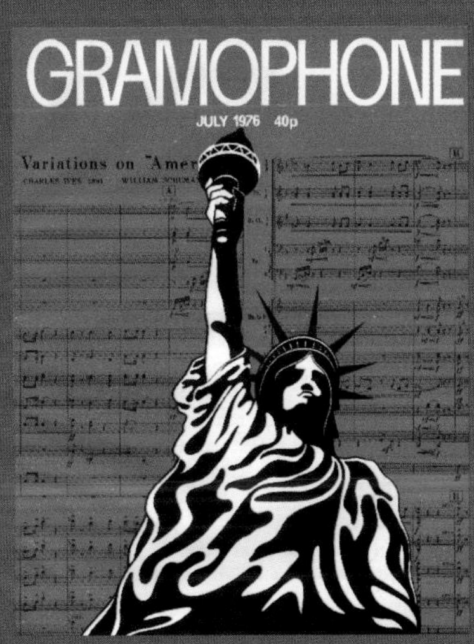

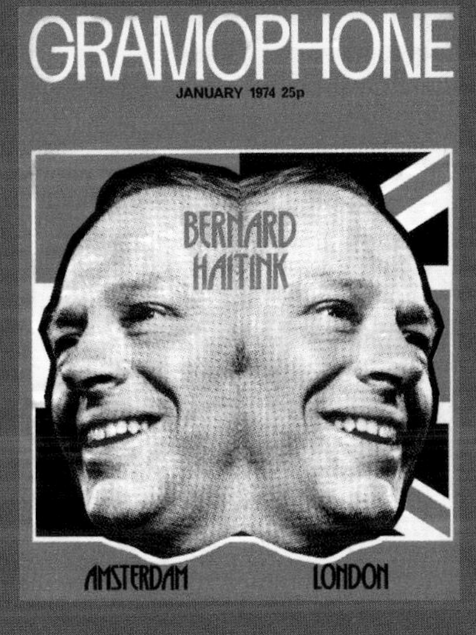

Challenging times

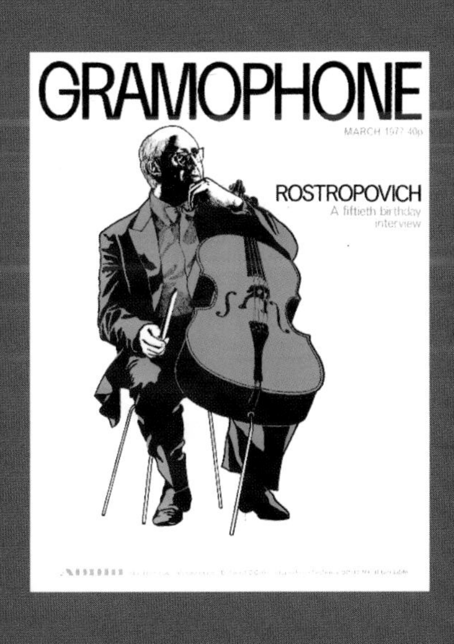

A *Gramophone* chronology

1970-1979

1970

January

- Decca begin their project to record all the Haydn Symphonies with Dorati and the Philharmonia Hungarica. Completed in 1974 the edition comprised 48 LPs in ten sets.
- First MIDEM Classique – but future plans shelved due to lack of support, to re-emerge in 1984.

April

- Philips launch their complete recording of *The Trojans* with Colin Davis.

May

- In Washington, County Durham, RCA open what is claimed to be the most modern record manufacturing plant in the world. The plant was closed in June 1981.

June

- Telefunken/Decca demonstrate TED video disc system in Berlin. Marketed in Germany in March 1975 as the first of its kind, but without success.

July

- Philip Brodie succeeds Ken East as MD of EMI Records UK.

September

- Deutsche Grammophon release their Beethoven Edition to mark the 200th anniversary of the composer's birth – 12 sets comprising 75 LPs plus illustrated book.

October

- Ken Glancy appointed MD of RCA Records UK.
- Dr Andreas Holschneider appointed head of DG Archiv Produktion.
- Classics for Pleasure launched.
- Decca release their first musicassettes.

Dr Andreas Holschneider *Photo DG*

November

- Decca introduce Dolby-B on musicassettes.

December

- Bhaskar Menon returns from the Indian company to be MD of EMI International Services Ltd.

1971

- DGG/PPI re-group to form PolyGram BV Netherlands and PolyGram GmbH Germany as management and holding companies for such repertoire divisions as Polydor International GmbH (including Deutsche Grammophon) and Phonogram BV (including Philips Classics).

January

- Rupert Perry joins EMI Records.
- MfP becomes a wholly owned EMI company.
- Electric and Musical Industries Ltd. becomes EMI Ltd.

Rupert Perry *Photo EMI*

April

- Bhaskar Menon becomes President and CEO of Capitol Industries Inc.
- Decca purchase Oiseau-Lyre label.
- Formation of Nimbus Records by Numa Labinsky and Michael Reynolds.

June

- American Vanguard catalogue is represented in the UK by RCA.

July

- Lord Reith, first Director General of the BBC, dies.

August

- David Bicknell retires from The Gramophone Company and is succeeded in the Classical A&R Department by Peter Andry.
- Philips demonstrate their VCR machine in London with production models to follow in the spring of 1972.

1972

- Richard Asher appointed MD, CBS Records UK.
- PolyGram Leisure UK formed with Stephen Gottleib as Chairman.

January

- Alec Robertson retires as Music Editor of ***G***.
- Reg Pollard retires as Advertisement Manager of ***G*** and is succeeded by Barry Irving.
- RCA introduce the "Dynaflex" LP – thinner disc with a raised rim and label area. Later adopted by other companies.

February

- Leonard Smith, Classical Manager of EMI Records and having 50 years' service in the record business, retires. He is succeeded by John Whittle who joined HMV in 1927.
- Geoffrey Bridge becomes first Director General of the British Phonographic Industry (BPI).

Leonard Smith *Photo EMI*

March

- Release of quadraphonic discs using SQ system from EMI and CBS; using CD-4 system from RCA; and using the QS system from Pye and a number of smaller labels.

September

- Philips introduce VLP video disc.
- Gerry Oord succeeds Philip Brodie as MD of EMI Records UK.

October

- Malcolm Walker appointed Editor of ***G***, Anthony Pollard becomes Managing Editor.
- Using a PCM recording machine, Denon make the first commercial digital recording – Mozart's String Quartet in B flat, K458, The Hunt.

November

- Sir Compton Mackenzie dies aged 89.
- Peter Andry becomes General Manager of EMI International Classical Division.

1973

April

- ***G***'s Golden Jubilee.
- Delos record label founded in the USA by Amelia Haygood.

May

- Reg Pollard dies.
- Goddard Lieberson becomes President of CBS Records Group.

L. G. Wood (left) and Bhaskar Menon, both EMI directors

June

- Bhaskar Menon appointed to Board of EMI.

September

- BIS records founded in Sweden by Robert von Bahr.

1974

January

- Ken Glancy leaves RCA UK and is appointed President and CEO of RCA Records in the USA. He is succeeded as MD of the UK company by Geoffrey Hannington.

July

- Ken Townsend succeeds Gus Cook as General Manager of EMI Studios.

October

- Ken East appointed MD of The Decca Record Company, leaving a year later.

November

- Sir Joseph Lockwood retires as Chairman of EMI but remains on the board until February 1980.
- Victor Olof dies.

1975

March

- Goddard Lieberson retires as President of CBS Records Group.

May

- George Lukan succeeds Geoffrey Hannington as MD of RCA Records UK.

June

- Maurice Oberstein is appointed MD of CBS Records UK in succession to Richard Asher.

November

- Maurice Rosengarten, Director of Decca Classical Recordings, dies.
- John Pattrick who joined EMI in April 1965, succeeds John Whittle as Manager of EMI Records Classical Division. Whittle retires.

John Pattrick *Photo EMI*

December

- Ray Minshull appointed Director of Decca Classical Recordings.

Ray Minshull *Photo Decca*

1976

August

- Leslie Hill becomes MD of EMI Records UK.

September

- Gerry Oord, previously MD of EMI Records UK, appointed MD of RCA Records UK.

October

- Enigma Classics launched by John Boyden.
- JVC announce VHS video cassette system in Japan.

1977

January

- Telarc Records founded in the US by Jack Renner and Robert Woods.

February

- Gilbert Wilson and Roger Wimbush die.

May

- Percy Wilson dies aged 84.
- Goddard Lieberson dies aged 66.

August

- F. F. Clough dies.

October

- Nonesuch catalogue transferred to WEA Records.

November

- First releases from Nimbus Records.
- Philips/MCA VLP video disc demonstrated.

December

- Dr Peter Goldmark, who developed the long-playing record with William Bachman, dies in a motor accident.

1978

January

- Gilbert Briggs, founder of Wharfedale Wireless Works, dies aged 88.
- Auvidis founded by Louis Bricard.

Louis Bricard
Photo Auvidis

February

- Presentation of the first ***Gramophone*** Record Awards with Decca's recording of Janáček's *Kát'a Kabanová* winning the Record of the Year.

March

- JVC introduce VHS video cassette system in the UK.
- Ramon Lopez succeeds Leslie Hill as MD of EMI Records UK.

April

- Anna Instone dies.

May

- Philips announce Compact Disc Digital Audio for early 1980s.

July

- Bhaskar Menon becomes CEO of EMI Music Worldwide.
- Decca's first experimental digital recording sessions at Walthamstow Assembly Hall – "Sylvia Sass sings dramatic arias".
- EMI launch "Listen for Pleasure", the first serious attempt to promote the spoken word on cassette.

October

- John Maunder, latterly with Shure but prominent in the British audio industry and founder with John Gilbert and Percy Wilson of the British section of the Audio Engineering Society, dies aged 62.
- Enigma Classics purchased by WEA.

1979

January

- W. R. Anderson dies aged 88.
- Decca make a live digital recording of the "New Year's Concert" with Boskovsky and the VPO.

David Fine

February

- David G. Fine is appointed MD of PolyGram UK.

March

- Press demonstration of Compact Disc Digital Audio in Eindhoven.
- Death of EMI record producer and impresario Walter Legge, aged 72.

June

- EMI make their first digital recordings – Debussy's *Images* and *Prélude à l'après-midi d'un faune* with Previn and the LSO.

July

- Sony "Walkman" launched in Japan.

September

- Geoffrey Bridge, first Director General of the British Phonographic Industry (BPI) retires after seven years and is succeeded by John Deacon.

Geoffrey Bridge *Photo BPI*

November

- EMI Limited merge with Thorn Limited to form Thorn EMI. The Chairman is Sir Richard Cave.
- First releases from Brian Couzens's Chandos Records.

December

- Reinhard Klaassen appointed to the Decca Board.
- David G. Fine succeeds Stephen Gottlieb as Chairman of PolyGram UK.

Reinhard Klaassen
Photo Decca

Challenging times

A difficult period

My notes for the 1970s bring back recollections of a particularly difficult period. With my father's death in 1965 I assumed responsibility for all his day-to-day financial work (of which I had no prior experience – I was always going to spend time with him but other, more pressing matters, always seemed to intervene) and this was in addition to my editorial work and liaison with the record and audio industries which was so vital to our ongoing success. Thus, all the Company's decision making was now my responsibility, although in this respect I was fortunate that my wife Margaret, by now a Director of the Company, was always ready to listen to my problems and so often was able to offer a fresh perspective – the old adage, 'a problem shared is a problem halved', has much truth in it.

Always ready with a smile, and no task too much, our Maintenance Engineer, H. A. "Sandy" Sandling, from 1968-79

After Prime Minister Sir Harold Macmillan reminded us that in the 1960s "we had never had it so good", the 1970s went very sour both in terms of monetary inflation and on the industrial front, and it seemed that hardly a month passed without some dispute – postal workers, transport drivers, printers, all had their strikes and in addition there was also the famous three-day working week in 1974 when relations between Edward (later Sir Edward) Heath's government and certain elements of the labour force broke down entirely. To cope with this we installed our own small electric generator in the car park so that at least we could have some power when the National Grid shut off. Goodness knows what the Health and Safety Executive would have made of the improvised wiring rig which was the work of our ever-resourceful Maintenance Engineer, H. A. "Sandy" Sandling (whose son Barry carries on his father's tradition in the Company to this day) but he managed to keep us all at work where others were falling by the wayside. It seemed that nearly every issue contained some apology for late delivery or reduced pagination. British readers, of course, understood the problems only too well but over 25 per cent of our sales were overseas and the patience of those readers was sorely tried.

A new printer

In March 1956, Gibbs & Bamforth, who had been our printers since 1938, were taken over by the Associated Iliffe Press. This was typical of much that was happening at the time (conglomerates were all the vogue) but posed us no serious problems and in fact it resulted in various plant improvements which were to be to our benefit. It also introduced us to the charming Claude Wallis and his Iliffe Board – and Bob Baker, who for many years was to advise us on print matters and played a key role in our investigation of the use of an electronic database for the production of our record catalogues in the late 1960s. However, in July 1960, a further take-over resulted in the International Publishing Corporation – run by Cecil King, and owners of *The Daily Mirror* – assuming control and eventually deciding to close Gibbs & Bamforth and, with effect from the issue dated February 1969, transferring the work to one of their more modern plants, Index Printers in Dunstable. Here we had to come to terms with the web offset printing press, a change from the flat-bed letterpress machine to which we were accustomed, but still in need of much development. Sadly, the quality of our print suffered enormously and this, coupled with the level of industrial disputes experienced, particularly in the London area, eventually confirmed my thinking that we should find a new printer for the magazine.

To a great extent the Company was top-heavy – not in the conventional sense but in that the volume of work necessary to maintain our various publications was not matched by the human resource available – the payroll through the 1970s for all departments (editorial, advertising, subscriptions, trade circulation, accounts and despatch) numbered on average no more than 20. Everyone had more than enough to do, and this was exacerbated by the problems resulting from the various industrial disputes. In the circumstances I was hesitant to disrupt a working arrangement with our printers which had existed for more than 40 years, to say nothing of leaving behind compositors and other skilled workers, many of whom I had known since I was a schoolboy in the late 1930s. None the less the situation had to be resolved.

During the late autumn of 1979 I let it be known that we were looking for a new printer and almost immediately Watmoughs of Idle, near Bradford in Yorkshire, indicated their interest. I was impressed with everything about the company, and particularly with Patrick Walker, the Managing Director, and his co-directors. As our discussions progressed my only point of concern, but one of critical importance, was the question of price. A facility to produce cost-effective colour sections, which at Index were prohibitively expensive, was most inviting (particularly from an advertisement point of view, as I was sure that in the 1980s the record and audio industries would need to improve the appearance of their advertisements which currently were either badly printed black and white, or carried a limited amount of spot-colour – full-colour was a rarity), but the creation of the all-important text, which was to be handled electronically, was very costly.

The situation was such that I wondered if it was really fair to accept Watmoughs' invitation to visit their works, in the knowledge that a final contract was highly unlikely. However, the fact that they had offered to run one of our colour sections, at their expense, left us with little alternative but to go. Thus, on a snowy January afternoon, Barry Irving and I arrived in Yorkshire and that evening had dinner with the Watmoughs' executives. Well after midnight, with Patrick Walker having retired to bed, I expressed my concern to Ken Lewis, their Sales Director: as a result, at 8.30 the next morning, meeting in Patrick Walker's office, a revised quotation was offered to us which I immediately recognized was much more attractive. It was agreed to move the job to Watmoughs with effect from the June 1980 issue, ironically as it transpired when Index Printers were in the grip of yet another strike. Thus we began an association with a new printer which would give us the opportunity to develop **Gramophone** along much more modern and visually attractive lines.

Celebrations and sadness

In April 1973 the magazine celebrated the completion of 50 years' publication: an event which was sadly marred by the death of our Founder, Sir Compton Mackenzie, OBE, on November 30th, 1972, just seven weeks short of his 90th birthday. He had been so full of enthusiasm for the Anniversary and had already written a lengthy piece as the Introduction to *The Gramophone Jubilee Book, 1923-1973*, which was also to appear in the April 1973 Golden Jubilee issue. In the *Jubilee Book* there was a Foreword by Sir Arthur Bliss, Master of the Queen's Musick, as well as specially commissioned articles from John Culshaw, Alec Robertson, Percy Wilson and Sir Adrian Boult, the last commenting, "I well remember the foundation of ***The Gramophone*** ... It seemed to me to mark the turning point: to establish the gramophone as an instrument of value whereas it had begun its life as an amusing toy with very squeaky results". In the magazine itself there was a letter of congratulation from The Prime Minister, Edward Heath, a reader of many years standing, whilst the issue itself also contained a facsimile, printed on yellowed paper, of the 28-page first issue.

Sir Compton Mackenzie in 1968

A party to celebrate the occasion was held on April 12th, 1973 at the Savoy Hotel in London. Those present included contributors past and present, together with executives from the international record industry. In

Three octogenarians celebrate ***Gramophone***'s 50th Anniversary – from the left, Alec Robertson (first contribution December 1923), Percy Wilson (September 1924) and W. R. Anderson (May 1925)

SIR ADRIAN BOULT

Sir Adrian Boult at a playback during Lyrita's first integral recording of the Elgar Symphonies with the LPO, completed in January 1968

Photo Lyrita

Sir Adrian Boult was always one of the most approachable of artists and showed the greatest interest in those around him. In 1972 I noticed that his subscription to ***Gramophone*** had lapsed and wrote to him suggesting that perhaps the time had come when we should add his name to our complimentary list. He replied (1).

On receipt of the February issue, which contained reviews of his recordings of the Berkeley and Williamson Violin Concertos, and Vaughan Williams's *Pilgrim's Progress*, he wrote again (2).

Obviously, I could not leave this letter unanswered and responded by expressing the hope that there may be many more wonderful recordings to come in the future – and added the rider that we would happily meet his hatter's account should this become a major problem (3).

1

Telephone 01-935 1387

38, WIGMORE STREET,
LONDON,
W. 1.

January 13th 1972

Dear Mr Pollard

Many thanks for your very kind letter. Of course I accept your kind offer. As a matter of fact I was rather reluctant to stop my subscription, but one has to cut things down now and then, and though I enjoyed the articles very often I felt that it would do me no harm to stop reading the very enthusiastic notices which my friends are so kind as to write about my work. I can remember the days when I used to read criticisms very carefully indeed and very often found really helpful things which the man pounced on and which I was able to improve. But now it all seems to be praise!

Many thanks
Yours sincerely
Adrian C Boult

Anthony C. Pollard, Esq.,
The Gramophone,
177, Kenton Road,
Harrow,
Mddx.

2

Telephone 01-935 1387

38, WIGMORE STREET,
LONDON,
W. 1.

February 2nd 1972

Dear Mr Pollard

I do not know whether you knew what was in store in the February number when you so very kindly offered me a subscription to "The Gramophone", but whether you did or you did not I must say how enormously touched I am with the notices in the three separate places in this number. I have had to get a much larger hat, and so the cost of the subscription, which you have so very kindly remitted, is going into the coffers of the hat shop.

Seriously I do want to thank Mr. Mann and Mr. Greenfield very much for what they have said and it is really true that this criticism seems to me to go much further than my worthiness.

Many thanks, and please do not trouble to answer this effusion.

Yours sincerely
Adrian C Boult

Anthony Pollard, Esq.,
General Gramophone Publications, Ltd.,
177, Kenton Road,
Kenton,
Harrow.

3

THE GRAMOPHONE

GENERAL GRAMOPHONE PUBLICATIONS LTD
177-179 KENTON ROAD · HARROW · MIDDX · HA3 0HA
Telephone: 01-907 2010

4th February 1972

Sir Adrian Boult,
38 Wigmore Street,
London, W1.

Dear Sir Adrian,

Thank you so much for your kind letter of the 2nd, which cannot go unanswered.

Whilst I cannot claim to have known in advance of my reviewers' reactions to your recordings discussed in the February issue I must admit to my extreme pleasure at reading such notices.

For the benefit of all concerned I can only hope for many more such recordings - and, with all due respect, if your hatters present a serious problem then I would be more than happy to meet them.

With kindest regards,
Yours sincerely,
Anthony Pollard.
(Anthony C. Pollard)

Directors A. C. POLLARD M. N. POLLARD G. G. BOXALL, F.C.A.

addition to a substantial amount of press coverage the event was celebrated by BBC Radio 3's *Record Review* in a programme of words and music compiled and produced by Anna Instone, with industry comment from Sir Joseph Lockwood and Sir Edward Lewis. BBC Radio 4's *PM* programme, Radio London and the World Service also celebrated the occasion.

Later in the year both EMI and Deutsche Grammophon celebrated their respective 75th anniversaries with various commemorative events and special recordings. These events, plus in 1977 the marking by the International Federation of the Producers of Phonograms and Videograms (IFPI) of the centenary of sound recording by Charles Cros, were fairly high-profile occasions whereas the 50th anniversary of Decca could well have passed unnoticed.

Sir Edward Lewis, the founding genius of Decca and one of the world's great record industry men, never sought publicity and thus he was happy to suggest that any celebration be related to the founding of the original company, Barnett Samuel (in which, of course, he played no part!), whose 150th anniversary was due in 1982. I was far from happy with this idea, as were a number of his Decca colleagues and others in the Industry. Initially, I asked John Culshaw as an ex-Decca man to write a commemorative piece and this appeared in the July 1979 issue. In conclusion Culshaw wrote, "I suspect that Decca's staff has more affection for Sir Edward than he supposes. He may not care for that word, but I don't think that admiration is a good enough substitute. Even the youngest member of Decca, if he stays for more than a year or two, must sooner or later become aware of what has happened in a mere 50 years and realize that in the first crucial ten years the firm survived only because of the tenacity and determination of the man who is still in charge. Some day a complete history of Decca will be written, but when it is the story of the first 50 years of the label will inevitably focus upon the personality of Sir Edward Lewis, and the initiative which led him, against all the odds, to create a record company which eventually stood in line with the giants – no matter how surprised they were."

Some members of *Gramophone* celebrating the 50th Anniversary: seated Mrs H. Dunbar (Accounts), Mrs H. Grimes (Accounts), Miss H. Goddard (Cashier), Mr H. A. Sandling (Maintenance), his wife, Mrs E. MacGillivray, Mrs J. Lavendels (Subscriptions), Mr E. MacGillivray (Despatch), Mr V. Dunbar (Circulation). Standing Mrs D. George (Reception) and her husband

Sir Edward Lewis – August 1976 *Photo Decca*

On June 16th, 1952 my father had arranged a dinner at the Savoy Hotel in London to celebrate Sir Compton's knighthood: he invited a number of people associated with the magazine as well as senior executives from Decca and EMI (at that time really the only record companies in the UK). The dinner was a great success but strangely enough many of the

A reception was held at the Royal Festival Hall in London on October 25th, 1973 as part of Deutsche Grammophon's international 75th anniversary celebrations. Cutting the cake are (from the left) Martin Lovett, Siegmund Nissel, Peter Schidlof, Eugen Jochum, Elizabeth Harwood and Norbert Brainin *Photo DG*

Sir Compton Mackenzie with Sir Alexander Aikman (MD of EMI) at the first "Founders' Dinner", held at the Savoy Hotel on June 16th, 1952

L. G. Wood, a Director of EMI
Photo EMI

record industry people knew their opposite numbers at best only as names, and as a result it was suggested that it should be perpetuated on an annual basis with us organizing it but the cost being shared by all three companies. To avoid any embarrassment, the rather exclusive event for some 25-30 people became known as "The Founders' Dinner" (EMI being founder advertisers from the first issue of the magazine and Decca joining from their inception in 1929) and it was to run from 1952 to 1978 with Sir Edward never missing a dinner.

By the 1970s there were many more companies in the business than just Decca and EMI but Sir Edward had been insistent that the dinner remained as originally conceived. However, in 1979 having talked with L. G. Wood of EMI, and executives from other companies, I decided to enlarge the event for the celebration of Sir Edward's Decca anniversary. The idea received positive approval and it was also proposed to use the occasion for the Industry to make a presentation to him. Fearing possible difficulties it was agreed to conceal the real nature of the evening from Sir Edward, and this was achieved with the help of his son Richard. However, it was a difficult moment when I greeted his arrival at the Savoy on May 10th and he asked, with obvious concern, "Who on earth are all these people?"

Happily, the dinner was a great success and afterwards his old friend Eric Gallo (Chairman of Gallo, Decca's African agents) wrote to me, "Am back in South Africa and wish to thank you for having me attend your dinner for Sir Edward. I think it was a great occasion ... with some very good speeches. Ted, of course, did not know anything about it, but has never stopped talking about it since and certainly enjoyed the evening." In many respects it marked the end of another era in the history of the British record industry.

Changes at Decca and EMI

Sir Edward was already seriously ill at the time of the dinner and would die on January 29th, 1980, at the age of 79. On October 30th, 1979, at his company's Annual General Meeting, he announced that discussions had taken place with the PolyGram Group (established in 1971 to co-ordinate the music business activities of Deutsche Grammophon and Philips) with a view to the acquisition of certain of the recording and music publishing activities of the Decca Group, and in fact such an agreement was signed on January 17th, 1980.

Parallel with this EMI were also in financial difficulties and on November 6th, 1979 a merger was announced between Thorn Electrical Industries Ltd. and EMI, to form Thorn EMI Limited. Thus, at the beginning of 1980 the status of Britain's two greatest record companies changed radically.

Sounds in Retrospect

For a while I must revert to more mundane matters and focus on the magazine itself. There has never been any question in my mind other than that the purpose of a classical recording was to capture the artistry and interpretative skill of a given performance; but our increasing ability to capture the real quality of the original sound and reproduce it in the home with greater realism, highlighted the importance of conveying this aspect of a recording to the reader. Terminology was all-important, to say nothing of an understanding of what one was actually listening for when reproducing a record. In December 1971 I therefore introduced "Sounds in Retrospect", a quarterly group-listening session with a panel which initially consisted of Edward Greenfield, Robert Layton, Malcolm Walker, John Borwick and John Gilbert, and represented both the musical and audio sides of the magazine. The cross-fertilization was invaluable to all those

January 1974 **Correspondence**

" D I S C O G R A P H Y "

In 1933 some friends and I brought out a rather highbrow quarterly in Hong Kong, which, naturally enough, only ran for two issues, in the second of which I wrote an article on Delius, and put in an impassioned plug for the Delius Society, which had been founded a few months earlier – in fact I drew attention to a notice about it which had appeared in the July 1933 issue of ***The Gramophone***.

My reason for writing this letter is that on re-reading my article recently for the first time probably for 40 years, I came across the following sentence: "Actually 18 recorded works exist, according to a very interesting article on Delius in the March number of ***The Gramophone*** by Mr Norman Cameron, which also contains an up-to-date discography – (I should like to think that I am the first in the field with this ugly, though now necessary, word)."

I'm quite certain that I made my claim in good faith, but I can't help feeling now that it is highly improbable that I was the first to use the word 'discography': and I wonder whether Roger Wimbush or any other of your contributors or readers can point to its first appearance in print.

T. W. Southam
Jupiter Recordings Ltd,
London W4

who took part, and in a slightly different format the feature still exists today under the title of "Soundings".

Two other new features were incorporated in October 1977 – a listing of all the month's new LP and cassette releases and "The Gramophone Collection" – both surviving to the present day.

Record Awards

Towards the end of the decade I was approached by the record industry to initiate an annual awards event. It was suggested that whilst there were other awards they generally lacked credibility and achieved little publicity for the winners. The perception was that such shortcomings could be eliminated if *Gramophone* was willing to grasp the nettle – and I was in no doubt that it was a prickly one! Many awards existed simply for the gratification of those directly involved, often with additional 'categories' being created to ensure that no one went home empty-handed, whereas I believed from the outset that the ultimate objective was to generate as much publicity as possible for the classical business and sell more records.

I indicated that any awards originating from *Gramophone* would be decided by our experienced panel of critics and in saying this pointed out that as a fiercely independent group of men and women there would be no question of any partisanship. This fact was happily accepted by the classical record companies and the first Awards were presented at the Savoy Hotel on February 28th, 1978. For many years the Awards have also had the invaluable support of the British Phonographic Industry, and in particular their long-serving and highly-respected Director General, John Deacon.

John Deacon, Director General of the British Phonographic Industry with (left) David Mellor, MP QC and Rupert Perry (right – CEO, EMI Europe) at the 1993 *Gramophone* Awards

February 1977

B E N

A Tribute to Benjamin Britten (1913-1976)
by John Culshaw

In this excerpt from John Culshaw's personal tribute to the composer, published in February 1977, he describes the founding of The Maltings, Snape

Benjamin Britten outside The Maltings *Photo Decca*

It was in the summer of 1965 that Ben and Peter [Pears] invited me to go and explore an old building at Snape which might, by a considerable stretch of imagination and a lot of money, be converted into the kind of multipurpose hall that was so urgently needed by the Aldeburgh Festival. We walked round The Maltings and then clambered inside. It was all but impossible to imagine what it would be like when gutted, because at that stage it consisted of floor upon floor with no through sight-line. We kept on descending until we reached the ovens in the basement. And yet ... there was a feeling about the place, about its setting by the river with the view of Iken Church through the reeds and across the marshes, that made it *right*. If Ben was to have a concert hall on his doorstep, this was it; and in 1967, thanks to a superb conversion job by Ove Arup and Partners who joined in close acoustical collaboration with Decca and the BBC, The Maltings at Snape was opened by the Queen. Two years later it burned down to a cinder, yet in 1970 it was open again and, if anything, better than ever.

The Maltings is Ben's monument, although I am not sure he would have liked me to put it that way. It is not a monument in the sense of Bayreuth, because it was not built to serve all music. It has proved to be a marvellous concert and recital hall; it can accommodate opera without strain; the many Decca recordings made there prove its quality as a recording location, and on at least three occasions – *Peter Grimes*, *Winterreise* and *Owen Wingrave* – the BBC turned it quite literally into a television studio. But, most important of all, its existence encouraged Britten to make many recordings which might otherwise not have been made at all, since they would have involved him in prolonged trips to London. At The Maltings he could work in peace, and in the environment that inspired so much of his work; the warmth and welcome of the building were, and will remain, a reflection of the man.

Gramophone Awards

The first *Gramophone* Awards ceremony was held at the Savoy Hotel on February 28th, 1978, a low-key affair attended mostly by representatives of record companies. Since then, it has become the most important and influential awards ceremony in the classical record industry's year, and an occasion on which *Gramophone* can salute the wealth of musical talent currently before the public. Over the years some of the greatest names in classical music have been recipients of *Gramophone* Awards: Herbert von Karajan, Bernard Haitink, Maurizio Pollini, Carlo Maria Giulini, Dietrich Fischer-Dieskau, Pierre Boulez, Jessye Norman, John Eliot Gardiner, William Christie, Charles Dutoit, Murray Perahia, Sir Simon Rattle, Luciano Pavarotti, Dame Kiri Te Kanawa, Sir Georg Solti, Anne Sofie von Otter, Krystian Zimerman, the list goes on.

1978. The first awards were presented by Lady Harewood, nobly standing in for her husband who was indisposed. Sir Charles Mackerras (centre) received the "Record of the Year" Award with his producer James Mallinson

The first "Record of the Year" winner was Sir Charles Mackerras's recording of Janáček's opera *Kát'a Kabanová* on Decca. Subsequent winners have included Karajan's Mahler Symphony No. 9 on DG (1984), Elgar's Violin Concerto with Nigel Kennedy on EMI (1985), the *Missa Pange lingua* by Josquin Desprez performed by The Tallis Scholars on Gimell (1987), Prokofiev's *Love for Three Oranges* conducted by Kent Nagano on Virgin Classics (1990), Nikolaus Harnoncourt's cycle of Beethoven Symphonies on Teldec (1993) and Puccini's *La rondine*, featuring Angela Gheorghiu and Roberto Alagna conducted by Antonio Pappano on EMI (1997).

Voting for the Awards is carried out by **Gramophone**'s panel of critics and the process falls into four parts. An initial list which runs to many hundreds of recordings reviewed in the magazine over the past year is drawn up. A committee of **Gramophone** reviewers work independently to reduce the list to a maximum of 40 discs per category. The revised list is then circulated to specialist critics in each category who add any discs they believe have been overlooked. This then forms the First Round nominations, voted on by the specialist reviewers. Their voting reduces the these nominations to just six discs per category, which become the Shortlist for all the critics to vote in the Second Round (with the specialist critics retaining a weighted vote). The "Record of the Year" is again voted on by a committee who consider a shortlist of six discs drawn from the winners in each category and then vote on the disc which carries off the ultimate accolade at the Awards ceremony.

1996. The Savoy Hotel, London

Alongside the prestige value, winning an Award also has a positive benefit on record sales. In December 1984 EMI's Eminence label released Nigel Kennedy's recording of Elgar's Violin Concerto. This had sold 19,000 copies in the ten months up to the end of September 1985. After

The staging of the Awards in the Savoy Hotel developed from a small, unadorned 9-inch high platform in 1978, with 70 guests standing in front, to a stage-set with A/V screens and 400 guests seated for lunch in 1996. In 1997 the need to present the event for television necessitated a move to London's Alexandra Palace, with Jill Dando as compère, the London Symphony Orchestra and Chorus, and 900 guests seated for dinner

being acclaimed "Record of the Year" in October 1985, it sold a further 10,000 copies in that month alone, and sales remained substantially higher than normal thereafter. Independent labels in particular report as much as tenfold increases in sales as a result of winning a *Gramophone* award, and continuing long-term sales. For example, the Chandos recording of Hummel's Piano Concertos performed by Stephen Hough, which won the Concerto award in 1987, had sold more than 50,000 copies on CD by 1996 and more than 20,000 on LP and cassette, and the recording continues to perform well. Perhaps the most striking success story, however, is that of Gimell's disc of Josquin's *Missa Pange lingua* which took "Record of the Year" in 1987. Gimell was founded in 1981 by Peter Phillips and Steve Smith to record The Tallis Scholars performing Renaissance masterpieces. The immediate result of winning the Award in 1987 was a doubling of the company's turnover before the end of that financial year, with the recording having sold four times the amount expected. It also opened new markets overseas, notably in Japan, where news of the Award stimulated interest in the label. The disc went on to sell over 100,000 copies worldwide by 1993 – an unprecedented figure for such apparently esoteric repertoire.

In 1997 the Awards ceremony was televised for the first time. The event, which took place on October 27th at Alexandra Palace, was broadcast the following evening to a television audience of almost 2·5 million viewers. It was a glittering occasion hosted by TV presenter Jill Dando, with the London Symphony Orchestra and Chorus in attendance. Recipients of awards who also performed live included Mstislav Rostropovich, Andreas Scholl, Murray Perahia, Angela Gheorghiu and Roberto Alagna. Sir Paul McCartney, Dame Kiri Te Kanawa, Christopher Lee, Darcy Bussell and The Rt Hon Sir Edward Heath MP were among the celebrity presenters, as was Luciano Pavarotti, who also received a Special Achievement Award.

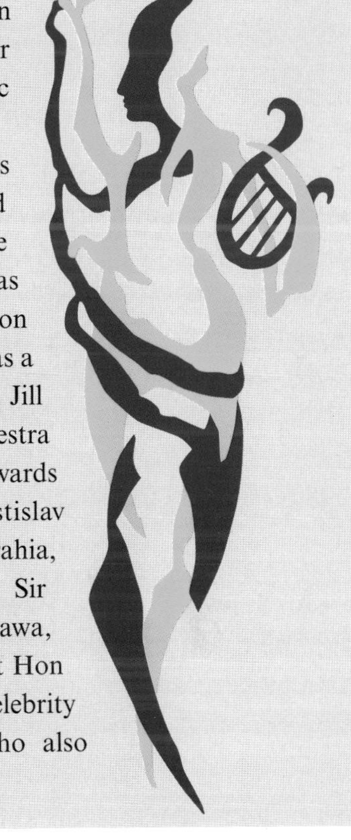

November 21st, 1995 **Los Angeles Times**

An American critic's view of the 1995 *Gramophone* Awards

MUSIC AWARDS THAT MEAN SOMETHING

by Herbert Glass

London – Picture this: In one place, at the same time – Elisabeth Furtwängler, widow of Wilhelm Furtwängler, king of the cult conductors, conversing with Myriam Scherchen, daughter of the late conductor Hermann Scherchen, whose spirit is beginning to attract its own army of rabid admirers. The frail and nearly blind composer Sir Michael Tippett, at 90 arguably the most honored living practitioner of his craft, making an entrance on the arm of actress Zoë Wanamaker (she of the harrowing encounters with Helen Mirren in the original *Prime Suspect*). The spry, 93-year-old composer Berthold Goldschmidt, last remaining survivor of the Nazis' "Entartete Musik" pogrom (directed chiefly against Jewish composers and their "degenerate" art) getting bear-hugged from behind by Simon Rattle – Sir Simon, the most lionized conductor of his generation. The twin kingpins of HIP (Historically Informed Performance), conductors William Christie and John Eliot Gardiner talking shop. The 21-year-old Siberian Sensation, violinist Maxim Vengerov, a model of casual chic in tight black jeans and tight white T-shirt, surreptitiously checking his pecs in a mirror.

1978. Ramon Lopez (EMI), Geoffrey Bridge (BPI) and Maurice Oberstein (CBS)

1983. Anthony Pollard and Alfred Brendel (whose Liszt recordings won the Instrumental Award)

(Below) 1985. Vernon Handley, Nigel Kennedy and Christopher Pollard (Nigel Kennedy having won "Record of the Year" for his recording of the Elgar Violin Concerto)

(Above) 1983. Anthony Pollard, Sir Colin Davis and Sir Michael Tippett who received the "Record of the Year" Award for his Triple Concerto (conducted by Sir Colin)

(Left) 1983. Sir Charles Mackerras who won yet another award in the Opera category for his Janáček

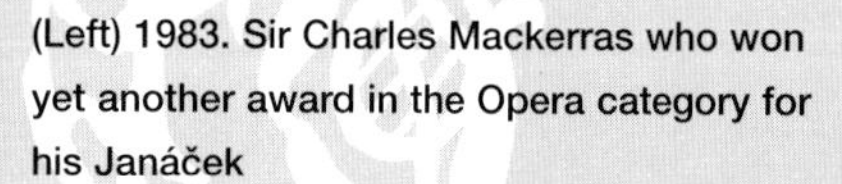

(Left) 1985. Sir Peter Pears, who presented the Awards

(Below) 1990. An airborne Richard Branson celebrates the "Record of the Year" Award for Prokofiev's *The Love for Three Oranges* with Louis Erlo and Jean-Pierre Brossman (both Opéra de Lyon), Nicolai Gedda (who presented the Award) and the conductor Kent Nagano. A representative of SARI (who sponsored the recording) and Simon Foster are obscured by the flying Branson

1991. Luciano Pavarotti and Dame Joan Sutherland both recipients of Special Awards

1992. The composer John Tavener and his Award for *The Protecting Veil*, with Steven Isserlis the cellist

1992. Sir Georg Solti received both the Opera Award for *Die Frau ohne Schatten* ("I have waited 20 years for this Award and I don't want to wait another 20 for the next"), as well as a Lifetime Achievement Award

(Right) 1991. Isaac Stern who collected the Chamber Music Award for his recording of the Brahms Piano Quartets with Laredo, Ma and Ax

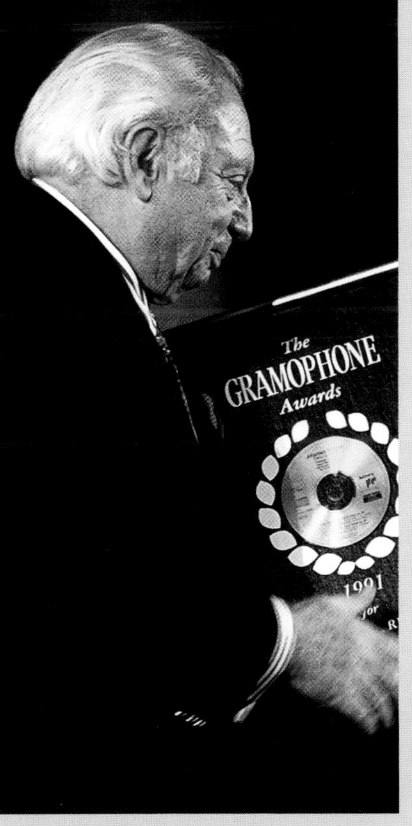

1992. Dame Kiri Te Kanawa, Artist of the Year, with Christopher Pollard

1993. David Mellor (right) presents Shura Cherkassky with his 80th birthday recital Award

(Left) 1994. John Eliot Gardiner (recipient of more *Gramophone* Awards than any other artist) receives his Artist of the Year Award from David (later Lord) Puttnam

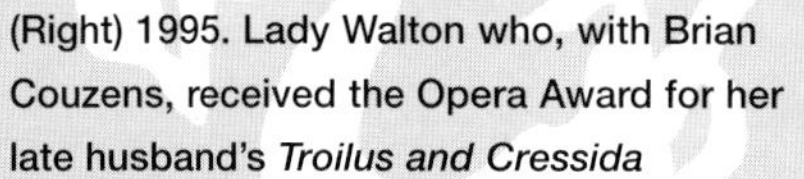

(Right) 1995. Lady Walton who, with Brian Couzens, received the Opera Award for her late husband's *Troilus and Cressida*

(Below) 1995. Live music featured for the first time when Maxim Vengerov, winner of the "Record of the Year" Award played to the assembled company. The picture shows him at the rehearsal

1995. William Christie with his Awards in the Early Opera and Baroque Opera categories

(Below) 1997. Mstislav Rostropovich received the Lifetime Achievement Award and delighted the audience by playing Bach

1997. Roberto Alagna, Angela Gheorghiu, Antonio Pappano, Mary Hegarty and William Matteuzzi take a bow following their performance of "Bevo al tuo fresco sorriso" from *La rondine*, "Record of the Year"

(Left) 1997. Roberto Alagna and Angela Gheorghiu, winners of Record of the Year, and the Opera and Classic fM's People's Choice Awards

1997. Luciano Pavarotti, who was presented with a Special Achievement Award by Dame Kiri Te Kanawa for his spectacular efforts in raising money for War Child, a charity established to aid children whose lives have been wrecked by the war in Bosnia. With him is Sir Paul McCartney, the finale of whose work *Standing Stone*, written to celebrate the Centenary of EMI, was performed as the closing item

October 1977

STOKOWSKI AND THE GRAMOPHONE

Following the death of Leopold Stokowski on Tuesday, September 13th, 1977, Edward Johnson contributed this appreciation of the conductor in the October issue of the magazine. He began by noting that in the last radio programme Stokowski heard, the day before he died, he was described as "the first conductor to take the gramophone seriously"

Leopold Stokowski

Unlike Toscanini and Furtwängler, both of whom disliked recording, Stokowski saw limitless possibilities in recorded music, and in his book *Music for All of Us* (1943) he predicted stereo ("Although records and radio, and their reproduction in the home, are at present monaural, they will undoubtedly be binaural in the future"), the need for noise reduction ("One important step forward is to do away with the scratching noise of the surface of records and all other sounds not part of the music"), and quadraphony ("By having loudspeakers around the walls and on the ceiling, the principles of antiphony can be developed in new directions and brought to new heights").

It is curious that Stokowski's sixty-year discography has so many extraordinary gaps and duplications. Although he recorded the works of well over a hundred composers (on twenty different record labels and with about thirty different orchestras) nowhere is there a complete Mozart symphony, only one (No. 53) of Haydn's, and nothing at all of Bruckner's. He recorded more Bach (in his own transcriptions) than any other composer, with Tchaikovsky and Wagner following more closely behind. He was the only great conductor never to have recorded a complete Beethoven cycle (the record companies having decided, apparently, that he was "not a Beethoven conductor") and it was not until 1974 that he first recorded the *Eroica*.

On the other hand, he recorded many works several times over: eight versions of Stravinsky's *Firebird* Suite (but no modern recording, alas, of the *Rite of Spring*); seven recordings of his own orchestration of Bach's Toccata and Fugue in D minor; six of the *New World* Symphony, and four each of Brahms's First and Schubert's *Unfinished* symphonies. Side by side with this duplication went a number of historic disc premières: Stokowski was the first to record Rachmaninov's Second Piano Concerto and *Paganini* Rhapsody (with the composer at the piano), Schoenberg's *Gurrelieder*, Shostakovich's Symphonies Nos. 1, 5, 6 and 11, Sibelius's Symphony No. 4, and many other recordings of works by American composers, including Charles Ives's Symphony No. 4.

He maintained his passion and feeling for music right to the end of his conducting career which concluded with Bizet's Symphony in C on June 4th, 1977 – his last recording for CBS with the National Philharmonic Orchestra. It will be coupled with his only recording of a Mendelssohn symphony (the *Italian*) which was taped a few days earlier. Had he lived, he would have made his first recording of Rachmaninov's Symphony No. 2 and, later on, a new recording of Beethoven's *Pastoral*.

Despite the frequent accusations that Stokowski lacked a sound musical taste, or that his approach verged on charlatanism, he was nevertheless a genuine musician with a deep love of music and an equal regard for both composer *and* listener. With his championship of the living composer, his achievements in the raising of orchestral standards, and his widespread propagation of classical music, he made a significant contribution to twentieth-century musical life. His vast recorded legacy undoubtedly contains some of the most exciting music-making ever committed to disc and the best of his recordings provide a lasting memorial to the legend of our time.

The event has developed in a typical *Gramophone* style; initially very low-key with minimal changes year-on-year, but carefully implementing all the lessons learnt. The artists honoured must now include virtually every great performer active over the past 20 years, and in 1995/6 there was an additional bonus in a series of most successful Award Winners concerts at the Wigmore Hall. Since 1990 the Awards have been the responsibility of my son, Christopher – who joined the Company in May 1981 – and for 1997 he achieved his goal of bringing the event to television, where it was seen by some 2·5 million viewers.

New layouts and other changes

In June 1974, to meet requests from the government to conserve paper, the review headings were reduced in size and layouts were tightened generally to make the best use of the available space. With some easing of the situation the following year we introduced a number of small line-drawings to caption the various features, similar to those which had decorated the pages in the 1920s and 1930s.

In January 1972 Alec Robertson retired after 48 years devoted service to the magazine. There were tributes from

Raymond Cooke (left – founder of KEF Loudspeakers) with Percy Wilson at The Science Museum in March 1975, seen alongside a vintage acoustic horn reproducer

Sir Compton, who recalled his first meeting with AR in 1922, and from Desmond Shawe-Taylor (to retire himself from the magazine in October 1973 after contributing the Quarterly for 22 years) who wrote in the February issue, "His pen was unstintingly at the service of music and never a vehicle for the parade of his own erudition. His love of music and his generosity of spirit shone through all he wrote and for years he set a standard in BBC music talks that will long be remembered." In June 1972, on his 80th birthday, AR received the MBE for his services to music and he was to enjoy a further nine years' retirement before his death on January 18th, 1982 at the age of 89.

A number of other old contributors died during this period and these included P. G. Hurst (March 1972), C. M. Crabtree (July 1976), Roger Wimbush and Gilbert Wilson (both February 1977), Percy Wilson (May 1977), F. F. Clough (August 1977) and W. R. Anderson (January 1979).

In the early 1970s I felt that the time had come to take a step backwards from my day-to-day involvement with the editorial side of the magazine and in October 1972 I appointed my assistant editor, Malcolm Walker, as Editor. Sheila Saxon, who had joined us in May 1962, was appointed assistant editor and served the Company with distinction in a number of capacities until her retirement in December 1988. Prior to this, in January 1972, Reg Pollard retired after 14 years as Advertisement Manager and he was succeeded by Barry Irving who would manage the department with great success for the next 24 years. Sadly, Reg Pollard's retirement was short-lived and he died the following May whilst swimming on holiday in Malta. In March 1974 Vic Dunbar, the Circulation Manager, also retired.

Sheila Saxon with Robert Layton celebrating *Gramophone*'s Diamond Jubilee on April 8th, 1983

The record industry

The 1970s were by no means static for the record industry. Stereo was fully established and the audio industry had developed a range of equipment, particularly pickup cartridges and carrying arms, which were capable of reproducing the sound more effectively than ever before. However, in a number of quarters an increasing dissatisfaction with the vinyl disc began to manifest itself and for much of the time our correspondence columns could have been fully occupied by readers' complaints about 'snap, crackle and pop'. Understandably, the main targets for

April 1970 **Correspondence**

Why we have stopped buying gramophone records

In spite of correspondence in your pages, and those of your contemporaries, the condition of gramophone records delivered by the suppliers continues to deteriorate.

Off-centre holes, dishing, warping, blisters, scratches and foreign bodies are all common, not to mention the 'snap, crackle and pop' of indeterminate cause. Replacements are as likely to be as bad if not worse than those returned as unsatisfactory. Records broadcast by the BBC have even necessitated apologies from the announcer – and these were recent issues.

Having no wish to acquire collections of records which give no pleasure in the playing, we have decided to stop buying until the situation appears to have improved.

D. A. Thoms
N. R. Wallis
Bristol

Malcolm Walker in 1973

Barry Irving in 1973

May 1975 **Correspondence**

MORE MISTAKES

I may perhaps have missed a previous discussion on my favourite misprint/mistranslation on a record sleeve. In case you haven't seen it, here it is. Westminster Gold 8219, Bartók: *Bluebeard's Castle*, has a reference to other works by Bartók in the sleeve-notes in which the author mentions the particularly popular suite from *The Wonderful Tangerine*.

Another recent ABC (formerly Westminster here in the States) release of reissued highlights of Beverly Sills's complete opera recordings has on the front and rear cover, "Beverly Sills: The Mad Scenes". But the spine reads, "Sills: The Mad Sills"!

Alison Ames
Classical Publicity Director, Polydor Inc,
New York, USA

John Borwick at a Press Conference in Japan in April 1976

attack were the large British manufacturing plants and whilst there was no doubt that they were suffering from the effects of the various industrial disputes (EMI at Hayes proposed to establish a bank of 'classical-only' presses but this was vetoed by the Unions), it was also clear that the vogue for thinner discs, and a number of cost-saving measures, were taking their toll. In all probability the retail price of records should have been increased to a greater degree than was the case, with additional resources being allocated to capital investment in terms of record presses, etc. but with the existing level of inflation there was understandably little enthusiasm for this line of approach – particularly as the majority of complaints were undoubtedly coming from the classical sector which only represented eight or nine per cent of the total sales.

None the less, the debate continued to resound in the magazine's pages and in 1978 John Borwick conducted a reader poll in an effort to obtain some measure of the problem. For quite a number of buyers the answer was to switch to cassettes – a compromise, as the ultimate quality was by no means as good as that obtainable from the disc, but of course there was an absence of 'snap, crackle and pop'! Ironically, in driving buyers towards the cassette the Industry damaged itself by increasing the number of people who, having cassette recorders, were now able to indulge in various forms of home-taping.

However, events were to overtake the situation for whilst the majors sought a palliative by pressing their classical records on the continent, and techniques such as Direct Metal Mastering (DMM) were introduced, a major new development was already in the wings.

Quadraphony and Video

Before we come to that major development I must mention quadraphony. This began to rear its head as early as 1970 and rumbled on until the latter part of the decade. The first quadraphonic discs were released in the UK in March 1972 but as far as record buyers were concerned this was a non-event. They were offered records based on three different non-compatible systems – EMI and CBS using SQ, RCA using CD-4, and Pye and a number of other small labels using QS. Decca, Deutsche Grammophon and Philips did not get involved.

Apart from the problem of compatibility, the average record buyer could see no real need for four-channel sound, even assuming the ability to accommodate four loudspeakers (which then were generally much larger than they are today). Beyond this a number of classical producers with whom I spoke at the time felt no need for an additional two channels and in truth didn't really know what to do with them if they had them – a famous Bernstein recording at Abbey Road had the orchestra in a circle around the conductor!

Why, one may reasonably ask, was the system ever launched? From a visit to Japan in 1972 I concluded that the idea was promoted by their electronic industry who

A Japanese CD-4 import, originating from the Victor Company (JVC), and reviewed by John Borwick in May 1973

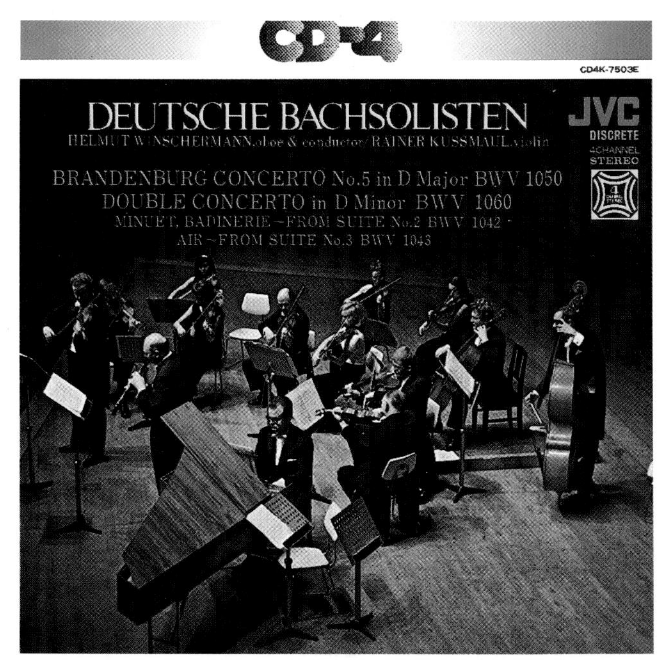

In September 1972 the Japanese convened an international conference in Tokyo to promote quadraphony. The British contingent consisted of Dr Keith Barker (left, Sheffield University), Anthony Pollard and Denys Killick (***Gramophone*** contributor)

recognized a need to keep the production lines flowing and saw quadraphony as the answer.

The 1970s also saw the development of the video tape recorder and the video disc, but the subject is not directly germane to these reminiscences except to note that as early as September and December 1970, John Culshaw and Humphrey Burton were debating the problems of accommodating classical music in the video context – a debate which still continues over 25 years later.

Digital arrives

The application of digital recording techniques to the record industry was an innovation of the 1970s. Using a pulse code modulation (PCM) machine, Denon in Japan made the first commercial digital record in October 1972 but this was not developed further in commercial terms until Decca's Sylvia Sass recording in July 1978, followed by their highly successful "New Year's Day Concert" from Vienna in January 1979. Then EMI produced their famous André Previn Award-winning recording of Debussy's *Images* and *Prélude à l'après-midi d'un faune* in June 1979 and the digital recording revolution was well underway.

However, the major signal came from Philips in Eindhoven and was contained in an announcement reported by John Borwick in the June 1978 issue. "The clouds of speculation about a new medium for sound recording and reproduction have just been pierced by an announcement from Philips Industries. On May 17th, 1978 they despatched a statement describing their revolutionary Compact Disc. This is a plastic disc measuring only 110mm (4·5 ins.) in diameter which will carry up to one hour of music on its single side. The programme is recorded digitally using the well proved PCM encoding system. The player will have a diode laser mounted in the pickup arm to scan the recorded signals optically instead of mechanically. Philips are forecasting that players and disc records will be available in the early 1980s at a price comparable with that of a good hi-fi player. It would be a great pity if this 'quantum leap' in audio standards were spoilt by the emergence of several conflicting, incompatible digital discs. We regard this Philips announcement as a momentous trail-blazer."

On March 8th of the following year I was invited to Eindhoven for the first press demonstration of the Compact Disc (combined with the launch of a new magnetic tape formulation!), an event of the utmost significance. From the outset I believed that Compact Disc was the ideal carrier for classical music and the demonstration only confirmed my thinking. The product was still in its early stages of development and the small player which stood in the centre of a table, covered with a green baize cloth, contained little more than the disc transport mechanism. Beneath the table, concealed from view, were several large boxes of electronics which would have to be developed and miniaturized before any further progress could be made. Ironically, the records used by Philips in the demonstration were all analogue recordings – at this stage their engineers had no original digital recordings available. Even so, the sound of excerpts from Colin Davis's *Tosca* left me in no doubt of the wonders to come.

A 1979 mock-up of the original concept of the packaging for Compact Disc, following closely the style of the gate-fold cardboard LP sleeve

Philips still had many problems to solve and an announcement dated October 8th, 1979 reported an agreement between themselves and Sony for the exchange of patent rights over a range of items including optical audio and video disc technology. The agreement was significant in that it indicated a move towards achieving interchangeability and a world standard. Hopefully, the lessons of quadraphony had been learnt.

Industry personalities

As new directions for the Industry unfolded so familiar names came and went. David Bicknell, who had joined The Gramophone Company in 1927 as an assistant to Fred Gaisberg, retired as Manager of EMI's International

July 1975

GODDARD LIEBERSON

One of the American record industry's major figures, who spanned a 36-year period from 1939 to 1975, was Goddard Lieberson. An interview which he gave to Alan Blyth, some months before his retirement in March 1975 as President of the CBS Records Group, is reprinted below. His memo to Bob Altshuler, Director of Publicity, is not without interest, as also is John Culshaw's tribute which followed his early death in May 1977

Goddard Lieberson talks to Alan Blyth

Goddard Lieberson *Photo Sony*

I knew when I went to see Goddard Lieberson, retiring President of the CBS Records Group, I was going to meet a piece of musical history, so in a sense I was surprised to meet such a dapper, youthful man, about as far removed as can be from an ageing, or *passé* executive. Yet Lieberson is old enough to have worked with Bartók, to have known Schoenberg and Ives, and what is even more important to have got some of their music on to record when anyone else in the business would have said that that way lay commercial suicide.

Lieberson is in fact English by birth – he comes from Hanley in Staffordshire – though in appearance, in aplomb you would guess that his upbringing was American. And you would be right. In fact, he went to the States as a boy and undertook his musical training at the University of Washington (the State not DC) and the Eastman School of Music at Rochester. He wanted to be a composer and looked all set to be one when he was caught by the record industry, but he is still proud of the fact that "I am the only person to attain my present status who started off as a serious musician".

He was interested in jazz just before the war and it was through a jazz convention – "Spirituals to Swing" in Carnegie Hall, 1939-40 – that he was persuaded by a friend [John Hammond] to join CBS. He began as an assistant to the director of the Masterworks Division, soon becoming director himself, graduating to executive vice-president in 1949, and to president in 1956. As he graphically points out, "Thirty years ago, the retail turnover was about 48 million dollars, today it's a 1·5 billion dollar business". But Lieberson is as interested in the music as much as the money – and the serious music at that, always realizing that a Streisand must be balanced by a Stravinsky.

In his early years he much preferred working with Bartók than Schoenberg, whom he described as "a very difficult man. If I didn't do anything for him, he complained that he was being neglected. But if I did try to help him, he took it as his due and gave me no thanks. Perhaps he was justifiably embittered because of all those years when he was absolutely ignored. We recorded *Pierrot Lunaire* under his supervision in California with a group that had just done a public performance in New York.

Alan Blyth

"Bartók I admired as much as a man as a musician. He was very dear to me, and I was connected with him right up to his death. I admired him for standing out against the Germans and Italians even when he had no need to. We recorded *Mikrokosmos* together, also *Contrasts* with the composer, Benny Goodman and Szigeti. In those days – that is just before the war – it was a little risky, or considered so, to record Ravel, so you can imagine how revolutionary it was to put Schoenberg and Bartók on disc. Personally, Bartók was quite charming and down-to-earth, as keen to tell a dirty story as talk about Wittgenstein's theories. Another work we did together was the Third Piano Concerto; in fact György Sandor learnt the piece in my apartment."

I asked him how long he had known Stravinsky. "I knew and worked with Stravinsky for nearly thirty years. At a certain period in his career he faced the terrible irony of deriving no income from his most popular pieces. From that period on, except for a very short interval, CBS Records continued a programme to record the entire *oeuvre* of Stravinsky as interpreted by him with the inestimable assistance of Robert Craft. I remade all the early great works with him so that he could derive some remuneration from these world-famous pieces which had gone into public domain."

Lieberson wrote an article on Ives as early as 1937. "At that time he was unknown except to other composers. I met him two or three times and recall that he was a generous, charming old man who talked rather a lot. There was no copyright in his music – it was simply available to anyone who'd perform it. He didn't care about the money because of what he had made in insurance. He was a real New England intellectual, rooted in Emerson and the like. You know, we made the first-ever record of his *Concord* Sonata."

CBS MEMORANDUM

FROM: Goddard Lieberson
TO: BOB ALTSHULER
DATE: May 17, 1974

Thanks for letting me see the proof of Alan Blythe's article. I must say Blythe has done one of the best, if not the best, pieces on me that I have seen. However, it's no less than what I would expect from the Gramophone, where their distinction of opinion is equalled by their distinction in writing.

Now, with my usual run of luck, this is, of course, the one article on me that is not appearing!

Then Lieberson returned to discussing Bartók, particularly in connection with him as an interpreter of his own music. "He was very calm, very calm as compared with Schoenberg when it came to the studio, and he took his music slower than it is marked. I think all composers tend to take their own music slowly in performance in order to explain it, if you see what I mean. Conductors, on the other hand, like excitement so they tend to take things too fast."

Of present day trends in America he commented: "Today the emphasis there seems to be towards avant-garde music, away from the heavy romantics. The music from Beethoven onwards to the end of the nineteenth century is not doing so well, and it's no accident I think, that a modern composer like Boulez who has turned conductor is making the running in the projection of the new music. I think we are at a critical moment of changing tastes, but I don't know how radical it is or whether old composers will eventually be forgotten".

He said that Britain was "one of the last bastions of the concert hall" and lamented the passing, as he saw it, of the Lieder recital. "After all, no songs are being written of any consequence to carry on the tradition. The last composer who is performed today in this field is, I suppose, Poulenc. Without a new literature it may die as an art form. To be replaced by what? The key to the whole of the future, of course, is the immense growth in population and the changing social structures. What the young people will go for is anybody's guess".

We moved on to the discussion of opera. "There you have the problem of maintaining a roster of singers, either as an opera house or a record company. So many so-called opera-lovers are no better than bull-fight lovers watching the latest matador. They want Caballé or Sutherland, or whoever's the latest star and never mind what the opera may be. It's a sort of half-world of music to me, a big sale based on names alone. As far as our company is concerned we are proud to have been the first to record *Wozzeck* and *The Rake's Progress*, proud to have done a *Pelléas* that is an integrated, fully rehearsed performance drawn from the opera house".

Back to the old days, reminiscences of his own time at the controls recording Adolf Busch, Serkin, Walter, Mitropoulos, the Budapest, the excitement of doing the *Hammerklavier* with Petri. "I think our relationship then was closer with the artists and there was inevitably more sense of excitement that we were doing something new; today everybody tends to be rather *blasé*. Besides, as techniques have advanced – and it was bound to happen – the engineer has inevitably become more important. Also, we are all aiming at mistake-free performances, which is ridiculous when you come to think of it. Is it more soulless, more cut-and-dried? I don't know, but I suppose something has been lost in spite of all the gains along the way. Personally, over the years I've missed being away from the creative side of the business, though I try to make my job as creative as possible, and a record business like any other is bound to express the personality of the man who runs it".

A Lieberson interview is far from being formal or cut-and-dried. A bizarre phone call from a friend, the interviewee lounging elegantly in his London suite (Claridges, of course), a sense of material as well as spiritual well-being are its possible appurtenances. But when he wants it to end, as other interviewers have testified, he makes sure you know, though in the politest, most gracious way. And that's not inappropriate to an executive whose incoming correspondence often begins 'Dear God'.

Goddard Lieberson died at the age of 66 on May 29th, 1977. John Culshaw contributed an obituary to the July 1977 issue

What brought his name unforgettably into my life was his 1951 recording of *Porgy and Bess*. For the first time that I could remember a record producer was accredited on the album, which would have mattered little if the result had not been so spectacular. Here at last was someone working in studio conditions and yet producing something that was bursting with theatrical atmosphere.

Nothing I can write can better his own statement in his notes accompanying *Porgy*: "I decided from the outset that *Porgy and Bess*, to be completely effective on records, must include not only the sounds of the music but the sounds of the drama – such sounds as a crap game, a fight, or footsteps, etc. – the theory being that throughout, the sound effects were to substitute for those stage actions that, when seen in the theatre, add tension to the poignant story that unfolds before us". In less than a decade such practices were commonplace, and all that had to be decided was whether they were well or badly handled; but in 1951 they were revolutionary, and Lieberson's *Porgy* (which was a mono recording) still seems to me to have more theatrical intensity than any of its rivals.

Lieberson's rapid promotion up the administrative ladder limited his studio work, but did not prevent him from producing some brilliant albums of musicals, including *My Fair Lady*, *South Pacific*, *West Side Story* and, more recently, *A Little Night Music*. He may have been a classical musician by training, but he was no snob. He was a formidable, almost an aristocratic character with a healthy scepticism towards anything that had been inadequately researched. I remember a lunch many years ago in his New York office when he talked enthrallingly about the early days of LP (in which he had always believed, artistically and commercially), and the current, wildcat predictions about pre-recorded video, in which he had no faith at all. That was more than ten years ago, and time so far has shown him to be right; but then Goddard Lieberson usually was right. He could be curt about something that did not appeal to him, but his enthusiasms were infectious. He will be sadly missed by his many friends all over the world.

[*Porgy and Bess* was originally issued as a mono LP (Philips, 5/55) and later reissued in "rechannelled" stereo (CBS, 9/69)]

The Grosvenor House in London, on August 31st, 1971, was the venue for a farewell luncheon to David Bicknell (left), seen with Victoria de los Angeles and his successor, Peter Andry *Photo EMI*

Artists Department in August 1971 after 44 years with the company. During this time, in addition to his role as a record producer, he acted as the Industry's principal negotiator with the Musicians' Union, establishing working arrangements for classical recording sessions in the UK which are still respected to this day. He was succeeded by Peter Andry, who had joined Decca in February 1954 and then moved to EMI in June 1956 with Victor Olof. Andry was also a most successful record producer but ultimately his greatest contribution was in adapting the framework of the EMI Artists Department to meet the increasingly stringent demands of the company and the changing nature of the classical business itself. Later, for Ramon Lopez, he was instrumental in establishing Warner Classics. Victor Olof, originally a professional musician and orchestral manager, was a successful producer for Decca and then for EMI: he was responsible for many of their major recordings in the post-war period and he retired from EMI in July 1963, although he continued to produce for the company in a freelance capacity until June 1969 (he died on November 3rd, 1974).

Sir Joseph Lockwood *Photo EMI*

In November 1974 Sir Joseph Lockwood retired as Chairman of EMI. From 1954 he had substantially reorganized the company, disposing of many loss-making operations and developing EMI's record business internationally in order to take full advantage of an increasingly impressive roster of artists. During his 20 years in office the company moved from a reputed annual loss of £500,000 to pre-tax profits in excess of £35m on a turnover of some £400m. He died on March 6th, 1991 at the age of 86.

The ultimate direction of Decca's post-war classical recording programme was for many years in the hands of Sir Edward Lewis's co-director, Maurice Rosengarten. Operating from Zurich and rarely seen publicly in classical music circles, he worked directly with Decca's classical recording managers – Harry Sarton, Victor Olof, John Culshaw and Ray Minshull. He died, very much in harness,

Maurice Rosengarten *Photo Decca*

on November 5th, 1975. Sir Edward said, "I cannot estimate the loss both as a friend and as a business colleague. He was a really great man", whilst Ray Minshull commented, "all the artists loved him, however hard may have been negotiations over terms – and there can be no doubt that he had one of the most brilliant and acute minds when it came to the negotiating table". One of his artists was Hans Schmidt-Isserstedt whose son, Erik Smith, had joined Decca in January 1957, ultimately producing more than 25 operas for the label, in addition to editing and recording all Mozart's wind music. Following John Culshaw's departure from Decca in 1967 he transferred to Philips in January 1969 where his first major project was Colin Davis's recording of *The Trojans*.

In September 1949, whilst working in America, I was fortunate enough to meet Goddard Lieberson. He was then head of the CBS Masterworks Division, which he had joined in 1939, and would eventually become President of the CBS Records Group, retiring in March 1975 after 36 years with the company. He was a record man to his fingertips with repertoire and artist interests having no boundaries. He worked with Bartók, Schoenberg and Stravinsky, and as early as 1937 was writing about Charles Ives, eventually making the first recording of his *Concord* Sonata, whilst in 1949 he led the Industry in recording plays, beginning with Paul Robeson in *Othello*. Later he invested in Broadway and produced famous recordings such as *My Fair Lady* and *South Pacific*. John Culshaw said that Lieberson's 1951 mono recording of *Porgy and Bess* was one of the most effective recordings he had ever heard "bursting with theatrical atmosphere" and it was later to influence much of his thinking when producing opera recordings. Lieberson died on May 29th, 1977, just a few months before his old colleague, Dr Peter Goldmark, who was involved in the development of the long-playing record in the late 1940s and who was to die in a road accident on December 7th, 1977.

The toll was not complete, for the decade was to see the passing of two other names who, in their respective areas,

Erik Smith (left) with Sir Michael Tippett and Colin (later Sir Colin) Davis at the recording sessions for *A Midsummer Marriage* at Walthamstow in July 1970 *Photo Philips*

Walter Legge (left) with Wolfgang Sawallisch during a playback at the *Capriccio* sessions (Kingsway Hall, September 1957)

had made substantial contributions to the record industry. The first was Walter Legge, of whom I have already written. After leaving EMI in June 1964 one felt that his enormous talent must surely be taken up by another record company, but that was not to be and as far as the record industry was concerned he was only to supervise a few recordings by his wife, Elisabeth Schwarzkopf, made for Decca and EMI. Perhaps he was too big a personality for the Industry as it was now developing? He died on March 22nd, 1979 leaving a legacy of some of the finest classical recordings ever to have been made.

Whereas Legge's name will remain, that of Anna Instone might well be overlooked – although that would have been impossible in her lifetime. She joined the BBC from the Guildhall School of Music in 1933 and was later to become Head of Gramophone Programmes, a post which she held with consummate success for 25 years. A daughter of Sir Samuel Instone, founder of Instone Airways (later to become Imperial Airways and eventually British Airways) she led something of a flamboyant life in her early days and for many years was the only woman to head a department in the BBC. She established the Gramophone Library and was responsible for all programmes using gramophone records, both classical and popular. For readers of **Gramophone** her founding of the Third Programme *Record Review* and editing for nearly 30 years the BBC's Sunday-morning *Music Magazine*, must surely say it all. Beyond this she formed a vital and understanding link between the BBC and the British record industry. She died on April 22nd, 1978.

Company for sale?

I suppose it was to be expected that over the years there would be offers to buy the Company, as there were occasional efforts to sell it. Compton Mackenzie toyed with this possibility more than once in the 1920s when the future of the Company looked very insecure but an incident in the late-1940s gave much concern to his co-Directors. In 1946-7 Mackenzie, still a major shareholder in the Company, was travelling on behalf of the Indian Government in the Middle-East, India, Burma, Malaya and Hong Kong preparing a history of India's contribution to victory in the Second World War, a journey of some 50,000 miles: given the problems of communication in those days he had provided an irrevocable power of attorney to his legal adviser. This manifested itself one weekend at Stanmore Golf Club, in north-west London, when my father, preparing to tee-off on the first hole, was confronted by one of his friends (a director of Odhams Press) who said, "Cecil, I hear your Company is for sale".

Anna Instone, Nicholas Boyle (EMI Classical Department and then Press Officer, Royal Festival Hall) and Anthony Pollard at a Music for Pleasure reception in 1965

What better way to ensure a muffed drive! Fortunately, with the help of Christopher Stone, who was as ignorant as my father as to what was going on, the matter was delayed until Mackenzie's return when the whole idea was quietly scotched.

However, after that there were any number of interesting offers made for the Company, in particular by Associated Iliffe Press (then publishers of *Autocar*, *Flight*, *Amateur Photographer* and a host of other titles) after they had purchased our printers in 1956; and then later by Cecil King, Chairman of the International Publishing Corporation who told me at a meeting in his office that he was anxious to buy two titles, ***The Gramophone*** and *Radio Times*. Respect for this giant of the publishing world prevented me from wishing him better luck with *Radio Times*!

Mention of *Radio Times* reminds me that in January 1987 my son and I were approached by the BBC to come to an arrangement whereby the BBC publication *Listener* and **Gramophone** would be operated under the same aegis. In the case of the earlier Iliffe offer my father suggested that the decision was really mine, and now I was to do the same with Christopher. As we walked away from their offices in Marylebone High Street we both recognized that, even though the BBC had had an abortive alliance with IPC in respect of *3 Magazine* (launched September 1982, closed April 1984), our rejection of their proposal would not be the end of the story! There were also discussions with Haymarket Publishing when the advantages of working under the wing of a much larger organization were recognized, but ultimately it was our belief that we should still retain our independence – an idealistic view, perhaps, and one which requires constant review in the light of the ever-changing economic climate.

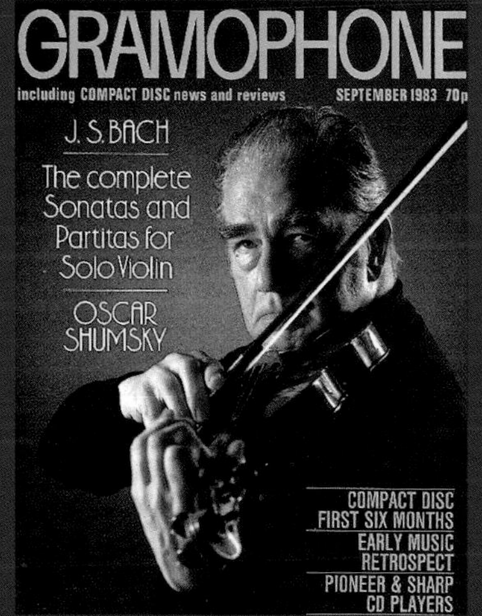

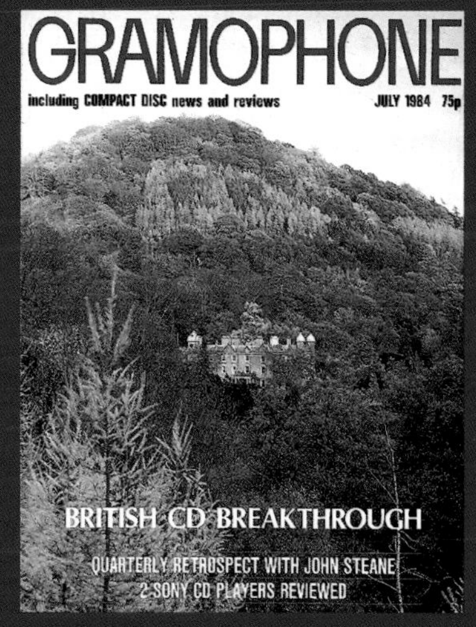

The Compact Disc

1980-1989

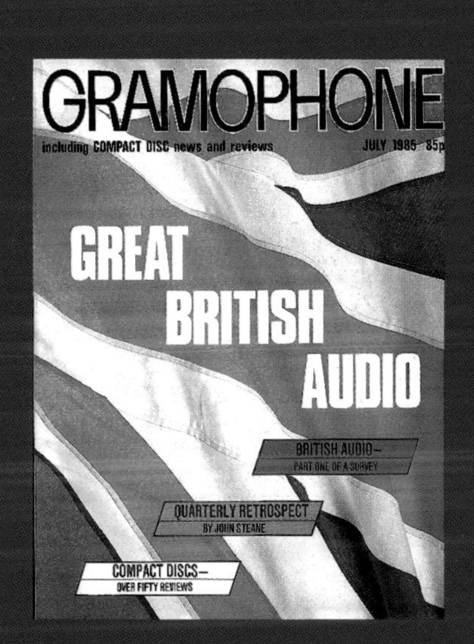

A *Gramophone* chronology

1980-1989

1980

January

- Malcolm Walker stands down as Editor of ***G*** due to ill health. Anthony Pollard returns to the editorial chair.
- The Decca Record Company acquired by PolyGram.
- Sir Edward Lewis, founder of Decca, dies at the age of 79.
- Reinhard Klaassen is made President of the new Decca/PolyGram company with Ray Minshull also appointed to the Board.

March

- W. W. Townsley retires from Decca after 54 years' service.
- Gunter Hensler appointed President of PolyGram Classics USA.

April

- Death of John Culshaw, aged 55.

May

- Ramon Lopez leaves EMI and joins PolyGram UK as MD. He is succeeded as UK EMI Records MD by John Bush.
- Kenneth Wilkinson retires from Decca after 49 years' service.

June

- Sony "Walkman" launched in UK, initially under the name "Stowaway".
- Cliff Busby succeeds John Bush as MD of EMI Records UK.

July

- The record industry abolishes recommended retail prices.

September

- L. G. Wood retires from EMI after 51 years' service.
- Formation of Classics International in the UK to represent DG and Philips. Peter Russell to be the General Manager.

October

- First releases from Ted Perry's Hyperion label.

November

- C. H. Thomas dies.
- Decca close their West Hampstead studios and establish a Recording Centre in Kilburn.

Gunter Hensler
Photo PolyGram

Kenneth "Wilkie" Wilkinson, Decca's Senior Recording Engineer, retires after 49 years' service. Celebrating the occasion, Sir Georg Solti (left) and Sir Clifford Curzon (right) *Photo Decca*

1981

February

- Paul Voigt, audio engineer, dies aged 80.

March

- First releases from Academy Sound and Vision (ASV) founded by Harley Usill, Jack Boyce and David Gyle-Thompson.

Harley Usill (left) and Jack Boyce at the presentation of the *Gramophone* Awards in February 1978

April

- Gimell Records founded by Peter Phillips and Steve Smith.
- Compact Disc conference is held in Salzburg.

May

- Christopher Pollard joins ***G***.

September

- Jan D. Timmer appointed Executive Vice-President, PolyGram International.

1982

January

- Alec Robertson dies aged 89.

March

- Capriccio label founded in Germany by Winfried Amel.

June

- DAT Conference in Japan sets standards for both stationary-head (S-DAT) and rotary-head (R-DAT) digital audio tape recorders.
- Direct Metal Mastering – DMM – introduced by Teldec.

Dr Winfried Amel
Photo Capriccio

August

- Europe's first Compact Disc manufacturing plant opened by PolyGram in Hanover.

September

- Gunther Breest succeeds Hans Hirsch as DG's A&R Director.

October

- Compact Disc system launched in Japan.

1983

January

- Jan D. Timmer becomes President and CEO of PolyGram International, David G. Fine becomes Executive V-P.
- Tim Harrold becomes Chairman, PolyGram Classics International (Decca, DG and Philips).

Tim Harrold (left) with Francisco Araiza at the 1988 Salzburg Summer Festival *Photo Philips*

- Ramon Lopez becomes President and CEO, PolyGram UK.
- Johannes H. Kinzl succeeds Ernst Th. van der Vossen as President, Philips Classics.

Johannes H. Kinzl (left) with Riccardo Muti in 1988
Photo Philips

- EMI licenced to use DMM technique for LP manufacture.

February
- Bob Fine, responsible for Mercury classical recordings, dies aged 60.

March
- Compact Disc system launched in UK.
- Peter Jamieson succeeds Cliff Busby as MD, EMI Records UK.
- Marco Polo Records founded in Hong Kong by Klaus Heymann.

April
- British Institute of Recorded Sound becomes the National Sound Archive, part of The British Library.

June
- Working groups established to consider viability of consumer digital tape medium.

September
- Compact Disc system launched in USA.
- EMI Eminence label launched.

1984

January
- DG record Puccini's *Manon Lescaut* in the final Kingsway Hall sessions.
- MIDEM Classique re-established.

March
- Sir Richard Cave retires from the Board of Thorn EMI.

April
- John Pattrick, General Manager of EMI Records UK Classical Division, moves to a similar post with Angel Records in Los Angeles and is succeeded by Simon Foster, who comes from the EMI Eminence label.

May
- Brown Meggs becomes President of Angel Records in the USA.
- Peter Andry becomes President of EMI International Classical Division.

June
- Christopher Pollard succeeds Quita Chavez as Editorial Manager of ***G***.
- Nimbus Records open first Compact Disc manufacturing plant in UK.

Brown Meggs
Photo Capitol

July
- RCA Records merge with Ariola to form RCA-Ariola. RCA owns 75 per cent, Bertlesmann 25 per cent.

November
- W. A. Chislett dies aged 89.

1985

January
- The BBC close the last of their 405-line TV transmitters, in use since November 1936 and superseded in 1969 by the UHF 625-line colour transmitters.

February
- James Jolly joins ***G*** as Assistant Editor.

April
- Colin (later Sir Colin) Southgate becomes MD of Thorn EMI.
- Ramon Lopez leaves PolyGram UK to join WEA.

Ramon Lopez (left) with Anthony Pollard and Maurice Oberstein (1979)

July
- Maurice Oberstein leaves CBS to become Chairman of PolyGram UK.

September
- Introduction of Philips LaserVision

December
- RCA Corporation sold to GE and with it the record division.
- George Fenwick, manager of EMI's 363 Oxford Street showrooms from 1935-61, dies aged 88. Fenwick joined HMV in 1911.

1986

January
- Andreas Holschneider appointed President of Polydor International.

February
- Ivor Humphreys joins ***G***.
- Chesky Records founded by Norman and David Chesky.

Andreas Holschneider (left) with Claudio Abbado *Photo DG*

March
- Nimbus close their LP manufacturing facility.

April
- Christopher Pollard succeeds Anthony Pollard as Editor of ***G***.
- Rupert Perry appointed MD, EMI Records UK and Eire in succession to Peter Jamieson.

May
- EMI open Swindon CD manufacturing plant.
- RPO Records is launched and distributed by ASV.

June
- *The Sunday Times* suggest DAT will offer a serious challenge to CD.

September
- RCA establish International Classical Division to embrace Red Seal, Eurodisc and associated labels.

December
- Bertlesmann acquire 100 per cent of RCA-Ariola and form BMG, the Bertlesmann Music Group.

1987

January
- George R. Marek, A&R Director of RCA from 1950-72, dies.

March
- Philips, Philips and Du Pont Optical, and PolyGram demonstrate the CD-Video system in Amsterdam.
- Reinhard Klaassen retires as President of Decca International and is succeeded by Roland Kommerell.

April
- PolyGram become wholly owned subsidiary of NV Philips Gloeilampenfabrieken.
- PolyGram launch medium-priced CDs.

Roland Kommerell

May

- Naxos Records founded in Hong Kong by Klaus Heymann.
- R-DAT digital audio tape recorders are launched in Japan.

Klaus Heymann *Photo Naxos*

July

- First pre-recorded DAT cassettes appear on the Capriccio label.
- Arabesque Recordings are formed in New York by Marvin M. Reiss and Ward Botsford.
- Olympia Records, founded by Distec Ltd. and Francis Wilson, are launched.

September

- BMG Classics are established.
- BBC introduce RDS (Radio Data Service) broadcasting.
- Ramon Lopez succeeds Nesuhi Ertegun as Chairman and CEO of WEA International.
- Jan D. Timmer returns to Philips in Eindhoven and is succeeded as President of PolyGram International by David G. Fine.

October

- Sony launch R-DAT digital tape recorders in Europe.

December

- First edition of the *Gramophone Good CD Guide*.
- John Bowers of B&W Loudspeakers dies.

1988

January

- Sony acquire CBS Records and Norio Ohga becomes President and CEO.

- John Pattrick returns from Angel to be Marketing Director, EMI International Classical Division.

April

- Ivor Humphreys succeeds John Borwick as Audio Editor of ***G***: John Borwick becomes Audio Director.
- Virgin Classics launched by Richard Branson, with Simon Foster as MD.

May

- James Fifield appointed President of EMI Music.

John Pattrick (left), Christopher Pollard and James Fifield *Photo EMI*

August

- George Mendelssohn, founder of Vox Records, dies aged 75.

September

- Death of David Bicknell, former manager of EMI International Artists Dept, aged 82. He joined The Gramophone Company in 1927.
- Colin (later Sir Colin) Southgate succeeds Sir Graham Wilkins as President and CEO of Thorn EMI.
- Chandos Records release a limited amount of repertoire on DAT.

October

- Philips launch CD-V.
- Dorian Recordings, founded in Troy, NY by Craig Dory and Brian Levine.

November

- Gunther Breest leaves DG and is appointed MD, CBS Masterworks. He is succeeded by Aman Pedersen as DG A&R Director.

December

- Andreas Holschneider appointed President of DG.

1989

February

- First releases from Collins Classics.
- Taiyo Yuden announce CD-R recordable CD.

March

- Peter Andry retires from EMI and is succeeded by Richard Lyttelton who first joined EMI in 1966.

Norio Ohga (right) on December 3rd, 1981 with Peter Andry. Ohga (a singer who had studied with Gerhard Hüsch) was at the time Deputy President of the Sony Corporation and he had brought a new Sony multi-track digital machine to Berlin for EMI's recording of *Der fliegende Holländer* with Karajan. Andry reported that the machine "was a marvel of science and it behaves simply splendidly"

- Gunter Hensler appointed President, BMG Classics in succession to Michael Emmerson.

May

- Peter Andry joins WEA – later Warner Classics International – as Senior V-P Classical Repertoire.
- Richard Lyttelton becomes President of EMI Classics.
- Peter Alward (joined EMI 1970) appointed V-P A&R, EMI Classics.
- Ken East retires from EMI.

June

- Industry agrees on SCMS (Serial Copy Management System) to legalize consumer digital recorders.

August

- Harold Leak, audio manufacturer, dies.

December

- Arthur Haddy, late Technical Director of Decca, dies aged 84.

Richard Lyttelton *Photo EMI*

Peter Alward *Photo EMI*

Arthur Haddy

The Compact Disc

Calmer waters for EMI and Decca

Seen from outside there were no obvious signs of the revised status of EMI and Decca, and such changes as might be deemed necessary by the new management teams were not implemented overnight. For EMI there were no conflicting music business interests in Thorn, but the financial gurus found difficulty in accepting that the purchase of EMI was anything but a short-term initiative and as a result there were recurrent rumours of a likely sale. The fact that nearly 20 years later a much enhanced music business still remains says much for Sir Colin Southgate's overall management of the company.

For Decca the situation was very different. The label was joining the PolyGram Group and would have to sit alongside two other classical companies – Deutsche Grammophon and Philips – both of whose cultures and backgrounds were quite different from Decca's.

Reinhard Klaassen (left) makes a presentation to Ray Minshull on the occasion of his 25th Anniversary with Decca (October 7th, 1982). The ladies are unidentified, but in the background is producer Chris Hazell *Photo Minshull*

Sir Colin Southgate, Chairman of Thorn EMI *Photo EMI*

Sir Edward Lewis had been consulted about the company's future management before his death and it was agreed that Reinhard Klaassen should be appointed as President – a particularly happy choice in that he had been Decca's distributor in Holland for many years and as such knew the label and its staff exceedingly well. He was supported by Ray Minshull, Decca's Classical A&R Director who had joined the company in 1957, and between them they ensured that in line with PolyGram's overall philosophy the character of the label was preserved.

The run-up to CD

The Philips CD player demonstrated at Eindhoven in March 1979 *Photo Philips*

The UK launch of LP in June 1950 was heralded by virtually no prior announcements, and similarly the advent of the stereo LP in May 1958 came as a surprise to the majority. However, as we have seen, the development of the laser-read Compact Disc was well documented and whilst there were alternative systems which gained some publicity – from Teldec, RCA and JVC – the Philips/Sony project soon emerged as the system of the future.

Following the initial low-key press briefing in March 1979, a major press conference was convened in Salzburg on April 15th, 1981, concurrent with the Easter Festival and also, as it happened, my annual golfing week at St Andrew's in Scotland. A few days before I was due to depart, Peter Russell (then General Manager of PolyGram's Classics International, representing Deutsche Grammophon and Philips in the UK) asked me to join the UK party in Salzburg. Needless to say, it fell right in the middle of my golf week but amazingly I missed only one day's play. Leaving St Andrew's on the Tuesday evening I flew down to London Heathrow and at 6·30am the next morning joined Peter Russell and several others in

S A L Z B U R G

During the 1970s and 1980s the Salzburg Festival became associated with a number of the classical record companies – initially Deutsche Grammophon and EMI, and then followed by Philips and Decca, with Sony coming in the late 1980s. Principally this related to the Summer Festival when press offices and hospitality suites were the norm, and virtually every shop window in the city tastefully displayed one or another record company's publicity material for an artist who would be featured in the Festival, with even the city's taxis providing mobile advertisement sites.

The driving force behind so much of this activity was Herbert von Karajan, who had been born in Salzburg and was the most influential member of the five-man Board of Directors until his resignation in 1988, one year before his death.

For many years performances at the Summer Festival promoted Karajan's latest recordings and in 1981 he used the backdrop of the Easter Festival to host an international press conference designed to accelerate the development and launch of the Compact Disc.

The invitation to Karajan's Sony/PolyGram press conference in Salzburg, Easter 1981

DG provided for Salzburg's capricious weather with their yellow complimentary shower coats, seen here being modelled by Peter Russell (left) and Bill Holland

Salzburg, summer 1988 – a vocal quartet with, from the left, Peter Russell (DG), Aman Pedersen (DG), Christopher Pollard (G) and Peter Czornyj (DG/Archiv)

Mitsuko Uchida arrives at Salzburg Airport, July 1989 *Photo Philips*

a private jet bound for Salzburg. Immediately after the conference it was back to Heathrow and then straight on to a scheduled flight for Edinburgh in readiness for the first tee the next morning. The conference gathered some 200 editors and journalists from all over Europe and was addressed by Akio Morita (Chairman of Sony), Joop van Tilburg (Senior Managing Director, Audio Division, Philips), Richard Busch (Deputy President, PolyGram Record Operations) and Herbert von Karajan who said that he had first been intrigued by the potential of digital sound when he had been in Japan in 1977 and visited Mr Morita's home, hearing a PCM recording of one of his own performances which had impressed him in terms of its overall quality. He previewed the release of CD with the now famous line, "Everything else is gaslight".

The conference was intended to show that Philips/Sony meant business, although it was still stated that the system would not be ready until the end of 1982. Compact Disc

David Fine (CEO, PolyGram UK, right) at the *Gramophone* Awards 1984 with his company's award winners. From the left – Bill Holland (DG), Lady Judy Mackerras, Peter Russell (PolyGram Classics), Jessye Norman and Hans Kinzl

players would come in the main from Japan, although Philips would manufacture theirs in Europe: pressing plants for the discs would initially be PolyGram in Hanover and two much smaller units in Japan – CBS/Sony and Technics. However, it did seem that as D-Day approached there was increasing concern on Sony's part that Philips were falling behind, and when the European launch date was deferred to 'early 1983' I had a telephone call from a UK-based Sony executive suggesting that, given the ready availability of Japanese manufactured players and discs, they were considering going ahead without their partners. Clearly, distribution of the hardware posed no problem for them but when I asked about the discs I was told that they would use Boots and Woolworths as their outlets. The thought that what I believed to be the finest reproduction system ever offered to the public was about to be launched in this way appalled me, and I suggested that he should talk at once with David Fine, Chief Executive Officer of PolyGram UK Ltd. Whilst the Japanese launch took place in October 1982, the European launch was delayed – by all parties – to March 1983.

Antipathy and doubts

There was also a high level of adverse publicity coming from the British hi-fi journalists and a number of others involved with the hardware side of the business. Viewed dispassionately, one could see that the substitution of the LP turntable, pick-up cartridge and carrying arm (all very fertile areas for journalists and manufacturers) by one 'non-adjustable', competitively-priced black box, could have major repercussions in a number of areas. Certainly, the hi-fi journalists were very uneasy, a situation not helped by the fact that broadly speaking they had not been included in the press conferences to date. There was even a suggestion that CD could be injurious to your health, and for good measure there were side-swipes at *Gramophone* which was seen by a number of them to be unreasonably espousing the case for Compact Disc.

I was surprised at the lack of foresight shown by the hi-fi industry generally, given the wonderful marketing opportunities which CD would offer. There were exceptions, of course, and both Peter Walker of Quad and Raymond Cooke of KEF had clearly given much careful thought to the whole matter, and on the evidence which was available to them expressed concerns to me regarding the actual sound quality of the few discs which they had heard. I referred their problem to Tony Griffiths, Manager of the Decca Recording Centre in North-West London, and on December 6th, 1982 he was able to arrange a full demonstration, with A-B tests using both original digital master tapes and the equivalent CD pressings (including the Solti/VPO Schubert Ninth). The

Jan Timmer, "Mr CD", President of PolyGram International *Photo PolyGram*

two carriers were considered to be indistinguishable and as a result both Peter Walker and Raymond Cooke came away confident in the system itself.

At this stage there was still no guarantee that Compact Disc would be accepted as a world standard but the appointment on January 1st, 1983 of Jan Timmer as President and Chief Executive Officer of PolyGram International would later be seen as crucial to the system's global acceptance. He drove his own organization exceedingly hard and ensured that by their financial investment and commitment other record companies were left in no doubt as to PolyGram's total belief in the system. In 1987 Timmer returned to the troubled parent-company, Philips Electronics in Holland, becoming President and CEO in 1990. He retired in December 1996.

The launch of CD

In the early 1980s the country was again in the grip of a recession which was affecting many companies, with even the long-established London record retailer EMG going out of business. In my usual monthly letter to the magazine's contributors on December 9th, 1982 I wrote, "As 1982 draws to a close it could be that it might prove to be one of those years best forgotten. Certainly, it was a bad year for the record and audio industries and among other things our advertising support suffered quite substantially. The problems set in at the end of the first quarter and showed little improvement until October when sales certainly began to pick up. However, it would be wrong to suggest that this indicates the demise of the record industry; a theory currently proposed by one of our leading newspapers and being 'researched' by them. Exercise care if you are drawn into any comment on this matter. Hopefully, the autumn/winter improvement will be maintained into 1983 when, of course, we have the launch of Compact Disc. No one is expecting an earth-shattering, overnight market success for this new system but we do know that the Japanese launch in October exceeded all forecasts." It was therefore not surprising that the UK launch of Compact Disc was to be a low-key affair.

Gramophone's new loudspeakers for CD were the 802s from B&W Loudspeakers

In the case of the long-playing record – as well as stereo and digital vinyl – it was

May 1983 **News**

THE NATIONAL SOUND ARCHIVE

Sir Edward Elgar once wrote "If ever there was a fairy story, the history of the gramophone is one". Had he been able to look ahead, he would surely have been delighted with the new chapter of the story that has just begun. From April 1st the British Institute of Recorded Sound, home of thc National Sound Archive, has become a department of The British Library. The merger brings with it administrative changes, but also the acceptance of a major principle: sound recordings are now recognized as a major element of Britain's national archive. In future the recordings of Elgar, to name but one, will be kept as documentary evidence of his life and times alongside his manuscripts, letters and biographies.

It is some 35 years since the idea of a sound archive in Britain was first explored. Led by Patrick Saul, founder and first Director of the Institute, a group of enthusiasts met to seek public and governmental support for the project. Among that gathering at Church House, Westminster in 1947 were Sir Compton Mackenzie, founder of ***The Gramophone***, and music critics Frank Howes and Desmond Shawe-Taylor. With the help of a few private donations the British Institute of Recorded Sound was launched. By 1955 it had acquired its first real home in London's Russell Square. Six years later it was awarded its first annual government grant-in-aid, recognition of a job well done.

The archive houses a collection of over 400,000 discs and 20,000 hours of tape recordings on all subjects. And, thanks to the invaluable help of the record companies who supply new releases free of charge, it continues to grow at a rate of about 18,000 discs a year. As well as commercial recordings the archive is able to make its own tapes of BBC broadcasts. It is possible, for instance to compare Britten's records of his *War Requiem* with a tape of the first performance given in Coventry Cathedral on May 30th, 1962. The many changes in technology can, of course, be seen as well as heard: every kind of format is kept here from the earliest cylinders to the most recent Compact Discs. **Richard Fairman** the classical buyer who was the first to embrace the new product and ensure its initial viability, and I was sure that Compact Disc would be no exception. My own enthusiasm for the system never wavered from that morning in Eindhoven in March 1979 when I first heard it, and very early on I resolved that the issue of *Gramophone* which carried news of the launch would do the product full justice. Obviously, I had no intention of trying to persuade the magazine's music critics to say anything which they did not believe but I was determined that this would not be one of those occasions when a snap judgement was called for, based on listening in unfamiliar surroundings and on equipment to which they were unused. I decided that a minimum of one month was necessary between our installing the equipment (which included new loudspeakers designed to take full advantage of the increased dynamic range offered by CD), providing the review pressings, and the date on which the manuscript would be required.

Once we knew that the March 1983 issue of *Gramophone* would carry the launch, John Borwick was able to make all the arrangements with Sony and Philips for the supply of the CD players and I started to pull every string I knew in PolyGram to get the review pressings! Our efforts were rewarded with an issue which carried the representation of a Compact Disc on the front cover and included a special two-colour 12-page section containing John Borwick's explanation of Compact

March 1983

WAC ON CD

In March 1983, the month that the Compact Disc was launched, the magazine's longest-serving contributor, W. A. Chislett, described his first impressions of the new system

My first session with the Compact Disc recalled a veritable cavalcade of earlier instruments and accessories, headed by the Puck phonograph, which was no more than the bare essentials for playing two-minute wax cylinders mounted on an iron frame, given to me 78 years ago. Some shops would give one of these to all who bought a dozen Edison records at 1s. 6d. [7½ p] each! Then followed an Edison Gem and later an Amberola for playing four-minute wax cylinders, an HMV table model, an Edison Diamond Disc phonograph with adapter for lateral-cut discs, one of E. M. Ginn's magnificent instruments with a huge horn, an HMV reel-to-reel tape player, and, finally, my present Quad/Garrard/SME/Technics link-up; and high spots recalled included the almost surreptitious stealing in of electric recording, the Lifebelt, the birth of the LP and the arrival of stereo and cassette. Harry Lauder singing *Roaming in the gloaming* in 1905 seemed marvellous. So did hearing something really resembling the ping of a drumstick on skin in an early electric recording of *The Merry Wives of Windsor* Overture 20 years later, and Peter Dawson's *On the road to Mandalay* in stereo on a reel-to-reel tape at the 1955 Radio Show.

W. A. "Bill" Chislett (right), who wrote for *Gramophone* from 1925 until his death in 1984, with Brian Rust who from 1948 contributed to the "Miscellaneous and Dance" and "Jazz and Swing" columns under a number of pseudonyms (Oliver King, John Oakland and "Ajax"), later to become a much-respected authority on the history and discography of popular recorded music

All these seem small beer now by comparison with the dazzling sonorities of the Compact Disc versions of, say, *The Rite of Spring* with Dorati conducting, and the fidelity and presence of the Pinnock/English Concert account of Vivaldi's *Four Seasons* and the Hogwood/Academy of Ancient Music version of Handel's *Water Music*. But despite these virtues and the vast dynamic range, I find the absolute, almost uncanny stillness in silent bars most impressive of all. At times I found myself holding my breath lest I disturb it. There is inevitably another side to the coin. Faults in performance or recording, such as coarse tone, stand out more prominently than in corresponding LP versions and the dynamic range sometimes is such that if the softest passages are not to disappear the *fortissimos* are almost overpowering and certainly un-neighbourly. All the same, having now listened seriously to recorded music for nearly 80 years I look forward with eager anticipation to the era of the Compact Disc.

Disc, his review of four CD players, reviews of 49 CDs from Edward Greenfield, Robert Layton, Richard Osborne, Lionel Salter and William Chislett, and a listing of the first classical releases from PolyGram, CBS, RCA, Erato, Chandos and Nimbus. On the basis of these independent assessments there could have been few readers who were not impressed with all that CD had to offer the classical record buyer.

LP or CD?

Once again, history was to repeat itself, although by now there was no one active in any of the record companies who was involved in the launch of LP 33 years previously. On the other hand there were still many readers who had agonized over the change from 78s to LP and they were now joined by thousands of others all debating if and when they should embrace CD, and what would be the future for LP. The magazine's correspondence columns provided the usual forum although I would say that the case for CD was far stronger than that which had been expressed originally for LP in the 1950s.

Initially, the growth of CD was controlled by very limited disc manufacturing facilities – the three operating plants having to serve a global market – and to ease the situation PolyGram even held back the release of anything other than single-disc recordings. There were also companies like EMI (who delayed entry until the end of the year) who objected to the three per cent royalty payable to Philips in respect of every record pressed. (Philips waived any royalty on their compact cassette provided the prescribed standards were observed, but when it came to CD they felt justified in requesting a royalty in order to defray their huge investment.)

Six months after the launch Andrew Keener assessed the overall position in an article which appeared in the September 1983 issue and in which he wrote, "The Compact Disc is half-a-year old and, apparently, doing very nicely. Reason has largely replaced euphoria at its alleged indestructibility: you cannot smear it with cereal and honey as breakfast television viewers were led to believe last March, and the drilling of a three-millimetre hole is to be strongly discouraged." He went on to discuss the co-existence of LP and CD, "The larger companies are unanimous in predicting many years of life yet for the LP. Both formats, says Peter Andry of EMI Music, can and will exist simultaneously for at least a decade or two and exploration of new possibilities in vinyl continues apace." On the question of sales parity Keener wrote, "All companies admit, however, that the forecasts are becoming shorter-term with regard to CD/LP parity. Not so long ago, says Peter Russell of PolyGram, people were talking about the end of the century for such a development; now he suggests that within three to four years sales of classical Compact Discs may be comparable with classical black discs [LPs]."

Shortages of CDs

By using approved white-label test pressings, provided in advance of the release date by the major companies, we had since the late 1940s been able to ensure that in the vast majority of cases review, advertisement and release date coincided – an ideal arrangement for all concerned. The system began to fall apart when, in the late 1970s, much of the classical LP production was transferred to the continent: not only did test pressings cease to exist but the companies often never seemed to know when the records would arrive. There were certainly no test pressings for CD and the supply of review pressings tended to be haphazard due to the shortage of pressing facilities. Within the few existing plants everything possible was being done to maximize output but even so readers were becoming more and more frustrated when they saw records advertised, and often reviewed, and yet were unable to find them in the shops.

The first British CD pressing plant established in 1984 by Nimbus at Wyastone Leys in Monmouth *Photo Nimbus*

With the launch of Compact Disc in March 1983, *Gramophone*'s readers once again ensured that the Editor would have a healthy postbag

CORRESPONDENCE

May 1983

What are we audiophiles, we gramophiles, to do now? The history of the gramophone, which began in Edison's laboratory about a century ago, ended on March 1st, 1983. Our exponential horns, our 'Lifebelts', our dynamic levelling, our fibre needles, our dust bugs, our playing decks founded on rock, our damping, our fineline styli – all these are now 'mere folly', overtaken at one stride and undermined by the virtual perfection of the Compact Disc. There is nothing left for us to strive for. Please, can somebody tell me I'm wrong?

F. W. Baldock
Harare, Zimbabwe

Thank you for the excellent coverage you gave in your March edition of the launch of the Compact Disc. The description of the technical merits of the system reminded me of a review I have in my possession, an extract of which I quote: "The machine represents an entirely new departure in the production of musical sounds and renders orchestral selections, songs and speech so naturally that one seems to feel the presence of the executants. All the scratching so common and detrimental to the music rendered by other disc machines has been eliminated. Anyone who has heard it will admit that its performance is as near perfection as it is possible to obtain. The records are unbreakable, light and practically indestructible and are predestined to absolutely revolutionize the Talking Machine industry. So far as these records have been seen they have created a most profound impression and it has been universally conceded that nothing has ever been brought out of such an astonishingly realistic nature and the demand from the public will be enormous. The elimination of all foreign sounds in reproduction is quite sufficient to win for them the admiration of everyone but there is much more than this: they represent the acme of perfect reproduction of vocal and instrumental music with no distortion or extraneous noises."

One would be excused for thinking that this is yet another rave review for the Compact Disc. It is in fact taken from a 1906 catalogue issued by the Neophone company for their wind-up gramophones and 78rpm records. It is my belief that in the years to come the claims made for the Compact Disc today will appear as ludicrous as the one above is now. I attend audio shows quite regularly and constantly update my equipment (I will no doubt eventually get a CD player because it is a major advance), but no one I think will convince me otherwise than that hi-fi is still only in its infancy!

Rick Hardy
Watford, Herts

June 1983

Though the quantity of recorded music is not deemed to be what matters most in a record, a recent Sony ad boasts of "60 minutes of perfect sound", while your reviewer RO rightly complains in your April issue of the "rather short measure: just 36 minutes" offered by the DG Compact Disc of Mozart's *Eine kleine Nachtmusik* and *A Musical Joke*. Indeed, with the very expensive new CDs and equipment, buyers and reviewers will pay more and more attention to the initiatives, if any, of the recording companies as regards the quantity of music offered per record. So far the attitude of these companies has been most conservative and the first CDs are only duplicates of the old LPs.

For instance, the three movements of Brahms's Violin Concerto, which last approximately 20, ten and ten minutes, and traditionally occupy two LP sides, leave room on a CD for the *Haydn* Variations or *The Song of Destiny* or the *Alto Rhapsody*, etc. But what we get on DG's Compact Disc of the work is the usual 20 minutes' loss. It is therefore to be feared that we shall continue to find *Don Giovanni* and *Figaro* on four CDs and *Rigoletto* on three when they could easily be fitted on to three and two CDs respectively.

Among the first batch of CDs on the market, there is a case in point where the new technique shows regression rather than progress: it takes Philips one whole CD to record *Also sprach Zarathustra* which Decca had managed beautifully to record on one old-fashioned LP side. In a few rare cases we did get a little more than 30 minutes of music on one LP side and it is true that CDs can also play for a bit more than 60 minutes. But I am afraid it will often be the reverse. I should like to suggest to your reviewers to make it a constant rule to mention the playing time of the CDs reviewed: it might deter the readers from buying partly blank records and the companies from promoting a policy turned towards the past rather than the future.

Gilles David
Paris

July 1983

Having decided last year to be in on the CD era from the very start, I have been proud owner of a Sony player for a few weeks now and, even though my collection of discs is still relatively small, I am very enthusiastic about the new medium.

There has been controversy over the playing time of CDs, some people feeling that a CD playing time of 35 minutes is short measure and that a CD should include more than a regular analogue release. I personally feel that the record companies are justified in pursuing a one-to-one treatment of recordings in analogue, cassette and CD form, but what happens when they start releasing multiple sets of operas? I note from Philips's list that Bernstein's *Tristan und Isolde* will appear as five CDs like the records and theoretically, therefore, at a price of less than £50. Even if this is still less than a couple of stalls seats at Covent Garden, at a playing time of three hours 50 minutes, the work would fit on to four CDs at a more attractive price of about £40.

The CD format has a playing time of up to 80 minutes. Would it therefore not be possible to release such works as *Der Rosenkavalier* (which Karajan has just recorded) on three CDs, the three acts having approximate running times of 75, 65 and 60 minutes respectively? It would certainly be glorious to sit back and enjoy each act uninterrupted. (The CD has already shown this great merit in the *Alpensinfonie* by Richard Strauss.) I would gladly pay the equivalent of four records to have such a major advantage.

Neil Headley
Zurich, Switzerland

Having previously read some jaundiced comments about Compact Discs and players from 'hi-fi' magazines, I was most interested to read the reviews of this equipment in your March edition. On the strength of these reviews I ordered a Sony CDP-101 machine and purchased some CDs. I waited two months for the player, but now that I have it I am not disappointed; the results are marvellous.

I have collected records (78s, mono and then stereo LPs) for 40 years and, of course, enjoyed the music tremendously. I have also tried to keep up, more or less, with the steady improvement in record-playing equipment that has taken place over the years. So I write as one who is already heavily committed, as it were, to LPs and conventional record-players of good quality.

Whereas the advent of quadraphonic sound and one or two other developments struck me as no more than mildly interesting, CDs offer a major breakthrough. They have the advantage over LPs in virtually every respect: size, silent surfaces, no wear, no side-change for 50-60 minutes, no danger of accidental damage, consistently excellent sound quality, etc. This means that there is an end to the dreaded problems of pickup tracking ("will the pickup get through the heavily modulated passages without distortion?") and hence end-of-side distortion. This problem may not be as acute today as it was some years ago, but tracking distortion has always been one of the most unpleasant drawbacks with LPs. Now also we no longer need have any 'snap, crackle and pop' nor any real worries about buying faulty record pressings, which means in turn that one can buy CDs by mail order with absolute confidence. No doubt superficial defects may appear occasionally but I have played ten or 12 discs and detected no single playing defect (i.e. extraneous noise, break in music or whatever).

Certainly CDs are at present relatively expensive, but that will probably change as supply catches up with demand: discounts are already beginning to appear in the market. Nevertheless, even if CDs remain at prices higher than those for LPs, they are (in my opinion) a much better product. I would prefer to buy, for a given money outlay, a smaller number of CDs rather than a larger number of LPs.

From the outset, Compact Disc playing time was a matter of some contention. The majority of readers seemed to believe that the manufacturers should utilize the full capacity of the disc and expected reviewers to comment accordingly, eventually persuading the Editor that playing times should become an integral part of the review heading. Initially, some manufacturers capitalized on the situation, as shown by this Denon sleeve from January 1984

Therefore I say to Philips and Sony: congratulations, and thanks for a great system. I will not be buying another LP. Maybe the mystique of putting needle into groove is going, along with the endless search for a better turntable, mat, arm and cartridge. Maybe the CD player is an electronic gadget that leaves the word 'gramophone' behind, but it is an excellent machine: the sound is fabulous.

Richard Platts
Belfast

To judge from your recent correspondence columns, gramophiles on all sides are talking of nothing but the new Compact Disc – it's very reminiscent of the margarine advertised on TV which apparently absorbs the South Australian legislative to the exclusion of all other business. Alas, from what I have seen of CD's impact on the great record-buying public, you could cut the apathy with a knife.

If we consider, of the various technological innovations introduced over the years, what the successful ones have in common, we find: (i) They offered the consumer an improved product for little or no increase in unit cost; (ii) Involved only a modest capital outlay for new hardware; (iii) Offered compatibility in so far as products of an earlier technology were accepted and even enhanced by the new hardware. It is also significant that those developments that did not possess these attributes succumbed with but little resistance, e.g. pre-recorded tapes in the 1950s and quadraphonics in the 1970s.

Considering the CD in the light of these historic desiderata we find that: (i) The unit cost is two to three times that of the LP equivalent; (ii) A major outlay on new hardware is required; (iii) There will be the continuing need to house and maintain existing playing systems for many years to come. I would suggest that with the anticipated future economic climate this would be at least 15 years.

I look at the serried shelves of my music room and there are 7,000 reasons why I balk at the thought of CD. True, I would be getting an everlasting product – and if I thought I might prove to turn out an everlasting person this might carry some weight. However, as – in over 30 years of LP collecting – I have never yet worn out a single record. I will settle for a lifetime's durability.

Alas, the current musical climate is hardly more propitious than that prevailing on the economic front – is there perhaps a link? Considering the conducting field, for example, I see an amplitude of competence and a dearth of genius – the one oasis in this desert of mediocrity being the emergence of the phenomenally-gifted Simon Rattle. (Long may he be issued on LP.)

John Gould,

London, SW15

June 1984

For the past 50 years, I have been an enthusiastic collector of recorded music of the great artists. In spite of my many years spent on tours of duty abroad, I have managed, via your admirable publication, to keep in touch with both new recordings and the latest audio developments. From the moment *Gramophone* appears on my desk, all else must wait whilst I eagerly devour its contcnts. Reviews, correspondence, news and views, quarterly retrospect and of course, the advertisements, are all of the utmost fascination. In particular, your correspondence columns cause me many a wry smile, for it would appear that in this ever changing world, the Canute-like attitude of some readers remains stubbornly resistant. How well I remember the appearance of the first long-playing record, and the *cri de coeur* from the avid 78rpm collector that the new sound was artificial and unnatural. Likewise, with the introduction of the stereo long-player, another apparent step back into the dark ages was made.

Now with the appearance of the Compact Disc the ultimate sin has been committed by the record companies in their efforts to antagonize the collector. They have produced a virtually indestructible record, which cannot be easily damaged, and reproduces, to my ear, with totally natural fidelity. However, this in itself is sufficient to provoke some of your correspondents to dismiss this most interesting audio innovation as being something either offensive, or at the least, musically subservient. One of your advertisers (April 1984), even dismisses the system as being old-fashioned and suggests that a recent price increase in 'black discs' by the PolyGram Group implies a pro-CD plot. The poor old record companies! How can they win, criticized both for their high prices on CD and for not increasing their CD prices in line with records and cassettes. What a strange breed we collectors are; it seems there's no pleasing us!

Anyway, I for one nail my colours firmly to the CD mast and urge your readers at least to attempt to experience what, for me, is the ultimate audio and musical experience. It does not mean one has to jettison one's 78s, mono LPs or stereo LPs. CD lives alongside most hi-fi systems and reproduces the next best experience to a live musical event.

Major Edgar Harrington

Hartley-Whitney, Hampshire

Although I dislike paying more for my gramophone records as much as anyone, I really must protest against the letter from Mr Weatherill in your April issue.

I don't think that some of my younger fellow enthusiasts realize what a tremendous bargain even Compact Discs at £16 are compared with what prices were 50 years ago. When I left school in 1931, I was lucky enough to receive as a prize, the Albert Coates recording of Beethoven's Ninth (which I still possess) recorded on eight fragile, scratchy shellac discs, which cost the school prize fund £2 8s. 0d. At about the same time I visited a well-known High Street tailor, and bought myself a suit which cost me £3 17s. 6d., and had I posted a letter it would have cost me 1½ d.

The last suit I bought from the same tailors cost me about £90, and a letter will, if I expect comparable service, cost me 16p. If the same price ratio were to be observed, today, Beethoven's Ninth would cost £55·75 compared with the suit, and £61·44 compared with the postage stamp, and yet the Compact Disc is only about a quarter of these sums, quite apart from the incomparable standard of the recording and reproduction.

E. C. Marsden

Blackburn, Lancashire

February 1985

The sonic honeymoon is over now and we've had time to face up to reality. The sound quality is much better than anything we've heard before and those dreadful faults of vinyl and tape are gone. CDs are much easier to use and less prone to damage, but do I hear little 'ticks' now and then and do I imagine tiny little 'drop-outs' here and there? I have had to return to the shop with discs that jump or 'skip' sections of music and what is most puzzling of all, if I hold the discs up to the light I can see lots of tiny little pin-holes. Can the laser play empty space?

It seems that it's the same old story again. Technology is once again being let down by the inevitable need for mass production. The software is flawed as it always has been and the problems of old are still with us, only with different names.

I do hope I'm wrong!

B. Harris

Plymouth

In May 1986 EMI opened their CD plant in Swindon which had been originally established to produce Video High Density (VDH) discs in conjunction with JVC. From the left Ken East (CEO, EMI Music Europe and International), Rupert Perry (MD, EMI Records UK) and Bhaskar Menon (CEO, EMI Music Worldwide)
Photo EMI

In time, matters would improve, but for the first three years demand for CD invariably exceeded supply. This hit many of the independents very hard, for having supported the new system from the outset and added valuable clout to the CD bandwagon, they now found it difficult to secure the pressing capacity they needed – although they would confirm PolyGram's even-handedness in coping with the situation.

The first British pressing plant was established by Nimbus, in Monmouth, who as early as March 1982 had signed a manufacturing licence with Philips. They produced their first CD on May 15th, 1984 and the plant came on stream on June 19th with initially a projected output of 30,000 discs per month. EMI were to follow with their Swindon factory which opened on May 15th, 1986, whilst other pressing plants gradually appeared elsewhere in the world.

'International' CDs

In one respect CD confirmed a change which affected the whole record business in the late 1970s and 1980s. Traditionally, records sold in the UK were manufactured in this country: from the earliest days there were imports but at a premium price which had to include carriage costs and import duty. This was very much the case during the LP era when it was almost impossible to sell imported records due to their price loading. With the coming of the Common Market, and the general relaxation of world trade tariffs, it was possible for all companies to press LPs in Europe and ship them into the UK at a competitive price. Among other things this gave rise to multi-lingual packaging and highlighted the need for the international currency of companies' trademarks. (This meant that the world-famous HMV 'dog and trumpet' had to give way to EMI Classics, the 'dog and trumpet' being the property of RCA/BMG in America and a number of other territories. There were similar problems with the Decca trademark which was not valid in America.)

With the coming of CD it was just as well that there was total flexibility of distribution, for initially the UK and the USA were totally dependent on discs pressed either in Germany or Japan. This also brought with it standard coupling arrangements and catalogue numbers which had an international currency. Whilst there are some records produced specifically for local markets, the majority of classical records are now designed for shipping anywhere in the world. In effect a small independent label in America can place its total pressing order with a plant, say in Austria, and then ship directly (invariably by air given the lightness of the CD) to its local distributors throughout the world. This has resulted in a near-total 'international' catalogue and explains to a great extent the wide range of repertoire now available in all major territories.

The famous 'dog and trumpet' which for international classical releases gave way to the EMI Classics logo, and the two redesigned Decca/London trademarks with the London logo progressively being given greater currency

The growth of CD

The growth of CD was matched by the increasing number of pressing plants coming on stream throughout the world and as the 1980s progressed so the sales balance between CD and LP was swinging in favour of the former, at a rate which had never been envisaged at the outset – in two months the DG/Bernstein *West Side Story* (a two-disc set released in April 1985) had sold in the UK 6,000 CD and 4,200 LP sets (with the impact of a BBC *Omnibus* programme still to come). Early in 1987 a full-price CD was selling for around £11 and the introduction of mid-price CDs on a number of labels, in the range of £6·50 to £9·00, was guaranteed to give a further fillip to the business. For the year ended September 1988

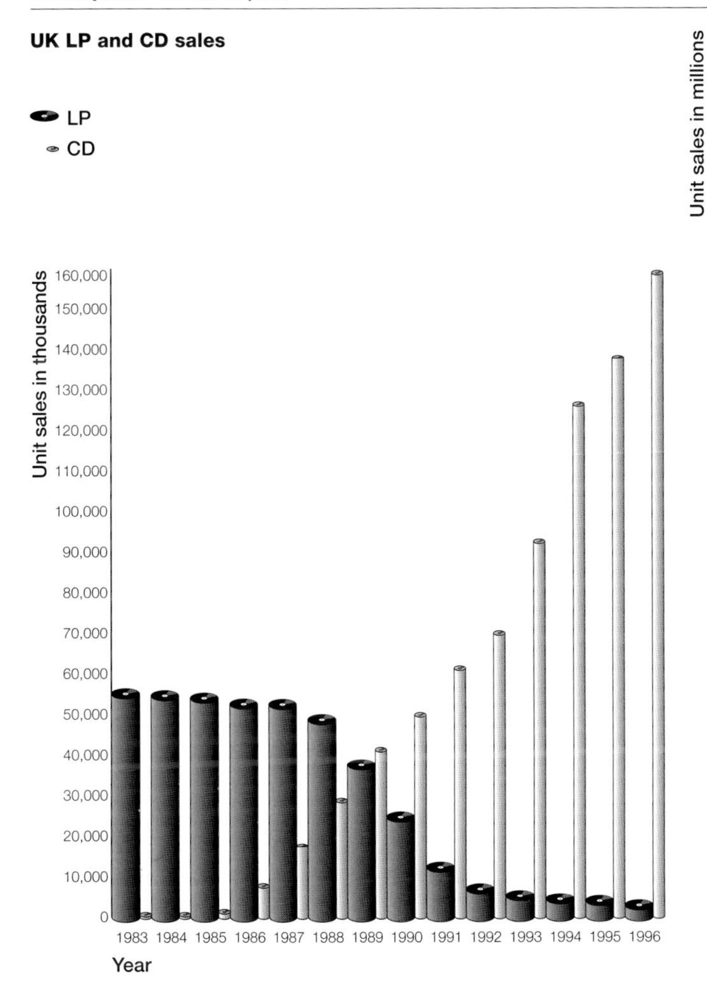

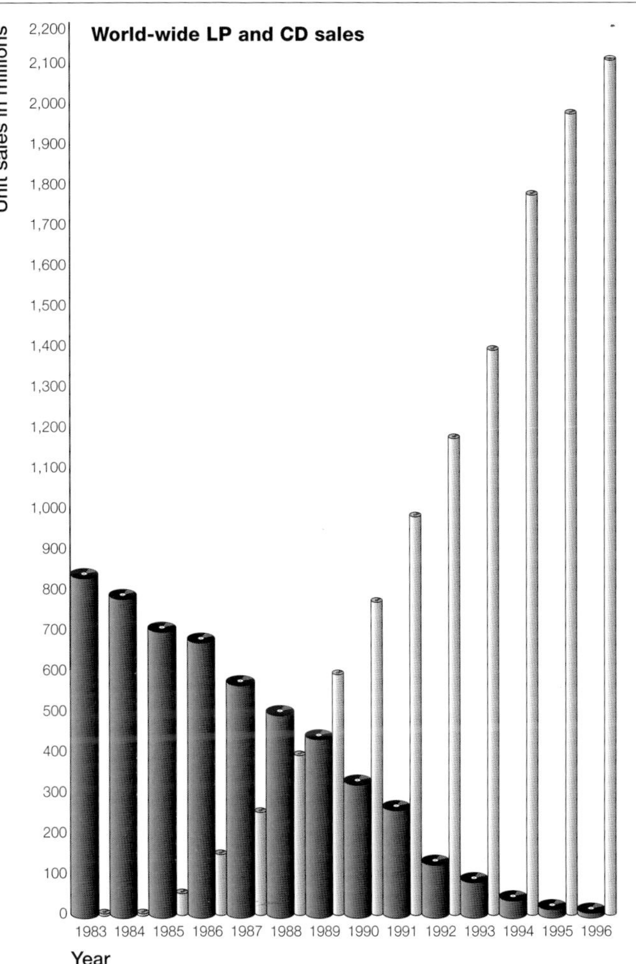

These two bar charts show the unit growth of CD and the decline of LP over the period 1983 to 1996, for both UK and world-wide sales
Source: Phil Hardy

the British Phonographic Industry (BPI) figures showed UK trade deliveries up by 17 per cent over the previous year, with CD responsible for over half of the increased revenue: by December it was suggested that CD would generate more revenue than LP. BIS Macintosh reported a CD growth rate in 1988 of 56 per cent, with 15 per cent of homes in the USA and Europe owning a CD player: the figure for Japan was slightly higher at 20 per cent.

In the March 1989 issue, under the heading "The LP's Future", Christopher Pollard conducted a survey which took into account feedback from readers and comments from various people in the record industry. His conclusions were as follows, "CD is clearly the medium of the immediate future and the average classical buyer has adopted it. The industry, buoyed by the greater profits to be made, is in good health and generally optimistic, a far cry from the dark days at the start of this decade. That leaves a vocal minority bemoaning the situation in strident and emotional terms; are they genuinely justified in their grievance or will posterity condemn them as just another group of 'flat-earthers'?"

The magazine had endeavoured to do all it could for those still wedded to LP but by December 1989, out of a total of 135 titled reviews only 23 indicated the availability of an LP equivalent. The writing was clearly on the wall.

LP, Cassette and DAT

Throughout the early part of the 1980s there were still efforts being made to improve the LP: apart from Direct Metal Mastering (DMM), for which EMI took out a licence in January 1983, there were any number of audiophile discs which found a ready market. The analogue cassette was also receiving attention and in April 1981 BASF were reporting increasing demands for the supply of their chrome tape. For the classical market the cassette maintained a relatively strong position until the launch of the Digital Compact Cassette (DCC) in April 1992 when it seemed that all the emphasis would switch to the new digital product. Regrettably the poorly-executed launch failed to convert the tape enthusiasts and sadly had the effect of undermining the existing classical analogue cassette market without establishing DCC as an alternative.

Apart from a scare concerning 'decaying' CDs, which the national press seemed to relish (in truth, they seemed increasingly intent on trying to kill off the Industry) the only other hiccup in the CD's progress was the DAT incident. On June 29th, 1986 *The Sunday Times*, under the headline "Digital taping may wipe out Compact Discs", wrote,

An EMI LP recording carrying the DMM logo

"Compact Discs are about to be made obsolete by a new generation of audio cassette dubbed Digital Audio Tape (DAT)". With CD having then only achieved a four per cent penetration in the UK a report such as this, emanating from what was seen as a responsible newspaper, resulted in considerable unrest – both for existing consumers, for those about to invest in CD, and the manufacturers themselves. The piece went on to say, "Most at risk in Britain are companies that have invested heavily in compact-disc production plants. Thorn EMI and Disctec have invested £25m and £15m respectively. Had they seen DAT coming, they might not have sunk such large sums into a technology that is likely to have a limited life." A complaint was lodged with The Press Council by The British Radio and Electronic Equipment Manufacturer's Association, claiming that the article was misleading and, in parts, factually incorrect and thus likely to have confused the general public. This was refuted by *The Sunday Times* and, notwithstanding the Industry's views, no retraction was forthcoming. Seen after more than 11 years have elapsed, during which time CD has fully established itself and DAT has assumed a role as an excellent professional recording medium, it may seem like a storm in a teacup, but at the time it certainly resulted in many people thinking twice about investing in CD.

Ramon Lopez, Chairman and CEO, Warner Music International *Photo WMI*

Peter Andry, who served Decca, EMI and Warner Classics before his retirement in 1996

Marco Bignotti (left), President of Warner Classics International, with Maxim Vengerov (right) and Niall O'Rouke (V-P Marketing) *Photo WMI*

Industry personalities in the 1980s

As we have already seen, Sir Edward Lewis died at the beginning of the decade, on January 29th, 1980 at the age of 79; on April 27th his able past-lieutenant, John Culshaw, died at the age of 55, a tragic loss for the music business to which he had so much more to contribute. David Bicknell, having joined Fred Gaisberg in The Gramophone Company in 1927, had given 44 years of his life to the business and was to die in September 1988 at the age of 82. Of the men who contributed to the world of audio Paul Voigt, once with Edison Bell, died on February 2nd, 1981; Harold

February 1983 **Correspondence**

RONALD PHILLIPS OF COLLECTORS' CORNER

Ronald Phillips, one of London's most respected record retailers, died in October 1981. Mr Watts's sentiments would be echoed by a host of other collectors [p. 59]

May I through your magazine express a personal tribute to the late Ronald Phillips. I first ventured into his Monmouth Street premises ("mind the two steps down") in 1957, fresh from school with a limited knowledge of great singers. Amidst much cigar smoke I was tutored on the art of operatic performances on record and allowed to browse through the vast stocks of 78s. His suggestions and advice to a young collector were to form the basis of enjoying opera and concerts to the present day. My visits were always on a Saturday morning and a postcard would summon me there to inspect the latest EJS records from Edward Smith in America. What treasures these were to me. Björling and Callas in *Trovatore* were promised but alas are still awaited. A visit to the New Oxford Street branch introduced me to Mrs Phillips and the Swedish X series records of Björling that were regularly stocked. My collection grew quickly and I recall many calls on the hot line to Monmouth Street with dear Ronald, cigar in hand, holding court and firmly ushering lost Pop collectors out whilst an aria was on the turntable. What a cornucopia of delight came from there and will remain with me and other collectors for ever.

V. R. Watts
Westerham, Kent

Leak, famous for his amplifiers and loudspeakers, died in August 1989 and Arthur Haddy, father of *ffrr* and so much other Decca wizardry, died on December 18th, 1989.

Happily, their successors remained to carry on the traditions of the business, and although Peter Andry (who ultimately worked for 42 years in the classical business) was to retire as President of the International Classical Division of EMI Music on March 31st, 1989, two months later he was appointed Senior Vice-President, Classical Repertoire of WEA Ltd. Under the wise guidance of Ramon Lopez – originally with EMI and PolyGram – WEA, then very much a 'pop-based' company, were intent on entering the classical business and it was Andry, respected internationally for his knowledge in this area, who would provide, among other things, the necessary artistic credibility. As Warner Classics International (with Andry as President until his final retirement in May 1996, when he was succeeded by Marco Bignotti) the company encompassed Teldec, Erato, Nonesuch, Finlandia and NVC Arts. In November 1988, Gunther Breest, who for many years had directed classical A&R for Deutsche Grammophon in Hamburg, moved to a similar role in what was to become Sony Classical, with the task of establishing a major classical presence for the company. He left the company in December 1994 and Peter Gelb took over the Presidency the following March.

Gunther Breest *Photo Sony*

Peter Gelb, President, Sony Classical *Photo Sony*

In March 1989 the Galerie Beaumont in Luxembourg hosted what was thought to be the first exhibition of "the classical record sleeve as art". The exhibition was based on the extensive LP collection of its creator, Michael Palmer, Director General for research at the European Parliament – and a *Gramophone* reader for over 40 years. Pictured at the opening (from the left), Giancarlo Bongiovanni (Bongiovanni Records), Martine Speller-Schneider (gallery owner), Christopher Pollard, Michael Palmer and Chevalier Antoine de Wouters d'Oplinter (Pavane Records)

Domestic matters in the 1980s

The decade started well with the move of the magazine's printing to Watmoughs. In addition to a major improvement in the overall quality of the print, Barry Irving was soon able to encourage more of our advertisers to take advantage of the excellent colour-printing facilities, as I had hoped, and by September 1986 we were also able to extend this to the editorial pages. In one other respect my hopes for the future were not fully realized; towards the latter part of 1979 Malcolm Walker's health posed problems for him and in January 1980 I had to resume my day-to-day editorial responsibilities. In June I appointed Quita Chavez (who had been with the Company briefly in the 1960s) as Editorial Manager for a period of four years. In July 1984 she was succeeded by my son Christopher but continued as an editorial consultant for a further 12 years. In April 1986 Christopher succeeded me as Editor.

Even more changes

In December 1984 Valerie Warburton, who had joined the Company in March 1978, became manager of the new computer-based Subscription Department and in February 1986 Ivor Humphreys joined us from *Hi-Fi News*, initially to support John Borwick and later to become Audio Editor himself in April 1988, as well as fulfilling a crucial role as our resident electronic publishing guru. As I have already noted, Alec Robertson died on January 18th, 1982 and the last of the original pioneers, William Chislett who had written for the magazine since February 1925, died on November 17th, 1984 at the age of 89. Typically, he worked to the end and the January 1985 issue contained the last of his reviews.

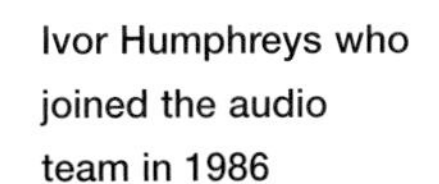

Ivor Humphreys who joined the audio team in 1986

The two Pollards in ACP's office at 177 Kenton Road in March 1989 *Photo Hanya Chlala*

Christopher's youthful enthusiasm. Initially, he brought fresh thinking to the magazine itself – the editorial colour sections and progressive 'modernization' of the layouts, etc., being but one aspect of this. He also took under his wing the record catalogues and *The Good CD Guide*, and later the annual Record Awards.

In fact, at a time when we were beginning to face much more significant competition in the market-place, and when the major players in the classical record industry were radically changing their marketing approach, it was none too soon for ***Gramophone*** to sweep away some of the accretions of the past and take a fresh look at the changing world in which we now had to live. As a result Christopher, who had become a Director of the Company in January 1988, was progressively to inject the whole operation with new thinking, happily respecting and preserving those characteristics which I had inherited from my predecessors and which we both believed epitomized so much of that for which ***Gramophone*** stood.

However, the business was changing in many respects (as were all businesses!) and parallel with an increase in the number of staff it was becoming obvious that my oligarchic style of management, however well it might have served the Company in the past, needed to be re-examined and adjusted. In much the same way as my father had been kind enough to suggest that the business had benefited from my arrival in the Company some 40 years previously, so I now certainly benefited from

Clive Portbury (BBC), Tara Guha (Warner Classics), James Jolly and Matthew Cosgrove (Warner Classics) *Photo Warner Classics*

But as 1989 drew to a close he realized that the ever-widening responsibilities which he was now accepting were prejudicing his ability to edit the magazine in the manner in which he wished. It was also true to say that, like me, his skills were not musically-based – that support traditionally came from those around us, the editorial staff and the contributors – and we recognized that the time had now come for ***Gramophone*** to have an editor who was musically qualified for the job. James Jolly, an avid reader of the magazine – and a pupil at Bradfield College before going on to Bristol University – had joined us on the recommendation of Richard Osborne (one of the College's masters and 'our' RO) as Assistant Editor in February 1985 and we were very happy when in January 1990 he accepted the role of Editor.

Christopher became Editorial Director, working very closely with James on a day-to-day basis, and I became Publisher – still with a deeply-rooted concern for all that happened to the paper which I held in trust for my illustrious predecessors.

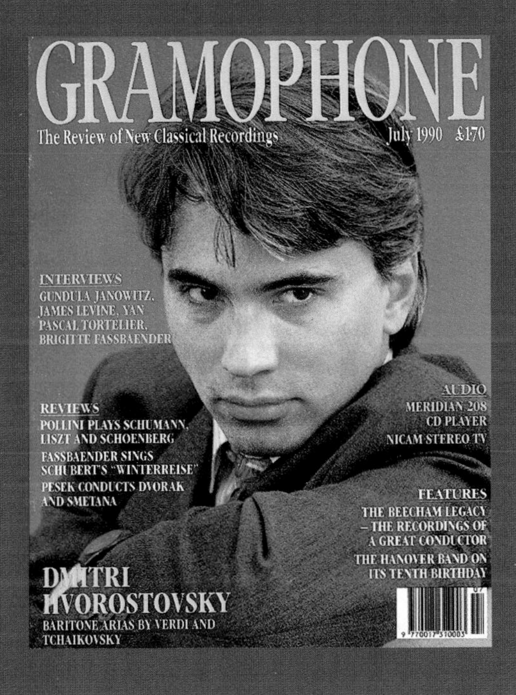

GRAMOPHONE
The Review of New Classical Recordings
July 1990 £1·70
INTERVIEWS
GUNDULA JANOWITZ, JAMES LEVINE, YAN PASCAL TORTELIER, BRIGITTE FASSBAENDER
REVIEWS
POLLINI PLAYS SCHUMANN, LISZT AND SCHOENBERG
FASSBAENDER SINGS SCHUBERT'S "WINTERREISE"
PESEK CONDUCTS DVORAK AND SMETANA
AUDIO
MERIDIAN 208 CD PLAYER
NICAM STEREO TV
FEATURES
THE BEECHAM LEGACY – THE RECORDINGS OF A GREAT CONDUCTOR
THE HANOVER BAND ON ITS TENTH BIRTHDAY
DMITRI HVOROSTOVSKY
BARITONE ARIAS BY VERDI AND TCHAIKOVSKY

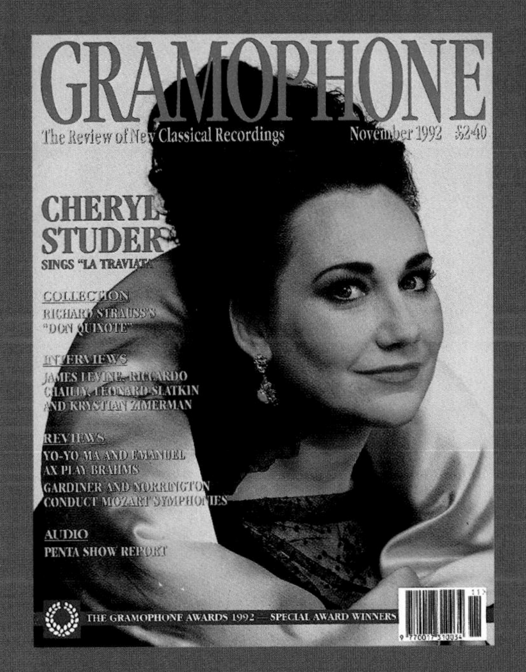

GRAMOPHONE
The Review of New Classical Recordings
November 1992 £2·40
CHERYL STUDER
SINGS "LA TRAVIATA"
COLLECTION
RICHARD STRAUSS'S "DON QUIXOTE"
INTERVIEWS
JAMES LEVINE, RICCARDO CHAILLY, LEONARD SLATKIN AND KRYSTIAN ZIMERMAN
REVIEWS
YO-YO MA AND EMANUEL AX PLAY BRAHMS
GARDINER AND NORRINGTON CONDUCT MOZART SYMPHONIES
AUDIO
PENTA SHOW REPORT
THE GRAMOPHONE AWARDS 1992 — SPECIAL AWARD WINNERS

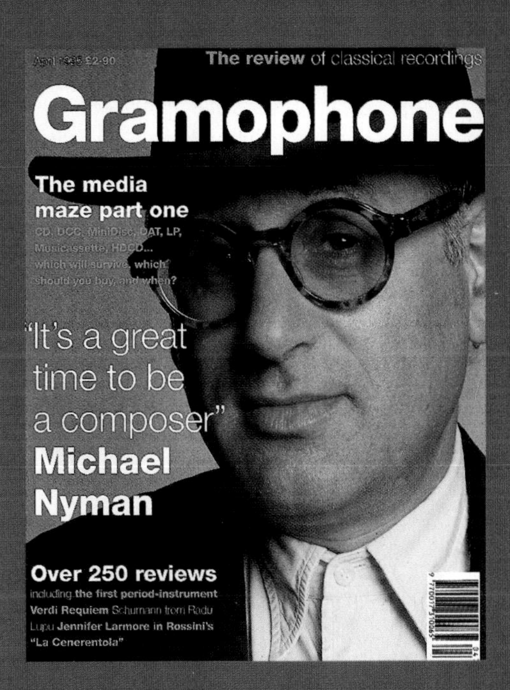

The review of classical recordings
Gramophone
The media maze part one
CD, DCC, MiniDisc, DAT, LP, Musicassette, HDCD... which will survive, which should you buy, and when?
"It's a great time to be a composer"
Michael Nyman
Over 250 reviews
including the first period-instrument Verdi Requiem Schumann from Radu Lupu Jennifer Larmore in Rossini's "La Cenerentola"

A changing world

The best classical music magazine in the world
Gramophone
EXTRA!
A film music special with interviews, news and reviews
Arvo Pärt
a portrait by Dennis Russell Davies Christophers Bowers-Broadbent Gavin Bryars Paavo Järvi Paul Hillier Neeme Järvi The Hilliard Ensemble
OVER 200 REVIEWS
Handel's "Orlando" from William Christie Pierre Monteux's classic "Daphnis" Bruckner from Sir Georg Solti A new Tchaikovsky First Piano Concerto with Martha Argerich and Claudio Abbado
The 1996 Gramophone Awards SHORT LIST
AUDIO
Celestion Home Theatre in a Box
Copland CDA 288 Compact Disc player
North American Edition

The best classical music magazine in the world
Gramophone
$7·50 US
NEW
Recommended recordings
Over 300 entries listing the best releases available
John Eliot Gardiner
Making it new
SPECIAL FEATURE
World music
Reviews
Bach Partitas from Angela Hewitt
Steven Isserlis in the music of John Tavener
Jean-Yves Thibaudet playing Bill Evans
A début on disc for composer and pianist Thomas Adès
James Levine conducts Wagner's The Flying Dutchman
PLUS
Audio
Quad in the groove
Sennheiser HD-600 headphones

The best classical music magazine in the world
Gramophone
£3·40
Barbara Bonney
Songs from back home
Reviews
Janáček's Kát'a Kabanová from Gabriela Beňačková
Richard Hickox conducts Haydn's Harmoniemesse
Handel's Ariodante from Marc Minkowski
Audio
Alan Parsons at Abbey Road
KEF/Meridian home cinema system
Rogers Minstrel SE loudspeaker

1990-1998

A *Gramophone* chronology

1990-1998

1990

- Brown Meggs retires as President of Angel Records.
- Bill Holland joins Warner Classics UK.

January

- James Jolly appointed Editor of *G*. Christopher Pollard becomes Managing Editor and Anthony Pollard becomes Publisher.

March

- Michael Fine starts Koch International Classics.

September

- North American edition of *G* launched.
- Philips Classical release their "Mozart Edition", a survey of virtually every work Mozart composed, eventually comprising 180 CDs in 45 volumes. The world sales by the end of 1997 had reached approximately six million discs.

October

- Warner's classical labels (Erato, Teldec, Nonesuch) now grouped as Warner Classics International.
- Yolanta Skura founds Opus 111 in Paris.

Alain Levy *Photo PolyGram*

November

- Roger Lewis appointed Director, Classical Division, EMI Records UK.
- Philips announce Digital Compact Cassette (DCC).

December

- David G. Fine retires as Chairman and CEO of the PolyGram Group and is succeeded the following month by Alain Levy who joined PolyGram in 1984.

1991

January

- Philips demonstrate DCC system in Las Vegas.
- Henceforth the classical CBS label becomes Sony Classical.

February

- Cala Records founded by Geoffrey Simon.

March

- All EMI's classical recordings to be marketed under the EMI Classics logo.
- Vanguard Classics relaunched by Seymour Solomon and Start Records.
- Sir Joseph Lockwood, former EMI Chairman, dies aged 86.

May

- Sony announce MiniDisc.

June

- David G. Fine becomes Chairman of the Board of the International Federation of the Phonographic Industry (IFPI).

July

- Jan D. Timmer appointed President of Philips, Eindhoven.

November

- Harley Usill, joint-founder of Argo and ASV, dies aged 66.

December

- Simon Foster leaves Virgin Classics.

1992

January

- Warner Classics International acquire remaining shares in Erato.
- Rupert Perry appointed President and CEO of EMI Records UK and Eire.

Rupert Perry *Photo EMI*

March

- EMI acquire Virgin Records and with it Virgin Classics, which in September make their new releases under the wing of EMI Classics.
- Simon Foster becomes Director of BMG Classics.

April

- UK launch of Philips Digital Compact Cassette (DCC).

July

- Zomba Group acquire a controlling interest in Conifer Records.

September

- Roger Ames succeeds Maurice Oberstein as Chairman and CEO of PolyGram UK.

October

- Gianfranco Rebulla appointed to succeed Dr Andreas Holschneider as President of DG.

November

- UK launch of Sony MiniDisc.

1993

March

- Martin Benge succeeds Ken Townsend as V-P, EMI Studios Group.

May

- *G* "Editor's choice" commences.
- *G* launch the "Blue riband" dealer scheme.

August

- Keith Howard joins *G* technical team.

September

- Death at the age of 94 of W. W. Johnson, founder of the NFGS.

October

- *G*'s John Gilbert dies aged 85.

December

- Finlandia Records acquired by Warner Classics International.

1994

January

- Numa Labinsky, joint-founder of Nimbus Records, dies.

March

- Ray Minshull retires as Executive V-P of Decca International and is succeeded by Evans Mirageas.

June

- Louis Benjamin, one-time MD of Pye Records, dies aged 71.

Evans Mirageas
Photo Decca

November

- National Video Arts Corporation becomes part of Warner Classics International.

December

- Gunther Breest leaves Sony Classical.

1995

March

- Raymond Cooke of KEF dies aged 70.
- Peter Gelb appointed President of Sony Classical.

Raymond Cooke

- John Pattrick retires from EMI.

April

- Peter Andry appointed President of Warner Classics International.
- Jean-Hugues Allard appointed Director of A&R for Sony Classical.

May

- Classics for Pleasure 25th anniversary.
- Rupert Perry appointed President and CEO, EMI Europe and Chairman, EMI Records Group UK and Ireland. He is succeeded as MD of EMI Records UK by Jean François Cecillon.

Jean-Hugues Allard
Photo Sony

Jean François Cecillon launches EMI's Centenary celebrations at London's Royal Lancaster Hotel on January 8th, 1996

June

- Keith Howard appointed *G*'s Consulting Audio Editor.

September

- Albert Imperato becomes V-P of DG in the USA.
- BBC inaugurate Digital Audio Broadcasting (DAB).

Albert Imperato *Photo DG*

October

- Alison Ames leaves DG to become V-P of EMI Classics, USA.

November

- BMG acquire Conifer Records from Zomba.

December

- Gianfranco Rebulla leaves DG.
- Tim Harrold retires as Chairman of PolyGram Classics and is succeeded by Chris Roberts.

Chris Roberts *Photo PolyGram*

1996

January

- ***GramoFile*** CD-ROM launched by ***G***.
- Bill Holland appointed MD, Warner Classics UK.
- Alison Wenham becomes MD of BMG/Conifer and Simon Foster A&R Director.

Simon Foster (left) with Bill Holland

Alison Wenham
Photo Conifer

John F. Pfeiffer *Photo RCA*

February

- John F. Pfeiffer, RCA producer, dies aged 75. He had been with RCA for 47 years.

March

- W. W. Townsley, who worked for Barnett Samuel and Decca for 54 years, dies.

May

- *G* offices move from Kenton Road to Sudbury Hill.
- Peter Andry retires as President of Warner Classics International and is succeeded by Marco Bignotti.

June

- Virgin Classics (EMI) move to Paris, with Alain Lanceron as President.
- Peter Alward becomes Senior V-P, Classical A&R for EMI.
- John Kennedy succeeds Roger Ames as Chairman of PolyGram UK.
- Roger Ames appointed President of PolyGram Music Group.
- Philips acquire a majority interest in Gimell Records.

July

- Music for Pleasure renamed EMI Gold.
- Karsten Witt appointed President of DG.

August

- EMI Music demerges from Thorn EMI.

September

- Bill Holland leaves Warner Classics UK to return to PolyGram UK as Director of Classics and Jazz.

October

- Sidney Shure, of Shure Bros Inc., pickup and microphone manufacturers, dies aged 93.

On January 21st, 1998 Deutsche Grammophon launched their Centenary celebrations with a Press Conference in Hamburg. Seen, from the left, are Karsten Witt (President, DG), Anne-Sophie Mutter, Michael Fine (V-P, A&R), Christian Thielemann, Christine Schäfer and Myung-Whun Chung *Photo DG*

Alain Lanceron *Photo EMI*

Cor Dubois *Photo BMG*

November

- Cor Dubois appointed President of BMG Classics in succession to Gunter Hensler.

December

- *G* commences a regular monthly covermounted CD.
- Peter Russell retires as Director, PolyGram Classics UK.

1997

January

- Iain Hutchison (who joined the Company in July 1991) becomes Advertisement Manager of *G* and succeeds Barry Irving who moves to a Business Development role.
- Roger Lewis leaves EMI to become President of The Decca Record Company, succeeding Roland Kommerell.

Roger Lewis *Photo Decca*

Costa Pilavachi *Photo Philips*

April

- Johannes H. Kinzl retires as President of Philips Classics and is succeeded by Costa Pilavachi.
- Chris Black appointed Director, Sony Classical & Jazz UK.

Chris Black *Photo Sony*

June

- Ken Berry, who joined the Virgin Group in 1973, appointed President of EMI Recorded Music.

James Fifield (left) President, EMI Music with Ken Berry, President, EMI Recorded Music *Photo EMI*

July

- Alan Parsons succeeds Martin Benge as V-P, EMI Studios Group.

October

- The ***Gramophone*** Awards ceremony, held at Alexandra Palace, is televised for the first time, achieving an audience of 2·5 million viewers.
- Brown Meggs dies.

November

- Rob Pell appointed MD of PolyGram Recording Services.

1998

February

- Classics for Pleasure relaunched by EMI.

April

- *G* celebrates its 75th anniversary.

A changing world

When I started to research and write these reminiscences in the spring of 1997 I might have been persuaded that comment on the 1990s would be largely academic. In fact, nothing could have been further from the truth. On reflection, I believe that the developments and consequent changes which have directly affected *Gramophone* over the past eight years have been greater than at any other time in the Company's history – and even when these words are first read the decade will still have a good 18 months to run – a long time in the history of the record and audio industries!

Change is something which everyone of us has to recognize, but to adapt to change is not necessarily the easiest of tasks. For a small company such as ours there is also the added complication that there is little room for error – the margins within which we operate are tight and a failure to perform effectively will swiftly precipitate major problems. It is in this context that the skills of management are paramount.

Writing at the end of the 1980s I indicated my transfer of executive responsibilities to Christopher, not the easiest of things if 'the old man' was still to have a function in the Company , but having benefited from my father's attitude I was anxious to follow his example. I would claim no sixth sense in the timing but seen even at this relatively short remove it came at very much the right moment. Progressively, Christopher was to implement a new management structure in the Company, largely consisting of younger people, which would be far more capable of resolving the challenges which the 1990s were to pose.

The record industry in the 1990s

By now Compact Disc was the established music carrier and its success generated a world-wide record industry far larger than anything which we had known in the past. The huge financial investment which was necessary resulted in many of the major record companies operating as integral parts of larger organizations and, as a result, being subject to performance expectations which, particularly in the classical business, had been absent in the past. For instance, the viability of individual recordings now had to be established before they could be undertaken, a requirement not exactly new but now being applied much more rigorously than in the past. In fact, Ken East had, much to the concern of some of those involved, instituted a similar arrangement when Managing Director of Decca (a post he held for one year from October 1st, 1974). Clearly, it was a logical discipline but one wonders whether Solti's *Ring* would exist today had it been applied in the late 1950s?

On October 2nd, 1985 Sir Peter Pears presented *Gramophone*'s "Record of the Year" award to a young Nigel Kennedy for his EMI recording of Elgar's Violin Concerto with Vernon Handley and the LPO. They are seen here in conversation after the presentation

Beyond this there was an increasing perception of the need to maximize sales, and in effect broaden the classical market. Nigel Kennedy's recording of Vivaldi's *Four Seasons* was released in November 1989 and with mass-media exposure it sold in excess of one million copies. Immediately, this was cited by chief executives in other record companies as an example of what could be achieved by a classical A&R department. The following September Decca released the "Three Tenors" recording which in its various formats was to sell in excess of 12 million copies world-wide and parallel with this came Pavarotti's "Nessun dorma" single and his "Essential Pavarotti" album which was to occupy the No. 1 position in the pop charts. The search was now on in all companies for similar products but it was not until 1992 that Nonesuch (part of Warner Classics) came up with Górecki's Third Symphony which would sell one million copies world-wide. As an almost unknown piece of contemporary music this was brilliantly marketed in the UK by Bill Holland (using, to a great extent, the Classic fM radio station), although as the composer himself was to say at a press conference in Brussels in February 1993, "It's a wonder, a miracle ... What has happened in America and London is very nice, but why? Please tell me." Sadly, there were no reported answers to the question that not only Górecki was asking! And at the time of writing no subsequent Górecki recording has sold even a tenth as many copies.

Perhaps as a result of all this activity – and the presence in the Industry of an increasing number of executives whose knowledge of, and interest in, the classical business was limited – sales of the core repertoire became progressively more difficult to achieve. To be fair, the classical record buyer was no longer required to replace worn, damaged or faulty discs (as had been the case with LP); there were no audio developments which established a major technical difference between a recording made in 1985 and another made ten years later and which demanded replacement of the former; with a few obvious exceptions there was a dearth of those artists who, for one reason or another, brought their charismatic qualities to the business; there were far too many records

News

ROMAN BATHS

October 1990

The Three Tenors in Rome

Take three of the most prominent singers in the world, add to that the public's penchant for the tenor voice, reserve the night of the eve of football's World Cup, July 7th, 1990, and throw in a concert in the beautiful surroundings of the Baths of Caracalla in Rome and you are guaranteed an enormous success. When José Carreras suggested that he join his colleagues Plácido Domingo and Luciano Pavarotti (who also share his passion for football) in a special concert for charity even he would have been hard-pressed to predict the impact the event would have. It was beamed around the world by satellite and the audience figures must have been staggering, but when released on disc as well as on video, the concert sailed into the pop album charts at No. 1.

Quite why there should be such a passion for tenors at the moment is difficult to explain, but the vocal splendour of hearing three of them simultaneously captured the imagination. It was an easy sport on the night mentally to weigh one against the other – yes, Domingo had the power and volume, Pavarotti the sweetness and exquisite *laissez-faire* (though as in all he does there was never a sign of less than thorough preparation) and Carreras had the passion and intensity. But more engaging still was the sense of everyone having fun: whatever competitive spirit exists between the three men (though, after all, they have totally different voices) there was no sign of it in Rome. If anything Carreras was the centre of affection, sharing a joke with his colleagues or simply linking arms for a good sing. Pavarotti audibly eased back the throttle when in duet with Carreras; it was a kind gesture and one that was not lost on the audience.

And then there was the audience; 6,000 people, paying around £200 each, were provided with the state-of-the-art in plastic tickets, and for a country that seems to thrive on bureaucratic complexities everyone was seated with quite remarkable speed and efficiency. Early comers were treated to a quick impromptu rendition by the soloists; Pavarotti in his flat-cap and scarf and Carreras in a mac that made him look as if he'd come to put out the music-stands – but when they started singing there were no confusions.

The programme was one of those judicious mixes that only tenors seem to be able to get away with – impassioned arias from ardent lovers served back to back with songs of distant lands. Even the medley, garnish courtesy of Lalo Schifrin, seemed in keeping with the event – the ripe orchestrations were needed to cut through the spontaneous rounds of applause. To Decca's considerable relief the medley was given twice, so what we hear on the record – beautifully edited – is a combination of the two. How they overcame the aeroplane that flew over during Carreras's first aria (and received from him a kiss blown up into the skies) or the motorcycle that weaved its way along the road behind the Baths is one of those technical feats one can only wonder at. **James Jolly**

and from another world

September 1963

I well remember sitting in the Baths of Caracalla in Rome one night in 1945. It is here that in summer the Rome Opera gives spectacular alfresco performances. The usual enormous audience, with British troops much in evidence, had assembled for a curious double bill – *Pagliacci*, preceded by the ballet *Scheherazade*. When the stage lights went on, there stood the cast in *Pagliacci* costumes while the orchestra began to play the Intermezzo from *Cavalleria*. Stupefaction! Then, rather dramatically, one whispered word spread through the night – "morto". Mascagni had died that day in Rome [August 2nd, 1945]. Since that other night in 1890 *Cav* has kept many a company on the road and has put a lot of money into a lot of pockets, including those of that old organ-grinder, who, it is said, was playing outside the composer's hotel when the great man himself rushed out, seized the handle, and speeded up the music. Next day, the organ reappeared carrying the message "Pupil of Mascagni". **Roger Wimbush**

"A load of gloomy piffle."
Alexander Waugh EVENING STANDARD (8/4/93)

"There is less to this music than meets the ear, sadly I don't think it will last."
David Mellor THE GUARDIAN (26/2/93)

"Henryk Górecki seems a very nice man, and it is because of perverse resentment of its popularity that I do not possess the now famous recording of his third symphony."
Stephen Pettitt THE TIMES (3/4/93)

"Hardly the stuff of which gold records are made."
Michael Walsh TIME MAGAZINE (8/3/93)

"Why this really rather dreary symphony has sent all those people into the record shops baffles me."
Michael Kennedy THE SUNDAY TELEGRAPH (11/4/93)

"To write down a few static harmonies in long notes takes only seconds. But if played very, very slowly and much repeated they can be made to last for hours...think up some politically correct (in Górecki's case syrupy emotional) title and you've got it made. The musically illiterate love it, because they think they are appreciating modern 'classical' music, and Classic FM and Radio 3 can both claim they are gaining new audiences."
Letter from Fritz Spiegel to THE GUARDIAN (2/1/93)

Henryk Górecki receiving silver and gold discs for UK sales of his Symphony No.3.

Over 300,000 copies sold.

No.1 in the UK and USA classical charts for a record-breaking number of weeks.

First recording by a living composer ever to reach No.1 in the UK classical charts.

The first recording of music by a living classical composer ever to enter the UK pop albums chart.

Highest climber in UK pop charts on two separate occasions.

Elektra Nonesuch

Marketed and Distributed by © WARNER CLASSICS UK, 46 Kensington Court, London W8 5DP A division of Warner Music UK. A Time Warner Company.

These two advertisements from Warner Classics, which appeared on consecutive pages of the June 1993 issue, highlight the enigma of Górecki's Third Symphony

released and too often duplication made the ultimate choice near-impossible – and, of course, there were an increasing number of cheaper recordings, both new and reissued, from which to choose.

The British Phonographic Industry (BPI) trade delivery figures reflect immediately the presence of something such as the "Three Tenors" (and Warner Classics had the trio's second offering in August 1994 with world-wide sales to date of all formats amounting to eight million) and without this impetus the picture which they paint is one which the prophets of doom in the national press are happy to translate as the imminent demise of the classical record business. In saying this one ignores the skills and resilience inherent in the business, with two major companies celebrating their Centenaries and a host of independents displaying a degree of creative flair for which one has nothing but praise. Later in this book John Borwick writes about the technical developments which we can expect to see in the near future and which, if managed successfully, may offer an opportunity to address some of those problems which today exercise the classical record business. We can but wait and see.

Whatever the case, the record industry first and foremost is all about people and its successes throughout history have been directly related to their endeavours. In these recollections I have said little about the artists, perhaps unjustly because without them there would be no record business. But much has been written and will continue to be written about them elsewhere by people far more qualified than myself. On the other hand I have tried in the context of this perhaps ungainly canvas to give some idea of those who made the recordings possible – the engineers, the producers and the record company

Following the success of his Third Symphony, Henryk Górecki (right) signed an exclusive recording agreement with Elektra Nonesuch (part of Warner Classics International) on February 12th, 1994. Robert Hurwitz, General Manager of Nonesuch who produced the Third Symphony recording, is seated left whilst Tony Fell, MD of Boosey and Hawkes, looks on *Photo Warner Classics*

executives. Whilst I would make no claim to have known all such people, it has been my very good fortune to meet and become acquainted, in varying degrees, with an enormous number of them. I have always felt privileged (a word I dislike as it is so often misused) to have enjoyed the friendship of Fred Gaisberg – a link which immediately establishes a connection with the very beginning of our Industry. One particularly happy incident occurred in May 1949 when he asked me to take him to the Abbey Road studios to hear a young singer who he believed had a great future – Victoria de los Angeles. Then there was Walter Legge, with my father, putting a somewhat inebriated young Subaltern on the milk train at 3am from Waterloo to return to my unit after celebrating ***The Gramophone***'s Silver Jubilee in June 1948; and C. H. Thomas of EMI – a wonderful man with, they might say, shellac in his veins – giving me a severe dressing-down following what he believed to be an unjust review in the 1950s; and recording sessions, particularly for *The Ring*, with John Culshaw ... memories abound!

Correspondence

THE LP REMEMBERED

December 1990

Does anyone out there remember the LP? Does anyone out there believe that the technological advantages of the CD make up for the lack of a decent album and booklet in the new marketing technology?

J. Paul Getty Jnr
London, SW1

January 1991

Why yes, Mr Getty, I remember LPs: I still retain a few.

Who could forget the pressing standards of the 1970s with more snap, crackle and pop than any breakfast cereal. Who could forget watching one's (expensive) stylus trying to stay in contact with the vinyl at all, as warps forced massive excursions of loudspeaker cones with every revolution of the disc. Then there was end of side distortion, with the prospect that every musical climax would be accompanied by levels of distortion hundreds of times greater than we have today. If all that was not enough, any piece of decent length was spread over several sides, and one had to leap to one's feet after the slow movement to turn the thing over.

C. S. Harrison
Halesowen, W. Midlands

March 1991

Since the major record companies stopped producing LPs and the "Last sale of vinyl" ads have disappeared, your magazine has been full of letters all doing their best to downgrade the LP and all that it stood for. No mention has been made of the second-hand market to which many true collectors subscribe. I have collected records since 1948. Most of my collection is still intact and I keep them in pristine condition and regard the many LP interpretations, as yet not available on CD and possibly never to be reissued, as in a class apart.

The people of my own age group – and, increasingly, youngsters as well – that I meet in second-hand dealers like Gramex and who really know their artists and repertoire, have very valid musical opinions. Like myself they collect both LPs and CDs and we feel that in order to enjoy classical records to the full we need the best of both worlds. The second-hand market is now the only source of LPs; as such it performs a very useful service.

Bill Newman
Edgware, Middx

In addition to the success of Górecki's Third Symphony, Warner Classics were at the forefront of the 'themed' compilation market, led by the ingenuity of their UK Director, Bill Holland. The series gained some notoriety as releases such as "Sensual Classics" matched romantic classical themes with the quasi-erotic marketing then employed by the up-market ice-cream makers. Never one to miss a PR opportunity, Holland distributed this photograph of himself within the industry to alert them to the release of Warner's response to EMI's runaway bestseller, "Canto Gregoriano"
Photo Warner Classics

One of the early Argo releases, reviewed in the March 1953 issue of *The Gramophone*

Harley Usill with Prunella Scales in the late-1950s *Photo Decca*

Decca's recording of *Les Troyens* was launched in Paris in November 1994. For Ray Minshull (left) it was his last recording for Decca as a member of the company; he is seen here with his successor, Evans Mirageas (centre) and Anthony Pollard *Photo Decca*

But to return to the 1990s it was sad to note the death of Harley Usill in November 1991. One of the original independents, he formed The Argo Record Company in December 1951 with Alex Herbage, coming under Decca's wing in 1957 and eventually departing to found ASV with Jack Boyce and David Gyle-Thompson in 1981. An Argo production involved Usill at virtually every stage and, as I knew to my cost, a poor review struck at the very heart of the man. Writing in the January 1992 issue, Ted Greenfield recalled meeting Usill after he had unfavourably dismissed his Marlowe Society recording of Shakespeare's *Macbeth*, "He told me to look at his back, 'Don't you see the dagger sticking out?' he asked vehemently, and he was only half joking". Another independent, in a somewhat larger context and also fiercely proud of his company's achievements, was Numa Labinsky. He had founded Nimbus Records in April 1971 (with Michael Reynolds) and not only developed a record label but established an enviable reputation as a manufacturer of LPs, later opening the first UK Compact Disc plant in June 1984. He died on January 28th, 1994.

Numa Labinsky

Jack Boyce started his career in the record industry as a salesman for EMI in 1956 and brought new thinking to Decca's classical marketing in 1959. Ultimately he founded ASV in 1981 with Harley Usill and David Gyle-Thompson. A true 'record man'

On March 27th, 1994 Ray Minshull retired as Executive Vice-President of Decca International, having joined The Decca Record Company in October 1957. He made Joan Sutherland's first major recording (for the Oiseau-Lyre label) in March 1958 and succeeded John Culshaw as Manager of the Classical A&R Department when he left the company in October 1967. With the able help of Jack Boyce, who in October 1959 had become Decca's Classical Marketing Manager, Culshaw's 15 years as a key producer were well publicized and established a pattern which would be copied elsewhere in the Industry.

However, Minshull chose to have a much lower profile and as a result it is easy to overlook the fact that he was producing recordings for Decca over a period of 36 years. For the whole of Culshaw's Decca career the ultimate guiding hand in the classical area was Maurice Rosengarten who died in November 1975, just eight years after Minshull succeeded Culshaw. At this point Sir Edward Lewis appointed Minshull as Director of Classical Recordings and for the next 18 years he was to have total responsibility for all decisions related to the Classical A&R Department. Minshull's last major recording as a member of Decca was the Berlioz *Trojans* with Charles Dutoit (released in December 1994). Shortly after the completion of Decca's *Ring*, Minshull had put this project on the agenda but for various reasons it was to be 30 years before it came to fruition. Such are the vagaries of the record business.

Gramophone in the 1990s

Notwithstanding our total independence it must be accepted that for the past 75 years our fortunes have been inexorably linked with those of the record industry, and the 1990s were no exception. The situation, however, was exacerbated for us when *Gramophone*'s position in the market-place, already plagued by the recession which affected the first three years of the decade, was challenged by two other magazine publishers.

August 1993 **Correspondence**

GRAMOPHONE AT 70

I have been a *Gramophone* reader since the early 1930s and can say without hesitation that no publication has come anywhere near to giving me consistently such richly informative and absorbing high-quality reading: each month one looks forward to the arrival of *Gramophone* with keen anticipation and not once has it failed to live up to its high reputation.

Full credit must go to Editorial policy and guidance in helping to maintain the very high standards shown by your contributors over the decades: I'm sure that when your 100th Anniversary comes *Gramophone*, like Johnny Walker, will be still going strong!

L. F. B. Gilhespy
Switzerland

THE TIMES

No 64,007 WEDNESDAY MAY 1 1991 40p

Constitutional clash over 131-109 vote

Lords defy MPs by rejecting war crimes bill

Down from the mountains: Kurdish children arriving in Zakho yesterday after weeks spent on the hills above the Iraq-Turkey border. Thousands were returning to their homes and the tent camps set up by the multinational forces

The price is right in the housing basement

Demand by Major for UN action

Appeal court ruling boosts Sunday trading

CBI offers hope of end to slump

The cost of being honest is 5,000 roubles

TODAY IN THE TIMES

INSIDE

Cyclone toll

Stormont hope

Hospital cuts

14 pages of top jobs in tomorrow's appointments section

INDEX

"It took me ten years before I dared walk on stage with Brahms's Second Concerto"

Krystian Zimerman in the May issue of

GRAMOPHONE

The Review of New Classical Recordings

ON SALE NOW

Since the early 1930s there had always been competitors but, apart from one very brief sortie by a major publishing house in the 1960s, their resources had always been similar to ours and there had been little difficulty in maintaining our supremacy.

However, in the early 1990s two large, well-funded publishing houses decided, quite independently, to challenge that supremacy and we found ourselves contesting a place in what was not only a recession-hit market but one in which three publishers were now competing.

Even in the days when we had the market virtually to ourselves I don't believe that we could ever be accused of complacency: the magazine was innovative and constantly looking for the best ways to serve both the readers and the industries depicted in our pages. None the less, the situation which we now faced called for a level of financial commitment and human resources unique in our history.

Our approach to magazine sales – both to the trade and by direct subscription – had to be reassessed, whilst advertisement sales had to assume a much more aggressive stance to match that of our competitors. The visual appearance of the magazine also had to be further enhanced to ensure its impact on the news-stands, and utilizing newspaper and commercial radio advertising the message had to be conveyed to all and sundry that for anyone interested in recorded classical music there was only one magazine to consider. In September 1993 the magazine contained more reviews that ever before (over 200) and in October 1994 we published the biggest issue in the magazine's history. To some extent we were in the 'numbers game' but we have been able to ensure, thus far, that *Gramophone*'s position remains intact without deviating from the long-established philosophies of the magazine.

However, at the same time as we were meeting the challenge from our competitors it was vital that our communications with the record and audio industries, both of whom were also under pressure in the marketplace, were maintained and even further developed. Under Ivor Humphreys' guidance, and with the support of John Borwick, Geoffrey Horn (who had joined us

Keith Howard, *Gramophone*'s Audio Consulting Editor, who joined in August 1993

August 1993

Correspondence

GRAMOPHONE'S FACE-LIFT

In September 1993, the appearance of the magazine was redesigned. The new look prompted several letters, both pro and con, from readers

October 1993

After receiving the September copy of *Gramophone* and reading through same, I feel compelled to write to thank you and your staff for the excellent new layout. All too often people are quick to complain and somewhat reluctant to give credit where it is due.

As a reader of *Gramophone* for the past 45 years I think that this is the easiest to read layout ever produced during that time, and I trust that you will now be staying with the format for some years to come (though probably not for the next 70 years!).

Robert Allen
Urmston, Manchester

... but

As a reader of *Gramophone* for 50 years I am well aware of (and have sometimes regretted) the many changes in its appearance which have crept in over recent years but I was quite unprepared for the culture-shock induced by the September issue. I never before realized so many typefaces actually existed and might all appear simultaneously between the covers of a single periodical. Surely such excess and eccentricities of typography and layout and the meretricious use of colour have no place in an influential journal of over 70 years' standing devoted to the serious appraisal of the more important forms of recorded music.

William McKnight Toner
Bridge of Weir, Renfrewshire

November 1993

I applaud the revised format of the magazine over the last two months and would suggest that it had become necessary, the 70th Anniversary being an opportune time. I would like to take this opportunity to congratulate yourself, staff and contributors on the consistently high standard attained in all sections over the years. The magazine has been avidly read by myself over the last 40 years.

N. Hughes
Llanelli, Dyfed

... but

The modified rapture apparently accorded the new-look *Gramophone* shamed me into reconsidering the somewhat intemperate views expressed in my recent letter. Having carefully examined the September issue and the current issue, with its cover expertly defaced by the attachment of a deeply unwanted CD, I can alas only marvel at my earlier restraint.

William McKnight Toner
Bridge of Weir, Renfrewshire

under Percy Wilson's aegis, first contributing to the magazine in February 1957) and Keith Howard (who joined in August 1993), the coverage of the audio pages was progressively enhanced both in terms of equipment reviews and a range of articles specially designed to keep all readers abreast of the increasing number of complex technical developments which were either directly (or indirectly) affecting (or likely to affect) the reproduction of sound and vision in the home. It was into this environment that Iain Hutchison was introduced in July 1991 to concentrate on advertisement sales to audio manufacturers, eventually assuming responsibility for all advertisement sales when in January 1997 Barry Irving, after 31 years in the Advertisement Department, switched to a Business Development role.

The 1990s saw the introduction of two new recording/replay systems, Philips's Digital Compact Cassette, announced in November 1990 and launched in April 1992; and Sony's Mini-Disc, announced in May 1991 and launched in the autumn of 1992 [pp. 241-3]. A limited amount of software was released to support both systems but neither effected any real market penetration, and neither was seen as a challenge to the Compact Disc. In discussing the analogue cassette on page 165 I have referred to the current position of DCC: however, a renewed marketing campaign for Mini-Disc in 1997 has emphasized its potential as an excellent recording medium (much like DAT) but there is still little evidence of any real software support. However,

Geoffrey Horn (left) and Barry Irving at *Gramophone*'s Diamond Jubilee in April 1983

typical of the complexity of the age in which we live, the situation has now been compounded by Philips's introduction of a £499 CD machine which offers not only high-quality replay facilities from audio CDs but also includes CD-R (record once and replay many times) and CD-RW (record many times and replay). Perhaps this is the extension of the exceedingly successful audio CD for which the market has been waiting? Or will it be DVD? [pp. 243-4]

Looking at the record industry, *Gramophone* took a number of initiatives which were designed to enhance the magazine's recognition beyond the actual readership and in so doing widen the support which we were providing for both record manufacturers and retailers. In May 1993 we launched the "Blue riband" scheme which set out to highlight and classify quality record dealers across the country: the initiative received support in all quarters and is also now used by record manufacturers for various specialized marketing exercises.

In the early days the Editor often reviewed the latest recordings but ultimately the responsibility for such comment was assumed exclusively by the reviewers. However, in the 1990s the huge number of reviews in each issue suggested the need to focus attention on just a few which had received outstanding notices, and this spawned "Editor's choice" which James Jolly initiated in May 1993. His selection of ten records each month, based upon the individual reviewers' comments, very quickly established itself and often creates sales levels well beyond manufacturers' expectations.

Another contribution from the Editorial Department is the specially compiled *Gramophone* monthly covermounted CD. Whilst covermounted CDs are nothing new – we have been using them at various times since November 1990 – they have formed a part (or perhaps more than just a part?) of the two magazines which invariably appear alongside *Gramophone* on the news-stands. Notwithstanding higher cover prices, the

Editor's choice

James Jolly selects ten outstanding CDs from this month's reviews

RECORDING OF THE MONTH

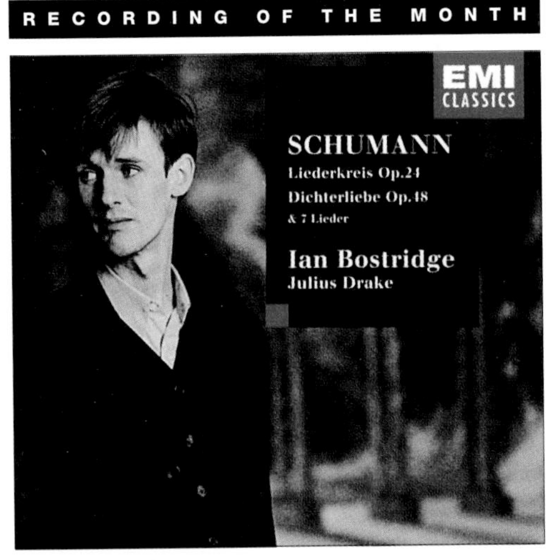

Schumann Dichterliebe. Liederkreis *Bostridge; Drake*
EMI
Choral and song reviews
Page 94

Adam Le toréador *Trempont; Jo; Aler; Welsh National Opera Orchestra / Bonynge*
Decca
Opera reviews
Page 108

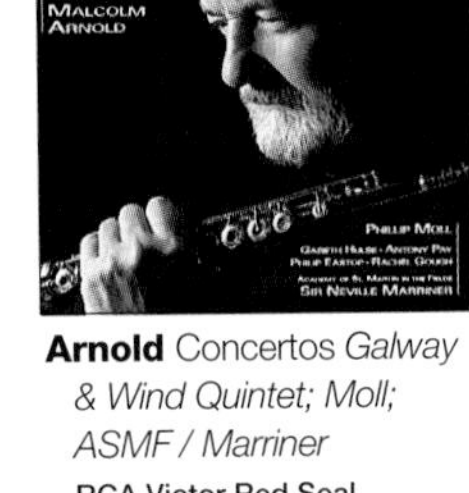

Arnold Concertos *Galway & Wind Quintet; Moll; ASMF / Marriner*
RCA Victor Red Seal
Orchestral reviews
Page 36

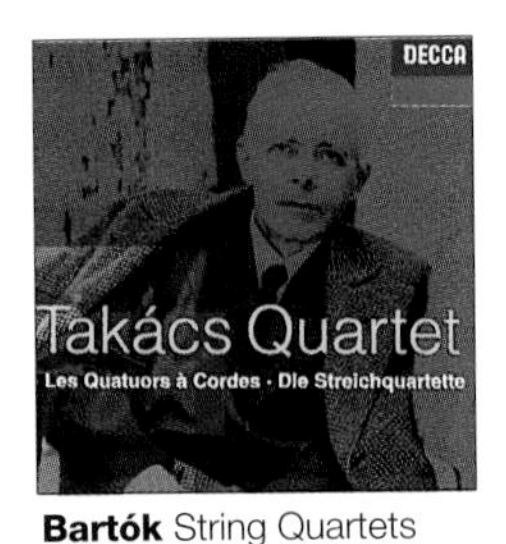

Bartók String Quartets *Takács Quartet*
Decca
Chamber reviews
Page 60

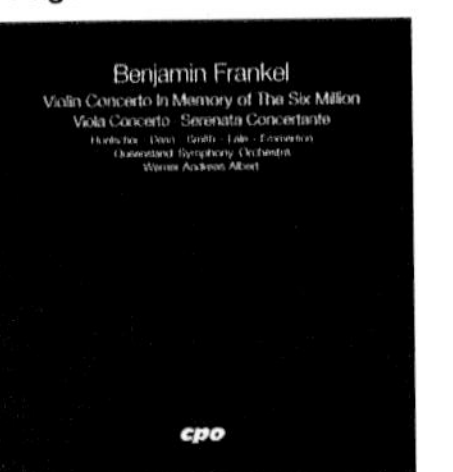
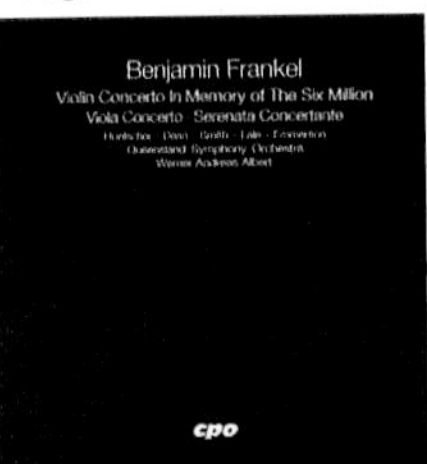

Frankel Violin & Viola Concertos, etc *Hoelscher; Dean; Queensland SO / Albert*
CPO
Orchestral reviews
Page 44

Korngold. J Marx Piano Concertos *Hamelin; BBC Scottish SO / Brabbins*
Hyperion
Orchestral reviews
Page 46

Mozart. R Strauss Lieder & Concert Arias *Schäfer; Berlin PO / Abbado*
DG
Choral and song reviews
Page 88

Rameau Les fêtes d'Hébé *Soloists; Les Arts Florissants / Christie*
Erato
Opera reviews
Page 112

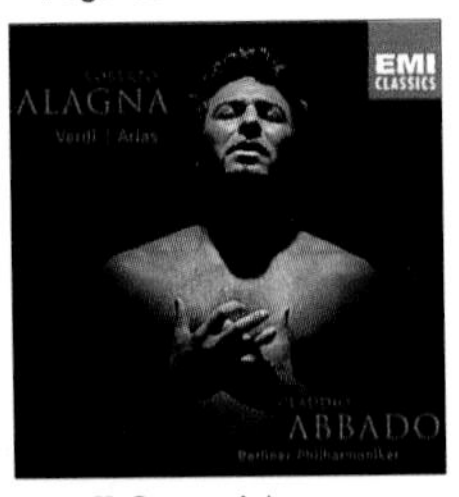

Verdi Opera Arias *Alagna; Berlin PO / Abbado*
EMI
Opera reviews
Page 118

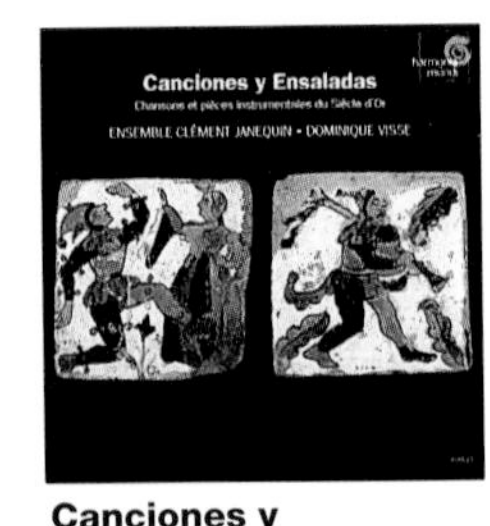

Canciones y Ensaladas *Ensemble Clément Janequin / Visse*
Harmonia Mundi
Choral and song reviews
Page 104

June 1997 **Correspondence**

G R A M O P H O N E   C O V E R M O U N T

I want to thank you for the enormous pleasure given by your new approach of highlighting monthly recommendations and supplying a trial disc. I have found more new music to enjoy than for many years. The recording companies should be paying you a substantial amount. Over the past few months I have bought at least three times as many CDs as I would have done otherwise. Each new find triggers a search for other music. While writing to you I am listening to Murray Perahia playing Handel – a disc I would never have bought without your recommendation (May, 1997) – and it is wonderful.

Anthony Yates,
Kew, Surrey

apparent advantage which accrues from the 'perceived added value' is such that in December 1996 we established a regular covermount. For some time we had solicited readers' views on the matter and the consensus was generally negative: however, when it was decided to proceed – specifically for the news-stand copies – and readers saw the resulting disc, there was a substantial change of opinion.

Also, back in September 1990, we introduced a North American edition of the magazine to provide a better service to the substantial number of influential readers resident in the USA and Canada – territories in which the magazine has enjoyed great success since the earliest days. The edition is identical to that sold elsewhere in the world but with the addition of a section designed specifically for North American readers.

Under the overall direction of Christopher, the Editorial Department – with James Jolly at the helm – currently fulfils an increasingly wide spectrum of responsibilities. In production terms all text is electronically keyboarded or scanned in the department and carried forward to final page layout, not just for the magazine but for the various Guides, the quarterlies, and what we euphemistically refer to as the "one-offs". Supporting James Jolly in these areas are Harriet Smith

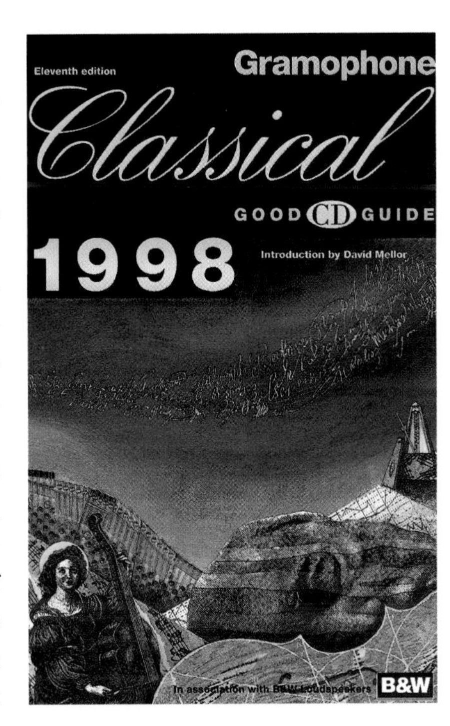

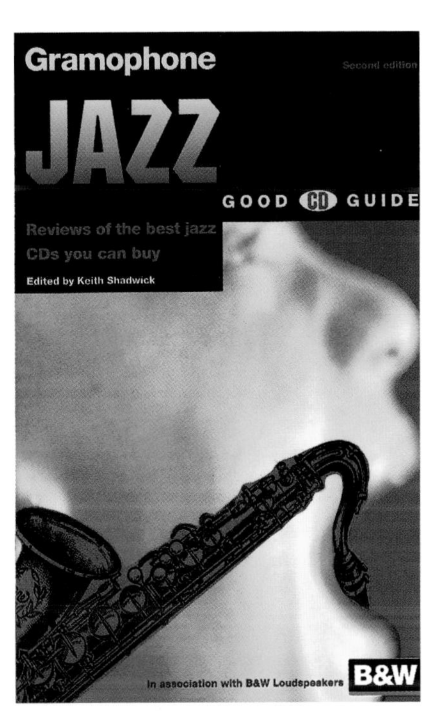

Gramophone staff February 1998

135 Greenford Road *Photo Bayley*

Reception: Maureen Coleman *Photo Bayley*

Subscriptions (left to right) : Janet Wiltshire, Val Warburton and Theresa Kelly *Photo Bayley*

Editorial Production and Design (left to right): Emma Roach, Katherine Bettley, Isabel Jagoe, Mark Walker, Lisa Druggan and Janis Nicholls (not in photo) *Photo Bayley*

Editorial (left to right): Alex Newby, James Jolly, Mark Wiggins, Harriet Smith, Vivian Stewart and Máire Taylor (not in photo) *Photo Bayley*

The Despatch Department: Jay Shah and Barry Sandling (Maintenance Engineer) *Photo Bayley*

Marketing and Circulation (left to right): Carol Gross, Nick Clements, Jennie King, Verity Batchelder, Robert Frumkin, Clive Regan and Tim Grocutt (not in photo) *Photo Bayley*

Finance and Administration (left to right): Jenny Savage, Janet Johnson, Anne Cains, Richard Phalp, Kerrie Cronin and Nicola McDonagh (seated) *Photo Bayley*

Advertising and Production (left to right): Iain Hutchison, Paul Geoghegan, Ivor Humphreys (Audio Editor), Dermot Jones, Patti Alvarez, Barry Irving, Oliver Wilson, Kathryn Giornali (not in photo) and Jo Frost (not in photo) *Photo Bayley*

Editorial Services (left to right): Diana Wray, Alan Worth, Richard Whitehouse, Kathryn Wolfendale, Malcolm Walker and Brian Godfrey (not in photo) *Photo Bayley*

(Deputy Editor, joined August 1991) and Mark Wiggins (Assistant Editor, joined February 1986), the whole under-pinned by the *Gramophone* database. Our first foray into electronic publishing came in January 1996 when we launched *GramoFile*, a CD-ROM which, at the time of writing, provides access to over 24,000 *Gramophone* reviews that have appeared since March 1983, the month we published our first CD reviews. This was followed in August 1997 by the establishment of an Internet site for the magazine (www.gramophone.co.uk) which includes access to the online version of *GramoFile*.

In June 1997, we introduced a monthly updated listing of some 300 "Recommended Recordings" as an integral part of the magazine. This is information which is invaluable to both the regular reader and those who might just select the magazine as an impulse buy – and who hopefully may join the 26,500 regular subscribers, many of whom have been reading the magazine for 30 years or more.

During the course of these reminiscences I have referred to a number of key people who have contributed to the Company's success over the past 75 years – a dangerous and invidious practice, since clearly one cannot mention everyone, but please understand that in a small company such as this one cannot afford to carry passengers. However, having referred to a number of the current team concerned with advertising, audio and editorial, I must mention several others without whom *Gramophone* would be a poorer place. In January 1972 Dermot Jones joined the Advertisement Department: his responsibilities have embraced selling, marketing and design, and today he is responsible for all aspects of production, together with print and paper buying. Another long-serving member of the Company since July 1978 is Jenny Savage who is principally responsible for the operation of our Sales Ledger accounts, whilst Verity Batchelder (who joined in September 1991) is concerned with all aspects of marketing, together with a direct responsibility for all sales, other than advertising. Last, but by no means least, is our Financial Director, Richard Phalp, who joined in April 1992. His role is one which originally I inherited from my father but ultimately it became clear that the increasing complexity of the business required a much more professional approach, one which Richard has embraced to the benefit of all concerned.

One of the major activities which he and Christopher undertook in May 1996 was the move from our old offices at 177-179 Kenton Road to new, larger and more suitable premises in Sudbury Hill. Although only a couple of miles from our old offices, the association with Kenton, dating back 55 years to 1940 when my father moved the office to his house in Ebrington Road, was now at an end – and makes perhaps a suitable point at which to conclude these reminiscences of *Gramophone*'s first 75 years.

My heartfelt thanks go to all those who have made this achievement possible – the loyal employees of *Gramophone*, our dedicated contributors, friends in the worldwide record and audio industries, our suppliers both large and small – and I wish all good fortune to those who will carry the traditions of our Founders forward to the next landmark. *Floreat!*

Records and reviewing

Chamber

Opera

Choral and song

Nostalgia

Orchestra

Soundbites

These short reviews, "Soundbites", are the musical equivalent of tasting-notes, a quick summing up of an impression made by one or two playings of a disc without, usually, carrying out the customary comparative listening. Not all discs currently have UK distribution (see the UK label distribution directory) but should be obtainable through international mail-order companies.

Borodin String Quartet No. 1 in A major. Piano Quintet in C minor[a]. [a]**Alexander Mndioantz** (pf); **Moscow String Quartet** (Alexander Detisov, Alexander Gelfat, vns; Igor Suliga, va; Alexander Osokin, vc).

CdM Russian Season Ⓟ Ⓓ RUS288 141 (66 minutes: DDD).

A long-breathed account of the marvellous First Quartet (1875-8) from this Moscow group: they take 39'27" as against 36'58" from the Borodin Quartet (EMI, 5/88 – nla). Secure though their playing is (and the recording's a good one, too), I find it a bit too laid-back and lacking in characterful profile for my tastes. The Piano Quintet is an earlier offering from 1862. Expertly dispatched on this occasion, its three movements serve up a delightful stylistic cocktail: the scherzo is clearly inspired by Glinka's Kamarinskaya and there are appealing echoes of Schumann and Brahms in the big-scale finale. **AA**

Bruch Concerto for Violin and Orchestra No. 2 in D minor, Op. 44[a]. Romance for Violin and Orchestra in A minor, Op. 42[a]. Adagio appassionata for Violin and Orchestra, Op. 57[a]. Concerto for Clarinet, Viola and Orchestra, Op. 88[bc]. [a]**Jacques Israelievitch** (vn); [b]**Donatus Katkus** (va); [c]**Guy Chadash** (cl); **St Christopher Chamber Orchestra of Lithuania / Arie Lipsky.**

Fleur de Son Classics Ⓟ Ⓓ FDS 57925 (66 minutes: DDD).

Concertmaster of the Toronto Symphony since 1988, Cannes-born Jacques Israelievitch brings plenty of affection and no mean panache to this repertoire, but Accardo and Masur's splendid Philips survey (7/91 – three discs) isn't seriously challenged, to say nothing of Heifetz, Perlman or Nai-Yuan Hu on Delos (12/95) in the Second Concerto. Moreover, Arie Lipsky's hard-working, unflatteringly recorded Lithuanian group sound uncomfortably weedy next to the glories of the Leipzig orchestra. The Double Concerto for clarinet and viola falls amiably enough on the ear, but

Chopin Etudes – Op. 10; Op. 25; Trois Nouvelles Etudes. **Yuki Matsuzawa** (pf).

Novalis Ⓟ Ⓓ 150 142-2 (67 minutes: DDD).

The longer you listen the better it gets: highlights among Matsuzawa's performances of these pinnacles of pianism include the tenderness of Op. 25 No. 7, the *Etude* in thirds, Op. 25 No. 6 and the *Trois Nouvelles Etudes*. If she seems a shade reticent in *Etudes* such as Op. 10 No. 12 then taken as a whole this is still a very impressive achievement. **Harriet Smith**

Corelli 12 Violin Sonatas, Op. 5. **Trio Veracini** (John Holloway, vn; David Watkin, vc; Lars Ulrik Mortensen, hpd).

Novalis Ⓟ Ⓓ 150 128-2 (two discs: 152 minutes: DDD).

The principal attraction of this set lies in the extensive ornamentation, which follows written-down versions as performed by Corelli and other contemporary virtuosos. Some sonatas are performed with harpsichord, others with just three strings. The ornaments are a new and welcome twist, a change from the overly slick Corelli often fashionable; yet intonation and security of tone are not of the standard usually associated with these musicians. A qualified recommendation. **FF**

Gesualdo Madrigali libro quinto. **Ensemble Métamorphoses / Maurice Bourbon.**

Arion Ⓟ Ⓓ ARN68388 (59 minutes: DDD).

Recordings devoted to one complete book of Gesualdo's madrigals are still thin on the ground. Here what strikes one (apart from the well-known chromaticisms) is the brevity of individual pieces. This French ensemble sing one to a part (sensibly enough). Though not quite on a par with the best ensembles for this repertory, Métamorphoses achieve a very nice blend, and tuning is mostly proof against the composer's wiles. A welcome issue. **FF**

Kenins Sonata for Cello and Piano[c]. Concertante for Flute and Piano[b]. Piano Quartet No. 2[a]. [b]**Robert Aitken** (fl); [a]**Paul Meyer** (vln); [a]**Steven Dann** (vla); [ac]**David Hetherington** (vc); **William Aide** (pf).

CMC Centredisc Ⓟ Ⓓ CCMCCD5997 (67 minutes: DDD).

Latvian-born Talivaldis Kenins is a composer of some distinction. The Cello Sonata is an uncommonly assured graduation piece, while the *Flute concertante* features a beautifully shaped *Lento*. The powerful Second Piano Quartet draws on the example of Shostakovich with discrimination and resourcefulness. Excellent performances, but the acoustic blurs the often intricate part-writing. **Richard Whitehouse**

Mendelssohn Violin Concertos – D minor; E minor, Op. 64. **Angèle Dubeau** (vn); **Orchestre Métropolitain / Joseph Rescigno.**

Analekta Fleur de lys Ⓟ Ⓓ FL2 3098 (51 minutes: DDD).

The booklet speaks of Angèle Dubeau's "warm tone and strong musical personality"; to my ears, however, her neat contribution falls short in precisely those selfsame departments! Surely the perennially fresh Op. 64 deserves solo playing of far greater personable warmth and charisma. Overall, there's nothing distinctive here. For this particular coupling, I'd turn to Mullova and Marriner on Philips (5/91) every time. **AA**

Paredes Permutaciones (versions 1 and 2). The Seventh Seed. **Arditti Quartet.**

Mode Records Ⓟ Ⓓ Mode 60 (61 minutes: DDD).

The Seventh Seed offers an intriguing update of the Persephone myth. While the libretto tends towards heavy-handedness, the music is subtly and imaginatively conceived for its modest forces, offsetting the contrived feel of the vocal writing. The semi-

THE INDEPENDENTS – AN INTRODUCTION

An aerial view from the late 1930s of the EMI factory at Hayes, Middlesex, with the various elements (record manufacturing and stores, cabinet factory, engineering, research, administration etc.) highlighted

With but few exceptions, history indicates that to be seen as part of the record industry it was necessary to own a recording studio and a manufacturing plant, as well as having the ability to market and distribute the records themselves. Thus, the world record business up to the late 1940s consisted principally of large, well-financed companies, established on a global basis: there was minimal evidence of what we now refer to as 'the independents'.

All this would change in 1948-9 when Columbia Records Inc. launched the LP in America. At the time they shared a substantial domestic market with RCA Victor, who chose not to support the LP but promoted an alternative in the form of the 7-inch 45rpm disc. The ensuing contest for market supremacy became known as the 'battle of the speeds' [pp. 84-5]: on the surface it was fought with advertisements in the media together with a range of in-store promotions designed to win the hearts and minds of record buyers.

There was, however, a major departure when Columbia took a gamble in a then unthinkable direction – they indicated to interested parties that in return for supporting the LP format they would waive any patent rights and provide a custom manufacturing facility with the costs kept to a minimum. Coming at a time when recordings could be made directly on to magnetic tape, and when for classical companies war-ravaged Central Europe offered the talents of a wide range of potentially interesting artists, this was an offer too good to refuse and resulted, directly and indirectly, in the greatest 'label explosion' then seen in the history of the record industry.

The practice of custom pressing led eventually to the establishment of independent manufacturing plants and a growth in independent recording and distribution facilities, thus creating the infrastructure which we recognize today.

Even so, as we shall see, the development of the independent labels during the LP era was nothing when compared to the situation which followed the launch of CD in 1983. For much of the time it was invariably the case that the independent label, whilst introducing original repertoire, lacked the investment and expertise consistently to produce the high-quality sound recordings which were originating from the major companies.

However, this was to change during the latter part of the 1970s when the technical initiative was seized by some of the independents with innovative techniques such as half-speed cutting (albeit used by the majors to a limited extent) and direct-to-disc recording, coupled with a concern for pressing quality and packaging too often seen as being given a low priority by the larger manufacturers. This was followed by the application of digital recording which, coupled with a range of improved microphones, ensured the likelihood of an acceptable sound quality, at the very least. In fact, the perceived technical inadequacies rapidly disappeared and the independents now had the ability to match the majors in quality of sound.

At much the same time many of the international trade barriers were coming down and it became feasible to supply the world from one manufacturing centre without incurring crippling import duties. Coupled with the advent of the ultra light weight CD in 1983, the opportunities for the independents were now greater than ever before.
ACP

The Sony PCM-F1 digital audio processor was discussed by John Borwick and Geoffrey Horn in the October and November 1982 issues of *Gramophone*. With its outstanding performance it was the successor to the faithful analogue tape machine. Weighing only 9lbs, measuring 12" x 3" x 4" and priced at under £1,000 it was the independent recording engineer's dream

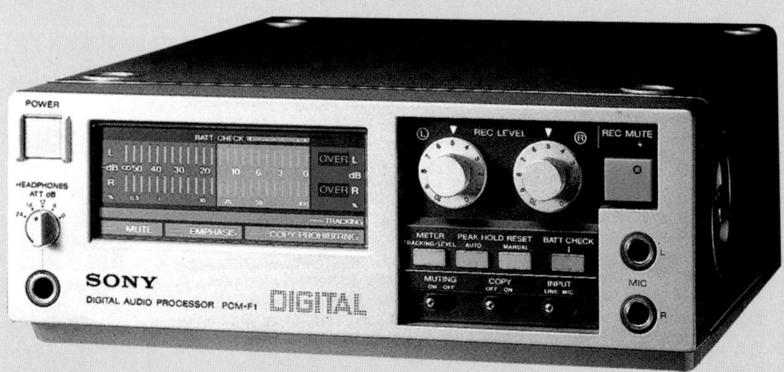

The independent labels

Christopher Pollard

What is an independent label? To me, it is a privately-owned company which doesn't control its own distribution, though this definition would currently exclude labels such as Harmonia Mundi, Naxos and Chandos as each owns distribution in at least some territories. It may be easier to say that the majors are PolyGram (Decca, Philips and Deutsche Grammophon), Sony, BMG (RCA, Conifer and Deutsche Harmonia Mundi), EMI (EMI and Virgin) and Warner (Teldec, Erato, Nonesuch, NVC Arts and Finlandia); the independents are thus all the others.

My brief is to discuss the background of the labels currently defined as independent and, with a respectful nod in the direction of those whose histories go back further, I will take the introduction of the Compact Disc as the catalyst for the robust growth of the independent sector which was to be such an uplifting feature of the classical industry in the 1980s and early-1990s.

The CD era

It would be wrong to credit the Compact Disc with all the responsibility for our independent labels, yet in one crucial way it changed the classical record industry to their lasting benefit.

Until CD, independent labels were rather the province of the hardest-bitten collector, the repertoire collector who knew that his interest in, say, English music could never be sated by EMI's offerings and that Richard Itter's Lyrita label was the place to find Moeran, Finzi and Bax. To the uninitiated these independent labels were risky, especially when so much emphasis in the later days of LP was placed upon the high quality which could be delivered by the German pressing plants so anxiously marketed by the major labels. The guarantor of quality in those days was, right or wrong, the label and not the medium.

With CD this was to change, instantly and irrevocably, and at that moment the majors' market share monopoly started to slip away. PolyGram, owned by the Philips electronics company which co-sponsored CD with Sony, were aware, much as were American Columbia in 1948-9, that for CD to succeed there would need to be plenty of product available quickly; as described elsewhere EMI were once again viewing the new technology with Luddite disdain so attractive pressing deals were offered to the smaller companies such as Chandos, BIS, Telarc, Hyperion and Nimbus.

The birth of the new sound carrier gave rise to a kind of feeding frenzy as the new CD buyers sought product to buy, and demand swiftly exceeded supply. As is usual with new technology classical buyers were at the forefront and, faced with browsers bereft of sold-out PolyGram material, they bought whatever was available in a strangely indiscriminate way. That isn't to say that the disproportionate quantities of Stanford and Stenhammar recordings which found their way into collections were poor – far from it – simply that there wasn't much else to buy.

Looking back, I wonder if Philips and Sony didn't reap a still greater benefit from the high profile taken by independent companies in the early days of CD. The critics, notoriously (and not always unreasonably) suspicious of big businesses, tend to be sympathetic towards independent labels and therefore perhaps had fears about the new medium, allayed by the substantial presence of Hyperion *et al.* On the face of it, critical sympathy towards independent labels is derived from the pioneering zeal traditionally shown in terms of rare repertoire and unsung artists; less overtly it is probably helped along by the feeling that the independents are not quite so commercially motivated as their bigger brothers; ironic when you consider that the biggest salaries in classical recording are drawn by independents.

Chandos and Hyperion

The absent labels paid a heavy price: with both Lyrita and EMI prevaricating, Brian Couzens's Chandos label was able to make the specialist British repertory very much its own, enjoying great success and contributing to the rapid growth of esoteric repertoire which would become a lasting feature of the CD market. Chandos itself grew rapidly, achieving the kind of financial muscle that, with CD pressing capacity at a premium, it advertised in *The Sunday Times* for a director to manage a new pressing plant based in Northern Ireland; the successful candidate was to be offered a six-figure salary, heady stuff in 1984. As it happened, enough new pressing capability came on stream elsewhere to dissuade Chandos from opening its

Brian Couzens, founder of Chandos Records in November 1979 *Photo Curzon/Chandos*

own plant; none the less, the fact that the project was so publicly mooted was evidence enough of the growth being enjoyed by hitherto marginal players.

Brian Couzens took the opportunity to develop his organization, eventually moving to large premises in East Anglia where some 50 folk now give the label in-house editorial, marketing, A&R, post-production, design and reproduction capabilities. Chandos also have a distribution capability in the UK and have at various times had their own offices in countries so disparate as the Czech Republic and the USA. Such a powerful facility contrasts starkly with Ted Perry's Hyperion label which still employs fewer than a dozen individuals and prefers to lean heavily on bought-in services. This philosophical difference is also evident in their relationships with artists and the type of repertoire development.

Hyperion have had lasting partnerships with a number of artists, among whom Emma Kirkby, Graham Johnson, Leslie Howard, Robert King and Matthew Best spring instantly to mind, yet the thrust of the label's activities remains unequivocally repertoire-based. Many retailers tell of customers who will buy all Hyperion releases, a stunning testimony to their faith in the consummate good taste of Ted Perry and his pianistic-inclined colleague Mike Spring, clearly willing to live with medieval polyphony or a Simpson symphony without demur. It is for this reason that artists have tended to take a lower profile in the Hyperion story; when their ambitions in respect of financial return or PR profile have become too much for Perry to cope with it has generally meant both parties moving on independently. Not for nothing do Hyperion's sleeves feature exquisitely chosen paintings.

Ted Perry, who drove a minicab by night to support the early days of Hyperion, which he established in October 1980 *Photo Hyperion*

Chandos, pursuing a different path, are closer in practice to some of the majors. Huge recording commitments to Neeme Järvi and Richard Hickox (both with over 100 items in their Chandos discographies), long-term relationships with orchestras (the Ulster, Scottish National and BBC Philharmonic key amongst them) and a willingness to engage with the core repertoire (no other full-price 'indie' has had the *chutzpah* in digital times to record modern-instrument symphonic cycles of Beethoven, Dvořák, Prokofiev and Brahms) all bear witness to Couzens's combative outlook. He will admit that neither the Beethoven nor the Brahms feature among the label's best-selling efforts, yet stoically and still credibly maintains his belief in, especially, Walter Weller's Beethoven with the CBSO ("the first time that I heard Karajan's early-1960s Beethoven symphonies on DG I knew that this was how those works were supposed to sound and resolved to record a cycle which gave me the same satisfaction myself"). If it is tempting to criticize Chandos for, perhaps, a hint of hubris when entering into significant contracts with the Detroit and Concertgebouw orchestras, then it must be added that the label remains hugely popular with collectors and critics alike, retaining a brand identity and loyalty which must be the envy of any major.

Both Perry and Couzens were hard-bitten veterans of the major labels when they set out on their own – the experience seems to have left each man with an extraordinary motivation to succeed – albeit by separate paths.

Independence maintained

No discussion of the world of independent labels can ignore the odd fact that so many remain precisely that, independent. In most industries a cycle of growth and regeneration sees successful upstarts quickly bought out by the major players, such acquisitions being one of the few easy ways for a mature corporation to increase its market share. Certainly, many of the old LP independents went that way, yet with the exception of Gimell (now part of PolyGram) and Finlandia (part of Warner Classics), the likes of Hyperion and Chandos, BIS, Telarc, Harmonia Mundi, Opus 111, Astrée Auvidis, ECM and, most remarkable of all, Naxos, remain not only in private ownership but in nearly all cases in the ownership of their founders; this more than anything demonstrates how recent a phenomenon we are considering and, given that few of those founders are in the first flush of youth, raises questions as to the future.

Nimbus

One label which has done anything but follow traditional paths is Nimbus. Initially a radically-minded recording operation, their acquisition in July 1975 of Wyastone Leys, an imposing mansion on the Welsh/English border, gave them space not only to establish their own studio but also to develop a very high-quality LP pressing plant. Their success in the field led to them becoming the first British manufacturers of CD and subsequently to the technical wing of the company taking responsibility for several dramatic advances in the world of optical disc technology before being hived off as a high-tech organization in its own right.

The label, meanwhile, eschewed any such conventional business development, producing recordings, principally of chamber or instrumental repertoire, which were not edited in any way and which were given a 'natural' acoustic. This fiercely held-to and, at that time, idiosyncratic path, denied them the easy plaudits won by many of their independent contemporaries and led to a number of uncomfortable discussions with *Gramophone* in which the brothers Michael and Gerald Reynolds, Numa Labinsky (*aka* Shura Gehrman) and Adrian Farmer expressed considerable unhappiness with the *Gramophone* review team and their criticism of "swimmy" acoustics and/or imprecise playing (not to mention the criticism elsewhere of the Count's bass-baritone *alter ego*).

Nimbus Records was founded by Numa Labinsky (left) and Michael Reynolds in April 1971. The photos date from c1960
Photos Nimbus

It has been my experience that when a label, major or independent, finds serious fault with *Gramophone* (roughly translated, the reviews aren't good enough, there aren't enough reviews, or front covers, or interviews with their artists, or Awards) then advertising support is often the stick that is waved. Nimbus were different; they withdrew editorial support but maintained their advertising. Every label should, of course, believe that they make the best recordings (and thereby hangs another tale, entitled "Where the classical record business went wrong 1988-92") but in the case of Nimbus it went two stages further than I've encountered elsewhere; they were neither prepared to acknowledge that anyone else was making any decent recordings at all, nor to tolerate any real criticism of their own efforts. This remains for me an example of utter self-belief and a kind of surreal integrity; they made life impossible at times but I continue to regard the label with great affection and respect – and, oh, they did, and still do, make some terrific recordings.

Adrian Farmer of Nimbus Records
Photo Nimbus

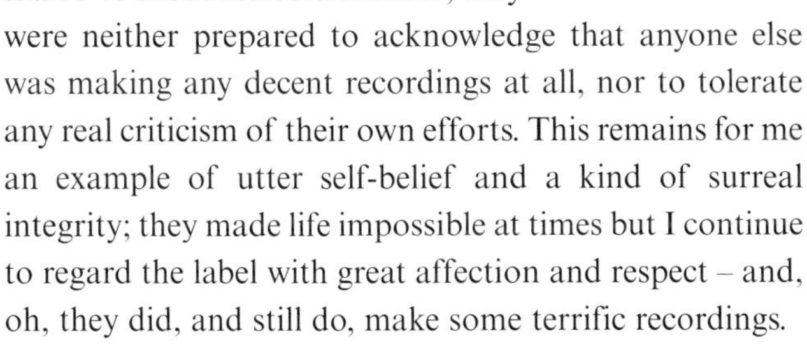

Telarc

An early feature of CD was the series of top-notch recordings from the Cleveland-based Telarc label. With Bob Woods and Jack Renner as founders, both renowned recording technicians, it was hardly surprising that their early digital recordings eclipsed most of what was being accomplished elsewhere. In retrospect it may be fair to comment that the 'sonic spectacular' with which the label became identified may in its turn have obscured the solid artistic worth of the label. Notwithstanding a crtically-acclaimed, and award-winning series of choral recordings from Atlanta under Robert Shaw, the label seems never to have enjoyed the share of international acclaim which appeared to be its destiny.

Robert Woods (left) and Jack Renner who formed Telarc in January 1977 and were pioneers in direct-cut and early digital recording
Photos Telarc

One not altogether welcome by-product of the culture of record criticism established by *Gramophone* in the UK has been a tendency to 'anglocentricity' among the critics whose words carry the most international weight of any. Up to a point this is inevitable – any publication must have some kind of geographic 'centre of gravity' – but when assessing the impact which a label like Telarc has had one feels duty-bound to comment that its standing might be higher were its home address a little (well, 4,000 or so miles) to the east.

Conifer

In 1977 advertisements began to appear in the classified section of *Gramophone* for Conifer Records, specializing in Lebanese imports. From this unlikely start John Deacon, then still Managing Director of EMI Greece (from whence an interest in matters eastern Mediterranean, and even a later collaboration to record Mozart's Da Ponte operas in Arabic), returned to insalubrious premises directly below the Heathrow flight path to develop his company into one of the more forward-thinking independent distributors. Later he was joined by Alison Wenham and Conifer went on to become an independent label in its own right and did much good work (John Rutter's Award-winning Fauré *Requiem* by way of illustration) without ever catching light in the way of some other British contemporaries.

Alison Wenham, MD of Conifer Records and then, in January 1996, MD of BMG/Conifer.
Photo Conifer

Virgin Classics

The rapid growth of the classical sector during the late-1980s occasioned, unsurprisingly, covetous looks from elsewhere in the industry. In 1986 murmurs abounded that Simon Foster, the UK classical head of EMI, was being wooed by Richard Branson to set up a classical label for Virgin; the rumours were true and on January 1st, 1987 Foster presented

Simon Foster, who has produced and marketed records for EMI, Virgin and BMG, and has been responsible for more *Gramophone* Award-winning recordings than anyone else

himself at the Ladbroke Grove headquarters of Virgin Records to take up his new post as Managing Director of Virgin Classics.

"Simon ooo?" demanded the receptionist. "Nah, never 'eard of yer". (Pop record companies had cornered the market in vacuous receptionists.) As it happened she was right, she had never heard of him and there was certainly no office at that address for Virgin Classics; two hours and three locations in West London later Foster found the small empty room which had been allocated to his new organization in an upstairs corridor of a little-known Virgin subsidiary. It did, if I recall, boast a phone point, but no chair, no desk and no light bulb.

The first releases came in April 1988 and two years later Virgin Classics had a catalogue of 120 recordings and had garnered critical plaudits from all around the world, including four **Gramophone** Awards (Britten's *Paul Bunyan* and *Prince of the Pagodas*, the Gabrieli *Venetian Coronation* and Prokofiev's *Love for three Oranges*). The label's acquisition by EMI in March 1992 removed it from the ranks of the independents but Foster's achievement in a short period undoubtedly ranks among the more remarkable chapters of recent years. What has to be acknowledged is that Foster's recordings, critically acclaimed though they were, did not match the critical billing with sales; how much this had to do with Virgin's naïvety in allowing their distribution to be controlled by various of their competitors and how much to do with a lack of sales appeal has never been properly established.

Midem

One definition of an independent has it that such companies do not own their own channels of distribution. Although some have dabbled in distribution it is fair to say that the growth of the independent labels was to a very large extent dependent upon a concomitant development in independent channels of distribution. Many independents were historically dependent upon major labels for their distribution but could never entirely disprove the notion that such arrangements rendered them perpetually second-class citizens. Only when companies such as John Deacon's Conifer in the UK and Avant Garde in Australia started to offer a sophisticated sales and distribution mechanism to smaller companies could the indies really come of age.

Once the idea had taken hold there was no end to the tide of independent distribution houses which sprang up throughout the world. Their global supermarket was Midem, the music industry jamboree which since 1967 had been oiling the contact between the record industry and music publishers each January in Cannes. The organizers had for years been desperate to create a classical element to the party, though without there being any clearly discernible reason for this other than their desire to put some kind of cultural gloss on the low-rent ambience which the rock industry carries with it. Following an unsuccessful attempt in 1970, Midem Classique was established in 1984.

With the notion that international distributors might be readily available at Midem the independent labels started to visit and by 1988 they came in their droves. The resultant action was wonderful to behold. Early on, anxious to be seen, the labels took stand-space of their own where they were then besieged by ravenous distributors from every corner of the globe; within hours the more sought-after labels were sheltering in the bars and hotels, terrified to return to their stands lest they be assailed by yet another Azerbaijani distributor keen to sell Rubbra to a new audience. Each evening label owners compared notes like schoolboys: one might just have signed up with a new company in Chile, others had probably never even thought of doing business in Chile, but now this would become the next morning's top priority.

Such headlong momentum caused the independent sector to grow quickly, labels discovering that even though some of their new foreign territories might be on the small side many of the same none the less amounted to good business. It is hard to imagine that without the cheap access to world-wide distributors allowed by Midem the independents could ever have grown so quickly, though it has to be said that a certain amount of the business done in that heady

Christopher Pollard, Peter Battershill (ex-Conifer and BMG, now a marketing consultant) and Jeremy Elliott at Midem in 1997. Elliott, MD of The Complete Record Company, is a distributor for a number of the independent labels

Gramophone's stand at Midem has become a meeting place for all visitors interested in the classical business. This picture of the 1998 stand was taken before the exhibition opened

atmosphere should be filed strictly under the "marry in haste, repent at leisure" heading.

The distributors found themselves in a similar situation as they reflected upon deals done which left them with more labels on their rosters than they could ever hope to cope with. For more than a few, Midem 1991-7 became a period of undoing the worst excesses of Midem 1986-90. None the less, strong businesses on both sides have emerged and Midem has become for the independents a reasonably cost-effective and civilized annual meeting place.

Naxos

The startling growth of Klaus Heymann's Naxos empire (established in Hong Kong in May 1987) almost defies belief, in particular in the fact that the major companies were so unsuccessful in, first of all, recognizing the encroachment into their markets made by this bargain-priced upstart, and then in dealing with it. PolyGram, it is true, made efforts to buy the label but by the time they got serious the asking price had risen further than they were prepared to pay and they chose instead to spend their money on developing the limp Belart brand, a budget label emasculated by being unable to display the Decca, DG or Philips logos from which the catalogue was drawn and hamstrung by internal politics which deprived the label of important repertoire.

The majors were certainly guilty of underestimating the threat posed by Naxos which initially sold largely undistinguished East European recordings of core repertoire through low-rent outlets such as Woolworths. In the late-1980s the majors saw their main challenge as coping with the threat to their artist rosters posed by the transmogrification of CBS Masterworks, the US-centric crossover label which then generated very little in terms of international A&R, into Sony Classical, a money-no-object DG clone run from an opulent villa in Hamburg. Terrified that Sony would sign up all the best artists – and to be honest, they did succeed in attracting Karajan, Bernstein and Horowitz, though all died within a year – the other majors became easy prey for artist managers who recognized their vulnerability and who, by playing the Sony threat shrewdly, were able to set up massive recording contracts for some of the most mediocre artists ever to see the inside of a recording studio; the short-term financial benefits to those managers and artists were undoubtedly immense, yet most of those careers are now long forgotten. This is the single biggest reason for the stagnation of the market for full-price core repertoire in recent years.

Further distraction for the major labels was provided in the form of Nigel Kennedy's huge success with his EMI recording of *The Four Seasons* (released in November 1989) and, for Decca, the "Three Tenors" phenomenon, whipped up during and after the soccer World Cup in Italy in 1990. Pop-orientated industry managers, long frustrated at their inability to understand the intricacies and long-breathed time-frames of the classical business, suddenly saw figures to which they could relate and instantly all wanted a share of the same pie; classical labels were expected to create chart successes.

On May 22nd, 1997 a party was held in London to celebrate the 10th birthday of Naxos. Here, with the cake, is the founder Klaus Heymann with his wife, the violinist Takako Nishizaki
Photo Naxos

The immediate effect of these new factors was to give all independents far greater elbow room. No longer was, for example, the local division of EMI fighting Chandos or ASV for British repertoire; it was far more concerned with punk fiddlers, Spanish monks and persuading the blameless and brilliant Peter Donohoe to grow a pigtail and have an 'image makeover' (happily, he refused). Hence the opportunity for independents to make hay and, more significantly, the opportunity for Heymann to build Naxos whilst his competitors were otherwise engaged. In theory the UK should have been a tough nut for Naxos to crack, because in Classics for Pleasure EMI had built a superb mid- and budget-price label, yet the early 1990s saw CfP starved of attention and investment, a cycle of neglect which would lead to the loss of the label's autonomy in 1995, Naxos having been handed the UK market on the proverbial plate. (A relaunch of CfP took place in February 1998.)

Heymann, initially derided by the majors for homespun sounding recordings and folksy packaging, moved on from core repertoire to begin an encroachment on the esoteric repertoire belonging to the independents, causing them to regard him as some kind of demonic force, hell-bent on destroying them. By 1992 the majors were well aware that Sony's European initiative had not succeeded and that they had been on a wildly expensive goose-chase, returned 'home' to discover that the independents' market share, led by Naxos, was reaching undreamed of heights all over the world; worse still, Naxos had ploughed much of its profit into better quality recordings with better quality artists while building further on the following which their founding artists such as Jenö Jandó and Idil Biret had attracted.

Heymann, a supremely shrewd character, had apparently allowed early criticism of the label's standards to wash over him, yet he confounded his critics by raising those standards dramatically and by achieving the kind of sales with 'difficult' repertoire, the Boulez Piano Sonatas for example, which seemed incredible. He, too, had created a

Bernard Coutaz, who founded the Harmonia Mundi label in October 1958 *Photo Harmonia Mundi*

label with which his customers were prepared to take chances and follow off the beaten track.

The development of Naxos brought a new dimension to the distribution of independent labels, traditionally restricted to the specialist classical retail market. Naxos brought a desire and ability to be sold through the bigger multiples as well as a willingness to try marketing gambits such as television advertising which would previously only have been considered by the majors.

The growth of Naxos's distribution business through the world has brought with it a new opportunity for the other independent labels to gain exposure beyond their traditional markets, though it remains to be seen how many will be able to take advantage.

Robina Young, a Yorkshire woman running A&R for a French company in America *Photo Harmonia Mundi*

Yolanta Skura (founder in October 1990 of Opus III), René Goiffon (Harmonia Mundi) and Christopher Pollard at Midem 1994

On January 16th, 1998, Harmonia Mundi celebrated their 40th Anniversary at a dinner in Arles. Surveying the cake (from the left) are James Jolly, Eva Coutaz, Christopher Pollard and Bernard Coutaz *Photo Harmonia Mundi*

Harmonia Mundi

Naxos's own distribution rather blurs the distinction between major and independent and in Harmonia Mundi there is another example of an independent label developing international sales and distribution capabilities. Harmonia Mundi, based in Provence, celebrated its 40th Anniversary in January 1998 and, with offices in London, Paris, Heidelberg, Los Angeles and Barcelona, is very much a model of the classical independent taking control over its own destiny. The label is owned by Bernard Coutaz, an idiosyncratic entrepreneur who goes very much his own way, even to the extent of building a chain of 25 Harmonia Mundi stores in France, launched in reponse to Coutaz's assessment of the unsympathetic direction of the French retail market.

Eva Coutaz, with Scott Butler and the 1985 *Gramophone* Award in the Early music (Baroque) category for William Christie's performance of Charpentier's *Medée*

Coutaz is not, however, the artistic leader of the label; that mantle fell for many years upon Eva, his German ex-wife, and is now partly shared by Robina Young, the ebulliently competitive Yorkshire woman who is the partner of René Goiffon, the President of the label's Los Angeles office. The artistic success of Harmonia Mundi in recent years undoubtedly owes much to the friendly rivalry between these two charismatic ladies. If the position can be summarized then it is probably fair to say that under Eva and Bernard the artistic policy, rooted in the work of Alfred Deller, William Christie and René Jacobs, was restricted in its appeal to francophile baroque lovers. Young's gift has been, via artists such as Nicholas McGegan, Lorraine Hunt and the Anonymous 4, to bring a more broadly cosmopolitan feel to things and, in the last named, to create commercial success, especially in the USA, of considerable significance.

Future independence?

In Chandos, Harmonia Mundi, Hyperion and Naxos I have introduced the most powerful figures in the independent market. Each depends to a large extent on a single individual and with none of Couzens, Coutaz, Perry or Heymann under 60 years old the issue of succession clearly becomes ever more critical. The logical progression is for some or all of these labels to be bought by the majors; it is, after all, unusual to find a market in which so few of the mature independent players have been swallowed up, especially as the majors have found it difficult to increase market share in recent years and all have at least talked aggressively about acquisition. If acquistion was genuinely part of the classical strategy of PolyGram, Sony or EMI then they seem to have failed. BMG, it is true, now own Conifer, Philips own half of Gimell and EMI own Virgin; however the first and last examples have more to do with deals driven by pop parents than any clear classical motivation, while Gimell's single artist policy, Peter Phillips and The Tallis Scholars, never appeared to be a serious long-term position. Warner Classics, the newest major player, acquired Teldec, Erato, NVC Arts and, most recently, Finlandia, to set alongside its own Nonesuch label and create a 1990s clone of PolyGram.

Steve Smith, Managing Director and Producer for Gimell, founded in April 1981 *Photo Barda*

A cursory check of the list at the back of ***Gramophone*** reveals that over 350 labels currently boast UK distribution. Most are literally one-man bands with no great ambitions – ambitions are, after all, likely to turn them into the kind of organizations from which most escaped to pursue their own particular artistic odyssey.

Robert von Bahr founded BIS in September 1973. Here, at the Finnish Ambassador's residence in London on April 19th, 1994, he celebrates the 21st anniversary of his company
Photo BIS

Younger pretenders

Do pretenders to the thrones of Hyperion and the rest exist? Smaller players include Robert von Bahr's admirably focused BIS; jazz-based ECM which Manfred Eicher has made into an object of desire for every major; Opus 111, run by the ex-Erato producer Yolanta Skura; and ASV, to which Hywel Davies has given point and purpose. Each successful independent either identifies, or more often creates a niche; some niches are straightforward, BIS and Scandinavian repertoire for example; it's not necessarily all that they do, but it defines where they come from. Some are less obvious – Ted Perry moves contentedly from medieval polyphony to modern British chamber music by way of romantic piano concertos but takes his audience with him – collectors who are patently happy to let Ted light their way.

Manfred Eicher, who founded ECM Records in November 1969
Photo ECM

Ultimately the indies are dependent upon the majors to make their market for them: perhaps this will change as new routes for retail open up; the Internet for example offers the chance for companies to avoid the need to be stocked by retailers, but for now the independents remain largely at the mercy of the market as a whole and need the majors to be healthy; interestingly, one route to good health for the majors may be through the acquisition of independents.

Hywel Davies, ex-string player in the Philharmonia and now MD of ASV (Academy Sound and Vision), the company formed by Harley Usill, Jack Boyce and David Gyle-Thompson in March 1981
Photo ASV

Ralph Couzens (left, Chandos recording engineer/producer and son of Brian), Ted Perry (Hyperion) and John Waite (Pavilion Records) at Midem 1995

Christopher Pollard

Christopher Pollard grew up in a garden with a house at each end; in one his mother's piano playing competed with his father's stereo, in the other lived his grandparents and the editorial department of ***The Gramophone***: it is reasonable therefore to conclude that he was fated to become part of the family company.

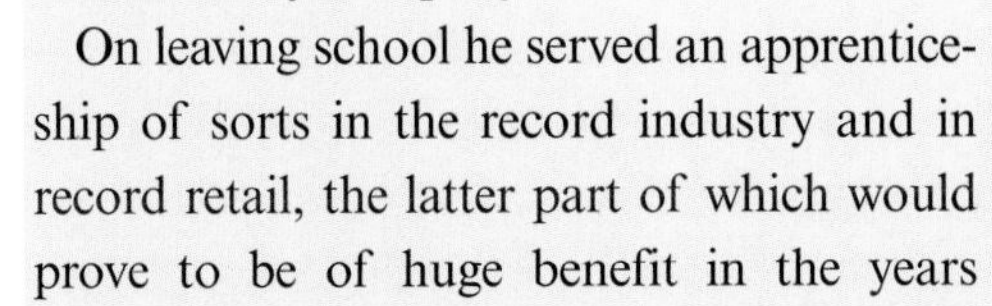

On leaving school he served an apprenticeship of sorts in the record industry and in record retail, the latter part of which would prove to be of huge benefit in the years ahead, interspersed with any travel opportunities he could find. In 1977, aged 20, he joined the Advertisement Sales Department. It is fair to say that whatever skills he may have had, advertisement selling was not one of them and it was with some relief that the Company bade him farewell a year later as he left to take a three-year Business Management course.

He returned in 1981 to work in the editorial department where a knowledge of, and interest in, the industry which had been so much a part of his early life was coupled with a knowledge that others would always know more about classical music. This allowed an objective approach to the Editor's role (to which he was appointed in 1986) which took the magazine through a developmental phase during which presentation was considerably changed and new features and writers were introduced. This process was greatly assisted by his deputy, James Jolly, who succeeded him as Editor in 1990.

Free from the day-to-day constraints of the Editor's chair, he turned his attention to the direction of the company as a whole, introducing new publications and in particular seeking to fulfil the potential of the annual Awards. The opportunity to pursue these objectives was largely created by the willingness of his father to devolve an increasing responsibility for the management of the Company, presumably on the basis that some of the ambitions which father held for son were now being fulfilled. In turn Chris looked more and more to his colleagues for their energies and inspiration and now considers that the young team who today run Gramophone Publications Limited are by far his proudest professional achievement.

When not fretting over the latest business developments he follows rugby union with a passion born of long years toiling in the front row of the scrummage (and thus deplores the modern tendency towards a faster and more fluid game, he favours extra watering of pitches and the abolition of fancy new drainage arrangements as a counterbalance) and competes modestly upon Britain's motor racing circuits. At home his wife and three daughters earn his undying affection by allowing him the pleasures of fine wine and good music, not always in that order but invariably in close juxtaposition.

From a critic's chair

Lionel Salter

Among the first classical music reviewers for ***The Gramophone*** were the genial and much-loved Alec Robertson and the operatic expert Herman Klein (both with long associations with the recording industry, the latter as early as 1904), and, fractionally later, Richard Holt and W. R. Anderson (who was responsible for many a pungent phrase), with W. A. Chislett and Roger Wimbush (both immensely long-service contributors) on the lighter side. From June 1930 jazz was in the hands of the ultra-laid-back Edgar Jackson, supported from August 1948 by that walking encyclopaedia Brian Rust (who wrote the "Miscellaneous and Dance" reviews as well as a number of jazz reviews under a variety of pseudonyms – in which he was by no means alone!). But when, a third of the way through its now 75-year history, I joined the magazine in 1948 (at the same time that Edward Sackville-West started his quarterly round-ups of records) there were – astonishing when one looks at the long list of reviewers today! – only three, besides myself, in the classical section: AR and WRA (both from educational backgrounds, and a couple of decades senior to me) and my slightly older contemporary Trevor Harvey, who after running music in the British Forces Network in Germany was then a conductor making his way in the musical world, and who had started writing for ***The Gramophone*** just six months previously.

Roger Wimbush puts the finishing touches to another *Gramophone* contribution, with his trusted Columbia acoustic horn reproducer providing a musical background (*c*1970)

It was to strengthen the team with more professional practical musicians that Christopher Stone recruited me (though later a few readers seemingly hankered after the old amateur-music-lover approach). I am still in the dark as to how much Christopher had known about me when he had approached me three years earlier: at that time, having just been invalided out of the army, I was trying to rebuild a career as a pianist and accompanist (which I had been for the BBC's pre-war television service) and, having had experience as a conductor in films (where I had also been an arranger and chorusmaster) and with the exiled Radio France Symphony Orchestra, I had taken a conducting job in the BBC: I had not yet emerged as a harpsichordist.

Trevor Harvey (left) with W. A. Chislett celebrating *Gramophone*'s Diamond Jubilee in April 1983

Early problems

Under the somewhat forbidding title of "Analytical Notes and First Reviews" – which persisted until May 1974, despite reappearances of some recordings that were then reviewed a second time (though from 1954 there was a separate section devoted to reissues) – we were expected to cover music of all types – orchestral, chamber, instrumental, vocal, operatic, classical and contemporary – and usually against the clock, with very tight deadlines; and we were by no means restricted to music with which we were known to be in sympathy! Records then came without any presentation material (we had to wait for the advent of LPs in June 1950 for that) and often in the form of advance single-sided 'white-label' copies with the baldest typewritten information (which frequently proved to be not even correct). I remember a set of about eight unidentified single sides, purporting to be of various Lehár overtures, which proved impossible to assemble in any sequence that made musical sense. It was very irritating when a few readers complained of our writing about the music on the discs, claiming airily that information about it (which often had to be laboriously researched from scores – which I always tried to procure – and sometimes obscure reference books) was easily available, and insisted that all that mattered was the sound quality. We tried to explain that even for knowledgeable listeners it was necessary to convey some idea of the music's character; and AR was moved to an unusually tart rejoinder when he wrote, "I relegate technical evaluation of a recording to second place, and if the unsophisticated

The Gramophone, August, 1939

ANALYTICAL NOTES AND FIRST REVIEWS

(Those marked with an asterisk (*) are additions to the H.M.V. Connoisseur Catalogue or Columbia Collector's List)

ORCHESTRAL

his head!) I grieve to inform you that Wm. Tell is completely mythical; but the gorgeous life of the music more than makes up for the ghostliness of the hero.

COLUMBIA

London Symphony Orchestra (Weingartner): **Concerto Grosso in G minor, Op. 6, No. 6** (Handel). Columbia, LX831-2 (12 in., 12s.).

This (also known as No. 17) was briefly described on page 428 of the issue of March, 1937. In the fugue there is a slight difference from my copy, bar seven having E flat *D*, D, instead of E flat

PSEUDONYMS

by Mark Walker

Some of the magazine's contributors, particularly in the early years when there were relatively few of them, chose to write under the guise of pseudonyms. Compton Mackenzie sometimes used his wartime codename "Z" (his chosen designation as head of counter-espionage in Athens); Christopher Stone wrote as "Peppering", while Faith Mackenzie was always "F Sharp". H. V. F. Little was "Piccolo" and W. S. Wild, one of the Expert Committe, "Indicator"; John Hope-Johnstone disguised himself as James Caskett; Alec Robertson wrote as Newman Passage (NP) while Peter Latham became Percy Passage (PP) – both named after side streets near ***The Gramophone***'s offices in Newman Street. Jazz reviewer Brian Rust had three other names: "Ajax", Oliver King and John Oakland; on occasion Lionel Salter was "PB", W. R. Anderson was "KK", Roger Wimbush was "Harlequin" and Walter Yeomans writing in the very first issue was Warren Monk.

Terpander

The most mysterious pseudonym of all was "Terpander" (named after the ancient Greek poet associated with musical innovation), who contributed a series of highly controversial articles to the magazine. In February 1932 the first piece was a strenuous defence of his musical hero, Stravinsky, whose music had recently been denigrated by the critic Ernest Newman writing in *The Sunday Times*. Terpander's article, however, contained an unfortunate reference to ***The Gramophone*** critic W. R. Anderson: "It is amusing to note", wrote Terpander, "that Mr Anderson, who perhaps realizes that the Stravinsky tide may turn, criticizes the *Symphony of Psalms* in a comparatively unbiased manner." This was taken as a slur on his professional reputation by WRA, who threatened litigation unless an apology from Terpander was forthcoming. The apology duly appeared in the next issue.

Terpander's fiery enthusiasm was undimmed, nevertheless, and he continued making occasional contributions to the magazine. In March 1933 a piece entitled "The Gramophone as Anarchist" argued that the gramophone, because it provides the opportunity to play the same piece of music over and over again, exposed an inherent weakness in "subjective" music (Beethoven, Wagner, Debussy, etc.) which soon exhausts its emotional appeal, in contrast to the objectivity of Bach or, of course, Stravinsky. Compton Mackenzie was so intrigued that he determined to make the experiment of listening to Stravinsky's *Histoire d'un Soldat* once a day every day for the next two months to see if its appeal would pall. Having adhered to his resolution, in due course Mackenzie admitted that "if I continue to play it over and over again I shall not easily get tired of it", but doubted whether "an ability to sustain infinite repetition is a mark of aesthetic superiority" (June 1933). Roger Wimbush, another contributor to ***The Gramophone***, incensed by what he referred to as Terpander's "latest heresy", labelled him "a professional poseur" in a letter to the Editor (July 1933).

In the early 1970s, an attempt was made to uncover Terpander's identity. In April 1973 it was reported that Peter Grant of Sussex had come up with the theory that Terpander was the musicologist Professor E. J. Dent. But in the next issue, Donald Loukes, Assistant Librarian of King's College, Cambridge, wrote that although Dent had indeed written a book entitled *Terpander, or music and the future* in 1926, there was no record of any pseudonymous articles by him. Furthermore, several short articles by Terpander in *The Musical Times* in the 1930s gave his address as 11 Cleveland Square, Lancaster Gate, W2. This turned out to be the residence of Bertram Jacobs, LL.B, not Professor Dent.

However, in the August 1973 issue, Roger Wimbush reported that another of ***The Gramophone***'s contributors, John Freestone, had served with Terpander during the war and he was in fact Manuel Jacobs, possibly the brother of Bertram. Reference to the Company's ledgers for the period in question show payments to a certain "M. K. Jacobs". Manuel Jacobs was invalided out of the army and went on to study composition with Lennox Berkeley. Some of his songs were sung by Peter Pears.

listener is more readily distressed by faulty engineering than by faulty interpretation it is part of our job to teach him not to put the cart before the horse".

However, in this regard one of the problems we had to keep in mind was the sort of equipment readers might possess: so should we aim at hi-fi owners who would hear (and pounce on) the slightest blemish, or general music-lovers with less critical ears and equipment? This in turn raised the question of what reviewers themselves were listening on – a point tackled in 1950 when, at the instigation of Arthur Haddy of Decca, shortly after the appearance of LPs, a standard reproduction system was provided for all reviewers, so that at least we should be working from the same criteria [pp. 94-5]. A constant source of trouble in 78rpm days was that there were frequently small differences of pitch between sides – exacerbated in one instance I recall where the chorus had started off afresh at the correct pitch for the second side regardless of the fact that it had gone flat in the course of the first; and change-over points in longer works were not

Malcolm Macdonald

John Warrack

always sensibly chosen. A procedure of fading out one side with an overlap fade into the next, adopted for a while, was generally regarded as unsatisfactory.

Expansion begins

New faces, several of whom had, like myself, previously written occasional articles, soon joined our little gang of four: the bluff and burly Ralph Hill, who, sadly, died in 1950, Basil Douglas (who was responsible for the BBC's much praised chamber-music series "Music in Miniature"), the ebullient Hubert Foss, and John Freestone, who had been a pupil of Blanche Marchesi. To complement the Sackville-West quarterly reviews, Desmond Shawe-Taylor began a quarterly "The Gramophone and the Voice" in July 1951, which he continued to write for 22 years: he quite often did not see eye to eye with other reviewers but was gracious enough to concede that his quarterly retrospect did not confer judicial authority on him. One 1951 reader, apparently unable to accept that critics' subjective views might legitimately differ, felt that reviewers should be drawn only from members of a special guild who would qualify by strict examination. (How interested I should have been to see how that would have been administered!) With increasing numbers of record issues, comparison between rival performances became necessary, which made the reviewers' task longer and in December 1954 comparative versions began to be listed at the head of reviews.

Meanwhile the provision of sleeve-notes sparked off all kinds of concerns. Some were utterly superficial, some mere puffs of the artist, some patently inaccurate about facts or dates; some, on the other hand, concentrated on scholarly niceties that probably left many record buyers cold. I led a campaign that notes should be signed, which would at least put a stop to plagiarism from existing writings; and criticisms were being made about the relevance of some notes to the music in question (though in fairness it should be said that commentators almost always had to write about the disc before it was available to be heard, so that some evasions were understandable). There was a justified insistence on proper identification of works – many companies were extremely lax or even irresponsibly inaccurate in this regard – and even of the edition used, which was highly germane when considering, for example, *Carmen* or the Bruckner symphonies. (Deutsche Grammophon's Archiv series initiated a welcome breakthrough in this matter – p. 97.) And many were the complaints about translations of sleeve-notes written by people with only the sketchiest idea of English or by musical illiterates who made ridiculous howlers (something still not unknown today, unfortunately). There was a constant call for texts of vocal music to be provided, with adequate translations: readers expressed their frustration at being kept in the dark about the meaning of songs.

William Mann (left) with Katharine Wilkinson (Philips) and Peter Goodchild (Decca) in 1970

Deryck Cooke (left) with Alec Robertson in 1970

I saw many reviewers arrive and depart (or stay). The 1950s brought much fresh blood: the young Andrew Porter who came on the recommendation of Shawe-Taylor and Sackville-West, my old friend Malcolm Macdonald (immensely knowledgeable over a wide range of music), the conductor Ivan Clayton (already stricken by the wasting disease that was eventually to kill him), effervescent Philip Hope-Wallace, the scholarly and judicious Roger Fiske, John Warrack (who also took over a quarterly review in May 1958), early music specialists Denis Stevens and Jeremy Noble, the scintillating William Mann and the quietly authoritative Deryck Cooke.

Critical considerations

Certain basic considerations had been coming to the fore. All critics know that enthusiastic or condemnatory reviews are relatively easy to write, though in the latter case fairness needs to be maintained in considering how much thought and effort may have gone into the recording, and where it has fallen short: far harder is it to talk about run-of-the-mill performances that contain no glaring faults but fail to rouse any enthusiasm. A critic has, of course, to be readable (some excellent musicians can mar the effect of their deliberations by being too academic), and a modicum of wit is always welcome; but the temptation to pen smart-alec put-downs or snide dismissals has to be resisted. Equally, young writers in particular need to be wary about proclaiming something or other "the finest performance I have heard" if a suspicion grows that he may not have heard many others. Compton Mackenzie was forthright on young critics "who try to leap in judgement before they can walk in education".

Looking back, we view with envy the amount of space then permissible for reviews. In early 78rpm days these had been very brief, but with the advent of LP a length of one-and-a-half pages was not unheard of. However, with the ever-increasing number of issues and the consequent pressure on space, more succinct writing became imperative. Decisions always need to be taken on what is really significant and how far to go into detail – bearing in mind that the readership extends from 'ordinary music-lovers' to highly informed listeners with an astonishing range of musical, technical and discographical knowledge (whose letters and corrections are much appreciated). Reviewers often float trial balloons when they find themselves short of information, and only rarely do our appeals go unanswered. (Caution has to be exercised when calling anything a "first recording", even when this is so claimed by the record company concerned, since knowledgeable readers, from many parts of the world, constantly alert us to a previous recording which has escaped our notice or has been unknown to us.)

Sometimes readers voice disagreements with our judgements – or we disagree among ourselves; but such independence is salutary since, while reviewers are extremely conscious of the responsibility of what they write (which has been shown to have a strong influence on record sales), they make no pretence to be taken as gospel. In any case, the passage of time, or repeated hearings, sometimes causes a change of mind – which it is only honest to acknowledge.

Candour

This question of honesty looms large in many aspects of reviewing. On occasion, accusations have been made that, because ***Gramophone*** relies heavily on its advertising, it and its writers are in the companies' pockets. This can be robustly denied; apart from being a slur on reviewers' probity, it would strike at the very roots of their credibility, as it would certainly be detected. Regular readers would be quick to spot any bias – they are extremely alert to any quirks in a writer's style or attitudes! – and would rightly withhold their trust. I am glad to say that I have always enjoyed complete freedom to express my views. When these have been highly critical or unpalatable to some record company, I am equally glad to say that, with very rare exceptions, they have accepted them philosophically as being, at least, honest opinions. And in some cases they have been grateful for having faults pointed out. It has been an accepted policy that if companies provide advance approved test pressings (on which we quite often, because of time factors, have needed to act) that contain recording faults, it is only fair to notify them of this before our review is published (one such case that I recall concerned a Curzon concerto disc where the recording pitch had slipped); but once the record is openly on sale we do not pull our punches. Then companies, often astonished to learn of the fault, are usually anxious to issue corrected versions. There was a celebrated instance when an unfortunate tape-editor was dismissed after I had pointed out that a bar had been omitted in an LP transfer of a Toscanini recording of a Brahms symphony; and there was a lengthy and incredulous discussion, referring back to the blameless recording log, when two distinguished artists unaccountably played an extra half-bar in a repetitive pattern in Beethoven's *Kreutzer* Sonata.

Another area where strict candour is essential is that of very famous artists, where any adverse criticism is taken by fervent admirers as a personal affront or as justifying denunciation of the offending writer. But even top artists can have off-days, and to dodge the issue – or to write an evaluation based on their public appearances rather than on the actual record in question (as a besotted fan – who chose to remain anonymous – once demanded in 1956 in the case of Callas) – would be to mislead purchasers. It is natural that reviewers should know many artists personally and even be their friends; but such personal relationships need to be put on hold if a review is to be entirely objective. (When I was a BBC producer I often did not engage artists with whom I was friendly but used others I heartily disliked, so long as they were artistically better for the job.) On a related topic, critics are usually reluctant to review records for which they have been engaged to write sleeve- or booklet-notes, since adverse comment would seem like knocking down their own wicket (besides alienating the record company!); but even this situation sometimes has to be faced (the reviewer then declaring an interest). Contemporary music is a particular minefield, where some commentators hasten to "embrace the new for fear of appearing reactionary" (as Robert Layton expressed it) or, in Desmond Shawe-Taylor's phrase, are "terrified of doing a Hanslick". It is as easy to jump on the band-wagon as to suffer from a hardening of the artistic arteries.

THE EARLY REVIEWERS

In the very earliest issues of the magazine many of the reviews were written by Compton Mackenzie and his associates in the spirit of the 'enthusiastic amateur'; but the necessity of establishing a more professional approach to record criticism was quickly recognized and a regular panel of music critics was gradually established. This team of reviewers has grown to in excess of 45 members during the 1990s, but in the years before the Second World War the bulk of the magazine's reviews were written by just six contributors who between them were responsible for setting the high standards which helped to consolidate *The Gramophone*'s reputation

W. R. Anderson

William Robert Anderson (WRA) was born in Blackburn in 1891, took his music degree at Durham University and became a music teacher and organist. He began reviewing records in 1920 when he was asked by musicologist Percy Scholes to write for *The Music Student*. WRA's first contribution to *The Gramophone* was in May 1925, when he wrote a piece on Berlioz entitled "The Byron of Music". He retired to Bournemouth, where he died on January 29th, 1979 aged 87. In his obituary notice (March 1979), William Chislett paid this tribute to his friend and colleague:

"I have been re-reading some of his reviews, especially some of the earlier ones, and how refreshing they are, with their tinges of his quirky humour never far away. Whether as critic, teacher, broadcaster or adjudicator WRA approached the subject in hand with enthusiasm. His praise had to be earned, and was all the more to be valued for that, and he would always stand up boldly for what he thought to be right, and be prepared to be counted, and while he set very high standards he was never unfair, unjust or unkind."

W. A. Chislett

The longest-serving contributor to *Gramophone*, William A. Chislett's experience of recordings began with cylinders and ended with Compact Discs.

Born in Rotherham, WAC attended Sheffield University and after qualifying as a solicitor he was appointed Deputy Town Clerk of Halifax in 1919. During the First World War he served as a gunner with the Royal Artillery. In 1927 he became Town Clerk of Barrow-in-Furness, and from 1935 to the beginning of the Second World War he was in private practice. An early convert to 'gramophony' (he was given his first phonograph aged nine) he began reviewing records in the *Halifax Courier* during the 1920s. After writing to the Editor of *The Gramophone* complaining about the standard of some reviews of band records, Christopher Stone engaged him to review for the magazine and his first article appeared in February 1925.

During the Second World War he commanded a Home Guard Infantry battalion, Anti-Aircraft batteries and Naval guns for coastal defence – for which he was awarded an OBE. He was also chief music critic of *The Oxford Mail* for 20 years and contributed to other journals including *The Bolton Evening News*. Oxford University conferred upon him an honorary degree in 1965.

In the December 1951 issue of the magazine, WAC began a regular round-up of light orchestral recordings under the heading "Nights at the Round Table", providing an opportunity to discuss music that didn't fit neatly into either the main classical reviews or the "Miscellaneous and Dance" section. The first column included Sir Thomas Beecham conducting Suppé's *Morning, Noon and Night in Vienna* Overture, two operettas – *A Thousand and One Nights* and *Gypsy Love* – and a selection of Christmas records. Operetta – Strauss, Lehár, Offenbach, Weber and Gilbert and Sullivan – was a common theme; records by artists such as Mario Lanza, André Kostelanetz and Arthur Fiedler made regular appearances; but increasingly WAC handed over other duties and concentrated on his much-loved band records, about which he was a recognized authority. He died aged 89 on November 17th, 1984.

Edgar Jackson

Edgar Jackson was born in London in 1895. His name was originally Cohen: his brother was a stockbroker, Kenneth Carr, who was killed motor racing in the 1930s. During the First World War Jackson was commissioned and served in the British Army. In January 1926 he founded and edited, for the music publisher Lawrence Wright, a magazine entitled *The Melody Maker* which happily still exists today. In November 1929 he left to become manager for the bandleader Jack Hylton, but this was short-lived and in June 1930 he began his 28-year association with *The Gramophone*, establishing the "Jazz and Swing" reviews. In June 1934, using his

experience from *The Melody Maker*, he persuaded Christopher Stone to redesign the magazine but the results caused universal ruptions and, for the most part, there was a quick reversion to the original designs. However, much more to the point, he set the most stringent standards for his record reviews (even building his own advanced record-playing equipment) and these soon became an integral and much respected part of the magazine. Ill health forced his partial retirement in May 1958 but he continued to edit and compile *The Gramophone Popular Record Catalogue* until 1966. He died on August 31st, 1967 at the age of 72.

Herman Klein

Born in Norwich in 1856, Herman Klein was a singing teacher and music critic. In Norwich he heard Jenny Lind and Tietjens sing in 1863, and later was taught by the great singing teacher Manuel Garcia. He also became a friend of Sir Julius Benedict, who had known Weber and Beethoven. He met Verdi and Gounod, and shook hands with Wagner. Between 1881-1901 he was music critic for *The Sunday Times*, and subsequently published a book, *Thirty Years of Musical Life in London* (1903). He travelled to America and contributed to *The New York Herald* 1902-9, before resuming teaching in London. He was chairman of the Critics' Circle, contributed to the second and third editions of Grove's *Dictionary of Music and Musicians*, and wrote, amongst other books on music, *The Reign of Patti* (1920), the biography of the soprano whom he had known personally. He joined **The Gramophone** team in June 1924. For almost ten years he contributed a monthly article, "The Gramophone and the Singer", and was the magazine's principal opera critic. He died on March 10th, 1934 at the age of 78. His collected writings from **The Gramophone** have been edited by William R. Moran and published by Amadeus Press (1990).

Alec Robertson

AR was educated at Bradfield and the RAM. He was a church organist, held a commission in the Hampshire Regiment, was ordained as a Priest, and made his name as a broadcaster. Passionately devoted to the music of Bach, he was also a great devotee of Wagner, and amongst his many books was a life of Dvořák and an introduction to plainchant. He was Head of the Education Department at The Gramophone Company when, alongside Walter Yeomans, he encouraged Compton Mackenzie to launch his new magazine in 1923. His first contribution to **The Gramophone** was an article entitled "Hints on Lecturing" which appeared in December 1923. He was appointed Music Editor in June 1955, a post he held until his retirement in January 1972. In December 1967, during **The Gramophone**'s regular Christmas gathering for its contributors, AR was presented with a gold disc by Leonard Smith of EMI for his services to the record industry over half a century. In the Queen's Birthday Honours of June 1972 he was awarded an MBE: this coincided with his 80th birthday and to celebrate the occasion the BBC's *Record Review* played Stravinsky's *Happy Birthday* and he appeared on Desert Island Discs. His autobiography, *More Than Music* (Collins), was published in 1961. He died on January 18th, 1982, aged 89.

Roger Wimbush

In June 1929 the first of three articles written by Roger Wimbush, entitled "A Gramophone Music Hall", appeared in **The Gramophone**, and these officially marked the beginning for him of a 48-year relationship with the magazine. Unofficially, he had already ghost-written two pieces concerning "Symphonic Jazz" signed by Fred Elizalde and Bert Ambrose in the February and March issues of that year (these were reprinted in the March 1998 issue of the magazine).

Born in Twickenham in 1909, RW began his career as the pupil of a freelance journalist in Fleet Street and 'ghosting' articles. He worked successively at Selfridges and Fishmongers' Hall before being appointed Managing Editor of the *Music Lover* – a job which involved him writing most of the articles, selling advertising space, seeing the issues through the Press and even selling copies by hand to those queuing for the Covent Garden Opera House.

At the beginning of the Second World War he was Press Secretary of the British Social Hygiene Council before joining the Royal Corps of Signals and then the Royal Norfolk Regiment where he was seconded to Press Relations duties. At the end of the war he was attached to the War Office and was responsible for taking British correspondents to the Nuremberg war trials. Numerous PR jobs followed, and he was elected President of the Institute of Public Relations in 1950-1.

Although lacking any formal musical education, Wimbush was devoted to old-time music hall, and he had a prodigious knowledge of live and recorded music in most of its forms. In March 1963 he inaugurated **The Gramophone**'s monthly news column, "Here and There", to which he continued to contribute until his death on February 22nd, 1977.

Joan Coulson (EMI Classical Promotion, 1954-85) with Edward Greenfield in 1978

The onward march

More and more reviewers were coming aboard, their names appearing on the masthead after a preliminary run where their reviews were signed with their full names before being promoted to the fraternity, when they were reduced to initials. The 1960s saw the arrival of Ted Greenfield (indefatigable and enthusiastic), Stephen Plaistow and Felix Aprahamian. Robert Layton sidled in with a regular Classical Reissues feature and then took over the Quarterly Retrospect from John Warrack before also settling down to monthly reviews. By this time there were 17 classical reviewers. There was then a distinct move towards specialization with the addition of Stanley Sadie, Julian Budden (though, like others of his fellow-reviewers who were on the BBC staff, he initially avoided the repertoire which he was handling there), Brian Trowell, Denis Arnold and Joan Chissell. The advantages of 'horses for courses' with certain categories of music were obvious, especially in view of increasing sophistication among readers; but two inherent drawbacks were less obvious – that those contributors might well become too pigeon-holed and feel, after a time, that they had already said, many times, everything that could be said about their particular field of interest; and the fact that if certain composers or musical areas became the province of one writer, however expert, it could result in a restricted view. There is still much to be said for a well-informed all-rounder.

By the late-1960s we had had about a decade to adjust to stereo, a technique which however had led to various concerns about correct placing, proportion and balance in the audio image – and discussions in the Correspondence columns about whether first and second violins should not be antiphonally positioned in the spectrum, as would have been the norm until well into this century – and, inevitably, to readers' grumbles that they needed to update their equipment. (An experiment in 1972 with quadraphonic recording, which presented producers with many additional headaches, met with a cool reception from the public.) The roster of reviewers had to be further extended because of the mounting flood of discs, many of out-of-the-way repertoire, that were pouring in. Alan Blyth, who had been contributing numerous interviews with artists, joined the reviewing panel in 1970; he was followed by the Elgar specialist Jerrold Northrop Moore and that perceptive and omniscient critic of singers John Steane, who also began a Quarterly Retrospect in July 1974 (another song expert, Eric Sams, came in for a while later in the decade); Mary Berry's calm authority on church music was invaluable, and Andrew Lamb, for long the undisputed expert on operetta, was allotted a slightly more extended field. Two other newcomers were Richard Osborne and Michael Oliver, both of whom became major figures in *Gramophone* (and on the radio). In the latter half of the decade still more experts were co-opted: Bryce Morrison on pianists, Nicholas Anderson on the baroque period, with a speciality of Vivaldi and Bach, Arnold Whittall for contemporary music, John Duarte on guitarists, David Fallows and Ian Fenlon on early music, Robin Golding on the Viennese classics, Gordon Reynolds on organists, and Ivan March, who for many years protected the interests of cassette buyers.

Margaret Pollard (left) with Joan Chissell in 1983

Richard Osborne

Michael Oliver

Ivan March

Questions that remain

The number of regulars – there were others who made more fleeting appearances – had now swelled to 26 and it is staggering that since the advent of the Compact Disc in March 1983 that number should have all but doubled. In theory that ought to lighten the load on individual reviewers, bearing in mind that one single two-disc issue will involve at least half a day's work (many people have no idea of the time that conscientious reviewing takes); but the result is that, with no let-up in the number of new releases from an ever-growing number of labels, we find ourselves contending for space even in the much enlarged magazine, enjoined to write briefer reviews and finding our material often held over for a month or more because of pressure of space. Groans predictably go up when yet another recording arrives of a much-duplicated work. When there are, for example, over 80 current recordings of Vivaldi's *Four Seasons* (leaving aside deleted versions) this puts an intolerable strain on a reviewer: a) to compare any new arrival with the formidable existing corpus, and b) to find something fresh to say.

In response to the demand for ever more information, record companies are now mostly disclosing details of the recording venue and the record producer; but unless there is some special reason for mentioning either, reviewers cannot afford the space to pass this on: on the other hand, purely musical details, such as which cadenzas are used, whether repeats are played, or what pitch is adopted, seem essential. (Gone are the days, fortunately, when arguments raged about 78rpm speeds, which affected pitch.) There are still arguments about 'authentic' instruments and performance practices. Initial dogmatism and pedantry have, to a large extent, been superseded by less rigid approaches, while 'historical' interpretations have been extended further and further forward in time. But not unexpectedly, there has been a backlash, with some polarization among reviewers and many readers left uncertain about which criteria should be applied. And of course opinions still differ about how much orchestral detail should be highlighted (or did the composer not wish for so clinical an approach?), about the proper balance between singers and orchestra in an opera (should every word be clearly audible or should the value of the musical phrase take precedence?), or about the importance or otherwise of singers' accents being idiomatic in foreign languages.

And so on, and so on. But this is what makes record reviewing remain a challenge; and I for one, after half a century on the job, still find the task enormously stimulating.

Lionel Salter

Lionel Salter has been reviewing for *Gramophone* since November 1948, making him the magazine's longest-serving current contributor. The first batch of reviews to which the initials LS were appended consisted of a *Blue Danube* from the VPO and Karajan, a new *Eroica* from Furtwängler, Ida Haendel playing Bruch's Violin Concerto and Delibes' *Sylvia* performed by the Hallé Orchestra under John Barbirolli.

A precociously musical child, he won numerous prizes and became a professional accompanist at the age of 12. He took degrees at Cambridge in music and modern languages, before working as an orchestrator and chorus-master in films (at the Korda Studios in Denham), as well as a music assistant in the early days of television. During the war he was chief guest conductor of the Radio France Symphony Orchestra, and on being invalided out of the army returned to the BBC as producer and administrator. He became successively Head of Opera for both radio and TV, and finally Assistant Controller, Music, at the same time pursuing a career as a harpsichordist, editing much eighteenth-century music and producing large-scale operas for the European Broadcasting Union. He has written books and innumerable programme-notes, edited the BBC Music Guides, was programme editor for the Edinburgh Festival for six years and the Proms for seven, has contributed to various works of reference and translated over 100 operas (some for performance, most for record booklets) and a couple of thousand song texts. LS is also well known as a broadcast speaker, adjudicator and a juror in international competitions.

Gramophone reviews

James Jolly

The review is the heart of *Gramophone*; for 75 years it has provided the lifeblood of the magazine. When Compton Mackenzie launched the publication it was to guide and, rather as his fellow Scot John Reith was to do at the BBC, educate in a field that was then in its infancy: classical music on record. Mackenzie set out to procure the finest opinions available and that desire holds true today, although the world in which we work has changed immeasurably.

Back in 1923 the catalogue was in many respects virgin territory – complete symphonies and operas were still a relative novelty. But guidance was needed and the role of guide was what fired Mackenzie all those years ago. In the early days the sound was of considerable importance; many of Mackenzie's editorials engaged with the new recordings not on the level of performance but for their technical quality (though Mackenzie, ever the enthusiastic amateur, was certainly not afraid of venturing opinions on the performance as well). Readers wanted to know whether to buy the new HMV disc or the Columbia rival, and even today the 'bottom line' is often "Do I go for the new Decca recording or stick to the older DG version?".

Gramophone's reviews operate on many different levels. The most basic is, of course, "Is this a performance I can live with?". Yet it is not as simple as that; the reader has to build a relationship with the reviewer, he (or sometimes she) has to know that what appeals to, say, RL will have the same appeal for himself. And over the years we all develop a special understanding. Indeed, such is the complexity of this relationship that it can operate on an even more sophisticated level – "I know that if RL doesn't like Maestro X's Sibelius then there's a chance that I may well like it myself". And that is the key to the ideal *Gramophone* review: to characterize a performance with such vividness that the reader takes over from the critic as the final arbiter. For me an ideal review is one where the critic clearly does not care for the performance himself but manages to convey the essence of the interpretation in a way that allows the reader to judge whether it is likely to fulfil his expectations. A composer who perfectly occupies this curious shadowland is Gustav Mahler, a man whose music seems to extract such a personal response from his interpreters – and one that can vary so dramatically from performer to performer – that the reader may hold a very different view of what Mahler is about from both the interpreter and the critic. A fan of Bernstein's Mahler or Tennstedt's is unlikely to respond to performances of a Boulez or a Dohnányi, and yet the ideal review of this music will alert the Boulezian to the attraction of a cooler more analytical response of another conductor. This is the irony of the 'good, bad review'.

One characteristic that has set *Gramophone*'s reviews aside from its rivals is the comparative element. T. S. Eliot argued that every time a new poem is written the entire canon of poetry is changed irreversibly and, similarly, every time a work is reinterpreted the entire history of that work is subtly altered. When Claudio Abbado records a new Bruckner Ninth, his version has to take its place not just alongside all the other versions with the Vienna Philharmonic, or all the versions that have been recorded by Deutsche Grammophon, but alongside every version that has ever found its way on to disc. Of course, space and time prevent such an all-embracing view but it is the task of the reviewer not only to characterize Abbado's Bruckner, offer a qualitative judgement, but also to place it in the context of the outstanding other recordings of the work: £15 is an expensive mistake to make!

The advent of the mid-price CD in the late-1980s brought the question of value-for-money into the limelight (not that it hadn't existed during the vinyl years), but to judge a new full-price recording alongside a budget-price reissue is of course a very real option, and more often than not to the detriment of the newcomer.

In the 'Good Old Days' life at *Gramophone*, as in so many other walks of life, was so much simpler. A visit to the (then relatively few) record companies would provide white label (test) pressings of the month's releases. Back at the office the 'titles' (or review headings) were prepared before the discs, and relevant comparative versions, were ready for delivery to the reviewers. This was a long day for Tony and Margaret Pollard who planned their route to take in all the contributors – starting in central London and usually finishing, late in the evening, in Hampshire with Margaret and Malcolm Macdonald, having visited Alec Robertson in Sussex *en route*, with time to discuss the records and enjoy some refreshment. No wonder Tony Pollard was a keen rally-driver! And then it was over to the critics.

James Jolly

James Jolly's love of music was awakened at his prep school and later developed at Bradfield College where he was not only taught by the composer Christopher Steel but also alerted to the infinite possibilities of the variety of musical interpretation by his English tutor, none other than *Gramophone*'s RO. (Bradfield College had other *Gramophone* links: Alec Robertson was also a pupil there and Cecil Bellamy, who reviewed spoken word for the magazine as well as edited the *Spoken Word Catalogue*, was a master at the College. A further link was also made through the late Christopher Headington, for about ten years a contributor to *Gramophone* but to Bradfieldians the composer of a setting of the Series 3 communion service and the music for the triennial Greek play.) A BA in English at Bristol University was followed by an MA at Reading University in "The Literary Response to the Visual Arts", essentially a course in aesthetics which fostered an interest in the writings of Walter Pater, the subject of his thesis. *Gramophone* was JJ's first job, as Editorial Assistant, then followed a spell at BBC Radio 3, producing *Record Review*, to all intents and purposes *Gramophone* in a different medium. In 1990 JJ returned to *Gramophone* as Editor and has steered the magazine through a period that has seen the first real competition for many years as well as overseeing a major redesign in 1993 and the launch of the monthly covermount CD.

Today with some 400 discs arriving each month, often in their finished state, the process is more complex, though in essence very similar. Review titles which carry all necessary information – besides detailing the work and the performers, they also reveal whether the disc is stereo or mono, full, medium, budget or super-budget price, whether texts are included and so on – still need to be prepared. In 1998 this also means logging the disc's existence on the *Gramophone* Database which then provides the electronic data that is required for the discographical needs of the whole range of *Gramophone* publications, including the *GramoFile* CD-ROM. Decisions as to what to select for review are taken with the knowledge that every so often something superb is going to slip through the net. Yet the modern age brings its compensations – first fax, then computer disks and now e-mail – everything to speed up the process and reduce the need for expensive typesetting bills.

And who are *Gramophone*'s critics? The review panel, now at its largest, numbers some 46 contributors whose interests span the entire musical gamut and whose professions are as varied as the types of music they write about. Matching repertoire to reviewers is for the majority of cases not complex: critic X specializes in the voice so the pairing of disc to reviewer is straightforward. With RO a world-renowned authority on Rossini and the author of a major biography who other to review recordings of the composer? Similarly with a track record as fine as DF's in research in Guillaume Dufay, the match of reviewer and repertoire is obvious. But where new repertoire is entering the catalogue at an exponential rate finding reviewers is a more complex task and requires some selective sampling. In addition, members of the panel can and sometimes do exercise their right to decline to review certain recordings – and their decision is always respected. This rarely presents insuperable difficulties: we are lucky to have 'on our books' some extremely fine writers with breathtakingly catholic tastes – is there nothing, for example, that LS or MEO won't review and engage with at a very high level of scholarship yet in a way that encourages exploration? School teachers and university lecturers form a hard core to the panel alongside full-time music critics. Yet what every single contributor brings is a passion not only for the music but for the world of music on record. Not for nothing is the magazine called *Gramophone*.

The reviewers

Andrew Achenbach
Nicholas Anderson
Mary Berry
Alan Blyth
Joan Chissell
Rob Cowan
Peter Dickinson
Duncan Druce
John Duarte
Adrian Edwards
Richard T Fairman
David Fallows
David J Fanning
Iain Fenlon
Hilary Finch
Fabrice Fitch
Jonathan Freeman-Attwood
Edward Greenfield
David S Gutman
Stephen Johnson
Lindsay Kemp
Tess Knighton
Andrew Lamb
Robert Layton
Ivan March
Ivan W G Moody
Bryce Morrison
David Nice
Patrick O'Connor
Michael Oliver
Richard Osborne
Stephen Plaistow
Nicholas A Rast
Guy S Rickards
Marc Rochester
Julie Anne Sadie
Stanley Sadie
Lionel Salter
Edward Seckerson
Robert Seeley
John B Steane
Michael Stewart
Jonathan Swain
John Warrack
Arnold Whittall
Richard Wigmore

An expanding universe

A personal view of recorded repertoire

Robert Layton

In the early years of the century the gramophone was less about repertoire than nostalgia. When this magazine was founded 75 years ago few musicians took the medium really seriously. Busoni was not alone in regarding it with scarcely disguised contempt – understandably so, when you remember that the bulk of its output would have been popular arias by celebrated singers, and piano pieces by famous instrumentalists. Of course, eventually there were complete symphonies and chamber works but they were relatively speaking few. Moreover before electrical recording arrived on the scene the medium could not do real justice to the orchestra. The early electrical recordings of Holst conducting *The Planets* made in 1926 (Columbia) or the excerpts from *The Dream of Gerontius* that Elgar conducted at Hereford in 1927 (HMV, 2/28), were among the first to make a realistic impression. Playing the 78s of the 1928 Bayreuth *Tristan und Isolde* conducted by Karl Elmendorff (Columbia, 12/28), one is astonished by the naturalness and depth of the sound. The great orchestral showpieces only became a really viable proposition after electrical recording was well established, but Stokowski's remarkable 78s of Stravinsky's *Le sacre du printemps* (HMV, 4/31) and the composer's pallid-sounding version (Columbia, 4/31), both recorded in 1929, show that the results could still be variable.

The Dream of Gerontius was recorded by HMV at Hereford Cathedral in September 1927
Photo Elgar Birthplace

The four-minute side

The 78rpm format naturally imposed its constraints. The recording companies thought in terms of its four-minute side, and many collectors would buy larger works piecemeal, one disc at a time. Moreover, the economics of record collecting and making were completely different in the 1930s. For the *Symphonie fantastique*, say, one would have paid 36s. [£1·80], an infinitely larger proportion of the monthly budget than a premium-price CD is now. In fact it would probably be nearer the cost of a night out in the best seats at Covent Garden or Glyndebourne! No one who has looked at Clough & Cuming's monumental *World's Encyclopaedia of Recorded Music* will doubt the riches that were already available, but more is probably released nowadays in one month than would then have appeared in two dozen. For example, the very first copy of ***The Gramophone*** magazine that I purchased (January 1946) reviewed only eight 'classical' records – and in this order: Ginette Neveu's recording of the Sibelius Violin Concerto, Walton's *Sinfonia concertante* for piano and orchestra (conducted by the composer), some of Moszkowski's *Spanish Dances*, Clifford Curzon and the National Symphony Orchestra with Falla's *Nights in the Garden of Spain*, Weber's *Euryanthe* Overture, a couple of Elgar's *Pomp and Circumstance* Marches, and Denis Matthews playing two *Nocturnes* by John Field. And that was all, save for a 10-inch Columbia 78 of Isobel Baillie and Kathleen Ferrier singing Purcell, which found Alec Robertson complaining that he could not "get at a collected edition of Purcell's music to find from where these duets came", and promising a review in the following issue! Of course the catalogues could offer alternative sets of Beethoven and Brahms symphonies from great conductors such as Weingartner, Toscanini and Furtwängler, and Walter Legge had founded the Beethoven Sonata Society, the Sibelius Society, the Mozart Opera Society, Hugo Wolf Society and so on [p. 46]; but the gaps were both legion and glaring. In January 1946 Mahler was represented by the Ninth Symphony and *Das Lied von der Erde* in the Society Editions; Eugene Ormandy's account of the Second was available to special order only; Bruno Walter's New York recordings of the Fourth and the Fifth were yet to come, as were Eduard van Beinum's records of the Seventh Symphony of Bruckner with the Concertgebouw Orchestra.

The new post-war world

To a certain extent of course, the gramophone reflects rather than creates changes in public taste and in the autumn of 1946, the advent of the BBC Third Programme served to introduce the British musical public to repertoire from which it had hitherto been cut off. A complete cycle of the Mahler symphonies, the first ever undertaken in Britain, kindled a flame that was to burn ever more brightly in the succeeding years; and a Bruckner cycle soon followed. Yet it was only in the mid-to late-1950s when LP had become firmly established that either composer came into his own. LP enabled a whole range of repertoire to reach a wider public that would have found it impossible to cope with countless side-changes and fibre-needle sharpening. Act 3 of *Die Meistersinger* had been recorded before the war on 30 sides, Mahler's Ninth on 20 sides, and Bruckner's Fifth on 18. Even so, it was still some time before either a Bruckner or Mahler canon was complete. The first *Gramophone LP Classical Record Catalogue* I possess, from June 1958 and now 40 years old, does not list Bruckner's First and Second symphonies or Mahler's Third, though there were by then no fewer than five LP versions of Mahler's First then available. The Sixth, Seventh and Eighth were available in single versions; 40 years on, of course, there are between 20 and 30 versions of each!

Vivaldi and Early music

The same process of expansion and exploration occurred in pre-classical music. Pioneers like Arnold Dolmetsch and Charles van den Borren had opened the eyes of the musical public to the riches of early music but the repertoire was not extensive. There were the French labels Anthologie Sonore and Louise Hanson-Dyer's Oiseau-Lyre, as well as the Columbia "History of Music through Ear and Eye" (twelfth to twentieth century, edited by Percy Scholes), the release of which started in April 1930 as a joint production with the Oxford University Press on 40 12-inch 78s. After the war came the HMV "History of Music in Sound", again produced in conjunction with the Oxford University Press and recorded in collaboration with the BBC's Third Programme. The first volumes appeared in June 1953 on 78rpm only, but from 1957 many of the items were re-recorded and issued simultaneously on a total of 27 LPs or 114 78s, with the tenth and final volume being reviewed in April 1959. Imagine such ambition in our current cultural climate! But generally speaking, the lacunae were conspicuous. Even Vivaldi was a rarity. When Alec Robertson gave an introductory talk to a series of seven programmes of Vivaldi's music on the Third Programme in the late-1940s, he had difficulty in illustrating it from commercial records and many of his music examples had to be specially recorded. There was no *Four Seasons* mania until the early days of LP and very little Monteverdi. Perhaps the most famous Monteverdi set was the five 78s of Madrigals recorded by a number of distinguished French singers under the direction of Nadia Boulanger (HMV, 6/38). The continuo part, played on the piano by Boulanger herself, sounds so poetic and alive that it leaves an indelible impression. However 60 years on, it is hardly likely that this repertoire will be reclaimed by the piano! But there is an authenticity of feeling that is quite special. Edward Sackville-West and Desmond Shawe-Taylor, who contributed Quarterly Retrospects to ***The Gramophone*** for many years, called it "one of the purest treasures the gramophone has given us".

By 1958 the representation of Vivaldi and the appetite for portmanteau baroque concertos had mushroomed to such an alarming extent that there was a backlash against the prevalent fashion. All these things are relative and the baroque boom would probably not raise an eyebrow from our present-day perspective. Vivaldi's *Four Seasons* was available in no fewer than eight different versions as opposed to over 80 in 1998! But that was fully commensurate with other areas of the repertoire, such as the symphonies of Brahms. There were nine versions of Nos. 2 and 4 then as opposed to about 60 now.

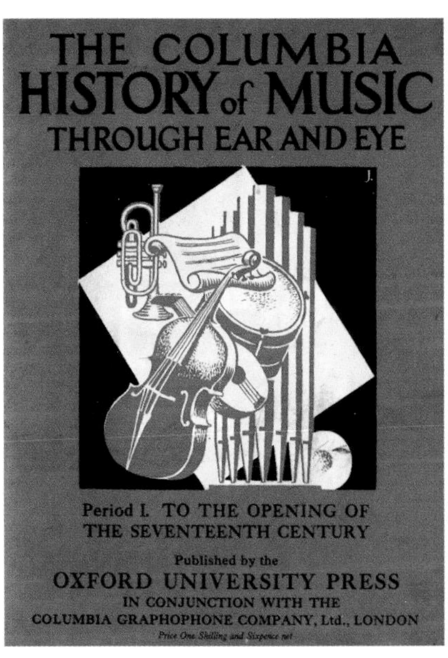
THE COLUMBIA
HISTORY of MUSIC
THROUGH EAR AND EYE

Period I. TO THE OPENING OF
THE SEVENTEENTH CENTURY

Published by the
OXFORD UNIVERSITY PRESS
IN CONJUNCTION WITH THE
COLUMBIA GRAPHOPHONE COMPANY, Ltd., LONDON
Price One Shilling and Sixpence net

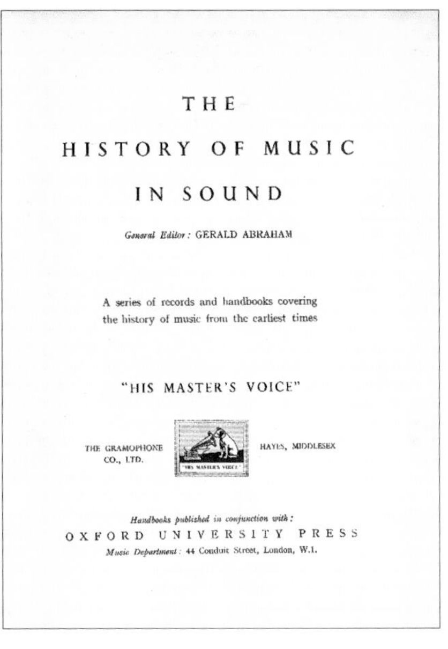
THE
HISTORY OF MUSIC
IN SOUND

General Editor: GERALD ABRAHAM

A series of records and handbooks covering
the history of music from the earliest times

"HIS MASTER'S VOICE"

THE GRAMOPHONE CO., LTD. HAYES, MIDDLESEX

Handbooks published in conjunction with:
OXFORD UNIVERSITY PRESS
Music Department: 44 Conduit Street, London, W.1.

New orchestral repertoire

In 1947 the Maharajah of Mysore established a Musical Foundation whose immediate objective was the recording of Medtner's Piano Concertos with the composer as soloist – the first album, produced for HMV by Walter Legge, was reviewed in February 1948. The Maharajah also invited wider participation and in the April 1950 issue there was a long list of readers' requests, together with the announcement that, among others, Balakirev's First Symphony (Columbia, 11/50) and Roussel's Fourth (1/51) had been recorded by Herbert von Karajan and the Philharmonia Orchestra – and I would venture to say that they have never been surpassed. Readers' suggestions included such diverse works as Berg's Violin Concerto (the pioneering Louis Krasner recording with Artur Rodzinski and the Cleveland Orchestra was never issued on this side of the Atlantic), the early symphonies of Roussel (Nos. 1 and 2), Franz Schmidt (Nos. 3 and 4), Szymanowski's *Hamasie*, Busoni's Piano Concerto and Janáček's *From the diary of one who disappeared*. All of these were to reach the catalogue, admittedly some later rather than sooner, and the only two works in

The Gramophone, January, 1948

H. H. The Maharajah of Mysore's Musical Foundation

(MEDTNER SECTION)

THE recording by His Master's Voice of the principal compositions of Nicolas Medtner is, perhaps, one of the greatest romances in the history of the Gramophone.

Christopher Stone, writing on Medtner, describes him as "gaunt, other-worldly, distinguished, neglected, living with his wife and his grand piano in the simplest seclusion in the north of London."

How fortunate, and indeed, wonderful that destiny should have brought Medtner's genius within the sphere of vision and great musical appreciation of H.H. the Maharajah of Mysore. For the Maharajah thereupon decided that Medtner must no longer languish in the desert of neglect, and that his genius and contribution to the world of music must be made known.

A star led man—a star that shone from the firmament into the life of Medtner. Let us for a moment consider and contemplate this remarkable happening. Medtner is 67 years of age. He was a close friend of Rachmaninoff, and he has that simple charm and trusting outlook which are usually found in one who has given his life to Art. He had moments of joy, when occasionally a work of his was performed or broadcast, but he now knows that all his toil was not in vain. The Maharajah has made funds available that Medtner's work might be recorded, and Medtner's star is aflame.

I shall not forget the look of wonder in Medtner's countenance as Captain Binstead, the Maharajah of Mysore's Commissioner, in my presence, put the proposal to him. What a service has been rendered to music, and oh! what joy for Medtner. I remember, too, my own wonder at the whole of the great project on my visit to the studios for the first of these great recordings.

Good Readers, you will now appreciate my reason for calling this a romance.

Since that day, some eight months ago, the greater part of Medtner's rich musical creation has been recorded, the Composer both supervising the recording, and playing the pianoforte parts. There has been a team of expert advisers behind these recordings, composed of Compton Mackenzie who was privileged in Mysore to discuss this project with the Maharajah in person, Walter Legge, of His Master's Voice, who brought Composer, Conductor, Artists and Recording Engineers together to make this an issue of the greatest artistic merit, Christopher Stone with his sage advice, and Benno Moiseiwitsch, whose friendship with Medtner and knowledge of his music are of paramount importance. The albums will be issued as Society Volumes, as directed by the Committee, of which I am privileged to be a member, under the capable management of my good friend Mr. C. H. Thomas, of His Master's Voice. I must again mention here Captain S. T. Binstead, who is, as I said before, the astute Commissioner for the Maharajah in this country. He has left no stone unturned to bring this project to fruition.

Let us then warm to this romance, for it is clear that Medtner, in the autumn of his life, has found recognition, that the reward of his life's labour has been made certain through the inspiration and timely intervention of H.H. the Maharajah of Mysore.

A service has been rendered to music, and to posterity which you will agree is unique.

On another page I give particulars of the first album and a photograph of Medtner.

FRED SMITH

RIMINGTON, VAN WYCK LTD., 42-43 CRANBOURN STREET, LONDON, W.C.2 *Telephone*: Gerrard 117[illegible]
Mail Order Department: 18a DEVONSHIRE STREET, MARYLEBONE, LONDON, W.1 *Telephone*: Welbeck 4695

that extensive list not yet recorded are Casella's *Il Couvento Veneziana* and Wellesz's Symphony – this must have been the First, Op. 62, of 1946, which I remember hearing broadcast with the Berlin Philharmonic under Celibidache.

Not all the public's enthusiasms met with an immediate response. In 1955, by which time the Bax Third Symphony recorded by Sir John Barbirolli and the Hallé Orchestra a decade earlier had long disappeared, there were eloquent pleas in the magazine for more of his music. They fell on deaf ears. My 1959 catalogue lists one version of his tone-poem, *The Garden of Fand*, two of *Tintagel*, his *Coronation March* and a song! The situation did not materially improve until Lyrita embarked on (though they never finished) the symphonies in the 1970s. Chandos put matters to right comprehensively in the 1980s with what is the best part of Bax's complete output.

The gramophone began to assume its exploratory role in real earnest with the advent of vinyl. In December 1949 Compton Mackenzie had noted the absence of any complete recordings of *Tristan*, *Meistersinger*, *Carmen*, *Fidelio*, *Otello*, *Boris* and much else besides. The enhanced playing time of the new format made all these practicable and in the early 1950s hardly a month passed without some important new addition to the recorded repertoire. In fact I am inclined to think this was the most exciting period of all, save perhaps for the early years of stereo. Every month brought new things such as Glière's *Il'ya Mouromets* Symphony, with Jacques Rachmilovich conducting the Orchestra dell'Accademia di St Cecilia, Rome (Capitol, 10/50), albeit abridged as it was when Ferenc Fricsay recorded it some years later. There was Ansermet conducting Prokofiev's Sixth (Decca, 5/52) and recording an abundance of Debussy and Ravel, the Nielsen symphonies and concertos, and then there was the Nixa label on which many of the records of the Haydn Society, the brainchild of H. C. Robbins Landon, appeared.

Oeuvres intégrales!

For the modern public which takes complete editions of the classical repertoire comfortably in their stride, it must be difficult to conceive of a period in which you could not buy all the Mozart piano concertos or all the Haydn symphonies – I recall collecting the latter piecemeal during the 1950s both on 78s, which were by then languishing in neglect and therefore cheap, and on LPs. By the early 1970s, when Decca embarked on its complete survey with Antál Dorati and the Philharmonia Hungarica, I must have acquired well over 70, though there were many unwanted duplications which one accepted less happily than one does today. It was the Vox label which catered for the collector who wanted *oeuvres intégrales* but they never managed to complete their early survey of the Mozart concertos with Ingrid Haebler. I recall that the D major, K451, was particularly shy and was not to be found in the British catalogues for some time until Walter Klien's stylish account appeared (Vox, 11/61). The first complete set from one ensemble was Géza Anda and the Camerata Academica of the Salzburg Mozarteum on DG, soon followed by Ingrid Haebler and Colin Davis on Philips. It goes without saying that there were advantages for the collector in not having cumbersome jumbo boxes. One could build up a collection of Beethoven quartets month by month as the Budapest Quartet or the Quartetto Italiano made their magisterial process through the canon, and similarly choose from among the various Bach cantata issues from Wolfgang Gonnenwein, Fritz Lehmann, Anton Heiller, Felix Prohaska, Karl Münchinger, Kurt Thomas and others. This was in 1958, shortly before Archiv embarked on their ambitious series with Karl Richter and his Munich Bach Choir and Orchestra which began in 1960, when there were roughly three dozen Bach cantatas listed in the catalogue, few of them in more than one version, as opposed to the comprehensive surveys now before the public.

The advent of stereo

I will never forget the thrilling effect made at the time by the very first stereo LPs which I bought in the late-1950s – *The Planets* of Holst played by the BBC Symphony Orchestra and Sir Malcolm Sargent (HMV, 1/59) and Debussy's *Jeux* and Dukas's *La Péri* with Ansermet and the Suisse Romande Orchestra (Decca, 5/59). They succeeded in capturing the space in which the music was being made, and involving you more directly in the musical experience. As the 1960s drew to a close the engineers were less inclined to allow the music to speak for itself and it still seems to me that those early stereo LPs offer some of the best sound – ever! One composer above all benefited from opening out the surrounding acoustic – Bruckner. Just as the LP had met the physical proportions of his musical thinking, so stereo did justice to the sonic dimensions. Even so, not all the symphonies were listed in catalogues from the early 1960s, but in terms of sound, some of those that were, are not only the equal of but superior to many modern rivals. I am thinking in particular of Carl Schuricht's account of the Ninth Symphony (HMV, 12/62) and the Third (HMV, 11/66), both with the Vienna Philharmonic.

Stereo gave the companies an opportunity to record *The Four Seasons* all over again and much other Vivaldi besides, but present-day music lovers will be surprised how low a profile a master like Telemann enjoyed in the catalogue. In 1958 there were not many more than a half-a-dozen LPs, though there was something of a turn-round in his fortunes in the mid-1960s when Archiv Produktion got to work on his behalf. Some composers are 'gramophone' composers, appearing seldom in the concert-hall but maintaining a peripheral but tenacious foothold on the catalogue. Forty years ago, the Swedish composer Franz Berwald, even now rarely found in our concert programmes, was represented by only one LP – Igor Markevitch's coupling of the *Sinfonie singulière* and the Symphony No. 4 in E flat – while Martinů, who was still alive, had only three works in the British lists – the Symphony No. 6, *Fantaisies symphoniques*, the Third Violin Sonata and the *Three Madrigals* for violin and viola. All that was to change in the 1960s and by the mid-1970s Martinů enjoyed decent if not handsome exposure on record, although not in the concert-hall or in broadcast programmes – at least not in the days when Sir William Glock was in charge of music at the BBC. Nor did Sibelius, but in his case the gramophone performed the service of "keeper of the flame", giving us complete cycles of the symphonies from Sir John Barbirolli (HMV), Lorin Maazel (Decca) and Leonard Bernstein (CBS) as well as Karajan's classic accounts of Nos. 4 to 7 (DG).

The 1960s saw one of the landmarks in the history of recording – the completion of Wagner's *Der Ring des Nibelungen* conducted by Sir Georg Solti and released by Decca. The first opera in the cycle, *Das Rheingold*, had been issued in March 1959 and the final work, *Die Walküre*, appeared in September 1966. Many of Berlioz's major works were also given complete for the first time, including *Les Troyens* and *Benvenuto Cellini*. Then there was the conquest of so much new repertoire and the discovery of composers unrepresented in the catalogue. The seventeenth-century French master, Marc-Antoine Charpentier, for example, whose currently available discography in 1998 runs to some 150 recordings of more than 170 separate works, was only just beginning to come into his own and in 1958 he had been represented solely by his *Messe de minuit* and excerpts from his opera, *Medée* conducted by Nadia Boulanger (Brunswick, 7/54). In 1958 Telemann's recorded *oeuvre* consisted of just 13 works; it now stands at over 300!

Much that was exciting in the music of our own century was also being put on disc; Decca embarked on the Britten operas, the middle symphonies of Prokofiev surfaced from neglect (though Charles Bruck had recorded the Second in the 1950s in France), and the foundations were being laid for the present interest in Szymanowski. None of his orchestral music was listed in 1958 (his only representation was the D minor Violin Sonata, Op. 9, the Chopinesque Etude, Op. 4, No. 3 and *The Fountain of Arethusa*), but the 1960s saw the Polish company Muza exploring his output in earnest.

The Compact Disc

The 1970s saw the expansion of the repertoire increase apace with the development of digital recording, and the launch of Compact Disc in 1983 started 'life' all over

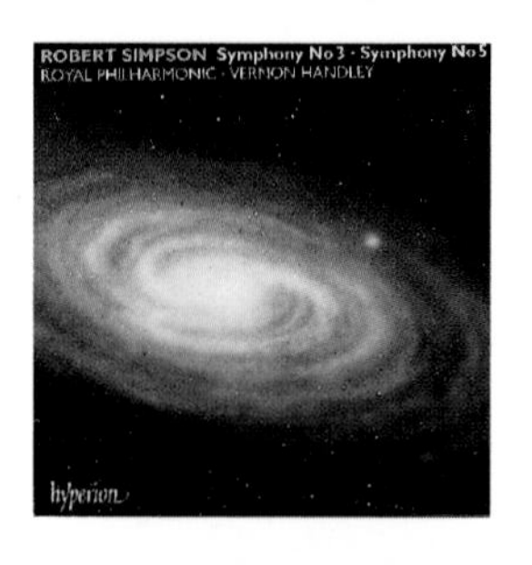

again! Initially there were fears that the ground won in the 1960s and 1970s might be lost, that repertoire would become narrower and enterprise stifled in an excess of caution. The new technology had involved an enormous investment and the major companies, understandably, wanted a positive return. I see that in my Quarterly Retrospect of May 1986, three years after the launch of CD, I wrote, "Few would now question the gains the new technology brings in its train, for the greater definition and range of the new medium are obvious, but the threat to the LP repertoire naturally gives cause for concern. Go into many retail outlets either here or on the Continent and you find the LP shelves occupying an ever-diminishing amount of space, as was the case [with 78s] in the early 1950s. But there the parallel between the present and the transition from shellac to vinyl stops, for whereas in 1950-4, the LP was the exploratory medium hungrily devouring new repertoire and blazoning new trails, the CD at the present stage of its development is still consolidating its basic catalogue." Earlier I had made a prediction that was nothing if not imprudent: "When the LP disc arrived in the early 1950s it was barely five or six years before its repertoire had overtaken the riches of the old shellac catalogue as enshrined in the *World's Encyclopaedia of Recorded Music*. Such has been the repertoire explosion since, that even with the most gargantuan and dynamic recording programme, CD is unlikely even to match the riches of the past three decades by the end of the century!" Further flights of prophesy and clairvoyance have been grounded! I had not counted on the ever accelerating pace of change, for this had virtually been accomplished within one decade. And there was an appetite for new repertoire, particularly among the smaller repertoire-driven companies without which we would be infinitely poorer. There is Hyperion's Robert Simpson Edition, their Purcell survey, Schubert Song Edition, BIS's symphonies of Eduard Tubin and Vagn Holmboe, not to mention the complete works of Schnittke; Chandos blazed a trail for Parry, Britten, Dyson and the symphonies of Edmund Rubbra. For all the explosion in repertoire it has taken the gramophone 60 years to get round to Rubbra's First and 50 to record the Third. But there is still a lot of good music left: Busoni's opera, *Die Brautwahl*, Frank Martin's opera *The Tempest*, Holmboe's *Nietzsche Requiem*, Alexandre Tansman's atmospheric radio opera *Le Serment*, Pizzetti's underrated *Assassinio nella cattedrale* and his Symphony in A, Wellesz's opera, *Incognita* – and I am sure readers of **Gramophone** could supply a rich and varied list of music from the eighteenth and nineteenth centuries.

Looking back over past issues of the magazine and browsing in its catalogues, it would have been as impossible to imagine the sheer extent of the post-war explosion of repertoire as it would be to predict its future in the coming years. The best analogy I can think of is astronomic: as our exploration of the repertoire expands, so there always seems more out there to discover.

Robert Layton

Robert Layton who has contributed a Quarterly Retrospect to **Gramophone** since the mid-1960s, abandoned the piano for the pen not long after leaving Worcester College, Oxford, where he studied composition with Edmund Rubbra and the history of music with Egon Wellesz. He had ambitions as a composer and in his twenties wrote a symphony. After leaving Oxford he gained a Swedish Government scholarship to study at Uppsala and Stockholm, where he wrote a study of Franz Berwald. He also worked briefly in the Swedish Film Industry archives and actually had some minuscule acting roles in some American soaps which were being made for economic reasons in Sweden. On returning to England he worked as a teacher in London's East End for a while, before joining the BBC's music division, first in succession to Deryck Cooke in Music Presentation and then becoming Music Talks Producer (a post previously held by two other **Gramophone** contributors, Alec Robertson and Roger Fiske). He produced among other things "Interpretations on Record" for the best part of two decades. In the 1980s he looked after various projects – a long series devoted to Szymanowski – and the BBC's Lunchtime Concerts at St John's, Smith Square. He is mainly identified not so much with Slavonic as Scandinavian music, writing a *Master Musicians* study of Sibelius, recently updated, and another *The World of Sibelius*. His translation of the first two volumes of Erik Tawaststjerna's *Sibelius* was awarded the Finnish State Literary Prize in 1984; he also holds the Sibelius Medal and was made a Knight of the Order of the White Rose, an honour accorded to such figures as Beecham, Ormandy and Heifetz.

Recording and reproduction

The acoustical era

John Borwick

From a vantage point 75 years on, sound recording technology in 1923 may fairly be described as primitive. It still relied on acoustic methods which had scarcely changed since the dawn of recording a quarter of a century earlier. How this made difficulties for recording artists, severely limited the choice of repertoire and degraded the sound quality of the records and the gramophones on which they were played was described at length in the pages of ***The Gramophone***. However, the technical reasons for these shortcomings were also researched by the Expert Committee [p. 26], and the magazine's Technical Editor Percy Wilson [p. 245] in particular, as a means of persuading the manufacturers to 'do better'.

Acoustic recording

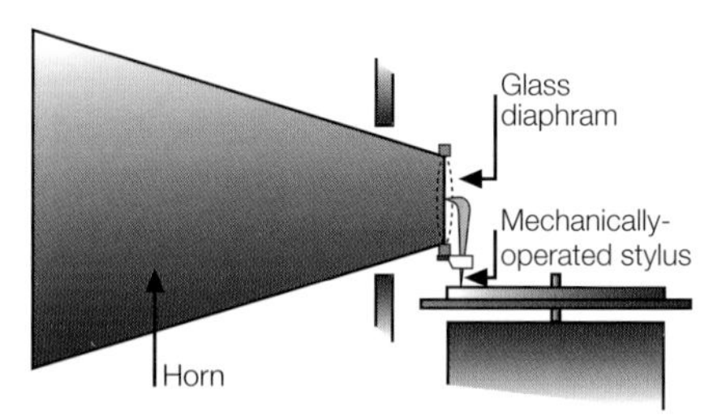

There were limiting factors at every stage of the process: Recording, i.e. capturing the sounds and storing them in a spiral groove on a wax master disc; Duplication, i.e. preparing a mould and using this to press quantities of records; Reproduction, i.e. retracing the groove in the record to recreate the original sounds with as little distortion as possible. These stages will be outlined in turn.

Recording

Since the acoustic energy produced by voices and musical instruments is very small, and the levels of spurious noise inherent in the gramophone record/play system were so high, everything possible had to be done to improve sound transfer efficiency.

Sound pick-up in the recording studio used a conical horn, often protruding from a wall and acting like an ear trumpet or a megaphone in reverse, to collect as much sound energy as possible and direct this to a glass diaphragm at the apex with a cutting stylus either attached directly at its centre or via a lever. As the diaphragm oscillated in response to the sound waves, the stylus, when lowered on to the surface of a revolving disc of 50-75mm (2-3in) thick wax, kept at a critical temperature, inscribed a lateral wavy line and the groove thus formed was caused to spiral from the outer edge towards the disc centre by means of a lead screw. This transported the whole turntable unit beneath the cutting stylus and maintained a predetermined groove spacing, or pitch, of about 100 grooves per inch. The machine was usually weight driven, using a 50 kilogram weight on a steel cable passing through one or more floors in the building.

An acoustic recording session in 1908, showing Stroh horn violins and (centre) the main and subsidiary recording horns. The conductor is Bruno Seidler-Winkler *Photo DG*

Already a host of problems can be identified. The horn ignored bass frequencies below a cut-off frequency determined by its dimensions, which also introduced a strong characteristic resonance effect, and was of low efficiency so that performers had to crowd close to the horn mouth. This suited solo singers, particularly loud ones, but was disastrous for instrumental ensembles. Balancing involved moving players around and

June 1924 **Correspondence**

RECORD SPEEDS

The primary consideration in getting the best from a record (assuming you have the best equipment) has always seemed to me to be the speed at which you play it. I'm afraid (from following ***The Gramophone*** for ten months) that we are prone to doubt the manufacturer's declarations regarding the best machines, sound-boxes, and needles, and yet accept wholeheartedly such statements as "to obtain the best results play all records at the speed of 78 (or 80)".

My doubts of the designated speed being the recording speed were first aroused by the Hayward-Bourne records of the Franck Sonata. It seemed rather slow and lifeless at 78. I was much surprised to find that it must be turned up to 83 to be in pitch, and at 83 you hear a fine rendition as they played it. Another record now aroused my suspicions, an old recording of the Overture from *Forza del Destino*, by La Scala Orchestra. It seemed too harsh, too brilliant. I tried it with the score, the pitch was clearly sharp, I began turning it down – 76, 74, 72, and finally at 70 did I find the recording speed. At 70 it is a pleasing recording.

Among the records in my library a number of interesting facts were soon discovered. I will mention some of the English records. The Columbia version of *Siegfried Idyll* begins at 79; part 2 should be played at 81; part 3, 81; part 4, 83; otherwise it rather dies out on one. Sir Henry Wood in the *Eroica* Symphony begins at the advertised speed of 80. The second movement, however, starts out at 83, and after a few bars (I believe eight measures) continues at 84, the second side goes back to 82. The third movement plays at 80, the last at 82. That these speeds must be observed for better results, no one can deny. Play the *Marche funèbre* of the aforementioned symphony at the advertised speed and note how heavily it drags, flatting after the opening measures.

I find that many artists have their own speeds, with many exceptions. Rachmaninov, for example, uses 75 and 77 in the American records and I believe the English are from the same recordings.

The following is a random list of records with their correct speeds. These speeds were obtained with an ordinary watch, and tested as to pitch with a piano and seem quite accurate.

Coates and Symphony Orchestra: Three Strauss Tone Poems, 78; *Der Freischütz* Overture, 78; Seventh Symphony (Beethoven), 76; Kreisler and Zimbalist: Concerto for two violins (Bach), 76. Coates and London S. Orchestra: *Le poème de l'extase*, 80; *Scheherazade*, part 2, 82, 80, part 4, 82. Rachmaninov: *Liebeslied*, 75; *Serenade*, 75; *Polka de W. R.*, 75; *Prelude in G minor*, 77.

K. Britzius
Minneapolis, Minn, USA

such devices as substituting a tuba for the string bass, a Stroh horn instrument for the conventional violin or placing an upright piano on a box with its back towards the horn.

The tonal extent of the recorded waveform was severely limited, compared with the 20-20,000Hz nominal range of hearing (Hertz = cycles per second) which modern systems encompass. The highest usable frequency (shortest wavelength) was no more than 3,000Hz, determined by the ability of the stylus tip to trace the radius of curvature, suppressing harmonics, so that all musical instruments tended to sound the same. Bass sounds, whose amplitude increases with decreasing frequency, had to be curtailed below about 200Hz for fear of breaking through into the neighbouring groove.

It would be possible to ameliorate these two restrictions by increasing the turntable speed to extend high frequency coverage and increasing the distance between grooves for deeper bass, but these changes would shorten the available recording time per disc. The compromise reached for a nominal running speed of 78 revolutions per minute (rpm) produced uncomfortably short playing durations of up to three or four minutes for 10-inch and 12-inch records respectively. In practice, running speeds were not standardized but varied between about 60 and 90rpm, so that a variable speed governor on the gramophone's spring motor was necessary.

Duplication

Whilst every copy of Edison's early cylinders needed to be recorded individually, the rival flat discs developed by Berliner had the advantage of replication from a master disc produced by a photographic process. Eldridge Johnson made the system more commercially viable by substituting a wax disc on which, after a dusting with fine graphite to make it electrically conducting, a thin metal 'father' could be formed by electrodeposition, having

February 1938 **Correspondence**

EDISON'S FIRST MACHINE

My attention has been called to Mr Wilson's most interesting article in your December issue, tracing the developments of the phonograph, in which he regrets not having known anyone who ever heard Edison's first machine.

This subject has always been one of great interest to me, and my memory goes back to the time, about 1912, when Mr Edison was conducting further experiments to improve his invention. I had the honour of working with Mr Edison at this time, my function being to sing certain arpeggios into the phonograph while Mr Edison measured the vibrations on a chart with a pencil. These experiments were conducted at the Edison Laboratories at Orange, New Jersey, over a period of months.

One day Mr Edison was listening with pleasure to some cylinders I had made for the company in 1908, and I told him that these were not the first Edison records I had made.

When I was a child in Brussels, about 1878, a talking machine was exhibited at the Brussels fair, in a building like the present 'penny arcades'. I spoke and sang into this machine, the sounds being recorded on a sheet of heavy tinfoil, which was afterwards snipped off with a pair of shears and handed to me. Mr Edison was delighted with this reminiscence, I remember, and said I had spoken into his first patented machine. The sounds emitted when the tinfoil was re-inserted into the machine and ground off by means of a crank were indeed primitive, in the light of the present day, but startling and miraculous enough for the time. Then, since the machine functioned by hand there was no adjustment of speed, and a soprano could turn into a squealing pig or a *basso profundo*, merely by cranking slower or faster. Yet the sounds approximated my voice and were recognisable as mine. It seems to me few realize to what a degree of perfection Mr Edison finally brought his invention. Even to-day, his improved cylinders are miracles of balance and pure, undistorted tone.

Blanche Arral
Grantwood, New Jersey, USA

April 1927 **News**

ACOUSTIC TILES

Emile Berliner, who shares (or declines to share – the controversy is futile) with Thomas Edison the honour of having invented the gramophone, has now patented the acoustic tiles on which he has been working for the last year and a half, and has demonstrated them in a practical way by putting them into a notoriously ill-sounding building in Washington and obtaining extraordinarily satisfactory results. Since old as well as new buildings can be treated with this invention, it is likely to be very thoroughly tested in the near future. What about the Albert Hall?

ridges instead of grooves. This in turn could be used to produce first a positive 'mother' and then one or more 'negative' moulds or stampers which could be used to press out large numbers of finished records.

Berliner's first discs were made of hard rubber or vulcanite but this had many faults, including an unacceptably high surface noise. A change to shellac produced a somewhat quieter background and provided the primary medium for recorded music for about half a century. The records were in fact made from a mixture of about 14 per cent shellac (from the shells of the lac, an insect which settled in very large numbers on certain trees in India, Burma and Siam – 'lac' means 100,000 in the Hindu language) plus carbon black, scrap and an abrasive limestone filler designed to grind the replay needle tip to the shape of the groove.

The pressing factories were more like Blake's "dark Satanic mills" than the clean-air rooms used for today's CD manufacture. A biscuit-steam-table type of press was used and quality varied widely. The 0·02-inch thick copper stampers were hardened by electroplating with nickel and chrome, then soldered to a 0·0625-inch steel backing plate, a process that took 22 hours to complete.

These shellac records had serious defects. There were no standards set for the mixture itself. The material was brittle and surface noise due to the filler and other coarse ingredients was very high. In a way the constant 'frying noise' was a blessing in that it helped to mask the myriad other ticks and plops due to blisters and unfilled grooves.

Improvements did come along, including a return to the idea of a laminated record by Columbia in 1922. This used a powder core bonded between two discs of kraft paper to produce a smoother, quieter surface. The company issued the new records without any publicity, so as not to prejudice sales of the older records, but the improvement was noted by Compton Mackenzie in the April 1923 issue [p. 21] and soon Columbia's "New Process" records of classical music gave the company a reputation for high quality.

Reproduction

The gramophone was easily the most popular medium for home entertainment in 1923. The rival cylinder had all but disappeared more than a decade earlier when Columbia ceased production in 1912 and Edison followed a year later, though continuing to produce small quantities until about 1929. Radio broadcasting had begun towards the end of 1922 but home reception relied mainly on hobbyist crystal sets, until in 1924 the superheterodyne valve circuit with loudspeakers and a volume control began to appear.

In October 1923, Christopher Stone described a new design of gramophone which used jets of gas in an attempt to improve sound quality

THE FLAMEPHONE

When we invited Scientific and Projections, Ltd., of Crawford Passage, Farringdon Road, London, EC1, to send a Flamephone to this office for our tests of portables we did not know that it was beyond the scope of the tests owing to its price and also because, though it is portable, it requires gas in order to obtain its especial effects, and is therefore hardly in the class of gramophones that can be carried and played *anywhere*. However, the makers very kindly sent us a model of the "semi-portable type" to see, and we are extremely grateful to them for having given us a chance of examining what is certainly a most interesting, and even exciting, invention. In a fine mahogany case it costs £17 10s. and weighs 22lb., and when put together is a distinctly handsome machine. But the fittings which make it specifically a Flamephone can be put on to any ordinary gramophone for £6, and this fact removes the invention at once from the realm of fantastic gadgets. It deserves the serious consideration of all gramophonists.

To quote from the description of it, "the mica diaphragm in the sound box is associated on one side with the horn, the mouth of which is directed upwards, and at the other with a gas chamber leading to two small upright burners, which are perforated with a number of very fine holes, gas being led into the chamber by a small rubber-tube attached to a cock at the back. The gas jets are directed horizontally across the mouth of the horn". There are a hundred jets, and in a darkened room these are very pleasantly reflected in the aluminium shield which protects the woodwork and also acts as a sounding-board. By a simple balancing device the weight of the soundbox and horn on the record can be adjusted to suit individual taste.

Mr Kitchen's invention is founded on the fact that a gas jet is extremely sensitive to sound waves over a very wide range, and it is claimed that though the Flamephone without any gas has a quality of tone "comparable with that of the average gramophone", the effect of turning on and lighting the gas is not only to augment the sound but to improve the quality of tone in a wonderful way. There can be no doubt about this improvement in volume and in tone. By many experiments of turning the office gas on and off as we tried the various records we satisfied ourselves that in some mysterious way the vibrations of the gas jets had a clarifying and strengthening influence on the soundbox.

A REAL REVOLUTION IN GRAMOPHONE CONSTRUCTION AT LAST.
The FLAMEPHONE
Something entirely new in acoustical science. By the application of a pulsating gas flame, the usual reproducing horn is entirely eliminated. The sound waves as they impinge the air are conducted through two columns of gas flame, thereby being reproduced in all their natural volume and tonal purity.
THE MOST REVOLUTIONARY DISCOVERY IN MODERN GRAMOPHONY.
A scientific method of transmission calculated to supersede every known form of gramophone reproduction.
The FLAMEPHONE proves incontestably that the records made by the best makers are perfect media for sound, and that actually it is merely that the gramophone hitherto encountered is not capable of eliciting the best from these records.
THE FLAMEPHONE OPEN.
Hear these same glorious records through the FLAMEPHONE, and learn how ideally perfect gramophone music can be made.
THE GREATEST REVOLUTIONARY PRINCIPLE IN GRAMOPHONE CONSTRUCTION.
Write for Brochure.
Agents Terms with exclusive Territory on application.
THE FLAMEPHONE CLOSED (SHOWING ITS COMPACTIBILITY).
Sole Manufacturers: SCIENTIFIC & PROJECTIONS, LTD.,
5, Crawford Passage, Farringdon Road, London, E.C. 1.
Telephone: HOLBORN 4783.

"If a long length of tube were not required in order to have the Flamephone out in the garden, one would say that it would be at its very best in the open air at night, with the picturesque illumination of the gas-jets"

The clearness of the tone was even more evident when the Flamephone was contrasted with the Orchestraphone in the office, which for the moment appeard to be almost woolly; and if a long length of tube were not required in order to have the Flamephone out in the garden, one would say that it would be at its very best in the open air at night, with the picturesque illumination of the gas-jets. On the whole, however, we felt that for normal purposes indoors it was slightly hard – not by any means harsh – in tone; it was not so comfortable, for instance, as the Kestraphone; but this must be largely a matter of individual taste, and it can at any rate hardly be doubted that the Flamephone principle applied to one's favourite make of gramophone would improve it. It is the principle rather than the semi-portable model submitted to us which won our respectful admiration, and the fact that a demonstration before the Royal Society was, we are told, greeted with unqualified approval, inclines us to recommend our readers to take an opportunity of judging the Flamephone if possible. Evidently this is one of those inventions which cost a good deal to start, but which, if able to establish themselves, may be offered to the public subsequently at a much reduced cost.

The anatomy of a sound-box

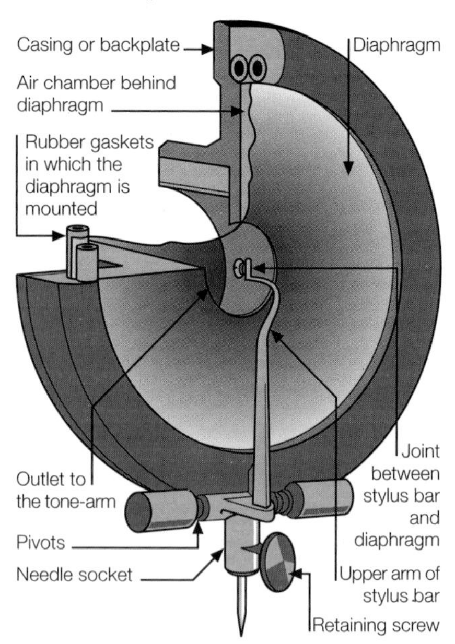

Gramophone designs varied widely, at prices ranging from 30s [£1·50] to £115, and were exhaustively put to the test by the Expert Committee and others. One essential component was the sound-box. This comprised a replaceable needle set into a socket and linked to a diaphragm by a stylus bar. In this way the needle oscillations set the diaphragm into sympathetic vibration. Diaphragms varied from about 30 to 75mm in diameter and were made of many different materials, including mica, wood and glass. The down-pressure was between 110 and 170 grams (4 to 6 ounces) for steel needles and even higher for fibre needles. The resulting air wave passed through a tonearm (a tubular extension on a pivot which transferred most of the weight carrying requirement from the surface of the record to the chassis of the machine to reduce record wear) to the attached expanding horn needed to 'amplify' the sound. Gramophone motors were mainly spring-driven and wound by hand. Double or quadruple spring motors would play two or four 12-inch sides without further winding.

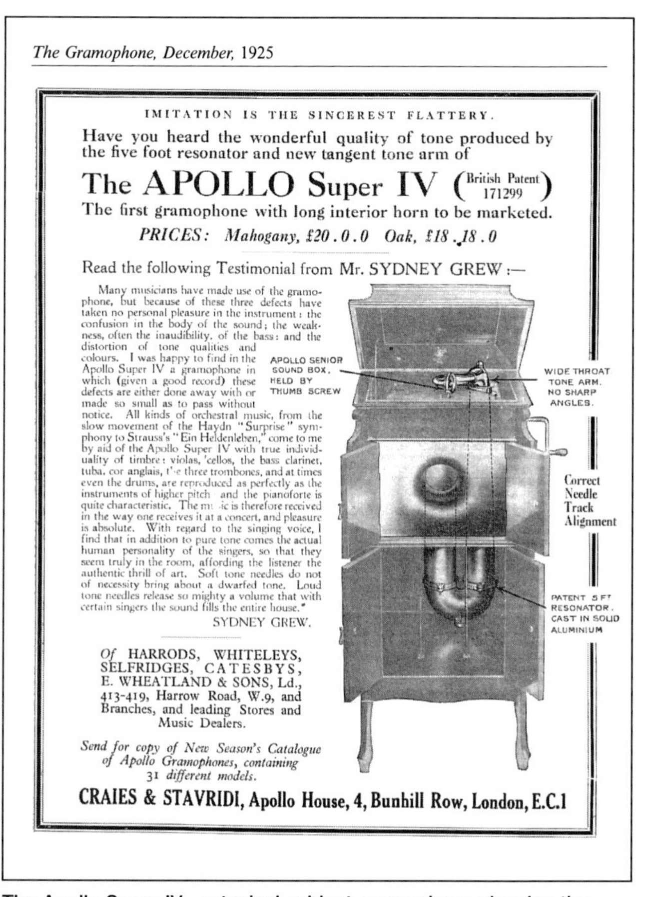

The Apollo Super IV – a typical cabinet gramophone showing the arrangement of its interior horn

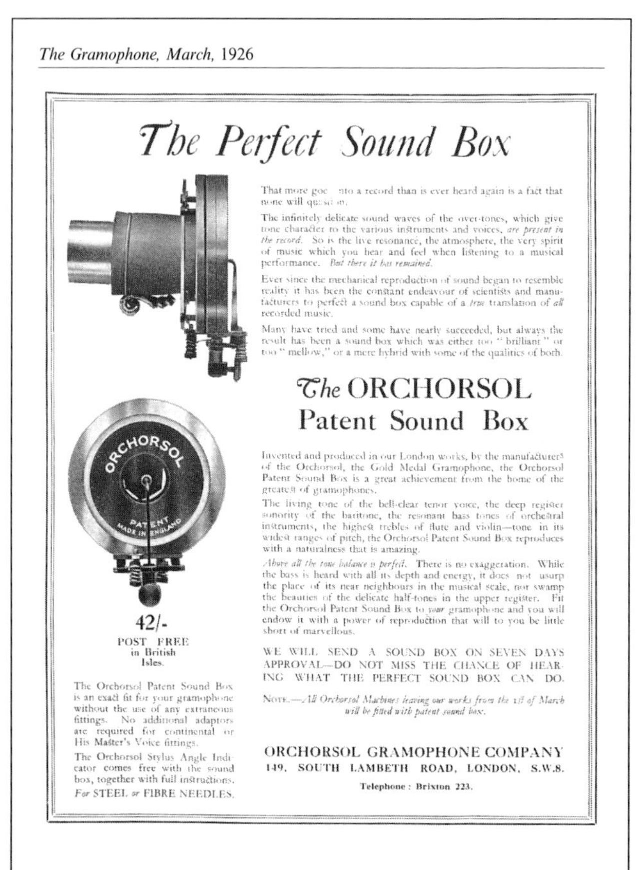

The Orchorsol sound-box – the company were judged victorious at the first Gramophone Congress organized by Compton Mackenzie and held in the Caxton Hall on July 9th, 1925

The need for an external horn was seen as a domestic nuisance, though some designs were very attractive, and cabinet gramophones became popular with concealed horns (sometimes referred to as "amplifiers") folded for convenience but at some loss of efficiency. However, Percy Wilson and other sound enthusiasts strongly advocated the use of well designed external horns, the bigger the better.

The Balmain model, for example, described in the March 1926 issue, consisted of a 60-inch (150cm) long horn carried on wheels and able to track in a straight path across the record and thus avoid the tracking distortion

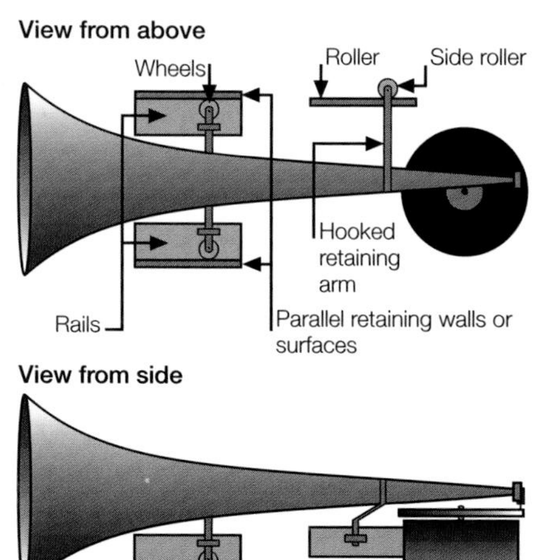

A cross-section of a Balmain straight horn which shows it being carried on wheels and running on rails. A version used by Compton Mackenzie was floated on baths of Mercury

introduced by all pivoted arms (and given detailed analysis by PW in the September and October 1924 issues). Tilting the track for the wheels reduced the force needed from the needle/groove contact to carry the horn and sound-box across the record, and permitted relatively low playing weights of 2 or 3 ounces (60-90 grams). The version of the Balmain horn used by the Editor of ***The Gramophone*** replaced the wheels and rails by floats on mercury.

In 1924 an intriguing device was introduced which eliminated the need for a horn, tonearm or sound-box. This was the Lumière pleated diaphragm but, along with a number of types of acoustic gramophone, it proved unsatisfactory for electrically recorded discs and was soon replaced by electrical pickups, amplifiers and loudspeakers.

Sound-boxes differed very much in quality and were the subject of lengthy debate by the Expert Committee. Needles (styli) could be ordinary steel, chromium plated steel (semi-permanent), diamond or sapphire (permanent), fibre or thorn. Of the last named, fibre needles were relatively soft and soon occupied the whole groove profile to spread the load of a heavy soundbox. They attenuated high frequencies, which reduced surface noise but also softened the musical tone. Thorn needles were harder and could play up to about six sides before being sharpened.

Feodor Chaliapin listening to an HMV Table Grand No. 460 fitted with a Lumière pleated diaphragm. Price £22 10s. Oak; £25 Mahogany
Photo EMI

In April 1925, William Wild (a member of the Expert Committee) gave some hints on the correct treatment of fibre needles

HOW TO USE FIBRES

By Mr "Indicator" Wild

Many use fibres. Alas! Many abuse fibres. "Abuse" them in more senses than the one of wrongly using them. What are some of the chief things to bear in mind? First, in the matter of apparatus. Pardon the platitudes, ye who know, for the sake of the many, oh, how many, who don't know.

1. The tone-arm. Short tone-arms are not suitable for fibre playing – shorter, at any rate, than eight inches over all.
2. Tone-arms must work free: free all the way across the playing portion of record. Goose-neck tone-arms ought to be able to be blown across with a good puff. Continental straight tone-arms' freedom must be guessed at by feeling with box suspended on point of finger.
3. Tracking must be as "Wilsonic" as possible. (See his articles in previous numbers.)
4. Instruments must be level; again use Wilson's method: Turn a single-sided record plain side up on a turntable, and whilst revolving put sound-box with needle down as if playing; should it run inwards or outwards, pack up instrument till it remains steady running in line.
5. Place fibre in first groove when starting, and cleanly lift at finish.
6. Get as near as 60 degrees as possible for playing angle, but point must come as near as possible to centre of turntable spindle.

Now, as to general practice. With difficult records, such as many Caruso's, sextets, bands, etc., first use the fullest length of fibre out of socket; later on you can find what shorter length will safely do. Léner Quartets and similar stuff can be played with quite a stump.

Slightly warm fibres before playing, especially if there is any tendency to dampness in room. A good plan is to have a metal air-tight box with a few fibres carried in waistcoat pocket; warmth without humidity is thereby obtained.

Finally, remember, if in spite of thus nurturing in one's bosom a fibre is still unsatisfactory in tone or performance, it is part of that innate cussedness of the inanimate, with which an individual fibre may be possessed, and gently consign it to that element to which all cussedness belongs – blazes. Fibres, unfortunately, have this individuality, ungovernable by mortals, that have driven many wild (or to Wild) in this matter.

In November 1925 the editor announced the arrival of a new 'gadget' invented by The Revd. L. D. Griffith, Rector of Silvington in Shropshire

THE LIFEBELT

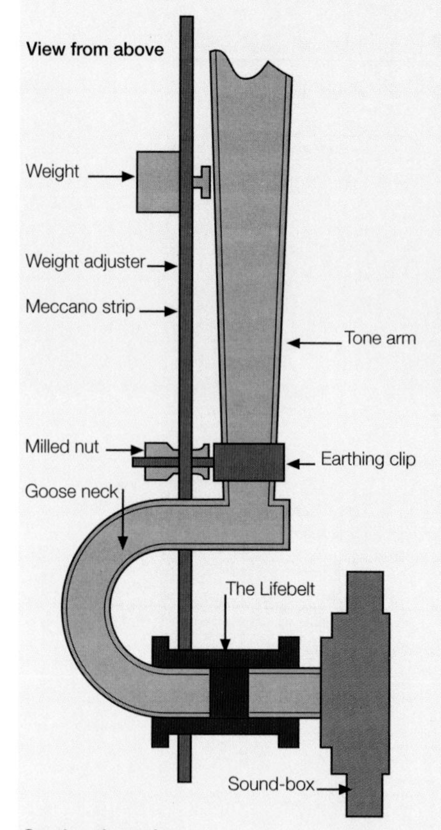

Section through a tone-arm showing a Lifebelt and weight adjuster

Christened "The Lifebelt" by Compton Mackenzie, it was a device intended to improve the tone of records by allowing greater flexibility of the tone-arm. This was achieved by means of a small rubber tube which, to quote the accompanying leaflet sent to all purchasers, "has been designed for insertion between the tone-arm and sound-box of a gramophone so as to give the reproducing stylus a certain quality of flexibility. By this means the reproduction is made less shrill and more resonant without loss of brilliance and without detraction from the quality of notes in the upper part of the musical register. At the same time the wear on records is reduced to a minimum".

After initial disappointing trials of an experimental prototype fashioned from a garden hose and two curtain rings, Mackenzie was ready to ascribe the inventor's enthusiasm to "another case of auto-hypnotism, produced this time by life in a solitary country parish". But when an improved model arrived the Editor reported that "it was a clear case of 'Eureka!'". He sent for Percy Wilson, knowing the Technical Editor would be sceptical. Wilson arrived on Jethou partially sea-sick but ready for testing. Two days of intensive record playing followed, after which Wilson went away "perfectly satisfied" of the Lifebelt's efficacy.

Not any piece of rubber tubing would do, as Mackenzie soon discovered from correspondence with gramophone manufacturers Balmain and Virtz, who had already tried the experiment. Once the Rev. Griffith was able to obtain a patent for his invention, Lifebelts were manufactured and sold exclusively through the pages of the magazine for a cost of five shillings [25p] each. Views from readers were solicited and glowing tributes from satisfied customers were printed in an intensive marketing campaign to promote this "miraculous" gadget.

A further refinement in the form of a weight adjuster was devised by Percy Wilson, this counterbalanced the additional weight on the record caused by the Lifebelt and was intended to reduce wear. This cost 7s. 6d. [37½p] plus 3d. postage.

But the Lifebelt phenomenon was short-lived. Within a few years the advent of electric recording and the introduction of electromagnetic pickups to replace tone-arms and sound-boxes obviated the need for such a device. The days when vicars in solitary country parishes could effect commercially viable improvements in record reproduction were gone. The age of the amateur gramophone inventor was passing.

December 1926 **A reader's contribution**

The Lifebelt in the Backveld by Leonard Flemming

I had read a great deal about the Lifebelt and, after studying very carefully all the opinions and suggestions given in *The Gramophone* by experts and others, I bought one.

At the very outset let me say that it was evident that one could not merely attach the Lifebelt to the gramophone – or the gramophone to the Lifebelt, much depends on whether you are left-handed or right-handed – and obtain perfect results at once. At first I simply pulled the two together. My gramophone had lacked a Lifebelt all its little life – the Lifebelt lacked a gramophone – and very solemnly I performed the sacred rite of joining these two together. I was not quite satisfied with the rendering of the "Fire music" from *Walküre*, and not having a weight adjuster – of which I had read a great deal – and being far away in the backveld where there are no shops or telephones, I attached, with a piece of string and some fencing wire, the carving fork to the tone-arm. There was a decided improvement, at least so I thought, but the string broke and brought the prongs of the fork somewhat heavily on to the record, one prong playing ten grooves ahead and one prong playing ten grooves behind the needle – an astounding performance. I decided that the Lifebelt was too long. So I cut off, with a pair of sheep shears, 1⅞ of an inch of the Lifebelt. Detaching the carving fork I replaced the Lifebelt and tried several records. There was no appreciable difference. Perhaps it was due to the drought and the dryness of the boards upon which my gramophone stands. Procuring four tins,

I half filled them with treacle, upon which I feed my stock in a drought, and after some difficulty placed the legs of my gramophone in them and tried a *Tristan* record. The result was disappointing. I now turned up past numbers of ***The Gramophone*** and gathered a few tips. I sawed off the legs of my gramophone and tried *Siegfried*. It was a complete failure; so also was *Less Than The Dust* and *I Want To Be Happy*.

I now sawed off, with a steel saw, one and three quarter inches of the tone-arm, and with my sheep shears sliced off one-and-a-half inches of the Lifebelt. I boiled the sound-box in glue for four and a half minutes, wrapped stiff brown paper round what was left of the tone-arm up to the goose neck curve, and tried half my records for two days, using 2,000 needles from fibres up to – when the needles were finished – tin tacks with the heads nipped off. The result was not quite what I had wished, but I felt that I was on the right road. I next sawed off the entire tone-arm – the new steel saw was a great joy – and I attached a length of hose-pipe in its place. The result was miraculous. A quartet sounded like a full orchestra, and an ordinary full orchestra like twenty massed bands. I felt, however, that the resonance was too great, so I cut off all the woodwork of the gramophone, took out my wooden floor, pulled down the bricks on one side of the house, bricked up the fireplace, bought a paraffin heating lamp to help me cool down after my trials with records, put what was left of the gramophone on a small table smeared with glycerine, pasted thin strips of red flannel on the mica of the sound-box and, using an axe this time, chopped off what seemed to be a superfluity of Lifebelt.

I built a hut to live in and continued my experiments. Of these I shall write later. From my hut I look at where my house was and where I once had a gramophone and Lifebelt. I shall get perfect results yet, but at present all that I have is half a house, the motor and turntable of the gramophone and an umbrella ring.

Photographs of a Lifebelt and weight adjuster in position on an HMV tone-arm

January 1926 **Correspondence**

The Lifebelt

My machine is a Columbia Grafonola Small Table Grand (No. 19a). The Lifebelt you sent had a brass fitting for attaching to the tone-arm; this I found did not fit tight enough and I tried packing with paper to make it firm, but the result was disappointing. I tried a variety of records with it, but my wife and I could not discern any appreciable improvement, except in a few orchestral records, notably Holst's *Planets* Suite, in which the basses seemed a little clearer; in the majority of cases, however, the results were disappointing, but we were buoyed up by the thought that at any rate the Lifebelt was saving the wear of our records considerably. On the 1st December when the December number of ***The Gramophone*** arrived, we hastily scanned its pages for criticisms of other readers that might help us in discovering any fault we might be making. No result at first, and then I read Mr Wilson's article on page 324, the last paragraph of which fetched me out of my easy chair with a bound, and ably supported by my wife, who backed me up in my resolve to take the risk of damaging the machine, we had the tone-arm off, put it in the workshop vice and with a hacksaw had the end of the tone-arm off, and the Lifebelt on again, tested it for needle-track alignment with Wilson's protractor, and trembling with excitement and fear that the result might be as indifferent as before or even worse, we put on a record. The result was magical and it was with difficulty that we could knock off and go to bed. The next evening we tried standing the machine on 2lb. jam jars, with even better results, and now it only remains for us to adopt Capt. Barnett's lead weight dodge to lighten the weight of the sound-box.

M. V. Le P. Trench, Lt.-Colonel.

Electrical recording

John Borwick

During the early 1920s, the idea began to be put about that a change from acoustic to electrical recording was inevitable and that it should happen sooner rather than later. The desire for change was principally driven by the rapid spread of radio broadcasting but was also inspired by developments in telephony. Thermionic valve amplifiers had extended the frequency range and electrical circuit technology had enhanced the quality of speech (and music) signals whether these were transmitted over landlines or over even longer distances by 'wireless'.

The electrical recording chain

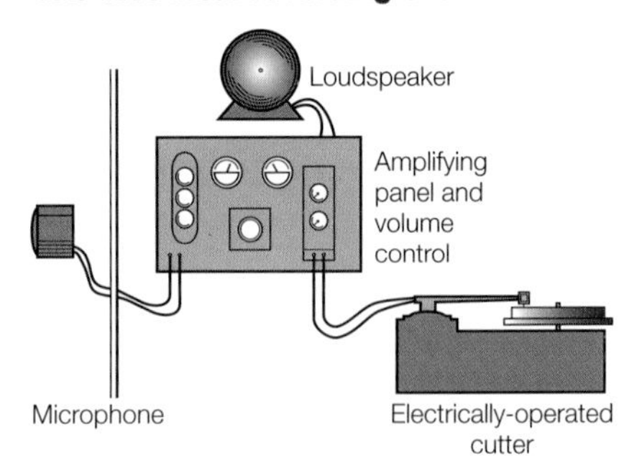

Bell Telephone Laboratories in America, owned by Western Electric, were well placed to apply electrical principles to sound recording. In a paper presented to the American Institute of Electrical Engineers in February 1926 (reprinted in the Journal of the Audio Engineering Society in May 1978) Bell engineers Maxfield and Harrison described their pioneering system for both recording and reproduction. The recording chain comprised a condenser microphone, as already used in broadcasting, connected by wire to the recording room. Here was installed an amplifier, with a volume indicator and an audible monitoring system, feeding the new electromagnetic disc-cutting mechanism. The latter consisted of a balanced armature transducer suspended in the field of a permanent magnet. Coils on the pole system received the amplified signal current and thus set the attached stylus into lateral vibrations, matching the original sound waves in level and frequency content.

Freed from the need to strive for energy transfer efficiency, electrical recording not only gave 'louder' records but a more consistent signal response over a wider frequency range. The system was fine-tuned to resemble a bandpass filter with a flat response between 200 and 6,000Hz. Above and below these limits the response was made to fall off gradually and then cut off sharply at 50 and 6,500Hz. This was a policy decision to secure the best ratio between groove spacing and playing time, as well as filtering off surface noise.

The cutterhead assembly was carried on a beam and driven by a feed screw at constant speed across a radius of the wax disc. The pitch of the groove spiral was set at about 100 turns per inch and the rotational speed was fixed at 78 revolutions per minute. This was the speed used at the time by Victor and some other labels, though it was by no means an industry standard. In practice, the use of an electrical motor synchronized to the 60Hz US mains supply and a 46:1 toothed gear ratio gave a speed of 78·26rpm (76·92rpm in 50Hz countries like the UK). The authors described a system of electrical playback but also showed a design for an improved acoustical player with refinements in both the sound-box and the folded exponential horn.

Independent research had also been carried out in England. Indeed what was possibly the first serious electrical recording anywhere was made by Guest and Merriman on Armistice Day, November 11th 1920 at the funeral service of the burial of The Unknown Warrior in Westminster Abbey. Both The Gramophone Company (HMV) and the Columbia Graphophone Company (English Columbia) developed electrical systems, as well as the Edison-Bell company using a system invented by Paul Voigt (and described by him in correspondence with PW quoted in the November 1965 issue). These British companies had the advantage that they were record-producing organizations and so prototype microphones and recorders could easily be tried out at scheduled acoustic recording sessions. Herbert C. Ridout described these early days in the April and May 1942 issues and how, to preserve secrecy, W. S. Purser (Columbia's chief Engineer in the Clerkenwell Road studios) set up in 1924 "a system of eavesdropping at the regular acoustic recording sessions taking place on the floor above. Inconspicuously, a microphone had been suspended in the recording studio, leading by a wire through the floor to Purser's workshop below".

The desire for secrecy extended to the labelling and promotion of the first electrically recorded 78rpm records reaching the shops. First public reactions to the new electrical recordings, which of course looked exactly like the acoustic ones, were very mixed. Sound quality on the new recordings was uneven, with all the inherent noise problems of shellac discs still much in evidence and new sorts of distortion associated with the relatively crude microphones, amplifiers and cutters. However, musical balance began to improve as the producers had a new freedom to place the artists in a more normal layout, instead of clustered around the ungainly acoustic horn.

The temptation to use the extra signal strength provided by the valve amplifiers to make 'louder' records, and thereby diminish the perception of background noise, increased the amplitude of the recorded waveform. This could make the records more difficult to track and, in the worst cases, cause a breakdown of the wall between the grooves. To put numbers to this, a pitch of 100 turns to the inch means a groove spacing of only 0·01in. Cutting a groove with the usual width of 0·006in (to suit a playback stylus of 0·003in tip radius) leaves a maximum lateral displacement of only plus and minus 0·002in if the running together of adjacent grooves is to be avoided.

An electromagnetic pickup

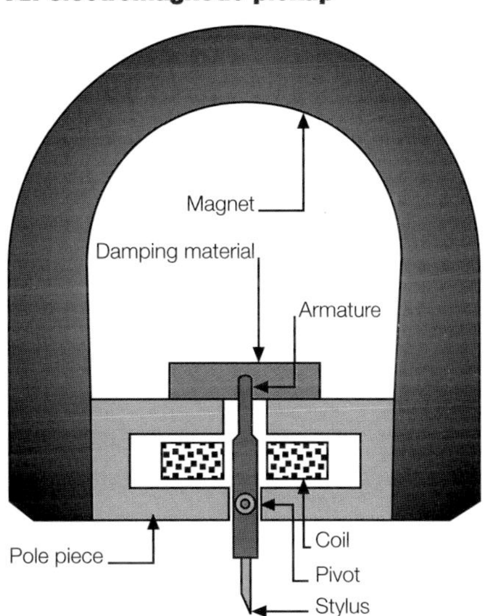

It should be remembered that the new discs had to be played on existing acoustic gramophones. In fact such players continued to be manufactured for many years, partly because of the limited availability of mains electricity (only one UK home in four had an electricity supply as late as 1931). The heavyweight sound-boxes had difficulty with the wider swings in the groove waveform. In addition, electrical recording achieved a greater frequency range up to 5,000Hz and beyond. This reinforced the impression that the new records were 'louder' but highlighted shortcomings in the reproduction of high frequencies on the part of sound-boxes and their associated tonearms and horns.

Electrical reproducers were the natural development and soon went on sale on both sides of the Atlantic. A normal tonearm was generally used, but the old acoustic sound-box was replaced by an electromagnetic pickup having a permanent magnet and fixed coils between which a light iron reed (armature) was suspended with the needle socket at the lower end. Needle vibrations set up changes in the magnetic field to generate an alternating signal in the coils. This was passed to an amplifier and a loudspeaker capable of converting the electrical signals back into sound waves.

The early loudspeakers used armature-driven cones and had a limited frequency response and low power handling capacity. However, in 1925 C. W. Rice and E. W. Kellogg in the USA described a viable 'direct radiator' loudspeaker which consisted of a light, rigid, conical diaphragm driven by a coil located in the radial field of a strong magnet. Energized magnets were used at first but in the early 1930s these began to be replaced by permanent magnets. This paved the way for the marketing of battery-driven radio sets and gramophones, the latter retaining spring-driven motors. Mains-driven radios still used energized magnet speakers right up to the Second World War as they could do double duty as smoothing chokes. The moving-coil is still the principal mechanism for loudspeakers to this day.

In the USA, Brunswick launched the Panatrope as their first "all-electric" phonograph in 1926 and, by offering this with or without a built-in radio, set the scene for separate record players, which could in fact be plugged into one's radio. Victor entered the market with their Electrola and Radiola models. In Britain, Columbia and HMV both introduced electrical players with a bifurcated horn inside table-top or floor-standing cabinets.

A bifurcated or "Stereoscopic" horn from a Viva-tonal Columbia Grafonola (1929)

The Expert Committee reported their tests on the Panatrope (£120) in the December 1926 issue. They described the "tremendous resonance in the bass" as "an

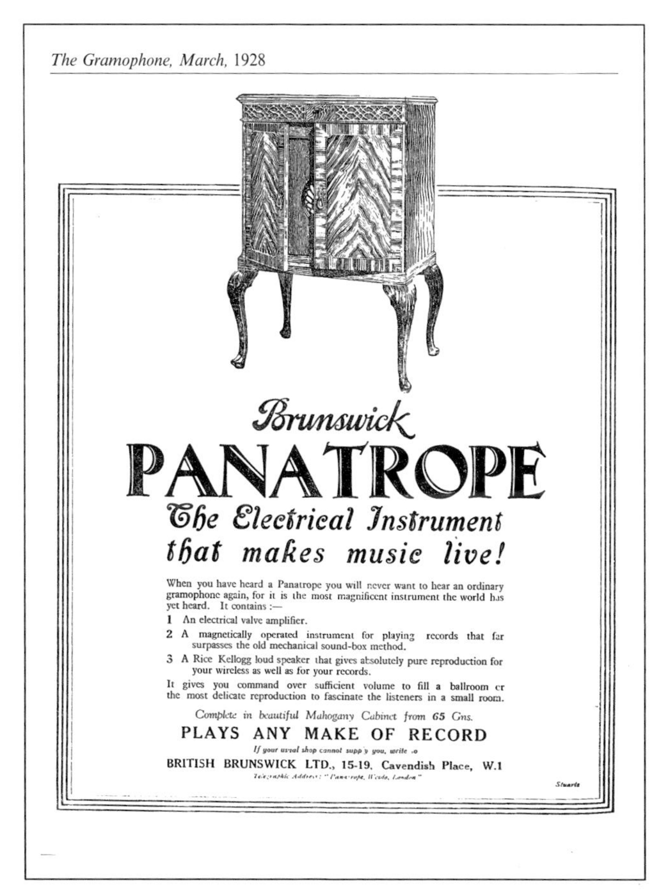

The Panatrope, launched in 1926, was the first all-electric gramophone and was fitted with a Rice/Kellogg loudspeaker

Following a detailed design for the Expert Committee's "Gramo-Electric Amplifier No. 1" published in the December 1927 issue, Compton Mackenzie responded the following month with an amused incomprehension concerning electrical reproduction that must have been shared by many of his readers

GRAMO-ELECTRIC AMPLIFIER NO. 1

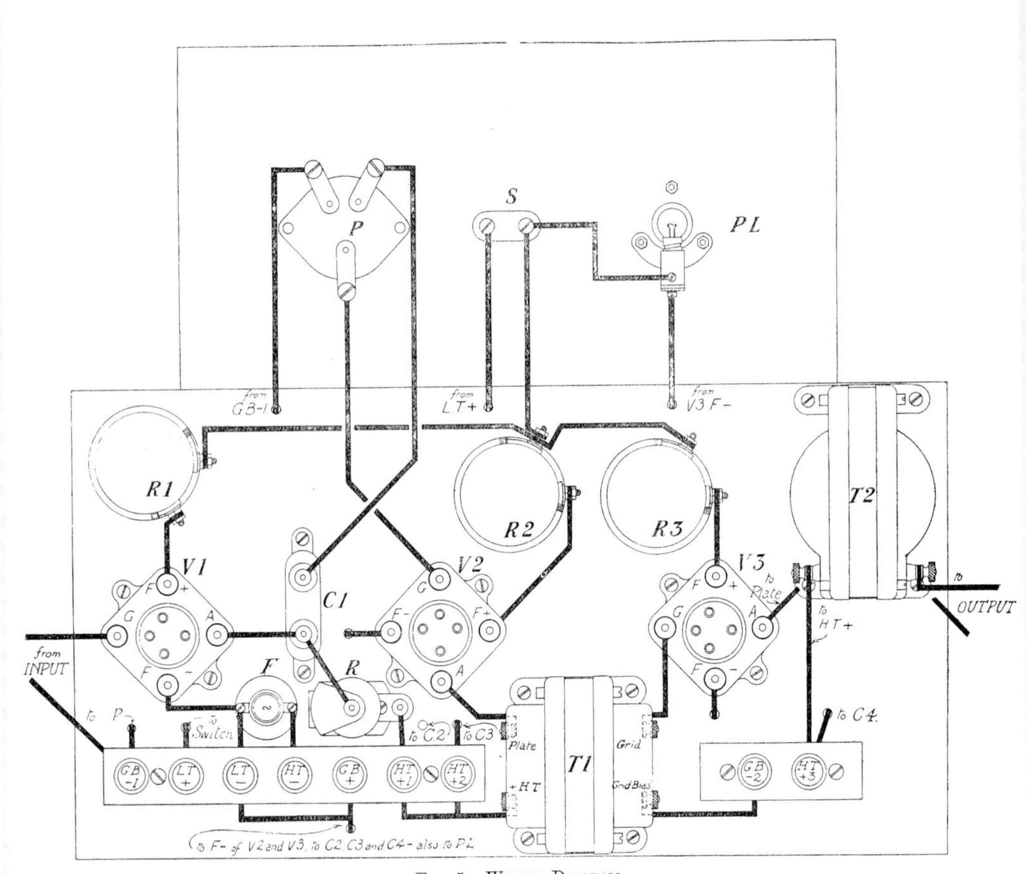

FIG. 5. WIRING DIAGRAM.

V_1, V_2 and V_3 Benjamin valve holders; R_1, R_2 and R_3 Igranic Pre-set Resistors, 10 ohms; R, R.I.-Varley Anode Resistance, 100,000 ohms; P, Igranic High Resistance Potentiometer, 1 megohm; C_1, Dubilier 0·1 mfd. Mica condenser; C_2, C_3 and C_4. T.C.C. or Dubilier Mansbridge Condenser under baseboard; F, Bulgin ·05 amp. 6 volt fuse bulb and holder; P.L., Bulgin Panel Light, ·05 amp. 6 volt and holder; T_1, Ferranti A.F.5 Intervalve Transformer; T_2, Ferranti O.P.1 Output Transformer; S, Igranic Push-pull switch.

My own feeling at the moment, after seeing the picture on page 307 of the Christmas number, is one of pious hope that when I see something like that looking at me in my library I shall be able to work without a gas mask. I can't help feeling a little nervous about that Igranic High Resistance Potentiometer, which looks uncommonly like the fifteen-inch guns of a battleship. The Bulgin Panel Light seems a nasty customer, and the Varley Anode has as sinister an expression as I have ever seen. Then there are some things called Dubiliers, which sound rather like Dublin Fusiliers of the Robot type, and when I read further that the resistance required for two ohms is 6 – 5·5/0·25 I am not surprised that the Varley Anode, which is prepared to resist 100,000 of them, looks so pugnacious. There is also a picture of a fuse bulb and holder, but I see no sign of the holder except a note of interrogation in the middle of the bulb. I expect that is what I shall turn into before this year is out. I now begin to appreciate all the implications of the phrase, "a martyr to science".

entirely new sensation so far as the reproduction of gramophone records is concerned". However, they found that the maximum setting of the five-step volume control gave higher sound levels than an actual performance, which distorted recordings of solo instruments and voices. Using a lower volume setting still gave coarser timbre than an acoustic gramophone. They concluded, "yes, the Panatrope is a very marvellous instrument. If we were asked to sum up its qualities in a phrase, we should say that it is to gramophone reproduction what electrical recording is to the making of a record. Which means that wonderful as it is in fact, it is even greater in its possibilities".

Exactly a year later, in the December 1927 issue, the Committee made similar observations on the performance of The Gramophone Company's first electrical reproducer which cost £200. There was full bass from its folded orthophonic horn (equivalent to a 9-foot straight horn) but also a more accurate rendition of the individual character of instruments and voices, though with a tendency to round off the edges. A 20-record changer system was included.

In that same December 1927 issue the Expert Committee published its design and detailed do-it-yourself instructions for the Gramo-Electric Amplifier No. 1. This was a battery-operated, three-valve design. The power output was only in the milliwatt range but, with a reasonably sensitive balanced-armature loudspeaker, it gave about the same sound levels as an acoustic gramophone. A later article in January 1928 described how to add a volume control between the pickup and the amplifier, since available pickups varied considerably in sensitivity, and a home constructor radio tuner unit was also described in the following month.

A formidable rearguard action was mounted by perfectionists like Percy Wilson and G. W. Webb; E. M. Ginn, with his famous EMG "Expert" hand-made gramophones, continued to demonstrate the superiority of external horns for realistic bass reproduction, when driven by a carefully set up acoustic sound-box. In January 1929, the Editor was still undecided on the subject, writing, "I do not intend to rush in at present with my ideas about electrical reproduction, because I require time in which to put these ideas in order and arrive at what I think about it". Indeed as late as May 1930, the Expert Committee were reviewing the EMG Mark X acoustic model (£30) with a curved 26-inch diameter exponential horn and a range of sound-boxes to suit the user's choice of needle. They felt that the sound projection was a little backward with fibre needles but "remarkably fine" when a Chromogram steel needle and appropriate sound-box were substituted. A review of the later Mark XA model followed in April 1932.

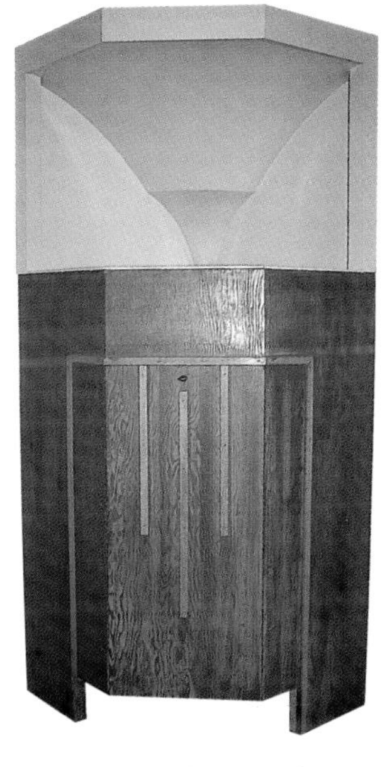
Voigt's late 1930s corner horn loudspeaker

However, when the best design techniques were eventually applied to electrical reproducers, for example by Paul Voigt in his Tractrix corner horn, electrical recordings, which had by then completely replaced the acoustic recording method, could be heard properly and the days of acoustic gramophones were really over.

During the next couple of decades, until shortly after the Second World War, electrically recorded discs and electrical reproducers enjoyed universal acceptance. Over 100 million records and nearly one million players were sold in the US alone during 1927. Though the 1929 stock market crash led to several very lean years, by 1946 about 400 million records were sold in the US. Refinements were introduced at every stage in the recording/reproduction chain. New high-quality microphones were linked to almost noise-free mixing desks. Improved loudspeaker designs provided a smooth response over the whole audible range, or at least up to 10,000Hz, which both helped recording engineers to monitor and adjust the signals sent to the disc-cutting lathe and encouraged sound enthusiasts to build ever more impressive home systems – the term 'high fidelity' coming into use as early as 1934.

The EMG Mark X Model

An important benefit of electrical recording and reproduction was the ability to impose a particular frequency response curve on the music signals on their way to the cutter-head and to 'equalize' this in the record player by introducing an EQ network giving a mirror-image response. Maxfield and Harrison had already noted the need to avoid large stylus swings by reducing the recording level progressively from about 200Hz downwards and then restore the original level on replay.

At the other end of the spectrum it became common practice to add treble emphasis on recording and to attenuate it on replay, along with much of the shellac surface noise which was predominantly high-frequency. Unfortunately the record companies chose a variety of EQ curves and so variable replay EQ networks were needed if records from all labels were to be played with something close to their original sound balance. In the mid-1940s, gramophone records improved

This brochure from January 1949 shows a typical post-war gramophone: the HMV Celebrity Reproducer Model 2000. Originally designed to play 78s and fitted with an auto-changer, it was adapted in the autumn of 1952, when EMI launched LPs in the UK, for three speeds 78, 33⅓ and 45rpm

The Columbia Playing Desk Model 228, launched at Radiolympia in 1939, was designed to be played through a mains radio. It was competitively-priced in an attempt to stimulate record sales

USE YOUR WIRELESS SET TO PLAY YOUR RECORDS
Its Popularity has Sent Record Sales Soaring!
THE best proof that this little Record-Player satisfies record-lovers is that RECORD SALES HAVE INCREASED wherever it has been sold. That means that the instrument has brought records in a new light to thousands—and that is what it will do for you.
For those who like something better, there are two other models—Standard, £3 19s. 6d. ; or Automatic Record-Changer Model, £9 9s. Both fitted with lids.
The model illustrated is No. 228 (A.C. only) at 39s. 6d.—a complete Electric Player with constant-speed motor, so no winding. Lead and plugs connect with pick-up sockets of any A.C. radio set and records are heard through the radio-set loudspeaker. Walnut-finish cabinet, fitted with needle container and hand and automatic brakes.

YOUR DEALER WILL GLADLY GIVE YOU A DEMONSTRATION

to such an extent that designers of record players were hard put to it to keep up. Both The Gramophone Company with its "Extended Range Recordings" and The Decca Record Company with its *ffrr* (Full Frequency Range Recording), announced on June 8th, 1945, claimed a response from 30Hz up to 14,000Hz. To match this, Decca launched their handsome Decola record reproducer at 165 guineas [£173] plus £43 6s. 3d. purchase tax (reviewed in September 1946). This housed a Garrard RC60 record changer capable of playing batches of up to eight 10- or 12-inch records mixed in any order, a new Decca miniature pickup fitted with a replaceable sapphire stylus, a 6 watts 8-valve amplifier with bass boost and treble cut in three steps, and three identical 12-inch loudspeakers fed in parallel, set at an angle to each other behind louvred panels (later there was an optional radio tuner). EMI similarly brought out the HMV "Electrogram de Luxe", first demonstrated at Abbey Road in August 1946 and then marketed and reviewed in June 1948 (£278 5s. 0d. plus £120 11s. 6d. purchase tax). An important change was heralded in 1930 when Union Carbide introduced a vinyl resin which was later seen to be well suited to record manufacture. It was compatible with existing shellac presses and, though relatively expensive, began to be used during the war for special issues such as the unbreakable "V Disc" for the American armed forces. These much quieter vinyl 78rpm discs showed up limitations in the temperature-sensitive wax masters and led to the introduction of lacquer coated aluminium discs, often referred to as 'acetates', by organzations such as the BBC, though EMI and Decca still used wax masters up to 1949. The lacquer discs had a quieter surface and for the first time allowed immediate playback to enable the producer and artists to check 'takes' for musical and balance accuracy.

The Decola – launched in September 1946 and designed to take full advantage of the reproduction possibilities of Decca's *ffrr* recording

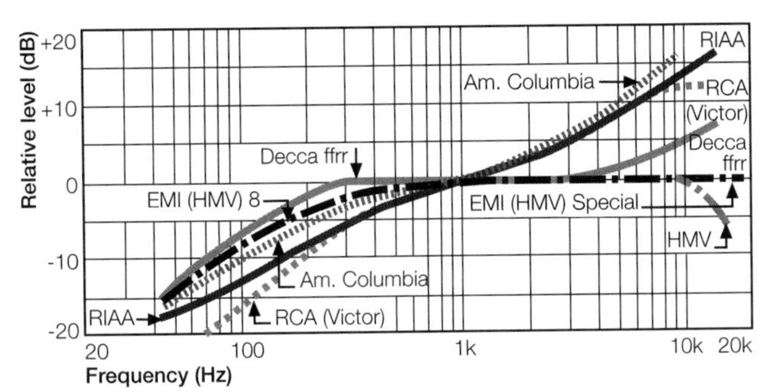

Examples of 78rpm recording characteristics

EMG continued to produce hand-made acoustic gramophones and their necessary accessories until the end of the 1930s

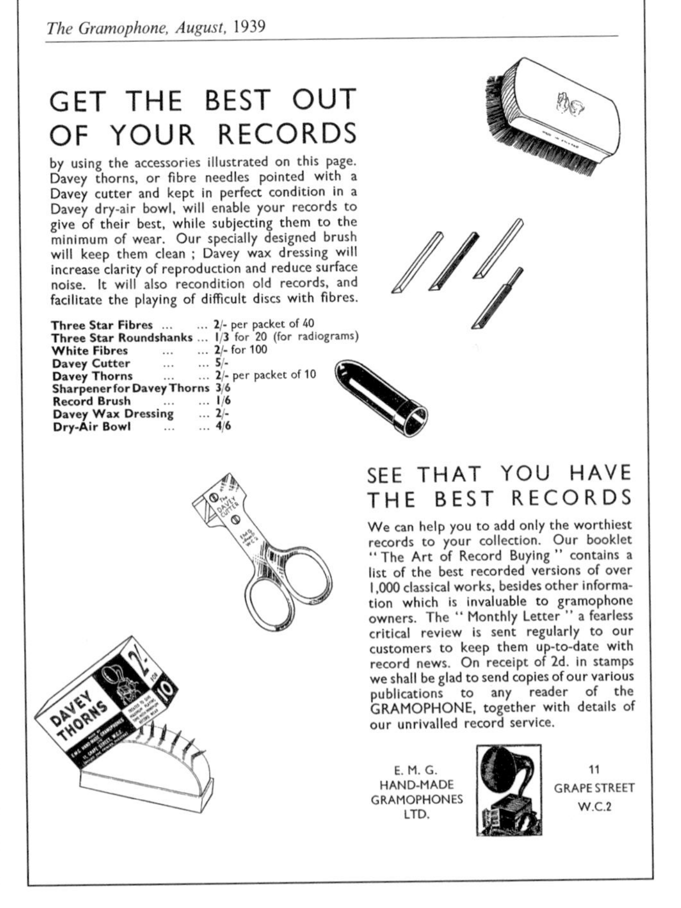

The Gramophone, August, 1939
GET THE BEST OUT OF YOUR RECORDS
by using the accessories illustrated on this page. Davey thorns, or fibre needles pointed with a Davey cutter and kept in perfect condition in a Davey dry-air bowl, will enable your records to give of their best, while subjecting them to the minimum of wear. Our specially designed brush will keep them clean ; Davey wax dressing will increase clarity of reproduction and reduce surface noise. It will also recondition old records, and facilitate the playing of difficult discs with fibres.
Three Star Fibres ... ... 2/- per packet of 40
Three Star Roundshanks ... 1/3 for 20 (for radiograms)
White Fibres ... ... 2/- for 100
Davey Cutter 5/-
Davey Thorns ... ... 2/- per packet of 10
Sharpener for Davey Thorns 3/6
Record Brush 1/6
Davey Wax Dressing ... 2/-
Dry-Air Bowl 4/6
SEE THAT YOU HAVE THE BEST RECORDS
We can help you to add only the worthiest records to your collection. Our booklet "The Art of Record Buying" contains a list of the best recorded versions of over 1,000 classical works, besides other information which is invaluable to gramophone owners. The "Monthly Letter" a fearless critical review is sent regularly to our customers to keep them up-to-date with record news. On receipt of 2d. in stamps we shall be glad to send copies of our various publications to any reader of the GRAMOPHONE, together with details of our unrivalled record service.
E. M. G. HAND-MADE GRAMOPHONES LTD.
11 GRAPE STREET W.C.2
DAVEY THORNS

The Long-Playing record

John Borwick

As early as the December 1926 issue of *The Gramophone*, Percy Wilson was writing about the need for a long-playing record capable of accommodating on one side much longer musical works than the four minutes or so provided by 78rpm shellac records. These short timings could be tolerated on vocal records or solo instrumental pieces but, since electrical recording had so improved the ability to record orchestral repertoire, changing sides every few minutes had become, in PW's words, a "harrowing interruption".

The dimensions of 78rpm and LP grooves and styli

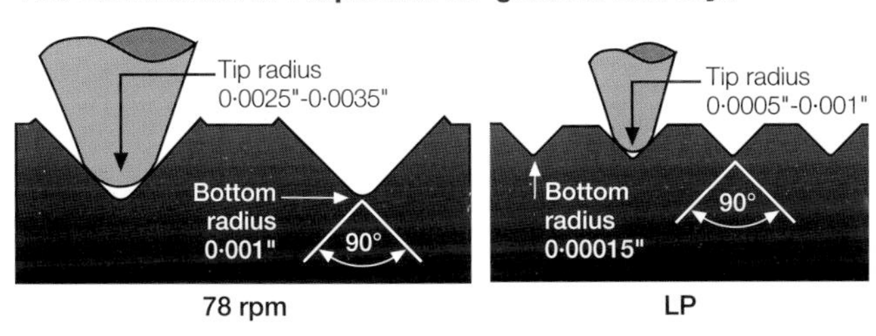

He postulated two ways that playing times could be lengthened: either by reducing the speed of the groove under the needle, or increasing the total length of the groove by inscribing more grooves per inch. Apart from visualizing "a flexible ribbon unwinding from a reel across a rotating drum" (in an inspired premonition of magnetic tape recording) PW concluded that current record materials were too granular for groove dimensions to be reduced without an intolerable increase in surface noise, and that acoustic gramophones needed the existing speed and groove amplitudes to produce loud enough sound levels.

The early years did see various short-lived attempts at solving this dilemma. In 1905 Neophone issued the first 20-inch 'long-playing' discs, which should not be confused with the little-known 20-inch 'loud-playing' records, with a larger groove and increased amplitude, introduced for public performance to large audiences on special machines. Edison recorded 450 grooves to the inch on his 40-minute discs in 1926 and Victor used a new Vitrolac material in 1931 to produce records running at 33⅓ rpm with a playing time of up to eight minutes. *The Gramophone* was sceptical of the Victor discs, commenting in the December 1931 issue, "it is rather premature now to wave flags about a long-playing disc which has to be made of a new and harder material and to be played with a special needle on an electrical reproducer with a new gear-clutch arrangement for its motor to enable the turntable to revolve at 33⅓ rpm or at 78rpm for the new or old records respectively".

The Columbia LP launch

The well-staged American launch of LP records, which had been developed by Dr Peter Goldmark of Columbia Broadcasting Systems (CBS) in collaboration with William Bachman of Columbia Records Inc., on June 21st, 1948 [p. 83] gave the world much improved sound quality and greater user convenience. Inevitably new types of record player had to be purchased, and indeed Columbia marketed an inexpensive 33⅓ rpm model to induce buyers to convert to the new speed. In the coming years, however, the LP provided an incentive for designers to produce record players and systems of true high fidelity standards to match the cleaner and more dynamic sounds on the new discs.

The 'long play' description referred to the almost six-fold increase in playing time per side to about 22 minutes. This was achieved partly by reducing the width of the groove, allowing the spiral to be packed at about 240

Dr Peter Goldmark (left), director of research at Columbia Broadcasting Systems (CBS), developed the microgroove system and in collaboration with William Bachman (right), director of research for the Columbia Recording Corp (later Columbia Records Inc) made it a reality *Photo CBS/Sony*

November 1926 **News**

LONG-PLAYING RECORDS

Dr Francis Mead of San Diego, California sends press cuttings about the new Edison records which have been demonstrated in America. They are 12-inch records, have 450 grooves to the inch, and are played with a diamond needle two thousandths of an inch in diameter. This implies about 20 minutes of music on each side of the record; but the newspaper reports are full of discrepancies. One of them claims 40 minutes for each side and quotes young Mr Edison as saying: "You see, an ordinary record would have to be four and a half feet in diameter to contain as much music as there is on this 12-inch one here."

grooves per inch instead of about 100. Clearly this move towards 'fine groove' or 'microgroove' records demanded new stylus dimensions, with a tip radius of about 0·001in instead of the old 0·003in, as well as new designs of pick-up cartridge and tonearm.

The rest of the playing time increase came from the slower turntable speed of 33⅓ rpm. This was seen by a few diehards as a retrograde step, since a slower running speed in any recording medium has the effect of compressing the recorded waveform and making it difficult to 'scan' the upper frequencies. However, as soon as properly specified players came on to the market, the LP record was demonstrably a considerable advance on the shellac 78 in terms of both frequency coverage and dynamic range. For the first time, playback equipment permitting, the full audible bandwidth of 20-20,000Hz could be reproduced and something approaching the scale of variation between quiet and loud passages, experienced at a live concert, could be heard.

A turnover cartridge suitable for playing both 78s and LPs

Perhaps the most spectacular improvement was the huge reduction in surface noise. Instead of coarse particle-filled shellac, essential for 78s if they were to withstand the tracking force of about 5 ounces (140g) imposed by the acoustic sound-boxes and heavy electrical pickups, the new records were made of a soft vinylite plastics material. This gave extremely low background noise levels and allowed the quietest passages in the music to be heard and appreciated as never before.

As a bonus, the new vinyl records were almost unbreakable but the soft surface was easily scratched, producing annoying clicks and plops, and of course required new lightweight pickups tracking at only a few grams. As well as scratches, vinyl records were soon found to be prone to attract dust and other deposits from the atmosphere or users' fingers. The problem was aggravated by vinyl's tendency to build up a static electrical charge which strongly attracted and held on to dust particles. Again, unwanted noise was the result and record cleaning plus antistatic treatment became part of the ritual of playing LPs for serious gramophiles. Cecil E. Watts researched this problem and produced the "Dustbug" tracking record cleaner and other products for combating surface noise.

The reduced groove dimensions made it imperative that the stylus was not only contoured very precisely but also made of the hardest material available so that it would keep its shape over many playings. Sapphire styli were used at first but, though more expensive, diamond styli eventually became the norm for all high-quality pickup cartridges.

To provide suitable styli for both the coarse-groove 78s and the new microgroove discs, various turnover stylus assemblies appeared, usually of the crystal or ceramic type, with a 0·003in stylus on one side and 0·001in on the other. Alternatively push-on styli could be used having one or other tip radius.

It took a year or two for the record companies to make the changeover to LP. Decca began supplying LPs in the UK in 1950 but EMI did not follow with LPs and 45s until 1952 [p. 86]. Equipment manufacturers had also to persuade consumers to buy the new products. To begin with there was the business of designing new three-speed turntables which could play at both 78 and 33⅓ rpm, plus the

The "Dustbug", a simple device designed to prevent the build-up of dust on the LP which caused surface noise

compromise 45rpm speed introduced in February 1949 for 7-inch vinyl 'singles' by Columbia's arch rival RCA Victor. The Garrard 301 transcription turntable, first shown at the BSRA Exhibition in May 1954, set new standards of performance. In 1956 there was a brief interest in adding a fourth speed, 16⅔ rpm, for which a small number of extra-long play discs were issued in America and Germany of the 'talking book' variety, where a frequency range of 200Hz-3kHz (i.e. the telephone range) was considered adequate (but deprecated by PW in the September 1956 issue). A few music discs on the American Vox label circulated in the UK in the late 1950s and the short-lived Top Rank label issued a single 16⅔ rpm disc of the tales of Edgar Allen Poe in January 1960, which played for 95 minutes, after which no more was heard of 16⅔ rpm. Record players became simpler still when in the early 1960s 78rpm was regarded as obsolete: 10- and 12-inch LPs covered most repertoire, whilst 7-inch 45rpm singles playing for up to four minutes per side (or 7½ minutes on the Extended Play version) gave added flexibility, particularly for the popular market and the juke-box industry for which they proved ideal.

As pickups, amplifiers and loudspeakers extended their response to lower frequencies, it became necessary to redesign certain features of turntables. Motor noise and AC mains hum became more noticeable and new types of suspension were needed as well as better magnetic screening. Low-frequency rumble and short-term speed fluctuations, referred to as 'wow and flutter', demanded accurate and smooth running bearings. The flywheel effect of the record platter, enabling it to iron out speed variations, was enhanced by making it much heavier and concentrating most of its weight at the perimeter.

The record factories had to pay even more attention to exact positioning of the centre hole at the epicentre of the groove, to avoid 'swingers' as off-centre discs were called. These introduced cyclic pitch changes and could even cause mistracking. Warped records were another source of annoyance as the new vinyl material could tend to 'flow' in storage, particularly at higher temperatures. The problem was increased if pressing plants tried to economize in vinyl by making thinner records.

Distortion and tracking error

The relatively noise-free and wide-ranging sounds obtainable from microgroove records drew attention to several forms of distortion inherent in the disc medium and designers made concentrated efforts to reduce the effects of these to a minimum. Pickup arms, for example, were refined to allow very precise setting of the tracking force which, as cartridges improved, fell to only one to three grams.

Any pivoted arm must inevitably introduce tracking error. This can cause quite severe distortion and arises from the misalignment of the stylus lateral axis as it tracks across the record. During recording the cutterhead is tracked in a straight line along a radius of the disc, with the stylus vibrations always at right angles to the groove. During playback the pickup on a pivoted tonearm traverses the disc in an arc and so is skewed at different angles with respect to the recorded waveform. The error can be minimized by procedures which were first analyzed by Percy Wilson as early as 1924 [p. 246]: arm length is increased to make the stylus overhang the centre spindle by a small amount, typically 0·7in (18mm); the headshell is offset by an angle of about 24 degrees. This reduces the tracking error overall and actually makes it fall to zero at two calibration points, normally set at 2·6 and 4·75 inches from the centre of the record. In a few later designs of linear pickup arm, tracking error was eliminated completely by mounting a relatively short arm on a carriageway which tracked along a radius. There were also some articulated systems which swivelled the headshell to maintain stylus/groove alignment.

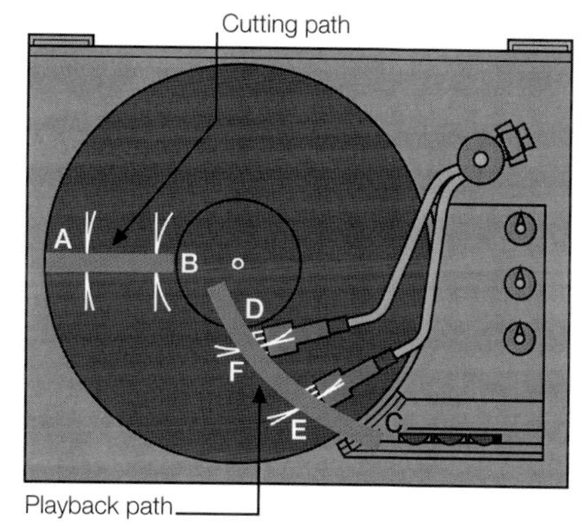

During recording the cutterhead is tracked in a straight line across the radius of the disc (A-B), but during playback the pivoted tonearm causes the stylus to move in an arc, thereby giving rise to tracking error. Points F and E indicate the two calibration points where tracking error falls to zero

Tracing distortion occurs because of the different shapes of the cutting and playback styli. The tip of the cutting stylus is necessarily wedge-shaped to produce a V-shaped groove and sloped at the back to allow free escape of the thread of cut-away material (called 'swarf' or 'chip'). By contrast, the tips of playback styli were conical (though oval 'biradials' came along later) with a radius designed to rest about halfway up the groove walls. However, when the recorded wavelength falls below the tip radius, the stylus can no longer follow the centre line of the groove and traces instead an inaccurate waveform. This leads to distortion and a loss of high frequencies which becomes more serious at high signal levels.

End-of-side distortion is also inherent in any disc medium where the rotational speed is fixed. The recorded

An early attempt to produce long-playing records was the World Record system. The discs were designed to be played on gramophones fitted with a special controller (a rubber friction wheel) which governed the rotation of the disc, ensuring constant linear speed throughout and thus increasing playing time. In July 1941 WRA recalled his experience of the system

WORLD RECORD

Mr Ridout's reference to the Pemberton Billing World Record [March 1941] made me bring out from its deep drawer the old controlling apparatus, which never would work with sufficient accuracy, but seemed to my unmechanical mind a little marvel. I have a few of the records: a whole quartet to a disc (thus in those days they made them). The surface was pretty noisy, but we were used to that. To put on such a record without the controller is to find a madhouse of shrill indecipherable sounds gradually sifting down, as the end approaches, into normal pace and pitch: the music was not recorded evenly all through, a great deal more being got upon the early grooves than the later ones. The controller so varied the speed as to produce the normal effect. I remember about twenty years ago going down to Twickenham to hear these marvels, and having an unbreakable disc put into my hand, whence it was suddenly tipped upon the floor by the demonstrator. It bounced cheerfully; how I wish many another ordinary disc that has come to grief had behaved so well.

iv

WORLD RECORDS
PLAY CONTINUOUSLY

Up to 15 minutes' uninterrupted music without repetition or attention. Naturally they afford a real entertainment and make listening to a gramophone a great pleasure. They are the same size and price as other records, yet contain 3 to 5 times more recorded music. World records are played by fixing a simple attachment to your present instrument. The attachment can be removed in a second to enable ordinary 3-minute records to be played.

FITTED OR DETACHED IN A SECOND

EVOLVED BY BRITISH BRAINS

Ask your Record Dealer to demonstrate them to you, failing which, write for Catalogue to

WORLD RECORD, Limited
Mortlake, London, S.W.

waveform at all frequencies becomes progressively more cramped as the pickup tracks towards the end of the record, leading to quite severe attenuation of treble frequencies. This can be avoided either by speeding up the motor from beginning to end (both for recording and playback), an idea which is in fact adopted in reverse for Compact Discs (which start at the inner radius) or by gradually introducing treble boost. Each of these solutions was tried but did not catch on. For example, H. Pemberton Billing promoted a linear recording speed idea back in 1922, which was briefly used by World Record. The running speed began at about 33⅓ rpm and then speeded up. A complicated and troublesome controller device was needed on replay and by 1924 the idea was dropped.

The duller sound at the inner grooves was very noticeable on 78s when musical works spread over more than one record side were played continuously (particularly when record-changers reduced the time gap).

Interestingly, American Columbia Records took account of this problem in the late 1940s. Prior to their planned launch of the LP record, they began recording in parallel with their 78rpm masters a 16-inch lacquer disc running at 33⅓ rpm, a format already used in the film and broadcasting industries. They used only the outer area of the disc to ensure that the difference in linear speed, and therefore the change in sound quality, would be small.

Standards

One sensible industry move which followed the launch of LP records was the standardization of virtually all parameters: physical dimensions, running speeds, groove contour and maximum signal level. Non-standardization had undoubtedly hindered progress during the 78rpm era, most particularly in regard to the equalization curves used to roll-off the bass and boost treble. This latter aspect of non-standardization continued with LPs but in the mid-1950s international agreement on a single characteristic was reached and published in the UK as

RIAA pickup equalization curves

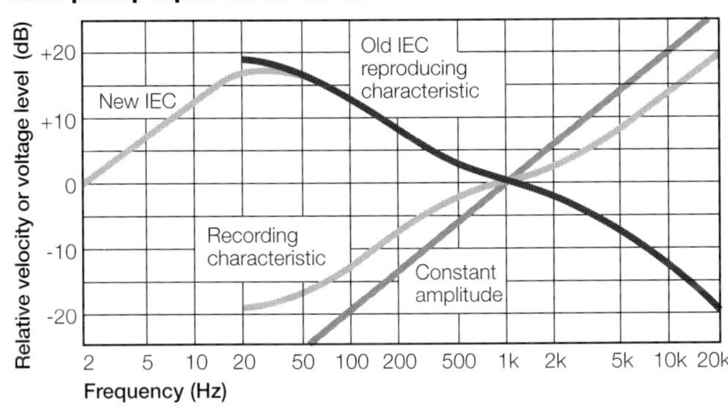

British Standard 1928 of 1955, now better known as the RIAA (and later IEC) characteristic, along with its reciprocal 'mirror image' curve for playback.

Hi-Fi progress

The decade 1948-58, which might be called the start of the hi-fi era when the public became sound conscious, witnessed considerable advances in the quality and variety of home equipment. Regular reviews in *The Gramophone* kept readers informed of the latest systems and separate units of special interest. At one end of the scale, for example, the Pye Black Box (reviewed in May 1954) was an elegant example of an all-in-one table-top record player. The basic model housed a BSR Monarch auto-changer, a two-stage amplifier with tone and volume controls and twin six-inch Rola speakers mounted one at each side. The price was 39 guineas [£41] but there was also a luxury model with a black enamel cabinet decorated with Chinese style paintings at 63 guineas [£66]. Versions with a non-changer turntable cost two guineas [£2·10] less.

Some of the individual units reviewed were indeed landmarks in the history of hi-fi. The original Quad Electrostatic loudspeaker was reviewed by PW in May 1958. He praised its transparent reproduction of orchestra and solo instruments but noted sibilance on voices, which he took to be a fault of the source rather than the loudspeaker, and a certain sensitivity to room placement.

Special events also demonstrated the march of high fidelity. On November 1st, 1954, for example, Gilbert Briggs of Wharfedale put on an extremely successful lecture/demonstration in the Royal Festival Hall in which he courageously included direct live versus prerecorded comparisons of organ solos, harpsichord and piano. Whilst the capacity audience could distinguish live from recorded examples with reasonable ease, there was high praise for the lifelike reproduction from Peter Walker's Quad II control unit feeding four standard Quad II amplifiers in parallel and three Wharfedale three-way speakers in corner cabinets. The recordings were played either on a Garrard turntable with Ferranti ribbon pickup or, in the case of the special recordings used in the comparisons, an EMI tape machine running at 30ips (76cm/s). A second Festival Hall demonstration was given in May 1955 and, as well as four other presentations in UK venues, Mr Briggs even took his show to Carnegie Hall in New York on October 3rd, 1956.

The Pye Black Box, a competitively-priced all-in-one table-top record player

The first London Audio Fair was staged in 1956, as a reshaping of the annual exhibitions organized by the BSRA (British Sound Recording Association), a group of amateur and professional sound enthusiasts founded as long ago as 1936. Intriguing exhibits included a prototype of the Quad Electrostatic full-range speaker mentioned above, as well as an electrostatic tweeter coupled with a 15-inch moving-coil woofer by Harold Leak, the HMV "Stereosonic" tape system [p. 111], the Kelly Ribbon tweeter used with a 12-inch Vitavox woofer, and a Connoisseur pickup with a retractable stylus and a tip resonance set above 20kHz.

Magnetic tape recording

John Borwick

The launch of microgroove long-playing records by American Columbia/CBS in 1948, to replace the four-minute 78rpm shellac discs, made it imperative to find a master recording system capable of longer 'takes' and seamless editing. The solution was provided by magnetic tape recording, only then emerging as a viable high-quality medium.

Up to that time, magnetic recording was something of an unknown quantity, yet its history goes back almost as far as that of the gramophone record itself. The Danish engineer Valdemar Poulsen (1869-1942) filed his patent "Method for the reception and temporary storage of news, signals and the like" in 1898, using ideas independently described in an American publication ten years earlier by Oberlin Smith.

Poulsen's Telegraphone was successfully demonstrated at the 1900 Paris Exposition where it was awarded the Grand Prix. It used steel piano wire wound around a horizontal cylinder along which a record/replay electromagnetic head could be made to track, first to record the signals from a telephone mouthpiece as a magnetic pattern along the wire spiral. The head was then made to retrace the wire and 'read' the signals for reproduction as sound from a telephone earpiece or other transducer.

Though the principle of magnetic recording was thus established, only limited numbers of Telegraphones were produced and occasionally used to record special events and telephone messages. The next two decades saw progressive backroom research into magnetic recording but very little commercial activity. Quality improvements were demonstrated such as the use of high-frequency erasure and AC bias. The German Kurt Stille, as noted by Henry Seymour in an article "The coming of the Telegraphone" in the December 1928 issue of the magazine, acquired patents for wire recorders as well as synchronized sound for films with sprocketed steel tape. These rights were sold to Louis Blattner and the BBC acquired two Blattnerphones in 1929 which were reportedly used to record King George V's Christmas message in 1931 and Lord Reith opening the BBC World Service in 1932.

Magnetic tape recording

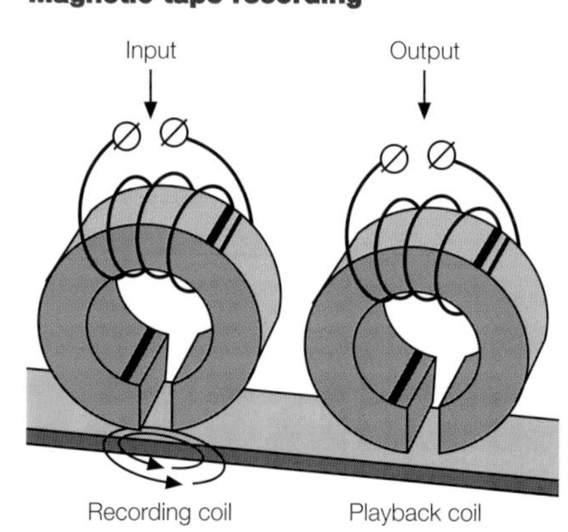

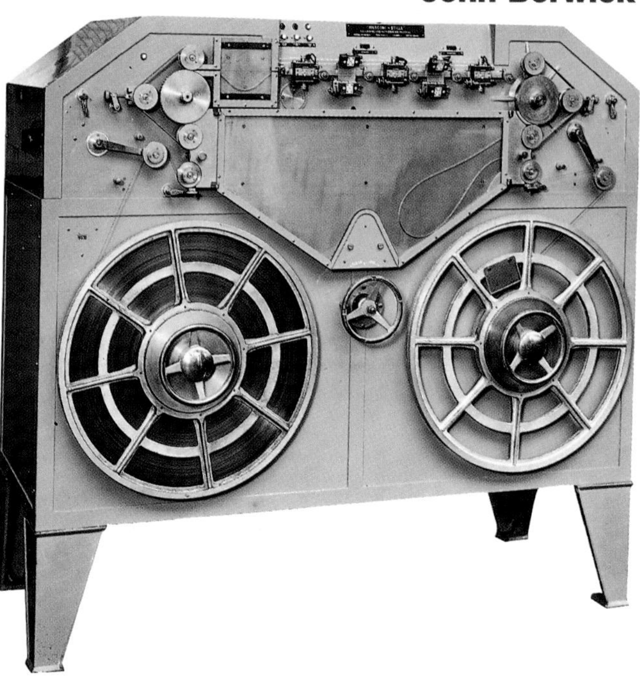

The Marconi-Stille MSR-3 steel tape machine

The Marconi Company bought out Blattnerphone and developed the Marconi-Stille steel tape machine which gave 30 minutes' running time at the very high speed of 1·5 metres per second (59 ips) and remained in BBC service up to 1950.

Tape in Germany

A potentially more profitable development had begun in Germany in 1929 when Fritz Pfleumer patented a recording tape having a flexible paper base to which magnetizable iron powder was fixed. AEG of Berlin took up his idea and recruited the help of the chemical firm BASF (then known as IG Farben). By 1934 the paper was replaced by a 0·03mm thick cellulose acetate base and coated with carbonyl iron. A prototype 'Magnetophon' recorder was produced and, after various adjustments, successfully demonstrated at the 1935 Berlin Show. The tape ran at one metre per second (39·4 ips) and was 6·5mm (0·26in) wide.

A year later the pure iron component was replaced by iron oxide and a new Magnetophon K2 model was got ready for the first tape recording of a live concert. This took place on November 19th, 1936 and featured Sir

Thomas Beecham and the London Philharmonic Orchestra who were performing in BASF's Concert Hall in Ludwigshafen as part of an eight-day tour in Germany. The occasion was described in the April 1984 issue in an article celebrating 50 years of BASF tape. Later improvements included a change to the gamma form of iron oxide (1939), use of high-frequency bias (allegedly discovered by accident by Walter Weber in 1940) and replacement of the cellulose acetate with pvc (polyvinyl chloride) developed by Karl Pflaumer and Rudolph Robl in 1940.

German Radio (RRG) adopted the Magnetophon for recording and transmission purposes in 1938 – few programmes were broadcast live, for political security reasons – but then the 1939-45 war brought a complete blackout of technical information.

Post-War developments

At the end of the war, the Allied Forces found a surprising variety of tape recording equipment in various German cities. There were Magnetophon models with DC or AC bias, and even with stacked stereo record and replay heads. Sound quality had been refined to the point where radio listeners could not detect whether broadcasts, by Hitler and others, were live or recorded. The occupying forces lost no time in 'exporting' samples of the Magnetophon K4 and other tape artefacts which soon led to a rapid rise in tape recording activity.

The first impact was in professional recording, where it took only a couple of years for magnetic tape to replace disc recorders for the storage of radio programmes and the preparation of studio masters. Things moved particularly fast in the USA where ex-servicemen Richard Ranger and John T. Mullin separately modified Magnetophon machines and persuaded Ampex and 3M, among others, to begin the manufacture of respectively professional recorders and "Scotch" tape – and given the Americans' need to network radio programmes across their three time-zones, tape recording could not come too soon. EMI in London were also quick off the mark, launching their BTR1 console recorder in November 1948, four of which were ordered by the BBC at £600 each, and setting up a tape factory soon afterwards at Hayes.

Producers and artists alike had to get used to a change in recording procedures. Tape machines were much easier to transport and set up than the ungainly disc-cutters and offered further benefits such as almost immediate playback and restart. This was both time-saving and confidence-boosting in the sometimes stressful conditions of a recording session. It became very easy to repeat a difficult passage, safe in the knowledge that the best 'take' – or even a single note – could be spliced in at a later date.

As W. S. Barrell, formerly Director of EMI Studios, recalled in Part six of his "I Was There" articles in the September 1960 issue, some engineers regretted the fact that they could no longer see, and with experience assess the quality of, recorded signals in a disc groove. They also feared that sound quality might be lost in the transfer from tape to the master disc required for record manufacture, or that the facility of editing tape, or 'soling and heeling', might be grossly abused. Early tapes were comparatively noisy and liable to overload with severe distortion. Short-term speed fluctuations (wow and flutter) were more noticeable than with the weight-driven disc recorders, and the tape running speed was found to be dependent on the sometimes unreliable mains frequency, requiring correction to be introduced to restore the musical pitch when transferring the tape to master disc.

However, all these problems – except perhaps the temptation to patch together indifferent performances – were solved by technical advances in both the tape and the machines. The fact that professional tape equipment was much cheaper and easier to operate had a very significant side-effect. Small entrepreneur record companies sprang up and were able to transport their recorders anywhere to track down new artists and explore previously ignored repertoire, with considerable artistic and commercial success.

The first tape recording of a live concert took place in the BASF Concert Hall in Ludwigshafen on November 19th, 1936, with Sir Thomas Beecham conducting the London Philharmonic Orchestra

Ferrograph Series 420 mono/stereo tape recorder with the Wright & Weaire deck

The heart-shaped Garrard cartridge, launched at the Earl's Court Radio Show in 1959, was an early British attempt to avoid the problems of open reel-to-reel tape machines. It was not a success

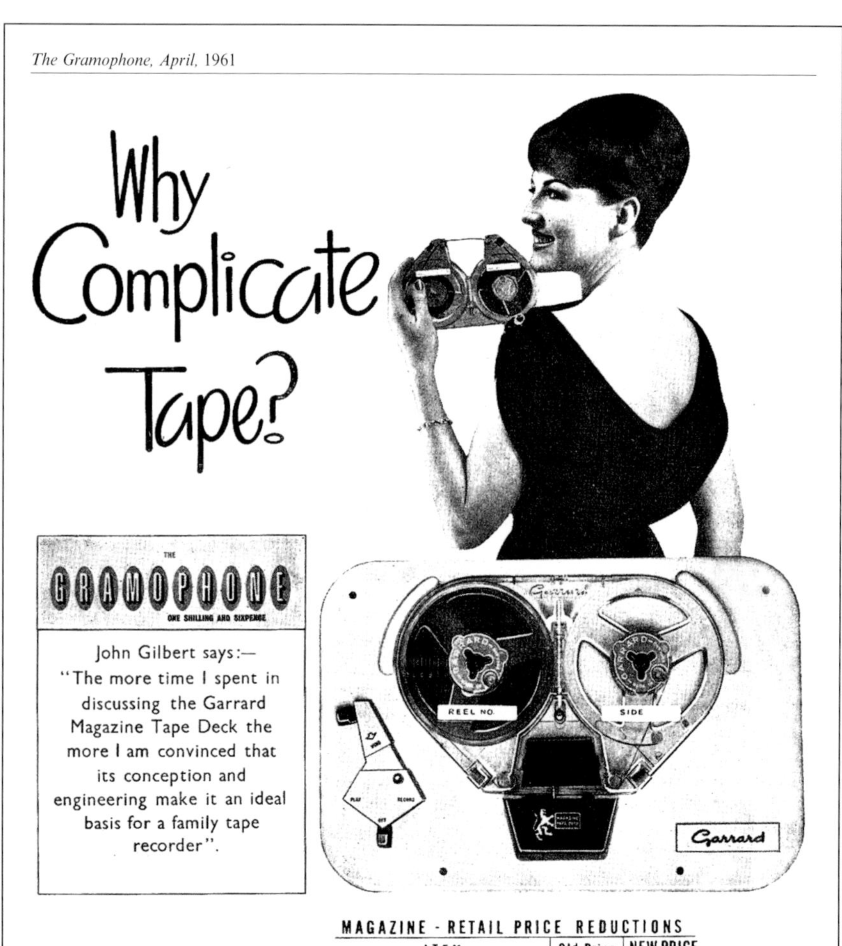

Tape in the home

The growth of amateur tape recording soon followed, as British home enthusiasts were quick to take up a new medium which allowed them for the first time to record music-making, birdsong, trains and off-air radio programmes, and edit them very easily. The early Wright & Weaire deck appeared in March 1949 and established the convention of half-track (turnover) mono reels running at 7·5 or 3·75 ips (19 or 9·5cm/s), though the slower speed was at first considered suitable only for speech. Recorder brand names soon proliferated in the UK and included Ferrograph (Wright & Weaire), Brenell, Reflectograph, Simon and Truvox.

By 1954, there were enough tape machines in people's homes to persuade the record companies to issue some of their new LP releases simultaneously on tape. PW made a mention of these in September 1954 when previewing HMV's exhibit at the Radio Show. They required the setting up of new multiple-recorder duplicating facilities and were on 7-inch reels running at 7·5ips half-track, to give 30 minutes playing time per side. They contained the same music as the equivalent LP and, in the same way, had to be turned over to play the second side. However, except for a flurry of interest in October 1955 when "Stereosonic" tapes made a brief appearance, the medium did not attract much public interest.

Successive moves included marketing 3·75ips tapes on 5-inch reels and changing to a quarter-track system with four interlaced tracks. However this led to some confusion and, as there was no music repertoire exclusively available on tape, the market for prerecorded tapes remained disappointing.

The awkwardness of threading open reel-to-reel machines was blamed for their non-acceptance and a succession of ready-threaded magazines, cartridges and cassettes were launched in the USA by RCA Victor (described in the July 1958 issue), Fidelipac and Earl Muntz, but with limited success. One British format was the Garrard heart-shaped cartridge introduced at the Earl's Court Radio Show in 1959 and designed to be used in a 'tape changer' like their popular auto-changer record-players. This had two small reels with the tape anchored at each end, but achieved no commercial acceptance.

The Philips Compact Cassette

Then at the Berlin Show in June 1963, Philips surprised everyone by unveiling their EL3300 portable "compact cassette" recorder. This new tape cassette format possessed all the right convenience features to enable it to hold centre stage for more than three decades – only recently giving some technical ground to digital media such as DAT, DCC and MiniDisc.

It says much for the extent to which tapes themselves had improved by 1963 that Philips were able not only to choose the slowest tape speed then considered viable, 4·76cm/s (1·88ips) but also to halve the tape width and adopt a compatible system of half-track mono/quarter-track stereo recording, which meant that any cassette could be played on any machine. They also freely licensed other manufacturers of machines and cassettes, provided they kept to the Philips standard specifications, and so ensured an immediate worldwide market for the cassette medium.

The Decca high-speed duplicating process in Bridgnorth: centre, facing camera, is Ivan March a great evangelist for the musicassette

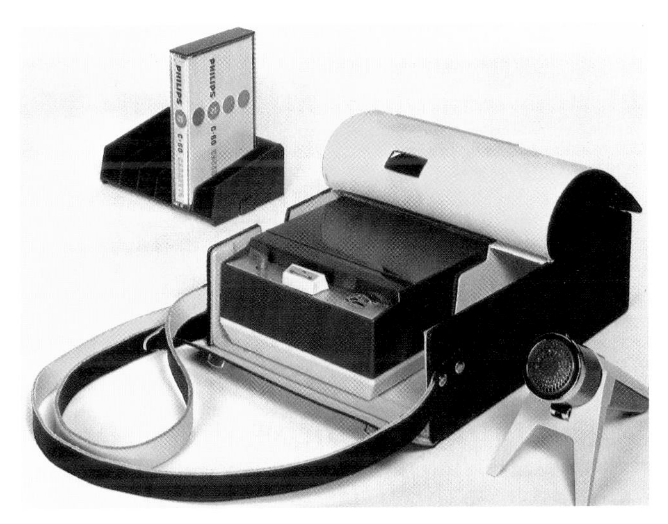

The Philips EL3300 portable compact cassette recorder, unveiled at the Berlin Show in June 1963, was the first machine to use the new compact cassette tapes

At first the record industry were in no hurry to produce prerecorded ‘musicassettes’. Then, in October 1966, when cassette decks and portables were being sold in large numbers and the sound quality had begun to match the needs of acceptable music reproduction, Philips and EMI started to issue stereo cassettes in parallel with their LPs. Decca delayed their marketing of musicassettes until October 1970 when they had refined the high-speed duplicating process to their own satisfaction and a month later pioneered the use of Dolby B noise reduction, as Arthur Haddy explained to me in an interview in the October 1970 issue.

The first musicassettes cost £2 each, slightly more than the equivalent LP disc, but had the advantage that they were compatible with both mono and stereo cassette players. They used ferric tape and fell well short of LP disc quality. However, the change to chrome tape (described in detail in the October 1971 issue) and Dolby B noise reduction, plus the use of a dynamic range enhancing technique called HX-Pro at the high-speed duplicating stage (from 1984), greatly improved quality and led to a steep rise in sales. A real boost to the popularity of cassettes came with the launch of the Sony “Walkman” lightweight portable (originally called the “Stowaway”) in Japan in July 1979 [p. 113]. From less than ten million units sold in the the UK in 1972, for example, the format achieved figures in excess of 80 million by 1989. Although sales have declined in recent years to just over 46 million by 1996, they continue to compare favourably with all other media except the Compact Disc.

It remains to be seen which of the various digital media being put forward for amateur recording and playback will achieve a comparable grip on the marketplace [for discussion of which see “The Media Maze”, page 241].

The Sony Walkman, originally called the “Stowaway”, was launched in Japan in July 1979 and gave a significant boost to the sale of musicassettes

Stereophony

John Borwick

By the mid-1950s, with professional tape recorders and LP records capable of capturing the full frequency range and (very nearly) the natural dynamics of musical sounds, any evolution towards greater realism had to depend on finding some method of recreating the spatial effect of being present at a live performance. Early attempts had been spasmodic and rendered non-viable by other limitations in the recording chain.

Even when the telephone was in its infancy, its inventor Alexander Graham Bell and such luminaries as Lord Rayleigh and Silvanus P. Thomson had experimented with 'binaural audition'. Using a pair of telephones, or even tuning forks and long rubber tubes, they explored the ear's ability to locate sounds and the effects of inter-aural phase differences.

The earliest public demonstrations of recreating a sense of space were organised by Clément Ader at the Paris Exposition of 1881. He set up primitive carbon-rod 'microphones' to left and right of the stage at the Paris Opéra and connected them by separate telephone lines to ranks of earpieces at the exhibition pavilion. By holding an ear-piece to each ear, visitors were astonished to find that they could follow the left/right movements of singers and enjoy a sense of spatial ambience.

In 1881 Clément Ader installed two groups of five primitive telephone-type microphones in the footlights of the Paris Opéra. They were connected to 80 telephone receivers at the International Exhibition of Electricity, three kilometres away, where listeners holding a left and right earpiece to each ear obtained a sense of spatial ambience

Skipping the next 50 years, during which any developments were mainly confined to laboratories, we come to the definitive British patent No. 394,325 (1931) in which A. D. Blumlein of EMI (1903-42) described all-embracing theories and practical designs for recording and reproducing two-channel sound on discs. He had solved the basic problems of dual-microphone techniques and of inscribing two mutually independent channels of information in a single record groove, and indeed supervised a number of experimental recordings at Abbey Road in 1932, later described by W. S. Barrell in the October 1959 issue.

One of his suggested microphone arrangements has come to be called the 'Blumlein method' and consists of a pair of bi-directional (figure-of-eight) microphones at right angles to each other and placed as close together as possible. This eliminates any time-of-arrival differences at the two microphone diaphragms but produces intensity differences because each microphone has its maximum sensitivity in different directions. Therefore a sound source at the left of centre, for example, will produce a greater signal level from the left microphone than the right. Then, when these signals are reproduced from a pair of suitably spaced loudspeakers, the listener will hear a 'phantom image' similarly spaced to the left of centre. An orchestra or other group of performers can therefore be made to appear spread out in their natural layout. Directional information from the rear of the microphones, however, is reversed.

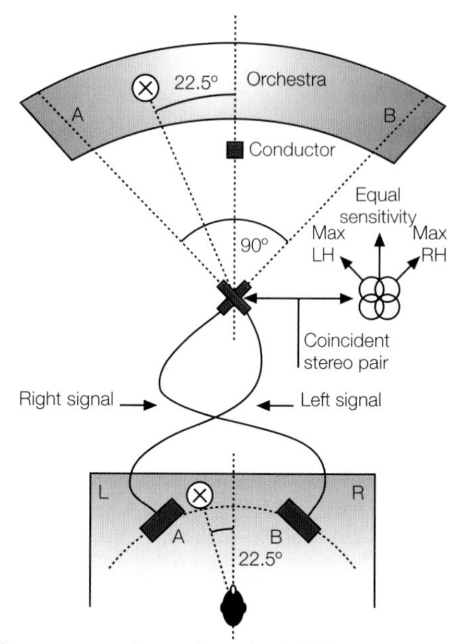

The 'Blumlein method' of stereo recording. By using a pair of bi-directional microphones, a sound source at X 22½ degrees from the centre line is reproduced in the listener's home at the same point

This kind of recording and reproduction has come to be called stereophony (or 'stereo' for short) after the Greek *stereos* meaning solid. One of the methods tried at Bell Laboratories in America used a pair of microphones at the ears of a tailor's dummy, affectionately called Oscar. This created a useful spread of sounds, particularly when listened to on headphones, and there are still dummy-head stereo enthusiasts around today.

With gramophone records still the only medium for pre-recorded music, any commercial application for stereo had to wait for a means of recording two independent channels of information in a single groove. Blumlein's patent did visualise inscribing two channels mutually at right angles each at 45 degrees to the record surface (the method finally adopted 25 years later). He also suggested using a pair of spaced cutterheads and gramophone pickups tracing

separate grooves (with an inevitable halving of the playing time of the disc), and this idea was briefly put into practice by Emory Cook in 1952.

In practical terms, the post-war spread of tape recording greatly simplified this two-track problem and the record companies began in the mid-1950s to stockpile stereo recordings in anticipation of some future stereo disc. As mentioned in the pievious chapter, this led to the first issues of "Stereosonic" prerecorded tapes by EMI in October 1955. These were launched at an Abbey Road demonstration on April 4th which was introduced by Sir Malcolm Sargent and described in the May 1955 issue. However these found little public acceptance and the industry stepped up its search for a viable stereo disc.

Arnold Sugden demonstrated a practical disc recorder at the London Audio Fair in 1956, using a combination of lateral and hill-and-dale signals. Arthur Haddy of Decca, in a development of their wartime ultrasonic recorders, produced an impressive system with two 12kHz bandwidth channels, one modulated on to a 14kHz carrier. Realizing that this system was probably too complicated for commercial exploitation, Haddy worked on refining the Sugden sum-and-difference method. He took this to meetings in America where a 45/45 system developed by Westrex (based on Blumlein's ideas) was adopted.

How record grooves are modulated

A Mono lateral

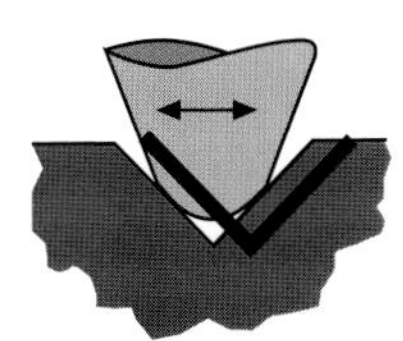

B Mono hill-and-dale

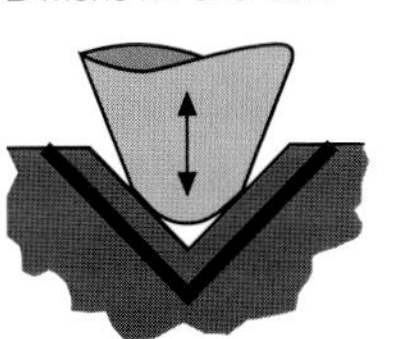

C Stereo left and right channels at ±45° to the record surface

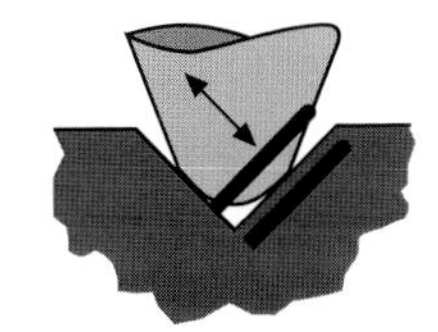

By 1958 international agreement was reached on the 45/45 system and this included the dimensions and other parameters needed for both discs and record-players to be produced in quantity, all discussed in detail in the April 1958 issue. In particular it was agreed that "The phasing and level of the two recorded signals shall be suitable for reproduction on equipment so connected that movement of the reproducing stylus parallel to the recorded surface (in the manner of a monophonic lateral record) produces equal and in-phase sound pressures at the right and left hand loudspeakers", i.e. stereo pickups would also be compatible and produce equal in-phase signals in both channels when playing a mono disc.

At first, the discs were cut with a constant groove spacing (pitch) but this set a limit to both dynamic range and playing time. The answer which Haddy brought to a successful conclusion was 'varigroove', a system which continuously adjusts the pitch so that the programme amplitude in each groove is just accommodated, without overlapping (an idea which was foreshadowed by a "Variable Micrograde" system used by Deutsche Grammophon for 78s described by F. F. Clough in the November 1950 issue, with further correspondence over the next two months: the records were never generally obtainable in the UK). This uses a preview head on the tape machine from which a master tape is being transferred to the disc-cutter, which sends a signal to the leadscrew motor altering the tracking speed as required. In the case of stereo, groove depth as well as spacing has to be adjusted in this way.

A Deutsche Grammophon "Variable Micrograde" 78rpm disc which could carry up to 7 minutes of music per side

The Westrex stereo cutterhead

Stereo progress

In some ways the eventual appearance of stereo LP records in 1958 was even more traumatic than that of the LP itself ten years earlier. The public had to be persuaded yet again to invest in new equipment and new records, if they wanted to take up this latest technical advance. The record companies, certainly EMI and Decca in England, were nervous in case sales of conventional mono records would plummet. Indeed EMI put out a

Custom-made hi-fi unit from the early 1960s with Decca pickup arm and stereo cartridge, Leak Stereo 30 integrated amplifier and control unit, and Garrard 301 three-speed motor

statement in January 1958 (reproduced in the February issue) playing down the likelihood of the immediate release of stereo records, saying, "It is no use putting stereo discs on the market – EMI could do that tomorrow – until the means of playing them is available in a form and at a price acceptable to a worth while section of the public" [p. 111].

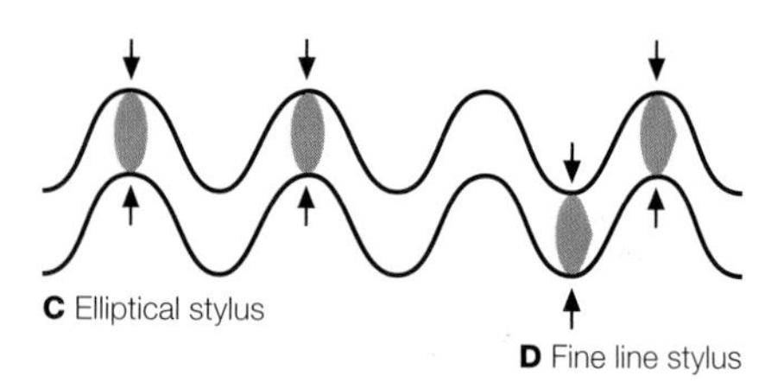

A record groove showing the angles of different stylus types in relation to the groove when tracing the modulation

The hi-fi companies were obliged to produce stereo pickups and amplifiers in quick time. In fact, many of the first stereo pickups were of poor quality, lacking the new requirement of vertical compliance and failing to ensure proper 90 degree angling between the two transducer elements, which discouraged many potential buyers from converting to the new system.

Exceptions to this rule were two high-quality stereo cartridges, designed by Decca and by EMI engineers, which reached the market respectively one year and three years after the launch of stereo discs: both were glowingly reviewed in *The Gramophone*. Having coped with recording and reproducing frequencies up to 28kHz during wartime, Decca were very well placed to go into production with a top class stereo pickup – and high performance cutterheads. The Decca *ffss* (Full Frequency Stereo Sound) pickup and arm, costing a little over £22 (reviewed in March 1959) had a combination of three fixed coils, two receiving signals from vertical movement of the stylus and one lateral. This cleverly used the sum-and-difference principle, already well established in the early Haddy experiments, was easily adapted to derive the 45/45 signals and tackled an important requirement for stereo playback, minimum interchannel crosstalk. It also meant that the lateral coil was suitable for mono records.

EMI's response was the Type EPU100, costing about £22·60. Reviewed in September 1961, it was a beautifully styled and engineered integrated cartridge and arm product. Its three-coil arrangement differed from that of the Decca but produced equally impressive crosstalk figures, wide frequency response and excellent tracking helped by viscous damping of the unipivot arm. Another British hi-fi product which helped to raise standards of record tracking was the SME pickup arm, launched in September 1959 and reviewed in January 1960.

In fact, tracking of stereo records was a vexed question. The recommended stylus tip radius had been reduced from 0·001in to 0·0005in to take account of the more complex groove shape on stereo records and the fact that groove depth varied constantly. Therefore, although the mono and stereo discs were nominally compatible, a mono stylus could inflict damage on a stereo record and the new stereo stylus tip sank low enough in a mono groove to introduce noise from debris. A compromise 0·0007in stylus became popular in the less expensive cartridges, but more exotic cartridges were often supplied with a stylus having a biradial elliptical tip contour. The major radius rested conventionally on the groove walls and the minor radius was better able to trace the shortest recorded wavelengths. More complex 'fine line' tip shapes came later.

Meanwhile, as existing mono pickups had little or no vertical compliance, the record companies felt obliged to produce both mono and stereo versions of new issues which, from all points of view, was a considerable nuisance. Then on April 13th, 1967 EMI issued a statement, reproduced in the May 1967 issue, that "from next July classical long-playing records will be released in stereo only". This was followed by other companies and led to a general adoption of the compromise 0·0007in stylus and a degree of vertical compliance in

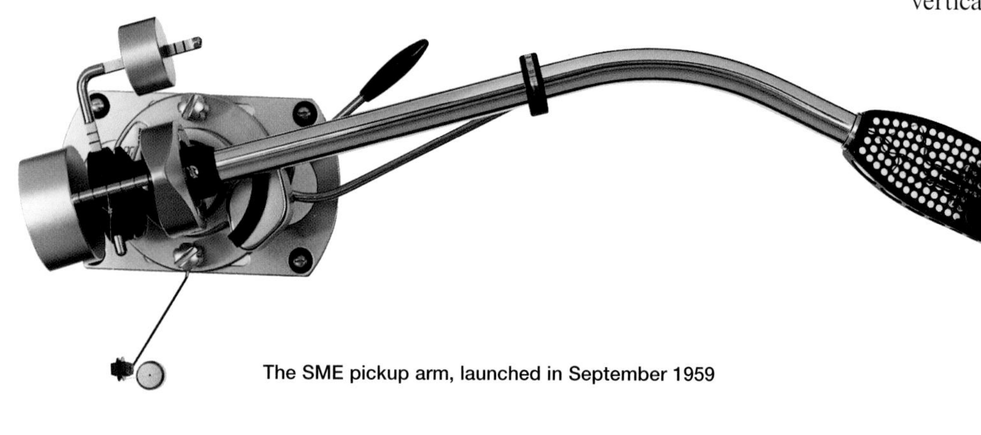
The SME pickup arm, launched in September 1959

even the least expensive mono cartridges and record-players.

History repeated itself to the extent that many record companies siezed the opportunity of stereo's arrival to re-record their star artists, just as they had done when LPs took over from 78s. But when successful artists were no longer available, there were attempts to reissue their performances in 'electrically created stereo'. This involved somehow making the signal in the left and right channels differ in such a way as to give the impression that sounds were emanating from different points along the line joining the two loudspeakers. Some degree of success was achieved on a few issues but in general the process was not liked and it fell into disuse.

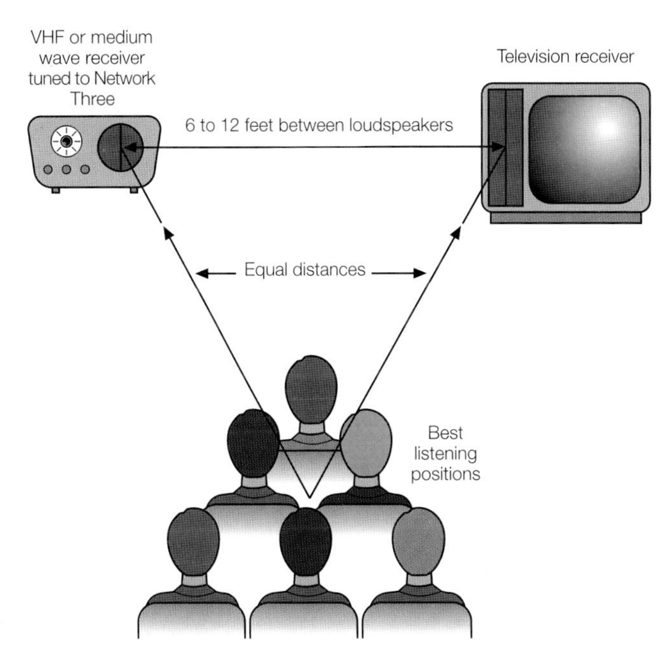

In 1958, the BBC began experimental stereo broadcasting with the left channel on the radio and the right channel on the TV speaker

Stereo broadcasting

After some intriguing but commercially unsatisfactory experimental stereo transmissions in 1958, on Saturday mornings with the left channel on radio and the right on TV sound, the BBC began regular stereo broadcasting of Radio 3 on VHF/FM in 1966, with Radios 2 and 4 following by 1972. The internationally agreed Zenith-GE multiplex system was used with the sum signal (L+R) modulated onto the carrier in the ordinary way, to provide a standard signal for mono receivers, and the difference (L-R) on a 38kHz subcarrier. Stereo receivers demodulated these signals by addition and subtraction to derive 2L and 2R to drive a pair of stereo speakers, as anticipated in the Haddy disc experiments.

Quadraphony

While stereo reproduction gives an acceptable spread of sound, the effect is confined to a narrow letterbox-shaped arc between the loudspeakers. Attempts to record and reproduce the full 360 degree sound field that surrounds a listener at a concert occupied engineers for many years and, for several years from 1972 onwards, the record companies did indeed issue so-called 'quadraphonic' records. They used arrays of four microphones or complex mixing arrangements to produce four signals to be reproduced through four speakers arranged in a square around the listener. The process was described in the April 1970 issue in a report on the CBS Records sessions in the Royal Albert Hall on February 22nd when the Verdi *Requiem* was recorded with Leonard Bernstein and the LSO [p. 144].

Unfortunately, for the process of reducing these four signals to the two which could be accommodated in the single groove of a stereo record, different record companies adopted three incompatible encoding systems, two multiplex and one discrete. The rival systems were described in the May 1972 issue, and explained in a booklet called "Quadraphony Now" which *Gramophone* published in October 1974. In the resulting confusion, very few homes bothered to invest in any of the decoders, four-channel amplifiers and extra speakers needed and eventually the industry cut its losses and gave up.

A reader's letter in the February 1971 issue summed up the negative attitude of most consumers, "The very idea of 'sitting in the middle of the orchestra' is ludicrous to a music-lover, much though it may appeal to the gimmick-merchants and equipment-showoffs". Dr Hans-Werner Steinhausen, the Technical Director of Deutsche Grammophon, was also sceptical in his article "Quadraphony – its Potential and its Limitations" in the November 1972 issue.

One British system called Ambisonics (described by one of its inventors, P. B. Fellgett, in the January and February 1976 issues) gave superior results and has continued in a small way, being used by Nimbus Records for example on all their recordings. In the last few years, surround sound has reappeared as an essential feature in the cinema, and on videos and television transmissions. A multiplex system is again used, though more recently replaced by separate discrete channels in a digital version, and careful mixing of dialogue (always on a centre channel), music and sound effects adds greatly to the realism.

The four speakers needed for quadraphonic reproduction failed to catch on in the 1970s, although surround sound has now become an important component of home cinema systems

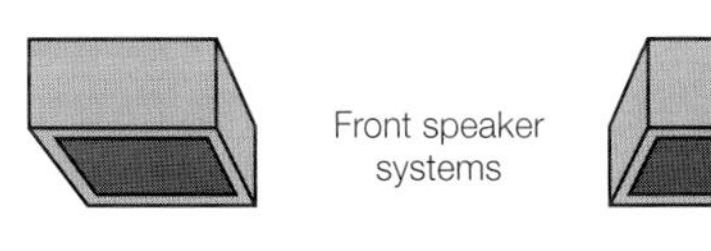

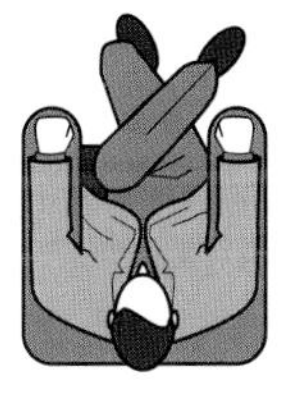

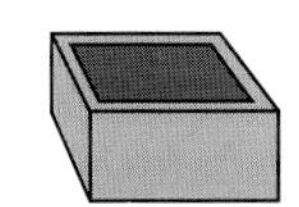

The Compact Disc

John Borwick

We have seen earlier that the recording and reproduction of sound using magnetic tape was first implemented for professional applications, and only later found its way into consumer media. In the same way, the revolutionary digital technology was adopted by professionals several years before the emergence of the first digital consumer music carrier, the Compact Disc in 1982.

Writing in July 1975 under the heading "A Digit on the Audio Pulse", I felt it necessary to explain the use of the word 'digital': "Just as Molière's *Bourgeois Gentilhomme* was delighted to be told that he had been talking 'prose' all his life (he had not needed a name for ordinary speech until it became necessary to distinguish it from 'poetry') so you may be surprised to learn that the electrical waveforms and groove modulations that we have been using to record and transmit sounds since Edison and Marconi are *analogue* signals. The name has been invented to distinguish ordinary continuous sound waveforms from a new discontinuous type made up entirely of on/off pulses encoded by numbers or digits and therefore called *digital*. The analogue form is so called because the rise and fall of signal amplitude with time imitates, or is analagous to, the changes in sound pressure level produced by the original sound waves".

For digital recording or transmission to take place, the audio signals must first be passed through an analogue-to-digital converter (ADC). This changes the analogue waveform into a stream of constant-amplitude pulses which are coded in such a way that the receiver or playback device has only to detect the presence or absence of a pulse, not its level, and pass this information through a digital-to-analogue converter (DAC) to reproduce the original data. This makes digital systems extremely impervious to interference and capable of operating at any desired order of accuracy.

The ADC operates by sampling the amplitude of the audio waveform at regular intervals and assigning to each sample a binary number of ones and zeros (or digital 'word') to represent the amplitude at that instant in time. For perfect results, enabling the waveform to be reproduced exactly, the sampling rate would need to be very high, as would the number of discrete levels capable of being encoded. Analysis has shown that a sampling rate of twice the highest desired audio frequency is enough to eliminate distortion. Similarly, the number of different amplitude levels sets a limit to fidelity since any wave amplitude falling between two usable levels (steps) will be assigned one of these and the small error will introduce a form of distortion.

Digital sampling of an analogue waveform

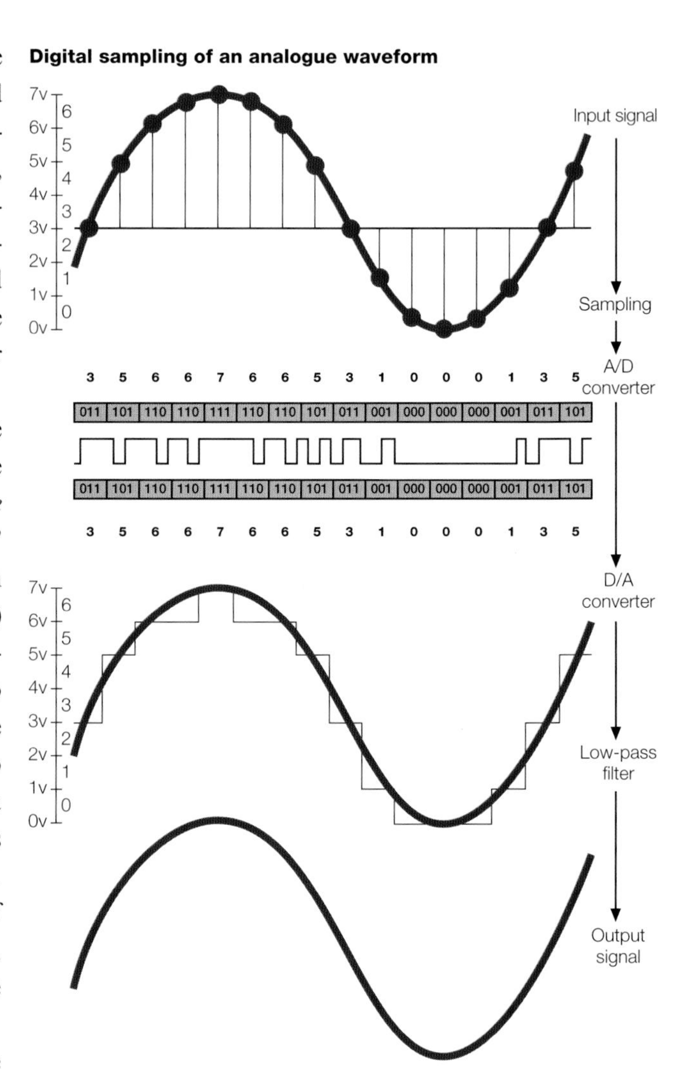

The BBC, one of the very first users of digital techniques, began using the Pulse Code Modulation (PCM) system for distributing their programmes to the various stereo VHF/FM transmitting stations in 1972. They chose a sampling frequency of 32kHz, to provide the required audio pass band of 15kHz, and a 13-bit word length ('bit' is short for binary digit) which provided an adequate signal-to-noise ratio of 78dB (the S/N ratio equals 6dB for each bit, i.e. 6 × 13 = 78dB). Critical listeners reacted favourably to the improved frequency and dynamic ranges from these PCM-distributed programmes, compared with analogue landline connections. A further benefit for stereo broadcasts was that digital distribution preserved the left/right channel phase relationships, previously degraded due to unequal time delays.

Digital recording

Within a few years, digital recorders began to come into use. Nippon Columbia (Denon), who had made the first commercial digital disc recording in October 1972, showed the way with a succession of PCM designs between 1972 and 1975, eventually spreading the digital signals over eight tracks on a 2-inch video-type tape recorder running at 15ips and giving a tape/head relative speed of 40 metres per second. When transferred to analogue LP, the results were still noticeably cleaner than the norm, with a complete absence of tape hiss or modulation noise, plus excellent transient response.

Telarc in America were soon up and running with digital recorders and LP transfer, including a spectacular version of Tchaikovsky's *1812* Overture played by the Cincinnati Symphony Orchestra and a battery of real-life cannons and church bells. The LP (reviewed in April 1980) had an unprecedented dynamic range and bass extending to about 6Hz, only trackable by the most sophisticated pickups.

In the UK, Decca were first off the mark with a Sylvia Sass studio session in July 1978, then taking their own design of digital recorder to Vienna for the 1979 "New Year's Day Concert". The LP was enthusiastically reviewed by Edward Greenfield in the April 1979 issue. He was impressed by the "truthfulness, particularly in the bass", but noted a degree of aggression in the treble (something that Decca avoided in later issues). In December 1979 EMI, having developed their own design of digital recorder based on an open-reel instrumentation deck, brought out their first classical LP made from a digital master. This was a recording of Debussy's *Images* performed by the LSO under André Previn (reviewed in December 1979) which impressed the "Sounds in Retrospect" panel who wrote in that same month, "It was not just that the background was virtually inaudible – as one would hope on a digital issue – but that the bloom on the sound told us both of exceptional fidelity and of truthful balancing". The LP went on to receive that year's Award in the Engineering category.

R.W. Bailiff of Decca contributed an article to the June 1979 issue in which he explained the digital tape recording technology and how Decca had settled on a sampling frequency of around 50kHz and a word length of 16 bits. He stressed, however, that Decca LPs made from digital masters were in every way equivalent to standard discs so far as their compatibility with existing record-players and hi-fi systems were concerned. However, the full benefits of digital technology can be experienced only when the music signals are kept in the digital domain all the way from the studio to a DAC in the listener's home. For this to happen, the record industry would clearly need to develop a digitally encoded gramophone record.

Compact Disc

The first ***Gramophone*** reference to Compact Disc appeared in the June 1978 issue, quoting a May 17th press release from Philips Industries on the development of a revolutionary 110mm (4·5in) optical disc – slightly smaller than the final version. It used the PCM digital encoding system with a 14-bit word and 44·1kHz sampling frequency, providing 84dB dynamic range and 20-20,000Hz frequency range. Philips forecast that players would be available in the early 1980s, and I commented, "We regard this Philips announcement as a momentous trail-blazer and we shall certainly follow up with more news as soon as it becomes available".

There was then a gap, but Philips did organize demonstrations of prototype discs and laser-beam players at an International Press Conference in Eindhoven, reported in the April 1979 issue [p. 145]. By January 1980, in an article called "The Shape of Discs to come", I was able to provide a detailed description of how CD works. I also referred to a number of rival digital disc formats which were then being promoted, but which were soon abandoned. These included a Sony 12-inch laser-scanned disc, the JVC VHD/AHD home video/audio disc which was briefly pressed in England by Thorn/EMI and became very popular in Japan, an RCA unit in which a stylus tracked a groove carrying digital signals to be read as capacitance fluctuations, and the Teldec (Telefunken-Decca) Mini-Disc. Fortunately, Philips and Sony agreed to cooperate on a single Compact Disc specification and the way ahead was clear.

A prestigious Press Conference jointly staged in Salzburg on April 15th, 1981 by Philips, PolyGram and Sony [p. 156] was fully reported in the June issue and, though the predicted launch date was still almost two years away, the demonstrations of the new medium were good enough to convince most of the 200 assembled journalists that its success was assured. The premiere appearance of a fair number of CD titles and CD players took place at the Tokyo Hi-Fi Show in October 1982, with a European launch following in March 1983.

Gramophone was uniquely placed to report and comment on the new music carrier, having acquired several players well in advance and persuaded the record companies to supply copies of every classical music title as soon as it became available (a number of faults detected by our reviewers were fed back to the manufacturers, and corrected in time for the main issue). Accordingly, the March 1983 issue contained a special 12-page section with reviews of four CD players and 49 discs. Reactions were very favourable, though a certain hardness of tone was detected on some discs and there was other evidence that the manufacturers still had a little to learn in disc mastering and pressing.

The joint Philips/Sony specification is laid down in a "Red Book" to which all disc and player manufacturers must subscribe. This establishing of a universal standard follows the successful policy adopted by Philips when they launched the Compact Cassette tape format about 20 years earlier. It has guaranteed that all CDs can be played on all makes of player, though naturally leaving scope for individual styling and extra features.

CD dimensions

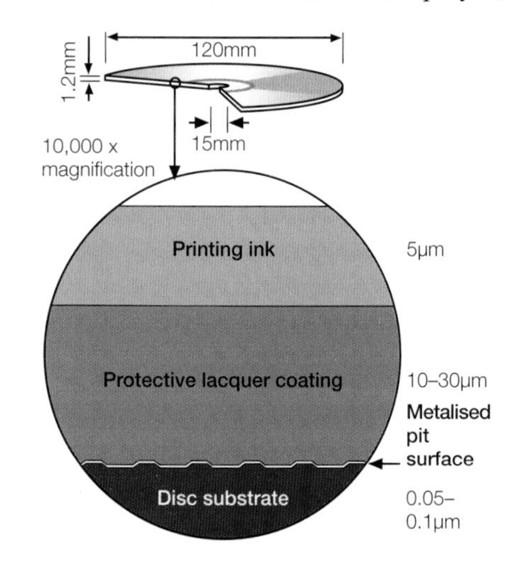

Again the word 'compact' highlights one of CD's principal benefits. The disc is only 120mm (4·7in) in diameter and 1·2mm thick, which saves on space and allows for the design of very small portables and in-car CD players. The digitally encoded signals are pressed into the upper surface of a transparent polycarbonate substrate in the form of a spiralling track of tiny pits; this follows a sequence of optical master recording on a glass disc, electroplating and mould (stamper) preparation not unlike that used for vinyl discs. The pitted surface is then given a thin reflective coating (usually of aluminium) and a final protective coat of lacquer on which the label can be printed.

The track begins near the disc centre with the Table of Contents and spirals outwards. Unlike vinyl discs, the linear tracking speed is kept constant at about 1·2 metres per second. The disc rotational speed has therefore to begin high, about 500rpm, and fall steadily to about 200rpm at the outer radius. The digital track contains both the left and right stereo channels and a synchronizing code (clock) which automatically locks the player's drive motor to the instantaneous speed as recorded at all points across the disc. Unwanted speed fluctuations (wow and flutter) are eliminated.

Playback head

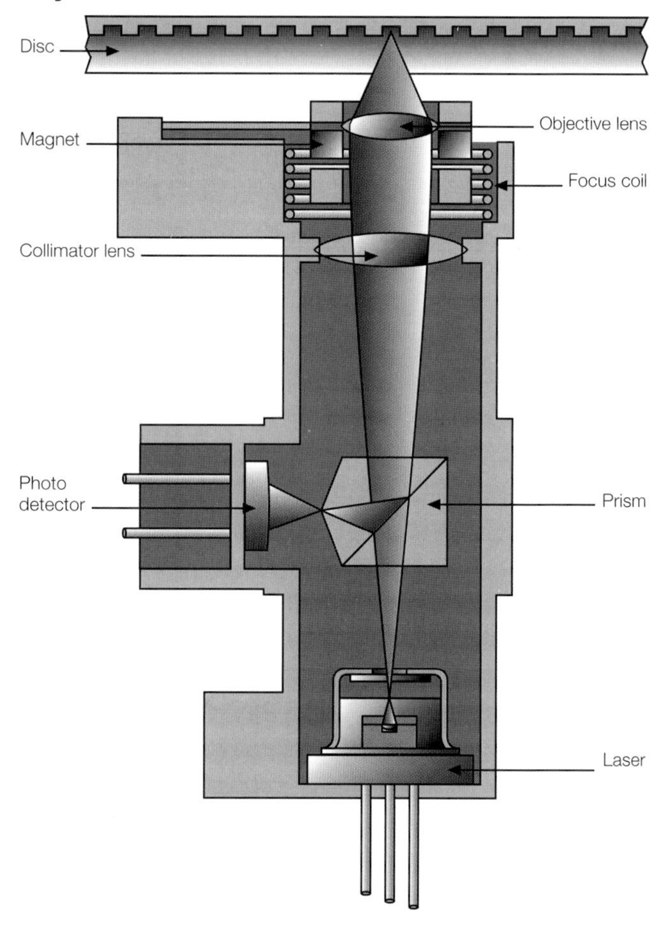

There is no mechanical contact with the record surface. The playback head scans the underside of the disc and comprises a laser light source sharply focused through the clear plastic substrate on to the metal-coated reflective layer, plus a light-sensitive photo detector on to which the reflected beam is directed. This registers the change in intensity of reflected light from the stream of pits and, after decoding, generates an electrical signal which recreates the original sequence of ones and zeros. This is passed through a digital-to-analogue converter which separates the L/R channels and sends them to a standard pair of analogue output sockets on the CD player for connection to a hi-fi amplifier. Some players also pass the digital signal direct to a 'digital output' socket for possible use with an external DAC unit or a digital recorder.

As well as the motor servo already mentioned which controls the instantaneous disc rotational speed, there is a focus servo, a tracking servo to keep the beam accurately centred on the narrow track, and a traversing servo to move the optical system radially across the disc steadily during play, or at high-speed in the fast search and cueing modes. The composite signals in the CD bitstream incorporate numerous coding features which add greatly to the medium's performance quality, stability and ease of operation.

These refinements would have been impossible to implement in an analogue system, as would the comprehensive error correction and concealment features which enable the player to ignore the effects of dust, scratches or external shocks, and the helpful display facilities, track selection and repeat/random/programmed sequence options. These user options were at first regarded as gimmicks but soon became an accepted part of the home music scene.

At a technical level, the Red Book set remarkable new performance standards. The chosen 44·1kHz sampling frequency ensured an effectively flat response from below 20Hz to 20kHz, and the use of a 16-bit word length provided a dynamic range of 96dB – much greater than in any analogue medium. To produce these parameters, plus a nominal playing time of 74 minutes per disc, involved the storing of some 15 billion bits of data, and required entirely new microprocessor electronics and thermoplastic pressing technology.

CD progress

From small beginnings, the Compact Disc made steady progress as the pressing factories took some time to get up and running, and consumers tended to wait for reassurance that the medium's claimed benefits would really materialize. Soon, however, the slow market growth accelerated until, in the late 1980s, CD sales actually passed those of the declining LP and eventually eclipsed LPs altogether.

CD players improved in sound quality and reliability. They were, of course, easily plugged into any home hi-fi and could enable even quite humble systems to produce clean and dynamic music signals at the touch of a key. The discs were robust enough to withstand any reasonable amount of manhandling. Though not "perfect", as misguided early advertising had claimed, the sound quality was the same at the one-hundredth playing as at the first – in marked contrast to vinyl discs which required frequent clearing away of dust from the disc and the stylus, both of which were subject to wear with repeated playing.

The discs themselves improved as new mastering and replication techniques were introduced. The recording equipment was progressively upgraded to provide 20-bit or more resolution, with some 24dB greater dynamic range and reduced distortion. At first, these improvements were of only marginal benefit on the actual CDs, since the high-bit master tapes (or the new digital optical discs which were used by some engineers) had to be downloaded in the standard 16-bit format.

Then techniques were developed which enabled some of the improved quality to be transferred to the CD. First came Sony's "Super Bit Mapping" technology, described in the February 1993 issue, which uses "noise shaping" to redistribute any ADC errors to parts of the sound spectrum where the ear is less sensitive. Then Deutsche Grammophon went over to an "Authentic Bit Imaging" process as part of the system which they, perhaps misguidedly, called "4D". This name did not refer to some extension of 3D (three-dimensional sound) but to a four-stage redesign covering microphone preamplifiers, built into special stage-boxes for placing close to the microphones, a 4 x 21-bit ADC and a new digital mixing console where the 16-bit downloading could take place to keep the music signals in the digital domain right through to the final CD itself.

CD spin-offs

It is doubtful if such wide-ranging researches into the Compact Disc medium would have been instigated if CD-Audio were the only end-product. An article in the August 1987 issue called "CD's Potential Progeny" explained how the original Red Book specification actually allowed for expansion in several different directions, and outlined the spin-off media already on offer. The extended family of CD-like disc formats now includes the following:

CD-ROM (Read-Only Memory): is one important derivative for use with computers to provide fixed programs, listings or instructions which cannot be altered. The main requirements for any ROM system are high storage capacity, fast access and an ability to display or

June 1993 **News**

LONGEVITY IN CD

No technology as complex as Compact Disc is entirely without its problems, but it is remarkable how reliable most CD players have been over the decade. There have of course been failures but the great majority of machines have proved themselves beyond question. Generally the failures, when they occur, concern disc tracking problems and in one guise or another these have afflicted machines from most manufacturers from time to time. But bearing in mind just how complex the technology is, it is remarkable how few problems there have been.

It was good to hear from one reader who has recently celebrated his player's tenth anniversary: Mr Terry Hooke of Dobwalls in Cornwall bought his Marantz CD-63 in the spring of 1983 as soon as the medium was launched in the UK. He has logged its 12,328 playing hours and the original laser is still going strong.

reproduce groups or sequences of data. CD-ROM meets these criteria ideally, which explains its rapid penetration into both business and home computer applications. A single CD-ROM, looking exactly like an audio CD, can store as much data as about 460 floppy discs, equivalent to 250,000 pages of text. Manufacturing of CD-ROMs requires greater precision and superior error correction, and so the development of the necessary technology has in turn fed back to CD-Audio.

CD-Video: made a brief appearance in 1988 and was described, along with reviews of two CD-Video players, in the October 1988 issue. However, the 5-inch disc could provide only six minutes of analogue video plus 20 minutes of digital stereo audio and, along with the planned 8-inch and 12-inch versions, was soon abandoned.

CD-R (Recordable): made gradual incursions into professional circles during 1991. Then, by the May 1992 issue when CD-R recorders costing about £3,000 were beginning to come from Marantz, Meridian, Micromega and Mission (all based on a Philips transport) it seemed timely to describe the new medium in some detail.

Like cassettes, blank CD-R discs are available in various 'lengths' – up to 74 minutes as shown here

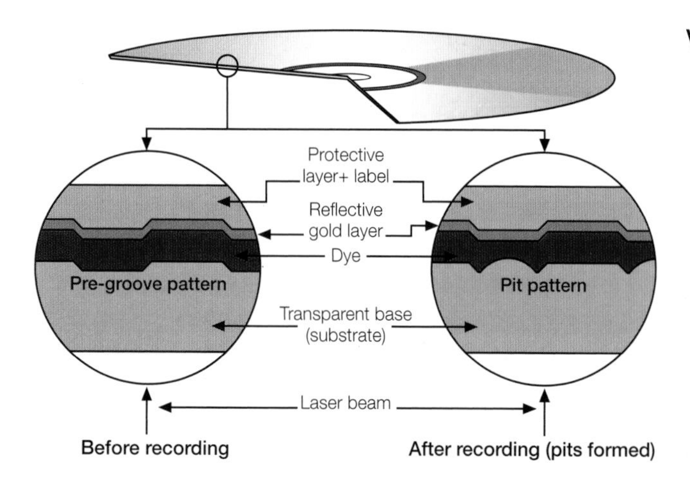

Cross-section of a CD-R before and after recording

CD-R is non-erasable (but see CD-RW in "The Media Maze"), which means that the discs are "Write Once Read Many-times" or WORM and the initial price of £19 for blank discs did at first seem prohibitive. Recording uses a layer of heat-sensitive dye embedded in a conventional disc which has first been pressed with a continuous spiral pre-groove containing a fixed frequency 'wobble' at 22·05kHz both to guide the recording laser and establish the correct running speed and 'absolute time' throughout the disc.

During recording, the stream of impulses from a high-power laser causes momentary heating at points along the groove and, in cooling, creates a tiny collapsed bubble at each point of light exposure. The substrate expands to take up these spaces and so establishes the desired series of pits as on a standard CD. A stop/start facility allows new recorded items to be added as required and, once completed, the CD-R disc can be treated in all respects like an ordinary CD.

CD-I (Interactive): first appeared in a few UK shops in April 1992. The idea was that users could 'interact' with the new format discs by pointing a computer-type cursor at various screen menus and options to play games, tour art galleries or listen to juke-box selections of music while viewing the lyrics, artist biographies or background information. However, the relatively high costs and scarcity of interesting programme material prevented CD-I from making much market progress.

The Kodak Photo CD: was launched in the summer of 1992. It allowed amateur photographers to take standard 35mm photographs and have them processed on to a CD-like disc for viewing on their television receiver. The special Photo CD players could also play audio CDs but were not bought in significant numbers. Instead, Photo CD has blossomed as a key medium for publishers of periodicals and books.

Video CD: as distinct from CD-Video already discussed, was jointly announced by Philips, Sony, Matsushita and JVC on June 29th, 1993. This was based on an existing "Karaoke CD" White Book standard and seemed to offer one important advantage over CD-I in that it could provide digital Full Motion Video. In the event, the proposal found itself in competition with other forms of 'high-density' 5-inch discs. After lengthy industry discussions, agreement was reached on DVD, variously taken to mean Digital Video Disc or Digital Versatile Disc, and the different applications of this are described in "The Media Maze" which follows.

The Media Maze

John Borwick

The meteoric rise and global penetration of CD took place despite the emergence of several rival formats each, at first, touted as a genuine break-through.

Digital Audio Tape (DAT)

The first was Digital Audio Tape (DAT) whose imminent arrival was heralded in a notorious article in *The Sunday Times* dated June 29th, 1986 which began with the words "Compact Discs are about to be made obsolete" and showed a photograph of an unidentified man holding a TDK blank DAT cassette to his ear! This spectre of a new all-powerful audio format, announced in a respected newspaper, did alarm many record collectors and certainly annoyed everyone in the record industry firmly committed to the continued promotion of the CD medium.

Regular ***Gramophone*** readers, hopefully, were not too upset by this false report, having been kept informed of DAT's progress since the original DAT Conference was held away back on June 14th, 1983 (the year of CD's launch in the UK). This Conference set up separate working groups to study the viability of a consumer digital tape medium based either on the stationary head (S-DAT) or rotary head (R-DAT) principle. Subsequent meetings during 1985 and 1986 did indeed sideline S-DAT (later to find application in the Philips DCC format discussed below) as being too technicaly complex, and agreed on an R-DAT standard.

Nevertheless, to 'put the record straight' following that *Sunday Times* story, ***Gramophone*** published an article in the December 1986 issue which retold the DAT development history and described how it worked. The cassette measures only 73 × 54 × 10·5mm yet contains enough tape for up to two hours recording. The drive is like a miniature videocassette mechanism with a tiny head drum rotating at 2,000rpm and two heads scanning a helical track as the tape runs at a linear speed of only 8·15mm/s. Three sampling frequencies are available – 32, 44·1 and 48kHz – and performance is basically equal to CD standards.

DAT was given the go-ahead in 1989 but promotion as a consumer product never really took off due to lengthy discussions on a copy inhibiting scheme which was finally incorporated as an SCMS (Serial Copy Management System) code. Professionals, however, were quick to see DAT's advantages as a portable recorder, backup machine or even for the preparation of CD masters. Though very few prerecorded DAT cassettes have been issued, falling prices may yet see DAT increase in popularity unless some rival format intervenes.

DAT tape path

Direction of head rotation (2,000rpm)
Drum 30mm in diameter
Pinch roller
90°
Capstan
Direction of tape travel

Two more promising, and certainly more affordable, consumer digital systems did indeed appear within a few months of each other in 1992. One was a tape medium and the other an optical disc, launched respectively by Philips and Sony who, despite having collaborated so successfully in the development of CD, now found themselves in conflict. The rival media had much in common, coming close to CD sound quality standards but employing data reduction techniques to economize in storage capacity requirements, and both seemed to have the same target – to provide a replacement for the ageing analogue compact cassette. They both offered a recording facility as well as playback.

Digital Compact Cassette (DCC)

The Philips approach (launched in the UK in April 1992) was to use a tape cassette of the same dimensions, tape width, running speed and playing time as the analogue cassette (their own invention 30 years earlier) and so enable the new machines to play (but not record) standard

A typical DAT recorder, the Sony DTC-55ES

DCC spreads its digital data across nine tracks as shown here. The replay head also caters for the conventional analogue compact cassette

DCC head configuration

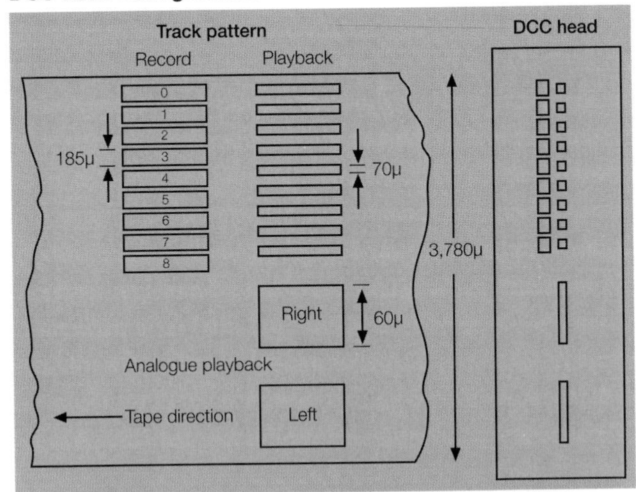

Technics RS-DC10 DCC recorder

cassettes. Digital Compact Cassette (DCC) uses a stationary head of a new design which spreads the digital data over nine tracks, with separate conventional L/R head gaps for analogue cassettes.

Though it was promoted by both the audio and music industries, DCC failed to generate a significant volume of software and the public stuck to their tried and trusted, though plainly less good, analogue cassettes. The almost simultaneous arrival of Sony's MiniDisc system in the UK (November 1992) didn't help and, by 1997, the system effectively ceased production.

MiniDisc (MD)

Sony's M2-1 Walkman, portable MiniDisc recorder

Sony preferred to continue with the CD laser-scanned disc approach. Their MiniDisc (MD) is only 64mm (2·5in) in diameter and contains 74 minutes of music just like a CD. Prerecorded MDs are manufactured on very similar production lines to CD, but the blank discs for user recording are of the more complicated magneto-optical type. Within the usual sequence of layers on a CD is added a pre-grooved layer of magnetic material sandwiched between two dielectric layers.

During recording, the focused spot from a laser-beam source momentarially heats the magnetic layer to the so-called 'Curie point' at which the individual mag-

MiniDisc recording

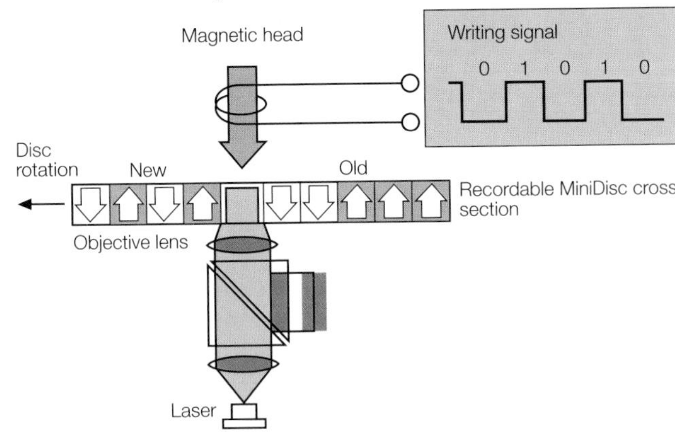

Playback of recordable MiniDisc

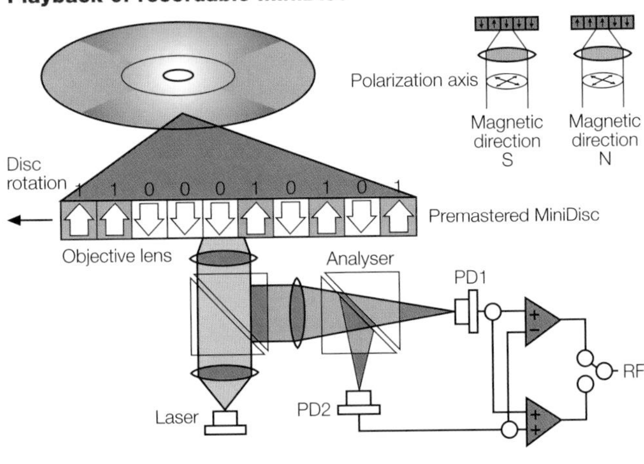

Playback of playback-only MiniDisc

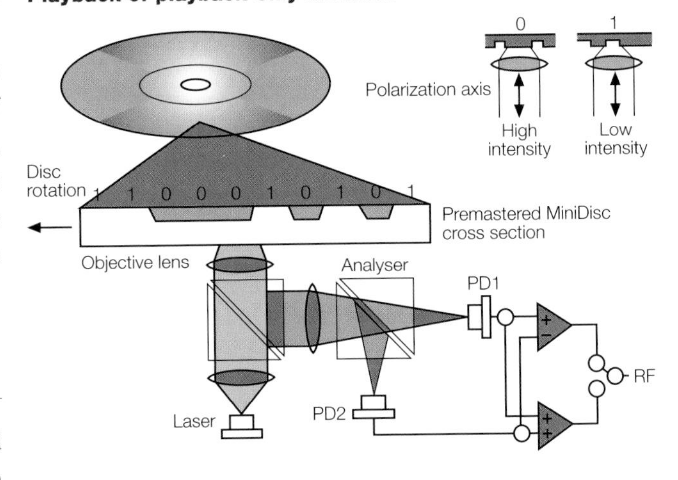

netic particles are susceptible to polarity reversal by a relatively weak external field. An electromagnetic recording head scans the track on the opposite side from the laser and the North/South pulses corresponding to the digital signal current through the head are recorded as a series of polarity reversals. Any previous recording is erased, giving MD the advantage of re-recordability which the recordable CD-R lacks. (The later CD-RW format, however, introduced Re-Writable CDs – p. 243).

For playback, the laser source acts as a conventional optical pickup with an additional magneto-optical readout analyser. The N/S magnetized pattern introduces alternating clockwise and anticlockwise rotation of the polarization of the reflected light which is converted into the required digital bitstream.

Unlike Philips, who began with mains-operated DCC machines, Sony first emphasized the small dimensions of MD by introducing battery-operated portables with a new buffer type of shockproof memory technology. It is fair to say that MD has established wider acceptance than DCC, amongst professionals as well as amateurs, and whilst it still has to generate a worthwhile software catalogue it certainly cannot be dismissed.

Philips CDD3610 CD-Recordable/CD-ReWritable machine

The Media Maze examined

In 1995, *Gramophone* decided to clear away some of the confusion which rival media and ill-informed press announcements had brought to all aspects of home entertainment and communications. A series of four articles entitled *The Media Maze* in the April to July issues, running to a total of 39 pages, sought to "help readers avoid expensive mistakes and move forward with confidence into the undoubtedly exciting entertainment and communications worlds of the future". The articles divided the subject into four parts:

1 **Audio discs and tapes**
2 **Video discs and tapes**
3 **Sound and television broadcasting**
4 **Computers and multimedia**

Part 1 discussed all the audio media mentioned above and hinted at the likely 'convergence' of every application in years to come: "Ten years from now all audio-only disc and tape media will be under threat from multimedia formats. Domestic gear will almost all embrace video as well as audio (with four or more channels of surround sound) and 'on demand' cable and satellite systems will be reducing our need to buy entertainment software across the counter. In another ten years the promised credit card sized, solid state media could be upon us offering a new scale in pocketable extra-long-playing, super quality multimedia".

Part 2 performed a similar function for video and home cinema. It concluded that video tape is ultimately doomed but, "it is going to be many years before new media offer the right combination of recordability, erasability, portability, and most of all very low cost that is already offered by video tape. So VHS VCRs have a definite, if finite, future which may be extended by the advent of digital video tape systems". The virtues of LaserDisc were outlined, including the expected move towards Dolby's AC-3 digital surround sound encoding. However a revolutionary new high-density CD, then being researched in various quarters, was tipped to be the real way ahead.

Part 3 summarized the state of play in Digital Audio Broadcasting and multichannel music distribution by cable and satellite. It also described the changes already in place to transmit stereo and surround sound within television programmes as a boost to home cinema which of course depended mainly on video cassettes and LaserDiscs. Any move towards High Definition TV, however, was seen as still being two or three years away.

Part 4 spelt out the numerous possibilities provided by the multimedia computer and the Internet, and concluded that "It is difficult to be anything but excited about an international system which promotes easy communication between individuals".

Even as these four articles were being written, new developments were taking place and, by 1997, it was already felt necessary to publish a series of articles in the same four categories entitled *The Media Maze Revisited* (September and October issues). Individual advances were noted, such as preliminary announcements of a digital version of the VHS videocasssette; the domestic equivalent of Dolby Stereo Digital encoding then being used increasingly in the cinema; the launch by the BBC on September 27th, 1995 of Digital Audio Broadcasting (DAB) and preparations for a UK start-up by British Digital Broadcasting in July 1998 of the long-awaited digital land-based (terrestrial) television service; the arrival of more powerful, yet affordable, multimedia computers and 'games on CD' with more than an hour of filmed content with major actors and surround sound, plus a huge growth in the use of the World Wide Web; and the imminent launch of an erasable version of CD-Recordable to be called CD-RW (ReWritable). In the event, Philips brought to the marketplace in November

Denon DVD-2000

1997 a CD-RW machine able to handle both CD-R and CD-RW (Re-Writable) discs. The CDR 870 recorder (reviewed in the January 1998 issue) also broke the recordable CD price barrier, coming in at only £499 complete with a starter pack of four blank CD-R discs and one CD-RW disc.

Digital Versatile Disc (DVD)

DVD has four possible disc formats, offering up to 17 gigabytes of storage – 25 times that of a conventional CD

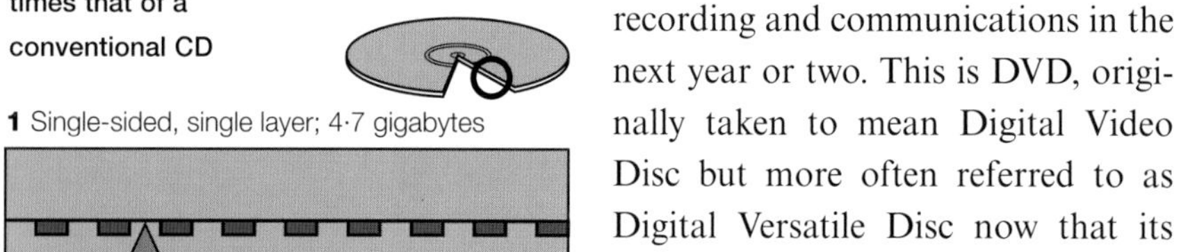

1 Single-sided, single layer; 4·7 gigabytes

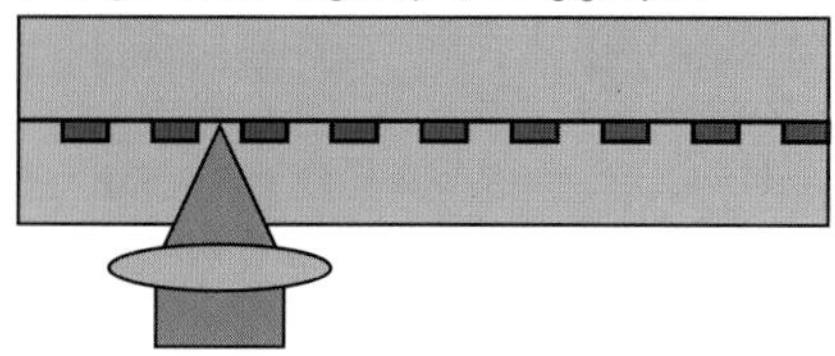

2 Double-sided, single layer: 10Gb

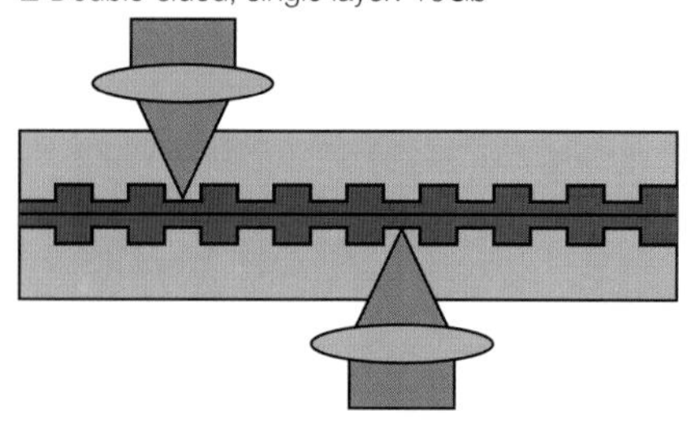

3 Single-sided, double layer: 9·4Gb

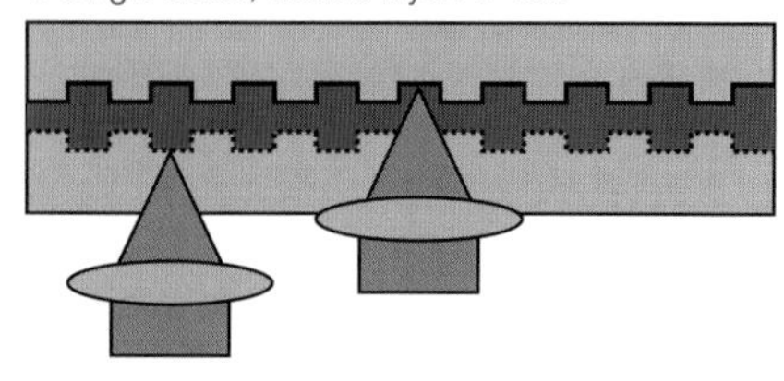

4 Double-sided, double layer: 17Gb

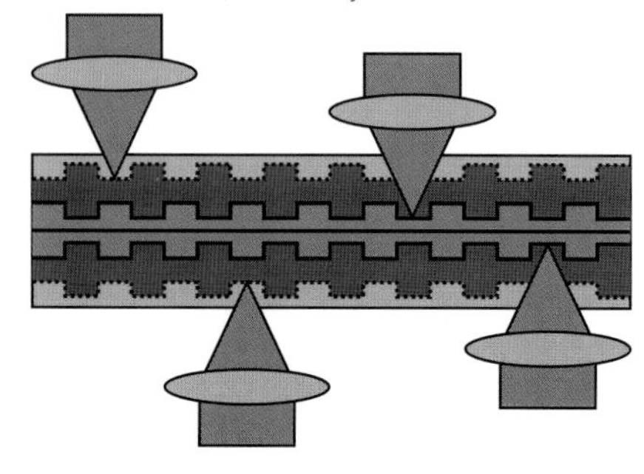

The most newsworthy item was a catch-all new version of the CD which seemed "destined to dominate all fields of recording and communications in the next year or two. This is DVD, originally taken to mean Digital Video Disc but more often referred to as Digital Versatile Disc now that its benefits for so many different aspects of the business have become apparent".

After wrangling amongst the interested parties through 1995-6 on the precise form of the next generation of high-density CD, agreement had been reached on DVD with a flexible specification that could be adapted to suit all foreseeable applications. In essence, DVD discs look very like ordinary CDs but achieve at least seven times more storage capacity by reducing both the size of the recorded 'pits' and the spacing between tracks by about half. Versions offering twice as much storage are produced by a dual-layer technique, and four times if a double sided dual-layer disc is employed.

The scanning laser beam has a shorter wavelength to enable it to 'read' this more tightly packed data stream and will automatically focus on the required layer on dual-layer discs. In addition, digital compression technology extends the programme capacity so that the single-layer, single-side disc, the first to put in an appearance in the marketplace, will accommodate up to the 133 minutes demanded by most feature films. Epic length films can be recorded non-stop on the dual-layer version.

Commercial considerations have given precedence to the needs of the video and computer industries, with DVD-Audio regarded as less urgent. A case for using this extra capacity to provide a greatly improved audio-only specification as a DVD option was strongly made by a hastily convened group called the Acoustic Renaissance for Audio (ARA), and outlined in our September and October 1995 issues. As it turned out, this need for a super-quality audio option is indeed written into the DVD specification. These Super CDs should offer a choice of 48 or 96kHz sampling with 16, 20 or 24 bit resolution and up to eight audio channels. The ARA Chairman, Bob Stuart of Meridian Audio, expressed himself, in an interview in the August 1997 issue, as basically satisfied with these provisions and so audiophiles everywhere have something to look forward to with interest.

JOHN BORWICK

John Borwick was born in Edinburgh in 1924. He served in the Royal Air Force before entering the British Broadcasting Corporation as a programme engineer in 1947. He balanced and supervised the recording and broadcasting of music programmes of all types, and later taught at the BBC Engineering Training School. Since leaving the BBC he has been a frequent broadcaster on audio/recording and has written or edited a number of books including *Microphones: Technology and Technique*, *Sound Recording Practice* and *Loudspeaker and Headphone Handbook*. He helped to set up the British AES Section in 1970 and was its first Secretary. In addition, he helped to formulate the four-year Bachelor of Music (Tonmeister) degree course at the University of Surrey in 1971 and was Senior Lecturer (Recording Techniques) for about ten years.

He joined ***Gramophone*** in December 1964 as Associate Technical Editor alongside Percy Wilson and has contributed to the Audio pages in practically every issue since, first as Audio Editor, then Audio Director and more recently Audio Consultant.

Percy Wilson, a gramophone man

Geoffrey Horn

Percy Wilson in the late 1960s with a Ferrograph tape recorder and an EMG Mk.10a gramophone

Percy Wilson's serious involvement with the gramophone began in his thirtieth year when he spent some £40, a considerable sum in the 1920s, on a handsome cabinet machine with internal horn. Born in Halifax on March 8th, 1893, he remained the consummate Yorkshireman all his days, although he spent most of them in the south. Leaving school he went to Queen's College, Oxford to take his BA in 1915. The Great War was then raging and his mathematics and science degree earned him a job as a Naval Instructor and later Lecturer in Applied Mathematics at the Royal Naval College.

In 1919, now married, he became an Administrative Officer in The Board of Education where he remained until 1938 when, with another war imminent, he transferred to the Roads Department of The Ministry of Transport as Principal Assistant Secretary; his long career in the Civil Service ending in 1953. But now, running in parallel with it, there was soon to be a second career with ***The Gramophone***. He recounts in Gilbert Briggs' celebrated book of *Audio Biographies* (Wharfedale Wireless Works, Idle: 1961) how his early view of the inadequacies of the gramophone was completely upset by a record bought as a Christmas present for his mother-in-law in 1919. On it were Caruso, Galli-Curci etc. singing extracts from *Lucia di Lammermoor* and *Rigoletto*. It "just bowled me over". He immediately started saving for that £40 machine.

The autumn of 1923 found him walking with his wife in Cheapside when he saw a copy of the third issue of ***The Gramophone*** in a music shop. Noting it was edited by Compton Mackenzie he bought it, was greatly intrigued and wrote off for the first two issues. Sadly issue number two was sold out, but in number three he had found that there was a continuing discussion about Needle Tracking Alignment and this intrigued Percy for, as he told me many years later, he had been over similar ground in his naval career. Apparently at some stage he had been required to produce formulae for the trajectory of the shells fired from the huge guns carried by our

An HMV cabinet gramophone similar to the one originally owned by Percy Wilson. Price £37 10s. in Oak or £42 10s. Mahogany

129 *The Gramophone, September*, 1924

NEEDLE-TRACK ALIGNMENT

By P. WILSON

1. At the present time there appear to be about five or six types of tone-arm in general use, *e.g.*,

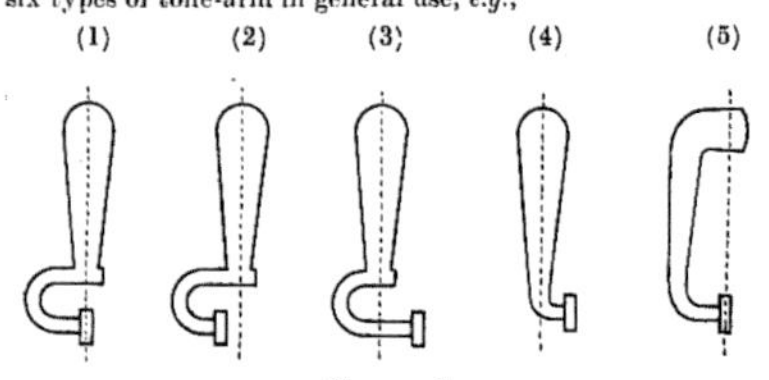

FIGURE 1.

Modifications of these types exist, but it is unnecessary to describe them here since, from a geometrical point of view, all types fall into one or other of three simple classes. In all rigid tone-arms the straight line joining the pivot to the needle is fixed relative to the plane of the diaphragm. The two important features (geometrically) of tone-arm design are, therefore:

(1) the length of this line, hereafter called the "vector";

(2) the angle which it makes with the plane of the diaphragm, hereafter called the "divergence."

The three fundamental classes of tone-arm are, therefore:

CLASS 1. CLASS 2. CLASS 3.

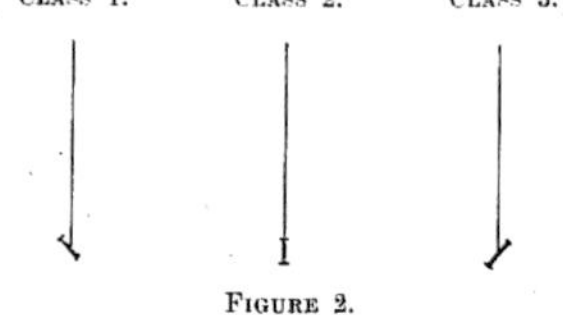

FIGURE 2.

Class 1 is usually seen in tone-arms with a short goose-neck (Type 2, Fig. 1), Class 2 in tone-arms with the normal pattern goose-neck (Type 1) and in the old Grafonola (Type 5), and Class 3 in the straight type of tone-arm (Type 4) and in tone-arms with an overhanging goose-neck (Type 3).

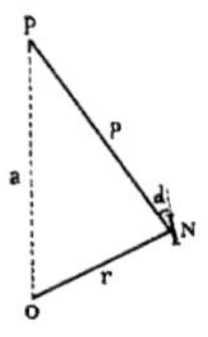

FIGURE 3.

In goose-neck tone-arms Class 1 may be converted into Classes 2 and 3, and Class 2 into Class 3, either by lengthening the goose-neck (*e.g.*, with a piece of garden hose) or by altering the orientation of the sound-box (see, for example, Mr. Little's letter on page 106, Vol. II., of THE GRAMOPHONE).

2. We can study the characteristic geometrical features of these three classes by considering the following diagram:

$OP = a$ is the distance between the pivot and the record centre, hereafter called the "base."

$PN = p$ is the distance between the pivot and the needle (the "vector").

$ON = r$ is the distance between the record centre and the needle in some particular groove (the "radius").

d is the angle which the vector makes with the diaphragm (the "divergence"). This will be considered positive in the position shown. This corresponds to Class 3. If $d = 0$ we get Class 2, and if d is negative we get Class 1.

The angle which the diaphragm makes with the radius is equal to $d +$ angle ONP. The diaphragm is tangential to the groove if this is a right angle. The "tracking error" is, therefore, $90° \sim (d + ONP)$. We will denote this by "x." If we agree that x may be either positive or negative in sign, we can write

$$x = 90° - d - ONP$$

so that $x + d = 90° - ONP$.

$$\sin(x+d) = \cos ONP$$

$$= \frac{p^2 - a^2 + r^2}{2pr} \text{ from the triangle}$$

$$= \frac{p^2 - a^2}{2p} \cdot \frac{1}{r} + \frac{1}{2p} \cdot r.$$

It is apparent from this equation that if p and a are both very large, and if p is equal or very nearly equal to a, then $x + d$ is very small. Hence, provided we keep the difference between the vector and the base relatively small, the longer the tone-arm the better chance we have of reducing tracking error. Practical considerations, however, place a limit on these lengths. For acoustical reasons it is essential that the tone-arm should have a definite taper, and should not be much less than ¾ inch at the sound-box end. The vector cannot, therefore, be much longer than 15 inches, since otherwise the width of the tone-arm at the pivot would be unmanageable. This condition can most easily be expressed mathematically by assuming that either a or p is of fixed length. We shall, therefore, assume that p is (a mathematical) constant.

The length of tone-arms varies a good deal. The normal length, I suppose, is about 9 inches; my own is nearly 13 inches. It cannot be too strongly insisted that very short pivoted tone-arms make for bad reproduction and ruined records: I have seen some which are barely 5 inches.

3. From the foregoing it is clear that there are two variables, a and d, which we can use to determine the best conditions for the reduction of tracking error. As they are independent, it would appear that we could determine values for these variables which would satisfy any two conditions. For example, we might determine "a" so that the tracking error is zero for some particular value of "r," and then determine "d" so that the mean value of "x" (neglecting sign) is as small as possible. Or we might try to find values which will make the greatest value of "x" as small as possible over a range of values of r, and at the same time make the rate of change of x as small as possible.

4. It is usually said (see, for example, page 5 of Capt. Barnett's "Gramophone Tips") that in order to get good

The first page of Percy Wilson's September 1924 article on needle-track alignment showing something of the mathematics involved

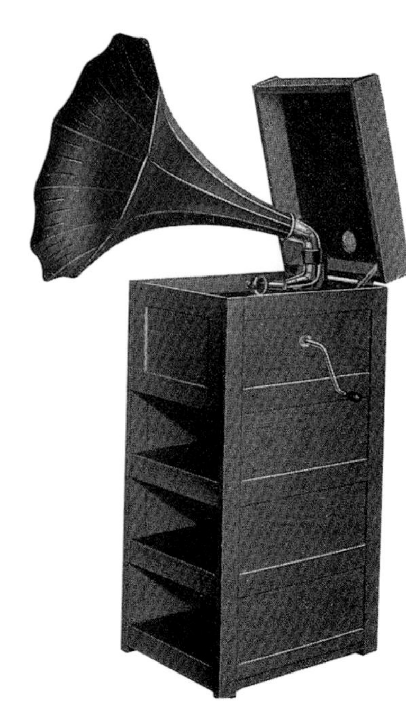

Percy Wilson's second gramophone, the HMV "Schools" model with external flared horn, so-called because the cabinet was designed "to harmonize with School furniture". Price £12

capital ships and this had proved to be an extremely daunting task pushing his considerable mathematical abilities to their limit. The similarities with needles working across non-radial transits of the disc immediately engaged his active brain.

His need to consult the missing second issue of the magazine took him one lunch hour to the editorial offices where he met Christopher Stone, the London Editor, who managed to find him a copy. It was the first of many visits and soon he was able to tell him that he had worked out mathematically the conditions for minimum tracking error. Stone immediately invited Percy to turn it into a form suitable for publishing and the result appeared in the issues for September and October 1924, running to six pages with a fair complement of mathematics which, although not difficult, would startle the modern reader. It also startled some of the readers of 1924 who had not experienced scientific theory applied to playing records before. It could be said that Percy was instrumental – with this and his subsequent writings on many allied subjects, not least his remarkable ability to think in terms of the future – in causing this burgeoning industry to take a much more professional approach to design. Those two articles in particular, with their subsequent additions, are classics and as valid today in the dying years of pickup arms as they were then; a memorial which has far outlasted its author.

Those early days saw the creation of many gramophone societies whose members included a fair sprinkling of highly placed professional people from all walks of life who found relaxation in music. The value of the tracking articles was not lost on them and resulted in invitations for Percy to talk at their meetings. In this way he made many influential friends who would help him progress the future of the gramophone over its growth years between the wars. A number of them persuaded him that his £40 gramophone had not been the wisest buy and he exchanged it for an HMV "Schools" model with an external flared horn and four-spring motor. Together they experimented with tuning the "Exhibition" sound-box and running melted wax down the joints in the 'flower petal' horn to prevent rattles. As he was to write, it became "easily the best gramophone I heard in those days". A rival was the machine later used by Compton Mackenzie which had been built by another part-time enthusiast, C. L. Balmain, then Deputy Controller of the Stationary Office; a note in the December 1924 issue invited interested readers to visit the Frith Street office to hear it. This ingenious model used a conical horn and sound-box which was arranged to float radially across the

December 1924 **News**

Mr Balmain is making one of his gramophones for the office, and this will be installed at Frith Street before Christmas. By the courtesy of the makers, to whom our best thanks are due, it will be fitted with (1) a Motophone, and (2) an HMV No. 2 Sound-box. If any of our readers are anxious to hear the machine, they will be very welcome at the office; but it is advisable to make an appointment beforehand.

March 1925

THE WILSON PROTRACTOR

Important notice Opposite will be found a Diagram, exact to scale, of a protractor prepared by Mr Wilson for the benefit of our readers. It will, if used, convince them how deceptive the naked eye can be in the estimation of errors of alignment. It is backed by an advertisement, like the Translations, and can be cut out and pasted on cardboard, so that each reader can judge for himself whether his machine is doing unnecessary damage to his records. If sufficient applications are sent to the London Office we are prepared to supply the protractor printed upon cardboard, and ready for use at a nominal charge to cover the cost of printing and postage.

Directions for assembling

1 Cut out the pointer and the protractor enclosed within the rectangle.
2 Paste the protractor smoothly on a piece of cardboard (or 3-ply) which is approximately the same thickness as a record.
3 When quite dry, cut out the slot of the protractor.
4 Paste the pointer on a piece of thin but stiff card.
5 Pivot the pointer on the protractor at the points marked by means of a drawing pin. Cut off or file down the point of the drawing pin so that it does not project through the card on the under side.

Directions for use

1 Place the slot over the spindle and the needle on one or other of the points x,y or z. The distances of the needle from the spindle are measured on the slot scales. If the point y is used the mean of the readings is taken.
2 Rotate the pointer until the lines drawn on it are parallel to the face of the sound box and read off the angle of error from the protractor scale.

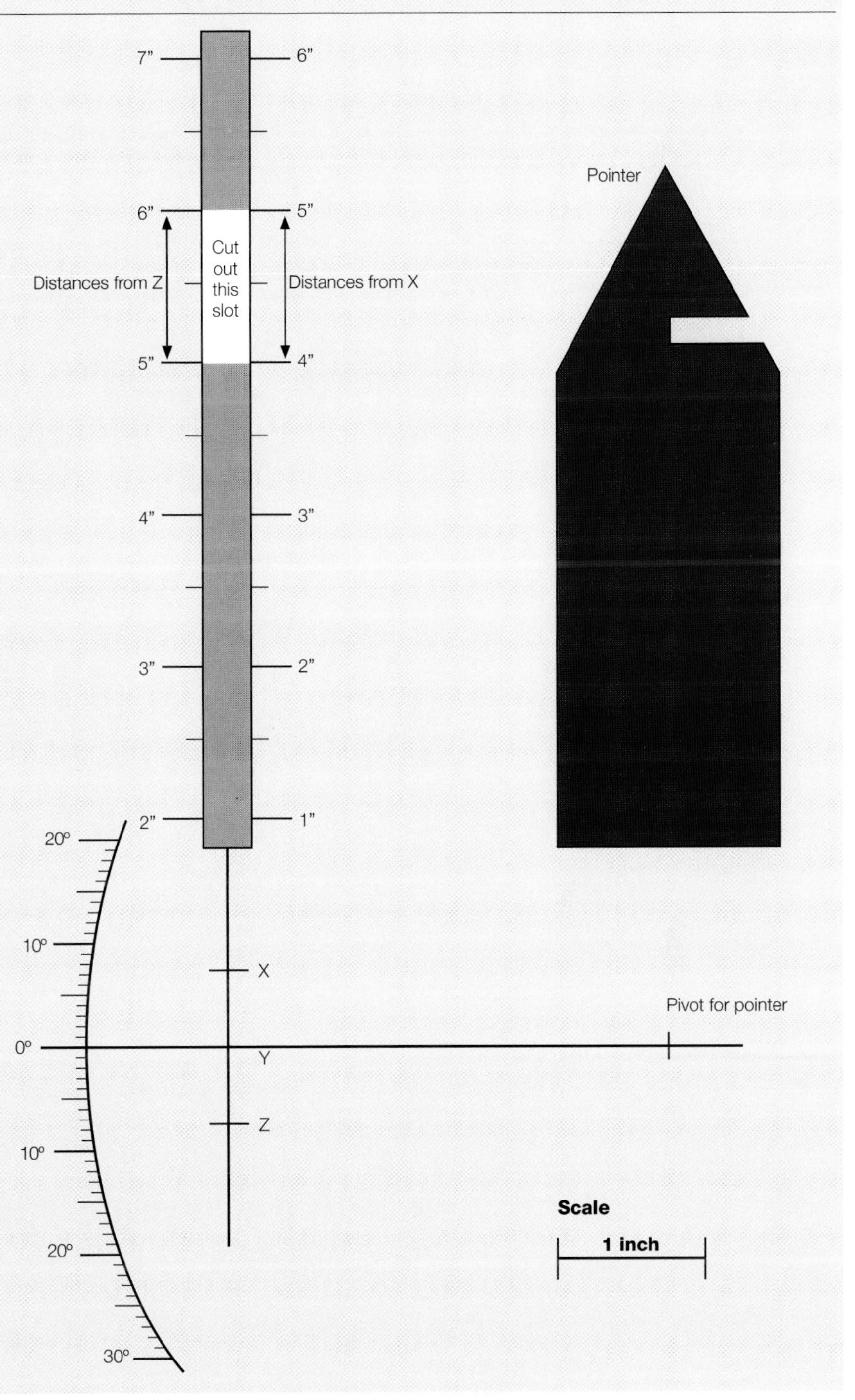

record on two open mercury baths – a material since known to be such a deadly poison that dire warnings are even packed with thermometers in case one is broken. How did we survive these dangers!

Percy became a regular contributor to the magazine and added the famous Alignment Protractor (March 1925) to his inventions; he was also aware of side pressure (or skating force) and suggested a simple remedy in the same issue. In November 1924 Christopher Stone proposed the setting up of an Expert Committee to advise on technical matters and this was easily formed from gramophone society friends, later joined in electrical recording days by more anonymous members from the National Physical Laboratory. Discussion had taken place about the shape of horns and George Webb, a member of the Committee and master builder with a huge collection of recording machinery, as well as a fine engineering workshop, had suggested 'exponential'. Percy was thus

October 1926

Compton Mackenzie Editorial

THE EXPERT COMMITTEE ARRIVE ON JETHOU

The arrival of the Expert Committee was heralded by the apparent conversion of my boat into a small steamship, due to the presence on deck of an enormous horn with which they arrived. This had been designed by Mr Wilson in strict deference to the higher mathematics, and had achieved, as is so often the case, a genuine beauty of form in consequence. A Triton blowing such a horn might make a Siren envious. The position of affairs, I may remind our readers, was that I had been inclined to suppose that no small sound-box could compete with electric recording, and that the Expert Committee had been inclined to suppose that the HMV No. 4 would inevitably be beaten in any competition with a properly tuned small sound-box. In the end we arrived at the conclusion that we were both right, or both wrong, whichever way you like to put it. In other words, while the Committee owned that for broad impressionistic orchestral effects the No. 4 sound-box was better than any small sound-box they had yet managed to produce, I was equally willing to admit that on every other kind of record the small sound-box was the victor. In a sense the Committe retired victors, because they were perfectly convinced that they could produce a small sound-box to beat the No. 4 in broad orchestral effects without losing any detail, and the adjustments they managed to make in existing sound-boxes during this week were so remarkable that I feel fairly confident in saying that they will produce this all-conquering small sound-box. I hope that this announcement will not plunge our readers into despair, because it must be remembered that for the Committe to produce these results they must carry with them yards of indiarubber tubing, enough mica to glaze a large greenhouse, dozens of spirit levels, gimlets, bradawls, pincers, and screwdrivers, not to mention a portmanteau full of sound-boxes waiting outside the fold, and another portmanteau full of sound-boxes which have been admitted. In addition to their own equipment, they had the tool-box of my carpenter, and a quantity of wood lying about for building purposes on which they fell like wolves. I should feel extremely chary about turning them loose in any house that was not already in the hands of builders, because I am convinced that nothing would deter them from tearing down partitions, unslating roofs, and even vivisection, if by such they could advance the millionth part of an inch along the road to gramophonic perfection.

OUR EXPERT COMMITTEE
Waiting for the first note

Certainly as things are at present it is clear that the various compromises in which gramophone makers have indulged are the only possible solution of the problem. One has to consider the sum total of rooms, the sum total of individual tastes, the questions of fool-proof working, and so many other considerations before one can produce a machine that will suit everybody's pocket, preferences, and house. I have no doubt whatever that with a Balmain machine refitted with the Wilson horn, and placed in Mackenzie surroundings, nowhere else at this moment in the whole world can even a faintly comparable performance be given of the latest recordings. But it would be ridiculous to suggest that such a performance would suit the conditions in which the majority of gramophiles spend their leisure. There are neighbours to be considered, sleeping children, and perhaps more than all the fact that the average person does not really enjoy the devil's own row in his room when he comes back tired from work amid the detestable surroundings of contemporary urban existence. Not that the new Wilson horn is merely a device to make more noise than any other. It gives a quality and fineness to the music when used with fibre needles which I have never heard equalled, and it is equally successful with the No. 4 sound-box, the new Orchorsol sound-box, and the special sound-boxes which the Expert Committee brought down with them in hundreds. You may be able to realise their prodigality with these sound-boxes when I tell you that most of my grates contain excommunicated members of the fold. What I am waiting for now is to hear of the arrest of the whole Committee at Weymouth, because I cannot believe that any Excise Officer will treat them as anything but a party of militant anarchists. "Have you anything to declare?" You can imagine the faces of the Customs officials when each of them declares a portmanteau full of sound-boxes tuned to favour anything from a bat's squeak to a stag-beetle's drone. Yes, I very much doubt if any of them get back to London on the evening of September 13th. If you could have seen the most Mozartian member listening for two hours to jazz played by the very loudest needle procurable, and heard him murmur at the end of it that, if we ever went to war with America, whatever his age he would be the first to join up, you would realise what an enthusiast is prepared to endure for the sake of truth.

inspired to investigate the theory of horns, a neglected subject left to the ingenuity of the makers of megaphones, trumpets and trombones. By the end of 1925 he had derived formulae for the curve based on the assumption that the expanding wavefronts were spherical and should pass the horn contour at a right angle. The method was explained in *Modern Gramophones* written with G.W. Webb (Cassell, London: 1929).

Making one was a different matter but a visit to a pattern maker provided a wooden former some five feet long on which layer after layer of parcel tape was pasted, dried out and varnished. The resulting horn was then mounted on a Balmain carriage so that it could be floated on the mercury in place of the original. The Expert Committee decided it should be demonstrated to Mackenzie then living on Jethou, one of the smaller Channel Islands. They took it down in the late summer of 1926 and, as Percy often gleefully narrated, completed the journey in a small boat with Percy in the stern holding all five feet of the precious horn between his knees.

It so happened that Mackenzie had just taken delivery of a new HMV machine fitted with the No. 4 sound-box which he had reluctantly found superior to his old Balmain. Choosing a Sousa march, one of the latest electrical recordings, they used the No. 4 on the new horn and floated it on Mackenzie's Balmain; the resulting sound was a revelation, a complete walkover and full justification of Percy's design. Back in England modifications were put in hand to make adaptors for the "Schools" and other machines and a firm with expertise in Papier mâché (Scientific Supply Stores) engaged to market it as the Wilson Panharmonic Horn. He later told me that as his colleagues had been so involved his Yorkshire canniness deserted him and he asked for no share of the profits, even when competing firms such as EMG and Bond used the design.

However, in the gramophone world the arrival of electrical recording and reproduction was beginning to make its mark. Percy was well aware that if any attempt was to be made to cover a full range of sounds, down to the lowest notes, the horn would have to be large and he commissioned an eight-foot straight horn of square section which exactly fitted the upper half of his hall doorway; it could be raised and lowered by a system of pulleys and ropes. This apparently produced a superb sound for its day but we have no record of his wife's comments when she had to bend double to pass under it. Allowing for the fact that doorways in older houses were at least three feet wide we can calculate that it would have maintained full (high) efficiency down to at least 100Hz. The need for ever lower frequencies spelt the eventual death of the horn for domestic purposes but there were one or two ingenious variants by Paul Voigt in England and Klipsch in America.

Percy however was to have one last fling: early in the 1930s the Science Museum in London decided to install a state-of-the-art wireless receiver and invited him to design a huge horn loudspeaker which would be fixed to propagate through a seven-foot square hole cut in the partition wall between two sections of the museum. This 27-foot-long monster was hung from the ceiling and provided with a Western Electric type 555 driver, a new and very advanced moving-coil design with a 2-inch aluminium dome diaphragm fed through a phase aligned coupling to the 1-inch horn throat. I recall as a boy hearing this magnificent effort which was fed from a receiver of considerable complexity and about the size of an old-fashioned telephone kiosk! It was switched on to the BBC London Regional programme, broadcasting from the new Brookmans Park transmitter at three o'clock every afternoon, and it was startling to hear the completely natural voice of the announcer sounding throughout the large hall.

The change to electrical reproduction made considerable organizational demands on the technical team and during the latter part of 1929 Christopher Stone decided to appoint Percy's younger brother Gilbert as Technical Editor. However, Percy continued as Technical Adviser and contributed a worthy series of articles which soon

Percy Wilson's horn loudspeaker mounted in one of the halls of London's Science Museum. During the last war this part of the Museum was bombed and in the post-war reconstruction the speaker was destroyed

acquired the generic title "Technical Talk"; they still make fascinating reading and contain many pointers to future developments which have since come to pass. Long-playing records and the possibility of stereophonic reproduction were among the subjects discussed. It was also the age of the radiogram and the annual autumn exhibitions at Radiolympia, but one common invention had really set the stage on which the whole industry performed and is still produced by the million today – the moving-coil cone loudspeaker.

War was declared in September 1939, in the middle of that year's Radiolympia. Much of the emphasis was on television, which had been inaugurated in November 1936 but was now to close-down for the duration of the war – although not before the TV sound-channel had been used to broadcast the Promenade Concerts from London's Queen's Hall, giving a tantalizing foretaste of the quality of sound to come. Percy and Gilbert ceased their activities for ***The Gramophone*** and technical comment in a much slimmed-down magazine was undertaken by Geoffrey Howard-Sorrell who held the reins until 1953, thus covering the important post-war years and the introduction of the long-playing record.

Percy, then with the Ministry of Transport, had a very busy time during the war but news of developments in audio and recording reached him from America via his friendship with David Sarnoff, later President of RCA. He learnt of the successful tests of FM broadcasting and of longer playing records – an early application of the latter took the form of the "V Disc" which was issued to US forces and used a flexible base material to avoid breakage and would later lead to the vinyl LP. Not much news emerged from the UK although progress in recording was being made, both to increase the frequency range for sound identification and in recording on acetate for broadcasting. However, informed listeners became aware that something novel was being used in Germany and at the end of hostilities the development of tape recording was revealed.

Retiring from the Civil Service in 1953 enabled Percy to relieve Geoffrey Howard-Sorrell of the burden he had carried so well and return as Technical Editor. Wartime pressures had resulted in developments in all fields of electronics and many people now found themselves immersed in and intrigued by the subject. Their wartime training, and the vast amount of surplus equipment sold off at ridiculous prices, encouraged an expansion of home electronics and as a result self-built amplifiers and other gear such as the emerging tape recorder proliferated. At the same time pre-war manufacturers, now with enlarged wartime facilities, came back into the field and produced some excellent products, such as the famous Decola. Percy, although *au fait* with electrical matters following his university years, never had the same inclination to involve himself in electronics; to him it was a means to an end. Although very much a hands-on man and inveterate experimenter, it was the mechanical side which had the greatest appeal. Therefore he had the foresight to recruit a number of people to help with reviewing equipment. This was complicated because they could not be directly employed by any particular manufacturer but fortunately there were a few consultants such as the late John Gilbert of the Northern Polytechnic and Stanley Kelly, happily still with us, who could be called upon.

In 1934 Percy had been involved with an early form of long-playing record required for Talking Books for the Blind: these had a duration of 24½ minutes per side at 24rpm. However, the stock held by the Royal National Institute for the Blind became unmanageable so in the early 1950s it was decided to change over to tape. Percy was again one of the team and helped to develop an early cassette player using half-inch tape travelling between two reels, one atop the other with 24 tracks giving 12 hours duration, later extended to 20 hours. This was probably the first cassette conception and produced an easily handled and readily transported medium. (A full description was given in *Wireless World* for January 1954.)

In the late 1950s Percy came to live in Oxford with his second wife and took a house in Headington. In 1949, on the other side of the city in Summertown, Philip Tandy and I had taken over a Radio and TV business which had been pioneered by my father. He had started up in the front room of his house in 1922 and two years later had been so successful that a shop front was put in and a proper business established, one of the first wireless-only shops in the country. We made an early decision to specialize in the growing field of high fidelity reproduction; it had always been a major interest and hobby of mine since boyhood – Philip's was music and 'ham' radio. My pre-war education was as an electronics man, initially with what was then the Post Office Engineering Department. Together we were innocents in the world of retailing but enthusiasm won the day.

Eventually we met Percy who was very pleased to discover a shared interest, and particularly to gain access to our workshop which was equipped with a good selection of test equipment. Entering with a carton containing some manufacturer's amplifier or whatever, he became a familiar sight, accompanied by his inevitable, "Would you run your rule over this?". Not infrequently in those days of hopeful cottage industries, and even large and established manufacturers trying to jump on this promising new bandwagon, the rule could not be made to fit and Percy, apprised by telephone, would come over in the evening to get the details which he would relay back to the manufacturer, often with suggestions for improvement. It was always his policy, still continued, to do this and not publish a negative review. As he often said, a bad review could put a small firm out of business when their next product might well have been a corker.

Percy became known to industry personnel on both sides of the Atlantic for he was a frequent visitor to the USA, where two of his academic sons held Professorships at State Colleges. Whilst visiting he joined the Audio Engineering Society, then a purely American group of which he was later to be a founder member of the British Section. He had the rare gift in this calling of being able to keep a secret so that he and I were often privy to developments months, sometimes years, before they became commercial. Typical examples were visits to Arthur Haddy at the Decca studios in West Hampstead where we heard early examples of stereo LPs, at first using a supersonic difference signal, a project later abandoned in favour of the Blumlein patent. Early work by Peter Walker on electrostatic loudspeakers was also fascinating.

Early in 1957 Percy passed me a book which he had been sent for review, and asked if I would like to read it and make a few notes for him as he was going away and was pressed for time. I have forgotten exactly what it was but I duly did as asked. When he eventually collected it he read my notes and proclaimed, "You can write!"; I replied, "Yes I know, they taught me at school", but this did nothing for his Yorkshire sense of humour for he carried on, "I shall publish it just as it is". Thus began my totally unexpected but long and friendly association with ***Gramophone*** which continues to this day.

Percy retired in 1966, but for some years had become engrossed with the problem of LP groove contamination by dust and airborne deposits of sticky particles from both domestic and outside sources. His development of an automatic washing and scrubbing arm with nylon bristles entering the groove, followed by suction drying, has since been incorporated in a number of commercial machines. However, none of them used his rather impractical but ingenious silent sucker, a suction pump in a wooden box buried in his front garden with a long length of tubing passing through a hole in the window frame. Unwary visitors could be seen nervously looking around for the source of the chugging noise!

But this was not quite the end of Percy's involvement with audio. He and his family were Spiritualists, and indeed for many years he had been Managing Director of the Psychic Press Ltd. As a result of this connection he became involved as a consultant in a number of unique sound reinforcement projects – both in major hotels and also in Spiritualist churches – in all of which I was also associated.

At the end of this varied and distinguished career Percy finally did accept retirement, and went to live in a Red Cross home. He presented the Common Room with his record collection and, as you might guess, installed a high fidelity gramophone. He died on May 1st, 1977 at the age of 84.

GEOFFREY HORN

Geoffrey Horn was born in 1921. His father was one of the pioneers of radio retailing and, being of a scientific mind, was also concerned with the various aspects of set design. GH inherited and developed these interests, and in the post-war period worked closely with Percy Wilson. His first contribution to ***The Gramophone*** appeared in February 1957.

Geoffrey Horn and Percy Wilson in Percy's garden at 56 Staunton Road, Headington, Oxford in the early 1960s

Chronology

1922

September

- Compton Mackenzie contributes an article entitled "The Gramophone" to *The Daily Telegraph*.

1923

March

- First recording made by the Royal Family – King George V and Queen Mary at Buckingham Palace.

April

- Compton Mackenzie founds ***The Gramophone*** (***TG***) on the island of Herm.
- Louis Sterling becomes MD of the Columbia Graphophone Company.

June

- First recording of a complete string quartet – Brahms's Op. 51 No. 1 by the Catterall Quartet for HMV.

July

- ***TG*** opens offices at 25 Newman Street, London.
- Compton Mackenzie moves from Herm to Jethou.

September

- *The Radio Times* first published following the beginning of regular broadcasting from 2LO, London Station of The British Broadcasting Company in November 1922.

November

- Gustav Holst completes the recording of his *Planets* Suite with the LSO for Columbia.

December

- Alec Robertson's first contribution to ***TG***.

1924

April

- First recording of a British symphony by Vocalion – Sir John McEwen's *Solway* with Cuthbert Whitemore and the Aeolian Orchestra.

May

- H. C. Harrison of Western Electric is granted patent for electrical recording.

June

- ***TG*** organizes Steinway Hall tests.
- Herman Klein, opera critic, joins ***TG***.

July

- First complete recording of an opera in English made by HMV – Puccini's *Madam Butterfly* with Rosina Buckmann in the title-role and Tudor Davies as Pinkerton.

August

- Edward "Chick" Fowler joins The Gramophone Company.

September

- ***TG*** moves to 58 Frith Street, London.
- Percy Wilson's first contribution to ***TG***.

October

- First Electrical Process record made by The Gramophone Company at Hayes – King Henry V's Prayer, read by Mr Pack – using B.E.G. Mittell's system.

November

- The Expert Committee is formed at the instigation of Christopher Stone.

1925

February

- W. S. Barrell joins the Columbia Graphophone Company as Chief Engineer to Recording Dept.
- W. A. Chislett contributes his first reviews to ***TG***.

March

- The American Victor company electrically record Alfred Cortot playing Chopin's Impromptu No. 2 in F sharp, Op. 36 at their Camden studios.

May

- W. R. Anderson's first contribution to ***TG***.

June

- First Western Electric process recording made by HMV in the UK – *Ah! Ha!* by Jack Hylton and his Band.

July

- ***TG*** organizes a Congress at The Central Hall, Westminster – forerunner of today's audio exhibitions.

October

- Rice and Kellogg introduce a dynamic loudspeaker.

December

- Electrical recording comes into general use, four years after Columbia had first made experimental attempts in Westminster Abbey during the burial service for The Unknown Warrior in November 1920. The first release of an electrically recorded symphony, made by HMV, is Tchaikovsky's No. 4 with Sir Landon Ronald and the Royal Albert Hall Orchestra.
- 78rpm turntable speed standardized.

1926

March

- Cecil Pollard joins ***TG*** as Business Manager.

May

- First actual performance recording by HMV at The Royal Opera House, Covent Garden – Boito's *Mefistofele* with Chaliapin in the title-role.

June

- Melba's Covent Garden farewell appearance recorded live by HMV.

July

- First recording by the Casals/Cortot/Thibaud trio of Schubert's Piano Trio in B flat, D898 by HMV.

August

- W. W. Townsley joins Barnett Samuel, predecessor of Decca.

December

- Kenneth Wilkinson joins World Echo Record Company and later Crystalate.
- Brunswick introduce the Panatrope, the first all-electric gramophone.

1927

March

- Walter Legge joins The Gramophone Company.
- To mark the centenary of Beethoven's death, Columbia release the first complete set of symphonies.
- Victor introduces the first record-changing phonograph.

May

- Columbia make first electrical recording of a complete opera in English – Leoncavallo's *Pagliacci* with the British National Opera Company.

July

- Christopher Stone begins broadcasting for the BBC.

July/August

- Columbia make the first-ever recordings in the Festspielhaus, Bayreuth of excerpts from *The Ring* and *Parsifal*.

August

- David Bicknell joins The Gramophone Company, Artists Department.

September

- John Whittle joins The Gramophone Company, Advertisement Department.
- HMV record excerpts from public performances during the Three Choirs Festival in Hereford Cathedral.

October

- Edison introduces 40-minute long-playing discs in the USA.
- Première of *The Jazz Singer*, first commercially successful talking picture.

1928

August

- Atterberg's Symphony No. 6 wins the Schubert Memorial Prize – Columbia record the work with Beecham and issue the results prior to the public première. This was the first known instance of such an occurrence.

1929

January

- RCA acquires the Victor Talking Machine Company.

March

- Alan Blumlein joins the Technical Department of the Columbia Graphophone Company.

April

- G. W. Cook joins the Technical Department of the Columbia Graphophone Company.

July

- C. H. Thomas joins the Columbia Graphophone Company.
- First release of recordings from The Decca Record Company, under the direction of Edward Lewis, which include Delius's *Sea Drift* with Roy Henderson, Grainger's *Jutish Melody* and *Offenbach's Orpheus in the Underworld* Overture.

September

- *TG* moves to 10a Soho Square.
- L. G. Wood joins The Gramophone Company.

November

- Gilbert Wilson, brother of Percy, appointed Technical Editor of *TG*.
- Edison Company cease issue of cylinder and diamond discs.

1930

May

- First release in Columbia's "History of Music" series, eventually comprising five sets containing 40 10-inch 78rpm discs.

June

- Edgar Jackson joins *TG* to review jazz records.

September

- Alfred Clark becomes Chairman of The Gramophone Company, while still retaining his position as MD.

October

- Formation of the BBC Symphony Orchestra, the first permanent London orchestra since the foundation of the London Symphony Orchestra in 1904. The new orchestra make their début in the Queen's Hall.

December

- Compton Mackenzie leaves Jethou.

1931

April

- The Gramophone Company and the Columbia Graphophone Company merge to form Electric and Musical Industries Limited – EMI. Louis Sterling is appointed MD and Alfred Clark Chairman.
- HMV introduce the first of their Society Editions, conceived by Walter Legge – Elena Gerhardt singing Wolf Lieder.

September/November

- RCA launch a short-lived series of 10- and 12-inch 33⅓rpm discs in USA. These include Beethoven's Symphony No. 5 with Stokowski and the Philadelphia Orchestra – the first symphony to be specially recorded for this medium.

November

- EMI open their new Abbey Road Studios (Chief Engineer, W. S. Barrell; Manager, W. S. Purser) with Elgar conducting the LSO.

December

- A. D. Blumlein (EMI) takes out British Patent No. 394, 325 embracing all aspects of two-channel stereo recording.

1932

- Garrard introduce first separate automatic record-changer, model RCI.
- Bell Laboratories use "Oscar", a tailor's dummy, to make binaural recordings.

February

- Christopher Stone appointed Co-Editor of *TG*.

April

- BASF and AEG, in collaboration with Fritz Pfleumer, produce magnetic tape in Germany.

May

- Harry Sarton joins Decca as A&R Manager.

October

- First concert by the newly formed London Philharmonic Orchestra under Beecham in Queen's Hall.

1933

February

- First American symphony recorded by American Columbia – Roy Harris's Symphony No. 1 by Koussevitzky and the Boston Symphony Orchestra.

May

- Robin Legge, music critic, dies.

September

- Anna Instone joins BBC Gramophone Department.

1934

January

- Beecham and the LPO make experimental stereo recording for EMI of Mozart's *Jupiter* Symphony, using Blumlein's system.

March

- Herman Klein dies aged 78.

June

- HMV make the first recordings in the new Glyndebourne Opera House with concerted items from Morart's *Le nozze di Figaro* under Fritz Busch, with the arias being recorded the following year.

August

- Decca Records Inc., a subsidiary of The Decca Record Company, founded in New York.

October

- RCA introduce the first record club in USA.
- The term 'high fidelity' comes into use in record and equipment advertisements.
- First release in series "L'Anthologie Sonore" in France which eventually comprised over 150 78rpm discs.

1935

- George Fenwick, who joined The Gramophone Company in 1911, working in the Cabinet Factory, is appointed manager of the famous 363 Oxford Street showrooms.

October

- Decca record their first complete opera, Purcell's *Dido and Aeneas*, with 20-year-old Nancy Evans in the title-role.

1936

July

- National Federation of Gramophone Societies (later Federation of Recorded Music Societies) formed by W. W. Johnson and F. E. Young.

November

- BASF record Beecham and the LPO in concert at Ludwigshafen on magnetic tape.
- The British Broadcasting Corporation opens the world's first regular television service from Alexandra Palace, London.
- The first edition of *The Gramophone Shop Encyclopedia of Recorded Music* by R. D. Darrell is published. Further editions appear in 1942 and 1948.

1937

March

- Decca purchase the Crystalate Company, and with it their recording studios at 165 Broadhurst Gardens, West Hampstead, together with two engineers, Arthur Haddy and Kenneth Wilkinson.

November

- Beecham makes the first classical recording by an English conductor in Berlin – Mozart's *Die Zauberflöte*, recorded by HMV. (Bandleader Jack Hylton had recorded there in November 1927.)

1938

January

- Mahler's Symphony No. 9 with Walter and the Vienna Philharmonic Orchestra recorded by HMV at a public concert in Vienna, prior to the Anschluss in March 1938.

November

- First NFGS "High Leigh" Conference.

December

- Columbia Broadcasting System (CBS) acquires the American Recording Company.

1939

- Goddard Lieberson joins CBS Masterworks as assistant to the Director.

January

- First releases on Louise Dyer's Oiseau-Lyre label reviewed in ***TG***.

April

- Fred Gaisberg retires from The Gramophone Company after 49 years in the Industry and is succeeded as Artists Manager by David Bicknell who joined the company in 1927.

May

- Sir Louis Sterling retires as MD of EMI and Alfred Clark continues as MD/Chairman.

October

- ***TG*** offices move to 49 Ebrington Road, Kenton, Middlesex.

1940

- *Fantasia*, filmed by the Walt Disney Studio with a stereo soundtrack, is released.

September

- ***TG*** leaves 10a Soho Square, London but retains a small basement office in Russell Square.
- George Winkworth joins ***TG*** as part-time Advertisement Manager.

October

- Walter Yeomans of The Decca Record Company dies.
- The British Chancellor of the Exchequer introduces Purchase Tax on gramophone records. Initially 33⅓ per cent on the price to the retailer. A 6s. [30p] 12-inch 78rpm disc is increased to 7s. 4d. [36p].

1941

May

- Cecil Pollard appointed London Editor of ***TG***.
- G. Howard-Sorrell joins ***TG***'s reviewing team.

1942

April

- EMI take advertising space on front cover of ***TG*** – continuing until May 1969.

May

- W. S. Purser, ex-Columbia Technical Manager, dies and is succeeded by Charles B. Gregory – who joined Columbia in 1895 – as Manager of the EMI Studios, Abbey Road.

June

- Capitol Records Inc is founded in USA by Glenn Wallichs, Johnny Mercer and Buddy DeSylva.
- Alan Blumlein and two other EMI research engineers are killed when a Halifax bomber crashes in the Wye Valley whilst carrying out airborne centimetric radar research critical to the war effort.

August

- James Caesar Petrillo, head of the American Federation of Musicians (AFM), introduces a ban on most recording activities in USA.

1943

September/November

- First recording sponsored by the newly created British Council undertaken by EMI – Moeran's Symphony in G minor by Heward and the Hallé Orchestra.

1944

June

- Decca commence the use of "Full Frequency Range Recording"– *ffrr* (the actual announcement was made in June 1945 – "in use over the past 12 months", the first important release being Stravinsky's *Petrouchka* with Ansermet and the LPO in 1946). EMI had a similar system which had been used when recording Holst's *Planets* with Boult and the BBC SO in January 1945 but it was not publicized at the time.

November

- AFM ban on recording in the USA ends.

1945

April

- Alfred Clark becomes President of EMI with Sir Alexander Aikman as Chairman and Sir Ernest Fisk as MD.

June

- RCA in America release the first 78rpm records pressed in vinyl – $2 as opposed to $1 – a limited exercise not copied elsewhere at the time.

August

- Founding of the Philharmonia Orchestra by Walter Legge.

October

- First public appearance of the Philharmonia Orchestra in the Kingsway Hall under Beecham.
- George Mendelssohn founds Vox Records in New York.

1946

January

- Charles B. Gregory dies and is succeeded as Manager of the EMI Abbey Road Studios by W. S. Barrell.

July

- Anthony Pollard joins ***TG***.

September

- Alfred Clark resigns as President of EMI.
- EMI make their first recording with Karajan and the VPO – Beethoven's Symphony No. 8.
- Founding of the Royal Philharmonic Orchestra by Sir Thomas Beecham.

November

- John Culshaw joins The Decca Record Company.

1947

- Limited introduction of magnetic tape for professional recording purposes.

August

- Deutsche Grammophon inaugurate their Archiv Produktion label under Dr Fred Hamel, initially covering the period from Gregorian Chant to circa 1800. The first recording was with Helmut Walcha at the small organ of the Church of St Jacobi, Lübeck.

1948

April

- ***TG*** Silver Jubilee is celebrated.

June

- The 33⅓ rpm long-playing record is introduced in the USA by Columbia Records Inc.

October

- Herbert Ridout dies.
- EMI introduce the use of magnetic tape for a number of their recording sessions.

November

- Lionel Salter joins ***TG***'s panel of reviewers.

1949

February

- 45rpm records introduced in the USA by RCA Victor.

April

- First release of Haydn Society 78s in the USA.

1950

- George R. Marek joins RCA as A&R Manager.
- Teldec is formed, a company jointly owned by Decca and Telefunken.
- Maurice Rosengarten becomes closely involved with Decca's classical catalogue.

January

- RCA Victor release LP records in the USA.
- First home tape recorders appear on the German market: UK follows 18 months later.

June

- Alfred Clark dies.
- Decca release its first 53 LP records in UK. The repertoire includes Beethoven's Symphony No. 5 (Schuricht and the Paris Conservatoire) and Piano Concerto No. 5 (Curzon/LPO/Szell) and Stravinsky's *Petrushka* (Ansermet and the Suisse Romande).
- Decca make their first opera in Vienna with the first-ever studio recording of Mozart's *Die Entführung aus dem Serail* with Krips and the VPO.

September

- First UK classical releases on Capitol label from Decca.

October

- The Nixa Record Company is established in the UK by Hilton Nixon – eventually to be called Pye Records.

1951

- Founding of the embryo British Institute of Recorded Sound by Patrick Saul. Fully established in 1955 and in 1983 to become The British Library National Sound Archive.

February

- First UK classical LP releases on the Telefunken label from Decca.

April

- Harry Sarton, Decca Artists Manager, dies.

July

- Nixa release LPs under licence from various American companies, including Concert Hall, Lyricord, Renaissance and Period.

July/August

- First Bayreuth Festival since 1943. Decca/Telefunken record *Parsifal* with Knappertsbusch, and EMI *Die Meistersinger von Nürnberg* and Act 3 of *Die Walküre* with Karajan.

September

- Cecil Pollard moves from Kenton to Green Lane, Stanmore and ***TG*** editorial office goes with him.
- Death of the pioneering recording supervisor and impresario Fred Gaisberg who had originally worked for Berliner in 1893 and came to London to make the first European recordings for the gramophone. He was 78.

December

- Argo Record Company founded by Harley Usill and Alex Herbage – first 78rpm releases.
- First LP release on Allegro label from Oriole.
- Sir Ernest Fisk resigns as MD of EMI.

1952

February

- First UK release of Haydn Society recordings on Parlophone 78s.

May

- Publication of the first volume of *The World's Encyclopaedia of Recorded Music: 1925-51*, compiled by Clough and Cuming. Further supplements appeared in 1953 and 1957.

July

- Compton Mackenzie is knighted in Queen Elizabeth II's first Birthday Honours List.

October

- L. J. Brown appointed MD of EMI.
- EMI release the first 45rpm records in the UK in addition to their first LP releases.
- First Argo LP releases.

November

- Vox release LPs in UK.
- American Vanguard label available in UK on Nixa.

December

- First Monarch LP releases.

1953

- French Erato label founded by Philippe Loury.

January

- First Philips popular 78s of British origin issued. Material from American Columbia followed in March on transfer of this label from EMI to Philips.

March

- First commercial stereo/binuaural recordings on tape made in Symphony Hall, Boston by Emory Cook.

June

- First edition of *The Gramophone Long Playing Record Catalogue* compiled by Stanley Day, comprised 112 pages and listed some 1,400 LPs and around 250 45s, priced at 2s. 6d. [12½ p].
- EMI launch their "History of Music in Sound". Completed in 1959 the series eventually comprised 10 volumes on 27 LPs.

August

- H. F. V. Little dies.
- Supraphon release LPs in UK.

September

- G. Howard-Sorrell hands back the technical editorship of ***TG*** to Percy Wilson.
- EMI Records Division moves from Hayes to Great Castle Street, London.

October

- Westminster release LPs in UK.

November

- Decca undertake their first experimental stereo recordings with Mantovani and his Orchestra at their West Hampstead studios.
- Oiseau-Lyre release LPs in UK.

1954

January

- Pye Black Box record-player introduced.

February

- Peter Andry joins Decca.

April

- EMI introduce extended-play 45rpm discs.

May

- Decca make their first commercial stereo recording in Victoria Hall, Geneva – Rimsky-Korsakov's *Antar* with Ansermet and the Suisse Romande Orchestra.

June

- Joseph (later Sir Joseph) Lockwood joins EMI as Chief Executive.
- Mercury release LPs in the UK – distributed by Oriole Records.

July

- First Philips LP release.

July/August

- First recordings of complete operas in stereo made by Decca in Rome – Verdi's *La traviata* and *Otello*, and Puccini's *Manon Lescaut*, all with Tebaldi.

August

- Reg Pollard joins ***TG*** to become Advertisement Manager in 1957.

September

- EMI introduce 7½ips pre-recorded reel-to-reel mono tapes.

October

- First Concert Artist LP release.
- RCA introduce "gruve-gard" LPs – raised rims and label areas.

November

- First Decca 45rpm releases.
- First Archiv/Heliodor LP release in the UK.
- Gilbert Briggs (Wharfedale) and Peter Walker (Quad) give first Royal Festival Hall demonstration of live and recorded sound.

November/December

- Decca make the first commercial stereo recording in UK – Grieg's Piano Concerto with Winifred Atwell, Stanford Robinson and the LPO.

1955

January

- ***TG*** joins Audit Bureau of Circulations.
- EMI acquire major interest in Capitol Records Inc.
- Emory Cook "Sounds of our Times" recordings released by Nixa.

February

- Deutsche Grammophon yellow label released in UK by Heliodor-Deutsche Grammophon Ltd.
- EMI's first commercial stereo recordings on tape, made in Kingsway Hall – Prokofiev's Symphonies

Nos. 1 and 7 with Malko and the Philharmonia.

March

- Isabella Wallich, niece of Fred Gaisberg, launches the Delysé label.

April

- Joe Batten, recording pioneer originally with Edison Bell and later Columbia, dies.

May

- Peter Dawson makes his final commercial recordings at EMI's Abbey Road Studios in stereo – the *Mandalay Scena* and *Clancy of the Overflow* with Mackerras and the LSO – over 50 years after his first cylinder recordings.

June

- Alec Robertson is appointed Music Editor of ***TG***.

October

- EMI release first "Stereosonic" 7½ips tapes in UK.

December

- First annual Critics' Choice feature in ***TG***.
- Amalgamations result in the formation of the Pye/Nixa label, to become Pye Records Ltd. in 1956.

1956

January

- First cover price increase for ***TG*** since June 1924, from 1s. [5p] to 1s. 6d. [7½ p].
- W. S. Barrell retires as Manager of EMI Studios, Abbey Road and is succeeded by Edward "Chick" Fowler, who joined HMV in 1924.
- World Record Club, the first UK record club, launched with Richard Attenborough (later Lord Attenborough) chairman of the selection committee.

April

- Mercury catalogue transfers to Pye Records in the UK.
- First European Audio Fair held in London at the Washington Hotel.

June

- First recordings made in UK by American engineers when Mercury undertook sessions with Barbirolli and the Hallé Orchestra in Manchester's Free Trade Hall. The works included the first recording of the new Vaughan Williams's Symphony No. 8 and Elgar's *Enigma* Variations.
- Record producers Victor Olof and Peter Andry leave Decca and move to EMI.

September

- Bhaskar Menon joins EMI as a management trainee.
- Gramophone turntables offering a fourth speed, 16⅔ rpm, now on the market but no discs so far.

October

- First recordings by a Soviet orchestra in Western Europe by DG – Tchaikovsky's Symphonies Nos. 5 and 6 with the Leningrad Philharmonic under Mravinsky.

December

- Karajan records Richard Strauss's *Der Rosenkavalier* for EMI at Abbey Road with Schwarzkopf as the Marschalin.

1957

January

- Erik Smith joins the Decca Classical Department.

February

- Geoffrey Horn's first contribution to ***TG***.

March

- Pye Records, in association with the British Council, record Tippett's *A child of our time* in Liverpool under Pritchard.

May

- George Winkworth, Advertisement Manager of ***TG***, dies.

June

- RCA Victor catalogue transferred in UK from EMI to Decca.
- Capitol label moves from Decca to EMI and introduces "Full Dimensional Sound" – FDS.

July

- Formation of EMI Records Ltd. – the first MD is C. H. Thomas.

September

- Quad Electrostatic loudspeaker introduced.

October

- Ray Minshull joins the Decca Classical Department.
- EMI introduce their "Great Recordings of the Century" series in UK.

November

- Argo acquired by Decca. They begin recording the complete works of William Shakespeare, completed in 1964 and totalling 137 LPs.

December

- W. S. Barrell retires from EMI.
- Dr Fred Hamel, who had directed the DG/Archiv label since 1947, dies: he is succeeded by Dr Hans Hickmann.

1958

January

- Philips introduce Fontana, in part a reissue label.

March

- Decca move from the Brixton Road to new offices on London's Albert Embankment.

May

- Edgar Jackson, Jazz and Swing reviewer for ***TG***, stands down after 28 years.
- First review of the Quad Electrostatic loudspeaker by Percy Wilson.

June

- Anthony Pollard becomes London Editor of ***TG***.
- Pye Records release first commercial stereo LPs in the UK, including Beethoven's Symphonies Nos. 1 and 8 with Barbirolli and the Hallé Orchestra.
- Decca introduce first budget-price LPs in the UK with their Ace of Clubs label.
- Sir Louis Sterling dies aged 78.
- Beecham records Bizet's *Carmen* in Paris with Victoria de los Angeles in the title-role (the recording is completed in September 1959).

August

- G. W. Webb, chairman of the Expert Committee (1924-30), dies.

September

- Decca begin the first-ever studio recording of Wagner's *Ring – Das Rheingold* with Solti and VPO.
- Saga Records launched by Wilfred Banks and W. H. Barrington-Coupe: initially a mail-order operation.
- Name of Heliodor Record Company changed to Deutsche Grammophon (GB).

October

- Harmonia Mundi founded in France by Bernard Coutaz.
- EMI, Decca and DG release their first stereo LPs.
- Mercury label transfers from Pye to EMI.

December

- First complete stereo recording of an opera by a 20th-century British composer made by Decca – Britten's *Peter Grimes* with Peter Pears in the title-role and conducted by the composer.
- Oscar Preuss, Parlophone A&R Manager until 1955, dies aged 69.

1959

February

- E. M. Ginn, designer of the EMG acoustic gramophones, dies.

March

- Karajan makes first stereo recordings for DG (Strauss's *Ein Heldenleben* in Berlin) and Decca (Strauss's *Also sprach Zarathustra* in Vienna).
- Solti's recording of Wagner's *Das Rheingold*, recorded in September 1958, is released.
- Decca discontinue the production of 78rpm records.
- First "March LP Weekend Conference" organized by Kathleen and Ivan March in Blackpool.

April

- American Audio Fidelity label available in the UK, with classical releases in September.

May

- L. G. Wood succeeds C. H. Thomas as MD of EMI Records.
- First releases on the Top Rank label.

June

- DG introduce the Heliodor bargain label in the UK.

September

- Garrard launch Magazine Tape Deck.
- SME launch their pickup arm.
- Nicolai Medal presented to the Decca Vienna recording crew by the VPO.

October

- John Gilbert, a contributor to ***TG*** for many years, joins as Audio Consultant.

November

- EMI introduce their budget-price "Concert Classics" label.

1960

January

- Maurice Rosengarten joins the Decca Board.
- First releases on the Lyrita label.
- First UK release at 16⅔ rpm on Top Rank label – tales by Edgar Alan Poe, reviewed in April 1960 – playing time 95 minutes.

April

- Associated Recordings market Westminster, Whitehall, Artia and Parliament labels in the UK.

July

- Lady Faith Compton Mackenzie dies at the age of 82.

August

- Top Rank label transferred to EMI.

October

- Associated Recordings market MK and Eros labels in the UK.

1961

- First classical LP to sell in excess of one million copies worldwide – Tchaikovsky's Piano Concerto No. 1 with Van Cliburn on RCA.

January

- W. S. Barrell dies aged 70.

May

- First release of Pye-Nonesuch spoken word recordings.

June

- ***TG*** masthead shows Sir Compton Mackenzie and Christopher Stone as Founders and Cecil and Anthony Pollard as joint Editors.

July

- ***TG*** open offices at 379 Kenton Road and amalgamate Subscriptions from Ebrington Road and Editorial from Stanmore.

1962

- W. W. Townsley appointed to the Decca Board.

February

- Decca introduce the Phase-4 label.

March

- Deletion of last EMI 78rpm records.
- Associated Recordings launch record club.

May

- Philips Records introduce the CBS label in the UK.
- EMI discontinue Top Rank label.

June

- Siemens and Philips combine their music businesses, Deutsche Grammophon Gesellschaft and Philips Phonographic Industries, by exchanging 50 per cent of each company's share. The venture is called DGG/PPI; both companies remain legally independent with their own repertoire.
- C. H. Thomas retires from EMI.

October

- EMI release "The Living Bible" on 12 LPs.

November

- Louise Hanson-Dyer, Australian-born founder of the Oiseau-Lyre label, dies.

1963

January

- Sir Isaac Shoenberg, a Director of EMI responsible for the British high-definition television system developed by the company in the 1930s, and other developments associated with recording, dies aged 82.
- Audio Fidelity label transfers to Philips in the UK.

February

- DG release Karajan's version of Beethoven's symphonies with the Berlin Philharmonic Orchestra – the first occasion in which all nine works were planned and packaged as an integral set.

April

- Decca release Solti's recording of Wagner's *Parsifal* – the first studio version of the opera ever to be made.

June

- Philips introduce new Compact Cassette recorder at Berlin International Audio Fair.

July

- Victor Olof retires from EMI.

September

- RCA introduce "Dynagroove" recordings to the UK.

1964

- Bhaskar Menon becomes Chairman and MD of EMI's Indian company.

January

- Mercury label transferred to Philips in the UK.

February

- Nonesuch Records formed in New York by Jac Holzmann.

April

- EMI and Decca confirm their intention to maintain a minimum resale price for their records.

June

- Walter Legge leaves EMI.

December

- John Borwick joins ***TG*** as Associate Technical Editor.

1965

- Lear introduce 8-track in-car cartridge in the USA.

February

- W. S. Meadmore dies aged 72.

March

- CBS (formerly American Columbia) commence independent operation in UK under the wing of Oriole Records, a CBS-owned company.

April

- Maurice Oberstein joins CBS UK from the USA.

May

- Christopher Stone dies aged 82.
- Saydisc founded by Gef and Genny Lucena.

July

- Barry Irving joins ***TG*** Advertisement Department.

August

- Joe Brogan, founder of The Gramophone Shop, New York, dies.

September

- Cecil Pollard dies aged 65.
- The "Music for Pleasure" label launched by Paul Hamlyn in association with EMI.

November

- Decca complete the first studio recording of Wagner's *Ring* with *Die Walküre*, featuring Solti and the VPO.

December

- Malcolm Walker joins ***TG*** as Assistant Editor.
- L. G. Wood joins the main board of EMI.

1966

February

- Percy Wilson retires as Technical Editor of ***TG*** and is succeeded by John Borwick, with John Gilbert continuing as Technical Consultant.

April

- Geoff Bridge becomes MD of EMI Records UK.

May

- Decca adopt the Dolby-A noise reduction system. The first sessions to utilize the system are held in Kingsway Hall, London – Mahler's Symphony No. 2 with Solti and the LSO.

July

- BBC radio commence regular stereo transmissions.

October

- UK introduction of Musicassettes by Philips and EMI.

1967

January

- "Stereo 8" tape cartridges introduced to UK.
- First MIDEM (Marche International du Disque de l'Edition Musicale) held in Cannes.

February

- Ken East succeeds Geoff Bridge and becomes MD of EMI Records UK.
- Live recording of Gerald Moore's farewell concert in London's Royal Festival Hall is made by EMI and released on LP three months later.

July

- EMI cease releasing LPs in both mono and stereo formats, other companies follow, although the Decca move did not come until March 1969.
- Decca delete all 10-inch LPs and discontinue their further production.
- The BBC introduce 625-line UHF colour television.

August

- Edgar Jackson dies aged 72.
- The Cleveland Orchestra under Szell becomes the first US orchestra to record in the UK while on a European tour. The recordings for CBS, made at EMI's Abbey Road Studios, include Mozart's Symphony No. 40.

October

- John Culshaw leaves Decca to join BBC-TV and is succeeded as Classical A&R Manager by Ray Minshull.
- Edward "Chick" Fowler retires from EMI Studios and is succeeded by Allen Stagg who had been MD of the International Broadcasting Company.

1968

May

- Nellie Pollard, Chairman of General Gramophone Publications Limited, publishers of ***TG***, dies aged 66.

July

- Freehold of 177-179 Kenton Road purchased by ***TG***.

September

- Dr Hans Hickmann, head of DG's Archiv label, dies. No successor is appointed until 1970.

October

- Pearl Records launched by Charles Haynes and John Waite.

1969

- G. W. Cook becomes General Manager of EMI Studios.

January

- Erik Smith leaves Decca and is appointed A&R Manager of Philips Classical Division.

June

- Definite article dropped from title ***Gramophone***. (References in this chronology now change from ***TG*** to ***G***.)
- RCA Records commence independent operation in UK.
- Victor Olof's last sessions for EMI.

July

- Resale Price Maintenance is abolished on gramophone records.

August

- John Goldsmith launches the Unicorn label.

November

- Sir Joseph Lockwood stands down as CEO of EMI and is succeeded by John Read. He remains Chairman.
- ECM Records founded in Germany by Manfred Eicher.

1970

January

- Decca begin their project to record all the Haydn Symphonies with Dorati and the Philharmonia Hungarica. Completed in 1974 the edition comprised 48 LPs in ten sets.
- First MIDEM Classique – but future plans shelved due to lack of support, to re-emerge in 1984.

April

- Philips launch their complete recording of *The Trojans* with Colin Davis.

May

- In Washington, County Durham, RCA open what is claimed to be the most modern record manufacturing plant in the world. The plant was closed in June 1981.

June

- Telefunken/Decca demonstrate TED video disc system in Berlin. Marketed in Germany in March 1975 as the first of its kind, but without success.

July

- Philip Brodie succeeds Ken East as MD of EMI Records UK.

September

- Deutsche Grammophon release their Beethoven Edition to mark the 200th anniversary of the composer's birth – 12 sets comprising 75 LPs plus illustrated book.

October

- Ken Glancy appointed MD of RCA Records UK.
- Dr Andreas Holschneider appointed head of DG Archiv Produktion.
- Classics for Pleasure launched.
- Decca release their first musicassettes.

November

- Decca introduce Dolby-B on musicassettes.

December

- Bhaskar Menon returns from the Indian company to be MD of EMI International Services Ltd.

1971

- DGG/PPI re-group to form PolyGram BV Netherlands and PolyGram GmbH Germany as management and holding companies for such repertoire divisions as Polydor International GmbH (including Deutsche Grammophon) and Phonogram BV (including Philips Classics).

January

- Rupert Perry joins EMI Records.
- MfP becomes a wholly owned EMI company.
- Electric and Musical Industries Ltd. becomes EMI Ltd.

April

- Bhaskar Menon becomes President and CEO of Capitol Industries Inc.
- Decca purchase Oiseau-Lyre label.
- Formation of Nimbus Records by Numa Labinsky and Michael Reynolds.

June

- American Vanguard catalogue is represented in the UK by RCA.

July

- Lord Reith, first Director General of the BBC, dies.

August

- David Bicknell retires from The Gramophone Company and is succeeded in the Classical A&R Department by Peter Andry.
- Philips demonstrate their VCR machine in London with production models to follow in the spring of 1972.

1972

- Richard Asher appointed MD, CBS Records UK.
- PolyGram Leisure UK formed with Stephen Gottlieb as Chairman.

January

- Alec Robertson retires as Music Editor of ***G***.
- Reg Pollard retires as Advertisement Manager of ***G*** and is succeeded by Barry Irving.
- RCA introduce the "Dynaflex" LP – thinner disc with a raised rim and label area. Later adopted by other companies.

February

- Leonard Smith, Classical Manager of EMI Records and having 50 years' service in the record business, retires. He is succeeded by John Whittle who joined HMV in 1927.
- Geoffrey Bridge becomes first Director General of the British Phonographic Industry (BPI).

March

- Release of quadraphonic discs using SQ system from EMI and CBS; using CD-4 system from RCA; and using the QS system from Pye and a number of smaller labels.

September

- Philips introduce VLP video disc.
- Gerry Oord succeeds Philip Brodie as MD of EMI Records UK.

October

- Malcolm Walker appointed Editor of ***G***, Anthony Pollard becomes Managing Editor.
- Using a PCM recording machine, Denon make the first commercial digital recording – Mozart's String Quartet in B flat, K458, The Hunt.

November

- Sir Compton Mackenzie dies aged 89.
- Peter Andry becomes General Manager of EMI International Classical Division.

1973

April

- ***G***'s Golden Jubilee.

- Delos record label founded in the USA by Amelia Haygood.

May

- Reg Pollard dies.
- Goddard Lieberson becomes President of CBS Records Group.

June

- Bhaskar Menon appointed to Board of EMI.

September

- BIS records founded in Sweden by Robert von Bahr.

1974

January

- Ken Glancy leaves RCA UK and is appointed President and CEO of RCA Records in the USA. He is succeeded as MD of the UK company by Geoffrey Hannington.

July

- Ken Townsend succeeds Gus Cook as General Manager of EMI Studios.

October

- Ken East appointed MD of The Decca Record Company, leaving a year later.

November

- Sir Joseph Lockwood retires as Chairman of EMI but remains on the board until February 1980.
- Victor Olof dies.

1975

March

- Goddard Lieberson retires as President of CBS Records Group.

May

- George Lukan succeeds Geoffrey Hannington as MD of RCA Records UK.

June

- Maurice Oberstein is appointed MD of CBS Records UK in succession to Richard Asher.

November

- Maurice Rosengarten, Director of Decca Classical Recordings, dies.
- John Pattrick who joined EMI in April 1965, succeeds John Whittle as Manager of EMI Records Classical Division. Whittle retires.

December

- Ray Minshull appointed Director of Decca Classical Recordings.

1976

August

- Leslie Hill becomes MD of EMI Records UK.

September

- Gerry Oord, previously MD of EMI Records UK, appointed MD of RCA Records UK.

October

- Enigma Classics launched by John Boyden.
- JVC announce VHS video cassette system in Japan.

1977

January

- Telarc Records founded in the US by Jack Renner and Robert Woods.

February

- Gilbert Wilson and Roger Wimbush die.

May

- Percy Wilson dies aged 84.
- Goddard Lieberson dies aged 66.

August

- F. F. Clough dies.

October

- Nonesuch catalogue transferred to WEA Records.

November

- First releases from Nimbus Records.
- Philips/MCA VLP video disc demonstrated.

December

- Dr Peter Goldmark, who developed the long-playing record with William Bachman, dies in a motor accident.

1978

January

- Gilbert Briggs, founder of Wharfedale Wireless Works, dies aged 88.
- Auvidis founded by Louis Bricard.

February

- Presentation of the first ***Gramophone*** Record Awards with Decca's recording of Janáček's *Kát'a Kabanová* winning the Record of the Year.

March

- JVC introduce VHS video cassette system in the UK.
- Ramon Lopez succeeds Leslie Hill as MD of EMI Records UK.

April

- Anna Instone dies.

May

- Philips announce Compact Disc Digital Audio for early 1980s.

July

- Bhaskar Menon becomes CEO of EMI Music Worldwide.
- Decca's first experimental digital recording sessions at Walthamstow Assembly Hall – "Sylvia Sass sings dramatic arias".
- EMI launch "Listen for Pleasure", the first serious attempt to promote the spoken word on cassette.

October

- John Maunder, latterly with Shure but prominent in the British audio industry and founder with John Gilbert and Percy Wilson of the British section of the Audio Engineering Society, dies aged 62.
- Enigma Classics purchased by WEA.

1979

January

- W. R. Anderson dies aged 88.
- Decca make a live digital recording of the "New Year's Concert" with Boskovsky and the VPO.

February

- David G. Fine is appointed MD of PolyGram UK.

March

- Press demonstration of Compact Disc Digital Audio in Eindhoven.
- Death of EMI record producer and impresario Walter Legge, aged 72.

June

- EMI make their first digital recordings – Debussy's *Images* and *Prélude à l'après-midi d'un faune* with Previn and the LSO.

July

- Sony "Walkman" launched in Japan.

September

- Geoffrey Bridge, first Director General of the British Phonographic Industry (BPI) retires after seven years and is succeeded by John Deacon.

November

- EMI Limited merge with Thorn Limited to form Thorn EMI. The Chairman is Sir Richard Cave.
- First releases from Brian Couzens's Chandos Records.

December

- Reinhard Klaassen appointed to the Decca Board.
- David G. Fine succeeds Stephen Gottlieb as Chairman of PolyGram UK.

1980

January

- Malcolm Walker stands down as Editor of **G** due to ill health. Anthony Pollard returns to the editorial chair.
- The Decca Record Company acquired by PolyGram.
- Sir Edward Lewis, founder of Decca, dies at the age of 79.
- Reinhard Klaassen is made President of the new Decca/PolyGram company with Ray Minshull also appointed to the Board.

March

- W. W. Townsley retires from Decca after 54 years' service.
- Gunter Hensler appointed President of PolyGram Classics USA.

April

- Death of John Culshaw, aged 55.

May

- Ramon Lopez leaves EMI and joins PolyGram UK as MD. He is succeeded as UK EMI Records MD by John Bush.
- Kenneth Wilkinson retires from Decca after 49 years' service.

June

- Sony "Walkman" launched in UK, initially under the name "Stowaway".
- Cliff Busby succeeds John Bush as MD of EMI Records UK.

July
- The record industry abolishes recommended retail prices.

September
- L. G. Wood retires from EMI after 51 years' service.
- Formation of Classics International in the UK to represent DG and Philips. Peter Russell to be the General Manager.

October
- First releases from Ted Perry's Hyperion label.

1981

February
- Paul Voigt, audio engineer, dies aged 80.

March
- First releases from Academy Sound and Vision (ASV) founded by Harley Usill, Jack Boyce and David Gyle-Thompson.

April
- Gimell Records founded by Peter Phillips and Steve Smith.
- Compact Disc conference is held in Salzburg.

May
- Christopher Pollard joins ***G***.

September
- Jan D. Timmer appointed Executive Vice-President, PolyGram International.

November
- C. H. Thomas dies.
- Decca close their West Hampstead studios and establish a Recording Centre in Kilburn.

1982

January
- Alec Robertson dies aged 89.

March
- Capriccio label founded in Germany by Winfried Amel.

June
- DAT Conference in Japan sets standards for both stationary-head (S-DAT) and rotary-head (R-DAT) digital audio tape recorders.
- Direct Metal Mastering – DMM – introduced by Teldec.

August
- Europe's first Compact Disc manufacturing plant opened by PolyGram in Hanover.

September
- Gunther Breest succeeds Hans Hirsch as DG's A&R Director.

October
- Compact Disc system launched in Japan.

1983

January
- Jan D. Timmer becomes President and CEO of PolyGram International, David G. Fine becomes Executive V-P.
- Tim Harrold becomes Chairman, PolyGram Classics International (Decca, DG and Philips).
- Ramon Lopez becomes President and CEO, PolyGram UK.
- Johannes H. Kinzl succeeds Ernst Th. van der Vossen as President, Philips Classics.
- EMI licenced to use DMM technique for LP manufacture.

February
- Bob Fine, responsible for Mercury classical recordings, dies aged 60.

March
- Compact Disc system launched in UK.
- Peter Jamieson succeeds Cliff Busby as MD, EMI Records UK.
- Marco Polo Records founded in Hong Kong by Klaus Heymann.

April
- British Institute of Recorded Sound becomes the National Sound Archive, part of The British Library.

June
- Working groups established to consider viability of consumer digital tape medium.

September
- Compact Disc system launched in USA.
- EMI Eminence label launched.

1984

January
- DG record Puccini's *Manon Lescaut* in the final Kingsway Hall sessions.
- MIDEM Classique re-established.

March
- Sir Richard Cave retires from the Board of Thorn EMI.

April
- John Pattrick, General Manager of EMI Records UK Classical Division, moves to a similar post with Angel Records in Los Angeles and is succeeded by Simon Foster, who comes from the EMI Eminence label.

May
- Brown Meggs becomes President of Angel Records in the USA.
- Peter Andry becomes President of EMI International Classical Division.

June
- Christopher Pollard succeeds Quita Chavez as Editorial Manager of ***G***.
- Nimbus Records open first Compact Disc manufacturing plant in UK.

July
- RCA Records merge with Ariola to form RCA-Ariola. RCA owns 75 per cent, Bertlesmann 25 per cent.

November
- W. A. Chislett dies aged 89.

1985

January
- The BBC close the last of their 405-line TV transmitters, in use since November 1936 and superseded in 1969 by the UHF 625-line colour transmitters.

February
- James Jolly joins ***G*** as Assistant Editor.

April
- Colin (later Sir Colin) Southgate becomes MD of Thorn EMI.
- Ramon Lopez leaves PolyGram UK to join WEA.

July
- Maurice Oberstein leaves CBS to become Chairman of PolyGram UK.

September
- Introduction of Philips LaserVision

December
- RCA Corporation sold to GE and with it the record division.
- George Fenwick, manager of EMI's 363 Oxford Street showrooms from 1935-61, dies aged 88. Fenwick joined HMV in 1911.

1986

January
- Andreas Holschneider appointed President of Polydor International.

February
- Ivor Humphreys joins ***G***.
- Chesky Records founded by Norman and David Chesky.

March
- Nimbus close their LP manufacturing facility.

April
- Christopher Pollard succeeds Anthony Pollard as Editor of ***G***.
- Rupert Perry appointed MD, EMI Records UK and Eire in succession to Peter Jamieson.

May
- EMI open Swindon CD manufacturing plant.
- RPO Records is launched and distributed by ASV.

June
- *The Sunday Times* suggest DAT will offer a serious challenge to CD.

September
- RCA establish International Classical Division to embrace Red Seal, Eurodisc and associated labels.

December
- Bertlesmann acquire 100 per cent of RCA-Ariola and form BMG, the Bertlesmann Music Group.

1987

January
- George R. Marek, A&R Director of RCA from 1950-72, dies.

March

- Philips, Philips and Du Pont Optical, and PolyGram demonstrate the CD-Video system in Amsterdam.
- Reinhard Klaassen retires as President of Decca International and is succeeded by Roland Kommerell.

April

- PolyGram become wholly owned subsidiary of NV Philips Gloeilampenfabrieken.
- PolyGram launch medium-priced CDs.

May

- Naxos Records founded in Hong Kong by Klaus Heymann.
- R-DAT digital audio tape recorders are launched in Japan.

July

- First pre-recorded DAT cassettes appear on the Capriccio label.
- Arabesque Recordings are formed in New York by Marvin M. Reiss and Ward Botsford.
- Olympia Records, founded by Distec Ltd. and Francis Wilson, are launched.

September

- BMG Classics are established.
- BBC introduce RDS (Radio Data Service) broadcasting.
- Ramon Lopez succeeds Nesuhi Ertegun as Chairman and CEO of WEA International.
- Jan D. Timmer returns to Philips in Eindhoven and is succeeded as President of PolyGram International by David G. Fine.

October

- Sony launch R-DAT digital tape recorders in Europe.

December

- First edition of the *Gramophone Good CD Guide*.
- John Bowers of B&W Loudspeakers dies.

1988

January

- Sony acquire CBS Records and Norio Ohga becomes President and CEO.
- John Pattrick returns from Angel to be Marketing Director, EMI International Classical Division.

April

- Ivor Humphreys succeeds John Borwick as Audio Editor of **G**: John Borwick becomes Audio Director.
- Virgin Classics launched by Richard Branson, with Simon Foster as MD.

May

- James Fifield appointed President of EMI Music.

August

- George Mendelssohn, founder of Vox Records, dies aged 75.

September

- Death of David Bicknell, former manager of EMI International Artists Dept, aged 82. He joined The Gramophone Company in 1927.
- Colin (later Sir Colin) Southgate succeeds Sir Graham Wilkins as President and CEO of Thorn EMI.
- Chandos Records release a limited amount of repertoire on DAT.

October

- Philips launch CD-V.
- Dorian Recordings, founded in Troy, NY by Craig Dory and Brian Levine.

November

- Gunther Breest leaves DG and is appointed MD, CBS Masterworks. He is succeeded by Aman Pedersen as DG A&R Director.

December

- Andreas Holschneider appointed President of DG.

1989

February

- First releases from Collins Classics.
- Taiyo Yuden announce CD-R recordable CD.

March

- Peter Andry retires from EMI and is succeeded by Richard Lyttelton who first joined EMI in 1966.
- Gunter Hensler appointed President, BMG Classics in succession to Michael Emmerson.

May

- Peter Andry joins WEA – later Warner Classics International – as Senior V-P Classical Repertoire.
- Richard Lyttelton becomes President of EMI Classics.
- Peter Alward (joined EMI 1970) appointed V-P A&R, EMI Classics.
- Ken East retires from EMI.

June

- Industry agrees on SCMS (Serial Copy Management System) to legalize consumer digital recorders.

August

- Harold Leak, audio manufacturer, dies.

December

- Arthur Haddy, late Technical Director of Decca, dies aged 84.

1990

- Brown Meggs retires as President of Angel Records.
- Bill Holland joins Warner Classics UK.

January

- James Jolly appointed Editor of **G**. Christopher Pollard becomes Managing Editor and Anthony Pollard becomes Publisher.

March

- Michael Fine starts Koch International Classics.

September

- North American edition of **G** launched.
- Philips Classical release their "Mozart Edition", a survey of virtually every work Mozart composed, eventually comprising 180 CDs in 45 volumes. The world sales by the end of 1997 had reached approximately six million discs.

October

- Warner's classical labels (Erato, Teldec, Nonesuch) now grouped as Warner Classics International.
- Yolanta Skura founds Opus 111 in Paris.

November

- Roger Lewis appointed Director, Classical Division, EMI Records UK.
- Philips announce Digital Compact Cassette (DCC).

December

- David G. Fine retires as Chairman and CEO of the PolyGram Group and is succeeded the following month by Alain Levy who joined PolyGram in 1984.

1991

January

- Philips demonstrate DCC system in Las Vegas.
- Henceforth the classical CBS label becomes Sony Classical.

February

- Cala Records founded by Geoffrey Simon.

March

- All EMI's classical recordings to be marketed under the EMI Classics logo.
- Vanguard Classics relaunched by Seymour Solomon and Start Records.
- Sir Joseph Lockwood, former EMI Chairman, dies aged 86.

May

- Sony announce MiniDisc.

June

- David G. Fine becomes Chairman of the Board of the International Federation of the Phonographic Industry (IFPI).

July

- Jan D. Timmer appointed President of Philips, Eindhoven.

November

- Harley Usill, joint-founder of Argo and ASV, dies aged 66.

December

- Simon Foster leaves Virgin Classics.

1992

January

- Warner Classics International acquire remaining shares in Erato.
- Rupert Perry appointed President and CEO of EMI Records UK and Eire.

March

- EMI acquire Virgin Records and with it Virgin

Classics, which in September make their new releases under the wing of EMI Classics.
- Simon Foster becomes Director of BMG Classics.

April
- UK launch of Philips Digital Compact Cassette (DCC).

July
- Zomba Group acquire a controlling interest in Conifer Records.

September
- Roger Ames succeeds Maurice Oberstein as Chairman and CEO of PolyGram UK.

October
- Gianfranco Rebulla appointed to succeed Dr Andreas Holschneider as President of DG.

November
- UK launch of Sony MiniDisc.

1993

March
- Martin Benge succeeds Ken Townsend as V-P, EMI Studios Group.

May
- ***G*** "Editor's choice" commences.
- ***G*** launch the "Blue riband" dealer scheme.

August
- Keith Howard joins ***G*** technical team.

September
- Death at the age of 94 of W. W. Johnson, founder of the NFGS.

October
- ***G***'s John Gilbert dies aged 85.

December
- Finlandia Records acquired by Warner Classics International.

1994

January
- Numa Labinsky, joint-founder of Nimbus Records, dies.

March
- Ray Minshull retires as Executive V-P of Decca International and is succeeded by Evans Mirageas.

June
- Louis Benjamin, one-time MD of Pye Records, dies aged 71.

November
- National Video Arts Corporation becomes part of Warner Classics International.

December
- Gunther Breest leaves Sony Classical.

1995

March
- Raymond Cooke of KEF dies aged 70.
- Peter Gelb appointed President of Sony Classical.
- John Pattrick retires from EMI.

April
- Peter Andry appointed President of Warner Classics International.
- Jean-Hugues Allard appointed Director of A&R for Sony Classical.

May
- Classics for Pleasure 25th anniversary.
- Rupert Perry appointed President and CEO, EMI Europe and Chairman, EMI Records Group UK and Ireland. He is succeeded as MD of EMI Records UK by Jean François Cecillon.

June
- Keith Howard appointed ***G***'s Consulting Audio Editor.

September
- Albert Imperato becomes V-P of DG in the USA.
- BBC inaugurate Digital Audio Broadcasting (DAB).

October
- Alison Ames leaves DG to become V-P of EMI Classics, USA.

November
- BMG acquire Conifer Records from Zomba.

December
- Gianfranco Rebulla leaves DG.
- Tim Harrold retires as Chairman of PolyGram Classics and is succeeded by Chris Roberts.

1996

January
- ***GramoFile*** CD-ROM launched by ***G***.
- Bill Holland appointed MD, Warner Classics UK.
- Alison Wenham becomes MD of BMG/Conifer and Simon Foster A&R Director.

February
- John F. Pfeiffer, RCA producer, dies aged 75. He had been with RCA for 47 years.

March
- W. W. Townsley, who worked for Barnett Samuel and Decca for 54 years, dies.

May
- ***G*** offices move from Kenton Road to Sudbury Hill.
- Peter Andry retires as President of Warner Classics International and is succeeded by Marco Bignotti.

June
- Virgin Classics (EMI) move to Paris, with Alain Lanceron as President.
- Peter Alward becomes Senior V-P, Classical A&R for EMI.
- John Kennedy succeeds Roger Ames as Chairman of PolyGram UK.
- Roger Ames appointed President of PolyGram Music Group.
- Philips acquire a majority interest in Gimell Records.

July
- Music for Pleasure renamed EMI Gold.
- Karsten Witt appointed President of DG.

August
- EMI Music demerges from Thorn EMI.

September
- Bill Holland leaves Warner Classics UK to return to PolyGram UK as Director of Classics and Jazz.

October
- Sidney Shure, of Shure Bros Inc., pickup and microphone manufacturers, dies aged 93.

November
- Cor Dubois appointed President of BMG Classics in succession to Gunter Hensler.

December
- ***G*** commences a regular monthly cover-mounted CD.
- Peter Russell retires as Director, PolyGram Classics UK.

1997

January
- Iain Hutchison (who joined the Company in July 1991) becomes Advertisement Manager of ***G*** and succeeds Barry Irving who moves to a Business Development role.
- Roger Lewis leaves EMI to become President of The Decca Record Company, succeeding Roland Kommerell.

April
- Johannes H. Kinzl retires as President of Philips Classics and is succeeded by Costa Pilavachi.
- Chris Black appointed Director, Sony Classical & Jazz UK.

June
- Ken Berry, who joined the Virgin Group in 1973, appointed President of EMI Recorded Music.

July
- Alan Parsons succeeds Martin Benge as V-P, EMI Studios Group.

October
- The ***Gramophone*** Awards ceremony, held at Alexandra Palace, is televised for the first time, achieving an audience of 2·5 million viewers.
- Brown Meggs dies.

November
- Rob Pell appointed MD of PolyGram Recording Services.

1998

February
- Classics for Pleasure relaunched by EMI.

April
- ***G*** celebrates its 75th anniversary.

Index

References in this index to chronology entries are given as month/year